Redundancy

Employment Law Handbook

July 2016

IDS

THOMSON REUTERS

Redundancy

Employment Law Handbook

Previous edition 2011

IDS
Floor 5
Friars House
160 Blackfriars Road
London SE1 8EZ
Email: ids.sales.support@thomsonreuters.com
Website: www.incomesdata.co.uk

ISBN 978 0 414 05611 4

IDS Employment Law Handbook, 'Redundancy', is published by Thomson Reuters (Professional) UK Limited (Registered in England & Wales, Company No. 16790446). Registered Office: 2nd Floor, 1 Mark Square, London, EC2A 4EG.

The information contained in this journal in not intended to be a substitute for specific legal advice and readers should obtain advice from a qualified adviser in relation to individual transactions or matters.

No natural forests were destroyed to make this product: only farmed timber was used and re-planted. A CIP catalogue record for this book is available from the British Library.

Printed in Great Britain by Hobbs the Printers Ltd, Totton, Hampshire, SO40 3WX

Contents

Abbreviations

Courts

ECJ	European Court of Justice
ECHR	European Court of Human Rights
PC	Privy Council
SC	Supreme Court
HL	House of Lords
CA	Court of Appeal
Ct Sess	Court of Session
NICA	Northern Ireland Court of Appeal
QBD	Queen's Bench Division
Div Ct	(Queen's Bench) Divisional Court
KBD	King's Bench Division
ChD	Chancery Division
NIRC	National Industrial Relations Court
EAT	Employment Appeal Tribunal
ET	Employment Tribunal

Case references

AC	Law Reports, Appeal Cases
All ER	All England Law Reports
Ch	Law Reports, Chancery Division
CMLR	Common Market Law Reports
COET	Employment Tribunal folio number
EAT	Employment Appeal Tribunal unreported case number
ECR	European Case Reports
ET	Employment Tribunal unreported case number
EWCA	Court of Appeal unreported case number
ICR	Industrial Cases Reports
IRLR	Industrial Relations Law Reports
ITR	Industrial Tribunal Reports
KB	Law Reports, King's Bench Division
QB	Law Reports, Queen's Bench Division
SCOET	Scottish Employment Tribunal folio number
SLT	Scots Law Times
TLR	Times Law Reports
UKSC	Supreme Court unreported case number
WLR	Weekly Law Reports

Legislation

EA	Employment Act 2002
EqA	Equality Act 2010
ERA	Employment Rights Act 1996
ETA	Employment Tribunals Act 1996
TULR(C)A	Trade Union and Labour Relations (Consolidation) Act 1992

Statutory references, unless otherwise stated, are to the Employment Rights Act 1996 (ERA), except in Chapter 12, where references are to the Trade Union and Labour Relations (Consolidation) Act 1992 (TULR(C)A).

Some of the cases mentioned in this Handbook were decided under legislation that preceded the ERA. Reference is made throughout to the corresponding provisions in the later statute and not to their antecedents in repealed legislation.

Introduction

The right of employees to receive a statutory payment when dismissed for redundancy was introduced by the Redundancy Payments Act 1965. That right, now found in Part XI of the Employment Rights Act 1996 (ERA), was the only redundancy protection enjoyed by employees at the time. Since then, however, a number of other employment rights have been introduced, many of which have a direct bearing on how redundancy dismissals should be carried out. Most notably, protection from unfair dismissal, first enacted in the Industrial Relations Act 1971 and now found in Part X of the ERA, requires employers to act fairly when dismissing employees for redundancy, and this includes a duty to follow fair procedures. In addition, the Equality Act 2010 prohibits discrimination in the redundancy process, while the Trade Union and Labour Relations (Consolidation) Act 1992 (TULR(C)A) imposes a duty on employers to inform and consult employees whenever 20 or more redundancies are proposed at a single establishment. Thus, any employer embarking on a redundancy exercise today has to take into account a range of legal considerations over and above the question of entitlement to statutory redundancy pay. This Handbook covers all of the relevant statutory provisions in detail. It does not, however, deal with contractual or ex gratia schemes in any depth (unless these have legal consequences for the statutory scheme), except in Chapter 6, 'Redundancy payments', where enhanced redundancy pay is considered.

One of the key questions to be addressed in any potential redundancy situation is whether the statutory definition of 'redundancy' is met. It is important to note in this regard that the TULR(C)A definition of 'redundancy' for collective consultation purposes differs significantly from the ERA definition that applies in respect of individual claims for redundancy payments or unfair dismissal. This difference has important implications as there will be circumstances in which the ERA definition of redundancy will not be met, and so no liability to make statutory redundancy payments will arise, but the wider definition in the TULR(C)A will apply, thereby triggering the statutory consultation procedure.

This Handbook updates and replaces IDS Employment Law Handbook, 'Redundancy', which was published in 2011, and takes into account changes in the law that have occurred since then. Economic instability has once again made redundancy a familiar feature of working life but the substantial law at the heart of this area has not changed significantly over the past few years. For example, the test of what amounts to a redundancy situation – first developed by Judge Peter Clark in Safeway Stores plc v Burrell 1997 ICR 523, EAT, and later approved by the House of Lords in Murray v Foyle Meats Ltd 1999 ICR 827, HL – has stood the test of time. However, the last five years have seen some important clarifications in the case law. For example, the question

i

of whether the dismissal of employees for refusing to agree to a reduction in hours amounts to a 'redundancy' dismissal was revisited by the EAT in Packman t/a Packman Lucas Associates v Fauchon 2012 ICR 1362, EAT. The EAT's conclusion that a reduction in headcount on a 'full-time equivalent' basis should be treated as redundancy reflects a modern understanding of redundancy that accords with industrial reality. There have also been significant developments in the area of collective consultation – notably, the European Court of Justice's judgment in USDAW and anor v VW Realisation 1 Ltd and ors 2015 ICR 675, ECJ, to the effect that employers' consultation obligations are only engaged where 20 or more redundancy dismissals are proposed at a *single* workplace. This has important implications for workers who are employed by large organisations planning mass redundancies across a number of separate workplaces.

Scheme of Handbook

The scheme of this Handbook is as follows:

- Chapters 1 and 2 describe the fundamental concepts of 'dismissal' and 'redundancy'

- Chapter 3 explains how an employer's liability to make a redundancy payment can be avoided if the employer makes an offer of suitable alternative employment that the employee unreasonably refuses

- Chapter 4 deals with the complex statutory scheme for claiming a redundancy payment when an employee is laid off or kept on short-time

- Chapter 5 examines who is and who is not entitled to claim statutory redundancy pay – i.e. the various classes of excluded employee and the different types of personal disqualification that can disentitle an employee to a redundancy payment

- Chapter 6 is concerned with the calculation of redundancy pay and considers the position of enhanced redundancy pay schemes

- Chapter 7 discusses the circumstances in which an employee may apply to the Secretary of State for payment of redundancy pay where the employer either refuses to make a payment or has become insolvent

- Chapter 8 explains the law governing unfair redundancies and describes the circumstances in which an employee unfairly selected for redundancy can bring an unfair dismissal claim

- Chapter 9 considers the circumstances in which discrimination may occur in the context of redundancy. It also looks at the special provisions prohibiting less favourable treatment on the grounds of part-time or fixed-term status

- Chapter 10 deals with the procedural requirements with which an individual must comply in order to be able to bring a claim under the redundancy legislation

- Chapter 11 sets out the statutory right of an employee under notice for redundancy to take time off to look for work or make arrangements for training

- Chapter 12 is concerned with the legal obligations on employers to consult 'appropriate representatives' and to notify the Secretary of State where collective redundancies are proposed.

It should be noted that where decisions cited in this Handbook are decisions of employment tribunals, these are intended to be illustrative only and are not binding on other tribunals, even if the facts and circumstances of the two cases appear to be identical.

The law is stated as at 30 May 2016. This Handbook completely replaces IDS Employment Law Handbook, 'Redundancy' (2011), which should now be discarded.

> **This publication aims to provide accurate, authoritative information and comment on the subjects it covers. It is offered to subscribers on the understanding that the publisher is not in business as a lawyer or consultant.**

1 Dismissal

To be entitled to a redundancy payment an employee will normally first have   1.1
to show that he or she has been dismissed. The exceptions to this rule are
where the employee has been laid off or kept on short-time. These special
situations are discussed in Chapter 4, 'Lay-off and short-time'. In this chapter
we examine the various situations that might amount to a 'dismissal' for the
purposes of the redundancy legislation. Then, in Chapter 2, 'Redundancy',
we go on to explain when such a dismissal will be categorised as being by
reason of redundancy: that is, where it arises because the business at which
the employee is employed closes, or closes in the place where he or she works;
or where the requirements of that business for employees to carry out work
of a particular kind, or work of a particular kind in a particular place, have
ceased or diminished – S.139(1) Employment Rights Act 1996 (ERA).

Definition of 'dismissal'   1.2

The basic definition of dismissal for the purposes of the statutory redundancy
scheme is found in S.136(1) ERA. (A similar, though not identical, definition
of dismissal for unfair dismissal purposes is found in S.95(1).) S.136(1) states
that an employee will be treated as dismissed if:

- his or her contract of employment is terminated by the employer, either with
  or without notice – S.136(1)(a)

- he or she is employed under a limited-term contract and the contract expires
  by virtue of the limiting event without being renewed under the same terms
  – S.136(1)(b), or

1

- he or she has been constructively dismissed – S.136(1)(c). A constructive dismissal occurs when an employee resigns, with or without notice, because of a repudiatory breach of contract by the employer. However, this subsection does not apply where the employee terminates the contract without notice in circumstances in which he or she is entitled to do so by reason of a lock-out by the employer – S.136(2).

To these basic definitions are added two further circumstances that also amount to dismissal for the purposes of the statutory redundancy scheme. These are:

- the resignation of an employee under notice of dismissal – S.136(3) (this also applies to unfair dismissal), and

- the termination of a contract by operation of law consequent on an act of the employer or an event affecting the employer – S.136(5).

1.3 The wording of S.136(1) indicates that this is an exhaustive list of the circumstances in which an employee will be treated as dismissed by his or her employer for the purposes of the statutory redundancy scheme. However, as discussed under 'Special dismissals by statute' below, dismissal may also be deemed in certain situations involving the termination of membership of specified bodies, even where the individuals concerned are not employees but statutory office holders – S.172 ERA.

1.4 Burden of proof

In a claim for a statutory redundancy payment, it is the employee who has to prove, on the balance of probabilities, that there has been a dismissal. Although there is a statutory presumption that a dismissed employee claiming a redundancy payment has been dismissed by reason of redundancy (see Chapter 2, 'Redundancy', under 'Presumption of redundancy'), there is no presumption that an employee has been dismissed in the first place. Thus, if an employee fails to prove that he or she has been dismissed, any claim for a redundancy payment (or for unfair dismissal) will fail.

In Morris v London Iron and Steel Co Ltd 1987 ICR 855, CA (an unfair dismissal case), M claimed that he had been unfairly dismissed while the employer claimed that he had resigned. The tribunal was unable to decide whose evidence was more likely to be true and so it rejected M's claim. The Court of Appeal upheld this decision, saying that, in such exceptional circumstances, the tribunal would have to fall back on the onus of proof, which lay on the employee to prove that he had been dismissed. As the employee had failed to do so, the tribunal had been entitled to reject his claim.

Dismissal by employer 1.5

Under S.136(1)(a) ERA termination of an employment contract by the employer, either with or without notice, constitutes a dismissal for redundancy purposes. If the employer says that the employee's job has come to an immediate end, that is a summary dismissal. If, on the other hand, the employer says that the contract will come to an end on a future date, that is a dismissal with notice (even if the employee is not required to work out that notice).

The question of whether there has been a 'dismissal' by the employer has a much wider importance than simply in relation to redundancy payments. Most significantly, an employee must establish that he or she has been dismissed by the employer in order to claim unfair dismissal. The ERA defines 'dismissal' in two places – the definition in S.136 applies exclusively in relation to redundancy payments and related matters, while the separate definition in S.95 applies when establishing the right to claim unfair dismissal (among other things). Although dismissal by the employer is defined in substantially the same way under both provisions, they are directed to different purposes and it is important to be clear about which provision applies. As Mr Justice Langstaff, then President of the EAT, noted in Francis v Pertemps Recruitment Partnership Ltd EATS 0003/13, S.138 ERA provides for a number of circumstances in which the employee, despite having been dismissed in circumstances covered by S.136, is treated as continuing in the same employment such that his or her entitlement to a redundancy payment is extinguished. Thus, in his view, 'the question upon which a claim for unfair dismissal is predicated is whether the contract is terminated, whereas the question upon which the right to a redundancy payment depends might be put broadly as the employment relationship being terminated'. Dismissal under S.95 ERA is considered in depth in IDS Employment Law Handbook, 'Contracts of Employment' (2014), Chapter 11, 'Termination by dismissal'.

Notice period 1.6

The amount of notice an employee is entitled to receive will depend on either the terms of the employment contract or S.86 ERA. S.86 lays down minimum periods of notice. Although the contract of employment may specify the period of notice which must be given, if it specifies a shorter notice period than is required by S.86 then it is the statutory minimum notice which applies. (Note, however, that it is open to an employee to waive his or her right to notice or to accept a payment in lieu of notice – S.86(3).)

The statutory notice period depends on the length of the employee's continuous employment. An employer is not statutorily bound to give any notice to an employee who has not been continuously employed for at least one month. To an employee who has been continuously employed for more

3

than one month but less than two years the employer must give at least one week's notice, and to an employee who has been continuously employed for more than two years the employer must give at least one week's notice for each year of continuous employment subject to a statutory maximum of 12 weeks' notice.

1.7 **Limited-term contracts.** The contract of employment of an employee who is on a limited-term contract terminates on expiry of the contract, without the need for notice, subject to S.86(4). This provides that an employee on a fixed-term contract of one month or less who has been continuously employed for three months or more should be treated as though he or she has a contract for an indefinite period.

1.8 **Remedy.** If an employer fails to give adequate notice then, unless it has made a payment in lieu of notice, the employee will be entitled to claim damages for breach of contract, either in an employment tribunal (for claims up to £25,000) or in the civil courts. Any such claim will not affect the employee's right to claim a redundancy payment in a tribunal, although, in practice, both claims will be heard together if the employee pursues the breach of contract claim in a tribunal.

For more information on contractual and statutory notice, see IDS Employment Law Handbook, 'Contracts of Employment' (2014), Chapter 11, 'Termination by dismissal', under 'Express dismissal – dismissal with notice'.

1.9 ## Withdrawal of notice

Redundancy decisions are often made as a response to volatile economic conditions. The fluidity of the situation can sometimes lead the employer to rethink the decision to make redundancies that have already been announced. However, an employer cannot unilaterally withdraw notice of dismissal once it has been given – Harris and Russell Ltd v Slingsby 1973 ICR 454, NIRC. Notice may only be rescinded if both parties agree, as the following cases demonstrate:

- **Hedley v J and J Nichol** ET Case No.2505828/09: H was given notice of dismissal for redundancy. The next day his employer heard from a contractor that a tender it had submitted for a project had been successful and it decided that redundancies were no longer required. At a meeting with H later the same day the employer purported to rescind the notice of dismissal but H refused to accept this. An employment tribunal held that the notice of dismissal for redundancy stood, since it could only be withdrawn by mutual agreement. However, by failing to accept reinstatement, H had failed to mitigate his loss and this had a significant impact on the level of his award for unfair dismissal

- **Coombe v East Lincolnshire Council** ET Case No.2602502/12: C was employed as an educational psychologist. In January 2012, the Council invited her and all other employees to apply for voluntary redundancy. C applied and on 30 March received a letter saying that approval had been given for her release and that her formal notice would take effect on 31 March and end on 22 June. The letter also confirmed her voluntary redundancy payment and her entitlement to take her pension without actuarial deduction. C took annual leave immediately before the termination of her employment and was overseas when, on 1 June, she received an e-mail from the Council asking her to contact it urgently. When she did so, the Council informed her that it had to rescind her redundancy because concerns had arisen about the proposed new structure of the psychological service. C objected and brought a tribunal claim to establish that she had been made redundant. The tribunal agreed, finding that the Council had given unconditional notice of termination, which it could not withdraw unilaterally.

As the Coombe case indicates, employers should not make any binding **1.10** agreements about redundancy terms until they are certain that the redundancies are going to go ahead. In British Polythene Ltd t/a BPI Stretchfilms v Bishop EAT 1048/02 difficulties occurred within a business that led to a call for volunteers for redundancy and B put himself forward. An agreement for B to be made redundant was reached but before it could be implemented the employer's needs changed and BP Ltd sought to revoke the agreement. B maintained that the agreement was binding. He resigned and claimed that BP Ltd was in breach of contract. A tribunal upheld his claim and awarded a sum representing the promised contractual redundancy pay under the agreement. On appeal, BP Ltd contended that the tribunal had failed to recognise that the agreement was subject to a condition precedent that the voluntary redundancy would only take effect if there was a genuine need for it prior to the date assigned for termination of B's employment. In rejecting this, the EAT held that there was nothing in the agreement to indicate any conditionality. It provided for dismissal on the ground of redundancy and B was entitled to rely on it. In the absence of any conditionality, the agreement could only be changed by the consent of both sides.

Date of dismissal
1.11

For the purposes of claiming a redundancy payment, a dismissal with notice generally takes effect on the date on which the notice expires and this remains so even if the employer does not actually require the employee to work out the notice – S.145(2)(a). Where, however, the employer dismisses summarily, i.e. without notice, the dismissal normally takes immediate effect – S.145(2)(b). This is the case even if a payment is made in lieu of notice – Dedman v British Building and Engineering Appliances Ltd 1974 ICR 53, CA.

In certain circumstances, though, where the employer has given no notice or inadequate notice, the date of termination of the contract may be postponed – for

5

specified purposes only – to the date when the proper statutory notice under S.86 would have expired – S.145(5)–(6). Notice will be postponed in this way for the following purposes in connection with the statutory redundancy scheme:

- calculating the two-year qualifying period for entitlement to a redundancy payment under S.155 (see Chapter 5, 'Qualifications and exclusions', under 'Qualifying service'), and

- computing the employee's total length of service in order to calculate his or her redundancy pay entitlement under S.162(1) (see Chapter 6, 'Redundancy payments', under 'Statutory redundancy pay scheme – relevant date and calculation date') – S.145(5).

1.12 So, for example, an employee with ten years and ten months of continuous service who is summarily dismissed because of redundancy will have a notional ten weeks of statutory notice added on to his or her length of service. This means that he or she will be treated as having completed 11 years' service and be entitled to a redundancy payment on that basis. (Note that it is only statutory notice under S.86 that can be added on in this way: more generous contractual notice terms are disregarded.)

It used to be the case that the termination date was also postponed for the purpose of ascertaining the maximum amount of a 'week's pay' in circumstances where, between an employee's actual dismissal date and the date upon which dismissal would have taken effect had the correct statutory notice been given, the Secretary of State raised the level of the maximum week's pay under S.227(3). However, S.227(3) was repealed by the Employment Relations Act 1999 and replaced by S.34 of that Act, which is not referred to in S.145(5) ERA. This seems to suggest that the postponement of the relevant date for the purposes of calculating a week's pay no longer applies (although the reference to S.227(3) in S.145(5) ERA still remains). In the many years since S.227(3) was repealed, we have not seen a case addressing this point.

1.13 Note that the ERA contains two provisions for calculating the date of dismissal – the 'relevant date' for redundancy payment purposes, as considered here, under S.145; and the 'effective date of termination' (EDT) under S.97. The EDT is the reference point for establishing a number of other important protections, such as the right to bring a claim of unfair dismissal, and it is the basis for setting the time limit running for a number of causes of action in the employment tribunal. Although the two provisions are substantially the same, such that the 'relevant date' for redundancy purposes will usually coincide with the EDT, it is important to establish the date under the provision appropriate to the situation under consideration. The EDT and the various factors that can affect its calculation are considered in depth in IDS Employment Law Handbook, 'Contracts of Employment' (2014), Chapter 14, 'Date of termination'.

Cutting short notice period. Where an employer gives notice but attempts to curtail the notice period by giving a payment in lieu of notice and asking the employee to leave early then, unless there is very clear evidence that both parties agreed to early termination, the courts will tend to hold that the original date for the expiry of the notice period has been preserved. In HW Smith (Cabinets) Ltd v Brindle 1973 ICR 12, CA, B was given a month's notice but after three days was told not to come to work any more. This was obviously not a consensual termination and B's date of termination was the date that her notice expired. **1.14**

The Brindle case was followed in Page v Telecom Protection Technologies Ltd ET Case No.1701930/09, where P was given notice of redundancy on 13 January 2009. On 29 January he was handed a letter which stated that he was entitled to receive 12 weeks' notice, that he was not required to work out his notice, that his employer would pay him a 'compensatory payment which is your net notice payment in lieu of working your notice', and that his last day of employment would be 30 January. P believed his dismissal was unfair and lodged a tribunal claim on 10 August. The tribunal found that his claim was made within the three-month time limit from his effective date of termination, which was the date on which the 12 weeks' notice expired.

The employer does, however, have the option of bringing forward the date of dismissal by issuing a new notice of termination. It might do this where, for example, it belatedly realises that the original notice period would give the employee sufficient continuous service to claim unfair dismissal and/or a redundancy payment. In Parker Rhodes Hickmotts Solicitors v Harvey EAT 0455/11 the EAT held that a clear notice dismissing an employee with effect from 28 August 2010 was valid and superseded an earlier notice that was due to end on 31 August. The employer's reason for bringing the dismissal date forward, which was to avoid the possibility of an unfair dismissal claim, was immaterial in determining the date of termination. In such a case the dismissal would be in breach of contract but the employer may consider that to be a more desirable (and cheaper) means of terminating the employment. **1.15**

Different rules apply where it is the employee who wishes to leave before the notice period has expired – see 'Leaving before notice expires' below.

Limited-term contracts. As indicated under 'Notice period – limited-term contracts' above, where an employee is employed under a limited-term contract which is not renewed before its expiry, the date of dismissal will be the date the limited-term contract expires – S.145(2)(c). **1.16**

Death of employee. If the employee dies during the notice period, the contract is treated as having expired by notice terminating on the date of the employee's death – S.176(1). If the employee dies after the contract has been terminated, but S.145(5) applies to postpone the date of termination to the **1.17**

7

end of the statutory notice period and this later date has not yet been reached, then the contract is also treated as having been ended by notice expiring on the date of the employee's death – S.176(2).

1.18 Warning of future redundancies

A warning of future redundancies is not a dismissal with notice (or at all) under S.136(1)(a). If an employee leaves following such a warning, he or she will be treated as having resigned and will not be entitled to a redundancy payment. A true notice of dismissal will not only inform the employee that his or her employment will end but will also inform him or her either directly or indirectly of the date upon which the employment will end. The leading case is Morton Sundour Fabrics Ltd v Shaw 1967 ITR 84, Div Ct, where S was warned by his employer that the department in which he worked would have to be closed down. S found another job, gave 28 days' notice and left. A tribunal awarded him a redundancy payment but the Divisional Court overturned this. As Mr Justice Widgery put it: 'As a matter of law an employer cannot dismiss his employee by saying "I intend to dispense with your services at some time in the coming months". In order to terminate the contract of employment the notice must either specify the date or contain material from which that date is positively ascertainable.' This had not happened and the event that actually terminated the contract was the notice given by S, not any action taken by the employer. It followed that S had not been dismissed and had no claim to a redundancy payment.

Similarly, in Kinmond v Rushton Connections Ltd EAT 799/97 the EAT ruled that a letter informing employees that, from a provisional date, the employer would be closing down its premises and relocating did not amount to a notice of dismissal. However, a later memo giving the actual date of the move did constitute such a notice.

1.19 A warning which states that employment will end on or after a certain date is not a notice of dismissal. An example:

- **Pritchard-Rhodes Ltd v Boon and anor** 1979 IRLR 19, EAT: the employees were sent a letter explaining that the company was in a perilous situation, but continuing: 'After careful consideration it is felt that the job which you are currently undertaking will last for at least seven months from 1.3.77.' The EAT held that all the employer was doing was giving a warning that the employment might well terminate at the end of the seven-month period but that it was not certain to do so. There was not enough certainty about the date when the employment would end for this to be a notice of dismissal.

Similarly, there is no notice of dismissal where the warning states that employment will end on or before a certain date. Two examples:

- **Burton Group Ltd v Smith** 1977 IRLR 351, EAT: S was told that he would be dismissed between 31 October and 26 December, the actual date to be confirmed later. On 24 October the unions and the employer agreed that the redundancies would take effect on 26 December but S died on 26 October without hearing of this. The EAT held that no formal notice of dismissal had been given to S, since all he knew was that the date of termination would be 26 December or such earlier date as the employer might select. There was an arrangement that S would be dismissed for redundancy, but no notice of dismissal

- **International Computers Ltd v Kennedy** 1981 IRLR 28, EAT: in October 1979 an employer told 900 employees that the factory where they worked would close by the end of September 1980 and that they would receive statutory redundancy payments and other severance payments. K found another job and left shortly afterwards. The EAT held that the employer's announcement was not a dismissal. The date of closure of the factory might have been stated clearly but it was quite unknown when K's individual employment would come to an end.

Even where it appears that the dismissal date is clear there may be no notice of dismissal. Two examples: **1.20**

- **Doble v Firestone Tyre and Rubber Co Ltd** 1981 IRLR 300, EAT: F Ltd proposed to close its factory on 15 February 1980 and issued a written statement informing the workforce of its intention. The statement went on to say that separate notices of dismissal would be issued to each employee at the appropriate time, and that although the employer intended to continue production until 15 February it would keep the matter under constant review. The EAT held that there was no firm date on which the employees' contracts were due to come to an end since those matters were to be kept under review. In any case, the proposal could not itself be a notice of dismissal because it had stated that notices of dismissal would follow at the appropriate time

- **Carder v Kvaerner Services Ltd** ET Case No.35933/95: C, a contracts manager involved in the supervision of building works contracts, received a letter from his employer on 23 February saying that it was obliged to consider him for an alternative position, and that if it were not successful in finding him alternative employment by 31 March 'then there will be no alternative but to terminate your employment by reason of redundancy'. An employment tribunal found that this letter did not amount to a dismissal. In reaching this conclusion, it took into account the fact that the employer wrote to C on 9 March stating that he, C, had not been notified of redundancy, which would only arise if the company failed to find him a suitable alternative appointment.

A valid notice of dismissal, if it does not specify the actual date of termination, must contain material from which that date is positively ascertainable. It is a question of fact for the tribunal whether a specific date was ascertainable. In

Wadham Kenning Motor Group t/a Wadham Stringer v Avery and ors EAT 405/91, for example, K, a director, told the workforce on 4 January 1991 that W's garage was to be closed down. Later that day, A, F and J were offered alternative employment at another garage. A and F resigned without taking up the offer and J resigned after trying out the new job. Thinking that their garage was to close, all three claimed redundancy payments. The tribunal found that either K had informed the staff on 4 January that the garage was to close on 28 February or it was common knowledge among the workforce that this was to happen. Letters to the garage's customers, for example, gave 28 February as the day of closure. The tribunal thought that a reasonable employee would have understood from all the events of 4 January that his or her employment was to terminate on 28 February. It found that A, F and J had been given valid notice of termination on 4 January. The EAT refused to interfere with that decision as there was some evidence to support the tribunal's finding.

1.21 Tribunals will take account of all the surrounding circumstances when ascertaining whether a valid notice of dismissal was given and, if so, when it was given. In Pole v NIACE ET Case No.22836/95, for example, the employer, embarking on a reorganisation, wrote to P on 12 December 1994 saying, in part, that it had decided 'to issue initial and precautionary notices of redundancy... This letter is formal notice that these decisions are to be implemented, and constitutes therefore a formal precautionary notice of redundancy, since your current post will be deleted from 1 April 1995.' P was later interviewed for one of the new posts that were available but was unsuccessful. The employer wrote to her again on 28 February saying that 'your present post has been declared redundant... therefore, I am writing to confirm formally the termination of your employment at NIACE on 31 March 1995'. P, who was entitled to 12 weeks' notice, claimed that the February letter was the notice of dismissal, while the employer argued that the December letter had been the notice of dismissal – meaning that P had been given more than adequate notice. A tribunal held that the December letter was ambiguous but, noting the use of the words 'initial' and 'cautionary', found that it was simply a warning of impending redundancies to take effect on 31 March. It found that the actual letter of termination was the February letter. It was influenced by its belief that the employer's intention had been to use the notice period to carry out interviews, thereby avoiding having to give notice once the interviewing process had been completed and risking having to make payments in lieu of notice.

There is no reason why an employee should not be given a very long period of notice. In Hicks v Humphrey 1967 ITR 214, ET, for example, a tenant employer told his employee in February 1966 that he had given notice to terminate the tenancy of the farm to take effect on 11 October of that year. The employee left before that date and claimed a redundancy payment. The tribunal held that the notice was a notice of dismissal, albeit a very long one.

Note that the rule in Morton Sundour Fabrics Ltd v Shaw (above) applies to notice given by an employee as well as to notice given by an employer. In Mabert v Ellerman Lines plc ET Case No.07680/83, for example, M and her husband were accepted as prospective adopters and she wrote to her employer to say that she intended to leave at short notice as soon as a child became available for adoption. A redundancy situation arose and M was made redundant. The employer claimed that she was not entitled to a redundancy payment because she had announced her resignation but a tribunal pointed out that all M had done was state her intention to resign in the future: this was not a valid resignation because no firm date had been set, so that what terminated M's employment was the employer's dismissal. M was therefore entitled to a redundancy payment.

Warning of redundancy and constructive dismissal. It has been argued   1.22
that a warning of redundancy amounts to a fundamental breach of contract that can give rise to a constructive dismissal (for the definition of which see 'Definition of "dismissal"' above). However, this argument was rejected by the EAT in Secretary of State for Employment v Greenfield EAT 147/89. In that case a tribunal found that there had been a constructive dismissal when an employer told all its employees, including the claimant, that they would be made redundant at some unknown time in the future. On appeal, the EAT overturned the tribunal's decision, saying that it was clear from the authorities that an indication of impending redundancy does not constitute a repudiation of contract or dismissal, actual or constructive.

However, in Greenaway Harrison Ltd v Wiles 1994 IRLR 380, EAT, the Appeal Tribunal appeared to suggest that a threat to dismiss with notice could be a fundamental anticipatory breach of contract, where the threat was made in the context of a unilateral variation of contract by the employer. In that case W was given notice that her hours of work were to be changed and that if she did not accept those hours she would be given notice of dismissal. W's manager informed her that she could speak to the managing director about the issue but that there was little possibility of him changing his mind. W decided that it would be pointless to do so and resigned. The EAT held that although the contract of employment had not actually been breached, the employer was in anticipatory breach of contract and that breach – the threat to terminate the employee's contract by giving notice of termination in accordance with the contract – was a fundamental breach of contract for the purpose of claiming constructive dismissal.

It is difficult to reconcile the Greenaway Harrison case with the Greenfield   1.23
case. The upshot of the two cases appears to be that where an employer informs employees that if they do not accept certain variations to their contracts of employment they will face redundancy, the employer may well be acting in fundamental anticipatory breach of the contract of employment,

11

allowing the employees to resign and claim constructive dismissal. However, if the employer merely informs the employees that they may face redundancy, but makes no suggestion of varying the employees' contracts, then that will not amount to a fundamental anticipatory breach of contract. Obviously, such an inconsistency in the law is highly undesirable and it is somewhat surprising that a definitive answer has yet to be provided by either the EAT or the Court of Appeal. In Kerry Foods Ltd v Lynch 2005 IRLR 680, EAT, the EAT considered the Greenaway Harrison case and expressed some concern at the decision but pointedly refused to reach a conclusion about whether it had been wrongly decided. In our view, Greenaway Harrison should be treated with some caution, not least because it appears to suggest that a threat to terminate a contract with notice in accordance with the terms of the contract can amount to an anticipatory breach of contract, while it is established case law that an actual termination in these circumstances can never amount to such a breach (see Haseltine Lake and Co v Dowler 1981 ICR 222, EAT).

Of course, if an employer clearly intends to commit a breach of contract, there will be scope for a constructive dismissal. For example, a warning that an employer would require an employee to move premises where it had no contractual right to do so would amount to a fundamental breach – see Maher v Fram Gerrard Ltd and anor 1974 ICR 31, NIRC.

1.24 In certain circumstances it may be possible to argue that a warning of future redundancies amounts to a breach of the implied duty of mutual trust and confidence inherent in an employment relationship. It is unlikely that a normal warning, such as in the above cases, would constitute such a breach. However, if the warning is couched in such a way that the employee is faced with a situation in which there is no prospect of his or her remaining in employment, it might lead to a finding of constructive dismissal. In Valor Heating Ltd v Nelder EAT 292/92 N, a regional service engineer, was selected for redundancy after 26 years' service. He was told that he had been selected because he had failed a Gas Regulation course. At a later meeting, he was offered the choice of taking over another region or accepting redundancy. N chose the latter because he did not want to move and he did not expect to remain in employment for very long after failing the Gas Regulation course. N brought tribunal proceedings, claiming that he had no choice but to accept redundancy. The employer gave a different version of events and said that N had been given the choice of accepting redundancy or remaining in the same job. The tribunal decided that N had been constructively dismissed. A situation was allowed to develop in N's mind in which he believed that, whatever happened, he would lose his job. Even if his belief was not in fact 'an accurate assessment of the situation', the employer had breached the implied term of mutual trust and confidence. The EAT, however, allowed the employer's appeal on the ground that the tribunal had failed to establish exactly what had been said to N at his meetings with management and whether he had, in fact, been faced with an intolerable choice. It remitted the case for the tribunal to make such a finding and then to determine whether there had been a breach of contract. In doing so, however, the EAT seemed to accept that it is possible for there to be a constructive dismissal in these circumstances.

Leaving before notice expires   1.25

An employee under notice of dismissal may wish to leave work before the notice expires, perhaps to go to another job. An important question, if the employee does leave early, is whether he or she is still entitled to a redundancy payment.

An employee can leave early and claim a redundancy payment only if he or she either:

- agrees with the employer to vary the notice period, or
- complies with the statutory provisions relating to counter-notice.

Agreement with employer. If the employer agrees that the employee can leave   1.26
before the expiry of the notice period then there is still a dismissal by the employer. All that has happened is that the employer has agreed to substitute an earlier termination date – McAlwane v Boughton Estates Ltd 1973 ICR 470, NIRC. It is important, however, that there is actual agreement between the parties. An employee's unilateral decision to leave early will amount to a resignation and, unless the employee has followed the counter-notice provisions (see below), he or she will have no right to a redundancy payment.

Statutory counter-notice. The basic requirements, which must be followed   1.27
precisely, are:

- the employer must have given notice to the employee to terminate the contract – S.136(3)(a) (a mere warning of a pending redundancy is not enough), and
- the employee must give counter-notice in writing, within the 'obligatory period' of the employer's notice, to terminate on a date earlier than the expiry of the employer's notice – S.136(3)(b). (A failure to provide the notice in writing will defeat a redundancy pay claim based on statutory counter-notice. Note, however, that for the purpose of an unfair dismissal claim, similar provisions under S.95(2) do not require the counter-notice to be in writing.)

Obligatory period. The 'obligatory period' is defined in S.136(4). It is the   1.28
period, ending on the date of expiry of the employer's notice, that is equal in length to the statutory notice period under S.86 ERA or to the employee's contractual notice entitlement, whichever is the longer. If, for example, an employee has three years' service, he or she will be entitled to a minimum of

13

three weeks' statutory notice under S.86. If the employer gives three weeks' notice, then the obligatory period and the notice period are one and the same. If the employer gives six weeks' notice of redundancy then – if the employee has no separate contractual entitlement to notice – the last three weeks of the employer's six weeks' notice will be the obligatory period. If, however, the same employee is entitled to four weeks' notice under the contract, then the last four weeks of the employer's notice will be the obligatory period. If the employer gives less than lawful notice, the obligatory period still ends on expiry of the employer's notice, meaning that the employee has a smaller window within which to give counter-notice.

There is a trap for employees where the employer gives longer notice than required. If an employee gives counter-notice during the notice period but before the obligatory period starts and then leaves his or her employment, he or she will be treated as having resigned and not as having been dismissed and will lose entitlement to redundancy pay. In Nicholas v George Payne and Co Ltd ET Case No.25139/95, for example, N was entitled to three weeks' notice. He was in fact given ten weeks' notice and told that he would get more than double his statutory entitlement to redundancy pay. N found a new job and his new employer wanted him to start seven weeks before the end of his notice period. N served his counter-notice. An employment tribunal found that he was not entitled to redundancy pay because he had failed to give his counter-notice during the obligatory period, which began three weeks prior to the end of his notice period.

1.29   *Length of counter-notice.* How much counter-notice should be given is uncertain as the length of the employee's counter-notice is not specified in the ERA, which only requires that notice must be given. It could be argued that the employee should be required to give the amount of notice that he or she would be bound to give in order to terminate the contract of employment lawfully. That would be either the statutory minimum of one week (see S.86(2)) or a longer period of contractual notice, if any. This proposition, however, was rejected in Ready Case Ltd v Jackson 1981 IRLR 312, EAT, where the Appeal Tribunal held that the word 'notice' in S.95(2) (the equivalent unfair dismissal provision) was to be construed not as 'valid notice' (i.e. not as the amount of notice the employee is obliged to give) but as notice of any period. In that case the employee had given five days' notice.

In Millington v Roberts and Hewett Agriculture Ltd ET Case No.00977/84 a tribunal held that it followed from Ready Case that a notice to leave immediately was a valid counter-notice. The tribunal, however, doubted whether Ready Case was correct and said that had it not been for that case it would have said that a counter-notice was only valid if it equated to the notice that the employee was either contractually or statutorily bound to give to terminate the contract.

What is clear is that an employee must give some notice. In Walker v Cotswold **1.30** Chine Home School 1977 12 ITR 342, EAT, a school cook was told that her job would end at the end of term, which was about seven weeks away. She simply left at the end of the afternoon, never returned to work and did not answer letters from the school. The EAT said there was no evidence of anything she said or did which could sensibly be construed as amounting to notice.

Employer's further notice. An employee who has served a valid counter- **1.31** notice is still deemed to have been dismissed by the employer but on the date of the expiry of the counter-notice and not of the original notice of the employer. However, if the employer wishes to stick with the original dismissal date, it may serve a further notice requiring the employee to work out the original notice period – S.142(1). This further notice must:

- be in writing and be given to the employee before the employee's counter-notice expires

- tell the employee that the employer requires him or her to withdraw the counter-notice and continue to work until the employer's original notice expires, and

- state that unless the employee complies the employer will contest any liability to pay a redundancy payment – S.142(1)–(2).

If the employee complies with the employer's further notice and withdraws his or her counter-notice, the employer's original notice of dismissal will remain in effect.

An employee who does not comply with the employer's further notice is **1.32** deemed to have been dismissed by the employer on the date specified in the employee's counter-notice. The employee is not, however, entitled as of right to a redundancy payment by reason of that dismissal. He or she must apply to a tribunal, which, having considered the reasons the employee had for leaving early and the reasons the employer had for wishing to retain the employee for the full notice period, must decide whether it is just and equitable for the employee to receive a payment. The tribunal may award the whole, part or none of the payment to which the employee would have been entitled but for the employer's further notice – S.142(3)–(4).

Two examples of tribunals' exercise of discretion in this regard:

- **Simon v HA Stradling and Sons Ltd** ET Case No.3926/85: S, a construction site agent, was given three months' notice of redundancy. He rapidly found two other jobs but in both cases the employer wanted him to start promptly, while his current employer needed him up to the end of the contract on which he was working. S gave counter-notice, refused to comply with the employer's further notice, and applied to a tribunal for a redundancy payment. Weighing

15

up the facts, the tribunal said that it was essential for S to safeguard his future given the difficult climate for the construction industry, and while the employer would be inconvenienced by the loss of a site agent, it could, at a pinch, hire a temporary replacement at no extra cost. In the circumstances it was fair for S to receive the whole of his redundancy payment

- **Harrison v Walsh t/a LLG Wheelchairs** ET Case No.2401814/98: H was under notice of redundancy, to expire on 31 March. On 17 March he gave notice to his employer that he was leaving on 25 March as he had new employment commencing on 26 March. The employer served a further notice requiring H to work until 31 March and stating that he would lose his entitlement to redundancy pay unless he did so. H left on 25 March. The tribunal ordered the employer to pay just 25 per cent of the redundancy pay. It found that the employer had compelling business and financial reasons for wanting H to remain until 31 March, and that H did not believe he would lose his new job if he delayed his start date – he simply believed that it would not be a good start to the employment relationship.

1.33 *Death of employee following counter-notice.* Note that if an employee dies after having served a counter-notice then the employer is deemed to have served a further notice under S.142(1), whether it has done so or not, and the employee is deemed not to have complied with it – S.176(5). The result is that a tribunal will have to exercise its discretion, under S.142(3), whether to award a redundancy payment (to the employee's estate).

1.34 ## Working on after notice expires

We have seen that the parties to an employment contract can agree to bring forward the employee's leaving date without the employee losing the right to a redundancy payment. It follows from this that the parties should also be able to set a new leaving date later than the original date without affecting that right. The ERA makes no provision for such an eventuality but the EAT in Mowlem Northern Ltd v Watson 1990 ICR 751, EAT, seemed to accept in principle that the leaving date can be postponed by agreement.

In the Mowlem case MN Ltd had a contract to carry out work at a particular power station where it employed W as a foreman. In January 1988 the contract was coming to an end and the company gave W notice of redundancy to expire on 11 March 1988. A few weeks before the expiry of that notice the employer asked W to transfer temporarily to another site, and to stay there beyond 11 March, in the hope that it would get a new construction contract at the original site to which W would then return. If the new contract failed to materialise, it would be up to W to decide what to do. W was told that, in the meantime, the redundancy notice would 'lie on the table'. In the event, the company failed to secure the new contract and W left in June 1989. MN Ltd refused to give him a redundancy payment, saying that the reason for the termination of employment was W's resignation and not redundancy. The EAT held that the employer's notice of dismissal stood but it had been suspended by mutual agreement. It became reactivated when it became clear that W would not be able to return to the original site.

Unfortunately, the reasoning behind this decision is not entirely clear. Presumably, the EAT was not saying that the parties varied the date of dismissal, since no new leaving date was fixed and Morton Sundour Fabrics Ltd v Shaw 1967 ITR 84, Div Ct (see 'Dismissal by employer – warning of future redundancies' above), makes it clear that there is no notice of dismissal where the exact date of leaving is not ascertainable. Rather, it seems that it was saying that the parties agreed to suspend the operation of the notice. The EAT went on to hold that in these circumstances there was nothing to prevent W claiming a statutory redundancy payment. It would appear that the EAT, in reaching this decision, did not consider S.138(1) ERA, which provides that where an employee's contract of employment is renewed, or he or she is re-engaged under a new contract of employment in pursuance of an offer (in certain circumstances which applied in this case), the employee will not be regarded as dismissed by reason of the ending of his or her employment under the previous contract. Although it is possible that W might have been able to argue that he never really accepted the offer because acceptance was dependent on a condition – that he would be able to return to the original site – which was not met, the EAT did not mention the section at all and therefore some doubt must be cast on the decision. **1.35**

The decision in the Mowlem case was relied upon by the employer in S Jones Industrial Holdings v Jarvis and anor EAT 641/93. There, J and W were employed as lorry drivers in the contracts division of a road haulage firm. They were given notice that they would be made redundant on 24 July. The employer did not want to lose them, however, and found them different driving duties after that date. J and W were then given a revised date of termination of 4 September but both left shortly before then. A tribunal found that the employees' original contracts had terminated on 24 July and that they were entitled to a redundancy payment. The employer challenged that decision on the basis of the Mowlem case and argued that the original notice of redundancy had been varied by mutual consent to take effect on 4 September. Therefore, as both employees had resigned before 4 September, they had not been dismissed and were not entitled to a redundancy payment. In contrast to the Mowlem case, there had been no agreement with the employees that the redundancy would 'lie on the table'.

The EAT held that the case was governed by ordinary contractual principles and found no agreement on the employees' part to accept a deferred redundancy date, even though they had been retained in a different capacity after 24 July. The EAT pointed out that an employee who continues to work **1.36**

17

after the date specified in the original redundancy notice and who has agreed to the continuation of his or her existing contract may, subject to the issue of suitable alternative employment, lose the right to a redundancy payment. Employers who wish to extend the contract beyond the expiry date should therefore make their proposals clear and obtain the employee's consent to them. In the instant case the employer had not made it plain what it was seeking to do. It was not clear that the contracts were being extended and, consequently, the employees remained entitled to their redundancy payments.

Unlike the Mowlem case, the question of suitable alternative employment does seem to have been raised before the tribunal in the Jarvis case. However, it is unclear from the EAT's decision how this issue was dealt with and since it does not appear to have been raised on appeal it is impossible to comment on whether S.138(1) might have applied in the circumstances. S.138 is discussed in more detail in Chapter 3, 'Alternative job offers'.

1.37 Expiry of limited-term contract

The Fixed-term Employees (Prevention of Less Favourable Treatment) Regulations 2002 SI 2002/2034 ('the FTE Regulations') made a number of changes to redundancy law, giving fixed-term and limited-term employees greater protection than they previously enjoyed.

Prior to the Regulations' coming into force, S.136(1)(b) ERA provided that where a fixed-term contract – which was defined as a contract with both a defined date of commencement and a defined date of expiry – expired and was not renewed on the same terms, then a dismissal had taken place. This definition did not cover a contract for a particular purpose designed to expire whenever the task in question was completed (hereafter referred to as a 'task contract'). As a result, such contracts – examples of which could include a sailor who is employed for a voyage of uncertain duration or a person who is engaged to fell an area of trees and whose employment will end when all the trees have been felled – came to an end by performance and there was no dismissal for ERA purposes.

1.38 However, task contracts are now included in the definition of 'fixed-term contract' found in Reg 1(2) of the FTE Regulations. In addition, S.136(1)(b) ERA was amended from 1 October 2002 to provide that an employee is dismissed if he or she is 'employed under a limited term contract and that contract terminates by virtue of the limiting event without being renewed under the same contract'. S.235(2A) ERA states that a contract of employment is a limited-term contract if:

- the employment under the contract is not intended to be permanent, and

- provision is accordingly made in the contract for it to terminate by virtue of a limiting event.

Subsection (2B) goes on to define a 'limiting event' as:

- in the case of a contract for a fixed term, the expiry of the term

- in the case of a contract made in contemplation of the performance of a specific task, the performance of that task, and

- in the case of a contract which provides for its termination on the occurrence of an event (or the failure of an event to occur), the occurrence of the event (or the failure of the event to occur).

Where an employee works under a succession of limited-term contracts he **1.39** or she may be dismissed for redundancy on the expiry of each contract and, if so, will be entitled to a redundancy payment provided he or she has been employed for at least two years. In Pfaffinger v City of Liverpool Community College and another case 1997 ICR 142, EAT, P had been a part-time lecturer under a series of fixed-term contracts, each for a single academic term, for 13 years. The last relevant contract was issued on 23 April 1993 and ran until 25 June, when term ended and the summer vacation began. Over the summer, P's employer introduced a new system of payment that had the effect of substantially reducing P's hourly rate. P did not return to work and claimed, among other things, a redundancy payment. Her employer argued that she had not been dismissed but that her employment had terminated by reason of the expiry of her contract on 25 June, and denied that she had the requisite continuity of employment. The EAT held that when P's contract expired at the end of each term she was dismissed for redundancy, since during a vacation the need for teachers ceases or diminishes. It said that, in situations like P's, a redundancy payment entitlement is not lost when the employee returns to work under a new contract the following term unless, in accordance with S.138, an offer of re-engagement was made before the previous contract had ended. The fact that P's fixed-term contracts gave her continuity of employment for the purposes of making certain claims in respect of her dismissal did not prevent the expiry of her fixed-term contract from being a dismissal or that dismissal being for redundancy. P was therefore entitled to a redundancy payment.

Note that a contract is still a fixed-term contract even if it can be brought to an end by notice within the term – Dixon and anor v BBC 1979 ICR 281, CA. Thus, a provision in a three-year fixed-term contract that it can be terminated by three months' notice on either side does not change its character.

Although it is now clear that the expiry of any type of limited-term contract **1.40** counts as a 'dismissal' for redundancy purposes, that does not mean that any such dismissal is necessarily by reason of redundancy. This issue is considered separately in Chapter 2, 'Redundancy', under 'Reason for dismissal – expiry of limited-term contract'.

19

1.41 Constructive dismissal

By virtue of S.136(1)(c) ERA there is a dismissal when 'the employee terminates the contract... (with or without notice) in circumstances in which he is entitled to terminate it without notice by reason of the employer's conduct'. This section refers to those cases where the employer has committed, or is threatening to commit, a repudiatory breach of contract, thereby entitling the employee under the law of contract to leave without notice. If the employee in fact leaves, with or without notice, there is a 'constructive dismissal': see IDS Employment Law Handbook, 'Contracts of Employment' (2014), Chapter 11, 'Termination by dismissal', under 'Constructive dismissal'.

The employer's reason for dismissal in a case of constructive dismissal is the reason for the employer's breach of contract that caused the employee to resign. Thus, as the Court of Appeal held in Berriman v Delabole Slate Ltd 1985 ICR 546, CA, if the reason for the breach of contract fits the statutory definition of redundancy, then the employee will be redundant.

1.42 Common breaches of contract that could lead to a constructive dismissal on the ground of redundancy include the following:

- laying off employees when there is no contractual right to do so. In Wootton v Quinney's Auto Services Ltd ET Case No.2465/96, for example, W's employer, acting in breach of the employment contract, laid him off on 11 December but refused to make him redundant, saying that there would be work for him in January. W, however, chose not to return and a tribunal found that he had been constructively dismissed. (Note that an employee who is laid off where the employer does have a contractual right to do so may be able to claim a redundancy payment under the special statutory scheme set out in Chapter III of Part XI of the ERA, despite the fact that he or she has not been dismissed – see Chapter 4, 'Lay-off and short-time')

- requiring employees to move to new premises when there is no contractual right to do so. For example, in David Webster Ltd v Filmer EAT 167/98 the depot at which F worked closed and he was moved, in breach of his contract, to another, more distant, location. F left and the EAT held that he had been constructively dismissed and the reason was redundancy

- changing terms of employment by, for example, switching an employee from one job to another because there is no longer a requirement for the former. In Melia v Green Contract Services Ltd ET Case No.2902217/08, for example, M was a time-served pipe fitter. The contract on which he worked was cancelled at short notice in February 2008 and he was given other work to do, such as gardening, since the employer had no further need for a pipe fitter. However, M was drifting further and further away from his trade so in July he accepted an offer from another company and resigned. An employment tribunal upheld his claim for a redundancy payment on the basis of a constructive dismissal. M had resigned in response to his employer's breach of contract in failing to provide him with the work he was employed to do.

Where the employer seeks to impose a change of role on the employee because **1.43** the employee's original role is no longer required, there will almost always be a constructive dismissal for redundancy. Mr Justice Langstaff noted in Lees v Imperial College of Science, Technology and Medicine EAT 0288/15 that such a situation will fall within the scope of S.136(1)(c) subject only to another term in the contract – such as a flexibility or mobility clause – preventing the employer's actions amounting to a breach. Thus, in that case, the tribunal had erred when it became 'sidetracked' into considering whether, in refusing to make the employee redundant and insisting on her taking up what it considered to be a suitable alternative role, the employer had breached the implied term of mutual trust and confidence. The tribunal had overlooked a more straightforward breach of contract – namely, the change of job content – in response to which the employee resigned.

It is important to stress, however, that a constructive dismissal will only amount to a dismissal on the ground of redundancy where the underlying reason for the breach of contract satisfies the statutory definition. See Chapter 2, 'Redundancy', in the section 'Diminishing need for employees', under 'Less work available – same work done under different terms and conditions', for a detailed consideration of when a change in an employee's terms and conditions in breach of contract may or may not amount to redundancy. It should also be borne in mind that a move to new premises or a change of job may rank as an offer of suitable alternative employment, so that the employee may forfeit any right to redundancy pay if he or she unreasonably refuses it – see Chapter 3, 'Alternative job offers'.

It is also important to bear in mind that a constructive dismissal is not **1.44** necessarily unfair, even though it involves a breach of contract. The question of unfairness is a separate one that takes into account numerous factors not confined to the contract of employment. For example, in David Webster Ltd v Filmer (above), the EAT held that the tribunal was entitled to find that the constructive dismissal for redundancy was nonetheless fair. A further example is O'Marra v Caldwell t/a Stevens Solicitors ET Case No.1501758/12, where the employer found itself in severe financial difficulties and asked employees to defer their January salaries until such time as it could pay them. OM said that she was unwilling to defer her salary and, although she carried on working, she obtained a judgment from a tribunal in May that the employer had unlawfully deducted her January wages. In June, the employer again informed employees that it could not pay them that month and OM resigned.

21

A tribunal found that she had been constructively dismissed but that the dismissal was fair. In its view, while other employers might have embarked on a redundancy consultation exercise when the financial difficulties arose, it was not outside the range of reasonable responses for the employer to hope to be able to ride out the financial difficulties and keep the business together.

The question of whether a constructive dismissal on the ground of redundancy is fair or unfair for the purpose of the unfair dismissal legislation is considered in Chapter 8, 'Unfair redundancy', under 'Unreasonable redundancy'.

1.45 **Affirming the contract.** An employee may be disqualified from claiming constructive dismissal if he or she works on without protest under changed terms and conditions – in such a case, the employee may be deemed to have 'affirmed' the contract, meaning that he or she has waived the right to rely on the employer's breach. Whether affirmation arises in any particular case depends on the facts. In Melia v Green Contract Services Ltd (above), for example, the tribunal considered that, although M had waited for over four months following the loss of his pipe-fitting work, in the circumstances he had not affirmed the contract. The new duties he was given changed from week to week and he continued to hope that he would be put back on pipe-fitting work; he did not accept that he would be doing unskilled work forever. For a detailed consideration of how affirmation arises following a repudiatory breach of contract, see IDS Employment Law Handbook, 'Contracts of Employment' (2014), Chapter 11, 'Termination by dismissal', under 'Constructive dismissal – affirmation of the contract'.

1.46 **Anticipatory breach.** As noted above, an employee may resign in circumstances that amount to a constructive dismissal not only where his or her employer has already committed a fundamental breach of contract but where the employer has indicated an intention to commit such a breach. This is known as an anticipatory breach. Where the employer's intention to breach the contract is clear, the employee does not have wait for the employer to carry out the threat before he or she can resign and claim constructive dismissal – Wellworthy Ltd v Ellis EAT 915/83. However, there is a risk that an employee may act too hastily in resigning before the nature of the threatened breach is clear. Furthermore, there will be no constructive dismissal if the employee resigns after a threat to breach the contract is withdrawn – Norwest Holst Group Administration Ltd v Harrison 1985 ICR 668, CA.

1.47 **Lock-outs**

The definition of dismissal *for redundancy purposes* is circumscribed by S.136(2) where there has been a 'lock-out' by the employer. 'Lock-out', as defined by S.235(4), means:

- the closing of a place of employment

- the suspension of work, or

- the refusal by an employer to continue to employ any number of persons employed by it in consequence of a dispute,

done with a view to compelling persons employed by the employer, or to aid another employer in compelling persons employed by it, to accept terms or conditions of or affecting employment.

Although a lock-out is a repudiatory breach of contract by the employer, if an employee resigns without notice because of that breach, S.136(2) expressly prevents a claim of constructive dismissal under S.136(1)(c). This does not prevent an employee claiming constructive dismissal at common law, or indeed pursuing an unfair dismissal claim. However, it means that an employee will not normally be able to claim a redundancy payment in these circumstances.

Note, however, that S.136(2) only applies when the employee resigns without **1.48** notice: if an employee gives notice of resignation, it seems on the literal wording of the statute that a claim for constructive dismissal under S.136(1)(c) can still be made. However, it will still be up to the employee to convince a tribunal that the reason for the employer's lock-out was redundancy, which may not be easy.

Dismissal by operation of law **1.49**

Section 136(5) ERA provides that certain events which operate to terminate a contract of employment, but which do not normally amount to a 'dismissal', should be treated as a dismissal for the purposes of the statutory redundancy scheme. The subsection applies where a contract is terminated automatically in accordance with an enactment or rule of law by:

- an act on the part of an employer, or

- an event affecting an employer (including, in the case of an individual, the employer's death).

In these circumstances, if the employee's contract is not renewed, and he or she is not re-engaged under a new contract, he or she will be taken to be dismissed by reason of redundancy if the circumstances fall within the definition of redundancy – S.139(4) and (5). Note that it is only the act of the *employer* or an event affecting the *employer* that counts under S.136(5). If an employee is prevented from working by an enactment – e.g. for health and safety reasons – or by death or injury, this does not count as a dismissal.

Section 136(5) may be relevant in many situations. For example, in London **1.50** Borough of Haringey v Reynolds EAT 1070/98 the junior school of which R was head teacher was amalgamated with its sister infant school to create a single 'primary school', pursuant to the requirements of the Education Act

23

1996. R agreed to accept premature retirement but, because her acceptance was based on misrepresentations by her employer, the tribunal found that her agreement had been rescinded. It went on to find that R had been dismissed by virtue of S.136(5). The closure of the junior school in accordance with provisions of the 1996 Act, in conjunction with the employer's erroneous insistence that R had resigned (a rule of law dictates that such insistence amounts to dismissal – see Ely v YKK Fasteners (UK) Ltd 1994 ICR 164, CA), were found to be 'acts or events' for the purposes of that provision. The EAT upheld the tribunal's decision.

1.51 At common law there are several situations where a contract of employment is regarded as having ended automatically as a result of some act or event done or suffered by the employer. These include:

- *death of employer.* At common law, where the contract of employment is with an individual employer, the death of that employer will automatically terminate the contract – Farrow v Wilson 1869 LR 4 CP 744, Court of Common Pleas. An employee who is not re-engaged by the person to whom control of the business passes will be taken to be dismissed for redundancy if failure to renew or re-engage him or her is wholly or mainly attributable to redundancy – S.139(4) and (5)

- *change in employing partnership.* In Brace v Calder and ors 1895 2 QB 253, CA, it was held that a contract of employment with two or more partners is brought to an end by the retirement from the partnership of one or more of the partners, unless the terms of the contract provide otherwise. It may be easy, however, to infer that the party contracting with the partnership is agreeing to work for the partnership as from time to time constituted and that therefore a change in the firm would not of itself automatically terminate the contract – see Briggs v Oates 1990 ICR 473, ChD. However, this may not be true where there is a major change in the partnership such as the splitting of a partnership with both parts remaining in the same business or where one of only two partners retires – see Tunstall and anor v Condon and anor 1980 ICR 786, EAT; Briggs v Oates

- *appointment of receiver by court.* Receivership by order of the courts automatically terminates the company's contracts of employment – Reid v The Explosives Co Ltd 1887 19 QBD 264, CA

- *appointment of receiver by debenture holders as agent of company.* Generally, the appointment of such a receiver does not automatically terminate the employees' contracts of employment – In re Foster Clark Ltd's Indenture Trusts 1966 1 WLR 125, ChD. There are, however, three exceptions to this rule. First, if the receiver sells off the business the contracts of employment are (probably – the position is not entirely clear) automatically terminated at common law. This situation, however, is

24

now altered by the Transfer of Undertakings (Protection of Employment) Regulations 2006 SI 2006/264 (TUPE), as explained under 'Transfer of business' below. Secondly, the appointment may terminate the contract of employment of a particular employee if the receiver and that employee enter into a new contract inconsistent with the contract between that employee and the company – In re Mack Trucks (Britain) Ltd 1967 1 All ER 977, ChD. Thirdly, the appointment may terminate the contract of an employee whose continued employment is in conflict with the role and functions of the receiver – In re Mack Trucks. This is most likely to be the case with the directors of the company, whose powers of control and management tend to be suspended during receivership

- *appointment of receiver by debenture holders as agent of themselves.* This will (probably) terminate the company's contracts of employment – Hopley-Dodd v Highfield Motors (Derby) Ltd 1969 ITR 289, ET; Deaway Trading Ltd v Calverley and ors 1973 ICR 546, NIRC

- *winding-up order.* Where the order is a compulsory order, the company's contracts of employment are terminated. Any employees kept on are regarded as employed by the liquidator in his or her personal capacity – see, for example, Golding and Howard v Fire Auto and Marine Insurance Co Ltd 1968 ITR 372, ET. A resolution for the voluntary winding up of a company, however, does not of itself automatically terminate employment contracts – Fox Brothers (Clothes) Ltd (in liquidation) v Bryant 1979 ICR 64, EAT. Whether or not the contracts are terminated will depend on the facts. Where the business is being discontinued there may well be a termination – Reigate v Union Manufacturing Co (Ramsbottom) Ltd 1918 1 KB 592, CA. Similarly, there may also be a termination of at least some of the employment contracts where the continued employment of the employees is incompatible with any restructuring of the business – Fowler v Commercial Timber Co Ltd 1930 2 KB 1, CA

- *statutory regulations* may have the effect that the employer must terminate contracts of employment and would therefore rank as an event affecting the employer

- *frustration.* A contract of employment may come to an end when an unforeseen event makes performance of the contract impossible or radically different from what the parties originally intended – Davis Contractors Ltd v Fareham UDC 1956 AC 696, HL. The contract is then said to have been 'frustrated'. When a contract is frustrated it ends automatically by operation of law, without a dismissal on the part of the employer or a resignation on the part of the employee, and the parties are discharged from further obligations under it. The employee cannot therefore claim unfair dismissal and is not entitled to any notice or payment in lieu – GF Sharp and Co Ltd v McMillan 1998 IRLR 632, EAT – but will be able to claim a redundancy

25

payment under S.136(5) ERA if the frustrating event affects the employer. Most cases on frustration in the employment context, however, turn on whether an employee's long-term sickness (or imprisonment) has frustrated the contract (see 'Non-dismissals and problem areas – frustration' below). These are obviously not events 'affecting an employer' and so S.136(5) will not apply. But what of, for example, the situation where premises have been destroyed by bombing, or burnt down during riots? These situations may well amount to frustrating events automatically terminating the contracts of the employees involved. They are also events 'affecting [the] employer' and as such presumably fall within the scope of S.136(5). It does not matter if the event also affects the employee – British Airports Authority v Fenerty 1976 ICR 361, QBD.

1.52   **Intervention of regulatory authorities**

In Rose v Dodd 2005 ICR 1776, CA, a legal secretary's contract of employment was found not to have been terminated by operation of law when the Law Society intervened in the affairs of the sole practitioner firm for which she worked. Having considered the earlier decision of the EAT in Barnes and ors v Leavesley and ors 2001 ICR 38, EAT, the Court of Appeal confirmed that the effect on contracts of employment of the Law Society intervening in the affairs of the employing firm is dependent on the facts of each individual case. Where the intervention leads to a cessation of trading, the contracts of employment are terminated. Where, however, the parties continue to work under the contract after the intervention, and attempts are made to dispose of the firm as a going concern, the contracts of employment continue. If contracts continue, liability for redundancy pay can transfer to a new employer under the TUPE Regulations (see 'Transfer of Undertakings Regulations' below).

In Merrick (formerly t/a Wm A Merrick and Co Solicitors) v Simpson EAT 0349/10 the EAT confirmed that the principle in Rose v Dodd applies just as much to a situation where a solicitor is suspended from practice as it does to a situation where the Law Society intervenes in a solicitor's practice. Neither situation automatically terminates the employment of any of the solicitor's employees.

1.53   Note that many of the regulatory responsibilities of the Law Society have now been transferred to the Solicitors Regulation Authority. However, this would not appear to affect the principle established in Rose v Dodd.

1.54   **Transfer of business**

When a business is transferred from one employer to another, the TUPE Regulations (see 'Transfer of Undertakings Regulations' below) will usually apply. The main effect of the application of TUPE is that the transfer of the business does not operate to terminate the employees' contracts of employment. Instead, the contracts automatically transfer to the transferee, who then takes responsibility for all the employees' contractual and statutory rights connected with the employment relationship – Reg 4(1)–(2). As a result, there is no dismissal and no redundancy situation.

However, where TUPE does not apply, the contracts of employment are automatically terminated at common law. The employees will then be able to rely on S.136(5) to show a dismissal and may claim redundancy payments if it can be shown that there is a redundancy situation falling within S.139(1). This will not normally be difficult, particularly where the transferor ceases to trade after the transfer has taken place.

Special dismissals by statute 1.55

Under S.172 ERA the Secretary of State may provide by regulations that the termination of certain employments by statute will be deemed to be dismissals by reason of redundancy and that the statutory redundancy scheme will apply to them. Under S.172(2) this may happen even when the individuals concerned are not employees as defined by S.230. S.172 applies when a person is unwilling to be transferred from one statutory body to another. In practice, it has been used in connection with problems that have arisen concerning the amalgamation of police forces and fire brigades – see Chapter 5, 'Qualifications and exclusions', under 'Employees and excluded employees – office holders'.

Transfer of Undertakings Regulations 1.56

Where the transfer of a business falls within the scope of the Transfer of Undertakings (Protection of Employment) Regulations 2006 SI 2006/246 (TUPE), special rules apply to automatically transfer the contracts of employees employed in the undertaking at the time of the transfer to the new employer (the transferee) – see Reg 4(1) and (2). These rules are discussed briefly below. For a detailed consideration of the TUPE Regulations, see IDS Employment Law Handbook, 'Transfer of Undertakings' (2015).

Pre-transfer dismissals 1.57

In order for Reg 4(1) and (2) TUPE to have the effect of automatically transferring an employee's contract to the transferee, the employee must have been employed in the undertaking 'immediately before the transfer' or 'would have been so employed if [he or she] had not been dismissed in the circumstances described in Reg 7(1)' – Reg 4(3). The second limb owes its existence to the House of Lords' decision in Litster and ors v Forth Dry Dock and Engineering Co Ltd (in receivership) and anor 1989 ICR 341, HL,

27

which established that a transferee cannot avoid TUPE liability by having the transferor dismiss unwanted transferring employees in advance of, but not 'immediately before', the transfer.

By virtue of Reg 7(1), dismissals because of the transfer itself are automatically unfair, while dismissals for an 'economic, technical or organisational' (ETO) reason, as set out in Reg 7(2), are potentially fair. Put simply, then, where an employer dismisses an employee on the ostensible ground of redundancy prior to a transfer to which TUPE applies, liability for unfair dismissal and any redundancy payment will pass to the transferee if the real reason for the dismissal was the transfer itself. If the reason for the dismissal was an ETO reason then there is no automatically unfair dismissal (although there may be an ordinary unfair dismissal under S.98 ERA). In these circumstances, liability usually remains with the transferor. In determining who is liable for a pre-transfer dismissal the key issue, therefore, is whether the employee has been dismissed by reason of the transfer or for an ETO reason. This is discussed in IDS Employment Law Handbook, 'Transfer of Undertakings' (2015), Chapter 4, 'Unfair dismissal'. The question of whether the classic redundancy situation involving a diminution in the requirement for employees can constitute an ETO reason is dealt with in Chapter 8 of this Handbook, 'Unfair redundancy', under 'Automatically unfair redundancy – transfer of undertakings'.

1.58 Effect of employee objecting to transfer

The European Court of Justice confirmed in Katsikas v Konstantinidis 1993 IRLR 179, ECJ, that, under what is now the EU Acquired Rights Directive (No.2001/23), which TUPE implements, an employee is entitled to object to the transfer of his or her employment. This is reflected in Reg 4(7)–(11) TUPE, which states that the rules in Reg 4(1) and (2) providing for the automatic transfer of employment and of contractual rights and liabilities 'shall not operate to transfer [the employee's] contract of employment and the rights, powers, duties and liabilities under or in connection with it if the employee informs the transferor or the transferee that he objects to becoming employed by the transferee'.

The consequences of expressing such an objection are set out in Reg 4(8), which states that, subject to Reg 4(9) and (11), 'where an employee so objects, the relevant transfer shall operate so as to terminate his contract of employment with the transferor but he shall not be treated, for any purpose, as having been dismissed by the transferor'. The effect of an employee's objection to a transfer, therefore, is to prevent his or her contract of employment from passing to the transferee and to terminate his or her contract with the transferor. However, that termination will not generally – as Reg 4(8) states – amount to a dismissal. It could not therefore be argued that a termination of employment under Reg 4(8) counts as a dismissal by operation of law under S.136(5) ERA – see 'Dismissal by operation of law' above.

28

As noted above, the objection provision of Reg 4(8) is subject to Reg 4(9) and **1.59** (11). Reg 4(11) states that Reg 4(1), (7), (8) and (9) are 'without prejudice to the right of an employee arising apart from these Regulations to terminate his contract of employment without notice in acceptance of a repudiatory breach of contract by his employer'. This reflects the Court of Appeal's decision in Humphreys v Chancellor, Master and Scholars of the University of Oxford 2000 ICR 405, CA, where H, who was employed to mark examination papers, left his employer prior to a transfer because the transferee planned to deprive him of the life tenure he had enjoyed under the terms of his employment contract with the transferor. The Court of Appeal found that he had 'objected' to the transfer under what was then Reg 5(4A) of the Transfer of Undertakings (Protection of Employment) Regulations 1981 SI 1981/1794, and that his objection resulted in the termination of his contract of employment, which therefore did not pass to the transferee. Nevertheless, the Court ruled that H's objection did not remove his right to claim constructive dismissal. Furthermore, the Court held that the appropriate respondent for H's constructive dismissal claim was the transferor, since H never had a contractual relationship with the transferee. Thus, in such circumstances, if the transferor's reasons for breaching the employee's contract amount to a redundancy situation, the transferor may be liable to make a redundancy payment.

Regulation 4(9) states that an employee who would otherwise transfer under Reg 4(1) may object to a transfer on the basis that it 'involves or would involve a substantial change in working conditions to [his or her] material detriment'. Such an objection has the effect that the contract of employment is terminated and 'the employee shall be treated for any purpose as having been dismissed by the employer'. In effect, Reg 4(9) provides for a new form of constructive dismissal that does not depend on a repudiatory breach of contract.

In many circumstances, Reg 4(9) and Reg 4(11) dismissals will be automatically **1.60** unfair, as they will be treated as dismissals by reason of the transfer, within the meaning of Reg 7(1). However, if the employer can show an 'economic, technical or organisational' (ETO) reason for the dismissals, they will not be automatically unfair, and might well be carried out by reason of redundancy.

Note that the workings of Reg 4 are exceedingly complex and it would be impossible for us to provide a thorough examination of them here. For further details, see IDS Employment Law Handbook, 'Transfer of Undertakings' (2015), Chapter 4, 'Unfair dismissal'.

Non-dismissals and problem areas   1.61

As was made clear at the outset of this chapter, dismissal is the gateway through which employees must pass in order to claim a statutory redundancy payment: if there is no dismissal, there is no right to such a payment. Certain specific situations do not count as dismissals and it is important to recognise these.

29

1.62 Frustration

As discussed under 'Dismissal by operation of law' above, frustration of a contract arises when an unforeseen event makes performance of the contract impossible or radically different from what was envisaged when the contract was made – Davis Contractors Ltd v Fareham UDC 1956 AC 696, HL. When an employment contract is frustrated there is no dismissal: the contract simply comes to an end and neither party has any further obligations under it. However, certain frustrating events affecting the employer are treated as 'dismissals' for redundancy purposes by virtue of S.136(5) ERA – see 'Dismissal by operation of law' above.

In the employment context, the situations in which frustration is most likely to occur are where an employee is incapacitated by illness; is prevented from working by a sentence of imprisonment; or is excluded from his or her workplace at the behest of a third party. These are considered briefly in relation to redundancy below. For a more detailed treatment of the circumstances in which frustration terminates a contract of employment, see IDS Employment Law Handbook, 'Contracts of Employment' (2014), Chapter 13, 'Termination by operation of law', under 'Frustration'.

1.63 **Employee's illness.** An employee's prolonged or sudden serious illness or disability is capable of frustrating the employment contract. Whether or not it does so depends on a number of factors. The EAT in Egg Stores (Stamford Hill) Ltd v Leibovici 1977 ICR 260, EAT, set out the following relevant considerations:

- the length of previous employment

- the expected future duration of employment

- the nature of the job

- the nature, length and effect of the illness or disabling event

- the employer's need for the work to be done and need for a replacement to do it

- the risk to the employer of acquiring employment protection obligations towards a replacement employee

- whether the employee has continued to be paid

- the acts and statements of the employer in relation to the employment, including the dismissal of, or failure to dismiss, the employee; and

- whether a reasonable employer could be expected to wait any longer for the employee to return.

The judgment in Leibovici was subsequently considered by the EAT in Williams v Watsons Luxury Coaches Ltd 1990 ICR 536, EAT. Having reviewed the concept of frustration in the field of employment law, the EAT made it clear that tribunals should guard against too easy an application of the doctrine, especially when redundancy occurs. Moreover, although it is not necessary to determine a specific date upon which frustration occurred, it may be helpful to attempt to do so as it may assist the tribunal in determining whether there is a true frustration situation. The EAT went on to endorse the factors identified in Leibovici, and added two more of its own:

- the contractual terms as to sick pay, and

- the prospects of recovery.

Where the contract expressly or impliedly makes provision for sickness **1.64** absence or long-term or permanent incapacity on the ground of ill health and envisages that the contract will continue to subsist, it will be harder to show that it has been frustrated. This is especially so in the case of long-serving employees whose contracts are expected to continue indefinitely – see James v The Greytree Trust EAT 699/95. As the High Court pointed out in Villella v MFI Furniture Centres Ltd 1999 IRLR 468, QBD, for frustration to occur there must be some outside event not foreseen or provided for by the parties at the time of contracting. Thus, since the employee's contract in that case expressly foresaw and provided for long-term incapacity under a permanent health insurance scheme, it followed that the fact that the employee subsequently became incapacitated was incapable of frustrating the contract.

The EAT also pointed out in Williams v Watsons Luxury Coaches Ltd (above) that as a result of the decision in FC Shepherd and Co Ltd v Jerrom 1986 ICR 802, CA, it is clear that a party alleging frustration should not be allowed to rely on the frustrating event if it was caused by the fault of that party. This would appear to prevent an employer treating an employee's contract of employment as frustrated in circumstances where the employee has become unable to work due to injuries sustained as a result of the employer's negligence. In Smith v Wingate Signs Ltd ET Case No.2408674/07, an unfair dismissal case, S was injured in an accident at work and went on sick leave. At the time, his employer had begun to have discussions with him about redundancy and the possibility of alternative work. There was little communication between S and his employer from April 2005, when his right to sick pay expired, until 27 July 2007, when S phoned to say he was fit to return to work. The employer maintained that S had resigned and was no longer an employee. S claimed unfair dismissal and an issue arose as to whether his contract had in fact been frustrated. However, the tribunal held that S had been unfairly dismissed. On the evidence the accident was caused by the employer's breach of duty to provide a safe system of work; that being so, the contract was not frustrated. S was dismissed on 27 July, when he was told that he was no longer an employee.

1.65 Three contrasting examples:

- **Marshall v Harland and Wolff Ltd and anor** 1972 ICR 101, NIRC: M was a shipyard fitter with 23 years' service who had been off work with angina for 18 months. There was no medical evidence of permanent incapacity and M himself expected to recover and return to work after an operation. His employment came to an end when the employer closed his workplace. The NIRC held that the contract had not been frustrated: there was no evidence that future performance would be impossible or radically different from what was originally envisaged

- **Hurst v Bailey Parkinson Tea Ltd and anor** EAT 842/95: H was off sick from mid-1991 with diabetes. In March 1992 the employer secured a report from H's doctor which said that H's condition was deteriorating and that it was unlikely he would ever work again. The employer took no steps to terminate H's contract. In 1994 the company ceased trading and all the staff were dismissed with redundancy payments. H claimed a redundancy payment. The tribunal decided that H's contract had been frustrated by his illness and that he had no entitlement to redundancy pay

- **Hanif v Secretary of State for Trade and Industry** EAT 1327/97: H was a 'stentor' at a textile firm. He had worked for his employer for nine years when he went off work with knee pain. Five years later the company went into administrative receivership and H had still not returned to work. He had been kept 'on the books' but not paid his salary. He claimed a redundancy payment from the Secretary of State, who refused to pay on the basis that his contract of employment had been frustrated. The EAT upheld this refusal, saying that while long-term sickness is something which every employment contract envisages, five years was so protracted a period that the contract was frustrated.

Once a contract has been frustrated, the parties to it cannot elect to keep it alive – GF Sharp and Co Ltd v McMillan 1998 IRLR 632, EAT.

1.66 *Disability discrimination.* Where an employee's ill health or injury amounts to a disability for the purposes of the Equality Act 2010 (EqA), not only must the employer refrain from discriminating against the employee on the ground of that disability but it has a statutory obligation to make reasonable adjustments to alleviate the disadvantage the employee experiences as a result of the disability. A finding that a contract has been frustrated would seriously undermine that protection. Addressing that issue in Warner v Armfield Retail and Leisure Ltd 2014 ICR 239, EAT, the EAT held that, in the case of a disabled person, before the doctrine of frustration can apply the tribunal must first consider whether the employer is in breach of a duty to make reasonable adjustments. If there is something which (applying the provisions of the EqA) it is reasonable to expect the employer to do in order to keep the employee in employment, the doctrine of frustration can have no application.

32

Imprisonment of employee. According to the Court of Appeal in FC 1.67
Shepherd and Co Ltd v Jerrom 1986 ICR 802, CA, a custodial sentence is
capable in law of frustrating an employment contract. Whether or not it does
so will depend on such factors as the likely length of absence, how necessary
it is to replace the employee, and whether it is necessary to find a permanent,
rather than a temporary, replacement. In the Jerrom case it was held that a
borstal sentence of between six months and two years, which was expected
to last nine months, frustrated the four-year contract of a single apprentice in
a fairly small company. However, the Court pointed out that such a sentence
would not necessarily frustrate the contract of a general labourer in a very
large company with a tradition of hiring temporary labour. In Mecca Ltd v
Shepherd EAT 379/78, on the other hand, the EAT held that a short prison
sentence of 20 days ('no longer than the period of an annual holiday') was
not enough to frustrate the contract.

In order for frustration to arise, the imprisonment must actually prevent the
employee performing his or her obligations under the contract. In Wills v
RWE npower plc ET Case No.2701870/13 W was told that his employment
was to end on 31 March 2013 on the ground of redundancy and that he would
be paid an enhanced redundancy payment of £30,803.18 on termination.
However, on 18 February 2013 W was convicted of ten counts of criminal
offences involving indecent photographs and images of children. He did not
tell RWE plc about his arrest or his court appearance. Instead, he arranged
to take leave from 11 March, the date on which he was sentenced to two
years' imprisonment. RWE plc found out about the conviction and sentence
from local press reports and, on 13 March, wrote to W saying that his prison
sentence frustrated his contract of employment and that he was not entitled to
notice or redundancy pay. A tribunal upheld W's claim for breach of contract.
It reasoned that, if W's contract were expected to continue after the end of
his leave, the two-year prison sentence would have frustrated the contract
but that was not the case here. W's authorised leave ran until the end of his
employment and so the length of the prison sentence was immaterial. The
simple fact of his being imprisoned did not frustrate the contract because it
made no difference to the contract's performance.

Exclusion from place of work. The employee's exclusion from his or her 1.68
place of work by a third party may also frustrate the employment contract.
In Stanley Wattam Ltd v Rippin EAT 355/98 R was employed by SW Ltd as
a chicken sexer. She was seconded to work at the employer's most important
customer, P, but was subsequently banned from their premises. With no other
possibility of seconding R to another site, SW Ltd eventually sent her her P45.
On appeal, the EAT ruled that the tribunal had erred in finding that R had
been dismissed. Since R had been excluded from her place of work by a third
party (P) and P had refused to change its mind, there were no alternative ways
of continuing R's contract.

33

The EAT's decision in Stanley Wattam is surprising in view of the fact that the employee's expulsion from the customer's premises did not bring her contract to an end automatically. On the contrary, as the employment tribunal found, the contract continued as the employer was prepared to go on employing her at other premises. It seems from the facts that the contract terminated because it was not practicable for the employee to take up the only alternative jobs available to her, which, arguably, is more akin to redundancy than frustration. However, a similar conclusion was reached in Manpower UK Ltd v Mulford EAT 0148/03, where the company on whose premises M worked removed him from his assignment after almost two years because of high levels of sickness. He was then offered different work by M Ltd but for various reasons he was only able to accept one job, after which he declined to do any further work for M Ltd. The EAT held that his contract with M Ltd had been frustrated when the company on whose premises he worked no longer wished to hire him.

1.69 Termination by mutual consent

Since a dismissal is the unilateral act of the employer, it follows that there is no dismissal where the employer and the employee agree to terminate the employment contract. In theory, the distinction between a dismissal by an employer and a consensual termination should be clear enough but in practice it is not always so easily made. The question of whether the employee was dismissed is a question of fact for the tribunal to decide – Scott and ors v Coalite Fuels and Chemicals Ltd 1988 ICR 355, EAT – and some situations that are presented as 'voluntary redundancy' may on examination turn out to be dismissals. There is still a dismissal for redundancy if the employee agrees to the employer's proposal of redundancy or if the employee volunteers for redundancy or even if the employee persuades the employer to dismiss him or her. In practice, however, the distinction between a situation where the employee and the employer agree to terminate the contract and the situation where the employee invites the employer to dismiss him or her may be narrow.

Some examples:

• **Optare Group Ltd v TGWU** 2007 IRLR 931, EAT: three employees volunteered to leave their posts at the start of a redundancy exercise. Upholding an employment tribunal's decision, the EAT held that these voluntary redundancies did amount to dismissals and that it was immaterial that the employees might have accepted a similar package even in the absence of a redundancy situation. However, the EAT noted that the result would have been different had there been evidence that the employees were anxious to leave and had expressed this wish independently of, or prior to, a redundancy situation arising

• **Burton, Allton and Johnson Ltd v Peck** 1975 ICR 193, QBD: P had been off work for several months and on his return it was found that there was no work for him. He claimed a redundancy payment. The employer argued that because P had been 'only too willing to be dismissed for redundancy' there had been a termination by mutual consent. The High Court held that an employee's agreement to redundancy is no ground for holding that a dismissal did not take place

- **Morley and ors v CT Morley Ltd** 1985 ICR 499, EAT: a father and two sons were employees and sole directors of a family business. The business was in financial difficulty and the directors decided that one of them would have to go. The father volunteered to leave and claimed a redundancy payment. Later, the two remaining directors agreed that the company would cease trading. The EAT held that: (i) the father had volunteered for redundancy and had been dismissed; and (ii) although the sons had taken the decision (as directors) to dismiss themselves (as employees), they had still been dismissed by the company

- **Walley v Morgan** 1969 ITR 122, Div Ct: M was employed on W's farm. In 1967 all the livestock was destroyed because of foot-and-mouth disease. M persuaded W to dismiss him and then claimed a redundancy payment. The Court held that the fact that W was persuaded to take the decision to dismiss did not mean that there was no dismissal.

A more recent example can be found in Francis v Pertemps Recruitment Partnership Ltd EATS 0003/13. F was employed by a recruitment agency, PRP Ltd, to work for a specific client. When the client no longer required F's services, PRP Ltd offered him two weeks' notice pay and the choice between PRP Ltd looking to find him another assignment or a redundancy payment. F accepted the second option and later complained of unfair dismissal. An employment tribunal found that the parties had mutually terminated the contract and that there was no dismissal. The EAT overturned the tribunal's decision on appeal. In its view, the employee did not have a choice between staying in employment with PRP Ltd on the one hand and his employment being terminated on the other. Unlike the contracts of employment of the majority of PRP Ltd's employees, F's contract required him to work for a specific client and did not entitle the agency to place him with any client on any assignment. Therefore, as soon as the client in question indicated that it had no further need for F's services, F's contract with PRP Ltd could no longer be honoured and – since F had not consented to it being altered – had to be terminated. According to the EAT, the crucial issue was who brought the contract to an end and where, as in this case, an employee is given two options, both of which involve dismissal, the only sensible conclusion is that the dismissal is intended by the person offering those options. **1.70**

In the above examples the tribunals and courts looked beyond what appeared to be a voluntary termination by the employee to find that it was in fact the employer who brought the contract to an end. However, there may be

35

circumstances where the tables are turned and a termination that is effected by way of dismissal is in fact found to be a voluntary termination. In Khan v HGS Global Ltd and anor EAT 0176/15, for example, the EAT upheld a tribunal's decision that there had been a consensual termination of K's contract when K opted for redundancy. K was a team manager in a call centre. His team was subject to a transfer under the Transfer of Undertakings (Protection of Employment) Regulations 2006 SI 2006/246, which meant that their workplace would move from Chiswick to High Wycombe. HGSG Ltd announced that those employees, like K, who thereby faced an increased journey time of over 75 minutes would have the option of relocating, applying for any available roles within HGSG Ltd, or taking redundancy. K opted for redundancy and received a statutory redundancy payment plus pay in lieu of notice and holiday pay. When he then sought to claim unfair dismissal, a tribunal found that he had not been dismissed for the purpose of S.95 ERA. It was satisfied that K understood that he was being offered a choice and that he did not feel pressured into leaving. On appeal, the EAT accepted that the tribunal had not fully appreciated that, following Optare Group Ltd v Transport and General Workers' Union (above), even a non-pressured termination may still amount to a dismissal. However, the EAT was satisfied that this was not a situation where K was volunteering for dismissal. He had made a free choice. Although HGSG Ltd had put K's decision into effect by formally dismissing him, that was merely the mechanism of the termination – it represented the form but not the reality.

1.71 Even where both employer and employee are willing to terminate employment voluntarily it is important that they agree on the details. In Manning v Metropolitan Police Authority ET Case No.2349913/11 M, who worked as a police community support officer, was placed on the MPA's redeployment list because of a series of sickness absences. In November 2010, the MPA began a voluntary redundancy scheme and M made an expression of interest and signed a voluntary redundancy declaration form. The form expressly stated that employees could withdraw their application for redundancy at any time until they received their exact statement of benefits and agreed a leaving date. M was away from work at the time and his manager agreed his leaving date with HR as 31 December 2010. It was only during the course of a telephone call on 31 December that M learnt of this and he was not told that he could change his mind about volunteering to leave. A tribunal upheld M's complaint of unfair dismissal, rejecting the argument that there had been a termination by mutual consent in the form of a voluntary redundancy. For termination to be mutual there would have to be an agreed leaving date, which was absent in this case – the MPA had simply assumed that M would leave on 31 December.

1.72 **Early retirement.** A common form of termination by mutual consent is termination on the ground of early retirement, whereby the employee seeks (or is offered) early retirement as an alternative to redundancy. A request for early retirement can lead to a dismissal if the request is clearly not voluntary. In Vanneck-Murray v Governors of St Mary's College, Twickenham EAT 611/82, for example, it was arranged that V, a teacher, would go on leave until she reached the age of 50 and then receive an accelerated, but reduced, pension. The alternative was disciplinary proceedings likely to result in her dismissal. The EAT upheld a finding that this was a constructive dismissal, not a termination by agreement, although it was justified in view of V's conduct. In Schoon v UNISON EAT 850/95, on the other hand, the EAT held that S had agreed to early retirement even though his employer had made it plain that if S did not agree to leave, investigatory procedures, preliminary to a disciplinary hearing, would be reinstated. The EAT said that the tribunal was entitled to find that this did not amount to holding a 'metaphorical pistol' to S's head.

However, the distinction between voluntary and enforced early retirement is not always an easy one to make. In Birch and anor v University of Liverpool 1985 ICR 470, CA, B and another employee made requests for early retirement under a scheme offered by the university in the context that compulsory redundancies would be needed if not enough volunteers were forthcoming. The requests were granted and the two employees were asked to make formal applications to retire on a stated date, after which the university wrote to them confirming that it was in the 'managerial interest' for them to retire and requesting them to do so on the stated date. The EAT and the Court of Appeal both held that this was not a dismissal but a termination by mutual agreement reached between the employer and the employees.

Where an employee has been issued with a notice of dismissal for redundancy and later takes early retirement instead, the position is not at all clear. In Scott and ors v Coalite Fuels and Chemicals Ltd 1988 ICR 355, EAT, written notices of redundancy were sent to the employees but in the ensuing negotiations they agreed to take early retirement as an alternative to redundancy. A tribunal concluded that the notices had been impliedly withdrawn by the employer and waived by the employees. A majority of the EAT held that there were no dismissals as the notices had been superseded by the subsequent agreement. The notice of dismissal did not prevent the parties agreeing to terminate the contract in some other way. By contrast, in Gateshead Metropolitan Borough Council v Mills EAT 610/92 M was given one year's notice of redundancy. He applied, and was accepted, for early retirement. A tribunal decided that he was also entitled to a redundancy payment on the ground that he had been dismissed and the notice had never been withdrawn. The Council relied on Scott and ors v Coalite Fuels and Chemicals Ltd (above) and argued that, once the agreement to take early retirement had been reached, it had impliedly withdrawn the notice. The EAT rejected this argument, holding that the notice could not be withdrawn without the consent of the employee. There was no express consent by M and no evidence that he had impliedly consented. The agreement to take early retirement was not inconsistent with a dismissal for redundancy and the tribunal had been correct to find that there had been a dismissal.

1.73

Employers would therefore be well advised to seek an employee's written consent to the withdrawal of a notice of redundancy when negotiating early retirement if they want to avoid making a redundancy payment to the employee.

1.74 Agreement not to renew fixed-term contract

In Manson and anor v University of Strathclyde and anor EAT 356/87 the EAT considered whether an agreement not to renew a fixed-term contract was a dismissal. In that case M and J had been employed on a series of fixed-term contracts by the University of Strathclyde. The latest contract was due to expire on 31 December 1985. In 1984 the university decided to seek outside funding to set up a company for the commercial exploitation of M and J's research. On 1 January 1986 M and J commenced employment with the new company and claimed redundancy payments from the university. In turning down their applications, the EAT found that the university had not told M and J that their fixed-term contracts would not be renewed; that they had agreed to leave the university and go to the company; and that at no time were they put under any pressure to leave. Although non-renewal of a fixed-term contract could be a dismissal (see 'Expiry of limited-term contract' above), in this case there was a termination by mutual consent.

1.75 Alternative employment

It is worth noting here that S.138(1) ERA provides that for the purposes of the statutory redundancy scheme, when an employee accepts a renewal of his or her contract or a re-engagement to take effect within four weeks of the old contract ending, there is no dismissal. The offer may be from the original employer or from an associated employer – S.146. However, S.138(1) applies only for the purposes of the statutory redundancy scheme and does not prevent an employee who has been re-employed from bringing an unfair dismissal claim – Jones v Governing Body of Burdett Coutts School 1997 ICR 390, EAT. Alternative job offers are discussed in Chapter 3, 'Alternative job offers'.

1.76 Mobility clauses

There will be no dismissal where an employer exercises a contractual mobility clause to move an employee to a different workplace. However, an employer seeking to exercise a mobility clause to avoid a redundancy situation should tread carefully.

First, the employer needs to ensure that the clause in question authorises its actions. In Smith and anor v Westside Day Nursery Ltd ET Case No.1802542/09 WDN Ltd operated four nurseries in Hull, and S and W worked in one of them. Their contracts of employment specified that they 'may be required to work at other locations'. The staff handbook, which neither was ever given, provided that employees might be required to relocate on a permanent basis.

38

In early 2009, WDN Ltd decided to close the nursery where S and W worked and informed them that they would be relocated to one of the other nurseries. A tribunal upheld their claims for a redundancy payment on the basis that they had not been told where to report for work once the nursery closed, and were thus dismissed. In any event, the tribunal considered that the wording of the mobility clause was ineffective to enable WDN Ltd to transfer employees permanently. The contract described their nursery as their 'usual' place of work. A power to transfer temporarily, however, would have been consistent with the wording of the clause.

Secondly, employers need to take care as to how they exercise the power to move the employee. In Curling and ors v Securicor Ltd 1992 IRLR 549, EAT, S Ltd had the benefit of a contractual mobility clause allowing it to relocate staff to Head Office or to one of its branch offices. When the company lost its tender to manage the detention centre where C worked it entered into negotiations over redundancies and alternative employment. At no time during the negotiations did the company seek to invoke the contractual mobility clause. However, when C and a number of his colleagues subsequently brought claims for redundancy payments in the tribunal, S Ltd argued that the existence of the mobility clause meant that there had been no dismissals and that no redundancy situation arose. Overturning the tribunal's finding that none of the employees had been dismissed, the EAT clarified that if an employer seeks to rely on the benefit of a mobility clause when making changes to jobs or the location of work, then it must make its position clear in that respect. It is not open to an employer to switch between applying redundancy procedures and invoking a mobility clause in the hope of settling on the most advantageous option. **1.77**

The Curling decision was considered by the Court of Appeal in Home Office v Evans and anor 2008 ICR 302, CA. In that case E and L were employed as immigration officers at Waterloo Station. Their contracts included a clause allowing them to be transferred 'anywhere' in the UK or abroad. When the Home Office decided that immigration services at Waterloo would be closed down, it considered invoking the redundancy procedures set out in a collective agreement. However, following legal advice, the decision was taken to invoke the mobility clause and affected staff were apprised of this at the time the closure was announced in spring 2004. When the Home Office informed E and L in August 2004 that they were to be moved to Heathrow, they resigned and claimed constructive dismissal. Both the tribunal and the EAT agreed that the Home Office was not entitled to change its mind on the redundancy/ mobility issue before finally and publicly announcing its position, since this amounted to the kind of switching identified in the Curling case. Allowing the appeal, the Court of Appeal stated that neither the tribunal nor the EAT had properly understood or applied Curling. In Curling, the employer had shifted from implementing a redundancy procedure to relying upon a mobility clause

39

at a much later stage of the proceedings – in fact, at the tribunal hearing itself. At that point, having already implemented the redundancy procedure, the employer's about-face was too late. By contrast, there was no question in the instant case of the Home Office switching from one contractual procedure to another, of leaving it too late to invoke the mobility clause or of waiving its right to invoke that clause. Rather, at all times after its staff announcement, the Home Office clearly and consistently followed the contractual mobility procedure and not the redundancy procedure.

1.78 It follows from these decisions that the announcement to staff that the workplace is to close is likely to be the point of no return. The employer must have made up its mind prior to that point as to whether it intends to invoke a contractual mobility clause or follow a redundancy procedure, which would include consideration of alternative employment.

(Note that mobility clauses may also be relevant when it comes to establishing the place of employment for the purpose of the statutory definition of redundancy. This is discussed in Chapter 2, 'Redundancy', under 'Closure of workplace – place of employment'.)

2 Redundancy

A dismissed employee is only entitled to a redundancy payment if he or she **2.1** has been dismissed wholly or mainly *by reason of redundancy*. 'Redundancy' is exhaustively defined in S.139(1) of the Employment Rights Act 1996 (ERA) and covers three broad scenarios: the closure of the business, the closure of the workplace, and where there is a diminishing need for employees to do the available work. In this chapter we examine the meaning of redundancy and consider when a dismissal will be 'by reason of' redundancy. The concept of 'dismissal' is discussed in Chapter 1, 'Dismissal'.

Presumption of redundancy   2.2

In the context of a tribunal claim for a statutory redundancy payment, there is a presumption that an employee who has been dismissed has been dismissed for redundancy unless the contrary is proved – S.163(2) ERA. In practice, therefore, if an employer wants to resist making a redundancy payment it must prove, on the balance of probabilities, that the dismissal was not for redundancy. That is not to say, however, that only the employer's evidence will be relevant to the question of redundancy, or that there is any formal burden on the employer. The tribunal will have regard to all the evidence, including that adduced by the employee, to decide whether the presumption has been rebutted. Thus, in Greater Glasgow Health Board v Lamont EATS 0019/12 agreement between the parties that the claimant's limited-term contract had ended because a seconded employee had returned to her usual job was sufficient to rebut the presumption of redundancy.

An example of the application of the presumption is given by Willcox and anor v Hastings and anor 1987 IRLR 298, CA. In that case the two claimants were employed by H. One of their posts became redundant and H wished to give the other to his son. Both claimants were dismissed and claimed redundancy payments. The tribunal was unable to decide which claimant had been dismissed for which reason and therefore dismissed the claims. The Court of Appeal held

41

that the tribunal had failed to have regard to the statutory presumption. If the presumption had been taken into account, the tribunal would have concluded that the employer had failed to rebut it in respect of both claims and that both claimants were entitled to a redundancy payment.

2.3 The presumption of redundancy only applies in claims for a redundancy payment and not in unfair dismissal cases. In an unfair dismissal claim, there is no presumption as to the reason for dismissal and it is for the employer to show that it had a potentially fair reason. This can cause curious results where the employee brings a claim for both redundancy and unfair dismissal. In Midland Foot Comfort Centre v Moppett and anor 1973 ICR 219, NIRC, for example, M brought claims for a redundancy payment and unfair dismissal. The tribunal was unable to determine from the employer's vague evidence what the real reason for the dismissal was so it held that the presumption of redundancy had not been rebutted and allowed M's redundancy pay claim to succeed. It went on to find that the employer had failed to show a reason for the dismissal (although redundancy would have been an 'acceptable' reason) and upheld M's unfair dismissal claim as well. The decision was upheld by the National Industrial Relations Court (the precursor to the EAT) on appeal.

2.4 Definition of 'redundancy'

Redundancy is defined in S.139(1) ERA and the definition applies both to claims for redundancy payments (see Chapter 6, 'Redundancy payments') and to unfair dismissal claims (see Chapter 8, 'Unfair redundancy'). The statutory words are:

'For the purposes of this Act an employee who is dismissed shall be taken to be dismissed by reason of redundancy if the dismissal is wholly or mainly attributable to –

(a) the fact that his employer has ceased or intends to cease –

 (i) to carry on the business for the purposes of which the employee was employed by him, or

 (ii) to carry on that business in the place where the employee was so employed, or

(b) the fact that the requirements of that business –

 (i) for employees to carry out work of a particular kind, or

 (ii) for employees to carry out work of a particular kind in the place where the employee was employed by the employer, have ceased or diminished or are expected to cease or diminish.'

This is a broad definition that covers a myriad of situations. One of the most common misconceptions about redundancy is that it only arises where the employer is in financial trouble or struggling to provide work. In Kingwell and ors v Elizabeth Bradley Designs Ltd EAT 0661/02 Mr Justice Burton addressed the confusion thus: 'It appears to us that there is a fundamental misunderstanding about the question of redundancy. Redundancy does not only arise where there is a poor financial situation at the employer's... It does not only arise where there is a diminution of work in the hands of an employer... It can occur where there is a successful employer with plenty of work, but who, perfectly sensibly as far as commerce and economics is concerned, decides to reorganise his business because he concludes that he is overstaffed. Thus, even with the same amount of work and the same amount of income, the decision is taken that [a] lesser number of employees are required to perform the same functions. That too is a redundancy situation.' For example, in Stephens v Franchill Ltd ET Case No.1304157/15 an employment tribunal accepted that there was a genuine redundancy situation even where the employer was turning down offers of work. The employer had taken the decision not to seek to grow the business and instead to wind down and this satisfied the statutory definition of redundancy.

However, not every business reorganisation will lead to redundancies. Where, **2.5** for example, an employer decides that its aims may be achieved by redeploying employees or by dismissing them and immediately re-engaging them on different terms and conditions, the definition of redundancy in S.139(1) may not be met – see 'Redundancy or reorganisation?' below. (Note, however, that the definition of redundancy for the purpose of collective consultation under the Trade Union and Labour Relations (Consolidation) Act 1992 is wider, so even if such a reorganisation does not fall within the definition of redundancy under the ERA, it may nonetheless trigger the statutory consultation procedure – see Chapter 12, 'Collective redundancies'.)

It is convenient for discussion to split the definition into three 'redundancy situations':

• closure of the business

• closure of the employee's workplace

• a diminishing need for employees to do the available work.

While these three basic descriptions are convenient for discussion, it is always important to have regard to the exact wording of S.139(1), as a dismissal is not a redundancy unless it falls within that section.

Temporary cessation and diminution   2.6
Section 139(6) ERA provides that the word 'cease' in S.139(1) means either a temporary or a permanent cessation of the business and 'diminish' means either a

43

temporary or a permanent diminution. Where a business is closed on a temporary basis, it is a question of fact for the tribunal whether the closure amounts to a 'cessation' of the business for the purposes of the redundancy scheme.

Two contrasting examples:

- **Gemmell v Darngavil Brickworks Ltd** 1967 ITR 20, ET: G was dismissed when his employer closed down the brickworks for machinery repairs. The closure lasted 13 weeks and G was unemployed for 11 of them before he found another job. This was a temporary cessation of the business which entitled him to a redundancy payment

- **Whitbread plc t/a Whitbread Berni Inns v Flatter and ors** EAT 287/94: F and others were dismissed when their employer closed the Berni Inn restaurant in which they worked. Four weeks later the business reopened as a brasserie and the employees claimed unfair dismissal. The EAT upheld the tribunal's finding that there was no redundancy situation because a four-week closure for refurbishment was not a temporary 'cessation' within the meaning of the statute. In the tribunal's view, S.139(1)(a), read with S.139(6), is 'restricted to situations where the business ceases for a significant period even if there is an intention in the future to open it, but not a situation where the operation is closed temporarily for refurbishment'. (The issue of whether the change in the type of restaurant amounted to a cessation of the old business is discussed under 'Closure of business' below.)

2.7 Associated employers

Section 139(2) ERA states that, for the purpose of the statutory definition of redundancy, the 'business' of an employer may be treated as one with the business of any associated employer. Two employers are 'associated' if one is a company controlled (directly or indirectly) by the other (who may be a company, but does not have to be) – S.231(a) – or if both are companies controlled (directly or indirectly) by another employer (who again may be a company, but does not have to be) – S.231(b).

'Company' means a limited company – Merton London Borough Council v Gardiner 1981 ICR 186, CA. However, this requirement has been modified to permit overseas companies to come within the definition – Hancill v Marcon Engineering Ltd 1990 ICR 103, EAT – and, indeed, partnerships consisting of limited companies – Pinkney v Sandpiper Drilling Ltd and ors 1989 ICR 389, EAT.

2.8 There is some judicial dispute as to what is meant by 'control' in the context of S.231. In Secretary of State for Employment v Newbold and ors 1981 IRLR 305, EAT, the EAT held that 'control' means control of more than 50 per cent of the votes attaching to shares, and is not a question of how or by whom the enterprise is actually run on a 'de facto' basis. However, in Tice v Cartwright 1999 ICR 769, EAT, the EAT ruled that an employment tribunal had been correct to hold that a partnership of two brothers had indirect control of a company in which the brothers each had a 50 per cent share, so that the partnership and the company were associated employers within the meaning of S.231(a) ERA. The EAT considered that in the circumstances of that case, 'control' dealt with practical rather than theoretical matters, and the correct legal test was of 'de facto' control. The EAT applied this analysis more recently in Schwarzenbach and anor t/a Thames-side Court Estate v Jones EAT 0100/15 to uphold an employment tribunal's decision that a company said to be 'at arm's length' from the respondent Schwarzenbach family was associated with them, even though it was owned by a chain of offshore companies the legal control of which was unclear. The tribunal had concluded that the companies were set up for an identifiable human beneficiary or beneficiaries and that it was reasonable to infer that this was a member or members of the Schwarzenbach family.

The question of 'control' for the purpose of defining an associated employer is discussed in greater depth in IDS Employment Law Handbook, 'Continuity of Employment' (2012), Chapter 4, 'Changes in employer', under 'Associated employer'.

2.9 The practical effect of S.139(2) is that a group of companies may, if it so chooses, select employees for redundancy from any part of the group, whether or not there is a redundancy situation in each individual company. The group can be looked at as a whole when applying a redundancy selection procedure. One further point to note: S.139(3) provides that, for the purpose of the redundancy scheme, schools maintained by a local authority may be treated as a single business. Thus, if there is a redundancy situation at any of them, all the local authority's maintained schools can be treated as if they were a group of associated companies. This applies whether the staff are employed by the local authority itself or by the governing body of the relevant school.

Lay-off and short-time   2.10
If an employee is laid off or kept on short-time, instead of being dismissed, he or she has no entitlement to a redundancy payment under S.139. A claim for a redundancy payment may however be made under the special provisions described in Chapter 4, 'Lay-off and short-time'.

Redundancy or reorganisation?   2.11
Confusion can arise as to the difference between a 'redundancy' and a 'reorganisation'. Often employers are uncertain as to whether the changes they are planning to make to working structures simply amount to a reorganisation or will give rise to a redundancy situation, in which case a proper redundancy exercise must be undertaken and redundancy payments will need to be made. However, redundancy and reorganisation are not

45

necessarily mutually exclusive. 'Redundancy' is a technical, legal definition; while 'reorganisation' simply means a change in working structures and has no specific legal meaning. As the EAT put it in Corus and Regal Hotels plc v Wilkinson EAT 0102/03: 'Each case involving consideration of the question whether a business reorganisation has resulted in a redundancy situation must be decided on its own particular facts. The mere fact of reorganisation is not in itself conclusive of redundancy or, conversely, of an absence of redundancy.'

A particular reorganisation may therefore involve making redundancies if the definition of redundancy is met; or it may not – where, for example, work is redistributed more efficiently without the need for a reduction in the number of employees doing a particular kind of work. (Conversely, redundancy may occur without the business being reorganised at all.) The EAT accepted in Barot v London Borough of Brent EAT 0539/11 that 'a reorganisation of a business that involves simply reshuffling the workforce may not create a redundancy situation if the business requires just as much work of a particular kind in question and just as many employees to do it, even if individual jobs disappear as a result'. There, it upheld an employment tribunal's decision that the significant restructuring of the Council's Children and Families Directorate entailed a reduction in the kind of work being done by B. The reorganisation involved a reduction in lower level, 'number-crunching' tasks and an increase in capacity for more senior and strategic work, which the tribunal was entitled to find met the statutory definition of redundancy.

2.12 Although business restructurings are often precipitated by financial crises and economic downturns, not all amount to redundancy. What is crucial, as the Barot case (above) affirms, is whether the restructuring essentially entails a reduction in the number of employees doing work of a particular kind as opposed to a mere repatterning or redistribution of the same work among different employees whose numbers nonetheless remain the same. So where, for example, a senior employee is dismissed because his or her work is to be done in future by an employee of lower status, the reason for dismissal will not be 'redundancy', although it may be for 'some other substantial reason of a kind such as to justify the dismissal' within the meaning of S.98(1)(b) ERA – see Pillinger v Manchester Area Health Authority 1979 IRLR 430, EAT. In contrast, where the purpose of a reorganisation is to reduce the size of the workforce overall as a reflection of the diminished business need for particular kinds of work, this will constitute redundancy.

The distinction between these different types of reorganisation is often difficult to draw in practice. The following cases illustrate just how subtle the distinction can be:

● **Excel Technical Mouldings Ltd v Shaw** EAT 0267/02: E Ltd's structure was headed by a general manager, S, and immediately below him were

46

six subordinate managers. When the company ran into severe financial difficulties, it decided to alter the management structure, resulting in a 'triumvirate' at the top made up of two of the previous subordinate managers and an external part-time consultant, and the retention of five of the previous six subordinate management positions immediately below. S, however, was dismissed, and his job functions were reabsorbed by the managerial team. An employment tribunal ruled that there was no redundancy because there had been no overall reduction in the number of managerial employees. On appeal, the EAT upheld that decision. It noted that the tribunal had identified the work of the particular kind carried out by S as being 'managerial work', and concluded that this type of work had neither ceased nor diminished. Although there had been a reshaping of the management structure and a consequential reshuffling of responsibilities, the work of the seven full-time managerial employees before the restructuring was still being carried out by seven employees after the restructuring

- **Corus and Regal Hotels plc v Wilkinson** EAT 0102/03: CRH plc embarked on a restructuring exercise of its hotel business involving the substitution of the post of general manager – held by W – with that of resident manager and the creation of the new position of area general manager. CRH plc contended that this restructuring rendered W redundant. An employment tribunal upheld W's claim of unfair dismissal on the basis that the business requirements for employees to carry out W's work had not ceased or diminished even though the identity of the persons carrying out his work had changed. The EAT approved that decision on appeal, ruling that the tribunal had not simply been influenced by the fact that the same number of (or indeed more) employees were employed after the reorganisation than before it, but also, crucially, by the fact that they were doing the same work as before. W was not therefore redundant and his dismissal for that reason was unfair

- **Lambe v 186K Ltd** 2005 ICR 307, CA: L was employed as a corporate finance manager (CFM) specialising in mergers and acquisitions. In 2002 he was told by the head of corporate finance that if he wished to remain with the company he would have to change roles and move into the finance control department. The reason was that the employer wished to transfer another employee, P, from that department and put him into a newly created position of senior CFM. These proposed changes took place in the context of the company having recently deleted two other CFM positions. L contended that his dismissal was not by reason of redundancy, but his contention was rejected by an employment tribunal. He unsuccessfully appealed to the EAT and then to the Court of Appeal, which concluded that the tribunal's finding that there was a diminution in the company's need for CFMs, and in particular for a dedicated employee responsible for mergers and acquisitions, was fully supportable on the evidence. The company had clearly been undergoing a substantial downsizing. Moreover, P's new role had not merely been to perform the job previously done by L but to deal with anticipated new business activities.

2.13 Another common scenario that reveals the complicated interface between 'redundancy' and 'some other substantial reason' for dismissal is where an employee is dismissed for refusing to agree to changes to his or her job. This was the situation that arose in Shawkat v Nottingham City Hospital NHS Trust (No.2) 2002 ICR 7, CA, a case which concerned a thoracic surgeon who was dismissed following a reorganisation for refusing to perform cardiac work in place of some of his thoracic work. In that case the Court of Appeal observed that where an employee is dismissed and his or her replacement performs a different kind of work from that which he or she was employed to perform, it will often be the case that the requirements of the employer's business for employees to carry out work of a particular kind have not diminished. So it was on the facts of the instant case: the requirements of the business for employees to carry out thoracic surgery had not ceased or diminished, which meant that, contrary to the decision of the employment tribunal, the employee had not been dismissed for redundancy within the meaning of S.139(1)(b) ERA.

A similar conclusion was reached by the EAT in Mitie Olscot Ltd v Henderson and ors EAT 0016/04 – a case in which a company sought to remedy its economic difficulties by seeking the employees' consent to a variation of their terms and conditions. Following their refusal, the employees were dismissed for what the employer claimed was redundancy. An employment tribunal, however, concluded that the evidence was insufficient to establish that there had been any diminution in the business requirements for employees to carry out work of a particular kind. The EAT subsequently upheld the tribunal's reasoning. In the words of Lord Johnson, 'the tribunal were more than entitled to conclude that the real reason behind the dismissal was economic problems and an attempt to renegotiate contracts, which, if it had been successful, would not have resulted in job losses to any material extent. That does not meet the definition of redundancy since the need for the employer was not lack of work but economic improvement.'

2.14 The remainder of this chapter concentrates on the statutory definition of redundancy, and the kinds of scenario caught by it. However, it is worth highlighting the variety of alternatives to redundancy that employers may wish to consider, assuming they are in a position to choose. These measures or reorganisations short of redundancy may include, for example:

- redeployment (i.e. moving employees to different roles or areas of the business)

- laying off employees (see Chapter 4, 'Lay-off and short-time')

- short-time working (see Chapter 4, 'Lay-off and short-time')

- restricting overtime

- cutting back on temporary staff/independent contractors, or using them more widely

- reducing business costs, such as by cutting non-essential business travel or finding more efficient ways of working

- monitoring absence more closely

- offering career breaks

- removing discretionary benefits

- changing employees' terms and conditions.

But it is vital, before any of these options is implemented, that careful consideration is given both to the terms and conditions of the affected employees' contracts, and to the implications of any changes to those contracts that the action taken may entail. For a detailed analysis of the implications of changing employment terms, and how to achieve this lawfully, see IDS Employment Law Handbook, 'Contracts of Employment' (2014), Chapter 9, 'Variation of contract'. For details of how to categorise dismissals that are consequent upon a reorganisation, but do not meet the definition of redundancy, see IDS Employment Law Handbook, 'Unfair Dismissal' (2015), Chapter 8, 'Some other substantial reason', under 'Business reorganisations'.

Closure of business   2.15

Section 139(1)(a)(i) ERA covers situations where the employer has ceased, or intends to cease, carrying on the business for the purposes of which the employee was employed. Complete closure of the business is the easiest sort of redundancy situation to recognise under this heading but other changes affecting the business can also result in a redundancy situation.

Change in nature of business   2.16

Where an employer changes the type of business which is carried on at the workplace, this may be regarded as a closure of the old business but only if the employer has replaced the business with a new one that is completely different in nature. Whether a new business is sufficiently different in nature to amount to a cessation of the old business is a question of fact for the tribunal. For example, in Whitbread plc t/a Whitbread Berni Inns v Flatter and ors EAT 287/94 (discussed under 'Definition of "redundancy" – temporary cessation and diminution' above), the employment tribunal decided that the closure of a Berni Inn and the opening of a brasserie four weeks later was not a cessation of the old business because both were 'middle range restaurants'.

The EAT upheld that finding. In Lewis v A Jones and Sons plc EAT 776/92, on the other hand, the shutting down of a family shoe shop that reopened over two months later as a fashion shoe shop targeting a much younger clientele did amount to a cessation of the old business. According to the tribunal, the new business was 'an entirely new venture targeting a different clientele and using a different approach'. The EAT dismissed the appeal.

A change in the way the business is run or the qualifications required of employees is not sufficient. In Kleboe v Ayr County Council 1972 ITR 201, NIRC, for example, K was an unregistered schoolteacher. Regulations were introduced that required all teachers to be registered, but K's application for registration was turned down and the Council dismissed him. K argued that the Council had given up the business of teaching by unregistered teachers, and this was therefore a redundancy situation. The NIRC disagreed, saying that the Council's business was simply teaching and that neither the business nor the requirement for employees to do it had ceased or diminished.

2.17 Transfer of undertakings

If the employer ceases to carry on a business because it has been transferred to a new owner, whether or not there is a potential redundancy situation will largely depend on whether the transfer is covered by the special rules contained in the Transfer of Undertakings (Protection of Employment) Regulations 2006 SI 2006/246 (TUPE). Where the transfer is not covered by TUPE, the common law will apply. Under these principles, the transfer of a business automatically terminates all existing contracts of employment. The reason for this is that, by ceasing to carry on the business, the employer commits a repudiatory breach of contract by putting it out of its power to continue employing the employees. The employees will then be able to claim constructive dismissal for redundancy.

If TUPE does apply, the Regulations replace the common law rule. Briefly, the contracts of employment of those employed in the business (or part of a business) that transfers automatically continue with the substitution of the transferee as employer. Thus, there is no dismissal and no redundancy situation. There are two general exceptions to this rule, both of which are addressed in more detail in Chapter 1, 'Dismissal', under 'Transfer of Undertakings Regulations'. The first is where there is an express dismissal before the transfer of an employee who would otherwise have transferred. In this case the dismissal takes effect but may be automatically unfair if the reason for the dismissal was the transfer itself – Reg 7 TUPE. The second exception is where the employee expressly objects to working for the transferee. In this case the employee's contract is terminated and TUPE does not apply. However, the employee will still be able to claim constructive dismissal against the transferor.

The considerations that determine whether TUPE applies are fully explained **2.18** in IDS Employment Law Handbook, 'Transfer of Undertakings' (2015). In cases where TUPE does apply, the most important question is whether the reason for dismissal is the transfer itself or some other reason. In order to avoid TUPE protection being undermined, the Regulations provide that it is automatically unfair for an employer to dismiss an employee by reason of the transfer itself – Reg 7(1). Courts and tribunals have generally interpreted this protection purposively, so that many dismissals that have some connection with a transfer are deemed to be unfair. This provision applies to dismissals both before and after the transfer, so it covers the situation where the transferee seeks to avoid liability for transferring employees by dismissing them, as well as where the transferor does so at the transferee's behest. If a dismissal is not by reason of the transfer itself but is somehow connected to or consequent upon the transfer, the dismissal may be fair if there is an 'economic, technical or organisational' (ETO) reason for the dismissal, as set out in Reg 7(2). Such a dismissal may be a redundancy dismissal, if the S.98(2) definition is satisfied, or a dismissal for 'some other substantial reason' within S.98(1) ERA if not. The question of whether a redundancy situation amounts to an ETO reason is considered in Chapter 8, 'Unfair redundancy', under 'Automatically unfair redundancy – transfer of undertakings'.

Despite the strong employment protection surrounding TUPE transfers, it is possible for a genuine redundancy situation to arise in the context of a TUPE transfer and for the employer to dismiss fairly for that reason. Three examples:

*   **Delaney v Profile Security Services Ltd and anor** ET Case No.1805774/09: D was employed by PSS Ltd as a part-time security guard, working on a site operated by TC Ltd. The contract was retendered in 2008 and part-time security guards were specifically excluded from the tender. An employment tribunal held that PSS Ltd was liable to pay D a redundancy payment. The transfer was within the scope of TUPE but, immediately before it, there was a requirement by TC Ltd that part-time working was not to be included in the service provision. This meant that D's contract of employment was not transferred under TUPE and he was dismissed as redundant by PSS Ltd

*   **Hayes v Concorde Interiors (Europe) Ltd** ET Case No.1202865/09: H was employed by C Ltd as a mobile maintenance engineer working on a contract held with Somerfield. C Ltd decided not to continue with the contract and CIE Ltd was asked to provide reactive maintenance services for some of Somerfield's stores. During due diligence, CIE Ltd discovered that C Ltd employed twice as many engineers as it believed were needed for the work. It concluded that there was a long-standing redundancy situation that had not been addressed. CIE Ltd accepted all of the engineers on the basis that the position would be reviewed after two months. At that point it established that the contract was running at a loss and some of the engineers, including

51

H, were made redundant. An employment tribunal found that the reason for dismissal was the redundancy situation that C Ltd had not addressed, and not the fact of the transfer

- **Davies v Droylsden Academy** ET Case No.2403451/15: D was employed by SP, which provided a service to educational institutions whereby they would let out school premises out of school hours and the rental income was split between SP and the school. One such school, DA, decided to take in-house the service provided by SP and so retain all the letting income. This would amount to a transfer under the TUPE Regulations. During the consultation period before the transfer DA informed SP that it envisaged it might need to make a reduction in staff following the transfer due to an anticipated overstaffing in the area in which D would be located and that this might put her at risk of redundancy. D's employment transferred to DA but she did not do any work for it. DA took the view that her role had been split between existing employees, that she was at risk of redundancy and that she was in a pool of one for redundancy selection, since no one else did the same work to anything like the same extent as D. DA therefore dismissed D for redundancy. An employment tribunal found that the dismissal was for an ETO reason and was fair.

2.19 **Proposed transfer.** In Downs v Landscape Institute ET Case No.2202349/09 an employment tribunal had to decide whether an archivist was dismissed as redundant in circumstances where, at the time of dismissal, it was proposed to transfer the entire archive to a new owner. However, the transfer never actually took place and the archive was mothballed. The tribunal decided that the dismissal could not amount to redundancy because, at the time, the Institute intended to transfer the archive to a new owner and envisaged it remaining available for consultation and continuing to be catalogued and organised. As the dismissal did not fall into any of the potentially fair reasons for dismissal, it was unfair, even though there was, shortly afterwards, a genuine redundancy situation.

2.20 ## Closure of workplace

Section 139(1)(a)(ii) ERA deals with the situation where an employer simply closes down a particular workplace. An employee who works at that particular workplace will be redundant if that was 'the place where the employee was... employed'. Even if the employer starts up the business again at a different location – i.e. simply moves that part of the business rather than closing it down completely – the employee will still be redundant. In deciding whether an employee is entitled to a redundancy payment on the closure of a workplace, two issues have to be considered:

- where the employee was employed to work

- any offer of suitable alternative employment at another workplace. If the employee unreasonably refuses such an offer from the employer, he or she will not be entitled to a redundancy payment – see Chapter 3, 'Alternative job offers', under 'Suitability and reasonableness', for details.

Place of employment   2.21

There is usually no difficulty in establishing where employees are employed to work. In most cases, it is where they report each day to carry out their duties. In the case of 'travelling' jobs, employees usually have a defined area – their 'patch' – in which their duties are to be carried out. Furthermore, most contracts of employment specify either one identifiable place or one identifiable area as the employee's place of employment. Thus, in the typical case, it will be clear whether the place where the employee was employed to work has been closed down or not.

In Exol Lubricants Ltd v Birch and anor EAT 0219/14 the EAT held that, in the case of someone like a delivery driver who has no fixed place where his or her duties are carried out, it is proper but by no means conclusive to have regard to any contractual provision setting out the employee's place of work. It is also appropriate to consider – depending on the facts of the case – any connection the employee may have with a depot or head office or similar. In that case, the EAT upheld an employment tribunal's decision that no redundancy situation arose when the employer decided to end an arrangement allowing two HGV delivery drivers to use employer-provided secure overnight parking for their HGVs in Stockport, near their homes. The employees' contracts of employment identified the place of work as a depot in Wednesbury, and it was at this depot that every working day began and ended. The need for delivery drivers in Wednesbury had not diminished, as evidenced by the fact that agency drivers were immediately engaged to replace the claimants.

The EAT decided in one case that a temporary change in location does not   2.22
alter an employee's place of work, even if the original workplace later closes down. In Kentish Bus and Coach Co Ltd v Quarry EAT 287/92 a driver was based at the Southwark depot. The employer decided to close down that depot and, until another one opened in the Southwark area, Q was asked to work from Leyton. The EAT upheld an employment tribunal's decision that Southwark remained Q's place of work for redundancy purposes while he worked temporarily elsewhere. He became redundant when the employer decided not to renew the operation in Southwark and asked him to stay at Leyton on a permanent basis.

Mobility clauses. Establishing the place of employment has proved more   2.23
problematic, however, where a contract contains a mobility clause that allows the employer to change the employee's place of work. Confusion has, in particular,

53

stemmed from the fact that there were originally two conflicting lines of authority on the correct test for determining the place of employment in these circumstances. Some decisions favoured the factual (sometimes called the geographical) test, which deems the place of employment to be the place where duties are actually carried out, while others applied the contractual test, which deems it to be the place or places where employees can be required to work under their contracts.

For many years, the contractual test held sway. For example, in United Kingdom Atomic Energy Authority v Claydon 1974 ICR 128, NIRC, C was employed under a contract whereby he could be required to work at any UKAEA establishment. The employer closed the unit where C worked in Suffolk and offered him a transfer to Berkshire but he refused to move and was dismissed. When he claimed a redundancy payment, the NIRC said that 'the place where [the employee] was... employed' meant any place where C could be required to work under his contract – i.e. any UKAEA establishment in Great Britain or overseas – and that, since there was work available, C was not redundant. Sir John Donaldson explained that: 'Many men and women are employed under contracts of employment which provide for transfers over a wide area. If work is short in one place but available elsewhere within the area, there will be no redundancy situation and the employer can dismiss without being liable to make any redundancy payment.'

2.24 However, the contractual test was always open to the criticism that it distorted the wording of the statute in that, instead of ascertaining the place where the employee was employed to work, it concentrated on the place where he or she might be required to work. The test was finally laid to rest by two decisions which made it clear that the contractual test should no longer be considered good law and that the factual test should be applied. In Bass Leisure Ltd v Thomas 1994 IRLR 104, EAT, T was employed by BL Ltd as a collector. She was based at the company's depot in Coventry and her work involved driving to a number of public houses to collect the takings from fruit machines. The employer shut down the Coventry depot and based T in Erdington, some 20 miles away. The extra travelling time disrupted T's domestic arrangements and she resigned and claimed a redundancy payment. T's contract contained two transfer clauses but the tribunal found that the employer could not rely on them because the conditions which were attached to them had not been satisfied. The tribunal held that T had been constructively dismissed and that she was entitled to a redundancy payment. The EAT upheld this finding on the ground that the place where T was employed was the Coventry depot and not the Coventry area. The mobility clause did not affect T's position because the employer had not complied with its terms. The EAT also held that T had not been offered suitable alternative employment.

While that was enough to dispose of T's case, the EAT nevertheless decided to address the issue of whether the test of the place of employment is factual or contractual. The EAT noted that the use of the word 'the' in 'the place where the employee was... employed' in S.139(1)(a)(ii) suggested that there was one identifiable 'place'. That place could, however, be widely defined in the contract to include a geographical area. Thus, for example, 'the place' where a steel erector is employed could be the area within which he can be required to attend at construction sites to perform his duties. The EAT also found considerable difficulty with any construction which treated 'the place where the employee was... employed' as any place the employee could be contractually bound to work. It reasoned that if a contract provides that an employee works at A, but could be moved on notice to B, then A must be the place of work until it changes to B. In the EAT's view, to hold that both A and B are the places of work would be contrary to the express wording of the contract. It concluded that the place where an employee was employed for redundancy purposes was a factual matter and one to be ascertained from the employee's fixed or changing place or places of work and any contractual terms evidencing this. Any contractual terms that make provision for the employee to be transferred to another place are irrelevant for these purposes.

The EAT's approach in the Thomas case was subsequently endorsed by the Court of Appeal in High Table Ltd v Horst and ors 1998 ICR 409, CA. In that case H, J and B worked for a contract catering company, HT Ltd, as silver service waitresses. Their contracts specified that they would be assigned to a catering contract with a particular firm in the City of London as their normal place of work but a mobility clause also provided that they could be transferred to other contracts if the needs of the business changed. In 1992 the company where H, J and B were located reduced its catering budget and informed HT Ltd that the catering contract would have to be scaled down accordingly. As a result, the roles of H, J, B and one other waitress were amalgamated into one post with longer working hours. H, J and B were not prepared to work the additional hours and so the post was given to the other waitress. H, J and B received redundancy payments but they brought claims of unfair dismissal. The tribunal hearing focused on the question of whether HT Ltd had acted reasonably in terms of consultation and in seeking to redeploy the employees. The tribunal decided that the dismissals were fair. The EAT allowed the employees' appeal on the basis that there was a question mark over whether the dismissals had in fact been for redundancy. The EAT took the view that, because there was a mobility clause in the employees' contracts, it could be argued that there was no diminution in the requirement for employees at the place where the employees worked, since the place where they worked was the whole of HT Ltd's operations. The employer appealed to the Court of Appeal, which held that the EAT had erred. According to the Court, the 'place' where an employee is employed should be determined primarily by a consideration of the factual circumstances pertaining prior to the dismissal. It was clear that the place where the employees were employed

2.25

in this particular case was the premises of the principal client for whom they were accustomed to work, and that the diminution in the needs of that client for the services of the employees meant that there was a redundancy situation at the employees' place of work for the purpose of S.139(1)(a)(ii).

In reaching its decision, the Court of Appeal specifically rejected the argument that the statute imposed a contractual test for the purpose of determining whether a redundancy situation has arisen. The Court acknowledged that, if the employee's work involved a change of location – as would be the case where the nature of the employee's work required him or her to go from place to place – then the contract of employment may be of assistance in determining the extent of the place where the employee was employed. However, it could not be right to let the contract be the sole determinant, regardless of where the employee actually worked. If an employee has worked in only one location during his or her employment, then there is no reason to widen the extent of the place where he or she was employed merely because of the existence of a mobility clause.

2.26 It follows from the Horst case that the contractual test for determining the place where the employee is employed for the purpose of S.139(1)(a) has now been laid to rest. This does not mean that the contract of employment is to be disregarded altogether, however. As was emphasised in both the Thomas and the Horst cases, the terms of the employee's contract may be of relevance under the factual test as one of the factors to be taken into account. For example, if an employee has worked at a particular site for the whole of his or her employment and is dismissed when that site is closed, then that will be a dismissal for redundancy regardless of the fact that the employer would have been entitled under the contract to move the employee to another site. But if the employee has been moved from place to place during the employment, the terms of a mobility clause may be of relevance in determining the place where the employee was in fact employed.

There are two other reasons why the existence of a mobility clause remains relevant. First, if the employer seeks to enforce the clause against the employee, it may be able to avoid making a redundancy payment, either by avoiding a dismissal in the first place or by establishing that the reason for dismissal was not redundancy but misconduct (i.e. the refusal to obey a lawful instruction to move to a different place of work). Secondly, it is possible that a tribunal may consider the existence of a mobility clause as relevant to the question of whether the redundant employee has refused an offer of reasonable alternative employment (see Chapter 3, 'Alternative job offers'), which would extinguish the right to a redundancy payment under S.141 ERA.

2.27 Care should be taken, however, to ensure that the wording of the mobility clause permits the employer's actions. In Smith and anor v Westside Day Nursery Ltd ET Case No.1802542/09 WDN Ltd operated four nurseries in

Hull, and the claimants worked in one of them. Their contracts of employment specified that they 'may be required to work at other locations' and the staff handbook, which neither claimant was ever given, provided that employees might be required to relocate on a permanent basis. In early 2009, WDN Ltd decided to close the nursery in which the claimants worked, as the numbers of children attending had declined, and informed employees that they would be relocated to one of the other nurseries. The claimants maintained that the offer of alternative work was not suitable for them in view of the increased travelling. An employment tribunal upheld their claims for a redundancy payment, on the basis that they had not been told where to report for work once the nursery closed, and were thus dismissed. In any event, the tribunal considered that the wording of the mobility clause was ineffective to enable WDN Ltd to transfer employees permanently. The contract described their nursery as their 'usual' place of work. A power to transfer temporarily, however, would have been consistent with the wording of the clause.

Territorial jurisdiction. The Court of Appeal's decision in High Table Ltd v   **2.28**
Horst and ors (above) was subsequently affirmed in the somewhat unusual case of Pitman v Foreign and Commonwealth Office 2003 ICR 699, EAT. P was an overseas security officer employed by the FCO under a contract which provided that he had to be prepared 'to serve anywhere in the United Kingdom or abroad'. In 1994 the FCO concluded that the number of overseas security officers should be reduced but that in some cases locally engaged security officers could be recruited to replace them. As a result, P was dismissed by reason of redundancy when his duties in New York were transferred to locally employed security officers. He brought a claim of unfair dismissal, arguing that there had not been a redundancy situation. In determining the claim in favour of the FCO, the employment tribunal first assumed that P was ordinarily working in Great Britain and that it therefore had jurisdiction to hear the claim under S.196 ERA. As a result, it concluded that P's place of work for the purposes of S.139 was within Great Britain, while his successor's place of work was New York. On appeal, the EAT held that the question of whether the tribunal has jurisdiction – and the determination in that context of whether somebody is ordinarily working abroad or in Great Britain – does not determine the question of where that person is employed for the purposes of S.139. Accordingly, the case was remitted to the tribunal to determine, inter alia, where the claimant was employed. (Note that S.196 was repealed in October 1999, leaving the ERA silent as to territorial jurisdiction. The question of territorial jurisdiction in unfair dismissal cases has since been governed primarily by the House of Lords' decision in Lawson v Serco Ltd and two other cases 2006 ICR 250, HL, and it is arguable that the principles established in that case apply to other claims, including claims for redundancy payments, under the ERA – see further Chapter 5, 'Qualifications and exclusions', under 'Employees and excluded employees – overseas

57

employment'. However, it would seem reasonable to assume that the general principle established in Pitman – that the question of whether there has been a redundancy is distinct from any question of jurisdiction – still applies even after the repeal of S.196.)

2.29 Transfer of undertakings

If the employer ceases to carry on business at a particular workplace because it has been transferred to a new owner, TUPE may come into play. This is discussed more fully under 'Closure of business – transfer of undertakings' above.

2.30 Diminishing need for employees

Section 139(1)(b) ERA states that there is a redundancy situation where the requirements of the business for employees to carry out work of a particular kind, or for employees to carry out work of a particular kind in the place where they are employed, have ceased or diminished. This covers three separate situations:

- where work of a particular kind has diminished, so that employees have become surplus to requirements

- where work has not diminished, but fewer employees are needed to do it, either because

  - the employees have been replaced by, for example, independent contractors or technology, or

  - because of a reorganisation which results in a more efficient use of labour.

It is the requirement for *employees* to do work of a particular kind which is significant. The fact that the work is constant, or even increasing, is irrelevant. If fewer employees are needed to do work of a particular kind, there is a redundancy situation – McCrea v Cullen and Davison Ltd 1988 IRLR 30, NICA.

2.31   In Hand Tools Ltd v Maleham EAT 110/91 M was production manager for HT Ltd. Following a management buy-out, he took on the role of general manager. His functions included supervision of the shop-floor, although he also took on some sales activity work, which was not successful. He was eventually dismissed for redundancy. An employment tribunal ruled by a majority that there was no redundancy situation as the work which M had been required to do – i.e. supervision of the shop-floor – continued to be a necessary function of the company. On appeal, the EAT held that the tribunal had erred in treating the continuation of M's supervisory functions as the determining factor. The proper test in M's case was whether the requirement of the business for employees to carry out that particular kind of work had ceased or diminished, not whether there had been an end to or reduction

58

in that kind of work. M had already conceded that the company could not sustain three executive employees where, before the buy-out, it had supported M working more or less on his own. By the proper definition of S.139(1)(b), M was redundant.

Note, however, that in cases of reorganisation where the overall number of employees remains the same or even increases, there may nevertheless be a redundancy situation where the requirements of the business for employees to carry out a *particular kind* of work have ceased or diminished, or are expected to do so. Such situations are discussed further under 'Less work available' below.

The EAT has made it clear that there is no need under S.139(1)(b) for an employer to show an economic justification (or business case) for the decision to make redundancies. In Polyflor Ltd v Old EAT 0482/02 an employment tribunal held that there was no redundancy situation partly on the basis that it was not satisfied that the employer's evidence showed an economic need to cut costs or make the employee redundant. The EAT overturned this decision on appeal – the facts were clear that the employee's role had disappeared and the employer was not required to show a business case for its decision. (Note, however, that the employer's motives may become relevant if it is alleged that the redundancy is a sham and that there is another, possibly discriminatory, reason for dismissal – see 'Reason for dismissal' below.) Similarly, in TNS UK Ltd v Swainston EAT 0603/12 the EAT overturned an employment tribunal's decision that TNS Ltd had failed to show that there was a genuine redundancy situation. The tribunal had concluded that 'the process which led to [S's] dismissal was entirely driven by costs implications' and that this was not the same as a diminishing need for employees to do work of the kind done by S. The EAT held that the tribunal's approach was contrary to authority. The tribunal had made clear factual findings that the unit in which S was employed was losing money and that TNS Ltd could do without the role performed by S in order to make savings. Those facts were tantamount to a finding of redundancy. The tribunal did not find that S was replaced or that the number of employees did not fall and, although there was no evidence that S's role in terms of work was diminishing, the fact that TNS Ltd considered that it could no longer afford to maintain her post created a redundancy situation.

2.32

Furthermore, there may be a redundancy situation under S.139(1)(b) even where the employer does not identify the 'particular kind' of work that diminishes. In Contract Bottling Ltd v Cave and anor EAT 0525/12 the EAT noted that, as a general rule, employers considering redundancies tend to look at each of the different types of work they have within their business. It is then easy to see that there is a diminution in the requirement of the business for employees to carry out work of a particular kind. However, sometimes there

59

is a diminution in the requirements of the business for employees to carry out work of several kinds. In the instant case, the employer's administration department was overmanned but, contrary to what the employment tribunal had found, the EAT did not consider it material that the employer had failed to identify the types of work within the department that were affected. In its view, applying the two-stage test derived from Murray and anor v Foyle Meats Ltd 1999 ICR 827, HL (discussed under 'Test of redundancy' below), there was no doubt that the definition of 'redundancy' for the purpose of S.139(1)(b) was satisfied, in that there was a diminution in the requirements of the business for employees to carry out work of particular kinds, and the dismissals were attributable to that diminution.

2.33 None of this, however, should detract from the obligation on the tribunal to apply the clear words of the statute. In Macquet v Naiade Resorts (UK) Ltd EAT 0495/10 the EAT held that an employment tribunal was not entitled to accept that there was a genuine redundancy situation on the basis of serious financial pressures without making any specific finding about a diminution in NR Ltd's need for employees to do work of a particular kind. The tribunal's decision was inadequately reasoned and so could not stand. Thus, while tribunals may readily accept an employer's case that financial concerns have led to the need to make dismissals, they must be clear about how those financial concerns translate into a situation that comes within S.139 ERA.

2.34 **Part-time employees.** In some circumstances, the diminution in the need for employees to carry out a particular kind of work may be minimal and the employer may only need to lose 'half a person'. This could be achieved by reducing an employee's hours, or by selecting a part-time employee for redundancy. It is important to note, however, that selecting someone who works part time for redundancy in preference to a full-time employee because of his or her part-time status may constitute a detriment for the purposes of the Part-time Workers (Prevention of Less Favourable Treatment) Regulations 2000 SI 2000/1551, unless that selection can be objectively justified. See further Chapter 8, 'Unfair redundancy', under 'Automatically unfair redundancy – part-time and fixed-term work'.

2.35 **Test of redundancy**

The question of whether an employee is redundant within the meaning of S.139(1)(b) was for many years dogged by a controversy over the correct test for determining the work which the dismissed employee was employed to carry out. According to one approach – the 'function' test – it was necessary to focus on the work that the employee actually did and it made no difference that under his or her contract of employment he or she could in fact be required to do other work. According to the rival 'contract' test, however, it was necessary to focus on the work which the employee could be required to do under the contract of employment. Thanks, however, to two decisions which took a bold and fresh look at S.139(1)(b), the whole contract/function controversy has been consigned to the dustbin of legal history. These two decisions established a test based directly on the statutory wording without any unnecessary gloss.

The first of these cases was Safeway Stores plc v Burrell 1997 ICR 523, EAT. In that case (the facts of which are given under 'Less work available – redeployment' below) the EAT stated that the function/contract debate was based on a misreading of both the statute and previous authorities. His Honour Judge Peter Clark set out a simple three-stage test. A tribunal must decide: (i) was the employee dismissed? (ii) if so, had the requirements of the employer's business for employees to carry out work of a particular kind ceased or diminished, or were they expected to cease or diminish? (iii) if so, was the dismissal of the employee caused wholly or mainly by the cessation or diminution?

HHJ Peter Clark stated that there are no grounds for importing into the **2.36** statutory wording a requirement that there must be a diminishing need for employees to do the kind of work *for which the claimant was employed*. The only question to be asked when determining stage (ii) of the three-stage test is whether there was a diminution in the employer's requirement for *employees* (rather than the individual claimant) to carry out work of a particular kind. It is irrelevant at this stage to consider the terms of the claimant's contract. The terms of the contract are only relevant at stage (iii) when determining, as a matter of causation, whether the redundancy situation was the operative reason for the employee's dismissal.

The test set out in the Burrell case was widely acclaimed as bringing light and clarity to a previously dark and muddled area of redundancy law and was subsequently endorsed by the House of Lords in Murray and anor v Foyle Meats Ltd 1999 ICR 827, HL. In that case (the facts of which are also given under 'Less work available – redeployment' below) Lord Irvine described the identical language used in the Northern Ireland equivalent of S.139(1) as 'simplicity itself'. The contract and function tests missed the point, he said, because the key word in S.139 was 'attributable' (in that the dismissal must be attributable to one of the three redundancy situations set out in the section – see 'Definition of "redundancy"' above) and there was no reason why the dismissal of an employee should not be attributable to a diminution in the employer's need for employees irrespective of the terms of the contract or the function which the employee performed. For Lord Irvine, S.139 asks two questions of fact. The first is whether there exists one or other of the various states of economic affairs mentioned in the section – e.g. whether the requirements of the business for employees to carry out work of a particular kind have ceased or diminished. The second question, which is one of causation, is whether the dismissal is

61

wholly or mainly attributable to that state of affairs. Naturally, in the case of a dismissal of an employee who could have been employed elsewhere, or who was not carrying out work the requirement for which had ceased or diminished, it may be more difficult to establish that the dismissal was indeed attributable to the redundancy situation. However, that is a question of fact, not law, for the tribunal to decide.

2.37 The advantage of the Burrell/Murray approach is that it removes the need to consider exactly what an employee can or cannot be required to do under his or her contract of employment and accords better with the wording of the statute. Another significant advantage is that it explains how a so-called 'bumping' dismissal – i.e. where an employee whose job is redundant is kept on at the expense of an employee in relation to whose work no redundancy situation exists – can be a redundancy dismissal within the wording of the statute. Bumping redundancies are discussed under 'Reason for dismissal' below.

Despite the clarity and simplicity brought by the Burrell/Murray approach, tribunals still fall into error by applying their own gloss to the test. For example, in Arnold Clark Automobiles Ltd v Mak EAT 0052/13 the EAT allowed an appeal against an employment judge's finding on the reason for dismissal where the judge had focused on the question of whether redundancy was the 'operative reason' for the employee's dismissal. There, ACA Ltd proposed to cease establishing contact centres, in which M worked as a training specialist. The employment judge found that this satisfied the statutory definition of redundancy and that the employer had permissibly decided that M was in a pool of one for redundancy selection. However, the employment judge went on to find that, had it not been for M raising a concern about the inappropriate behaviour of a manager, ACA Ltd would have found her an alternative role elsewhere within the business. The judge concluded that ACA Ltd's efforts in this regard were superficial because of the difficulty between M and the manager and that this was the real reason for dismissal. Allowing the appeal, the EAT held that, following Burrell/Murray, the judge should have focused on the statutory question of whether the dismissal was wholly or mainly attributable to the diminution or cessation in the requirements of the business for employees to carry out work of the kind carried out by M. The EAT rejected the claimant's argument that this was merely a matter of semantics. The employment judge had glossed the words of the statute and thereby failed to apply them to the situation. On the facts, the employment judge was bound to conclude that redundancy was the reason for dismissal.

Having set out the test for redundancy, it is now necessary to look further at the different types of circumstances giving rise to a redundancy situation under S.139(1)(b).

Less work available   2.38

Where the number of employees needed has declined because the work required from those employees has declined, there is clearly a redundancy situation. In Short v PJ Hayman and Co Ltd EAT 0379/08, for example, the EAT upheld an employment tribunal's finding that the loss of a major contract which had provided 75 per cent of the work dealt with by the employer's insurance claims department gave rise to a redundancy situation, and that the dismissal of the claims manager was wholly or mainly attributable to the diminution in work.

The situation is less clear cut where the business requires less work of a particular kind but the number of employees remains the same overall. These difficult cases tend to fall into the following categories:

- reallocation of duties

- same work done under different terms and conditions

- same work done by different kind of employee

- work changes but remains work of the same particular kind

- redeployment.

We examine these in turn.

Reallocation of duties. There are two possible approaches to the question   2.39
of whether a redundancy situation arises where a job disappears when an employer redistributes the same amount of work among the same number of employees: the 'requirements of the business' test and the 'jobs' test. The difference between these tests is best illustrated by an example:

- two individuals are employed as 'packer/stackers'. Following a reorganisation, the employer decides that he now requires one packer and one stacker. The overall requirements of the business are the same, in that the employer requires the same number of employees to do the same amount of work. The 'requirements of the business' test therefore suggests that there is no redundancy situation. The 'jobs' test, on the other hand, requires the tribunal to consider whether there has been a reduction in the requirement for employees to do work of a particular kind. If, therefore, packing and stacking can be categorised as two discrete kinds of work then this will lead to the conclusion that the employees are redundant.

A number of older cases adopted the 'requirements of the business' approach – see, for example, North Riding Garages Ltd v Butterwick 1967 2 WLR 571, Div Ct; Jones v Star Associated Holdings Ltd 1970 ITR 178, Div Ct; and Frame It v Brown EAT 177/93. In the Brown case, the EAT preferred to focus on the company's overall requirements, expressing the view that the problem

63

with the 'jobs' test is that it would hamper any reorganisation or reallocation of duties within a business enterprise.

2.40 However, more recent cases have tended to follow the 'jobs' approach, which now has the greater weight of authority. In Murphy v Epsom College 1985 ICR 80, CA, M was one of two plumbers but he also did some engineering work. Later, M declined to perform the engineering tasks and the college decided to dismiss him and employ an engineer who would also undertake some plumbing. The evidence suggested that the college still needed two employees, one plumber and one who would do both plumbing and engineering work. On the 'requirements of the business' test, therefore, it appeared that there was no redundancy situation. Both the EAT and the Court of Appeal held, however, that M's dismissal was for redundancy: whereas previously the business required a plumber who could do some engineering, now it required an engineer who could do some plumbing. The EAT justified its approach by reference to the wording of S.139, which defines redundancy as a diminishing need for 'employees to carry out work of a particular kind'. In this case, the employer no longer needed an employee to carry out work of the particular type done by M and he was, therefore, redundant. The Court of Appeal upheld this finding, saying that a reorganisation creating a substantial change in the kind of work required by the employer can result in redundancies even though the employer's overall requirements for work or employees remain the same.

The Murphy decision is open to criticism in that the Court of Appeal did not take account of the earlier authorities when reaching its decision. Nevertheless, we would suggest that the 'jobs' test is entirely in line with the statutory wording, which speaks of a diminution in the requirements of the business 'for employees to carry out work of a particular kind'. It is significant that in Safeway Stores plc v Burrell 1997 ICR 523, EAT (see 'Test of redundancy' above), the EAT emphasised that the new test set out in that case was consistent with the decision in Murphy. As His Honour Judge Peter Clark put it: 'The employer originally had two plumbers, now it only required one. The employee was dismissed by reason of redundancy.'

2.41 The Murphy decision was also followed in BBC v Farnworth EAT 1000/97 where F, a radio producer, was replaced by a more experienced producer. The EAT upheld the tribunal's decision that her dismissal was for redundancy, stating that an employee is redundant when his or her particular specialism is no longer required, even if the employee is replaced by an employee with a different specialism so that the overall requirements of the business for employees have not diminished. Just as in the Murphy case a plumber who could do the work of a heating engineer was replaced by a heating engineer who could do plumbing, so in the instant case the post of 'Mark 1' producer had been replaced by that of 'Mark 2' producer. (The facts of the case are outlined in more detail under 'Same work done by different kind of employee' below.)

The issue was revisited by the Court of Appeal in Shawkat v Nottingham City Hospital NHS Trust (No.2) 2002 ICR 7, CA. S worked exclusively as a thoracic surgeon for the Trust. However, the Trust decided to merge the cardiac and thoracic surgery departments in the hospital where S worked and subsequently informed S that he would be required to carry out both forms of surgery. He refused to carry out any cardiac surgery and was eventually dismissed. An employment tribunal found that S had been unfairly dismissed on the ground that the Trust had attempted to impose unreasonable duties on him that he had reasonably declined to carry out. However, the tribunal dismissed S's claim for a redundancy payment. It held that the Trust's requirement for employees to carry out thoracic surgery had not diminished and, therefore, there had been no diminution in the Trust's requirement for employees to perform 'work of a particular kind' within the meaning of S.139(1)(b)(i). Upholding this decision on appeal, the Court of Appeal confirmed that the correct approach is for a tribunal to decide, as a question of fact, whether the employer's need for employees to carry out work of a particular kind has diminished. It is, therefore, the kind of work that must be defined (such as, in the instant case, 'thoracic surgery') rather than the kind of employee (such as, in the instant case, '100 per cent thoracic surgeon'). Accordingly, although the effect of the Trust's reorganisation of the cardiac and thoracic departments changed the work that its employees in the thoracic department were required to carry out, since the Trust still needed the same amount of thoracic surgery to be carried out, S was not redundant despite being asked to reduce the amount of thoracic surgery that he himself performed.

The Shawkat decision may appear, at first sight, to adopt a contrary position **2.42** to that of the Court of Appeal in Murphy v Epsom College (above). However, the Court in Shawkat incorporated into its judgment Sir Denys Buckley's statement in Murphy that: 'Every case of reorganisation must, I think, depend ultimately on its particular facts. In each case it must be for the individual tribunal to decide whether the reorganisation and reallocation of functions within the staff is such as to change the particular kind of work which a particular employee, or successive employees, is or are required to carry out, and whether such change has had any, and if so what, effect on the employer's requirement for employees to carry out a particular kind of work.' Furthermore, the two judgments are distinguishable on the facts. In Murphy the employer required 'a different kind of tradesman... to perform functions and assume responsibilities in connection with the college's heating installations of a more extensive and more responsible kind than the functions which Mr Murphy was competent to perform' but who would also be able to assist with general plumbing work, meaning that the employer's need for plumbers was reduced from two to one. In Shawkat, on the other hand, while the employer's reorganisation changed the work that S personally was required to carry out, this change had no effect on the employer's requirement

65

for employees to carry out a particular kind of work. Indeed, the EAT in Corus and Regal Hotels plc v Wilkinson EAT 0102/03 confirmed that there is no conflict between Murphy and Shawkat, and the then President of the EAT, Mr Justice Langstaff, cited both in Brunel University v Killen EAT 0403/13. The question of whether or not there is a diminution in the requirements of the business for employees to carry out a particular kind of work is a matter of fact for the tribunal to decide in each case.

2.43   **Change in duties.** A reallocation of duties may entail a fundamental change in the duties of employees so that the work to be done after the reallocation is quite different from that done before. This may create a redundancy situation. In Robinson v British Island Airways Ltd 1978 ICR 304, EAT, the posts of 'Flight Operations Manager' (R's job) and 'General Manager Operations and Traffic' were abolished and a new job of 'Operations Manager' was created. Both holders of the existing jobs were considered unsuitable for the new one and they were dismissed. R claimed that his dismissal was unfair but the EAT said that he was fairly dismissed because of redundancy. It based its judgment on the finding that the work in the new job was 'in a different league' (because it was far more important) from that in the old jobs. (Note that fewer employees were needed because two posts were replaced by one and the EAT could have held R to be redundant for this reason, although it did not.)

Three more recent cases confirm that this approach is consistent with the current state of the law following Murphy v Epsom College and Shawkat v Nottingham City Hospital NHS Trust (No.2) (above):

- **Hakki v Instinctif Partners Ltd (formerly College Hill Ltd)** EAT 0112/14: H, an HR administrator who carried out administrative tasks for the HR manager, as well as providing administrative assistance to the CEO and the Financial Director, was dismissed consequent on a reorganisation that created two new full-time posts, one of HR adviser and one of PA to the CEO/Financial Director. The reorganisation reflected not a decrease but an increase in the work formerly done by H but both new roles required different skill-sets from those that she had demonstrated and involved greater responsibility. An employment tribunal found that there was a redundancy situation and the EAT agreed. The tribunal had permissibly found as fact that the requirement for an employee to do H's old job was going, to be replaced by two materially different jobs, and that there was therefore a redundancy situation even though the work increased. The present case was consistent with the situations in the Robinson and Murphy cases

- **Wright v Sungard Public Sector Ltd** ET Case No.1403103/10: W had worked for SPS Ltd as a commercial contracts administrator for 11 years when he was dismissed as redundant. He had a law degree and a Masters in law but no professional legal qualification. A new commercial director was appointed in May 2010 and she decided that rather than employing two contract administrators, SPS Ltd needed one commercial consultant and a commercial lawyer with a professional qualification to provide weightier representation at high-value contract negotiations. W and a colleague were made redundant. He argued that there was no redundancy since the new role was no different from the role he had been carrying out and he was capable of performing it even though he was not professionally qualified. The employment tribunal rejected this claim. It found that there was a business requirement for a different skill-set and qualification, which meant that the work W was employed to do had diminished

* **Kellett v Key Retirement Solutions Ltd** ET Case No.2406457/15: K worked for KRS Ltd as an annuity broker, selling annuities to customers of pensionable age. Following the Government's announcement in March 2014 that those aged 55 and over would no longer be obliged to use their entire pension fund to purchase an annuity, KRS Ltd decided that all of its brokers should be capable of selling a wide range of regulated financial products, which meant that they would need to retrain and pass exams in order to gain regulatory approval. An employment tribunal found that this business decision meant that there was a genuine redundancy situation affecting K's role, since KRS Ltd had no further requirement for unqualified annuity brokers.

Same work done under different terms and conditions. The Court of Appeal has held on a number of occasions that work and the requirement for employees to do it do not change simply because the work is carried out under different terms and conditions. Changes in terms and conditions are relevant to the fairness of a dismissal but they do not create a redundancy situation. In Chapman and ors v Goonvean and Rostowrack China Clay Co Ltd 1973 ICR 310, CA, the employer withdrew free transport to work because it was uneconomic and some employees lost their jobs because they could no longer get to work. The Court of Appeal held that there was no redundancy situation. The fact that the terms of employment had changed did not mean that the requirements for work and for employees to carry it out had changed, so that the statutory definition of redundancy was not satisfied. The result would have been different if the statute referred to the requirements for employees 'on the existing terms of employment' but the statute does not contain these words. As Lord Clyde put it in Murray and anor v Foyle Meats Ltd 1999 ICR 827, HL: 'The contractual provisions which the employer may make with the employees are not necessarily a requirement of the business: they are rather a means whereby the requirements of the business in respect of the workforce may be met.'

2.44

A similar point was considered in Johnson v Nottinghamshire Combined Police Authority 1974 ICR 170, CA. There the employer introduced a double-shift system for two clerical workers at a police station but the new hours did not suit them and they were dismissed and replaced by two different employees. They claimed redundancy payments but the Court of Appeal held that the dismissals were not for redundancy. The same work still remained to be done by the same number of employees, the only difference being in the hours during which the work was to be done.

2.45   The point was emphasised again in Loy v Abbey National Financial and Investment Services plc 2006 SLT 761, Ct Sess (Outer House), where L argued that, following a takeover, certain aspects of his job were sufficiently different to indicate that his previous job had come to an end. Rejecting this contention, the Court re-emphasised that changes to an employee's terms and conditions, even changes that would entitle the employee to claim constructive dismissal, do not mean that the employee is redundant. The only test for redundancy is that found in Safeway Stores plc v Burrell 1997 ICR 523, EAT, and Murray and anor v Foyle Meats Ltd (above). Since, in the present case, the requirements for employees to do work of a particular kind had neither ceased nor diminished, L was not redundant. A similar conclusion was reached in Shawkat v Nottingham City Hospital NHS Trust (No.2) 2002 ICR 7, CA (discussed in full under 'Reallocation of duties' above), in which the Court of Appeal held that even though S had been unfairly dismissed on the ground that his employer had attempted to impose unreasonable duties on him that he had reasonably declined to carry out, he was not redundant because the Trust's requirements for employees to perform work of a particular kind had not diminished.

Two further examples:

- **Mitie Olscot Ltd v Henderson and ors** EAT 0016/04: the company tried to remedy its economic difficulties by seeking its employees' consent to a variation to their terms and conditions. When the employees refused, they were dismissed. The EAT upheld the employment tribunal's decision that the attempt to renegotiate the contracts, if successful, would not have resulted in job losses and that the real reason for the dismissals was the economic problems. This did not meet the definition of redundancy since the need for employees had not diminished

- **Martland and ors v Co-Operative Insurance Society Ltd** EAT 0220/07: the dismissal of the entire sales workforce, followed by an offer of re-engagement on new terms, was held to be for 'some other substantial reason' under S.98(1)(b) ERA and not for redundancy under S.98(2)(c). In the view of both the employment tribunal and the EAT, the work which was required both before and after the dismissal was 'selling' and neither changes in the method of performance nor a reduced level of contact with clients could justify an inference that the work was of a different kind.

2.46   A case that does not rest easily with the above authorities is McCafferty v Rankin Park Club EAT 205/90. M was the manager of a social club and was responsible for day-to-day tasks, including the engagement and payment of casual staff. The club found itself in financial difficulty and decided to terminate M's existing employment and to offer him a job as bar manager. As bar manager he would still have been responsible for the day-to-day running of the club and for the engagement of casual staff but not for their payment. His salary would also have been reduced and he would have been responsible for his own national insurance and income tax contributions. In other respects his work would remain the same. M rejected the job and claimed unfair dismissal. The employment tribunal held that M had been dismissed for redundancy and the EAT upheld that decision. With respect, it is difficult to see how the statutory definition of redundancy had been satisfied in this case. The evidence seems to show that the requirements of the business for a person to carry out the type of work which M had done previously had not diminished; all that had altered were some of the terms on which that type of work was to be carried out. The EAT did not refer to the Court of Appeal's judgment in either the Chapman or Johnson cases (above) and the decision must therefore be treated with some caution.

There are two situations where a change in the terms of employment can lead to **2.47** redundancy, however. These were recognised by the Court of Appeal in Johnson v Nottinghamshire Combined Police Authority (above). The first is where the change is caused by a redundancy situation. This can happen where a change in terms is accompanied by a reduction in the number of employees, as in:

- **Kykot v Smith Hartley Ltd** 1975 IRLR 372, QBD: two weavers working on the day-shift left and the employers decided to abolish the night-shift and transfer two weavers from the night-shift to the jobs vacated on the day-shift. They refused the transfer and were dismissed. An employment tribunal said that since there would have been no change in the work they did there was no redundancy. The High Court disagreed and pointed out that the reorganisation was caused by a general fall-off in trade and led to an overall reduction in the number of employees. This was enough to distinguish the case from Johnson and the Court held that the dismissal of the night-shift workers was caused by redundancy

- **Dacorum Borough Council v Eldridge and anor** EAT 608/89: E and T were employed by the Council in the refuse collection department. As a result of the Local Government Act 1988 the Council was obliged to put its refuse collection service out to competitive tendering. The Council wished to submit a tender on behalf of the workforce and decided it would have to reduce the workforce and change working conditions. The changes entailed the ending of a working practice whereby employees worked substantially fewer hours than they were contractually obliged to do. Both E and T volunteered for redundancy but their requests were not accepted. They refused to accept the new terms and conditions and were dismissed. On

69

the question of whether E and T were entitled to a redundancy payment an employment tribunal held that a redundancy situation had existed from the time the Council was statutorily obliged to put the services out to tender and the Council had failed to rebut the presumption of redundancy. E and T were therefore entitled to redundancy payments. The EAT held that the tribunal was entitled to come to that conclusion.

2.48 The second situation where a change in the terms and conditions of employment can lead to redundancy is where the nature of the changes means that the work could be described as being of a different kind. One question that sometimes arises is whether a change from the night-shift to the day-shift or vice versa is a change in the kind of work done. In Macfisheries Ltd v Findlay and ors 1985 ICR 160, EAT, the claimants worked night-shifts for domestic reasons and refused to change to day-shifts when the night-shift was terminated. They were dismissed and claimed redundancy payments. An employment tribunal held that the claimants' work on the night-shift was 'work of a particular kind' and that since the requirement for that work had ceased they were redundant. The EAT upheld this decision, saying that the tribunal had not assumed that working at night automatically made the work 'of a particular kind' – a view which would have been mistaken – but had looked at all the relevant factors such as the nature of the work done on the two shifts, the impact of night work on the claimants' personal and domestic lives, and the fact that they had a contractual right not to be compelled to change to day-working. (Note, however, that in Barnes v Gilmartin Associates EAT 825/97 another division of the EAT stated that it did not find the reasoning in Findlay 'altogether compelling'.) A different conclusion was reached in Maher v Photo Trade Processing Ltd EAT 451/83, where the EAT held that there was no redundancy situation when the night-shift workers were all offered work on the day-shift and where the work on the day-shift was substantially the same as on the night-shift. The business required the same number of employees for the same tasks but at different hours.

2.49 **Part-time to full-time work.** A similar question arises if an employer demands that a part-time worker becomes full time. One argument is that part-time work is 'work of a particular kind' and therefore if an employer requires fewer part-time workers there is a redundancy situation. An employment tribunal in Brown v Dunlop Textiles Ltd 1967 ITR 531, ET, rejected that submission, however, as did the Court of Appeal in Johnson v Nottinghamshire Combined Police Authority (above). In Brown the tribunal did nonetheless find that there was a redundancy situation, because the employers needed fewer employees overall to do the work for which B had been employed. However, that decision would be unlikely to stand today, especially in light of the EAT's decision in Barnes v Gilmartin Associates (above). In that case a part-time secretary was dismissed and replaced by a full-time secretary. A tribunal found that the employer had a requirement for a full-time secretary and could not afford to employ both a full-time and a part-time secretary. Accordingly, the post of part-time secretary was redundant. The EAT overruled the tribunal. Citing Johnson, the EAT held that it was bound to conclude that there was no diminution in the requirement for employees to carry out work of a particular kind – i.e. secretarial work. (The EAT went on to hold, however, that in the circumstances the dismissal was fair for some other substantial reason – namely, a business reorganisation.)

Of course, if a part-time employee is to be replaced by a full-time employee the nature of whose work will be of a different kind, there is a redundancy situation. Thus there was a redundancy situation where a part-time audiotypist was replaced by a full-time secretary whose duties were wider than audiotyping – Ellis v GA Property Services Ltd ET Case No.13453/89.

Reduced hours. A complicated question arises where, in response to a   **2.50** diminished level of work, the employer decides to reduce all employees' hours instead of making dismissals. In such circumstances, would someone who resigns and claims constructive dismissal, or who is dismissed for refusing to comply, be entitled to redundancy pay? On one reading, the statutory definition would appear to be met, in that the requirements of the business for employees to carry out work of a particular kind have diminished and dismissals are the result. If the dismissal is a constructive dismissal, the reason for it is the reason for the employer's breach of contract that caused the employee to resign – Berriman v Delabole Slate Ltd 1985 ICR 546, CA – which, in these circumstances, would be redundancy. The opposing view is that, even though the level of work may have diminished, there cannot be a redundancy situation where the employer does not seek to reduce the number of employees doing the work. Its requirements for employees to carry out that kind of work remain the same. On this reading, redundancy only occurs where the requirements of the business for employees doing the work have diminished, not where the requirements of the business for the amount of work to be done have diminished.

Until recently, the latter view has had the support of authority at EAT level following Aylward and ors v Glamorgan Holiday Home Ltd t/a Glamorgan Holiday Hotel EAT 0167/02. In that case the claimants were employed by a company that provided respite care and holidays for elderly, disabled and disadvantaged people. The business consistently traded in profit for the ten months from March to December but suffered losses in January and February. In March 2000, the company's accountant advised that it would need to take drastic action to avoid imminent insolvency and the company decided to close the hotel for the months of January and February each year. Due to local authority requirements, it was unable to reduce staffing levels during the period the hotel was open, so instead the company proposed to change the employees' terms and conditions by reducing their weeks of paid

71

work from 52 to 42 per annum. Nine out of the 29 permanent members of staff objected and were dismissed and replaced by new members of staff. An employment tribunal dismissed their claims for redundancy pay and the EAT upheld that decision. It said: 'We are in no doubt that the tribunal decision in this case was correct, focusing as it did on the requirement for employees to do work of [a] particular kind rather than the amount of work to be done. The requirement for employees at this hotel had not altered. The number working there was to be the same before and after reorganisation. What occurred was a business reorganisation which involved a change in the terms and conditions and particularly the number of days that were to be worked by the same number of employees.'

2.51 A similar approach was adopted in Mitie Olscot Ltd v Henderson and ors EAT 0016/04, where the Appeal Tribunal accepted that the real reason for dismissal was 'some other substantial reason of a kind such as to justify the dismissal of an employee holding the position which the employee held' under S.98(1)(b) ERA and not redundancy under S.98(2)(c). Indeed, tribunals have long recognised the right of employers to dismiss employees who refuse to go along with a business reorganisation. While a refusal to agree to changes that the employer is contractually entitled to impose may constitute misconduct, which is a discrete reason for dismissal under S.98(2)(b), dismissals of employees who refuse to accept a business reorganisation are generally pleaded as being for 'some other substantial reason' within S.98(1)(b). For example, in Garside and Laycock Ltd v Booth EAT 0003/11 the EAT accepted that SOSR was established when an employee was dismissed for refusing to accept a pay cut that the employer had proposed as an alternative to compulsory redundancies. It was 'common ground' in that case that the dismissal did not fall within the category of redundancy. (For more examples of SOSR dismissals in the context of business reorganisations, see IDS Employment Law Handbook, 'Unfair Dismissal' (2015), Chapter 8, 'Some other substantial reason'.)

However, the Aylward interpretation has been open to some criticism in that the EAT based its decision on a misreading of the ratio in Safeway Stores plc v Burrell 1997 ICR 523, EAT. The EAT in Burrell held that the correct test for redundancy is whether there was a diminution in the employer's requirement for employees generally to carry out work of a particular kind, not just the individual claimant. In reaching this conclusion, it was primarily concerned with whether S.139 ERA implies a 'function' or 'contract' test – see 'Definition of redundancy – diminishing need for employees' above – and was not actually required to address the distinction between the amount of work to be carried out by employees and the number of employees needed to carry out that work, which was the issue in Aylward.

2.52 These criticisms of Aylward were endorsed by another division of the EAT, presided over by its then President, Mr Justice Langstaff, in Packman t/a

72

Packman Lucas Associates v Fauchon 2012 ICR 1362, EAT, when upholding the decision of an employment tribunal that an employee dismissed because she refused to agree to reduced hours in the face of a drop in the need for employees to do book-keeping work had been dismissed by reason of redundancy. Not only had the EAT in Aylward relied on a misunderstanding of Burrell, it had also reached a decision that was inconsistent with earlier observations of the Court of Appeal in Johnson v Nottinghamshire Combined Police Authority 1974 ICR 170, CA. Langstaff P concluded that the S.139 test requires an 'holistic' view to be taken of a situation that involves two linked variables: the employees and the work. Thus, where an employer's business needs fewer employees to do the same amount of work, employees dismissed as a result are dismissed by reason of redundancy; and where the number of employees stays the same but the amount of work available is reduced, then that is also a redundancy if dismissals result, such as where employees resign or are dismissed as a result of changes to hours or pay. In contrast, if there is just as much work for just as many employees, then a dismissal arising out of that situation would not be for redundancy, because there would be no reduction in the requirements of the business for employees to carry out work of a particular kind.

Following the Packman decision, we now have conflicting authorities at EAT level and a definitive judgment on the matter from the Court of Appeal would be welcome. However, until that happens, there can be little doubt that Packman is the correct decision to follow – its reasoning is fuller than that of Aylward, it is the later of the two decisions, and it was given by the President of the EAT. The Packman decision should therefore be treated as definitive until the Court of Appeal rules otherwise.

2.53 It is clear that the Packman approach increases the burden on employers in so far as it raises the possibility that a wider class of reorganisations should now be treated as redundancy situations. Employers should be aware that they cannot necessarily avoid making redundancies by reducing employees' hours because any employees who resign and claim constructive dismissal may be entitled to a redundancy payment. Furthermore, in any case where such a dismissal leads to a claim for unfair dismissal, the procedural fairness of the dismissal would be judged by the redundancy standard rather than the 'some other substantial reason' standard. Given that redundancy dismissals generally entail different procedural requirements – such as a transparent selection process and a search for alternative employment – the employer may have a more difficult time establishing reasonableness than in the case of an SOSR dismissal.

On the other hand, the Packman approach is justified in the interests of increasing employment protection and, moreover, accords with industrial reality. Langstaff P noted in his conclusions in Packman that the lay members of the EAT were convinced that the result was the right one, 'not least because, from an industrial background, one would approach the question of hours and number of employees by adopting an FTE (a full-time equivalent) approach'. When measured on an FTE basis, a move from full-time to part-time work is clearly a redundancy situation even though it can be implemented while preserving employee numbers. HHJ Peter Clark, who had previously presided over the EAT in Burrell, referred to Packman when he returned to the question of 'what is redundancy' in the later decision Servisair UK Ltd v O'Hare and ors EAT 0118/13. He summarised the relevant question as being 'whether there has been a relevant reduction in FTE headcount'.

2.54 **Same work done by different kind of employee.** There is no reduction in 'work of a particular kind' merely because there is a change in the kind of employee required to do it. In Vaux and Associated Breweries Ltd v Ward 1968 ITR 385, Div Ct, the employer dismissed a barmaid because it wanted somebody younger and more attractive. There was no change in the work to be done, so the Court said that dismissal was not by reason of redundancy. Similarly, in Pillinger v Manchester Area Health Authority 1979 IRLR 430, EAT, P, a scientific research officer, was dismissed because the work on which he was engaged would be done in future by a scientist of a lower grade. The EAT held that this was not redundancy: there was no change in the work to be done simply because it would be done by an employee of lower status (but compare BBC v Farnworth EAT 1000/97 below).

Two more examples of the same work being done by different employees:

• **Excel Technical Mouldings Ltd v Shaw** EAT 0267/02: E Ltd was headed by S, the General Manager, who had six managers working under him. A reorganisation resulted in a management triumvirate consisting of two of the subordinate managers and an external part-time consultant, plus the retention of five of the six subordinate management positions. S, however, was dismissed and his duties absorbed into the management team. A tribunal and the EAT both ruled that there was no redundancy. S had been carrying out managerial work, the need for which had not declined – the work of seven full-time managerial employees was still being carried out by seven employees after the reorganisation

• **Corus and Regal Hotels plc v Wilkinson** EAT 0102/03: CRH plc embarked on a restructuring exercise of its hotel business which involved the substitution of the post of general manager – held by W – with that of resident manager and the creation of a new position of area general manager. CRH plc contended that this restructuring rendered W redundant. An employment tribunal upheld W's complaint of unfair dismissal on the basis that the business requirements for employees to carry out W's work had not ceased or diminished even though the identity of the persons carrying out W's work had changed. The EAT approved that decision on appeal, ruling that the tribunal had not simply been influenced by the fact that the same number of employees (or indeed more) were employed after the reorganisation than before it, but also, crucially, by the fact that they were doing the same work as before. W was therefore not redundant and his dismissal for that reason was unfair.

While status or qualifications per se cannot mark the work out as being of a particular kind, the experience or greater competence of an employee may do so. In BBC v Farnworth EAT 1000/97 F was employed in the post of Radio Producer, 'Mark 1'. The BBC decided that the programme on which she worked needed a more senior producer. It therefore appointed a 'Mark 2' producer and dismissed F. An employment tribunal found that the reason for the dismissal was redundancy. It noted that the BBC required a wide range of producers of different experience and ability and the need for as many producers at the dismissed employee's level had diminished. The EAT pointed out that it is a question of fact for the tribunal to determine whether an employee's work is sufficiently specialised for him or her to be regarded as different from other comparable employees. It stressed that it is the work and not the person that is important, so that personal attributes are not relevant except in so far as they reflect upon the employee's ability to perform relevant tasks. Similarly, an employee's qualifications are irrelevant except in so far as they imply special skills, attributes or knowledge. **2.55**

Work changes but remains work of the same particular kind. There is no redundancy situation if the new work is of the same kind as the old work. If the new work is of a different kind, however, there is a redundancy situation. **2.56**

In Amos and ors v Max-Arc Ltd 1973 ICR 46, NIRC, the NIRC considered how such work was to be distinguished. The employer had decided to reorganise by subcontracting stainless steel work and expanding black metal work (which was less well paid). Some employees refused to do the black metal work and claimed redundancy payments. A tribunal held that all the work – both stainless steel and black metal – was 'sheet metal work' and was work of the same particular kind and that there was no diminution in the overall requirement for employees to do it. The NIRC decided that work of a particular kind meant work which is distinguished from other work of the same general kind by requiring special aptitudes, skill or knowledge: if steel work could be distinguished from metal work on those grounds, then a redundancy situation was created when the employer decided to subcontract it.

A redundancy situation was found to exist in Lambe v 186K Ltd 2005 ICR 307, CA. There, L, an accountant, was employed as a corporate finance manager (CFM) specialising in mergers and acquisitions. In 2002 he was told by the head of corporate finance that if he wished to remain with the company he would have to change roles and move into the finance control department. The reason was that the employer wished to transfer another **2.57** employee, P, from that department and put him into a newly created position of senior CFM. These proposed changes took place in the context of the company having recently deleted two other CFM positions. L turned down the new job on the ground that it was unsuitable and he was dismissed for redundancy. He contended that his dismissal was not by reason of redundancy but his claim was rejected by an employment tribunal. He unsuccessfully appealed to the EAT and then to the Court of Appeal, which concluded that the tribunal's finding that there was a diminution in the company's need for CFMs, and in particular for a dedicated employee responsible for mergers and acquisitions, was fully supportable on the evidence. The company had clearly been undergoing a substantial downsizing. Moreover, P's new role was not merely to perform the job previously done by L but to deal with anticipated new business activities.

2.58 **Suitable alternative employment.** It is important to note that an offer of different work may be an offer of suitable alternative employment and if the employee unreasonably refuses to take up the offer he or she will not be entitled to a redundancy payment – see Chapter 3, 'Alternative job offers', under 'Suitability and reasonableness', for details. In Denton v Neepsend Ltd 1976 IRLR 164, ET, for example, the employer replaced a cold saw with an abrasive cutting machine. Although the purposes of the two tools were identical – cutting metal – the tribunal found that work on the new machine needed a much more sophisticated operational technique and was much more onerous because the machine worked at a higher speed. Work on the new machine was of a different particular kind and there was a redundancy situation. However, the tribunal went on to find that the offer of work on the new cutting machine was an offer of suitable alternative employment (although D had not acted unreasonably in rejecting it).

2.59 **Redeployment.** Problems have arisen where an employer seeks to redeploy an employee who appears to be redundant because the duties that he or she is actually performing have diminished. An employee's contract of employment may cover tasks that the employee does not actually perform and the question arises whether, if there is work available which an employee could be required under the contract to perform, that person can still be redundant. As has already been noted in the introduction to this section under 'Test of redundancy', there was a long-standing conflict between the 'function' test (under which there is a redundancy situation in respect of the employee if there is a diminution in the work which he or she actually did) and the 'contract' test (under which there is no redundancy unless there is a diminution in all work which the employee could be required to do under his or her contract of employment).

Until the late 1990s, the contract test was generally held to embody the correct approach. It was considered to derive from the case of Nelson v BBC

(No.2) 1980 ICR 110, CA, where Lord Justice Brandon stated, obiter, that the question of whether the employee was redundant focused on 'the work which he was employed to do'. Although this statement of the contract test was unsupported by further explanation, it was subsequently endorsed by the Court of Appeal in Cowen v Haden Ltd 1983 ICR 1, CA, and has been treated as binding authority by the EAT in a number of cases, including Pink v White and anor 1985 IRLR 489, EAT.

Since then, however, as we have already seen, both the function and contract **2.60** tests have been held to be unnecessary glosses on the wording of the statute and a new approach was put forward by the EAT in Safeway Stores plc v Burrell 1997 ICR 523, EAT. In that case B was employed by Safeway as a petrol filling station manager. As part of a restructuring exercise, the post of filling station manager was abolished and replaced with the post of filling station 'controller' – a lower-status job attracting a lower salary. B decided that he did not want to apply for the job of filling station controller and he was dismissed with a redundancy payment and pay in lieu of notice. He claimed that his dismissal was unfair. The employment tribunal decided, by a majority, that he had been unfairly dismissed because redundancy was not, in fact, the reason for his dismissal. The tribunal found that, under B's contract, Safeway could lawfully have called upon him to exercise many more functions and responsibilities than he actually did. However, the majority held that what mattered was the work that B was required to do in practice and concluded that the work he was actually doing was still being done, albeit by someone with a different job title. In their view, the requirements of Safeway for B to carry out work of a particular kind had not diminished and he had not been dismissed by reason of redundancy. The chairman of the tribunal, on the other hand, considered that it was the terms of B's contract that were decisive. In his view, the job that B was employed to do as a manager no longer existed and he was therefore redundant. Safeway appealed, arguing that the majority of the tribunal had applied the wrong test in deciding that there had been no redundancy.

The EAT held that both the majority of the tribunal and the tribunal chairman had adopted the wrong approach because both the function and the contract tests were predicated on a misreading of the statutory provisions and previous authorities. The EAT stated that determining whether an employee has been dismissed for redundancy involved a simple three-stage test:

- was the employee dismissed?

- if so, had the requirements of the employer's business for employees to carry out work of a particular kind ceased or diminished, or were they expected to do so?

- if so, was the dismissal caused wholly or mainly by the cessation or diminution?

2.61 In deciding at the second stage whether there was a redundancy situation, the terms of the individual employee's contract of employment were irrelevant. The contract would only be relevant when enquiring whether the redundancy situation was the operative reason for the dismissal. The EAT pointed out that, even where a redundancy situation exists, if that does not cause the dismissal then there is no dismissal by reason of redundancy. Thus in Nelson v BBC (No.2) (above) the employee was directed to transfer to another job as provided for by his contract. It was his refusal to do so, and not the redundancy situation, that was the operative cause of the dismissal.

The Burrell decision was subsequently endorsed by the House of Lords in Murray and anor v Foyle Meats Ltd 1999 ICR 827, HL. In that case M and D were employed by FM Ltd, which carried on business as livestock slaughterers in Northern Ireland. Under their contracts of employment M and D could be required to work elsewhere in the factory, such as the boning hall or the loading bay, and occasionally they did so. All the company's employees were engaged on the same terms. In 1995, following a downturn in business, the company needed to reduce the number of employees working in the slaughter hall by 35. M and D were among those selected and they were dismissed by reason of redundancy. Both employees complained of unfair dismissal. The industrial tribunal found in favour of the company on the basis that the dismissals were by reason of redundancy as defined by statute in that the company's 'requirements for employees to carry out work of a particular kind' – i.e. work in the slaughter hall – had diminished. The Northern Ireland Court of Appeal upheld the tribunal's decision and M and D appealed to the House of Lords. The employees argued that the company's requirements for employees to carry out work of a particular kind related to those employees who were contractually employed to carry out work of a particular kind. As all the company's employees were engaged under the same terms, they were all contractually obliged to work in the slaughter hall. In the employees' view, therefore, the company should have included all their employees in the pool for selection for redundancy and should not have limited it to those actually working in the slaughter hall at the time. The House of Lords held that the tribunal had not erred in holding that the employees were dismissed for redundancy, notwithstanding that under their contracts of employment the employees could be required to work in any part of the employer's factory. The tribunal had been right to hold that the company's requirements for employees to carry out work of a particular kind had diminished within the meaning of the statutory definition of redundancy.

2.62 Lord Irvine, who gave the leading judgment, boiled the test down to two questions: the first is whether the requirements of the business for employees to carry out work of a particular kind have diminished. The second, which is one of causation, is whether the dismissal is wholly or mainly attributable to that state of affairs. Naturally, in the case of the dismissal of an employee who could have been employed elsewhere, or who was not carrying out work the requirement for which had diminished, it may be more difficult to establish that the dismissal was indeed attributable to the redundancy situation. However, that is a question of fact, not law, for the tribunal to decide.

It follows from the Burrell and Murray decisions that, in cases involving employees who have flexibility clauses in their contracts, the question of whether the employee was dismissed for redundancy will focus on whether the redundancy situation was the reason for the employee's dismissal. If it was, then it will be irrelevant that, instead of dismissing the employee for redundancy, the employer could have required the employee to move to another kind of work. Where the employer does invoke a contractual right to redeploy the employee, it may be able to establish that the reason for the dismissal was the employee's misconduct in refusing to obey that lawful redeployment order, rather than any redundancy situation.

Fewer employees needed to do the work   2.63

Where the overall amount of work that needs to be done has not diminished, a redundancy situation may nevertheless arise where fewer employees are needed to do the work. This situation will typically arise where the employer has introduced technological changes to working practices that have the effect of requiring fewer employees to do the same amount of work. The situation may also arise where the employer uses independent contractors to perform part or all of the work needed to be done; or where the employer reorganises the work so that it can be done by fewer employees. We discuss these situations, in turn, below.

Technological advances. An obvious example of redundancy is where   2.64
employees' roles are rendered obsolete by technological advances. Thus in Trevillion v Hospital of St John and St Elizabeth 1973 IRLR 176, NIRC, there was a redundancy situation where a stoker ran out of work when the last two of an original 12 solid fuel boilers were converted to oil.

In that case the work (stoking) disappeared altogether. However, new technology may mean that the work remains, but can be done by fewer employees. This also gives rise to a redundancy situation. Sir Hugh Griffiths gave an illustration of this in Scarth v Economic Forestry Ltd 1973 ICR 322, NIRC: 'Suppose a business has managed to produce a million cardboard boxes per year by the use of old machinery and ten men. It is intended to continue to produce a million cardboard boxes per year, but new machinery is bought which is capable of producing that number of boxes, but is satisfactorily operated by two men. The requirements of the business remain the same, namely the production of a million cardboard boxes per year; but the business no longer requires employees to produce those cardboard boxes in the numbers that it had previously done. So, eight employees become surplus

79

to the requirements of the business... and when they are dismissed they are entitled to redundancy payments.'

2.65   A distinction must be made, however, between cases where the new technology results in fewer employees (a redundancy situation) and where the new technology is simply a new way of performing the same job (no redundancy). The important question here is whether the work remains of the same particular kind or whether the change in the manner of performance of the work is such that the job itself is different. The amount of retraining necessary for the employees to take on board the new technology may well be relevant here.

In Cresswell and ors v Board of Inland Revenue 1984 ICR 508, ChD, the High Court had to consider whether the Inland Revenue's introduction of a computerised system of clerical procedures to replace a manual clerical system amounted to a breach of contract. The employees argued that the change was such that they were being required to work under new contracts of employment. Mr Justice Walton, giving the judgment of the High Court, identified two key questions: what was the employee employed to do? And, was the job so altered as to fall outside the original job description? The High Court took the view that no employees had the absolute right to have the manner in which they carry out their employment maintained throughout their employment. Furthermore, the Court thought that an employee is 'expected to adapt himself to new methods and techniques introduced in the course of his employment'. This latter point was subject to the duty of the employer to provide any necessary training or retraining. Commenting on the nature of the training which may be involved, the Court stated that it would be a question of fact whether the necessary training involves the acquisition of such esoteric skills that it is unreasonable to expect the employee to acquire them. However, in Walton J's opinion, 'in an age when the computer has forced its way into the schoolroom and where electronic games are played by schoolchildren in their own homes as a matter of everyday occurrence, it can hardly be considered that to ask an employee to acquire basic skills as to retrieving information from a computer or feeding such information into a computer is something in the slightest esoteric or even, nowadays, unusual'.

2.66   In the High Court's view, the job done by the employees was still the same after computerisation, albeit that the methods of doing the job had changed. Consequently, the employer was not in breach of contract in requiring that the job be carried out by way of computerised, as opposed to manual, methods.

There may, however, be a trap for employees who accept a job change brought about by new technology and then find that they cannot cope. The following case illustrates the point:

*   **Luckhurst v Kent Litho Ltd** EAT 302/76: L was a very experienced worker in black-and-white photographic printing. He agreed to convert to

colour printing but the quality of his work was never adequate and he was eventually dismissed after the black-and-white work dried up. The EAT held that this was a fair dismissal for capability reasons. L could have claimed a substantial redundancy payment when the changeover to colour took place but he lost the right when he accepted reclassification and there was no longer a redundancy situation at the time of his dismissal.

Independent contractors. There may also be a redundancy situation where an employer replaces employees with independent contractors. This is because the employer requires fewer employees – even though it may still need the same number of workers to do the work. In Bromby and Hoare Ltd v Evans and anor 1972 ICR 113, NIRC, the employer dismissed two decorators because their work could be done more efficiently by independent contractors. The NIRC said that this was a dismissal for redundancy. **2.67**

A reorganisation bringing in outside contractors to do work previously done by employees does not have to be forced on the employer before it amounts to redundancy. As Lord McDonald said in Noble v House of Fraser (Stores) Ltd EAT 686/84: 'If an employer chooses to engage outside contractors instead of employees to do work of a particular kind he no longer requires employees to do it. That in our view clearly falls within the definition of redundancy.' Furthermore, even where the use of outside contractors is associated with an increase in work, the definition of redundancy may be satisfied. In Wallace v Localstars Ltd ET Case No.2201889/15 an employment tribunal accepted that there was a redundancy situation where two quality control analysts were dismissed when the company outsourced its graphic design work. This was so even though the outsourcing increased the company's ability to fulfil orders and so led to an increase in work – the need for 'employees' had nonetheless diminished.

Note, however, that under the provisions governing 'service provision changes' in the Transfer of Undertakings (Protection of Employment) Regulations 2006 SI 2006/246, many 'contracting out' scenarios are covered by the Regulations, meaning that employees who formerly carried out the work will automatically transfer to the new contractor. For more details, see IDS Employment Law Handbook, 'Transfer of Undertakings' (2015), Chapter 1, 'Identifying a "relevant transfer"', under 'Service provision changes'. **2.68**

Reorganisation of work. This is the third type of situation where there is a diminishing need for employees: the employer reorganises and redistributes the work so that it can be done by fewer employees. The leading cases are: **2.69**

• **Sutton v Revlon Overseas Corporation Ltd** 1973 IRLR 173, NIRC: S was chief accountant. The employer reorganised, dismissed S as redundant and split the work he had previously done between three existing employees. There was no reduction in the work because business was increasing generally.

81

S claimed that he was not redundant and that the dismissal was unfair. The NIRC held that S was redundant. Reorganisation enabled the existing work to be done by fewer employees and changes in job specifications eliminated the need for one employee, the chief accountant

- **Carry All Motors Ltd v Pennington** 1980 ICR 806, EAT: the employer decided that a transport depot was overstaffed because the work of the transport manager and the transport clerk (P) could be done by one person. The transport manager was retained but P was dismissed. A tribunal thought that this was not a statutory redundancy situation because there was no diminution in the work, and found P's dismissal unfair. The EAT held that the tribunal had applied the wrong test by concentrating on the requirements for work and ignoring the requirements of the business for employees to carry out the work. Fewer employees were needed so that P was redundant (and his dismissal was not unfair)

- **McCrea v Cullen and Davison Ltd** 1988 IRLR 30, NICA: M was the manager of CD Ltd. He went into hospital and his work was taken over by the company's managing director, who discovered that he could do both his own work and M's work. Accordingly, M was dismissed. The tribunal held that M was not redundant because the amount of management work had not diminished. The Northern Ireland Court of Appeal held, however, that M was dismissed for redundancy because the company needed fewer employees and the fact that the work had not diminished was irrelevant.

2.70 **Temporary understaffing.** In Sutton v Revlon Overseas Corporation Ltd (above) the NIRC added a refinement by saying that there would not be a redundancy situation if the business became temporarily understaffed through the shedding of employees during a reorganisation. This would mean that the requirement for the employees had not diminished. Two examples of temporary understaffing:

- **Harding v NUM** EAT 316/76: H was dismissed after a series of disputes with the NUM and his work was thereafter done on an ad hoc basis by the president. The NUM did not intend to replace him permanently until all claims H had brought against it had been disposed of. The EAT upheld a tribunal finding that H was not redundant: his work was only being done by an existing employee on a temporary basis until the coast was clear for the appointment of a permanent successor

- **O'Grady v Cookshop Supplies** ET Case No.31001/83: the employer was under pressure to stem losses in its shops. O'G, a full-time assistant, was abruptly dismissed to cut costs. However, the manager found that she could not cope on her own, so a month later a full-time junior was engaged to replace O'G (at less pay). When O'G complained of unfair dismissal the employer pleaded redundancy. The tribunal decided that there had been no redundancy. All that had taken place was an unsuccessful experiment which showed that there had been no decrease in the requirement for employees to do O'G's work. (Even if there had been a redundancy, O'G's dismissal would have been unfair because she would have settled for lower pay or fewer hours if she had been consulted.)

However, this approach appears to conflict with S.139(6) ERA, which states that 'diminish' in S.139(1) means to diminish 'either permanently or temporarily and for whatever reason'. A better view, in line with the legislative definition, is that a temporary diminution in the requirement for employees can lead to redundancy dismissals but it will be for employment tribunals to decide, on the facts, whether the definition is met (see Whitbread plc t/a Whitbread Berni Inns v Flatter and ors EAT 287/94, discussed under 'Definition of redundancy – temporary cessation and diminution' above).

Lack of capability. If the dismissal is simply for reasons of economy – because the employer cannot afford to keep the employee on any longer – but the employer has made no decision to reorganise so as to reduce the number of employees, then the dismissal will not be for redundancy. In Hindle v Percival Boats Ltd 1969 ITR 86, CA, the employer dismissed H, a very capable woodworker, because he was uneconomically slow when working with fibreglass. The Court of Appeal (by a majority) held that this was not redundancy: it was a dismissal because of H's personal deficiencies. (Under the unfair dismissal legislation, not then introduced, it would have been a dismissal on the ground of capability.)
2.71

Expected job losses. Section 139(1)(b) ERA states that there is a redundancy situation where the requirements of the business for employees to carry out work of a particular kind, or for employees to carry out work of a particular kind in the place where they are employed, have ceased or diminished or are expected to cease or diminish. Thus, an expectation that the need for employees will cease or diminish at some point in the future will amount to a redundancy situation in the same way as an actual cessation or diminution and any dismissals carried out as a result of that expectation will be for redundancy. In Strathclyde Buses Ltd v Leonard and ors EAT 507/97 an employment tribunal held that the dismissal of employees following a merger was not for redundancy because, although the merger had created a redundancy situation, the tribunal was not satisfied that that situation applied to the dismissed employees. The tribunal accepted that it had been known for some time that the employees' jobs would disappear once new technology had been installed but it noted that that day was still a long way off. Moreover, the employer had had to bring in temporary workers to do much of the work formerly performed by the employees. The EAT overruled the tribunal and held that the employees were redundant. The tribunal had erred in focusing on the fact that temporary staff had been brought in, rather than on the fact that the dismissals occurred in the context of a merged company where
2.72

83

redundancies were inevitable. The tribunal should have given more weight to the fact that the whole process of merging with another company involved an expectation of job losses and it was that which created the reason for the dismissals. (There was a further appeal to the Court of Session in this case – see Leonard v Strathclyde Buses Ltd 1998 IRLR 693, Ct Sess (Inner House) – but this concerned compensation only and did not challenge the EAT's conclusion on the reason for dismissal.)

2.73 Reason for dismissal

Even if there is a redundancy situation a dismissed employee is only entitled to a redundancy payment if the dismissal was 'wholly or mainly' by reason of that redundancy – S.139(1). It has already been noted that a dismissed employee who is claiming a redundancy payment is presumed to have been dismissed by reason of redundancy – see 'Presumption of redundancy' above. If a party wishes to establish that there was no redundancy dismissal, that presumption must be rebutted either by proving that there is no redundancy situation or by showing that the dismissal was not wholly or mainly by reason of it.

In McGibbon and anor v O.I.L. Ltd EAT 747/95 a company had to reduce its North Sea oil fleet from 14 vessels to 11 because of a downturn in business. A number of ratings were warned that redundancies would have to be made but were offered new contracts to do the same job on less favourable terms. Those who did not accept the terms were to be put into a redundancy pool out of which the eventual redundancies would be made according to a number of criteria. M was among the 40 ratings who were eventually dismissed for redundancy. The EAT was prepared to accept that there was a redundancy situation and that the employer's need for ratings had diminished. However, the EAT did not think that the employment tribunal had been entitled to hold that the actual dismissals – or that all of them – were attributable to redundancy. The reason for this was that the numbers did not add up: the number of ratings dismissed exceeded the number displaced by the removal of three vessels. One possible explanation for the dismissals was, as the ratings themselves claimed, that they were dismissed for refusing to accept the offer of new terms. The EAT held, therefore, that the company had failed to establish that the dismissals were by reason of redundancy.

2.74   Tribunals are only concerned with whether the reason for the dismissal was redundancy and not with the economic or commercial reason for the redundancy itself – James W Cook and Co (Wivenhoe) Ltd v Tipper and ors 1990 ICR 716, CA. In Moon and ors v Homeworthy Furniture (Northern) Ltd 1977 ICR 117, EAT, H Ltd closed a factory on the ground that it was not economically viable. The employees sought to demonstrate that the factory was viable and the dismissals unfair but the EAT ruled that there was no jurisdiction to consider the reasonableness of the decision to create a redundancy situation in the first place.

On the other hand, tribunals are entitled to examine the evidence available to determine what was the real or, if there was more than one, the principal reason for the decision to dismiss and to ensure the genuineness of a decision to dismiss for redundancy. Tribunals are not bound to accept the reason given for the dismissal, as the following case shows:

- **Hartwell Commercial Group Ltd v Brand and anor** EAT 491/92: B and J were employed as the managing director and accountant respectively of a company that formed part of the FS Group. When H plc took over the FS Group, the business was running at a loss. A report seen by W, the chief executive, recommended that B and J be made redundant but warned that, under a covenant entered into by the FS Group, the cost in enhanced redundancy payments would be £125,000. B and J were then criticised for their performance and soon afterwards both were dismissed for insubordination and poor performance. An employment tribunal found that W was not a truthful witness and that the dismissal letters were pretexts for the real reason, which was redundancy. The EAT upheld the decision, stating that where there is more than one possible reason for a dismissal the correct approach is to ask what was the real or primary reason. The test required the tribunal to consider all the available evidence and to bear in mind that a reason not communicated to the employees at the time could be a reason for dismissal.

The economic and commercial reasons for the dismissal may therefore be relevant in so far as they enable the tribunal to be satisfied that redundancy is the true reason for dismissal. In Bly v Sheffield and Hallamshire County Football Association Ltd ET Case No.1805035/13 B was employed as senior football development officer. In 2012, he acted as staff representative in a dispute over contractual holiday entitlement. Then, in February 2013, SHCFA Ltd made B redundant and redistributed his responsibilities among other staff at a time when it was expecting to receive funding for a new post that might well have appealed to B. An employment tribunal upheld B's claim for unfair dismissal. It found that there was no documentary evidence as to the need to make B's post redundant, no financial justification for the redundancy and no evidence whatsoever as to why he could not have been retained until funding for the new post was clarified. All the evidence pointed to the true reason for dismissal being connected to B's acting as staff representative.

2.75

There are several situations where difficulties may arise in determining whether the dismissal was by reason of redundancy. These are discussed in turn below.

85

2.76 ## Industrial action

Industrial action may force an employer to close the business or cut the workforce. The question has arisen as to whether the employees who took the action and thus, in a sense, caused the redundancy situation remain entitled to redundancy payments. As pointed out earlier, the reason for the redundancy situation is irrelevant to the question of whether a redundancy payment is due. It is the reason for the dismissal which counts. Therefore, if the employees were truly dismissed for redundancy they are entitled to redundancy payments. It is possible, however, that they were actually dismissed for taking part in the industrial action. This is a matter for the tribunal to decide on the evidence. Two illustrations:

* **Fenn v Mirror Group Newspapers Ltd** EAT 28/81: after a long history of unofficial action the company decided to dismiss the participants in one particular strike. It also closed down the magazine on which the strikers worked and made the rest of the staff redundant. The EAT held that the reason for the dismissal of the strikers was that they were a disruptive influence. Although they had caused other people to be made redundant, the reason for their dismissal was not redundancy

* **Sanders and ors v Ernest A Neale Ltd** 1974 ICR 565, NIRC: some employees took industrial action and the employer threatened to dismiss them unless they undertook to work normally. No such undertaking was given and the threat was carried out. The employer subsequently closed the factory and wound up the business altogether, giving redundancy payments to those employees who had not taken part in the industrial action. The NIRC said that there was clearly a redundancy situation but it had not caused the dismissals of those taking industrial action.

2.77 In Webb and ors v Sundaw Products Ltd and Hall Foundries Ltd EAT 477/79 the EAT had to consider a lock-out by the employer, followed by closure of the business, when the employees refused to accept new terms and conditions of employment. It upheld the tribunal's finding that action meant to compel the acceptance of new terms was inconsistent with an intention to close the business, so that it was the refusal of the new terms that caused both the closure and the accompanying dismissals, and not the closure that caused the dismissals. It followed that the employees had not been dismissed because of redundancy.

Where an employer may have more than one motive in deciding to dismiss employees involved in industrial action it is a question of fact which was the dominant or principal reason. In Baxter and ors v Limb Group of Companies 1994 IRLR 572, CA, the employees imposed an overtime ban after a long-running dispute with management over bonus payments. The employer warned them that the action might lead to their dismissal and when the employees refused to call it off they were summarily dismissed. Subsequently, the employer decided to dispense with directly employed labour and the work done by the dismissed employees was contracted out. A tribunal held that the employer's decision to contract the work out meant that there was a redundancy situation at the time of the dismissals and awarded the employees a redundancy payment. The EAT overturned this decision and a majority of the Court of Appeal also thought that the tribunal had erred. In Lord Justice Dillon's view, the test was quite simple – if the employer dismisses all the employees who refuse to call off industrial action and engages new employees, the reason for the dismissal is industrial action. In his opinion it made no difference to that reason that the employer chose to obtain the replacement workers as contract labour from another company, rather than directly employ new staff.

It is clear in the above case that there was a redundancy situation as soon as the **2.78** employer made the decision not to replace the workforce with directly employed labour. The difficulty only arises in determining the real or principal reason for the dismissals. If the employer dismissed the employees simply because it could no longer tolerate industrial action from employees, that was the real reason and the employees were not redundant. If, on the other hand, the employer simply chose that moment to change the means by which labour was bought, and that was the dominant motive, then a redundancy situation would be the cause of the dismissals. The Court of Appeal concluded, on the facts of the case, that the industrial action was the principal cause of the dismissals.

Note that where an employee is dismissed for taking part in industrial action, he or she may have the right to claim unfair dismissal under special provisions contained in the Trade Union and Labour Relations (Consolidation) Act 1992. An in-depth discussion of these provisions can be found in IDS Employment Law Handbook, 'Industrial Action' (2010), Chapter 8, 'Industrial action dismissals'.

Concurrent reason for dismissal

2.79

If different reasons for dismissal are alleged, an employment tribunal may have to decide, on the balance of probabilities, which was the real, or main, reason for dismissal. Two contrasting examples:

- **Jolly v Haynes and anor t/a Interlink Kings Lynn** ET Case No.1502403/10: J received a letter from her employer on 1 March 2010 giving notice that her employment would end on 27 August, and saying 'as you are now over the statutory retirement age we review your employment every six months'. J had received a similar letter the previous year and simply carried on working, so she expected the same to happen this time. However, on 25 April the employer informed all employees that the depot was to close and that they would all be laid off with effect from 3 September. J claimed a redundancy payment but the employer maintained that her employment was terminated because of retirement. An employment tribunal found in J's favour. The employer had met none of the requirements then in place

87

for retirement dismissals under the ERA. Moreover, S.163 ERA provides that there is a presumption that an employee who claims a redundancy payment is dismissed for redundancy, and that it is for the employer to rebut that presumption. In this case the employer had failed to do so. J had not expected her employment to end on 27 August. She was sent the same letter of redundancy as all the other employees and she was paid to 3 September

- **Terry v Bevan Funnell Ltd** ET Case No.3103104/09: T began working for BF Ltd in 1974 and by 2008 had become its operations director. The MD was a friend and was protective of T but the proprietor took a more robust attitude when, in 2009, BF Ltd was going through a difficult time. The proprietor considered that T was out of his depth. The MD was told to make redundancies in order to effect cost savings and he decided that T had to be dismissed. T brought a claim of unfair dismissal, arguing that he was dismissed on the proprietor's instructions. The employment tribunal rejected his claim. There was no doubt that the proprietor wanted to see T removed from the business but it was clear that BF Ltd was in a parlous state and this had led to a genuine redundancy situation. The tribunal noted that, in a redundancy situation, employees are frequently selected on performance grounds and dismissal can result much more quickly than would be the case in non-redundancy situations. The tribunal was satisfied that the principal reason for T's dismissal was redundancy, not performance.

2.80 If the redundancy situation consists of a closure of a business or workplace and dismissals are left until the time of the closure, they are likely to be presumed to be because of redundancy. The date of dismissal will be a pointer to the reason. Some contrasting cases:

- **Marshall v Harland and Wolff Ltd and anor** 1972 ICR 101, NIRC: M had been on sick leave for about 18 months when the company decided to close his workplace. It sent him notice of dismissal and resisted his redundancy pay claim in part on the ground that he had been dismissed because of sickness, not redundancy. The NIRC held that the company had taken no action to dismiss M before the closure, although it could have done so. The fact that it left it until the closure indicated that the closure was the reason for dismissal – i.e. there was a redundancy situation

- **Guest v Wallis and Linnell Ltd (in liquidation)** EAT 636/80: G had been off sick for about ten months when the employer gave her 12 weeks' notice of dismissal because of her sickness. During the notice period the employer closed the factory where she had worked and all the employees were made redundant. The EAT held that closure of the factory did not act as a redundancy situation for G because she was already under notice of dismissal for sickness. The reason for her dismissal was sickness, not redundancy

- **Curtis and anor v Worcestershire County Council** ET Case No.1304610/09: C and B were employed to work in a primary school.

The school had difficulties and the Council decided it should close on 31 December 2008. By the time the decision was made C and B were both over normal retirement age and had been granted permission to remain in employment until 11 and 7 December 2008 respectively. In mid-2008 C and B both requested further extensions of their retirement dates. The Council advised the school that it should not grant an extension of their employment beyond 31 December 2008, in view of the school's closure. The school accordingly informed C and B that their employment would only be extended to 31 December, and that they would not be entitled to redundancy payments as their employment was terminating on the ground of retirement. The employment tribunal held that C and B were entitled to redundancy payments since, had their dismissals really been on the ground of retirement, the Council would have simply refused their request to have their employment extended. Redundancy was the main reason they were dismissed on 31 December.

Misconduct. Difficulties can arise where the employee's misconduct is a factor **2.81** in the dismissal. In Watters v Thomas Kelly and Sons Ltd EAT 626/81 an elderly lady who ran the business closed it down, apparently because she thought closure was the only effective way of getting rid of W, of whom she was frightened because of his conduct. The EAT said that the reason for dismissal was the closure of the premises – i.e. a redundancy situation under S.139(1)(a). But it pointed out that S.140(1), which excludes the right to a redundancy payment in certain circumstances, might operate to reduce or eliminate the employee's entitlement in these circumstances – for further details, see Chapter 5, 'Qualifications and exclusions', under 'Disqualification – misconduct'.

Change of reason for dismissal 2.82

In Waters v Stena Houlder Ltd EAT 145/94 W, an offshore rig electrician, was injured at work and off sick between April and September 1991. In May 1992 the injury troubled him again and he was off work from then onwards. In September the employer gave him ten and a half months' notice of redundancy but hoped to find him alternative employment before the notice expired. W went to great lengths to get himself fit but the company doctor said that, under the guidelines operating in that industry, he was not fit enough for offshore work. Acting on this doctor's advice, the employer dismissed W for incapacity one week before he was due to receive his redundancy payment. An employment tribunal found that the employer had acted reasonably. W appealed. He relied on W Devis and Sons Ltd v Atkins 1977 ICR 662, HL, in which Viscount Dilhorne held that evidence of conduct which is discovered after a dismissal is irrelevant to the issue of whether the dismissal was reasonable. On the basis that subsequently discovered conduct could not have influenced an employer's decision to dismiss, his Lordship concluded that the reasonableness of a dismissal has to be determined in

89

the light of facts known to the employer at the time of dismissal. Applying this reasoning, W argued that, once the employer had given him notice of dismissal for redundancy, the subsequent discovery of his incapacity did not permit it to substitute a different reason.

The EAT saw nothing in the authority which required it to hold that an employee could not be summarily dismissed, or dismissed with shorter notice, for conduct or incapacity which occurred during the original notice period. Since an employer would be entitled to dismiss summarily for vandalism, for example, while an employee was on notice for redundancy, the EAT could see no reason why the same should not apply if an employee became incapable of performing the contract. However, the EAT did consider that it was necessary for the tribunal to determine, as part of the reasonableness test, whether the employer had acted in good faith in bringing W's employment to an end in the way it did. As the tribunal had not expressly done this, the EAT remitted the case for that point to be determined.

2.83 A similar situation arose in Bottoms v Futuresource Consulting Ltd ET Case No.1200162/13. There, B was under notice of dismissal for redundancy, which was due to expire on 26 November 2012. On 15 November FC Ltd wrote to him calling him to attend a disciplinary hearing convened to consider allegations of misconduct during the notice period. B did not attend the meeting and FC Ltd decided in his absence that he should be summarily dismissed for gross misconduct. A letter setting out that decision was sent to him by e-mail at 17:14 on 26 November but B maintained that he did not read the e-mail until the next day. An employment tribunal found that, since 26 November would ordinarily have been B's last day, it could be assumed that he would have finished work at the usual time of 17:30 and that it was not reasonable to expect him to have read the e-mail within the 16 minutes after it was sent. The redundancy dismissal, rather than the misconduct dismissal, was therefore effective to terminate the contract and so B was entitled to a redundancy payment.

It may also be the case that an employee under notice of dismissal for redundancy can be dismissed during the notice period for misconduct that occurred before the redundancy decision was taken. In Williams v Leeds United Football Club 2015 IRLR 383, QBD, LUFC gave W 12 months' notice of termination by reason of redundancy on 23 July 2013. However, on 24 July, LUFC discovered, thanks to a 'fishing expedition' that was undertaken with the purpose of finding something to justify W's summary dismissal and so save a substantial amount of money, that W had forwarded a pornographic e-mail using LUFC's e-mail system over five years earlier. LUFC dismissed W summarily for that reason and W claimed wrongful dismissal. The High Court rejected the claim, finding that LUFC had not known about the breach when it occurred and was entitled to take action when it was discovered.

The Court rejected the suggestion that LUFC should have been prevented from relying on the breach because it was actively looking for misconduct that would justify summary dismissal – it considered that LUFC's motive was irrelevant to the contractual position.

The Williams case was not concerned with the unfair dismissal or redundancy payment schemes, only with the contractual implications of the employer's conduct, and so it does not necessarily mean that an employer could avoid statutory redundancy liabilities towards an employee by the same means. Viewed in the light of Waters v Stena Houlder Ltd (above) there seems no reason why an employer could not rely on past misconduct, discovered during the redundancy notice period, to bring forward the termination date and displace redundancy as the reason for dismissal. However, as the EAT noted in Waters, if such a dismissal gave rise to an unfair dismissal claim, the tribunal would have to consider whether the employer acted in good faith in dismissing under such circumstances. In such a case, the employer's motive would be highly relevant. **2.84**

Voluntary redundancy **2.85**

Voluntary redundancy is a recognised category of dismissal for redundancy and normally presents no problems provided there is a genuine redundancy situation. Once an employer has made a decision that redundancies are needed, the fact that an employee agrees to, or volunteers for, redundancy does not mean that the contract is terminated by mutual consent. The employee is still considered to have been dismissed for redundancy – Burton, Allton and Johnson Ltd v Peck 1975 ICR 193, QBD.

Voluntary redundancy or voluntary retirement? A distinction must be drawn between voluntary redundancy and voluntary (early) retirement. In Birch and anor v University of Liverpool 1985 ICR 470, CA, the university offered an early retirement scheme but with a threat that enforced redundancies would be made if the scheme did not produce the required results. The Court of Appeal, reversing the tribunal's decision, held that there was no dismissal of those who opted for early retirement; their contracts were terminated by mutual consent. In Optare Group Ltd v TGWU 2007 IRLR 931, EAT, on the other hand, three employees volunteered to leave their posts at the start of a redundancy exercise. Upholding the employment tribunal, the EAT held that these voluntary redundancies did amount to dismissal, and that it was immaterial that the employees, all of whom were close to retirement age, might have accepted a similar package even in the absence of a redundancy situation. However, the EAT noted that the result would have been different had there been evidence that the employees were anxious to leave and had expressed this wish independently of, or prior to, a redundancy situation arising. **2.86**

If an employee is under notice of dismissal for redundancy and then agrees to take early retirement, he or she will still be considered to have been dismissed for the purposes of the redundancy scheme, provided there has been no express agreement to a withdrawal of the notice. In Gateshead Metropolitan Borough Council v Mills EAT 610/92 M was under notice for redundancy from his lecturing post. He applied, and was accepted, for early retirement. An employment tribunal found that M had been dismissed for redundancy and that he was entitled to a redundancy payment. The EAT held that the tribunal had been entitled to find that there had been a dismissal. The EAT did not accept the Council's argument that M's contract had been terminated by mutual consent when his application for retirement was accepted. Nor did the EAT accept that M's agreement to early retirement had the effect of impliedly withdrawing the notice. The EAT held that notice could not be withdrawn without M's consent. As the Council had failed to secure that consent, M was entitled to a redundancy payment.

The question of whether there is a dismissal in these circumstances is discussed in more detail in Chapter 1, 'Dismissal', under 'Non-dismissals and problem areas – termination by mutual consent'.

2.87 Bumping

Selection criteria for redundancy are sometimes applied to a class of employees wider than the class to which the redundancy situation relates. This may mean that employee A is dismissed and replaced by employee B, when it is really employee B's job that has become redundant. This is known as 'bumping' or 'transferred redundancy'. The leading case is:

- **W Gimber and Sons Ltd v Spurrett** 1967 ITR 308, Div Ct: S was a warehouse manager who was dismissed and replaced by a sales representative who had become surplus to requirements (and who was not replaced). The Divisional Court endorsed as sound in law the tribunal's view that: 'If there is a reduction in the requirements for employees in one section of an employer's business and an employee who becomes surplus or redundant is transferred to another section of that business, an employee who is displaced by the transfer of the first employee and is dismissed by reason of that displacement is dismissed by reason of redundancy.' The Court also held that the tribunal had been entitled to find that the employer had not displaced the presumption of redundancy.

2.88 Despite the above decision, for many years the lawfulness of bumping redundancies remained in doubt. This was because, under what was known as the 'contract' test, an employee was only redundant if there was a diminution in the work which the employee could be required to do under his or her contract of employment – see 'Diminishing need for employees – test of redundancy' above. In a bumping situation, there is no diminution

92

in the work on which the dismissed employee was employed. However, the more recent test of redundancy set out in Safeway Stores plc v Burrell 1997 ICR 523, EAT, and Murray and anor v Foyle Meats Ltd 1999 ICR 827, HL, places the emphasis on causation – i.e. was there a redundancy situation and, if so, was the employee's dismissal on account of that redundancy situation? Under this test, bumping dismissals are no longer problematic, although, as the House of Lords pointed out in Murray, where an employer dismisses an employee whose work was unaffected by any drop in demand it will naturally be more difficult to establish the necessary causal link between the redundancy situation and the dismissal. Tribunals will tend to look carefully at the reason for dismissal and if the predominant reason is, say, the unsuitability or conduct of the dismissed employee, then the reason for dismissal will not be redundancy. An example:

- **Leung and anor v Elements Oriental Buffet House Ltd** ET Case No.2101669/08: L and T, who were both in their fifties, were employed as chefs at a restaurant near Chester. In late 2007 or early 2008 their employer closed its restaurant in Southport, leaving the jobs of three men in their thirties redundant. L and T were dismissed as redundant with immediate effect and without consultation, in order to retain the younger men, who were paid at a lower rate than L and T. An employment tribunal upheld L and T's claims of unfair dismissal and age discrimination. The employees in Southport were significantly younger than the claimants, and the employer did not provide a satisfactory explanation as to why the claimants were bumped. The tribunal noted: 'Certainly and especially since this was a case of bumping, we wanted to hear far more than we did of the respondent's reasoning.'

The EAT placed a limitation on the scope of bumping in Babar Indian Restaurant v Rawat 1985 IRLR 57, EAT, by saying that bumping can only occur within one business, so that where an employer closed down one business and dismissed an employee in another business to make way for a transferred employee from the closed business the dismissal was not because of redundancy. The EAT applied the test of whether the two businesses could really be viewed as a 'single enterprise' or not. However, it ignored S.139(2) ERA, which states that 'the business of the employer together with the business or businesses of his associated employers *shall be treated as one*' (our stress). (It made no difference to the result, however, since there was an alternative finding that if the dismissal was because of redundancy it was still unfair.) **2.89**

Note that, in some cases, the reasonableness of a redundancy dismissal may depend upon whether the employer has properly considered and consulted on the possibility of bumping – Fulcrum Pharma (Europe) Ltd v Bonassera and anor EAT 0198/10. This is discussed fully in the context of procedural fairness in Chapter 8, 'Unfair redundancy', under 'Unreasonable redundancy'.

2.90 **Chain of events leading to dismissal**

Where a chain of events occurs that eventually results in an employee's dismissal it may be difficult to determine which event actually caused the dismissal. In Runnalls v Richards and Osborne Ltd and anor 1973 ICR 225, NIRC, for example, R, a long-distance lorry driver, was disqualified from driving. The employer looked around for other work and R was given the job of carrying materials on a lorry on private land. Later the employer decided to cease carrying materials in this way and R was dismissed. He claimed a redundancy payment. The NIRC held that the cause of the dismissal was R's disqualification from driving. There was no diminution in the requirements of the business for employees to carry out driving and therefore no redundancy situation.

Similarly, in Norris v Nottingham City Council ET Case No.2602440/13, an employment tribunal found that while a genuine redundancy situation had arisen it did not cause the employee's dismissal. There, N worked for the Council as a policy officer. He was elected as an official of the UNISON trade union and, from August 2007, spent all of his time fulfilling his union duties. In 2009 his policy officer role was deleted but he remained in employment as a full-time union official. When in May 2013 he resigned from his union position he had no role to which to return within the Council. He did not seek redeployment and the Council dismissed him at the end of June. An employment tribunal rejected his claim for a redundancy payment. If he had been dismissed in 2009 when his post was deleted then he would have been entitled to redundancy pay. However, the cause of the termination of his employment in 2013 was his voluntary decision to resign from his trade union role. Thus, the reason for his dismissal was not redundancy because the Council's need for trade union officials had not ceased or diminished.

2.91 **Selection criteria and reason for dismissal**

When an employer decides that a number of employees must be dismissed in a redundancy situation, it will have to apply selection criteria to decide which employees are to lose their jobs. In such circumstances redundancy will normally be the main reason for dismissal and the reasons for selection will be subsidiary reasons. So if employees are selected for redundancy on the basis of their attendance records, for example, the reason for dismissal will be redundancy and not absenteeism.

It is only in exceptional circumstances that a tribunal will hold otherwise. In Timex Corporation v Thomson 1981 IRLR 522, EAT, the employer put forward T's incapability as a reason for his selection for redundancy. An employment tribunal found that incapability, not redundancy, was the real reason for dismissal. The EAT upheld the tribunal's decision and said that it was a matter of fact for the tribunal as to whether a redundancy situation was merely a pretext for a capability dismissal.

94

Expiry of limited-term contract

2.92

Statute expressly provides that there may be a dismissal for redundancy pay purposes if a contract is for a limited term and that contract terminates by virtue of the limiting event without being renewed under the same contract – S.136(1)(b) ERA. This covers fixed-term contracts, contracts made in contemplation of the performance of a specific task and contracts that terminate on the occurrence (or non-occurrence) of a particular event – S.235(2A) (see Chapter 1, 'Dismissal', under 'Expiry of limited-term contract').

If the reason for non-renewal is redundancy, this is treated as a dismissal by reason of redundancy. In Pfaffinger v City of Liverpool Community College and another case 1997 ICR 142, EAT, for example, the claimants were lecturers who had been employed for many years on a series of fixed-term contracts, each of which was for a single academic term. When the employer tried to renegotiate the terms of the contracts the claimants brought claims for redundancy payments. The EAT noted that the combined effect of the definition of 'dismissal' and the definition of 'redundancy' is that, where an employee is employed on a succession of fixed-term contracts, the employee may be dismissed for redundancy on the expiration of each contract. The EAT concluded that the claimants were dismissed when their fixed-term contracts expired at the end of the academic term and that the reason for the dismissals was redundancy, in that the employer had no need for part-time lecturers to carry out the function of part-time lecturing during the vacation. (Note that the fact that the claimants may have had continuity of employment throughout the series of fixed-term contracts for other statutory purposes did not prevent the expiry of each fixed-term contract being by reason of redundancy. See Chapter 1, 'Dismissal', under 'Expiry of limited-term contract'.)

By contrast, in Shrewsbury and Telford Hospital NHS Trust v Lairikyengbam 2010 ICR 66, EAT, a locum consultant cardiologist who was employed on a series of fixed-term contracts was not dismissed for redundancy when his contract was not extended. There remained a requirement for the work of a consultant cardiologist on the expiry of L's contract: the position of locum consultant was essentially the same as the substantive consultant post for which L had unsuccessfully applied.

2.93

It makes no difference that the employee knows in advance that the contract is unlikely to be renewed because the work is diminishing. If the reason for non-renewal is a reduction in the need for employees to do work of a particular kind, then non-renewal is a dismissal for redundancy – Nottinghamshire County Council v Lee 1980 ICR 635, CA.

Temporary cover. The non-renewal of a temporary contract to cover for an absent employee – for example, one who is suffering long-term illness – does not fall within the definition of redundancy. If the absent employee

2.94

95

later decides not to return, thus creating a job vacancy, and the temporary employee is not offered the post, dismissal is still not for redundancy but may be for 'some other substantial reason' (SOSR) – Whaite v Dumfries and Galloway Regional Council EAT 223/92. Similarly, where the limited-term contract is to replace an employee who is away on secondment, the return of the seconded employee will be the reason for dismissal, not redundancy – Greater Glasgow Health Board v Lamont EATS 0019/12. In that case, it was accepted that the job in question was only ever a 'single employee job', so that there was no question of any diminution in the employer's requirement for employees to carry out work of a particular kind within the meaning of S.139 ERA.

Indeed, where an employee is engaged in order to cover for another employee who is, or will be, absent because of pregnancy, childbirth, adoption leave, additional paternity leave, or medical or maternity suspension, S.106(1) ERA provides that his or her dismissal upon the resumption of work by the original employee will be treated as being for SOSR – S.106(1). However, S.106(1) will only apply where the employer informed the employee on his or her engagement, in clear and unambiguous language, that the employment would be terminated on the return of the permanent employee – Victoria and Albert Museum v Durrant 2011 IRLR 290, EAT. In that case, which concerned maternity leave cover, the EAT also observed, in passing, that where another reason for dismissal exists (such as redundancy), S.106 will not always displace that reason in favour of SOSR. That will only happen where there is no other reason for dismissal than to facilitate the return to work of the woman from maternity leave. For example, if an employee is 'bumped' out of a post so as to accommodate somebody whose post had disappeared, and the bumped employee is then given work covering for somebody on maternity leave and subsequently dismissed on her return, that employee might still be dismissed for redundancy.

2.95   **Expiry of apprenticeship.** There are some limited-term contracts which, by their very nature, cannot be renewed – for example, contracts of apprenticeship or training. In North East Coast Shiprepairers Ltd v Secretary of State for Employment 1978 ICR 755, EAT, an apprentice's contract expired and he was not offered further employment as a journeyman because there had been a diminution in the employer's requirements for journeymen in his trade. The EAT held that, while there was a redundancy situation, redundancy was not the reason for dismissal. The real reason was the expiry of the fixed term and the fact that an apprenticeship contract is a 'once in a lifetime agreement' which cannot be continued under the same contract when it comes to an end. Dismissal was bound to occur when the contract ended, whether or not there was a redundancy situation in the employer's business. It followed that the apprentice was not entitled to a statutory redundancy payment.

96

3 Alternative job offers

Offer and acceptance

Trial periods

Suitability and reasonableness

Death of employer or employee

Offer during period of family leave

There is no legal obligation on employers to search for suitable alternative **3.1** employment for employees whose roles have become redundant. However, the statutory redundancy payments scheme, contained in the Employment Rights Act 1996 (ERA), encourages employers to do so where alternative work is available. Failure to offer a redundant employee an available alternative role may convert a dismissal for redundancy into an unfair dismissal – see Chapter 8, 'Unfair redundancy', under 'Unreasonable redundancy – alternative employment'. On the other hand, an employer may avoid liability for a redundancy payment altogether if a redundant employee accepts an offer of alternative employment (subject to the employee's right to a four-week trial period), or if the employee unreasonably refuses an offer of suitable alternative employment.

Briefly, the statutory scheme works as follows:

- the employee must be given notice of dismissal because of redundancy and the employer must make an offer of re-employment *before* the old employment ends. This may be an offer of the employee's old job back again – where for example, work has picked up after notice of redundancy has been given – or, more commonly, it may be an offer of a different job. The new job must start, or be due to start, either immediately after the old job comes to an end or after an interval of not more than four weeks (give or take a weekend). (Note that there is one possible exception to the rule that an employee must have been given notice of dismissal, which is where the employee has been laid off or kept on short-time – see Chapter 4, 'Lay-off and short-time', under 'Eligibility for redundancy payment')

- if the employee accepts the offer, he or she is treated as not having been dismissed and the question of a redundancy payment will not arise. This is subject to the employee's statutory right to a trial period of four weeks where the job is different to the one that the employee previously carried out, or where it is the same job but the terms and conditions are different. If the employee decides against the job and leaves during the trial period, he or she is treated as having been dismissed when the old job came to an end and as having refused an offer of new employment

97

- if the employee refuses an offer of new employment, he or she will lose the right to a redundancy payment if the offer constituted an offer of suitable employment and the refusal was unreasonable. He or she will still, however, be regarded as having been dismissed by reason of redundancy

- if the offer was for unsuitable employment, or if it was suitable but the employee's refusal of it was reasonable, then he or she will be entitled to a redundancy payment.

3.2 Note that this chapter is concerned with the statutory mechanism for offering alternative or renewed employment. The circumstances in which a failure to offer such employment can lead to a redundancy dismissal being unfair or discriminatory are examined in more detail in Chapter 8, 'Unfair redundancy', and Chapter 9, 'Discriminatory redundancy'. Note also that S.138(1) applies only to the statutory redundancy scheme contained in Part XI of the ERA. It does not, therefore, prevent an employee who has accepted an offer of alternative employment from bringing an unfair dismissal claim under Part X of that Act.

3.3 Offer and acceptance

It is clear that an offer must be made in the case of re-engagement in a new job, but an ambiguity in the statutory wording means that it is not absolutely clear whether an offer needs to be made in the case of a renewal of a contract on the same terms and conditions. S.138(1) ERA states that:

> 'Where... an employee's contract of employment is renewed, or he is re-engaged under a new contract of employment in pursuance of an offer (whether in writing or not) made before the end of his employment under the previous contract, and... the renewal or re-engagement takes effect immediately on, or after an interval of not more than four weeks after, the end of employment, the employee will not be regarded... as dismissed.'

It has been suggested that there should, in fact, have been a further comma after the words 'under a new contract of employment' in the second line, as was the case in the Redundancy Payments Act 1965, which introduced the statutory scheme. The comma disappeared when the Employment Protection Act 1975 amended the scheme and was not reinserted when the RPA was consolidated into the Employment Protection (Consolidation) Act 1978 (EP(C)A). There followed two obiter opinions of the EAT in which the absence of that comma was interpreted as meaning that 'in pursuance of an offer' only applies to 're-engagement' – see SI (Systems and Instruments) Ltd v Grist and anor 1983 ICR 788, EAT, and Ebac Ltd v Wymer 1995 ICR 466, EAT. When the EP(C)A came to be consolidated into the ERA, a Parliamentary committee opted not to reinsert the comma, noting that, following Grist and Wymer, to

98

do so would offend the principle that a consolidating statute should not change the law.

If the obiter views of the EAT are correct, then while an employer who fails **3.4** to make an offer to re-engage an employee before the end of the previous contract will not be able to rely on S.138(1) to deny the employee a redundancy payment, an employer who fails to make an offer to renew in these circumstances will still be able to rely on S.138(1) (provided the renewal takes effect within four weeks of the ending of the old contract).

In our view, the distinction, if it exists, is best ignored in practice and employers should assume that an offer is always necessary. There are three reasons for this:

- S.141(1), which governs the situation where the employee either refuses the offer of re-employment or terminates the contract during the trial period, refers to an offer to renew or re-engage, indicating that an offer is required in either case for the purposes of this section

- there is no convincing or generally accepted definition of the difference between 'renewal' and 're-engagement'. One might think that 'renewal' meant the same job on the same terms, whereas 're-engagement' involved a different job on different terms. But this cannot be right because S.138(2) says that there must be a trial period where the contract is renewed on terms and conditions which differ (wholly or in part) from the corresponding provisions of the previous contract. The explanation may be that 'renewal' refers to the same job, which may be with different terms and conditions, such as a new workplace, while 're-engagement' means a different job, but this is not certain

- in any event, the employer will not be able to rely on an employee's unreasonable refusal of an offer in order to avoid liability for a redundancy payment unless it has actually made an offer – see S.141(1) and (2). Nor, it seems, will the employer be able to rely on the employee's unreasonable termination of the contract during the trial period unless an offer was made – see S.141(1) and (4).

In practice, most tribunals accept that an offer is necessary and do not try **3.5** to distinguish between renewal and re-engagement. In the case of Coombe v North East Lincolnshire Council ET Case No.2602502/12, for example, the tribunal did not make any such distinction and found that because the Council had not made an offer to C of either renewal or re-engagement – but had simply sought to rescind the notice of C's redundancy dismissal (which it could not do unilaterally) – the terms of Ss.138 and 141 were not engaged. Therefore, it was not open to the Council to argue that C was not entitled to a redundancy payment. In any event, the tribunal found that even if an offer had been made it would not have been unreasonable for C to refuse it.

99

3.6 Timing of offer

As pointed out above, the offer must be made *before* the end of the employee's employment under the previous contract – Ss.138(1)(a) and 141(1). For an offer to be made it must be communicated to the employee. In Smith and anor v Brown Bayley Steels Ltd 1973 ITR 606, ET, the employer posted an offer of another job to S's house on 29 March. It arrived on 31 March. S's notice of dismissal for redundancy expired on 30 March and so the offer was made one day too late.

In any case, it is advisable not to leave an offer of alternative employment until the last minute, particularly if there has been a long notice period. The employee may prudently have found another job and the lateness of the offer may be a factor in deciding whether he or she acted reasonably in refusing it – see 'Suitability and reasonableness' below.

3.7 The offer must be for new employment to start either immediately after the end of employment under the original contract or after an interval of not more than four weeks – Ss.138(1)(b) and 141(1). A weekend can be added on to the four weeks. Thus, if the employment ended on a Friday, Saturday or Sunday, the four weeks are calculated as if the employment had in fact ended on the following Monday – S.146(2).

An offer made before a notice of dismissal has been given is not a valid offer for these purposes. In McHugh v Hempsall Bulk Transport Ltd EAT 410/90 M worked as an HGV driver for HBT Ltd and was offered employment with the purchaser of its business, the offer to take effect on 1 January, the day of completion of the sale. M did not want to work for the transferee, R Ltd, and remained an employee of HBT Ltd, although his services were hired out to R Ltd. Two months later R Ltd said that it no longer required M's services and HBT Ltd, having no other employment to offer him, dismissed M on 9 February. Furthermore, it refused to give him a redundancy payment on the ground that he had been offered suitable alternative employment under the old S.94 EP(C)A (now repealed) on the transfer of the business. The EAT held that no offer of suitable alternative employment had been made to M because there was no offer which took effect either on termination of his employment or after an interval of not more than four weeks as required by what is now S.141(1). It was necessary to consider the situation at the time M's contract was actually terminated and, at that time, there was no alternative employment on offer. He was therefore awarded a redundancy payment.

3.8 Contents of offer

The offer need not be in writing – Ss.138(1) and 141(1), but it must be made by the employer or by an associated employer – S.146(1). The associated employer does not have to have any employees at the time the offer is made so a subsidiary or dormant sister company can make the offer for the purposes of the statutory scheme – Lucas and anor v Henry Johnson (Packers and Shippers Ltd) and anor 1986 ICR 384, EAT.

Two employers are 'associated' in this context if one is a company controlled (directly or indirectly) by the other (who may be either a company or an individual) or if both are companies controlled by another employer (who again may be either a company or an individual) – S.231. 'Company' means a limited company and 'control' means control of more than 50 per cent of the votes attaching to shares. An offer of employment with another employer with whom the original employer has business dealings will not count unless the two employers are associated as defined – see, for example, Farquharson v Ross 1966 ITR 335, ET.

Although an offer need not be in writing, it is usually preferable that it is, **3.9** particularly when the job offered is of a different kind, or on different terms and conditions, from that previously done by the employee. The onus is on the employer to show that an offer has been made, and if it cannot do so it cannot rely on the employee's refusal in order to avoid a redundancy payment – Kitching v Ward and ors 1967 3 KIR 322, Div Ct. An offer in writing will be the most convincing evidence.

According to the High Court in Watson v Sussex NHS Foundation Trust 2013 EWHC 4465, QBD, the offer of employment must be capable of acceptance by the employee so as to give rise to an immediately binding contract. That condition was not met in the instant case as the offer letter contained no start date and was conditional on satisfactory references and occupational health reports being obtained. W was therefore entitled to a redundancy payment.

An offer should specify the material terms in sufficient detail to show where **3.10** the new employment differs from the old. The statute does not actually say this, but the Divisional Court applied the general law of contract to reach this conclusion in Havenhand v Thomas Black Ltd 1968 1 WLR 1241, QBD. This was a case in which the provisions about notice and overtime were different under the new contract, but were not specified in the offer (which at that time had to be in writing). The High Court ruled that the offer was inadequate and that H, despite having started employment under the new terms, was entitled to a redundancy payment because no valid offer of a new job had been made to him. Similarly, if the employer is offering an employee the choice between several different jobs, it should provide sufficient detail for the employee to clearly distinguish between them. A series of vague offers is no substitute for one precise offer – Curling and ors v Securicor Ltd 1992 IRLR 549, EAT.

This does not mean, however, that every 'i' must be dotted and every 't' crossed. In McKindley v William Hill (Scotland) Ltd 1985 IRLR 492, EAT, the Appeal Tribunal said: 'To be intelligible the agreement must embody important matters such as remuneration, status and job description.' It was

101

not necessary for it to contain all the items that were required to be specified as written particulars of terms of employment under what is now S.1 ERA. Thus trivial omissions could be overlooked. In Kaye v Cooke's (Finsbury) Ltd 1974 ICR 65, NIRC, for instance, the National Industrial Relations Court (the predecessor to the EAT) thought that an offer was not invalidated simply because it did not refer to a 19p travel allowance.

3.11 Normally, however, an offer of alternative employment should make clear the financial prospects of a new job – Modern Injection Moulds Ltd v Price 1976 ICR 370, EAT. This point was emphasised in Fisher v Hoopoe Finance Ltd EAT 0043/05, where HF Ltd, which was part of a group of companies, employed F as a new business manager and paid him approximately £40,000 per annum. At the same time as acquiring a new company – SF Ltd – the group decided to wind up HF Ltd, which ceased to trade. As a result, a redundancy situation arose in which F was in danger of dismissal. The employer kept F informed about the situation and drew his attention to a sales account manager vacancy within SF Ltd. It did not, however, give him details of the financial package and F decided not to pursue it. He was therefore made redundant in April 2004. The following month, SF Ltd advertised the sales account manager position, offering a salary of £40,000 per annum. F brought a claim of unfair dismissal against HF Ltd, arguing that his employer's failure to provide him with financial information about the proposed alternative role had rendered his redundancy dismissal unfair. The tribunal rejected F's claim, concluding that since he had expressed no interest in the alternative job, there had been no need for the employer to make further enquiries of the vacancy at SF Ltd. Accordingly, HF Ltd had discharged its obligation to investigate and bring to F's attention any suitable alternative employment. The EAT, however, overturned this decision.

In the EAT's view, the law should be that 'where there are one or more possibilities of suitable alternative employment available to an employee who is to be made redundant then the employer should normally inform the employee of the financial prospects of those positions'. The EAT accepted that it may not always be practicable for an employer to provide such information because the financial prospects of the positions in question might not have been determined. However, in this case, given the short period between F's dismissal and the advertisement of the sales account manager post, there was a 'clear indication' that HF Ltd either had the relevant financial information available to it when referring F to the vacancy, or could easily have obtained that information from SF Ltd. In view of this, the EAT held that the tribunal erred in concluding that HF Ltd had discharged its duty to bring suitable alternative employment to F's attention.

3.12 An alternative job offer must be recognisable as an offer of a new job and must be more than a general statement of intent to find alternative employment on the employer's part. In Byers v British United Trawlers (Aberdeen) Ltd SCOET S/738/81 B was a deck-hand on the trawler Pindaris. His employer wrote to him saying: 'It has... been decided to lay up Pindaris and offer alternative employment to the... crew in our Oil Rig Standby Fleet.' A tribunal held that this was not a valid offer. It did not state any of the essential terms and conditions and amounted to no more than a statement of intention to make an offer. A similar result occurred in Metanodic Engineers Ltd v Whitehouse EAT 695/78. There, W was a shop foreman who became redundant when the galvanising shop in which he worked closed down. He was then put onto other work, which consisted largely of painting the premises, although he never knew from one day to the next what he would be doing. The EAT held that there was nothing that could be fairly described as an offer, but only 'day-to-day acceptance by the employee of functional directions as to what he should do'.

An instruction to report for work at new premises on a specified date was held to be a valid offer by the House of Lords in McCreadie v Thomson and MacIntyre (Patternmakers) Ltd 1971 SLT 242, HL. The only difference between the new contract and the old was the change of workplace and that was adequately stated by specifying the new location address. Similarly, in Lonmet Engineering Ltd v Green 1972 ITR 86, NIRC, the employer posted a notice to say that it would be moving premises to Hemingfield. The notice contained two columns, one headed 'Coming to Hemingfield' and the other 'Not coming', and employees were invited to decide whether or not to move by putting their names in one of the two columns. The NIRC followed the McCreadie case in saying that this was a valid offer.

3.13 An offer must be for 'employment'. An offer of work on the condition that the employee accepts self-employed status is not a valid alternative for these purposes – see, for example, Okuda v Photostatic Copies (Southern) Ltd and anor ET Case No.23253/92. Note also that where a collective offer is made to a number of employees and has to be accepted by all or none of them, the jobs must be suitable for all. If not, there will have been no offer of suitable alternative employment in respect of any of the employees – E and J Davis Transport Ltd v Chattaway and ors 1972 ICR 267, NIRC.

Communication of offer

3.14 An offer need not be made to each affected employee individually. In McCreadie v Thomson and MacIntyre (Patternmakers) Ltd 1971 SLT 242, HL, their Lordships stated that an offer posted on a noticeboard is valid 'so long as the offer is in writing, brought to the notice of the employee, capable of being understood by him and in fact read by him'. There was no doubt in McCreadie that the employee had read and understood the offer because he wrote a letter to one of the employer's directors refusing it. However, the offer must actually

103

be seen and read by an employee. In Maxwell v Walter Howard Designs Ltd 1975 IRLR 77, ET, for example, M was absent on sick leave when a notice containing an offer of work in new premises was put up on a noticeboard. Since he neither saw nor heard of the offer until after the employer had moved, a tribunal held that no offer had ever been made to him.

There is a trap here for employers. If an employee refuses to listen to an offer of another job, or simply says that he or she is not interested in receiving one, no valid offer will have been made if the employer takes the employee at his or her word. However, the employer cannot rely on the employee's unreasonable refusal of an offer of suitable alternative employment unless it has actually made an offer – so it will be left with liability for a redundancy payment. Two illustrations:

- **Simpson v Dickinson** 1972 ICR 474, NIRC: S, a shop assistant, became redundant when the shop changed hands. At an interview with the new owner, she made it clear that she was not interested in working for it or anybody else, but would instead take a holiday and then look for work in a hospital. Due to S's lack of interest, the employer never made her an offer. The NIRC held that because no offer had been made, she was entitled to a redundancy payment

- **Pearson v Stan Wharton Ltd** ET Case No.27715/85: P, a car salesman, worked for a company that ceased trading because of financial difficulties. The employer tried to offer him a similar job with an associated car leasing company, but P immediately indicated that he did not want to know about it. The tribunal held that no offer had been made because P refused to hear it. In any case, it would not have been unreasonable for him to have refused it because of the general financial uncertainty surrounding the employer's enterprises.

3.15 Acceptance

If an employee accepts the alternative job on offer, he or she is treated as not having been dismissed from the previous contract – S.138(1). This is subject to the right to a trial period, for which see 'Trial periods' below. Just as an offer need not be in writing, there is no need for any particular formality over the employee's acceptance of the offer. An employee can accept an offer by simply turning up to work in the new job.

Note that S.138(1) applies only to the statutory redundancy scheme contained in Part XI of the ERA. It does not, therefore, prevent an employee who has accepted an offer of alternative employment from bringing an unfair dismissal claim under Part X of that Act. In Jones v Governing Body of Burdett Coutts School 1997 ICR 390, EAT, for example, J, a school caretaker, became redundant and accepted an offer of alternative employment as a site manager. While still employed as a site manager, he complained that he had been unfairly dismissed from his caretaker post. A tribunal rejected his claim on the ground that, by virtue of S.138(1), he was regarded as not having been dismissed from that post. The EAT overturned this decision, stating that S.138 was only concerned with the employer's liability to make a redundancy payment. The case was therefore remitted for the tribunal to reconsider J's unfair dismissal complaint.

Re-employment must be 'in pursuance of' offer   3.16

The statute refers to re-employment taking place 'in pursuance of an offer' made by the employer – S.138(1). If the terms and conditions of the new job turn out to be different in practice from those that were offered, the re-employment will not have been 'in pursuance' of the offer. As a result, the original dismissal for redundancy will stand. Two cases illustrate this:

- **Eaton v RKB (Furmston) Ltd** 1972 ICR 273, NIRC: E became redundant through the closure of his workplace. He accepted a move to new premises and his employer arranged to collect him near his home. After E had started the new job, the employer shifted the pick-up point to a mile further away from his home and he left and claimed a redundancy payment. The NIRC held that, because of the change in pick-up point, the new employment was on significantly different terms from those offered, so that re-employment had not been 'in pursuance' of the offer. E was therefore entitled to a redundancy payment

- **Clarke and ors v Wolsey Ltd** 1975 IRLR 154, ET: redundant hosiery department operatives were offered new jobs in the fashion knitwear department. The offer said that they would be working on a piece-rate system which would allow for average earnings of £27 per 40-hour week. After six months a typical operative was only earning around £14 per week. A tribunal held that the actual terms on which the operatives were re-employed had been significantly inferior to the terms offered, so that they were never genuinely employed under the offer. Thus, they were entitled to redundancy payments.

While the statutory trial period is limited to four weeks, this limitation does not apply when the employer fails to uphold the terms of the offer. However, the employee must still leave within a reasonable time, otherwise he or she may be taken to have agreed to a variation of those terms.

Trial periods   3.17

Three kinds of trial period might apply where a potentially redundant employee tries out a different job – a statutory trial period, a 'common law' trial period and a contractual trial period.

105

3.18 **Statutory trial period**

The statutory trial period is mandatory and always arises when the provisions of the new or renewed contract differ, wholly or in part, from the corresponding provisions of the previous contract as to the capacity and place in which the employee is employed and the other terms and conditions of employment – S.138(2)(a) ERA. The Divisional Court considered what is meant by this provision in Rose v Henry Trickett and Sons Ltd (No.2) 1971 ITR 211, Div Ct, and made three points:

- all differences count unless they are trivial or insignificant

- it is individual terms and conditions that must be looked at, not the whole contract as a package to be weighed against another contract as a package, and

- it is irrelevant that the new terms may be more favourable than the old terms.

If the contract is renewed on the same terms, there is no need for a trial period and no statutory right to one. This most commonly happens where business picks up during the notice period and the employer decides that it need not make employees redundant after all.

3.19 The trial period begins when employment under the old contract terminates, and it ends four weeks after the date on which the employee starts work under the new contract – S.138(3)(b)(i). (This is subject to a general proviso that the new contract must take effect not more than four weeks – give or take a weekend – after the old one ends – Ss.138(1) and 146(2).) 'Four weeks' in this context means four consecutive calendar weeks. In Benton v Sanderson Kayser Ltd 1989 ICR 136, CA, B's trial period began on 22 December and the ensuing four calendar weeks included 11 days when the employer's premises were closed for Christmas. B argued that in such circumstances, 'four weeks' should be read as 'four working weeks', since otherwise an employee would have no proper chance of assessing the new job. The Court of Appeal rejected this contention, stating that the statute was quite unambiguous and that 'four weeks' could only mean 'four consecutive calendar weeks'.

3.20 **Termination or notice during trial period.** The Act does not set down any method by which the employer or employee should terminate, or give notice to terminate, the trial period. Therefore, given that it takes place after the old contract of employment has ended, it is arguable that either party may terminate the trial period summarily, or give notice to terminate without having to observe any statutory notice requirements or any analogous requirements that may have existed under the old contract.

In any event, if the *employee* terminates – or gives notice to terminate – the new contract during the trial period 'for whatever reason', and the contract is

106

then terminated, he or she will be treated as having been dismissed when the original contract came to an end and for the same reason that that contract ended, i.e. redundancy – S.138(2)(b)(i) and (4). The employee is also treated as having refused the offer of a new job. If the new job was suitable in relation to the employee and the employee acted unreasonably in leaving it, he or she will not be entitled to a redundancy payment – S.141(4). However, if the job was not suitable or, even if it was suitable, the employee was not unreasonable in leaving it, he or she will be entitled to a redundancy payment. 'Suitability' and 'reasonableness' are considered in the next section of this chapter – see 'Suitability and reasonableness'. Note that if an employee indicates in writing during the trial period that he or she is not happy in the new job, but delays formally terminating the contract or giving notice until after the trial period has ended, he or she will not be treated as having been dismissed for redundancy – see, for example, Bodman v Hays Logistics UK ET Case No.1200619/02.

If the *employer* dismisses the employee or gives notice of dismissal during the trial period 'for a reason connected with or arising out of any difference between the renewed or new contract and the previous contract', then the employee is treated as having been dismissed when the original contract ended and for the same reason that that contract ended, i.e. redundancy – S.138(2)(b)(ii) and (4). The employee will then be entitled to a redundancy payment. 'A reason connected with or arising out of' any difference between the two contracts would certainly cover the employer deciding that the employee is incapable of doing the new job. For instance, in Bailey v Whitehead Bros (Wolverhampton) Ltd ET Case No.1317/82 a redundant works manager took a job as a librarian/storekeeper with an extended trial period. Unfortunately, he was not physically capable of doing the new job and he was dismissed for this reason when the trial period ended. A tribunal decided that the dismissal arose out of a change to the new employment and that B was entitled to a redundancy payment because his old employment terminated. **3.21**

In Hook v Day and anor ET Case No.15806/78 H was employed as a maintenance worker at two hotels. One of them was sold and the new owner hired H as an odd-job man and relief barman. After three weeks – i.e. within the statutory trial period – the owner decided that he could do most of H's work himself and dismissed him. A tribunal held that H's dismissal arose out of a change to his new employment – in that he proved to be superfluous to requirements – and he was to be treated as having been dismissed for redundancy when his original contract ended. This case, like the Bailey case, was decided under the slightly different wording of S.84(6) of the Employment Protection (Consolidation) Act 1978 (which preceded S.138(2) ERA), and which talked about dismissal 'for a reason connected with or arising out of the change to the renewed, or new, employment'. However, given that the ERA was simply a consolidating Act and did not profess to make any substantial changes to the law, these cases are likely to still be relevant.

3.22   Dismissal of the employee for another reason – e.g. misconduct – would not be 'for a reason connected with or arising out of' any difference between the two contracts, and would simply be an ordinary dismissal unconnected with the redundancy scheme. Such a dismissal would not have the artificial effect of reviving the employee's original dismissal for redundancy and he or she would not be entitled to a redundancy payment.

To summarise, if an employee is dismissed for redundancy but then enters a trial period in a new job:

- if he or she leaves or gives notice within the trial period, the employee will get a redundancy payment only if the job was unsuitable and/or he or she did not act unreasonably in leaving it

- if the employer dismisses the employee or gives notice within the trial period, the employee will get a redundancy payment unless the dismissal was for a new reason unconnected with the fact that he or she was on trial in a new job.

3.23   But even if the employer dismisses the employee, or gives notice during the trial period, for a reason connected with or arising out of any difference between the renewed or new contract and the previous contract – thus entitling the employee to a redundancy payment – the employee will still have the right to bring an unfair dismissal claim in respect of the termination during the trial period. This is because, as previously stated, the statutory provisions about trial periods are contained in, and restricted to, part XI of the ERA, which covers the statutory redundancy scheme only. They have no relevance to the unfair dismissal provisions contained in Part X of the Act. In Hempell v WH Smith and Sons Ltd 1986 ICR 365, EAT, H was made redundant and given a redundancy payment. She then had a trial period in a new job, but the employer decided that H was unsuitable and dismissed her within the trial period. Under the statutory redundancy scheme H was treated as having been dismissed for redundancy when her original contract ended. There was nothing she could claim over this because she did not contend that the original redundancy dismissal was unfair and she had already received a redundancy payment. However, the EAT held that H was entitled to bring an unfair dismissal claim over her dismissal during the trial period.

3.24   **Extension of trial period.** The parties can agree to a statutory trial period of longer than four weeks, but only in strictly limited circumstances: the extension must be to retrain the employee for employment in the new job – S.138(3)(b)(ii). If the change in employment only consists of a change in workplace and the employee will be doing the same work, there is no need for retraining and the parties will be limited to the statutory four weeks.

An agreement for an extended trial period must:

- be in writing and be made before the employee starts work under the new contract
- specify the date on which the period of retraining will end
- specify the terms and conditions of employment that will apply to the employee after the end of the retraining period – S.138(6).

The EAT has held that an 'agreement' need not be a formal legal document or contract, but a unilateral document signed only by the employer will not suffice. To constitute an agreement, the employee must do something to indicate acceptance – e.g. by counter-signing the employer's letter – McKindley v William Hill (Scotland) Ltd 1985 IRLR 492, EAT.

3.25 If the statutory conditions for an extended trial period are not met, the employee will lose the entitlement to a statutory redundancy payment if he or she stays on beyond the normal four-week trial period. In Higton v Wiggins Teape Paper Ltd ET Case No.13814/86, for example, H's employer gave him an extended trial period of four months in a new job. There was a written document recording this but the tribunal doubted whether any other statutory requirements were met. Furthermore, the document looked more like an offer than an agreement – it specified the length of the trial period but not the date on which it would end, and was silent on the terms and conditions that would apply to H after it ended. Also, the extended trial period did not seem to be for retraining, as H had no apparent need for this. However, what finally put paid to H's claim for a redundancy payment was that he did not give notice until after the four months had ended.

3.26 **Further trial periods.** The parties are not limited to one statutory trial period. Any number of trials in different jobs may take place, provided the new contract differs from the previous one, is made before the previous one ends and starts immediately, or within four weeks thereof. If they all prove abortive and the employment is finally terminated, the employee is still deemed to have been dismissed for redundancy when the original contract ended.

There is a six-month limitation period for a redundancy pay claim and that time normally runs from the date of termination of employment. However, if there has been a trial period, the limitation period runs from the end of the trial period or, if there has been more than one trial period, the last trial period – S.145(4)(a). This applies only for the purpose of calculating when the limitation period for a claim starts.

Common law trial period

3.27 Employees may be entitled to a 'common law' trial period. This arises in constructive dismissal cases where the employer, faced with a redundancy situation, imposes new terms and conditions in breach of the employment contract. If the imposed changes amount to a fundamental breach, the employee has three choices: (i) terminate the contract and claim constructive dismissal; (ii) accept the new terms, in which case there is an agreed variation of contract and the question of a trial period does not arise; or (iii) continue working (perhaps registering a protest) for a reasonable trial period. This is known as a common law trial period. It may be longer than the statutory trial period of four weeks, but not too much longer or the employee may be taken to have accepted the new terms and conditions.

The question of a common law trial period does not arise if there is an express termination by the employer and an offer of a new contract. Nor does it arise if dismissal is through expiry of a fixed-term contract followed by re-employment under a new contract. In such cases the employee is allowed the statutory four-week trial period and no more. This is illustrated by Meek v (1) J Allen Rubber Co Ltd (2) Secretary of State for Employment 1980 IRLR 21, EAT, where M was dismissed following the closure of his workplace and offered another job on a trial period to last not less than six months. M did not like the job and left it after about seven months, leaving the employment altogether shortly afterwards. He claimed a redundancy payment, arguing that the common law trial period applied and that he had left within a reasonable time of the trial period agreed with the employer. Upholding the tribunal's decision that M was not entitled to a statutory redundancy payment, the EAT stated that he had been expressly dismissed and had accepted an offer of alternative employment. This meant that he was only entitled to the statutory four-week trial period. Since he had not left within that period, M was to be treated as not having been dismissed in the context of the statutory scheme. The extended trial period agreed with the employer – which was not for the purposes of retraining – was irrelevant to the statutory redundancy scheme.

3.28 The distinction between statutory and common law trial periods can be summarised as follows:

* where there has been an express dismissal, followed by re-employment under a new contract, the employee is entitled to the statutory four-week trial period only (unless he or she is retraining)

* where there is no express dismissal and the employer tries to deal with the redundancy situation by imposing new terms and conditions in breach of contract, the employee is allowed a reasonable period – the common law trial period – to make up his or her mind whether to accept the changed terms or to treat him or herself as constructively dismissed and leave. For example, in Bevan v CTC Coaches Ltd EAT 107/88 B was ordered to move his workplace from Monmouth to Cardiff. Some weeks later the employer proposed to remove paid travelling time from his hours and to make changes in transport provision. B resigned and claimed that he had been

constructively dismissed. A tribunal held that he had accepted the employer's breach of contract by agreeing the move to Cardiff. The EAT, however, ruled that B was entitled to a common law trial period – which it described as 'thinking time' – after the employer's breach of contract in moving him to Cardiff. There had been further repudiations during the trial period and B was entitled to resign when he did. There had been a constructive dismissal.

One question that has arisen is whether an employee can claim both a common law and a statutory trial period. Two old cases that addressed this issue:

- **Air Canada v Lee** 1978 ICR 1202, EAT: L was a switchboard operator. The employer moved to new premises where the switchboard was in a basement. L tried out the new premises, did not like them and resigned two months later. The EAT held that the employer was in breach of contract by requiring L to move. She had a reasonable time at common law in which to make up her mind. As L had left within a reasonable time, she had been constructively dismissed, the reason for the dismissal being redundancy because her workplace had closed. The statutory trial period was irrelevant because it comes into play only when there has been an express dismissal. The only dismissal here was a constructive dismissal when L resigned, and once she had resigned there could be no further trial period

- **Turvey and ors v CW Cheyney and Son Ltd** 1979 ICR 341, EAT: when work in the employer's polishing department declined the employees, whose contracts did not oblige them to work anywhere else, were offered new jobs in other departments. They accepted the offer on a trial basis but left more than four weeks later having not liked the work. A tribunal rejected their claims for redundancy payments as they had exceeded the statutory trial period. However, the EAT held that where there is a breach of contract by the employer, the employee is entitled to a reasonable common law trial period for making up his or her mind whether to accept the new job or not. If the employee decides to take the job, he or she will then be entitled to a statutory trial period in addition to the common law trial period.

So far as a straightforward application of the common law rules is concerned, the two cases produced the same result: in both, employees left after trying out the new jobs and the EAT held that they had been entitled to a reasonable trial period. But the Turvey case suggests that an employee is entitled to two trial periods – a 'reasonable' common law trial period plus the statutory four weeks. This is questionable as, once an employee has chosen to accept a variation of terms by staying in a new job for a reasonable time, the question of constructive dismissal should surely vanish. The employee has affirmed the new contract and so there is no dismissal which would trigger the right to a statutory trial period. Nevertheless, the Turvey case was cited with approval by the EAT in Kentish Bus and Coach Co Ltd v Quarry EAT 287/92. In that case Q worked as a bus driver based at the company's Southwark depot. When that depot closed

3.29

the employer asked him to work at its Leyton depot until another depot was opened in Southwark. There was no mobility clause in Q's contract and the journey to Leyton took 1½ hours each way, but despite this Q agreed to give it a try. Five months later, he was asked whether he would stay permanently in Leyton and given two weeks to decide. Q was then dismissed for disobeying an instruction to work a late shift, but he claimed that the dismissal was really for redundancy. A tribunal found in his favour and awarded a redundancy payment. The EAT upheld this decision despite the long gap between closing the Southwark depot and Q's dismissal. He had acted reasonably in not deciding whether to accept the employer's breach until the new arrangement was offered on a permanent basis. In response to the employer's argument that the tribunal had failed to consider – or had misapplied – S.138, the EAT held that the trial period envisaged by that section had never started. Citing the Turvey case, it said that the statutory trial period does not come into operation until an employee has a reasonable amount of time to consider whether or not to accept the employer's repudiatory breach of contract.

According to the EAT in Optical Express Ltd v Williams 2008 ICR 1, EAT, a common law trial period cannot run concurrently with a statutory trial period. In that case W managed a dental and optical store for OE Ltd in Bolton, but his position became redundant when the company decided to close its dental service. OE Ltd offered W the position of manager at the Bolton optical store and at her current protected salary. As the contractual provisions differed from those of her previous contract, the four-week statutory trial period applied. During that period, W's solicitor wrote two letters outlining her concerns and reservations regarding suitability of the new role. Two weeks after the trial period ended W resigned, alleging that OE Ltd had committed a repudiatory breach of contract in eroding her position and status and in failing to answer her solicitor's letters, which entitled her to treat herself as constructively dismissed. She then claimed a statutory redundancy payment.

3.30   Before the tribunal, OE Ltd disputed that W was entitled to the redundancy payment because she had unreasonably refused an offer of suitable alternative employment. In response, W argued that she had preserved her right to claim a statutory redundancy payment because her solicitor had terminated, or had given notice to terminate, the new contract during the statutory trial period, with the result that she was to be treated as having been dismissed for redundancy from the date that the original contract came to an end in accordance with S.138(4). The tribunal found that the letters neither gave notice to terminate nor did in fact terminate the new contract during the statutory trial period. Nevertheless, relying on Turvey and ors v CW Cheyney and Son Ltd (above) and Air Canada v Lee (above), it held that there was a common law trial period which ran alongside the statutory procedure, meaning that W was entitled to a redundancy payment. Overturning this decision on appeal, the EAT held that where there was an express offer and

112

acceptance of a S.138 contract of re-engagement, triggering a statutory trial period, it was impossible to suggest that a common law trial period ran alongside it. The tribunal had been wrong to rely on the decisions in Turvey and Lee in finding that a common law trial period applied when in neither case had a statutory trial period actually operated.

The application of the common law trial period also came under scrutiny in East Suffolk Local Health Services NHS Trust v Palmer 1997 ICR 425, EAT. There, P's employer decided to close the hospital where she worked and she accepted an offer to transfer to a new hospital. However, before commencing that employment, P realised that the travelling involved would be too difficult and told her employer that she would prefer redundancy. A tribunal upheld her claim for a redundancy payment. On appeal, the employer conceded that P would have been entitled to a redundancy payment had she declined the offer of alternative employment and been dismissed. She would also have been entitled to a redundancy payment had she commenced work at the new hospital and resigned during the statutory trial period. However, on the facts of the case, no formal dismissal had occurred; P had simply been warned that the hospital was to close. Since there was no dismissal, there could be no right to a redundancy payment. The EAT accepted that the tribunal had failed to identify a dismissal and allowed the appeal on that basis. However, it pointed out that it would, in principle, be open to the tribunal to find that an employee who accepts alternative employment but resigns before starting work under the new contract can claim a redundancy payment on the basis that there has been a constructive dismissal. In such circumstances, the employee is entitled to a period in which to decide whether to accept the new terms. The EAT therefore remitted the case to the tribunal to decide whether the proposed change in job location constituted a fundamental breach of contract which the employee had accepted.

3.31 In practice, the problems raised in the above cases may be avoided if the employer expressly terminates the old contract – thus effecting a dismissal – and offers a new job under a new contract. Then the employee will only be entitled to the statutory trial period and no question of a common law trial period will arise.

Contractual trial period

3.32 Nothing in case law or the ERA prevents an employer and employee from entering into a contractual arrangement whereby the employee undertakes an alternative role on a trial basis. In Inchcape Retail Ltd v Large EAT 0500/03 L was told that his role of parts manager at a car dealership was to become redundant, but that IR Ltd was keen to retain his services. It offered him the alternative role of operations manager in aftersales. L expressed doubts as to his suitability for the role, in response to which he and IR Ltd agreed a plan of action whereby he would do the role as a 'designate post' for six

113

months while simultaneously undergoing a personal development plan to bring his skills into line with those needed to be operations manager. It was also agreed that if L did not develop those skills, the redundancy process would be restarted. During the six-month trial period, L did not receive the training he had expected and it became clear that he would not develop the necessary skills to do the job on a permanent basis. He sought to restart the redundancy process, but IR Ltd resisted, prompting him to resign and claim constructive dismissal.

The tribunal found that L had a contractual right for the redundancy process to be restarted and by failing to recognise this IR Ltd had acted in breach of contract, in response to which L had resigned. Upholding this decision on appeal, the EAT noted that the tribunal had not found that the statutory provisions were re-engaged when it became clear that the trial period was going to be unsuccessful. Rather, it found that IR Ltd had agreed to restart a redundancy process which included all possible outcomes, including the offer of alternative employment or dismissal with a payment equivalent to a statutory redundancy payment. In finding that the constructive dismissal was unfair, the tribunal had correctly taken the approach of assessing the suitability of offers of alternative employment.

3.33 Note that any contractual agreement for a trial period cannot waive an employee's entitlement to a statutory trial period, since this would offend S.203 ERA, which renders void any provision of an agreement or contract which purports to waive or exclude an employee's rights under the Act.

3.34 Suitability and reasonableness

An employee will lose his or her entitlement to a redundancy payment if he or she refuses an offer of an alternative job, or resigns, or gives notice during the trial period if:

- the job was identical to the old one or, if not identical, was 'suitable employment in relation to the employee', and

- refusal of the offer, or resignation during the trial period, was unreasonable – S.141(2)–(4) ERA.

The employer must show both that the job offered was suitable and that the employee's refusal of it was unreasonable – Jones and anor v Aston Cabinet Co Ltd 1973 ICR 292, NIRC. This means that an employer is expected to discuss an offer of alternative employment with the employee concerned since, if this is not done, the employer can only guess at the employee's reasons for refusing it.

3.35 This is an area in which case law is largely of illustrative rather than instructive value. There are two reasons for this. First, the two matters

114

to be judged – 'suitability' and 'reasonableness' – are questions of fact for the tribunal. The words are ordinary English words with no special legal significance. For example, the courts have rejected the contention that the 'reasonableness' of an employee's refusal of alternative employment should be judged in line with the 'range of reasonable responses' test used for determining whether or not a dismissal is unfair under S.98 ERA – see Hudson v George Harrison Ltd EAT 0571/02 and Devon Primary Care Trust v Readman 2013 IRLR 878, CA. It follows that there is little scope for tribunals to misdirect themselves in law and appeals against their decisions are rarely successful, although see below on the need for tribunals to assess reasonableness from the subjective view of the employee.

Secondly, suitability is assessed objectively by the tribunal. However, there is also some subjectivity in this matter because it must assess whether the job offered is suitable 'in relation to the employee' concerned. In Chalmers v Northamptonshire Teaching Primary Care NHS Trust ET Case No.1902049/08, for example, the ward where C worked as a nurse was closed and she was offered an alternative role working in a hospice. She refused the job, maintaining that she was incapable of working in an environment where death was an inevitable outcome. The Trust refused to give C a redundancy payment, stating that she had unreasonably refused an offer of suitable alternative employment. In subsequent tribunal proceedings, it contended that it was ludicrous to suggest that a nurse with C's experience would be unable to cope with death. However, the tribunal held that she was entitled to a redundancy payment. C had spent most of her nursing career working in a rehabilitation ward and she did not have the 'psychological mindset' to work in a hospice. Moreover, when her father died seven years previously, she was absent for a year and had bereavement counselling. The tribunal accepted that C had a degree of emotional fragility when it came to dealing with death which could be exacerbated in the context of a hospice. Accordingly, the role was not suitable for her.

The reasonableness or unreasonableness of a refusal also depends on factors **3.36** personal to the employee and is assessed subjectively from his or her point of view at the time of the refusal – Executors of JF Everest v Cox 1980 ICR 415, EAT. Accordingly, a tribunal will fall into error if it substitutes its own view about the reasonableness of a refusal. In Bird v Stoke-on-Trent Primary Care Trust EAT 0074/11 B's post, which was 80 per cent managerial and 20 per cent clinical, was at risk of redundancy due to restructuring and she was invited to apply for whatever posts were available. At that time the only jobs available were exclusively managerial and so she did not make any applications. The Trust later offered B three alternative roles. The first was a purely clinical role, which B rejected as being unsuitable because she would have been required to work in a clinical setting alongside colleagues for whom she had previously been responsible. (The Trust later accepted that this was not a suitable alternative role.) B also rejected the two other posts that were offered to her by the Trust: one was 15 per cent managerial and 85 per cent clinical; the other was 20 per cent managerial and 80 per cent clinical. B was eventually made redundant but without being paid a contractual or statutory redundancy payment as the Trust considered that these other two roles were suitable alternatives and that B's refusal of these roles was unreasonable. A tribunal dismissed B's subsequent claim for a redundancy payment on the basis that she had unreasonably refused these offers of suitable alternative posts. However, the EAT overturned this decision. The tribunal had wrongly substituted its own view about the reasonableness of B's refusal, finding that her view that the offered roles involved a demotion was irrational, rather than considering whether someone in B's particular circumstances could reasonably have taken that view. If B had taken one of the two posts it would have meant moving from managing a team of physio- and occupational therapists to being managed within a team, with the result that she could no longer call herself manager within the NHS. The EAT was unable to say what conclusion the tribunal would have reached if it had approached the issue in the correct way and therefore remitted the case to a differently constituted tribunal.

3.37   The need to assess reasonableness subjectively makes it difficult to extract general principles from the cases, as tribunals must always consider the employee's individual circumstances. An apparent minor change in terms and conditions of employment may affect employees very differently. Two examples:

- **Day v Premier Grocery Products Ltd** ET Case No.1500344/08: D's post became redundant when the employer closed down its plant in King's Lynn where he worked, and he was offered an alternative job in Wisbech. However, the new job would have required him to work 15 weekends each year, which he was unable to do because he was a Colour Sergeant in the Territorial Army and in order to maintain and further his career in the TA he was required to commit to 25 weekends a year. In his subsequent tribunal claim for a redundancy payment, D pointed out that the new contract would significantly affect his ability to continue with his TA career (he was just two years away from reaching the position of company sergeant major, an objective that had taken him 25 years to achieve), and argued that swapping his rostered weekends when necessary would have been a major problem. The tribunal held that D was entitled to the payment. Given his particular circumstances, namely his commitment to the TA, his refusal of the alternative job was reasonable

- **Goodwin v Total Security Services Ltd** ET Case No.1500931/09: G was posted by the employer to work as a security guard at Tesco in Saffron Walden. The store eventually decided that it no longer needed the employer's services and G's post became potentially redundant. The employer offered G alternative jobs in Great Dunmow, Bishops Stortford and London but he

116

rejected all of them. In subsequent proceedings, the employer maintained that G had unreasonably refused the offers and so was not entitled to receive a redundancy payment. The tribunal accepted that the jobs constituted suitable alternative employment – it was not uncommon for security officers to be moved about. However, G was unable to drive; could not read or write, and had difficulty with written signs, notices and timetables, so using public transport would have presented particular difficulties for him. Accordingly, he did not have the skills to respond to events that people with reading skills would take in their stride, and so he had not acted unreasonably in refusing the offers of alternative employment.

Given the difficulty in distilling general principles from the cases, all that we can do here is point out some of the factors that tribunals may take into account, repeating our warning that decisions cannot normally be taken as precedents applicable in other cases.

Interrelation of 'suitability' and 'reasonableness'   3.38
A tribunal will first consider whether the alternative job offered is suitable. Only if it is will it then go on to consider whether the employee was reasonable in rejecting it. Where a suitable job offer is made, the employee would be well advised to carefully consider and to respond to the offer before rejecting it. This is because the way in which an employee considers a suitable offer and responds (or does not respond) to it will be a relevant consideration in the overall assessment of reasonableness – Lincoln and Louth NHS Trust v Cowan EAT 895/99.

In practice, tribunals often treat 'suitability' as covering factors relating to the nature of the job on offer as they affect the particular employee – e.g. job content, status, terms and conditions, while 'reasonableness' will generally cover factors relating to the employee's personal circumstances – e.g. domestic problems, housing, health. Nevertheless, in Spencer and anor v Gloucestershire County Council 1985 IRLR 393, CA, the Court of Appeal said (obiter) that drawing too rigid a distinction between the issues of a job's suitability and the employee's reasonableness or unreasonableness in turning it down would lead to confusion. Some factors may be common to both aspects and tribunals are entitled to look at them in either context.

A case that illustrates this point is Cambridge and District Co-operative   3.39
Society Ltd v Ruse 1993 IRLR 156, EAT. There, R was the manager of a butcher's shop until it closed down. He was then offered the position of butchery department manager in a supermarket. However, R did not like the new position, feeling that he had suffered a loss of status. He was to some extent under the store manager's control, did not have his own key, and no longer had responsibility for banking money. The tribunal held that the post constituted suitable alternative employment but that R's perceived loss of

117

status made it reasonable for him to refuse that offer. The employer appealed to the EAT on the ground that once an objective finding of suitability had been made, the employee could not rely on his or her subjective perception of that employment to refuse the offer. If the offer was suitable, R could only rely on factors extraneous to the job, such as personal factors affecting him. The EAT rejected this argument as there was nothing in S.141(2)–(3) that restricted an employee's reasons to factors unconnected with the employment itself. Accordingly, as a matter of law, it was possible for an employee to reasonably refuse an objectively suitable offer of alternative employment on the ground of his or her personal perception of the job.

Rather helpfully, the EAT considered the interrelationship between suitability and reasonableness once more in Commission for Healthcare Audit and Inspection v Ward EAT 0579/07. W's role was to be deleted in a reorganisation and she was offered a new job which she rejected because, in her view, it would have seen the size of her department reduced by 75 per cent; her budget would have been halved; and the future job prospects were not as good. She claimed a redundancy payment, which the Commission resisted on the basis that she had unreasonably refused suitable alternative employment. The tribunal found that, since the new job did not involve a loss of status nor impact adversely on her future job prospects, the employment was suitable, though it did recognise that suitability was marginal, a factor that it took into account in finding that W's refusal of the offer was reasonable. On appeal, the Commission argued that the tribunal could not take into account suitability of the new post when determining whether the refusal was unreasonable. Rejecting this contention, the EAT confirmed that there is no requirement for suitability and reasonableness to be considered in isolation. Simply put, a tribunal is entitled to have regard to the issue of suitability when considering the question of reasonableness.

3.40 The upshot of Ward is that, where a new job is overwhelmingly suitable for the employee, it may be less of a challenge for the employer to demonstrate that the employee's refusal is unreasonable than it would be if, for instance, suitability is only marginal.

We now consider the following factors that tribunals have taken into account in assessing suitability and reasonableness:

- job content and status
- pay, including fringe benefits
- hours
- workplace
- job prospects, and
- timing of offer.

118

It should be noted that the willingness of an employee to undertake a trial period is not evidence that he or she considers it suitable. To determine otherwise would undermine the very reason for providing a statutory trial period in the first place – Laing v Thistle Hotels plc 2003 SLT 37, Ct Sess.

Job content and status

3.41

The fact that an employee's pay is preserved in a new job will not be sufficient to make the job suitable. A drop in status will most likely make a job unsuitable, even if earnings are maintained. In Taylor v Kent County Council 1969 2 QB 560, Div Ct, a long-serving headmaster was offered a job as a schoolteacher. The Divisional Court held that this was like asking a director to work as a navvy and that the job was manifestly unsuitable. However, an employer should not refrain from offering alternative employment if the only job available involves a loss of status. In Green v GA Transport Ltd (t/a Allens Transport Services) EAT 306/79 the employer failed to offer an operations manager at risk of redundancy the position of HGV driver where there was evidence that he would have accepted it. The employer's failure to offer G the alternative job demonstrated that it had not acted reasonably in treating redundancy as a sufficient reason for dismissing him. However, contrast this decision with Barratt Construction Ltd v Dalrymple 1984 IRLR 385, EAT, where it was held that if a relatively senior employee is prepared to accept a lesser position instead of being made redundant, he or she ought to make this clear to the employer. Although Green and Dalrymple appear to represent conflicting authorities on the question of whether the employer should offer a lower status job, there are important differences between the two cases. The employee in Green had done the lower status job in the past and there was evidence that he would have accepted it as an alternative position had it been offered. These factors, which strongly suggest that the alternative job was suitable, were not present in the Dalrymple case.

The importance of status is further emphasised by the following cases:

*   **Harris v E Turner and Sons (Joinery) Ltd** 1973 ICR 31, NIRC: H was a joiner who was promoted to apprentice instructor, a position which carried with it staff status and higher pay. After six years the employer discontinued the joinery apprenticeship scheme and offered H alternative employment, on the same pay, as a bench hand in the joinery production shop. H refused the offer and sought a redundancy payment. A tribunal held that because H was a skilled joiner, this was a suitable offer which he had unreasonably refused. On appeal, the NIRC held that employment is not necessarily suitable simply because the employee has the skills necessary to perform it. For example, an offer of employment as a teller would not be suitable for a bank general manager. The tribunal had misdirected itself by not giving enough weight to the instructional content of H's work and to the status that went with it, which made the alternative work offered to him unsuitable

119

- **Marsden v Cambridge County Council** ET Case No.1500819/02: M was employed as a field social worker by the Council. She had reached the grade of senior practitioner prior to it being phased out in 1998 and was paid on a management band. The Council opted to withdraw social worker assistance from the service for which M worked and she was offered alternative employment as a social worker (rather than as a senior social worker), with her pay protected for three years. In determining that she had not unreasonably refused an offer of alternative employment, an employment tribunal found that she was entitled to treat the offer as a demotion and to be concerned by the loss of her 'senior' status.

3.42 By way of contrast, in Browning v White Knight Products Ltd ET Case No.3100413/98 a quality control technician's refusal to accept alternative work as a machine operator, on the ground that he had originally been employed as a machine operator and did not want to take a retrograde step in status, was held to be unreasonable. The tribunal was influenced by the fact that part of B's job as a quality control technician had been to stand in for machine operators on a routine basis while they took breaks.

Loss of job content may make a new job unsuitable where, for example, it fails to utilise the employee's skills. In Koch v Hoverlloyd Ltd ET Case No.428/82 the terms and conditions of K's new job were better, but the range of duties was much narrower and she estimated that she had lost two thirds of the content of her previous job. That made the job unsuitable and K's resignation during the trial period not unreasonable. A similar conclusion was reached in Morgan v Global Solutions Ltd ET Case No.2407066/04. There, M's role as a senior custody officer at Preston Crown Court was made redundant and she was offered the same position at Accrington Magistrates Court. Though her terms and conditions were identical, she had fewer supervisory responsibilities and spent much of her working day completing crossword puzzles. The tribunal held that, given the high regard M had for job satisfaction, it was not unreasonable of her to refuse the offer of alternative employment.

3.43 Conversely, extra job content may make it reasonable for an employee to reject an offer of alternative employment. In Patchett v Buck and Hickman Ltd ET Case No.34883/81, for example, a redundant stock record clerk was given a 10 per cent rise and switched to a new job requiring more flexibility. A tribunal thought that her resignation was not unreasonable – but she was 60 years old and it would have taken a different attitude had she been younger.

A substantial change in job content may also make it reasonable for an employee to refuse an offer of alternative employment. In Horsley v British Fuels Ltd ET Case No.57257/95, for example, an employee's 24 years of experience and extensive contacts in the wholesale side of the employer's business were factors taken into account by a tribunal in holding that he had

120

reasonably refused an offer of suitable alternative employment in industrial sales. The employee was entitled to refuse the change in career direction after so many years.

Pay and other benefits

3.44

Any significant drop in earnings is likely to make a job unsuitable. It is not only basic pay that counts but the whole package on offer, including the opportunity to earn overtime and bonuses – Kennedy v Werneth Ring Mills Ltd 1977 ICR 206, EAT. In Carron Co v Robertson 1967 SC 273, Ct Sess, the Court of Session said that fringe benefits such as staff status, sick pay and holiday entitlement were all elements to be considered when determining the suitability of a job.

In Grainger v White ET Case No.1168/85 the manageress of a hairdressing salon, who had 40 years' experience in the industry, was offered alternative employment as an assistant in a sports shop on the same pay. Among other things, the tribunal held that, while her pay was to remain unchanged, G would have lost the tips which she had received as a hairdresser. This made the offer unsuitable.

Employees offered lower-paid roles are sometimes given 'pay protection' for a specified period. However, such protection, particularly if it is for a limited time, will not necessarily mean that an employee will have acted unreasonably if he or she refuses the offer. In Marsden v Cambridge County Council (above), one of the factors which influenced the tribunal's decision that M had reasonably refused an offer of suitable alternative employment was that her pay would be frozen for three years, but then reduced to a lower grade. However, that decision can be contrasted with Wiseman v Central Lancashire Primary Care Trust ET Case No.2408405/08, where W worked as patient service manager, a Band 7 post. Following a merger and consequent restructuring process, her post became redundant and she was offered the alternative job of programme support officer, a Band 6 post. Although W's pay was set to reduce under the proposal, it would have been protected for two years. She refused the offer on the ground that her pension would be affected and she was set to retire in three years' time. The Trust refused to give W a redundancy payment, saying that she had unreasonably refused an offer of suitable alternative employment. A tribunal agreed. W's anticipated retirement date was only two months beyond the date when her pay protection would have ceased and so the loss in salary and its impact on her pension was negligible.

Redundancies are often made when an employer's business is facing hard times and uncertainty over its ability to continue paying wages may be a relevant factor in considering suitability or the reasonableness of a refusal to accept suitable alternative work. In GD Systems Ltd v Woods EAT 470/91 W worked for a small company as a computer programmer. On 31 March he was given

3.45

121

one month's notice of termination. He had little work to do and on 24 April he was denied access to the employer's premises. Various offers of alternative employment were made to him orally but W refused them. A tribunal decided that his refusal was reasonable because there was no guarantee that his salary would be paid. His March salary had not been processed until May and he had brought a Wages Act claim (now a claim under Part II of the ERA) in respect of his April salary. The EAT upheld the tribunal's findings.

3.46   ## Working hours

A change in shift patterns will be a relevant factor for tribunals to consider. In Morrison and Poole v Cramic Engineering Co Ltd 1966 ITR 404, ET, the employer closed a night-shift and offered the employees work on a double day-shift (on less pay). The tribunal appreciated the difficulty that long-serving night-shift workers would have in reacclimatising to day work and found the offer unsuitable. Similarly, a change in the number of hours worked may be relevant. In O'Connor v Montrose Canned Foods Ltd 1966 ITR 171, ET, for example, a maintenance fitter worked a 40-hour week plus 14 hours of overtime. He was made redundant and offered new employment with no overtime. The offer was held to be unsuitable.

As mentioned above, the question of reasonableness is to be judged from a subjective rather than objective standpoint. As a result, family and caring considerations can be extremely relevant. Two contrasting illustrations:

- **Saggers v East Gloucestershire NHS Trust** ET Case No.18145/96: S's part-time clerical post became redundant and she refused an offer of alternative employment because it involved some work on Fridays. One of the reasons she took her original job was that it left her free on Fridays, when she had a long-standing commitment to visit an elderly neighbour. A tribunal held that S had unreasonably refused suitable alternative employment. There was no reason why she could not have fitted her neighbourly duties around work on Fridays, or rearranged them for another day of the week

- **Weston v A Welcome House Ltd** ET Case No.2301444/00: W worked in a care home from 7.30 pm to 7.30 am. AWH Ltd announced that the care home would close and offered her employment at another of its homes which was a 20-minute drive from her house. However, she would have to work until 8 am. W refused the offer – she needed to finish at 7.30 am to see her daughter off to school. A tribunal held that the offer of alternative employment was suitable but, considering the importance that W placed on seeing her daughter off to school, she had not unreasonably refused.

3.47   ## Change of workplace

In Chapter 2, 'Redundancy', under 'Closure of workplace – place of employment', we discuss the impact of a contractual mobility clause on the

122

question of whether a redundancy situation has arisen. In this section, we proceed on the basis that no such clause exists (or, if it does, that it has not been invoked). The question then is whether a change of workplace might make an alternative job offer unsuitable, or enable the employee to reasonably refuse the offer if it is suitable.

A mere change of workplace is unlikely to make a job unsuitable if the nature of the job itself is unchanged. Rather, if an employee turns down an offer of identical work at a different location, his or her reasonableness will generally be in issue. In Payler v Douglas Wemyss LLP ET Case No.3501678/10, for example, the employer had its main office in Leicester, but for many years also had an office in Loughborough. P had worked as a fee earner in the Loughborough office for 15 years until the employer decided to close it and begin consulting with staff on relocating to Leicester. P was offered an increased salary to offset her extra travelling costs, as well as the ability to work from home two days a week. However, she refused the offer and claimed a redundancy payment. A tribunal found that the employer had tried to counter every objection that P had raised to the move – it had even offered to pay for a dog-walking service. In refusing even to countenance the offer of suitable alternative employment, P had acted unreasonably.

The question of reasonableness will depend very much on the personal **3.48** circumstances of the employee, since a change of workplace may affect employees differently. To illustrate this point, here are two cases decided by the same tribunal on the same day:

- **MacGregor v William Tawse Ltd** 1967 ITR 198, ET: M, who worked in the civil engineering and contracting industry, was offered work at a site in the Hebrides from which he would only get home one weekend every six weeks. He refused the offer. A tribunal held that the work was suitable – a degree of mobility was to be expected in the industry – and M's refusal was unreasonable

- **MacCallum v William Tawse Ltd** 1967 ITR 199, ET: M received an identical offer to that in the above case. However, he had a wife and five children, two of whom were in poor health, and his wife could not cope with prolonged periods of caring for the family alone. The tribunal held that while the work was suitable, M's special domestic circumstances made his refusal of the offer reasonable.

Generally, significant extra travelling time and cost will make a refusal to relocate reasonable. In Gibbs v Gardner ET Case No.2540/86 an employer closed its shop in Paddington and offered G identical work at another shop in Radlett. This would have increased his daily travelling time by nearly two hours and cost him an extra £17 per week. The tribunal held that G's refusal was reasonable. Similarly, in Landry v Wedlake Saint Solicitors ET Case

No.3300098/10 L worked as a legal secretary near her home in Hertfordshire until the employer closed that office and relocated to London. She was offered a job in London but, after visiting the office and finding that her travelling time would be 2 hours and 15 minutes, L declined the offer. The employer claimed that L had unreasonably refused a suitable alternative post and had therefore forfeited the right to a redundancy payment. The tribunal disagreed. The employer had failed to show that L had made an unreasonable decision in rejecting the London job offer. She had made a lifestyle choice in refusing to commute to London: she was 57 years old – an age when many people are looking for ways to reduce time spent at, or going to and from, work.

3.49   An employer may offer to reimburse any increase in fares or the move may be a minor one involving little or no extra cost. Even so, an employee with special domestic circumstances could still be acting reasonably in refusing to move. For example, in Cahill v Keith Prowse and Co Ltd and anor ET Case No.33490/76 C's employer changed its premises in Central London meaning that C would have to switch from a few minutes' walk to work to a half-hour bus ride. C suffered from claustrophobia and could not use public transport. Furthermore, she had a small son at home. A tribunal held that her refusal was not unreasonable. Similarly, in Charlwood v KPK (Sheet Metal) Ltd ET Case No.22786/79 the employer moved only four miles and offered C enhanced benefits. However, the four miles meant significant extra travelling because of traffic conditions and caused domestic problems for C, who was a widower with daughters aged 12 and 16. The tribunal held that his refusal was not unreasonable.

However, employees will not always succeed, even where large distances are involved. In Gotch and Partners v Guest 1966 ITR 65, ET, for example, an architect was offered a move from Bournemouth to Bristol at an increased salary and with a contribution to his removal expenses. A tribunal thought that this was a suitable offer and that his refusal was unreasonable. And in Little v Beare and Son Ltd EAT 130/80 a warehouseman refused a move that would have increased his daily travelling from 32 to 72 miles. A tribunal found his refusal unreasonable: it thought that the travelling was not excessive for Greater London, and noted that the employer had provided L with a van to assist with his journey. The EAT refused to interfere because no point of law was involved.

3.50   The nature of an industry is also a factor to be taken into account. In Thompson v Moroc Construction Ltd COET 1463/36 T worked as a van driver for a construction company at sites around 15 minutes' drive from his home. When work dried up at these sites he was offered new employment involving an extra 12 hours' travelling time (which would be paid) but he refused. The tribunal thought that it was usual in the construction industry to travel to distant sites and that T's refusal was therefore unreasonable.

124

However, in McGurrell v Garrett and Campbell Ltd ET Case No.32273/83 M, a printer, worked in Kingston, which was around 15 minutes by car from his home, and he was offered an equivalent job in Central London when the Kingston premises closed. This would have meant an hour's journey each way by underground, which M disliked, and he refused. The employer argued that this was unreasonable because an hour or so each way was par for the course for London commuters. The tribunal, however, held that what others were willing to do was irrelevant. The move would have introduced an unacceptable feature into M's daily life and it was not unreasonable for him to refuse.

An employee may have personal objections to new premises, in which case a refusal to move may be reasonable if the objections are justifiable. In Flannery v Tetley Walker Ltd ET Case No.27541/79, for example, a redundant barmaid refused a move to a pub which was known to be frequented by rowdy customers and where the police were often called in. A tribunal found her refusal reasonable. And in Bates v North West Anglia Healthcare Trust ET Case No.1901514/98 B, a school nurse, lived and worked in King's Lynn, where she was a 'pillar of the community' and knew all the families with whom she worked. A tribunal held that she had reasonably refused a move to a town about half an hour away – she felt isolated in strange territory and her pre-existing disposition to depression was exacerbated. In Fuller v Stephanie Bowman (Sales) Co Ltd 1977 IRLR 87, ET, on the other hand, F refused a move to new premises because they would be shared with a sex shop. The tribunal said that this could be a reasonable objection in some circumstances but, having visited the premises, it decided that F was being over-sensitive and that her refusal was unreasonable.

Job prospects

3.51

If the new employment on offer is only temporary, with no guarantee for the future, that may make it unsuitable even if the terms and conditions are otherwise identical. In Ireland v Fairfield-Rowan Ltd 1966 ITR 191, ET, for example, the employer offered to renew I's contract, but only for two months and with no certainty as to what would happen after that. A tribunal thought that I's refusal was reasonable. However, in Morganite Crucible Ltd v Street 1972 ICR 110, NIRC, an offer of work which the employee expected to last only 12–18 months was described by the NIRC as an offer of 'regular' rather than 'temporary' re-employment. It overruled a tribunal and held that the employee's refusal was unreasonable.

The fact that new employment is only temporary may, on the other hand, be the one factor that makes it suitable. In Dutton v Hawker Siddeley Aviation Ltd 1978 ICR 1057, EAT, D, a wood machinist, was asked to move temporarily to another department to train as a capstan operator. His pay

125

and conditions would be unchanged and this was deemed a purely temporary move until work picked up in his original department. It was held that in the circumstances this was an offer of suitable alternative employment and D's refusal was unreasonable.

3.52 Reasonable suspicion that a job offer is not genuine may also justify an employee's refusal. In Woodcock v J and G Meakin Ltd 1968 ITR 164, ET, a written job offer was made to W. However, the same job – and only one was available – was simultaneously offered to another employee. There was also evidence that the job had already been filled by a third employee. A tribunal thought that W's refusal of the offer was reasonable because he had grounds for believing that no job was in fact available. Similarly, in Page v Thorn Lighting Ltd ET Case No.66259/93 a redundant employee believed that an alternative job had been 'manufactured' for him so that he would not leave and work for a competitor. He raised concerns about the genuineness of the job with his employer but received no reply. P left at the end of the trial period and a tribunal held that he did not act unreasonably in rejecting the offer.

3.53 Timing of offer

The timing of an offer of re-employment may be a relevant factor in considering reasonableness. In Bryan v George Wimpey and Co 1967 3 KIR 737, ET, an offer was not made until the evening before B's notice expired and after he had prudently found another job. His refusal was held to be reasonable. The facts were similar in Thomas Wragg and Sons Ltd v Wood 1976 ICR 313, EAT, in which the Appeal Tribunal held that the lateness of an offer was a relevant, but not decisive, factor. However, when combined with the employee's worries about future redundancies in the industry and the fact that he had found another job, it did make his refusal reasonable in this case.

In Gregory v Hanning Ltd ET Case No.1900771/98 H Ltd, a small company in the mining industry, gave notice of redundancy to all employees but made it clear that it hoped to rescind some of the notices if the industry picked up. Towards the end of his notice period, G was told that his employment could continue and that, to the best of the employer's knowledge, there was no further risk to his job. However, G rejected the offer as he had secured employment elsewhere. A tribunal rejected H Ltd's argument that G was not entitled to a redundancy payment because he had unreasonably rejected its offer of re-employment, pointing out that he had endured two months of uncertainty and that the future of H Ltd remained in doubt. G's new employer appeared to be a much more stable company and most people in G's position would have acted as he did.

3.54 Similarly, in Tavistock and Summerhill School and anor v Richards and ors EAT 0244/13 the EAT upheld a tribunal's finding that the claimants were entitled to a redundancy payment. In March 2011 all six claimants

126

were given redundancy notices when the school where they worked had to close due to financial difficulties. The effective date of termination of their employment was to be the end of the summer term in July 2011. The school was subsequently saved and the new Board of Governors offered continuing employment to the claimants before the notices were due to expire. The EAT held that the claimants – five of whom had by then found new employment, the other one having planned for retirement – had acted reasonably in refusing the offer, which was made shortly before the termination date. Each of them was therefore entitled to a redundancy payment.

Option to accept redundancy payment

3.55

It seems that if the offer of suitable alternative work also contains an option to accept a redundancy payment, then an employee who chooses the payment will not have unreasonably refused the offer of work. In Armstrong v NATS Ltd ET Case No.2701583/09 A, who was at risk of redundancy, had been given a letter stating that if suitable alternative work could not be found, or if he did not want to be considered for any alternatives, then his employment would terminate, leaving him entitled to benefit from the employer's redeployment and redundancy agreement. A interpreted this as an offer to choose between redeployment and a redundancy package. He refused the offer of work and was given notice of termination, but the employer refused to give him a redundancy payment, stating that he had unreasonably refused an offer of suitable alternative employment. A tribunal held that the offer was indeed suitable, but that the letter A had received provided him with an option, and in choosing the redundancy payment he did not unreasonably refuse an offer of alternative employment. He was therefore entitled to a statutory redundancy payment.

Constructive dismissal

3.56

In Sennitt v Fysons Conveyors Ltd EAT 297/93 the EAT held that an offer of alternative employment cannot, as a matter of law, be suitable if it could give the employee grounds for claiming constructive dismissal. S and others were dismissed by administrative receivers on the day that FC Ltd was due to complete the purchase of the employer's business. Immediately after the dismissals, the employees were offered new employment by the purchasers, but on less favourable terms regarding pay and fringe benefits. Also, the guaranteed hours were shorter – FC Ltd considered that the generous terms of employment given by the previous employer probably contributed to the downfall of the business. S refused the offer and claimed a redundancy payment. The EAT held that S had not received a suitable offer in law, as he had grounds for claiming constructive dismissal by FC Ltd. In reaching this conclusion, it relied on what is now Reg 4(11) of the Transfer of Undertakings (Protection of Employment) Regulations 2006 SI 2006/246, which preserves

127

an employee's right to treat him or herself as constructively dismissed if, on a transfer, changes are made to the working conditions that amount to a fundamental breach of contract. As there was no suitable offer in law, there was no need to consider whether S had acted reasonably in refusing it and he was entitled to a redundancy payment.

This case is open to criticism because it is not specifically justified by any part of the ERA and runs counter to the rest of the statutory redundancy scheme provisions. It suggests that where, on a transfer, a redundant employee is offered conditions of employment which are sufficiently detrimental to give rise to a claim of constructive dismissal, a claim for a redundancy payment will automatically succeed. The usual defence open to an employer that the employee unreasonably refused the offer is not available in these circumstances. However, if S's claim had been for unfair dismissal, then the employer's reasons for seeking a change to terms and conditions would have been a relevant factor going to fairness of the dismissal and, on the facts of the above case, the employer might have succeeded.

3.57 Time off to look for work

If a tribunal finds that a redundant employee has unreasonably refused an offer of suitable employment, he or she is not entitled to a redundancy payment. However, the employee is still treated as having been dismissed by reason of redundancy, and so retains the statutory right under S.52 ERA to time off during the notice period to look for work or to make arrangements for training – see Chapter 11, 'Time off during notice period', for details.

3.58 Denial of employee's right to statutory trial period

In Elliot v Richard Stump Ltd 1987 ICR 579, EAT, the Appeal Tribunal held that E had reasonably refused an offer of alternative employment when his employer refused to allow him a trial period. The same conclusion was reached in Parsons and anor v Shaw Healthcare (North Somerset) Ltd ET Case No.1400014/13, where the tribunal held that it was not unreasonable for G, one of the two claimants, to reject an offer of alternative employment because, while the alternative role was suitable, the employer had denied her the right to a statutory trial period. G had a number of family caring responsibilities which she carefully synchronised with her work commitments and hours. Both of her parents had health issues and she attended their house each morning to get them up, give them their breakfast and medication. In her old job she worked ten hours, for one day a week, finishing at 7.45 am. The alternative job involved an additional five-mile drive, and would not finish until 8.00 am. Without a trial period, G was in no position to know what the alternative job might mean for her and her family caring responsibilities.

128

Death of employer or employee

3.59

Slightly different rules apply where an individual employer, or the employee, dies. These rules, contained in Ss.174 and 176 ERA, are discussed below.

Death of employer

3.60

The death of an individual employer operates to terminate a contract of employment at common law. To reinforce the point, S.136(5) ERA states that the death of an individual employer is to be treated as a dismissal of his or her employees for the purposes of the statutory redundancy scheme. The business passes to the deceased employer's personal representatives, who may or may not have the power to continue running the business, depending on the terms of the will. If there is no such express or implied power in the will, the personal representatives may only keep the business running until it can be sold as a going concern.

The policy behind the legislation is to encourage continued employment and under the ERA personal representatives can offer to renew or re-engage employees as in any other redundancy situation. Indeed, S.174 has much the same effect as the normal scheme. If the employee accepts an offer of continued employment with the personal representatives, he or she is treated as not having been dismissed and consequently as not being entitled to a redundancy payment. If the terms of the offer differ from those under the old employment, the normal trial period will apply. If the offer is suitable and the employee unreasonably refuses it or leaves unreasonably during the trial period, he or she loses any right to a redundancy payment. The only differences between the normal scheme and the provisions of S.174 are that the new employment must begin within eight weeks (not four) of the old job finishing and the offer of new employment need not, for obvious reasons, be made before the previous employment came to an end.

Where no offer of renewal or re-engagement is forthcoming, it follows from S.136(5) that the employee may claim a redundancy payment from the deceased employer's estate.

3.61

The mere substitution of personal representatives as the employer does not count as a significant difference in terms and no account is to be taken of such substitution in assessing the reasonableness or otherwise of the employee's refusal of a job – S.174(4).

It may not always be easy to tell whether there has been an offer of renewal or re-engagement when employees simply carry on working in the business for a period after the death of an employer. In Ranger v Brown and ors 1978 ICR 603, EAT, the Appeal Tribunal held that tribunals should not infer the

3.62

129

existence of an offer and acceptance in such circumstances. Instead, they should look to see whether there was any express or implied agreement, having regard to the length of time involved and the circumstances of the case generally.

It is possible for an employee to become his or her own employer on the death of the original employer. In Rowley, Holmes and Co v Barber and anor 1977 ICR 387, EAT, a sole trader left his business to his employee, who was also his sole executor. The employee was not professionally qualified and could not carry on the business himself, so he sold it and reverted to being an employee of the business. The EAT held that during the interval between the employer's death and the sale of the business, the employee was acting in two capacities – one as executor and the other as employee. Hence he was employing himself with the consequence that there was no break in the continuity of his employment.

3.63 **Domestic servants.** In the case of domestic servants in a private household, the personal representative is deemed to be the person to whom management of the household has passed in consequence of the employer's death – S.174(6). Typically, this may be a surviving spouse, who need not necessarily be an executor or personal representative. But this does not apply if the new head of the household is a purchaser for value. A house buyer does not incur any liability for redundancy payments to the domestic staff.

3.64 **Does TUPE apply?** As a general rule, the Transfer of Undertakings (Protection of Employment) Regulations 2006 SI 2006/246 (TUPE) will apply to the transfer of a business from one employer to another, so that contracts of employment are not terminated and transfer automatically to the new employer. The contracts continue as though they had always been made with the new employer, who 'inherits' all the liabilities and duties in connection with the employment relationship transferred.

However, the question arises as to whether the Regulations apply to the transfer of a deceased employer's business to his or her personal representatives. There is a strong argument against the application of TUPE in this situation as the wording of Reg 4(1) provides only for the automatic transfer of contracts 'which would otherwise be terminated by the transfer'. The contracts of the deceased employer's business would not otherwise have been terminated by the transfer, because they have already been terminated by the employer's death. This point is reinforced by S.136(5) ERA, which provides that the death shall operate as a dismissal. On this analysis, the Regulations do not apply and S.174 comes into play instead.

3.65 The main argument to the contrary was inspired by Reg 3(2) of the now-repealed Transfer of Undertakings (Protection of Employment) Regulations 1981 SI 1981/1794, which provided that a transfer could be effected 'by operation

130

of law'. This was drafted as a 'catch-all' provision and would seem to involve some sort of automatic legal process applying to effect a legal transfer from one person to another. Thus, the automatic succession from a deceased sole trader to his personal representatives for the purpose of administering the estate could perhaps be considered a transfer by operation of law. It was accepted by an employment tribunal in Fitch v Secretary of State for Employment and ors ET Case No.24292/84 that an executor who runs a sole proprietor's business in an identical fashion after the latter's death would be subject to TUPE. However, there are difficulties with this analysis. First, it means that S.174 is superfluous. Secondly, it would have the effect of compelling the personal representatives to continue employment, a situation which might be at odds with their powers (or conflict with their duties) under the Administration of Estates Act 1925. The situation might also be problematic where, for example, the deceased employer's estate is bankrupt and has to be wound up. Most crucially, when the 2006 TUPE Regulations were drafted, the reference in Reg 3(2) to a transfer being effected 'by operation of law' was removed, as the growth in case law from the European Court of Justice had made a 'catch-all' provision unnecessary. Since there has been no indication from the ECJ that the EU Acquired Rights Directive (No.2001/23), which the Regulations implement, applies upon the death of an individual employer, the effect of removing this wording seems to fatally undermine the argument that TUPE applies on the death of an individual employer.

Nevertheless, until there is an authoritative ruling on this point, uncertainty over whether TUPE applies in these circumstances will continue. The issue becomes most significant when considering the position of employees who are not offered renewal or re-engagement by the personal representatives. If the Regulations were to apply, such employees would automatically have their contracts continued, at least for a time, which would probably be preferable to compensation for the loss of employment. If, as seems likely, the Regulations do not apply, the death of an employer would take effect as a dismissal and the employees' only remedy would be a claim for a redundancy payment against the deceased's estate.

Note that, where the business is continued by the personal representatives and later sold as a going concern, TUPE will apply to that later transfer.

Death of employee
3.66

If an employee who is under notice for redundancy dies after receiving an offer of re-employment, there is a further modification to the normal scheme. Three situations are covered:

- an offer has been made to the employee, but the employee dies before having made up his or her mind whether to accept or reject it. The employee is treated as if he or she had refused the offer. If the offer was suitable and it would have been unreasonable for the employee to have refused it, the deceased employee's estate will not be entitled to a redundancy payment – S.176(3)

- the employee accepts an offer of re-employment, but dies during the trial period without having given notice to terminate the trial. The estate will not be entitled to a redundancy payment if the new employment was suitable and it would have been unreasonable for the employee to terminate the trial – S.176(4)(a)

- the employee has given notice to terminate the trial during the trial period, but dies before the notice expires. He or she is treated as if the notice had expired and the contract had been terminated at the date of death. Again, the estate will not be entitled to a redundancy payment if the employment was suitable and the employee acted unreasonably in giving notice – S.176(4)(b).

An employee may have died intestate with the effect that there are no personal representatives to claim on behalf of the estate. If so, the tribunal may appoint an 'appropriate person' as an ad hoc personal representative for the purpose of carrying on tribunal proceedings – S.206(4) and (5). This may be somebody, such as a union representative, who had been authorised by the employee before death to act in connection with the proceedings. Alternatively, it may be the surviving spouse, parent, child or sibling of the deceased employee.

3.67 Offer during period of family leave

Regulation 10 of the Maternity and Parental Leave etc Regulations 1999 SI 1999/3312 ('the MPL Regulations') contains special provisions that apply where, during an employee's maternity leave, it is not practicable by reason of redundancy for her employer to continue employing her under her existing contract of employment. Almost identical provisions relating to employees on adoption leave and shared parental leave are to be found in Reg 23 of the Paternity and Adoption Leave Regulations 2002 SI 2002/2788 ('the PAL Regulations'), and Reg 39 of the Shared Parental Leave Regulations 2014 SI 2014/3050 ('the SPL Regulations') respectively. (Similar provisions used to apply to those on additional paternity leave. However, following the introduction of the shared parental leave scheme, the entitlement to take additional paternity leave was abolished in respect of children born or adopted on or after 5 April 2015.)

Where there is a suitable available vacancy, the employee on maternity, adoption or shared parental leave is entitled to be offered such a vacancy with the employer, the employer's successor or an associated employer before employment ceases under the employee's existing contract – Reg 10(2) MPL Regulations, Reg 23(2) PAL Regulations and Reg 39(2) SPL Regulations. This duty appears to be absolute, in that if suitable alternative employment is

132 ⎯⎯⎯⎯⎯⎯⎯⎯⎯⎯⎯⎯⎯⎯⎯⎯⎯⎯⎯⎯⎯⎯⎯⎯⎯

available, it *must* be offered to the employee on maternity, adoption or shared parental leave in preference to any other employee who is similarly affected by the redundancy situation but who is not on such leave.

Note that the SPL Regulations use the term 'suitable alternative vacancy' rather than 'suitable available vacancy'. However, we respectfully suggest – given that the rest of the clause is almost identical in formulation to the corresponding clauses in the MPL and PAL Regulations – that nothing turns on this difference in wording and that the clause should be construed as referring to a 'suitable available vacancy'. **3.68**

Where an employee's role is to be removed from the organisational structure because the employer makes a decision to merge it with another role, the obligation to make an offer of available employment arises once that decision to merge the roles has been made, not after a decision has been made as to who should get the newly merged position – Sefton Borough Council v Wainwright 2015 ICR 652, EAT. In that case the EAT rejected the Council's submission that there was no redundancy until such time as it had decided who was to have the new role and that W, who was on maternity leave, was not entitled to special treatment under Reg 10 until that point. The right to be offered a vacancy arises when the redundancy situation affecting the employee's job becomes known, and is extinguished when either the dismissal takes effect at the end of the notice period or the maternity leave ends. In accordance with the definition of redundancy contained in S.139(1)(b) ERA, an employee is redundant when the requirements of the business for employees to carry out work of a particular kind 'have ceased or diminished or are expected to cease or diminish'. In the instant case the employer had sought to avoid the effect of Reg 10 by relying on its restructuring process and the displacement and redeployment stages that this involved. That did not, however, avoid the conclusion that W's post was redundant and that she was entitled to be offered a suitable available vacancy. It would undermine the protection afforded by Reg 10 if it was left to the employer to determine when the redundancy arose; employers could state that there was only a redundancy after others had been 'redeployed' into what might otherwise have been suitable available vacancies. W's redundancy arose once the Council had made the decision to delete and merge the two posts. A vacancy was simply a position that was 'not presently occupied' and the fact that the role was not open to a wider pool of employees did not mean it was not a vacancy. While the Council might have preferred to give the vacancy to another employee, P, it was obliged by Reg 10 to offer it to W unless it was in a position to offer her some other suitable available vacancy. The newly merged role was a suitable available vacancy when W's role became redundant. Therefore, she should have been slotted into the job without the need to compete. The Council's failure to offer her the vacancy was a breach of Reg 10, which rendered her dismissal automatically unfair.

133

3.69 Had the Council found a different suitable available vacancy at the time it merged the two roles, the EAT suggested that the Council may have avoided liability under the MPL Regulations by offering W that role instead. That would have been the case even if W had rejected such an offer on the basis that she should have been given the merged role, since the employer's obligation under Reg 10 is met once it has 'offered' the vacancy.

The new contract must take effect immediately on termination of the previous contract and must be such that:

- the work to be done is of a kind which is both suitable in relation to the employee and appropriate for him or her to do in the circumstances, and

- its provisions as to the capacity and place in which the employee is to be employed, and as to the other terms and conditions of employment, are not substantially less favourable to the employee than if he or she had continued to be employed under the previous contract – Reg 10(3) MPL Regulations, Reg 23(3) PAL Regulations and Reg 39(3) SPL Regulations.

3.70 For a vacancy to constitute a 'suitable available vacancy' it must satisfy both limbs of the test – i.e. it must be suitable and appropriate for the employee to do and not be on substantially less favourable terms than his or her previous position. It is for the employer to decide whether a vacancy is suitable, taking into account the claimant's personal circumstances and work experience, given that there was no requirement for the claimant to engage in that process – Simpson v Endsleigh Insurance Services Ltd 2011 ICR 75, EAT.

If a suitable available vacancy exists (i.e. a vacancy that is suitable, appropriate and not substantially less favourable than the employee's previous job) and the employer fails to offer it to the employee, the dismissal will be automatically unfair under S.99 ERA if the reason or principal reason for the dismissal is redundancy – for more detail, see Chapter 8, 'Unfair redundancy', under 'Automatically unfair redundancy – family-friendly cases'. If, however, the employer does offer such a vacancy and the employee unreasonably refuses it, his or her dismissal will almost certainly be fair and the employee will lose the right to a redundancy payment – S.141 ERA.

3.71 If there is no suitable available vacancy, the employment (and the maternity, adoption or shared parental leave period) will come to an end by reason of redundancy. However, the employee will be entitled to his or her notice period and to a written statement of the reasons for the dismissal (S.92(4) ERA). The employee will also be entitled to a redundancy payment (statutory or contractual) provided that he or she has sufficient qualifying service.

For a more detailed discussion of redundancy during maternity leave (and, by extension, adoption leave and shared parental leave), see IDS Employment Law Handbook, 'Maternity and Parental Rights' (2015), Chapter 4, 'Returning

134

to work after maternity leave', under 'Redundancy during maternity leave'; Chapter 6, 'Adoption leave and pay', under 'Redundancy and adoption leave'; and Chapter 8, 'Shared parental leave and pay', under 'Employment protection during and after SPL – redundancy during SPL'.

4 Lay-off and short-time

Overview of statutory scheme

Duration of lay-off or short-time

Notices and counter-notices

Employee's resignation

Eligibility for redundancy payment

Death of employee or employer

In most cases an employee can only claim a redundancy payment if he or she **4.1** has been dismissed for redundancy – see Chapter 1, 'Dismissal'. This chapter is concerned with the one exception to that rule. Chapter III of Part XI of the Employment Rights Act 1996 (ERA) (Ss.147–154) sets out a scheme that allows an employee who has been laid off without pay or put on short-time to claim a redundancy payment, provided that he or she complies meticulously with the statutory procedure. An employee may be laid off or put on short-time where, for example, the employer temporarily closes its operation because of a depleted order book or lack of supplies.

This scheme does not apply if the employee has been dismissed – S.151 ERA. Furthermore, it is not necessary for the employee to be redundant within the statutory definition, but only that he or she should have been laid off or put on short-time for the requisite period. He or she must, however, have been employed for at least two years – S.155.

Overview of statutory scheme   4.2

The provisions of the ERA governing lay-offs and short-time working are no less complicated than their predecessors in the Employment Protection (Consolidation) Act 1978, which were described as 'labyrinthine' by Lord McDonald in Kenneth MacRae and Co Ltd v Dawson 1984 IRLR 5, EAT. He went on to say that 'the provisions… have been the despair of all who have been concerned with the interpretation of industrial legislation since the scheme of statutory entitlement to a redundancy payment was introduced in 1965'. Therefore, before considering the scheme in detail, it may be useful to set out a brief overview of it.

The basic features of the scheme are as follows:

- the employee must have been laid off or kept on short-time (or a mixture of the two) either for four or more consecutive weeks, or for a total of six weeks (no more than three being consecutive) in any period of 13 weeks – S.148(2) ERA

- the employee must give the employer a written notice of intention to claim (NIC). This notice must be given within four weeks of the last of the weeks of lay-off or short-time working on which the claim is based – S.148

- if the employer wishes to contest liability then it must serve a written counter-notice to that effect within seven days of service of the employee's NIC – S.149 ERA. Provided that the employee has fully complied with the requirements of the scheme, an employer can only defeat a claim at this stage if, at the date of service of the NIC, there is a reasonable expectation of a return to normal working within the next four weeks – S.152

- if the employer has served, and not withdrawn, a valid counter-notice, then the employee must apply to a tribunal to decide the matter – S.149

- finally, if the employer fails to serve (or serves and then withdraws) a counter-notice or a tribunal upholds the employee's claim, the employee must terminate his or her contract of employment by giving either one week's notice or contractual notice – whichever is the longer – within three weeks –S.150.

4.3 Where the employee is entitled to a redundancy payment under the lay-off or short-time provisions, the payment will be calculated in the normal way under S.162 ERA – see Chapter 6, 'Redundancy payments'. The statutory procedure under Ss.147–154 can only be used to claim *statutory* redundancy pay. The employer may also operate a contractual scheme that offers an enhanced redundancy payment, but most contractual schemes will only apply when there has been a dismissal for redundancy. Therefore, they are unlikely to come into play when an employee has been laid off or kept on short-time.

4.4 Definition of lay-off

For the purposes of the statutory scheme, a week of lay-off occurs when an employee, whose contractual remuneration depends on his or her being provided by the employer with work of the kind which he or she is employed to do, is not provided with such work, with the result that he or she is not entitled to any remuneration for that week – S.147(1) ERA. If the employee's remuneration does not depend upon his or her being provided with work, the lay-off provisions do not apply – see further 'Contractual right to withhold pay if no work available' below.

The employer 'provides' work if it offers the employee work within the terms of the contract of employment – Spinpress Ltd v Turner 1986 ICR 433, EAT. The fact that no work is done does not mean that work has not been provided. In Dunlea v Adecco UK Ltd ET Case No.3302701/12, for example, D was employed by A UK Ltd under a zero-hours contract and was assigned

138

to work at Xerox in Welwyn Garden City. Her contract provided that she could be moved from one assignment to another by consent. Her work at Xerox ended on 29 June 2012 and she was then offered a further assignment within London. She refused it because it was at a lower grade and would mean a drop in her hourly rate of pay and increased travelling costs. On 30 July she e-mailed R claiming a redundancy payment as she had been laid off for four weeks. R sent a counter-notice saying it had offered her work of the kind she was employed to do. The tribunal found that D had not been laid off within the meaning of S.147 and so was not entitled to a redundancy payment. There was no contractual obligation on A UK Ltd to provide D with a job commensurate to that which she formerly held. Furthermore, the new assignment was within commuting distance of her home and therefore fell within the scope of the contract. The situation might have been different, however, if the assignment had been outside a reasonable commuting distance.

4.5 An employee will not be treated as being laid off if he or she was not available for work anyway – e.g. because of sickness. In Johnson v Knowsley Caravans Ltd ET Case No.5071/74, for example, the rest of the workforce was laid off during J's sickness absence, but the employment tribunal held that sickness, not lay-off, was the reason that J had no work.

Equally, an employee will not be regarded as laid off if the reason for not working is that he or she has frustrated the employer's attempts to offer work that is available. In Coombs v Total Security South West ET Case No.1402601/06, for example, a client told the employer that it no longer wanted C, a security guard, to work at its premises owing to his unreliability. Having left, C made no serious attempt to contact the employer about alternative work, and although the employer wrote two letters to him about the availability of other work, C did not receive them as he had not provided details of his current address. In these circumstances, the tribunal rejected C's claim for a redundancy payment, commenting that 'a worker cannot invoke the lay-off provisions simply by going to ground, staying out of contact, and then claiming that the respondent never actually offered work so there was no work to do. You cannot (metaphorically) lie in bed and switch the telephone off and claim you are laid off.'

Definition of short-time working

4.6 A week of short-time working occurs if there is a diminution in the work provided by the employer and, as a result, the remuneration for any week is less than half a 'week's pay' as defined by Chapter II of Part XIV of the ERA – S.147(2). Short-time working is often described as a form of partial lay-off and can occur where the employer maintains its operation on a reduced scale, e.g. on two out of five days, in order to eke out what little work is available. The method of calculating a week's pay and the definition of a 'week' are explained in IDS Employment Law Handbook, 'Wages' (2016), Chapter 9, 'A week's pay'.

4.7 **Contractual right to withhold pay if no work available**

The statutory scheme only applies where the employee's pay is dependent upon his or her being provided with work to do by the employer – i.e. the employer must have a contractual right (whether express, implied or by way of incorporation) to withhold remuneration if there is no work. Few employees have a 'right' to work but many have a right – often implied – to be paid when they are not provided with work, in which case a failure to pay wages during a period of lay-off or short-time working would amount to a breach of contract but would not invoke the statutory lay-off/short-time provisions – see further 'Lay-off in breach of contract'. In Cornwall Aluminium Windows Co Ltd v Dawidiuk EAT 1405/96 D was laid off in June 1996 after 17 years. After being away from work for six weeks, he resigned. The employer offered to take him back but D claimed that he had been dismissed and was entitled to a redundancy payment. The employer argued that the statutory provisions on lay-off applied. D's contract simply provided that 'your wage is £108 per week'. The EAT upheld a tribunal's decision that D was entitled to be paid during the period in which he remained an employee but was not being provided with work by the employer and that the lay-off provisions did not therefore apply.

Similarly, in Powell Duffryn Wagon Co Ltd and anor v House and ors 1974 ICR 123, NIRC, the employer repaired railway wagons and guaranteed its employees a minimum weekly wage, whether or not work was available. Business dried up when British Rail staff prevented wagons from reaching the employer's repair shops and, having no work to do, H and his fellow employees were laid off without pay. Upholding the tribunal, the NIRC held that there was no statutory lay-off because the employees were entitled to a guaranteed minimum salary.

4.8 Note, however, that statutory guarantee payments made by an employer under Part III of the ERA (Ss.28–35) do not prevent an employee claiming to have been laid off or placed on short-time working, as such payments do not constitute remuneration to which the employee is entitled under the contract. If a lay-off lasts long enough, the employer may be obliged to pay both guarantee payments and a redundancy payment in respect of the lay-off. In Spencer v Purdy and anor t/a Kelco ET Case No.67371/95, for example, S's employment was terminated when the factory where she worked closed down. P made an offer of alternative employment which involved S working at home, but she refused and was consequently denied a redundancy payment. The tribunal held that S was entitled to a redundancy payment as, in its view, P did not make an offer of suitable alternative work. P was also ordered to make a guarantee payment to S in respect of one workless day. (Guarantee payments are discussed in IDS Employment Law Handbook, 'Wages' (2016), Chapter 6, 'Guarantee payments'.)

140

Piece workers and time workers. Piece workers, whose remuneration varies **4.9** according to the amount of work done, fall under the statutory scheme, as do employees whose contractual terms either expressly or impliedly allow the employer to lay them off without pay or introduce short-time work. Such terms may be found in the contract itself, be incorporated into the contract by virtue of a collective agreement, or be implied by custom and practice.

It has been suggested that time workers whose remuneration does *not* vary according to the amount of work done are not covered. However, under S.147(1) it is the payment of remuneration, not the amount of remuneration, that must be dependent on the provision of work. Thus, in our view, a time worker who is contractually entitled to a fixed salary, irrespective of how much work he or she does, will still be covered by the scheme if he or she can nonetheless be laid-off without pay where there is no work available. The decision in Powell Duffryn Wagon Co Ltd and anor v House and ors (above) would seem to support this view but ultimately, of course, whether or not an employer has a right to lay off is a question of fact to be decided by the tribunal in each case.

Lay-off in breach of contract. As we have seen, the right to lay off must **4.10** be permitted by the contract of employment. If an employer lays off an employee or puts him or her on short-time without having an express or implied contractual right to do so, this will amount to a fundamental breach of contract leaving the employee entitled to resign and claim constructive dismissal. If the reason for dismissal was redundancy, which is likely in a lay-off situation, the employee may claim a redundancy payment in the normal way (provided that he or she has at least two years' continuous service), thereby avoiding the intricacies of claiming a redundancy payment by way of the lay-off and short-time provisions – Waine v R Oliver (Plant Hire) Ltd 1978 IRLR 434, EAT. He or she can also claim that the dismissal was unfair. In Stevenson and anor v Good Stuff Ltd EAT 572/94 two part-time sales assistants were laid off despite the fact that a right to lay-off was not provided for in their contracts of employment. They resigned and claimed that they had been constructively dismissed. The EAT ruled that they were each entitled to a redundancy payment. There had been a decline in trade which reduced the employer's requirements for employees to perform work of a particular kind. That led to the lay-off and was the reason for the constructive dismissal.

A term permitting lay-off will only be implied into a contract if there exists for that employment a custom of laying off that is 'reasonable, certain and notorious' and is such that 'no workman could be supposed to have entered into service without looking to it as part of the contract' – Bond v Cav Ltd and anor 1983 IRLR 360, QBD.

141

4.11   Of course, an employee who has been laid off or kept on short-time in breach of contract may elect to keep the contract going and claim any shortfall in wages as a breach of contract claim or under the protection of wages provisions contained in Part II of the ERA – see IDS Employment Law Handbook, 'Wages' (2016), Chapter 2, 'Unlawful deductions from wages'. The Acas advice leaflet, 'Lay-offs and short-time working', makes it clear that an employee in these circumstances has four options. He or she may:

- choose to accept the breach of contract and treat the contract as continuing, while claiming a statutory guarantee payment

- sue for damages for breach of contract in the civil court or, in certain circumstances, at an employment tribunal

- claim before an employment tribunal that there has been an unlawful deduction of wages under Part II of the ERA, or

- claim that the employer's action amounted to a dismissal (constructive or otherwise), giving rise to a potential claim of unfair dismissal and/or, if eligible, redundancy pay.

4.12   **Unreasonable lay-offs.** In A Dakri and Co Ltd v Tiffen and ors 1981 ICR 256, EAT, the Appeal Tribunal held that there is an implied contractual term that any lay-off will only be for a 'reasonable' period and that, in the circumstances of the case, a lay-off lasting more than four weeks was a fundamental breach of contract entitling the employee to claim constructive dismissal by reason of redundancy. However, that case was called into question by the later decision of Kenneth MacRae and Co Ltd v Dawson 1984 IRLR 5, EAT, where the Appeal Tribunal held that a contractual right to lay off indefinitely is not normally subject to any test of reasonableness. The employer cannot be regarded as in breach of contract simply by virtue of the passage of time. The EAT went on to say that if an employee thinks that he or she has been laid off for too long, the remedy is to follow the statutory procedure for claiming a redundancy payment based on lay-off.

Dawson was followed in Craig v Bob Lindfield and Son Ltd EAT 0220/15, where the tribunal rejected the claimant's argument that he was entitled to regard himself as constructively dismissed after a four-week period of lay-off. The tribunal did not accept that the employer was subject to a term of reasonableness, and in any event considered that the period of lay-off was clearly reasonable. Upholding that decision on appeal, the EAT held that the reasoning in Dawson was to be preferred: contrary to what was said in Tiffen, the EAT did not accept that there is an implied term that a period of lay-off will be not more than is reasonable. The EAT did, however, acknowledge that there may be situations where the employer's behaviour was such that it amounted to a breach of the implied term of trust and confidence, thereby giving rise to a constructive dismissal claim. However, that was not the case here.

142

It was the case, though, in Bowman v Key Enterprises (1983) Ltd ET Case **4.13**
No.2501214/09, where B was employed by KE Ltd from April 2003 as a
computer supervisor. KE Ltd offered employment and training to people with
mental health problems and/or employment needs and in February 2008 a
service user made a complaint about B. KE Ltd produced an action plan
aimed at improving B's attitude towards service users. However, on 17 April
she was called to a meeting and accused of belittling her clients. She alleged
that her manager had fabricated the complaints, at which point her manager
became angry and stated that she, the manager, had had lots of complaints
about B and, when pressed, confirmed that she believed the clients over B.
During the first half of 2008 KE Ltd lost a number of contracts and B was
called into a meeting in June without any prior warning and told she was laid
off. A few days later she arranged to have lunch with some of her colleagues
and while in the office she spoke to another colleague and spent some time on
a computer dealing with a question from a client about matters she had been
working on with him. She then received a letter from the company telling
her she was not allowed to visit the premises without permission and could
not use any of KE Ltd's equipment. B resigned in response to the lay-off and
the letter. Her claim of unfair constructive dismissal was upheld. Although
the lay-off was contractually lawful, as was the exclusion from company
premises, the way that they had been implemented – without consultation,
warning or proper explanation – taken together with KE Ltd's actions in
accepting complaints against B at face value without asking for her side of the
matter so undermined B's trust and confidence as to amount to a fundamental
breach of contract.

For the circumstances in which terms may be implied into contracts of
employment see IDS Employment Law Handbook, 'Contracts of Employment'
(2014), Chapter 3, 'Contractual terms', under 'Implied terms'. For further
discussion on the implied term of mutual trust and confidence, see the same
Handbook at Chapter 4, 'Implied term of mutual trust and confidence'.

Holiday rights
4.14

Statutory holiday entitlement is unaffected by any period of lay-off or short
time working and an employee can therefore take holiday during this time
and be paid his or her normal rate of pay. Briefly, all employees are entitled
to 5.6 weeks' paid annual leave under the Working Time Regulations 1998 SI
1998/1833 – see IDS Employment Law Handbook, 'Working Time' (2013),
Chapter 4, 'Annual leave'. A week's pay for these purposes is calculated
according to Chapter II of Part XIV of the ERA, although these provisions
need to be read in light of case law interpreting the EU Working Time Directive
(No.2003/88) and the Working Time Regulations – see IDS Employment Law
Handbook, 'Wages' (2016), Chapter 9, 'A week's pay', under 'Calculating
statutory holiday pay'. It is highly arguable that a week's pay for an employee

on short-time working should be calculated according to his or her normal working hours, not the short-time hours, unless the employee has agreed to a variation of his or her employment contract – see Dutton v Jones (t/a Llandow Metals) 2013 ICR 559, EAT.

4.15 Duration of lay-off or short-time

The statutory scheme comes into play when either:

- the employee has been laid off or kept on short-time for four or more consecutive weeks – S.148(2)(a) ERA, or

- the employee has been laid off or kept on short-time for a total of six or more weeks in a period of 13 weeks. No more than three of the weeks can have been consecutive – S.148(2)(b).

For these purposes, it does not matter whether the weeks relied upon by the employee are weeks of lay-off, short-time working, or a combination of the two – S.154(a) ERA. A 'week' for these purposes is a week ending with a Saturday, unless the employee's pay is calculated weekly by reference to a week ending with a day other than Saturday, in which case it means a week ending with that other day – S.235(1).

4.16 The stipulation in S.148(2)(b) that not more than three of the weeks claimed for should be consecutive may be important in the context of the time limit for making a claim. An employee must give a notice of intention to claim (NIC) not later than four weeks from the end of the last of the weeks of lay-off or short-time working on which the claim is based – S.148(2). Suppose that in the course of a 13-week period an employee:

- is laid off for four weeks

- works again for four weeks

- is laid off again for three weeks

- works again for two weeks.

By the end of those 13 weeks it will be too late for the employee to claim a redundancy payment. He or she cannot rely on S.148(2)(b) by adding the four-week lay-off to the three-week lay-off and saying that the claim is within four weeks of the end of the latter. This is because the first period of lay-off was of more than three consecutive weeks. The claim should have been made within four weeks of the end of the first period of lay-off.

4.17 An employee who has not been laid off or kept on short-time for the full qualifying period may not present an NIC – see 'Notices and counter-notices' below – and any such notice that is presented will be invalid. In Allinson

144

v Drew Simmons Engineering Ltd 1985 ICR 488, EAT, A was placed on short-time working on 26 September. On 20 October he gave notice that he intended to claim a redundancy payment. The EAT held that this notice, served before A had been on short-time for a full four weeks, was invalid and his claim for a redundancy payment failed.

Strikes and lock-outs   4.18

An employee cannot rely on any week of lay-off or short-time working that occurs wholly or mainly as a result of a strike or lock-out – S.154(b) ERA. Note that the employee does not have to be a participant in the strike or lock-out, and the strike or lock-out need not be in the trade or industry in which he or she is employed. Indeed, the strike or lock-out need not even take place in Great Britain. The only requirement is that it should be the main cause of the lay-off or short-time working.

'Lock-out' and 'strike' are defined in S.235(4) and (5) ERA. These definitions are restricted to action taken to compel the other side to accept or reject terms and conditions of or affecting employment. Political or sympathy strikes do not count in this context. Furthermore, lay-offs or short-time working caused by industrial action short of a strike – such as a work-to-rule – are not excluded from the scope of the statutory scheme.

Tribunals have come to different conclusions about when a lay-off is deemed   4.19
attributable to a strike or lock-out. Here are two cases concerning the famous 1984 miners' strike:

- **Ward v SH Ward and Co Ltd** ET Case No.9977/85: W, a hotel waitress in Barnsley, was laid off following a serious downturn in business during the miners' strike. An employment tribunal held that the lay-off was mainly caused by the strike. Although W would otherwise have qualified for a redundancy payment, the weeks of lay-off could not be counted

- **Cooke v Hayden Nilos Conflow Ltd** ET Case No.13049/85: C was laid off during the miners' strike by HNC Ltd, which manufactured mining equipment. An employment tribunal found that there had been a 43 per cent reduction in business within the UK, but that export sales were unaffected. It was still possible for the employer to carry on with its business – even though it had a sound economic reason for the lay-off. In the tribunal's view, it had not been established that C's lay-off was mainly attributable to the strike.

Notices and counter-notices   4.20

A central feature of the lay-off and short-time working scheme is the strict requirement for a notice of intention to claim (NIC) from the employee and – if the claim is to be opposed – a counter-notice from the employer. Notice

145

is given by an employee to an employer if it is delivered to the employer or posted to the employer at the employee's workplace. Alternatively, the NIC may be given to a person designated by the employer, or left for such a person at a designated place, or posted to that person at a designated address – S.179(2) ERA. Counter-notice is given by an employer to an employee if it is delivered to the employee, left for the employee at his or her usual or last-known place of residence, or posted to the employee there – S.179(1).

If a notice is 'left' for a person at a place as specified above, it is presumed to have been received by that person on the day on which it was left there, unless the contrary is proved – S.179(4) ERA. As far as a notice sent through the post is concerned, S.7 of the Interpretation Act 1978 comes into play. This provides that, where an Act authorises a document to be served by post, then service is deemed to be effected at the time when the letter would be delivered in the ordinary course of post unless the contrary is proved. When posting a notice, it is advisable to obtain some proof of posting, but there is no requirement to send documents by registered post or recorded delivery. It should be remembered that the time limits for giving notices cannot be extended, even if the notices are lost in the post.

4.21   Notice of intention to claim

The employee's NIC must be given in writing. It need not be in specific terms but must indicate the employee's intention to claim a redundancy payment in respect of lay-off or short-time working. The NIC must be served not earlier than the last day of the last week of lay-off or short-time working relied upon and not later than four weeks starting with that date – S.148(2) ERA. Employment tribunals have no discretion to extend this latter time limit for any reason. However, if an employee sends the employer an NIC which is premature or defective in some way, he or she can cure the defect simply by sending another one, provided that this is done within the four-week time limit.

4.22   Employer's counter-notice

The employer's counter-notice must also be in writing. It must be given to the employee within seven days of service of the employee's NIC and must state, as a minimum, that the employer intends to contest any liability for a redundancy payment – S.149(a) ERA. As with the employee's NIC, the time limit cannot be extended for any reason.

The employer's counter-notice need not set out the details of the grounds upon which a redundancy payment is opposed. However, it must state that the employer intends to contest liability for a redundancy payment. In Fabar Construction Ltd v Race and anor 1979 ICR 529, EAT, the employer sent a letter that simply stated: 'We confirm our offer made to you on Friday, April 21, 1978, to commence work at our Chowdene site on Monday, April

146

24, 1978.' The EAT held that this was not a valid counter-notice because it did not indicate an intention to contest liability for a redundancy payment. Similarly, in Bradley v International Quality Control Laboratories Ltd ET Case No.9657/84 the employer sent a letter indicating its expectation of substantial work coming in and then said: 'Please consider this letter as a counter-notice under the redundancy payments scheme.' An employment tribunal held that this was inadequate.

The employer may withdraw a counter-notice by giving a subsequent notice **4.23** of withdrawal in writing. There is no time limit for this. If the employer does not do so, the question of the employee's eligibility for a redundancy payment must be decided by a tribunal – S.149 ERA. The only ground upon which the employer can defeat a claim at this stage is discussed under 'Eligibility for redundancy payment – employer's defence to contested claim' below.

Employee's resignation   4.24

Once an employee has served a valid NIC, the final thing that he or she must do to secure a redundancy payment – subject to any defence raised by the employer – is resign by giving notice – S.150(1) ERA. An employee will not be entitled to a redundancy payment if his or her contract of employment still exists. However, if the employee decides to terminate the contract and take a redundancy payment, continuity of employment will be broken in the event that he or she resumes work with the same employer. Note that the employee's resignation is not a constructive dismissal. This scheme does not apply to employees who are dismissed (whether constructively or otherwise) – S.151 ERA – as they could then simply rely on the fact of that dismissal to claim a redundancy payment in the normal way (or compensation for unfair dismissal).

Notice requirements   4.25
The employee must give one week's notice, or full contractual notice if the contract stipulates a longer period – S.150(2) ERA. A week's notice means a full week's notice. In Homson v FMS (Farm Products) Ltd 1967 ITR 326, ET, the employee gave notice on a Monday to terminate her employment the following Saturday. Her claim failed because this was not a full seven days' notice. Notice to terminate on a Saturday must be given on the previous Saturday to amount to a week's notice. Similarly, in Broadhurst v Brockhouse ET Case No.21734/86 the employee gave notice on a Monday to terminate his contract on pay-day (Friday). The tribunal held that for the notice to be valid it should have been given on the preceding pay-day. And in Hurdley v Fretwell and ors ET Case No.23337/95 H had already been laid off for nearly two months when, having obtained new employment, he served notice that he was applying for a redundancy payment as a result of the lay-off. However, he did not allow one week between leaving and starting his new

147

employment and so the tribunal concluded that he was not entitled to a redundancy payment.

But provided sufficient notice is given, the form of the notice would appear to be less prescriptive. In Walmsley v C and R Ferguson Ltd 1989 SLT 258, Ct Sess (Inner House), for example, W wrote to his employer saying: 'If you do not wish to do any of the above... then I am left with no option but to resign and instigate... tribunal proceedings against you. I look forward to hearing from you within seven days.' In subsequent proceedings, W admitted that he had not intended to give one week's notice because he did not know that this was necessary. The tribunal, however, construed the reference to 'seven days' as constituting a week's notice. The EAT overruled this, but, notwithstanding W's admission, the Court of Session restored the tribunal's original decision, holding that it was possible to read W's letter as giving one week's notice and that the tribunal had been entitled to read it in this way. The legal effect of the language used was important, not the intention of the writer. Furthermore, W was a workman not familiar with the statute.

4.26 The employee's notice to terminate need not be in writing. In Fabar Construction Ltd v Race and anor 1979 ICR 529, EAT, an oral offer to give a week's notice coupled with a request for the employee's P45 was held to be adequate notice.

The timing of service of the employee's notice to terminate is crucial since the time limits cannot be extended and a failure to serve the notice within the applicable time limit will deprive the employee of entitlement to a redundancy payment – S.150(1). There are three circumstances to consider:

- the employer does not serve a counter-notice within seven days of service of the NIC. The time limit here is three weeks after the end of those seven days – S.150(3)(a) ERA. This covers both the situation where the employer does not serve a counter-notice at all and the situation where one is served late. It will also apply when the employer's counter-notice is invalid because it does not state the employer's intention to contest liability for a redundancy payment. This is treated as the equivalent of not giving a counter-notice at all, so that the same time limit applies – see, for example, Vennard v Deal 1969 ITR 315, ET

- the employer gives a counter-notice within the seven-day time limit, but withdraws it by a subsequent notice in writing. The time limit here is three weeks after service of the notice of withdrawal – S.150(3)(b) ERA. There is no time limit for service of an employer's notice of withdrawal

- the employer gives a counter-notice within the seven-day time limit and does not withdraw it. This means that the case must go to a tribunal. The time limit here is three weeks after notification to the employee of the tribunal's

148

decision – S.150(3)(c) ERA. This means that an employee in a contested case does not have to resign until a tribunal has decided that he or she is eligible for a redundancy payment. But there is a catch, in that the three-week time limit applies even if the employer appeals – S.150(4). This means that if an employer's appeal is successful, the employee may be both out of a job (through having resigned within three weeks of the tribunal's decision) and unable to claim a redundancy payment.

Note that these are the *latest* dates on which an employee's notice to terminate may be given. It does not matter how early notice is given, provided that the employee is still employed at the date of service of the NIC and can show the requisite period of lay-off or short-time working. In Armstrong and ors v Barber and Nicholls Ltd ET Case No.21247/75 A was laid off on 7 February. She served an NIC on 15 June and the employer did not serve a counter-notice. A gave notice of termination on 15 August – which was outside the time limit. However, she remained laid off and then served a second NIC on 20 August. Once again, the employer did not serve a counter-notice and A's notice of termination was held to have been presented in time – it did not matter that it predated the valid NIC. **4.27**

Pay during notice period
4.28

There are specific statutory provisions that protect an employee's pay during the notice period if the employee is, inter alia, ready and willing to work but no work is available – see Ss.87(2), 88 and 89 ERA. These provisions are fairly narrow in scope but where they do apply, they guarantee full pay during the statutory notice period to employees who have resigned while being laid off or kept on short-time – see IDS Employment Law Handbook, 'Contracts of Employment' (2014), Chapter 11, 'Termination by dismissal', in the section 'Express dismissal', under 'Dismissal with notice – right to be paid during notice'.

Eligibility for redundancy payment
4.29

If the employer does not serve a counter-notice, or serves one and then withdraws it, or if the employer serves a counter-notice but is unable to rely on the defence in S.152(1) (see 'Employer's defence to contested claim' below), then it can only challenge the employee's claim on the basis that the employee has failed to follow the statutory procedure (or the lay-off or short-time working was mainly caused by a strike or lock-out).

Where the employer does not serve a counter-notice, or serves one and then withdraws it, and the employee *has* followed the statutory procedure and the lay-off or short-time working was not mainly caused by a strike or lock-out, the employee will be eligible for a redundancy payment just as if he or she had

149

been dismissed for redundancy. The same qualifying conditions apply in these circumstances – see Chapter 5, 'Qualifications and exclusions'. This means, for example, that the employee must have at least two years' qualifying service. For these purposes, the period of qualifying service is calculated up to the last day of the last week of lay-off or short-time working on which the employee is relying – S.153 ERA.

4.30 Employer's defence to contested claim

If the employer has served a counter-notice (and the employee has followed the statutory procedure and the lay-off or short-time working was not mainly caused by a strike or lock-out), the issue must be decided by a tribunal. At this stage, only one defence is available to an employer under a counter-notice. This is that, at the date of service of the employee's NIC, it was reasonably expected that the employee would, not later than four weeks after that date, enter into a period of employment with the same employer of at least 13 continuous weeks during which he or she would not be laid off or kept on short-time for any week – S.152(1) ERA. Note that the relevant date for these purposes is the date of service of the employee's NIC: it will not necessarily help the employer if business has picked up and there is plenty of work available at the date of the tribunal hearing, which may be several months after the date of service of the NIC.

This defence is only available to an employer if it has served a valid counter-notice. In Reid v Arthur Young and Son EAT 714/82 R served an NIC on the employer after he was laid off. The employer wrote back to R saying that his job was still available, but the EAT held that this did not constitute a valid counter-notice. Consequently, the statutory defence was not open to the employer.

4.31

The employer's defence will fail automatically if the employee continues to be laid off or kept on short-time during each of the four weeks after the date of service of the NIC – S.152(2) ERA. The only exception will be if the lay-off or short-time working is wholly or mainly attributable to a strike or lock-out – S.154.

The criterion for establishing the employer's defence is what was reasonably to be expected at the date of service of the employee's NIC. Four examples:

- **Dixon and ors v John Watson Fabrications Ltd** ET Case No.315/75: D entered a period of 13 weeks' continuous employment two days after service of his NIC. An employment tribunal commented that this would not necessarily be conclusive. However, on the facts there was a reasonable expectation of continuing work at the date of service of the NIC, so D's claim for a redundancy payment failed

- **Spencer v Thomas B Ramsden and Co (Bradford) Ltd** ET Case No.1800743/98: S was laid off from 8 January to 10 February, when she was telephoned at home and told to return to work the following day. During the conversation, S was told that she would be working for two weeks, after which the situation would be reviewed. She served an NIC on 11 February and the employer served a counter-notice on 12 February, saying that within the next four weeks it expected to be in a position to give her continuous employment for at least the next 13 weeks. S worked from 11 February and remained in continuous full-time employment up to the date of the hearing – a period of approximately ten weeks. The employment tribunal found that, on the date that S served her NIC, there was no reasonable expectation that she would, within four weeks, enter into a period of employment of at least 13 weeks during which she would not be laid off. The tribunal based its decision on the fact that, on 11 February, the employer had told S that she would be working for two weeks after which time the situation would be reviewed. In the tribunal's view, on 11 February there was only a reasonable expectation of two weeks' work for S

- **McAloon v Moette Ltd** ET Case No. 2507065/09: McA was employed as a machinist and started working for M Ltd in 2002. Due to a downturn in work she was laid off from 27 January 2009. On 20 March she sent M Ltd a letter claiming the right to be paid a redundancy payment and M Ltd replied with a counter-notice on 25 March, stating that it would be able to provide her with appropriate work in the near future. In fact, on the evidence, M Ltd was in the process of tendering for new work but no contracts had been agreed. McA did not accept the counter-notice and her claim for a redundancy payment was upheld. The tribunal could not conclude on the evidence that work was due to pick up in four weeks from the end of March to such an extent that McA would not be laid off or kept on short-time working for at least 13 weeks. It accepted that the employer believed that work would pick up at some point but that was not sufficient

- **Cole v Adecco UK Ltd** ET Case No.3304037/11: C was employed by A UK Ltd and worked at Xerox. Her assignment there ended on 12 August 2011 and A UK Ltd wrote to her saying her employment was not terminated and it would be in touch to discuss opportunities for her as they arose. On 12 September C served an NIC. A UK Ltd responded on 16 September with a counter-notice stating that it believed it had suitable work for her which would last for at least 13 weeks, and some ten days later it sent her details of a two-week assignment and a one-day assignment. She refused them, as they were not for 13 weeks. In early October she was offered a part-time assignment, which she rejected as she wanted full-time work. A further offer of work was made but C did not believe she was qualified for the role and on 26 October she submitted her claim. In finding that C was entitled to a redundancy payment, the tribunal emphasised that it was concerned with the point in time at which the NIC is served and that in determining what was likely to happen it was appropriate to look at what actually happened.

151

4.32 The 'period of employment' that the employee is expected to enter must be employment under the same contract of employment – Neepsend Steel and Tool Corporation Ltd v Vaughan 1972 ICR 278, NIRC. In that case, N, a skilled form tool grinder, was laid off but then offered less skilled work. This was at lower pay and involved night-shifts, which N had not previously worked. The NIRC held that this would not have been employment under the contract from which he was laid off and the employer had therefore failed to make out the statutory defence.

4.33 ## Alternative work

There is a question-mark over whether an employer can defeat a claim under the lay-off and short-time working scheme by making an offer of suitable alternative work under S.141 ERA – see Chapter 3, 'Alternative job offers'. S.82(5) of the Employment Protection (Consolidation) Act 1978 (EP(C)A), the predecessor to S.141(2) ERA, provided that an employee who unreasonably refused an offer of suitable alternative work would not be entitled to a redundancy payment 'by reason of his dismissal'. These words led the employment tribunal in Cluett v Rawlings Builders (Canford Cliffs) Ltd ET Case No.31618/86 to conclude that the question of alternative job offers only arose where there had been a dismissal for redundancy. It had no relevance to a redundancy claim based on lay-off or short-time working.

In Reid v Arthur Young and Son EAT 714/82 the EAT made the same point and laid great emphasis on the reference to a 'dismissal' in S.82(5) EP(C)A. However, S.141(2) ERA makes no specific reference to a dismissal, providing merely that an employee who unreasonably refuses an offer of suitable alternative work will not be entitled to a redundancy payment. This suggests that once a tribunal has ruled that the employee is eligible under the scheme, and the employee then gives notice of termination, it may be open to the employer to oppose a redundancy payment on the basis that an offer of suitable alternative employment had been made in accordance with S.141. However, the 1996 Act was intended merely as a consolidating Act and did not profess to make any changes to the substantive law. As a result, the courts and tribunals are likely to treat any putative changes with considerable caution.

4.34 # Death of employee or employer

There are special rules contained in Ss.175 and 176 ERA dealing with the effect of the death of the employee or employer on a claim for redundancy pay based on lay-off or short-time working.

152

Death of employee

If an employee dies after serving an NIC but before he or she has given notice to terminate the contract and he or she is still within the period allowed for a notice to terminate, the requirement for a notice to terminate disappears – S.176(6)(a) ERA. This means that the deceased employee's estate may still claim a redundancy payment, subject to any statutory defence raised by the employer.

If an employee dies within seven days of serving an NIC, the employer is treated as having served a counter-notice even it has not in fact done so – S.176(6)(b) ERA. The employer may then contest any tribunal proceedings.

Death of employer

Death of the employer is only relevant in the case of a personal employer, as opposed to the normal case of a corporate employer. If an employee is laid off or kept on short-time for one or more weeks before the death of the employer but has not yet served an NIC, and he or she is then taken on by the deceased employer's personal representative(s) but laid off or put on short-time again for one or more weeks, the week in which the employer died and the week in which the employee was taken on by the personal representative(s) are treated as consecutive weeks – S.175(2) ERA. This means that any weeks which elapse between death of the employer and re-employment by the personal representative(s) are disregarded for the purposes of accruing weeks of lay-off or short-time.

If the employee has served an NIC and the employer dies within four weeks of service and the employee has either not given any notice of termination, or has given notice but it has not yet expired, then the position depends upon whether the employee is re-employed by the employer's personal representative(s) within four weeks of the date of service of the NIC. If he or she is not re-employed, the statutory scheme operates as if the employer had not died and the employee had terminated the contract by giving the notice required under the scheme (see 'Employee's resignation' above). However, the personal representative(s) cannot use the employer's statutory defence under S.152 in these circumstances, and they cannot serve a counter-notice – S.175(3) and (4).

If the employee is re-employed in these circumstances, and was laid off or kept on short-time by the deceased employer for one or more weeks between service of the NIC and re-employment by the personal representative(s), and he or she is laid off or kept on short-time for at least one week following the start of employment with the personal representative(s), then the statutory scheme operates as if all the weeks of lay-off or short-time working were consecutive and in the same employment – S.175(5). The time limit for service of the employee's notice to terminate is extended by any weeks between the death of the employer and the date of re-employment.

Note that the death of a personal employer operates so as to terminate a contract of employment – S.136(5). If an employee is not re-employed by the personal representative(s), he or she will have a claim for a redundancy payment, provided the failure to re-employ was due to redundancy – S.139(4). This will apply whether or not he or she was laid off or kept on short-time. The provisions are discussed in Chapter 1, 'Dismissal', under 'Dismissal by operation of law'.

5 Qualifications and exclusions

Employees and excluded employees

Qualifying service

Disqualification

Contracting out

This chapter deals with the qualifications to and exclusions from the right to a statutory redundancy payment. Exclusions from the right to claim unfair dismissal, whether by reason of redundancy or otherwise, are dealt with in IDS Employment Law Handbook, 'Unfair Dismissal' (2015), Chapter 2, 'Exclusions from right to claim'.

5.1

The statutory redundancy pay scheme, which is set out in Part XI of the Employment Rights Act 1996 (ERA), applies only to *employees* – i.e. those working under a contract of employment or apprenticeship – Ss.135 and 230. However, not all employees are entitled to redundancy payments when made redundant:

- certain categories of employment are specifically excluded

- only employees with sufficient qualifying service can claim

- employees who would otherwise qualify may become disqualified because of personal factors: failure to work out notice, misconduct or unreasonable refusal of suitable alternative employment can (in certain circumstances) lead to disqualification

- employees may have been collectively contracted out of the statutory redundancy scheme

- an employee may have failed to claim a redundancy payment within the statutory time limit.

Note that S.209 ERA gives the Secretary of State wide powers to vary or revoke these exclusions or to create new ones by order. In this chapter, we consider the excluded categories of employment, qualifying service, specific disqualifications and collective contracting-out. Failure to work out notice is considered in Chapter 1, 'Dismissal', under 'Dismissal by employer – leaving before notice expires'; refusal of suitable alternative employment is considered in Chapter 3, 'Alternative job offers'; and the time limit for claiming a redundancy payment is considered in Chapter 10, 'Enforcement', under 'Statutory redundancy payments – time limits'.

5.2

In addition to the statutory restrictions, certain exclusions from the right to claim a redundancy payment may arise under general law owing to:

155

- illegality in the contract, or
- state or diplomatic immunity.

5.3   These general law exclusions are large topics in themselves and are outside the scope of this Handbook. They are, however, dealt with in other IDS Employment Law Handbooks: see IDS Employment Law Handbook, 'Contracts of Employment' (2014), Chapter 7, 'Void terms and illegality', under 'Illegality', and IDS Employment Law Handbook, 'Employment Tribunal Practice and Procedure' (2014), Chapter 2, 'Tribunals' jurisdiction', under 'State and diplomatic immunity'.

5.4   ## Employees and excluded employees

Normally, only employees will be entitled to redundancy payments. 'Employee' is defined as 'an individual who has entered into or works under (or, where the employment has ceased, worked under) a contract of employment' – S.230(1) ERA. 'Contract of employment' is, in turn, defined as 'a contract of service or apprenticeship, whether express or implied, and (if it is express) whether oral or in writing' – S.230(2).

5.5   Whether or not a person is an 'employee' for the purpose of qualifying for employment rights protection is ultimately a question of fact for the court or tribunal. Employment status is discussed in depth in IDS Employment Law Handbook, 'Contracts of Employment' (2014), Chapter 2, 'Employment status'.

The limitation of the statutory scheme to employees means that certain categories of worker are not covered because they do not work under contracts of employment. These are:

- independent contractors and the self-employed (including many casual workers)
- office holders (subject to exceptions – see 'Office holders' below), and
- partners (i.e. individuals carrying on a business in common with a view to profit – Cowell v Quilter Goodison Co Ltd and anor 1989 IRLR 392, CA).

5.6   ### Employee shareholders
The Growth and Infrastructure Act 2013 introduced a new category of excluded worker – the 'employee shareholder' – with effect from 1 September 2013. S.31 of the Act inserted new S.205A into the Employment Rights Act 1996, creating 'employee shareholder' status. This is a new breed of worker who, in return for a minimum of £2,000 of shares in the employer's business, forgoes some of the employment protection rights to which an 'employee', as defined by the ERA, would otherwise be entitled. One such right is the right to a statutory redundancy payment – S.205A(2)(d) ERA.

156

In response to widespread concern that the new employee shareholder regime could give rise to abuse, the Government imposed conditions and procedural requirements on the establishment of employee shareholder status. Among other things, whenever an employer proposes hiring an individual on an employee shareholder basis, the employer must provide the individual with a statement detailing the employment protection rights affected and giving details of the entitlements and restrictions that attach to the shares – S.205A(1) and (5). Furthermore, the individual must receive independent advice on the terms and effects of the proposed employee shareholder agreement (S.205A(6)) and the employer must pay the individual's reasonable costs in obtaining that advice (S.205A(7)). For further details, see IDS Employment Law Handbook, 'Contracts of Employment' (2014), Chapter 2, 'Employment status', under 'Specific categories of worker – employee shareholders'.

Agency workers   5.7

In the absence of contractual provisions granting 'employee' status, agency workers – i.e. those supplied to an 'end-user' by an employment business – are not usually classed as 'employees' of either the end-user or the employment business. In James v Greenwich London Borough Council 2008 ICR 545, CA, the Court of Appeal held that a tribunal is only entitled to imply a contract of employment between an agency worker and an end-user where it is necessary to do so to give business reality to the situation and there is no such necessity where agency arrangements are genuine and accurately represent the relationship between the parties. Similarly, in Consistent Group Ltd v Kalwak and ors 2008 IRLR 505, CA, the Court of Appeal held that, where an express term in the contract between an agency worker and an employment business describes the former as self-employed, a contract of employment cannot be implied in direct contradiction unless it is necessary to do so. Although the Supreme Court modified this straightforward approach to a limited extent in Autoclenz Ltd v Belcher 2011 ICR 1157, SC, holding that a court is entitled to disregard contractual terms that negate employment status where such terms do not represent the true agreement between the parties, it remains the case that few agency workers will be able to establish that they are 'employees' of either the end-user or the employment business for the purposes of S.230 and thus have the right to claim redundancy pay.

Note that, since 1 October 2011, agency workers with at least 12 weeks' continuous employment in the same role have been entitled to the same basic working and employment conditions that they would have been entitled to had they been directly recruited by the hirer. However, Reg 6(2) and (3) of the Agency Workers Regulations 2010 SI 2010/93 specifically excludes any payment referable to the worker's redundancy. The employment rights and protections available to agency workers are explored in more detail in IDS Employment Law Handbook, 'Atypical and Flexible Working' (2014), Chapter 1, 'Agency workers'.

157

5.8 Office holders

Some workers who are not employees may become eligible for redundancy payments by virtue of regulations made by the Secretary of State under Ss.171 and 172 ERA. The Redundancy Payments Office Holders Regulations 1965 SI 1965/2007 extend the statutory scheme to certain holders of public offices who do not rank as employees. These are clerks of the peace, justices' clerks, British Airports Authority police, rent officers and immigration medical inspectors. (Note that registrars of births, marriages and deaths are also covered by the Regulations but, with effect from 1 December 2007, such registrars ceased to be office holders and became employees of the relevant local authority – S.69 Statistics and Registration Service Act 2007.)

Under the Redundancy Payments Termination of Employment Regulations 1965 SI 1965/2022, chief constables and chief or assistant chief fire officers may be treated as employees eligible for redundancy payments in certain circumstances following the reorganisation of police forces and fire brigades.

5.9 Some public servants are 'employees' as defined but are excluded from the redundancy scheme because they are regarded as being analogous to Crown servants (see 'Crown servants, etc' below) and are protected under a separate scheme. By virtue of S.159 ERA, any employee who is treated as an office holder for the purposes of the Superannuation Act 1965 or as a civil servant for pension purposes has no right to a redundancy payment.

5.10 Crown servants, etc

Whether Crown servants – such as members of the Civil Service – can be said to have contracts of employment is unclear. However, the question is largely academic in the context of redundancy payments since Crown servants have their own redundancy pay scheme and are specifically excluded from the statutory scheme – Ss.159 and 191. Disputes about entitlement under Civil Service schemes may be referred to an employment tribunal – S.177. (Note that at the time of writing, the Government is considering reforms to the Civil Service Compensation Scheme. The Government has committed to introducing a number of measures aimed at curbing civil servants' entitlement to redundancy payments, including a cap of £95,000 on public sector exit payments. The Government has also confirmed that it will invoke the power under S.154 of the Small Business, Enterprise and Employment Act 2015 to make regulations requiring public sector employees to repay exit payments if they return to the public service within 12 months. A consultation on these proposals, including draft regulations, ran between December 2015 and January 2016.)

It should be noted that although the Trade Union Reform and Employment Rights Act 1993 extended a number of employment rights to parliamentary staff – who have never been regarded as employees – and paved the way for similar provisions in respect of members of the armed forces, these rights do not include a statutory right to a redundancy payment – see Ss.192, 194 and 195 ERA. These workers, therefore, have to rely on the severance terms forming part of their terms of engagement. National Health Service employees were formerly excluded from the statutory scheme but that exclusion was repealed on 1 April 1991 by S.66(2) of the National Health Service and Community Care Act 1990.

Employees of overseas Governments   5.11
Employees of the Government of any overseas territory are excluded from the statutory redundancy scheme – S.160. An overseas territory is any territory or country outside the UK – S.160(3).

Domestic servants   5.12
Domestic servants who are close relatives of their employers are excluded from the statutory scheme – S.161. This covers cases where the employer is parent, grandparent, step-parent, child, grandchild, step-child, sibling, or half-sibling of the employee. Otherwise a domestic servant in a private household can claim a redundancy payment in the normal way as if the household were a business carried on by the employer.

Share fishermen and women   5.13
Share fishermen and women are excluded from the redundancy scheme (and from many other statutory rights under the ERA). A share fisherman or woman is one 'remunerated only by a share in the profits or gross earnings of the vessel' on which he or she is employed – S.199(2). In Goodeve v Gilsons 1985 ICR 401, CA, the Court of Appeal held that a fisherman was not excluded when he was remunerated by a share in the profits of the fleet of vessels in which he was employed.

Overseas employment   5.14
It used to be the case that an employee was not entitled to a redundancy payment if he or she was working outside Great Britain on the 'relevant date' (usually the date on which the dismissal took effect – see Chapter 6, 'Redundancy payments', under 'Statutory redundancy pay scheme – relevant date and calculation date' for further details) unless under his or her contract of employment he or she ordinarily worked in Great Britain – S.196(6) ERA. However, this provision was repealed by the Employment Relations Act 1999.

The ERA is now silent on the entitlement of overseas employees to redundancy payments. Guidance can be found, however, in the House of Lords' decision in Lawson v Serco Ltd and two other cases 2006 ICR 250, HL. There, their Lordships stated that the statutory right to claim unfair dismissal under the ERA now covers 'employment in Great Britain', and that in general an

159

employee would be able to claim unfair dismissal if he or she were working in Great Britain at the time he or she was dismissed. In addition, employees working and based abroad may in exceptional circumstances be entitled to claim unfair dismissal, even though they are not employed in Great Britain at the time of dismissal, provided their employment has sufficiently strong connections with Great Britain and British employment law. It is arguable, by extension, that employees who are able to satisfy the Lawson test on the relevant date should be entitled to a redundancy payment under the ERA. For a detailed discussion of the Lawson test, see IDS Employment Law Handbook, 'Employment Tribunal Practice and Procedure' (2014), Chapter 2, 'Tribunals' jurisdiction', under 'Territorial reach – unfair dismissal and other ERA rights'.

5.15 Power to extend rights
Section 23 of the Employment Relations Act 1999 gives the Secretary of State power to extend the scope of existing employment rights, including the right to a redundancy payment, to a wider category of individuals than just 'employees'. The Act itself does not identify the intended beneficiaries of this provision but the Explanatory Notes to the Act state that the Government is committed to ensuring that 'all workers other than the genuinely self-employed enjoy the minimum standards of protection that the legislation is intended to provide, and that none are excluded simply because of technicalities relating to the type of contract or other arrangement under which they are engaged' (para 232). No regulations have yet been made under this provision.

In addition, as noted above, S.209 ERA gives the Secretary of State wide powers to vary or revoke exclusions or to create new ones by order.

5.16 Qualifying service

An employee needs to have two years' continuous employment in order to qualify for a redundancy payment – S.155. In general, continuity will remain unbroken as long as the contract of employment governs the whole or part of consecutive weeks – S.212. However, some breaks in employment count as periods of continuous employment despite the fact that there is no contract of employment in existence. In addition, some breaks in employment do not break continuity even though they do not count as periods of continuous employment. See IDS Employment Law Handbook, 'Continuity of Employment' (2012), Chapter 2, 'Breaks in employment where there is no contract', and Chapter 3, 'Non-counting weeks that do not break continuity', for further details.

5.17 Two years' service at 'relevant date'
For continuity purposes, two years means two calendar years, each of 12 calendar months – S.210(2). (Note that this is not the same as 104 weeks, since

four weeks are not the same thing as a calendar month and 52 weeks fall just short of a calendar year.) It used to be the case under S.211(2) that any period of continuous employment before the employee's 18th birthday did not count for redundancy purposes. However, that provision was repealed with effect from 1 October 2006 by the Employment Equality (Age) Regulations 2006 SI 2006/1031 (which were themselves replaced by provisions in the Equality Act 2010) – see 'Disqualification' below. Therefore, an employee made redundant may now count weeks of employment under the age of 18 as part of his or her total period of continuous employment. This is the case even if those weeks preceded the change in the law because the period of continuous employment must be calculated according to the rules in force on the 'relevant date' – normally the date on which employment comes to an end (S.145).

Although the 'relevant date' is normally the date on which employment comes to an end, if the employer has dismissed without notice or with less than the minimum statutory notice laid down in S.86(1), then the relevant date is the date on which the proper statutory notice would have expired had the employer given it on the date the employee was dismissed – S.145(5). In such circumstances there may be an interval of up to 12 weeks – the maximum statutory notice – between the termination of employment and the relevant date. S.213(3) provides that that interval counts as a period of continuous employment for the purpose of determining the employee's entitlement to a redundancy payment. See Chapter 6, 'Redundancy payments', under 'Statutory redundancy pay scheme – relevant date and calculation date' for further details.

Overseas working
5.18

Section 215(2) provides that weeks during the whole or part of which an employee was employed outside Great Britain do not count in calculating his or her period of employment for the purposes of the redundancy scheme, unless the employee remained an employed earner for national insurance purposes.

The test is whether the relevant NI contributions were payable, not whether they were actually paid. The Department for Work and Pensions will advise should there be any doubt as to whether an employee meets this condition.

A week of overseas employment that does not count under this provision does not break continuity of employment, however – S.215(3). Instead, the start of a period of continuous employment is deemed to be postponed by seven days for each week that does not count – S.211(3).
5.19

The above provisions do not apply to mariners employed on British ships who are ordinarily resident in Great Britain – S.215(6). In their case, overseas weeks do count whether or not NI contributions were payable.

161

5.20   **Receipt of redundancy payment**

In general terms, receipt of a redundancy payment breaks continuity of employment for the purposes of the statutory redundancy scheme – S.214. However, such a payment does not break continuity of employment for any other purpose. This means that employees must start counting again as far as future entitlement to redundancy payment is concerned (and will need to wait another two years before becoming so entitled) but not for other purposes, such as claiming unfair dismissal (as long as continuity has otherwise been preserved).

Section 214 has limited application in practice because payment of a redundancy payment will usually only occur as a result of a dismissal for redundancy. In such circumstances, an employee's employment will normally have come to an end altogether, so the question of future continuity will not ordinarily arise. One situation in which S.214 might apply is if an employee is dismissed for redundancy but business then picks up unexpectedly and within four weeks of dismissal he or she is given the old job back. It appears from S.138(1) that the employee may then be treated as not having been dismissed at all, thus preserving continuity of employment during the interval between 'dismissal' and re-employment (see S.213(2)). In such circumstances S.214 would break continuity for the purposes of the redundancy scheme. The employee does not have to pay back the redundancy payment but does lose the accrued service if he or she should be made redundant again. S.138(1), and alternative job offers generally, are discussed in Chapter 3, 'Alternative job offers'.

5.21   **Genuine statutory redundancy payment.** For the purposes of S.214 it is irrelevant whether the redundancy payment was paid in respect of dismissal, lay-off or short-time – S.214(2). S.214(5) provides that a redundancy payment is treated as having been paid if:

- the whole of the payment has been paid to the employee by the employer

- a tribunal has determined liability and found that the employer must pay part (but not all) of the redundancy payment and the employer has paid that part. This will happen when claims are brought under Ss.140(3) or 143 – see 'Disqualification – misconduct' below, or

- the Secretary of State has paid a sum to the employee in respect of the redundancy payment under S.167 – i.e. where the employer is insolvent.

In order for S.214 to break continuity for redundancy purposes, the employer must have been liable to pay a redundancy payment under the legislation. A 'redundancy' payment made when in fact there is no statutory liability to make it – because, for example, the employee has not been genuinely dismissed by reason of redundancy – does not break continuity of employment for the purpose of the statutory redundancy payment scheme – Rowan v Machinery Installations (South Wales) Ltd 1981 ICR 386, EAT. Thus, if there is a transfer of an undertaking under the Transfer of Undertakings (Protection of Employment) Regulations 2006 SI 2006/246 (TUPE) from one employer to another, continuity of employment will not be broken even if a 'redundancy payment' was made. This is because if TUPE applies there is no dismissal and so no liability to make a statutory redundancy payment. In Senior Heat Treatment Ltd v Bell and ors 1997 IRLR 614, EAT, some employees received severance packages from the transferor in return for 'opting out' of a transfer of the business. However, before the date of the transfer the employees entered into contracts of employment with the transferee to take effect immediately after the transfer. When the transferee dismissed them less than two years later, the issue was whether they had sufficient continuity to claim redundancy payments. The EAT decided that they did, commenting that not every severance payment breaks continuity under S.214. In this case TUPE applied, which meant there was no dismissal on the transfer and so no right to a statutory redundancy payment. The employees had simply received a voluntary severance payment from the transferor and they clearly had no objection to the transfer since they had in fact agreed to go and work for the transferee. For further analysis of this case, see IDS Employment Law Handbook, 'Transfer of Undertakings' (2015), Chapter 2, 'Who transfers?', under 'Objecting to transfer – meaning of "objection"'.

Payments made by Secretary of State. Where an employee is dismissed by   5.22
an insolvent company by reason of redundancy and an employer is unable to make a redundancy payment, the Secretary of State will make a payment out of the National Insurance Fund under S.167 ERA – see Chapter 7, 'Payments from National Insurance Fund'. By virtue of S.214(5)(c), continuity of employment is broken where such a payment is made.

Whereas continuity under S.214(5)(a) is not broken by a 'redundancy' payment made by the employer in circumstances that do not, in fact, amount to redundancy, a payment made by the Secretary of State under S.214(5)(c) may break continuity even if there was no genuine redundancy situation. In Lassman and ors v Secretary of State for Trade and Industry and anor 2000 ICR 1109, CA, R Ltd became insolvent. On 29 March 1988 T Ltd signed an option agreement to purchase R Ltd and, two days later, L and a number of other employees were dismissed for redundancy. However, they accepted jobs with T Ltd to commence on the next working day. The then legal position led the Secretary of State for Trade and Industry to conclude that the employees were not protected by TUPE and, in June 1988, the employees received redundancy payments from him in respect of their 'dismissals' by R Ltd. However, owing to a subsequent decision of the House of Lords, it became clear that the employees had, in fact, transferred automatically to T Ltd under TUPE and had thus not been dismissed by R Ltd. Matters came to a head some years later, when T Ltd also became insolvent and the employees were dismissed by that company. They claimed a payment from the Secretary

163

of State based on their period of employment with R Ltd as well as with T Ltd. In their view, since TUPE had applied to the 1988 transaction, the Secretary of State had not been liable to make the payments in respect of their 'dismissals' by R Ltd, meaning that S.214 had not broken continuity for redundancy purposes. The Court of Appeal observed that S.167 does not actually require an employee to be entitled to a redundancy payment for that payment to be valid. Rather, it requires the Secretary of State to be satisfied that the employee is so entitled, which is a subjective test, not an objective one. The question to be decided, therefore, was whether the Secretary of State had been satisfied that the payment should be made, not whether he had been entitled to reach the decision he did. On that basis, the Court held that the Secretary of State had properly concluded (on the basis of the law as it stood at the time) that the employees' contracts of employment had not transferred under TUPE, and that consequently they had been entitled to redundancy payments. This meant that continuity had been broken by S.214.

5.23 **Reinstatement and re-engagement.** Regulations made under S.219 ERA – the Employment Protection (Continuity of Employment) Regulations 1996 SI 1996/3147 – provide that where an employee is reinstated or re-engaged in consequence of any act to which the Regulations apply, and the employee repays in full the amount of the redundancy payment, S.214 does not apply and that employee's continuity is preserved.

The actions to which the Regulations apply are set out in Reg 2:

- a claim made in accordance with a designated 'dismissal procedures agreement' under which employees are collectively contracted out of their statutory protection against unfair dismissal – see S.110 ERA (such agreements are rare)

- the presentation of a 'relevant complaint of dismissal' to a tribunal

- intervention by an Acas conciliation officer under Ss.18A–18C of the Employment Tribunals Act 1996 to settle a case – see IDS Employment Law Handbook, 'Employment Tribunal Practice and Procedure' (2014), Chapter 3, 'Conciliation, settlements and ADR', under 'Early conciliation' and 'Acas-conciliated (COT3) agreements'

- entry into a 'relevant settlement agreement' – see IDS Employment Law Handbook, 'Employment Tribunal Practice and Procedure' (2014), Chapter 3, 'Conciliation, settlements and ADR', under 'Settlement agreements', or

- an agreement to submit an unfair dismissal dispute to Acas arbitration in accordance with an Acas scheme approved by the Secretary of State – see S.212A of the Trade Union and Labour Relations (Consolidation) Act 1992.

5.24 (Note that Reg 2 refers to two further actions – a decision arising out of the use of one of the statutory disciplinary or grievance procedures contained

164

in Schedule 2 to the Employment Act 2002 and a decision arising out of the 'statutory duty to consider procedure' contained in Schedule 6 to the Employment Equality (Age) Regulations 2006 SI 2006/1031, under which employees had a right to request to continue working beyond their intended retirement date. However, both these procedures have been repealed so these provisions no longer have any effect (although Reg 2 has not yet been amended to reflect this).)

Change of employer
5.25

Continuity of employment normally applies only to employment with a single employer – S.218(1). However, there are a number of exceptions where employment with one employer can be carried forward and added to employment with a successor employer. A change of employer will not break continuity of employment in the following circumstances:

- there is a transfer of a business or undertaking – S.218(2). Note that this protection of continuity consequent on a 'transfer' is not the same as the protection offered by the Transfer of Undertakings (Protection of Employment) Regulations 2006 SI 2006/246. Although the two schemes have much the same effect in terms of entitlement to a redundancy payment, the meaning of 'transfer' under S.218(2) is not informed by the detailed definition of a 'relevant transfer' for the purposes of the Regulations. For a full consideration of the meaning of a 'transfer' under S.218(2) and the differences between the two statutory schemes, see IDS Employment Law Handbook, 'Continuity of Employment' (2012), Chapter 4, 'Changes of employer'

- an employer who is a 'body corporate' is substituted by statute for another body corporate – S.218(3)

- the employer dies and the employee continues working for the employer's personal representatives or trustees – S.218(4)

- there is a change in the composition of an employer partnership or trust – S.218(5)

- there is a transfer of employment between associated employers – S.218(6)

- an employee of the governing body of a school maintained by a local authority is taken into the employment of the authority – S.218(7) and (11)

- health service employees are undergoing professional medical or dental training which involves their being employed by different health service employers – S.218(8)–(10).

Local government service. The Redundancy Payments (Continuity of Employment in Local Government, etc) (Modification) Order 1999 SI 1999/2277 provides a further statutory exception for employees in local government service or in other related sectors. The effect of the Order is that
5.26

165

virtually the whole of the local government service is to be treated as a single employer for the purposes of the redundancy scheme. If a local government employee is made redundant, his or her period of continuous employment is calculated by reference to his or her length of service in local government as a whole, rather than simply the length of service with the particular authority that has made the redundancy. This applies only in the context of the redundancy scheme. So, if an employee works for five and a half years for John O'Groats Council and then moves to Land's End Council and is made redundant after six months, he or she will be entitled to a redundancy payment based on six years' service. But he or she will not have the two years' service needed to bring an unfair dismissal claim against Land's End.

'Local government service' covers over 100 institutions in Great Britain, all of which are listed in the Order. Only service that falls strictly within the scope of the Order counts. In West Midlands Residuary Body v Deebank 1990 ICR 349, CA, D's local government service was interrupted by a period of ten months during which he had been compulsorily transferred to a regional water authority, which had taken over functions previously exercised by Birmingham City Council, D's employer. Water authorities (as they then were) are not listed in the Order. However, the Order does apply to 'any other body... established by or under any enactment for the purpose of exercising the functions of' a local government authority and D argued that this wording fitted the water authority. The Court of Appeal disagreed. It decided that in this context 'functions' meant 'current functions' and that the statutory wording only applied to bodies that carried out the current functions of local authorities as contractors or agents. It did not apply to a body established to take over completely the functions of a local authority. In any case, so many specific institutions are listed in the Order that it was surprising that water authorities should not have been listed if it had been intended to include them. D's continuity of employment was therefore broken by his spell with the water authority.

5.27 Similarly, in Scales v Suffolk Careers Ltd ET Case No.1501080/97 S began working in the careers service of various local authorities in 1992. In 1996 he began working for Suffolk Careers Ltd, which had won the contract to supply the careers service on behalf of Suffolk County Council. His employment terminated on 31 March 1997. S claimed his service was continuous from 1992 by virtue of the Order. Although Suffolk Careers Ltd was not named in the Order, it had applied to be included and its application was being processed. The tribunal dismissed S's claim. It said that the statutory framework had to be strictly applied and unless an employer is named in the Order, employees cannot benefit.

(Note that both of these cases were in fact decided under the Redundancy Payments (Local Government) (Modification) Order 1983 SI 1983/1160, which preceded the 1999 Order. The principle established in the cases is, however, equally applicable to the later Order.)

National Health Service. As we have seen above, S.218(8) specifically provides   5.28
that professional training undertaken with different health service employers
does not break continuity. In addition, the Redundancy Payments (National
Health Service) (Modification) Order 1993 SI 1993/3167 provides that the
entire National Health Service is treated as a single employer for redundancy
purposes. The employers covered are listed in Schedule 1 to the Order.

Renewal or re-engagement   5.29
As discussed above (under 'Receipt of redundancy payment'), if an employee
is dismissed for redundancy but then re-employed after not more than four
weeks, he or she will be treated as not having been dismissed at all – S.138(1)
(see Chapter 3, 'Alternative job offers', for full details of the conditions which
must be satisfied before S.138 applies). By virtue of S.213(2), the interval
between dismissal and re-employment in such a case counts as a period of
continuous employment, although continuity will still be broken under S.214
if the employee has received a redundancy payment.

When an employee is deemed to have been dismissed by the death of his or
her employer the ERA allows an interval of eight weeks for him or her to
be re-employed by the deceased's personal representative. The employee will
then be regarded as not having been dismissed and the interval will count as
a period of continuous employment – Ss.174(2) and 213(2).

Disqualification   5.30

An employee who would otherwise be entitled to a redundancy payment may
be or become disqualified by factors that are personal to him or her. For
example, entitlement to redundancy pay may be affected if an employee who
has been given notice of redundancy wishes to leave before his or her notice
expires. This is dealt with in Chapter 1, 'Dismissal', under 'Dismissal by
employer – leaving before notice expires'. Another form of disqualification,
covered in Chapter 3, 'Alternative job offers', is the unreasonable refusal of
an offer of suitable alternative employment.

In this chapter we consider the employee's misconduct as a special factor
which may bar his or her right to a redundancy payment. We then go on to
explain the special treatment of strikes, as a form of industrial misconduct,
that take place after notice of redundancy has been given.

Note that a number of age-based disqualifying factors contained in the ERA   5.31
were removed by the (now repealed) Employment Equality (Age) Regulations
2006 SI 2006/1031. These were:

167

- lower and upper age limits (18 and 65) on the right to claim redundancy payments (Ss.211(2) and 156 ERA), and

- an exclusion from the right to a redundancy payment in certain circumstances where the employee was also entitled to claim a pension (S.158).

However, as noted above, the two-year qualifying period for claiming a redundancy payment remains in place, despite its potentially indirectly discriminatory effect upon younger workers, as does the age-based calculation of the statutory redundancy payment – see Chapter 6, 'Redundancy payments', under 'Age discrimination'.

5.32 Misconduct

Section 140(1) ERA provides that an employee loses the right to a redundancy payment if his or her conduct is such that the employer is entitled to dismiss without notice – i.e. if the employee is guilty of gross misconduct – and the employer does dismiss in one of the following ways:

- without notice

- with shorter notice than required by contract or statute, or

- by giving full (or more than full) notice accompanied by a written statement that the employer would, because of the employee's conduct, have been entitled to dismiss without notice. (Note that the employer does not have to provide such a written statement when it gives no notice or shorter notice – apparently even if short by just one day.)

This is a rather puzzling provision. As stated in the introduction to this chapter, a dismissed employee is only entitled to a redundancy payment if he or she is dismissed *because of redundancy*. So, if the employee is dismissed for gross misconduct, it stands to reason that he or she will not be in a position to claim a redundancy payment. Quite simply, the principal reason for the dismissal will be the misconduct, not redundancy – see Chapter 2, 'Redundancy', under 'Reason for dismissal – change of reason for dismissal'. At first glance, then, S.140(1) appears redundant in itself.

5.33 However, it seems that S.140(1) will be applicable where the employee is given notice for redundancy but is then dismissed for gross misconduct in the prescribed manner (i.e. the employer gives no notice, short notice or provides a written statement when giving full notice). Note that in these circumstances, S.140(2) and (3) provides limited exceptions to the operation of S.140(1) – see 'Misconduct during notice period' below.

Another point worth making is that, strictly speaking, S.140 does not actually require an employee to be dismissed by reason of gross misconduct. It merely requires that the employer be *entitled* to dismiss by reason of gross

168

misconduct. So, it appears that S.140(1) will apply where the employer in fact dismisses for redundancy but is entitled to dismiss for gross misconduct (of which the employer may not be aware at the time of dismissal). The employee will then be disqualified from receiving a redundancy payment if he or she has been dismissed in a prescribed manner under S.140. In X v Y Ltd 1969 ITR 204, ET, X was dismissed summarily, with pay in lieu of notice, because of redundancy. It was then discovered that he had been guilty of misconduct which would have entitled the employer to dismiss him summarily. The tribunal held that the employer had been entitled to dismiss X summarily because of his conduct, although it did not do so because it was unaware of it at the time. Since it had (fortuitously) dismissed without notice, X was not entitled to a redundancy payment. This type of situation is unlikely to occur very often since an employer that dismisses an employee by reason of redundancy, unaware of his or her gross misconduct, is likely to dismiss with full notice and will not send an accompanying written statement precisely because it is unaware of the misconduct. It seems odd that an employer can profit from its failure to give sufficient notice whereas an employer who dismisses with full notice loses the benefit of this provision if it has not sent an accompanying statement. However, on a strict interpretation of S.140(1), this appears to be the case.

5.34 Section 140(1) may also apply where it is unclear whether the reason for dismissal is redundancy or misconduct. In these circumstances, S.163 means that it is likely that the employee will be presumed to have been dismissed by reason of redundancy. However, the employer may be able to rely on S.140(1) to counter this presumption provided it has dismissed in the prescribed manner.

The main policy reason behind S.140 appears to be that an employee guilty of gross misconduct has repudiated the contract of employment and rendered it voidable at the option of the employer, leaving him or herself vulnerable to dismissal without notice. Consequently, if that employee happens to be coincidentally redundant, there should be no entitlement to a redundancy payment. It should be noted that when statutory redundancy rights were first introduced by the Redundancy Payments Act 1965, it might well have suited the employer to contend that a dismissal was for some reason other than redundancy because there was then no statutory right for employees to claim unfair dismissal. If, however, the employer runs that argument today, it risks a finding of unfair dismissal that could well be more costly than a redundancy payment.

5.35 **Objective test.** The test under S.140(1) is an objective one – the employer must be factually entitled to dismiss summarily. This means that the employee's misconduct must be gross misconduct – i.e. misconduct amounting to a repudiatory breach of contract warranting dismissal without notice. It is for the employer to prove that the employee was in fact guilty of the misconduct in question. This contrasts with the test for unfair dismissal, which is whether

169

the employer acted reasonably in deciding to dismiss, and it is important not to confuse the two issues. In Bonner v H Gilbert Ltd 1989 IRLR 475, EAT, a tribunal decided that an employee was not entitled to a redundancy payment because his employer had an honest belief in his guilt, had reasonable grounds for that belief, and had carried out reasonable investigations. The EAT held that the tribunal should have asked whether the employer had shown that the employee had been guilty of a fundamental breach of contract, not whether it reasonably believed that he had committed misconduct.

5.36 **Misconduct during notice period.** As explained above, S.140(1) removes the entitlement of an employee guilty of gross misconduct to a redundancy payment, provided the employer dismisses in a prescribed manner. However, there is an exception in the case of an employee who is already under statutory or contractual notice of redundancy and who is then dismissed for misconduct during 'the obligatory period of notice' in one of the ways described in S.140(1) – S.140(5)(a). S.140(3) provides that in such a case (provided the employee is not dismissed for taking part in a strike – see below) the tribunal has a discretion to order the employer to make an 'appropriate payment' to the employee if it thinks it just and equitable to do so. That payment may be either a full redundancy payment or whatever portion of it that the tribunal thinks fit – S.140(4).

The policy behind this would appear to be that where an employee's claim to a redundancy payment has already crystallised (because he or she has already been given notice of dismissal for redundancy) then he or she should not necessarily lose the right to claim at least some of it if dismissed for some other reason in his or her final days of employment. It should be noted that under S.140(3) the employee is not technically entitled to any redundancy payment unless he or she refers the question to an employment tribunal. However, if it appears that there are circumstances which might justify the tribunal awarding some or all of the redundancy pay to the employee, it is clearly open to the employer to make an appropriate payment to the employee to save the time and expense of going to tribunal.

5.37 The 'obligatory period of notice' is the period of notice required by statute or contract (whichever is longer) and ends on the date the employer's notice expires – S.136(4). Since the obligatory period is likely to differ from one employee to the next, it follows that some employees will forfeit their redundancy pay while others will not, even if they are given the same amount of notice. For example, if an employer gives 12 weeks' notice of redundancies as representing the maximum statutory notice, then the obligatory period will be the whole of the 12 weeks for an employee (A) with 12 years' service, who is statutorily entitled to 12 weeks' notice. But only the last two weeks of the notice period will be the obligatory period for an employee (B) with only two years' service because he or she will be statutorily entitled to only

170

two weeks' notice (assuming there is no differing contractual right to notice). Therefore, if B is dismissed summarily for gross misconduct during the eighth week of his or her actual notice period, S.140(1) will apply to exclude his or her entitlement to a redundancy payment, and the S.140(3) exception will not apply so the tribunal will have no discretion to award redundancy pay even if the circumstances would otherwise appear to warrant it. However, if A were dismissed at the same time in identical circumstances, the S.140(3) exception would apply, and the tribunal's discretion to award a payment would crystallise.

The tribunal's discretion under S.140(3) is a wide one and is to award what it considers 'just and equitable' in the circumstances, up to the full amount of the potential statutory redundancy payment. In Lignacite Products Ltd v Krollman 1979 IRLR 22, EAT, K was summarily dismissed for stealing shortly before the expiry of his redundancy notice. The EAT refused to interfere with a tribunal's award of 60 per cent of K's statutory redundancy pay, although it thought that the award was high. The tribunal had looked at the relevant factors, including K's length of service (24 years), and the EAT could not substitute its own decision.

Other factors that tribunals may consider are the seriousness of the misconduct, the employee's previous record, whether the misconduct was a one-off offence, and whether the employee has lost other benefits besides the statutory redundancy payment. In Danson v Capper Pipe Service Co (Western) Ltd ET Case No.8142/82, for example, an employee who had been given notice of redundancy was dismissed for refusing to obey an order. The tribunal thought that he should have been warned that he was endangering his redundancy payment. It also took account of the employee's previous trouble-free record and made an award of 50 per cent of his statutory entitlement.

5.38

Some other examples:

- **Fenton v Samuel Webster and Wilsons Ltd** ET Case No.8298/85: F, who had been accepted for voluntary redundancy, stole a number of crates of drinks during his notice period. He was summarily dismissed and forfeited ex gratia severance payments of £9,258. The tribunal awarded 35 per cent of his redundancy payment

- **Peirson v Courtaulds Ltd** ET Case No.21015/79: P stole scrap material from his employer during the notice period. The total value was over £500 and the tribunal thought that he had been stealing systematically for over six months. Nothing was awarded

- **Phelps v Butler (1843) Ltd** ET Case No.51066/96: P was dismissed for redundancy in April 1996. He agreed with his employer that he would remain on 'garden leave' until 30 April and would receive a redundancy payment. The employer then discovered that P had been diverting customers to a competing firm with which he had obtained work. The employer stopped the cheque for redundancy pay and notified P that his employment was terminated with immediate effect on 30 April, the last day of his employment under the earlier agreement. A tribunal found that by virtue of S.140(1) P had forfeited his right to a redundancy payment. However, it also found that the employer had given notice to P within the obligatory period and that it was just and equitable under S.140(3) to award P one half of his redundancy payment. It took into account P's distress at his redundancy, which he felt to be unjustified; P's failure to make personal gain from his disloyalty; and the fact that the incidents involving the diversion of customers had since been put right.

5.39 In a more recent case – Knox v Biotechnology and Biological Services EAT 0066/06 – where S.140 was briefly considered, the EAT stated that a tribunal might also consider whether the employer adopted the course of action that it did as a device to seek to bring itself within the provisions of S.140 so as to avoid making a redundancy payment.

5.40 **Strike during notice period.** Section 140(1) does not apply if an employee who has been given notice of redundancy is dismissed for taking part in a strike during the obligatory notice period (see above) in circumstances which entitle the employer to treat the contract of employment as terminable without notice – S.140(2). Where this provision applies, the employee's right to a redundancy payment will be unaffected by participation in the strike.

Unlike S.140(3), S.140(2) is not dependent upon the tribunal's discretion, and the employee automatically retains his or her right to redundancy pay, provided the conditions under S.140(2) are satisfied. However, the position becomes more complicated if the employer serves a written notice of extension requesting the employee to extend the notice period by the number of working days lost because of the strike (see below).

5.41 Section 140(2) only applies when the employee participates in a strike and not when he or she participates in any other type of industrial action (although industrial action short of a strike could fall under S.140(3) – a provision discussed under 'Misconduct during notice period' above). 'Strike' in this context means a strike about terms and conditions of employment – S.235(5). Participation in a strike about something other than terms and conditions does not count for the purposes of S.140(2) (although, again, it could fall under S.140(3)). In addition, the ERA is explicit that taking part in the strike must constitute a repudiatory breach of contract, although it is hard to conceive of circumstances when such action would not do so. The ERA does not appear to impose a requirement that the strike be official (or protected) so it is assumed that unofficial (and unprotected) strike action would also fall under S.140(2) – see IDS Employment Law Handbook, 'Industrial Action'

(2010), Chapter 8, 'Industrial action dismissals', for a description of the different types of industrial action.

The decision in Simmons v Hoover Ltd 1977 ICR 61, EAT, suggests that S.140(2) only applies when an employee goes on strike *after* having been given notice of redundancy – it does not operate if an employee is dismissed for redundancy when already on strike, which continues after the notice has been given. In that case 150 employees, including S, had been on strike for some two and a half months when the employer sent them letters giving one week's notice of redundancy. The strike was settled a few weeks later and the other employees returned to work but S had found another job and claimed a redundancy payment instead. The EAT held that striking was a repudiatory breach of contract entitling the employer to dismiss S without notice. He was barred, therefore, from any entitlement to a redundancy payment by virtue of S.140(1) (then S.2(2) of the Redundancy Payments Act 1965), and that S.140(2) (then S.10 RPA) did not apply.

However, it is arguable that this interpretation of S.140(2) is contrary to the wording of the provision, which refers to the employee 'tak[ing] part' in a strike after having been given notice of redundancy, not 'going on' strike at that time. Interestingly, S.143(1) – which governs extension of the notice period after a strike (see below) – specifically applies to the situation where the employee 'begins to take part in a strike' after notice of termination has been given. **5.42**

Extension of notice period after strike. We have seen above that if an employee goes on strike during the obligatory period of notice, his or her right to a redundancy payment is unaffected, and that this is not dependent upon the tribunal's discretion. However, the employer is entitled to require the employee to make up the working days lost due to the strike by working through an extended notice period as a prerequisite to the employer agreeing to pay a redundancy payment. **5.43**

Section 143 contains the rather complicated statutory scheme that regulates this procedure. Briefly, if an employee goes on strike when under notice of dismissal for redundancy, the employer may serve a written notice of extension requesting him or her to agree to extend the notice period by the number of working days lost because of the strike – S.143(1). 'Notice period' in this context means the notice given by the employer and is not limited to the obligatory period. The employer's written notice must:

- indicate the employer's reasons for making the request, and

- state that the employer will contest liability to make a redundancy payment if the employee does not comply with the request, unless the employer is satisfied that the employee could not comply with the request – e.g. because of sickness or injury – or that it was not reasonable in the circumstances for the employee to comply with it – S.143(2).

173

5.44 If the employee complies with the notice, then the notice of termination is deemed to have effect as if the period specified had been extended by the period set out in the employer's written request and the employee will be entitled to a redundancy payment calculated as at that date. If the employee only partially complies, by coming to work on one or more, but not all, of the days within that period, the notice period is then treated as continuing up to the last day on which the employee turns up to work – S.143(7)–(8). The employee is then entitled to redundancy pay calculated as at that date.

If the employee does not comply with the employer's request – for example, by not turning up for work on any of the days requested – he or she will lose entitlement to a redundancy payment (unless the employer agrees to pay one anyway – S.143(4)) and must apply to a tribunal for an 'appropriate payment'. The tribunal may then award a redundancy payment in whole or in part if it is satisfied that the employee was unable to comply with the employer's request or that it was reasonable for the employee not to comply with it – S.143(3)–(6). The amount of the award is a matter for the tribunal's discretion.

5.45 Lay-off and short-time

Note that S.140(2) and (3) also apply as exceptions to S.140(1) where an employee who has given a notice of intention to claim a lay-off or short-time redundancy payment under S.148 is then dismissed for taking part in a strike or for misconduct after the service of the notice. However, once the employee is dismissed, he or she is then barred from claiming lay-off or short-time redundancy – S.151. Any claim for a redundancy payment would have to be based on the express dismissal by the employer and would be dependent upon one of the exceptions to S.140(1) applying (i.e. S.140(2) or (3)). Lay-off and short-time redundancies are discussed in Chapter 4, 'Lay-off and short-time'.

5.46 Contracting out

The general rule is that any provision attempting to exclude an employee's rights under the statutory redundancy scheme or to preclude his or her right to claim a redundancy payment in a tribunal is void – S.203(1) ERA. It used to be the case that fixed-term employees could waive their rights to a statutory redundancy payment where their employment was to last two years or more but S.197, which made provision for this, was repealed with effect from 1 October 2002 by the Fixed-term Employees (Prevention of Less Favourable Treatment) Regulations 2002 SI 2002/2034. All employees may, however, settle a complaint or agree not to bring proceedings to seek a redundancy payment by entering into an Acas-conciliated settlement or a settlement agreement – see IDS Employment Law Handbook, 'Employment Tribunal Practice and Procedure' (2014), Chapter 3, 'Conciliation, settlements and ADR'.

174

Collective contracting out

5.47

Under S.157 ERA unions and employers may enter into a collective agreement whereby employees are, in defined circumstances, entitled to severance payments on the termination of employment. If the Secretary of State is satisfied with the scheme, he or she may issue an exemption order stating that the statutory redundancy scheme will not apply to the employees covered by the collective agreement.

It is a condition for making an exemption order that the collective agreement specifies that disputes under a contracted-out redundancy scheme should be referable to an employment tribunal – S.157(4). The tribunal will then have to apply the terms of the contracted-out scheme instead of those of the statutory scheme. An agreement between an employer and a union will not displace the statutory scheme unless it is the subject of an exemption order. In Godridge v Yorkshire Imperial Metals Ltd 1968 ITR 30, ET, there was an agreement between union and management that purported to displace some of the statutory provisions about alternative job offers in a redundancy situation. The tribunal held that the agreement was invalid because it had not been made the subject of an exemption order and applied the provisions of the statutory scheme instead.

The Secretary of State may revoke an exemption order by making a subsequent order – S.157(5). He or she may do this on the application of all or any of the parties to the agreement or without any application having been made. The Secretary of State is not, however, obliged to revoke an exemption order even if all the parties to it ask him or her to do so.

5.48

6 Redundancy payments

An employer must pay a redundancy payment to an employee who is dismissed **6.1** by reason of redundancy, or is eligible for a redundancy payment by reason of being laid off or kept on short-time – S.135 Employment Rights Act 1996 (ERA). This rule is subject to some exclusions and qualifying conditions, which we discuss in Chapter 5, 'Qualifications and exclusions'.

In this chapter we look at the method of calculation for payments under the statutory redundancy scheme, and consider entitlements that may arise under an employer's enhanced redundancy pay scheme. We also examine the impact that the age discrimination legislation has had on redundancy pay.

Statutory redundancy pay scheme **6.2**

According to the Government, the statutory redundancy pay scheme, which was originally introduced in 1965, exists to ensure that employees who are made redundant receive at least a statutory minimum severance payment that recognises the degree of their past commitment to the employer's business, and to promote labour market flexibility by easing the process of job transition. The current scheme governing statutory redundancy payments is set out in Part XI of the ERA. As explained below under 'Formula for calculating statutory redundancy pay', the amount of redundancy pay to which an employee is entitled depends in part on his or her age and length of service. This could be considered discriminatory on the ground of age but, when the prohibition on age discrimination was introduced by the Employment Equality (Age) Regulations 2006 SI 2006/1031, the Government decided to retain the statutory scheme, as it considered it to be objectively justified – see 'Age discrimination' below.

Formula for calculating statutory redundancy pay **6.3**
The amount of statutory redundancy pay an employee is entitled to depends on his or her age, length of service and pay. The employee is entitled to:

- one and a half weeks' pay for each complete year of service after reaching the age of 41

177

- one week's pay for each complete year of service between the ages of 22 and 40 inclusive, and

- half a week's pay for each complete year of service below the age of 22 – S.162(2) ERA.

Note that the actual wording of S.162(2) refers to 'a year of employment in which' the employee 'was not below' the relevant age. This makes it clear that the year in which an employee turns 22 would fall into the lower band, and the year in which he or she turns 41 would fall into the middle band for the purpose of the calculation.

6.4 The maximum length of service that may be taken into account in a redundancy pay claim is 20 years – S.162(3), a year being a period of 12 complete calendar months – S.210(2)(b). The total amount of a week's pay is also subject to a statutory maximum – S.227. S.34 of the Employment Relations Act 1999 provides that the statutory maximum limit for a week's pay is set by the Secretary of State each September by reference to the Retail Price Index. The current limit is £479 (with effect from 6 April 2016). It follows that the absolute maximum statutory redundancy payment an employee can hope to receive is currently £14,370, i.e. (£479 x 1½) x 20.

An employee is not entitled as of right to a statutory redundancy payment if:

- the employee under notice of dismissal for redundancy has served a counter-notice on the employer to terminate the contract on a date earlier than the expiry of the employer's notice and the employer has served a further notice requiring the employee to work out the whole of the notice period, and the employee has refused to do so – S.142 (see Chapter 1, 'Dismissal', under 'Dismissal by employer – leaving before notice expires')

- the employee has been dismissed for misconduct while under notice of dismissal for redundancy or after giving notice of an intention to claim redundancy arising from a lay-off or short-time situation – S.140(1), (3) and (4) (see Chapter 5, 'Qualifications and exclusions', under 'Disqualification – misconduct')

- the employee has been on strike and fails to comply with an extension notice properly issued by the employer in respect of the days lost because of strike action – S.143 (see Chapter 5 under 'Disqualification – misconduct').

6.5 However, in each of the above scenarios, an employment tribunal may order the employer to pay an 'appropriate' payment – that is, either the whole of the redundancy payment to which the employee would ordinarily have been entitled, or such part of that payment as the tribunal thinks fit.

Some employees may, because of statutory provisions, be paid by a person other than their employer. In such a case the person responsible for paying the

178

remuneration is treated as the employer for most purposes of the statutory redundancy scheme – S.173. This will apply, for example, to a teacher who is employed by a school's board of governors but paid by the Local Authority. The governors hire and fire but the authority will be responsible for redundancy payments.

Relevant date and calculation date   6.6

In order to work out an employee's statutory redundancy entitlement, it is necessary to ascertain two key dates: the 'relevant date' and the 'calculation date'.

Relevant date. The relevant date is the date by reference to which: 6.7

- an employee's entitlement to a redundancy payment is established (i.e. whether the employee has two years' continuous service – see Chapter 5, 'Qualifications and exclusions', under 'Qualifying service'; is not otherwise disqualified from receiving such payment as a result, for example, of gross misconduct – see Chapter 5 under 'Disqualification'; and is not the subject of an exemption order issued under S.157 – see Chapter 5 under 'Contracting out')

- the amount of the redundancy payment is calculated under S.162 (and S.168 in respect of a payment by the Secretary of State in the event of the employer's insolvency or refusal or failure to pay – see Chapter 7, 'Payments from National Insurance Fund')

- the six-month time limit for making a claim begins to run (see Chapter 10, 'Enforcement', under 'Statutory redundancy payments – time limits'), and

- the current statutory maximum week's pay (£479, with effect from 6 April 2016) is ascertained – see IDS Employment Law Handbook, 'Wages' (2016), Chapter 9, 'A week's pay'.

The relevant date is generally equivalent to the effective date of termination of the contract of employment, that is:

- where the contract is terminated by notice (by either the employer or the employee), the date on which that notice expires – S.145(2)(a)

- where the dismissal is without notice, the date on which the termination takes effect – S.145(2)(b)

- where the employment is under a limited-term contract which terminates by virtue of the limiting event without being renewed under the same contract, the date on which the termination takes effect – S.145(2)(c).

There are three cases where the relevant date will differ – either for all or for   6.8
some purposes – from the effective date of termination of the contract:

- where the employee is treated as dismissed under S.136(3) (where he or she has given notice to leave earlier than the expiry of the employer's notice – see Chapter 1, 'Dismissal', under 'Dismissal by employer – leaving before notice expires'), in which case the relevant date is the date on which the employee's notice expires – S.145(3)

- where the employee has accepted an offer of alternative employment and leaves during the trial period (or a subsequent trial period for another alternative job), the relevant date is the date of termination of the original contract – S.145(4)(b). However, the six-month time limit for claiming a redundancy payment will run from the date of termination of the most recent contract – S.145(4)(a)

- where the contract is terminated by the employer with either no notice or insufficient notice, the relevant date for the purposes of assessing the employee's qualifying service in relation to S.155 (period of continuous employment) and S.162(1) (calculation of the amount of redundancy pay due) is the date on which the proper statutory notice under S.86 would have expired had it been given – S.145(5). Prior to the Employment Relations Act 1999, this later date was also the relevant date for the purpose of ascertaining the level of the maximum week's pay. However, this no longer seems to be the case. Note that the relevant date can be extended by the period of the statutory minimum notice due even if the employee has waived his or her right to notice and accepted pay in lieu – Staffordshire County Council v Secretary of State for Employment and another case 1989 ICR 664, CA.

Where an employee has been laid off or put on short-time, the relevant date is the last day of the last week of the lay-off or short-time relied upon – S.153.

6.9 If an employee dies during the notice period, the contract of employment is treated as having expired by notice terminating on the date of the employee's death – S.176(1). If the employee dies after the contract has been terminated, but S.145(5) applies to postpone the date of termination to the end of the statutory notice period and this later date has not yet been reached, then the contract is also treated as having been ended by notice expiring on the date of the employee's death – S.176(2).

6.10 **Calculation date.** The 'calculation date' is the second key date in the statutory redundancy pay scheme and is the date on which an employee's 'week's pay' is calculated. It will be either:

- where the employee was dismissed with no notice, or with less than the minimum statutory notice, the date on which the contract of employment ends – S.226(5)(b), or

- in all other cases, the date on which notice would have been given by the employer in order to comply with the minimum notice requirements under S.86, working backwards from the relevant date – S.226(5)(c) and (6). (In other words, the date x weeks before the relevant date, where x weeks is the minimum statutory notice required.) This includes cases where the contract has been terminated by the giving of contractual notice which is longer than that required under the statute.

Similarly, where an employee has been laid off or put on short-time, the calculation date is ascertained by reference to S.226(5) and (6). However, the date for determining whether an employee is on short-time working is the day immediately preceding the short-time relied upon – S.226(4). This date has no bearing on the calculation date for the redundancy payment and relates only to the issue of whether there is short-time working – Dutton v Jones (t/a Llandow Metals) 2013 ICR 559, EAT. The EAT also held that an employee who goes on to short-time working is not to be regarded as having accepted a permanent variation to his or her terms of employment involving a reduction in normal working hours. Thus, a 'week's pay' is the amount provided for by the original employment contract, notwithstanding the short-time working (see 'Week's pay' below).

Where a pay increase is awarded after the calculation date, the redundancy **6.11** payment is calculated on the lower wage in force at the calculation date. This is so even if the pay increase is expressed as being backdated to a date prior to the calculation date – see, for example, Jones v Cammell Laird Shipbuilders Ltd ET Case No.34115/84; or there is an implied contractual term that this will be the case – Leyland Vehicles Ltd v Reston and ors 1981 ICR 403, EAT.

Examples of relevant dates and calculation dates. Taking an employee who **6.12** has been in employment for six years and eleven months:

- if on 7 March she is given eight weeks' contractual notice of dismissal for redundancy, the relevant date by reference to which her age, length of service and statutory maximum week's pay will be calculated will be the effective date of termination of her contract – i.e. 2 May. The calculation date on which her week's pay will be measured is six weeks (her statutory notice period) before the expiry of her contract – i.e. 21 March. If on 22 March she received a pay rise, her statutory redundancy payment would still be calculated by reference to her wage prior to the increase

- if on 7 March she is given only one week's notice of dismissal for redundancy, the calculation date on which her week's pay would be measured is the date on which that notice expires – i.e. 14 March. The relevant date for the purposes of calculating her length of service and the amount of her redundancy entitlement is the date on which her statutory period of notice would have expired – i.e. 18 April. She will therefore have seven years' continuous service and, if she turned 42 before this date, she will be entitled to one and a half weeks' pay in respect of her final year. However, the maximum week's pay applicable will be the rate in force on 14 March

- if on 7 March she is dismissed for redundancy without any notice, the relevant date for the purposes of calculating her length of service and the amount of her redundancy entitlement will again be that date on which proper notice under S.86 would have expired – i.e. 18 April. The maximum week's pay applicable, however, will be the rate in force on 7 March, the date her contract terminated. The calculation date will also be 7 March. The same is true if she is constructively dismissed for redundancy on 7 March and leaves without notice

- if on 7 March her fixed-term contract expires and she leaves because of redundancy her calculation date will be six weeks before 7 March – i.e. 24 January. Her relevant date will be 7 March and the maximum week's pay in force on that day will apply.

6.13 **Variations before calculation date.** The amount of a week's pay is assessed at the calculation date, subject to the applicable statutory maximum (usually that in force at the relevant date – see 'Relevant date' above). If an employee accepts a genuine variation in wage just before the calculation date, this is the wage upon which the redundancy pay will be calculated. In France v Aldridge Brownlee Solicitors LLP ET Case No.3103356/12, for example, an employee with 24 years' service agreed to reduce her hours from five to three days per week when the department in which she worked started making a loss. The reduction was stated to be subject to a review after three months and the parties agreed that if that review resulted in the employee's redundancy, her redundancy pay would be calculated on the basis of her full-time hours. When the review took place, the employee was not made redundant, but agreed to continue working three days per week. After two years, she was issued with a revised contract which stated that her working hours were 21 per week. The employee expressed her unhappiness with the new contract, stating that she wished to remain on her full-time contract, but continued to work 21 hours per week until she was made redundant almost a year later. A tribunal rejected her claim that her redundancy pay should be calculated on the basis of her full-time hours. The temporary arrangement to protect her redundancy pay had ceased after the first three months, and the employee had accepted a permanent variation to her contract.

As in the France case, tribunals will generally distinguish between a temporary expedient and a contractual variation. If the change can be characterised as a temporary expedient, the tribunal will be able to avoid finding that a period of lower-paid work put an employee at a disadvantage when it comes to the calculation of his or her redundancy payment. Two examples:

- **Nelson and ors v Ryley and Co (Shipping) Ltd (in liquidation) and anor** ET Case No.24061/84: employees were put on 'emergency' short-time work which, in the event, lasted for over two years before they were made redundant. The tribunal calculated their redundancy pay on the basis of their full-time salary, ruling that their contractual wages had not been varied

182

- **Friend v PMA Holdings Ltd** 1976 ICR 330, EAT: upholsterers' hours were cut during the three-day week caused by the miners' strike in early 1974 and were not increased before they were made redundant some months later. The EAT ruled that the employees had not agreed to a variation of their original contract and that their redundancy payments should be based on their wages under that contract.

Where an employee's hours and wages have been increased shortly before the calculation date, a tribunal may be more inclined to see a contractual variation. In Hart v John Blundells Ltd ET Case No.04341/84, for example, the claimant had worked full time during the last three months of her employment, having worked part time for the previous nine years. Her hours had originally been increased on a temporary basis when her manager went on holiday and had remained that way as a result of an injury he had sustained. The tribunal awarded her a redundancy payment based on her full-time wage, ruling that her contractual hours had been varied until such time as the manager was fit to return to work. **6.14**

The practice of calculating redundancy pay on the basis of an employee's 'terminal pay' – i.e. his or her salary at the time he or she ceased to work for the employer – has been criticised on the basis that it discriminates unfairly against women, since more women than men reduce their hours in order to bring up a family. In Barry v Midland Bank plc 1999 ICR 859, HL, B had been employed by Midland Bank plc as a full-time clerk from 1979 to 1990, when she left in order to have a baby. She returned to work on a part-time basis until she accepted voluntary redundancy in 1993. Her severance payment under a contractual redundancy scheme (which reflected the calculation method adopted by the provisions of the ERA) was calculated on the basis of her part-time salary. B complained to a tribunal that the failure to take account of her 11 years' full-time service amounted to a breach of Article 119 of the EC Treaty (now Article 157 of the Treaty on the Functioning of the European Union) and the Equal Pay Act 1970 (now the Equality Act 2010). The House of Lords found that the scheme was not indirectly discriminatory against women even though it made no allowance for employees whose hours of work fluctuated. Their Lordships took account of the fact that the primary objective of the scheme was to provide support for lost income during the period following redundancy – not to remunerate for past service.

Some indirect support for the Barry decision may be found in the ECJ's ruling in Grau-Hupka v Stadtgemeinde Bremen 1994 ECR 1-5535, ECJ. In that case the ECJ ruled that the EC Social Security Directive (No.79/7) does not require that a pension scheme compensate a woman for the 'lost years' while she was not working for family reasons. **6.15**

Week's pay **6.16**

Once the relevant date and the calculation date have been established, the next step is to calculate the employee's 'week's pay'. The rules governing the

183

calculation of a week's pay are set out in Chapter II of Part XIV of the ERA, and vary depending on whether the employee can be said to have a set number of 'normal working hours' and whether he or she is a shift-worker or a piece-worker, or simply paid a set wage for a given number of hours. Basically, a week's pay is the gross contractual remuneration for working the normal working hours in a week, capped at the applicable statutory maximum rate. What constitutes a week's pay is covered in detail in IDS Employment Law Handbook, 'Wages' (2016), Chapter 9, 'A week's pay'.

6.17 Tax treatment of statutory redundancy pay

Statutory redundancy payments are calculated on the basis of gross pay, and there are no deductions for income tax or national insurance – S.309(1) Income Tax (Earnings and Pensions) Act 2003 (ITEPA).

Note, however, that while statutory redundancy payments made under the ERA are specifically exempted from general earnings under S.62 ITEPA by virtue of S.309, such payments do fall within S.401 ITEPA and are chargeable to tax under that section on any amount exceeding £30,000 – see S.403. The maximum possible statutory redundancy payment (from 6 April 2016) is £14,370. Therefore, unless the value of other taxable elements of a termination package causes the £30,000 limit to be exceeded, statutory redundancy payments will usually be exempted in full.

6.18 Written particulars of redundancy payment

Unless the exact amount of the redundancy payment has been determined by a tribunal, the employer must provide the employee with a written statement indicating how the amount has been calculated – S.165(1) ERA. An employer who fails to provide the statement without reasonable excuse is guilty of a criminal offence and liable on summary conviction to a fine not exceeding level 1 on the standard scale (currently £200) – S.165(2). While the level of the financial penalty may not act as a deterrent for non-compliance with S.165(1), providing a breakdown of the sums paid to the employee in respect of his or her entitlement to a redundancy payment will provide proof that the employer has discharged its obligation in this respect, thus preventing an employee from subsequently arguing that no redundancy payment has been made.

In the event that the employer has failed to provide a written statement, the employee can give written notice requiring it to provide one within a given period (which must be at least one week from the date the notice was given) – S.165(3). Failure to comply with the notice without reasonable excuse is an offence punishable on summary conviction by a fine not exceeding level 3 on the standard scale (currently £1,000) – S.165(4).

184 ───

Enhanced redundancy pay

6.19

Many employees are entitled to contractual redundancy payments in excess of the statutory payments made under S.162 ERA. These are commonly referred to as 'enhanced' redundancy payments.

Like the statutory scheme, an employer's enhanced redundancy scheme might use multipliers based on an employee's age and/or length of service, and thereby advantage older and long-serving employees. Provisions in the Equality Act 2010 (which replaced similar provisions in the Employment Equality (Age) Regulations 2006 SI 2006/246 with effect from 1 October 2010) specifically provide that this is allowed, as long as the enhanced scheme is modelled on the statutory scheme – see 'Age discrimination – enhanced scheme modelled on statutory scheme' below. This means that a scheme that has age-related elements that do not mirror the statutory scheme will be discriminatory on the ground of age unless the employer can show that the discriminatory elements of the scheme are objectively justified as a proportionate means of achieving a legitimate aim – see 'Age discrimination – enhanced scheme not modelled on statutory scheme' below.

Entitlement to enhanced redundancy pay

6.20

An employee's contract of employment or written statement of particulars may contain an express term that entitles him or her to a payment on redundancy that is in excess of the statutory redundancy payment. Alternatively, a term to that effect may be implied by virtue of the parties' conduct or by the custom or practice of a particular employer. (Express and implied contractual terms are discussed at length in IDS Employment Law Handbook, 'Contracts of Employment' (2014), Chapter 3, 'Contractual terms'.)

Often, enhanced redundancy payment schemes are contained in staff handbooks or collective agreements. Where this is the case, an employee will only be able to enforce those terms if he or she can show that they have been incorporated into the individual contract of employment. Incorporation may be express (e.g. where the individual employment contract states that certain of its terms are regulated by, for example, a collective agreement) or implied (e.g. where there is a clear custom that terms of collective agreements are incorporated into the contract). For a detailed discussion of the general principles in relation to incorporated terms, see IDS Employment Law Handbook, 'Contracts of Employment' (2014), Chapter 5, 'Incorporated terms'.

Express incorporation. In Keeley v Fosroc International Ltd 2006 IRLR 961, CA, the Court of Appeal noted that provision for redundancy is a widely accepted – and important – feature of an employee's overall remuneration

6.21

185

package, and as such is 'particularly apt for incorporation' into an individual's contract of employment, even if couched in terms of information or explanation, or expressed in discretionary terms. So, for example, if an employee's employment is expressly made subject to the terms of a collective agreement or a staff manual which itself sets out the terms of the policy, then the policy will be incorporated into the employee's contract of employment. However, the Court of Appeal noted that it does not necessarily follow, in the event that another document has been expressly incorporated into a contract of employment, that *all* its terms will be incorporated and therefore amount to legally enforceable rights.

In Keeley, K's contract of employment consisted of a written 'statement of employment terms', which expressly incorporated the company's staff handbook by reference. The handbook dealt with various matters, such as annual leave, equal opportunities, grievances, parental leave, maternity rights and retirement, and also contained five pages setting out the company's redundancy policy. As regards compensation, that policy provided: 'Those employees with two or more years' continuous service are entitled to receive an enhanced redundancy payment from the company, which is paid tax free to a limit of £30,000.' The provision did not explain how the payment should be calculated, but did state that the details would be 'discussed during both collective and individual consultation'.

6.22 In July 2004 K was made redundant and claimed that the company was in breach of contract in failing to make him an enhanced redundancy payment. The High Court held that, although the relevant provision of the staff handbook used the word 'entitled', few of the other provisions in the redundancy section had the character of contractual terms because they were statements of principle or procedure. Accordingly, the enhanced redundancy payment provision, in its context, did not denote any contractual right. The Court of Appeal overturned this decision, holding that there were a number of factors which pointed strongly to the provision being contractual in nature; namely, the wording of the provision described the employee as being entitled to the payment; the provision was included in a section of the staff handbook headed 'Employee benefits and rights', which set out other entitlements such as the right to annual leave, parental leave and paternity leave; and the redundancy section itself also provided for entitlements – such as the right to paid time off to look for new work and the right to appeal against dismissal – which were distinct from the procedural, aspirational or discretionary elements of the section and amounted to 'close supporting context for concluding that statements of entitlement in that section were intended to have contractual effect'. The fact that the method of calculation of the payment was not specified – it was expressed to be decided on a case-by-case basis – did not prevent it from being an enforceable contractual right.

The Keeley case was followed in Harlow v Artemis International Corporation Ltd 2008 IRLR 629, QBD, where H's employment contract stated that 'all other terms and conditions are as detailed in the staff handbook as issued to you and subject to its most recent update'. The staff handbook had originally been a hard copy manual distributed to all staff but had later been replaced by a number of policies (including an enhanced redundancy policy) stored in electronic form on AIC Ltd's intranet. The High Court held that the enhanced redundancy policy contained in a part of the staff handbook which also dealt with matters such as holiday and sickness leave was apt for incorporation into an employee's contract as an express term. The Court noted that the Court of Appeal in Keeley had identified two significant factors to take into account when determining the nature of a provision:

- first, the importance of the provision in the overall bargain; and

- second, its precise wording.

6.23 The High Court had no doubt that the redundancy provisions would be of importance in the overall bargain, as part of the remuneration package. It noted that not all handbook provisions will be contractual – some are merely 'declarations of an aspiration'. However, that was not the case here – the calculation method of the redundancy payment was clearly stipulated and there was provision in the policy itself for time off work to look for new employment. Furthermore, the policy was included in a section of the handbook dealing with entitlements – such as annual leave and sick leave – which must have been contractual.

The fact that AIC Ltd appeared to have varied its practice in making redundancy payments to other employees did not affect H's rights to his redundancy terms contained in the published policy in force at the time of his redundancy. The High Court cited the cases of Solectron Scotland Ltd v Roper and ors 2004 IRLR 4, EAT, and Jones v Associated Tunnelling Co Ltd 1981 IRLR 477, EAT, in support of the proposition that where an employer purports unilaterally to change the terms of a contract that do not immediately impinge on the employee (and changes in redundancy terms do not impinge on an employee until he or she is in fact made redundant), the fact that an employee continues to work knowing that the employer is asserting that a change has been effected does not mean that the employee can be taken to have accepted the variation.

6.24 The situation may be different, however, where redundancy is a real and present threat. In Mears and anor v Shropshire Council ET Case No.1316640/12, for example, an employment tribunal considered that where an employer imposes a change to its enhanced redundancy terms at a time when the workforce is aware that redundancies are not a vague or hypothetical concept but a real possibility, the fact that employees continue to work without raising any objection to these changes *can* be an indication of their acceptance.

187

The fact that other employees have rarely taken up the option of a redundancy enhancement does not mean that it ceases to be a contractual right. In Arkley v Sea Fish Industry Authority EAT 0505/09 the EAT held that a redundancy policy was couched in mandatory – not discretionary – terms, with the result that a provision providing for ten years' enhanced pension benefits to redundant employees was a contractual right. Clause 1 of the policy provided that 'compensation in accordance with the scheme will be payable' and clause 2(e) referred to staff 'entitlement' to immediate payment of pension benefits. The EAT, relying on the Supreme Court's guidance in Chartbrook Ltd v Persimmon Homes Ltd 2009 1 AC 1101, SC, on the construction of contractual terms, noted that the proper construction of A's contract was what a reasonable person, having all the background knowledge available to the parties, would have understood the language in the contract to mean. Applying that test, the EAT held that the reasonable person would have concluded that redundant staff in A's position would be offered ten years' enhanced pension benefits. This conclusion was reinforced by the employer's custom and practice of offering redundant employees the enhancement – although this option was rarely taken up – and the fact that it had not sought to amend the policy. It therefore followed that A had a reasonable expectation that he would be offered the enhancement when made redundant and that the employer's unilateral withdrawal of that option amounted to a breach of contract.

6.25 Where enhanced redundancy terms contained in a collective agreement have been incorporated into employees' individual employment contracts, they may continue to apply even after the collective agreement ceases to have effect or the employer has de-recognised the relevant trade union – Framptons Ltd v Badger and ors EAT 0138/06. The EAT in that case considered that there would be 'a very strong presumption that the parties to the individual contract will have intended that terms should continue to be derived from the collective agreement, even after that agreement has ceased to have effect, if the consequence of not so doing is that there would be no binding contractual terms at all.' However, the EAT noted that it is possible that enhanced redundancy terms that have been incorporated from a collective agreement into individual employment contracts could be varied to the employees' detriment if the trade union were to negotiate new terms with the employer – for example, reducing the benefit of enhanced payments in return for greater job security. Furthermore, where it is clear that enhanced redundancy terms have been agreed to apply for a limited period or to a particular redundancy exercise only, employees will be unable to claim the benefit of them at a later date or in respect of a separate redundancy exercise.

6.26 **Implied incorporation.** The main route by which redundancy terms are impliedly incorporated into employment contracts is where they are regularly (but not necessarily universally) adopted in a particular trade or industry or by a particular employer – commonly referred to as 'custom and practice'. The traditional requirement for implication via this route is that the custom in question must be 'reasonable, notorious and certain'. This means that the policy's terms must be fair and not arbitrary or capricious, must be generally established and well known, and must be clear cut. The onus of proving that redundancy terms have been impliedly incorporated falls on the employee. Any claim for an enhanced payment is likely to fail if the employee cannot adduce sufficient evidence of the custom or practice he or she is relying upon. Essentially, the custom or practice has to be so clear and obvious that, in effect, the parties knew they had to adhere to it and did not consider it necessary to set it out expressly – see Stenhouse and ors v First Edinburgh Ltd EAT 0017/04.

Probably the most important factor in determining whether an implied right to enhanced payments has arisen is whether a clear and certain policy of making such payments has been *communicated* to employees. If that has not happened, it is difficult to see how they can have a reasonable expectation that they will receive enhanced payments if made redundant, and it is equally difficult to see how the redundancy policy could be regarded as being sufficiently 'notorious' in the sense of being well known.

The facts of Albion Automotive Ltd v Walker and ors 2002 EWCA Civ **6.27** 946, CA, provide a useful example of how, in practice, courts and tribunals approach the issue of whether employees have acquired an implied contractual entitlement to enhanced redundancy payments. There, the Court of Appeal held that an employment tribunal had correctly concluded that there was such an entitlement, in view of the following findings of fact:

- the redundancy terms, when first applied, had been the outcome of high profile negotiations

- it was likely that the terms had been approved by the employer's parent company

- the terms had subsequently been applied to further redundancy exercises with little or no consultation with the parent company

- the availability of the enhanced terms had been drawn to the attention of all the employees in writing at the time of each redundancy exercise

- the policy had been followed for an extensive period of time and had affected 750 employees, amounting to three quarters of the workforce

- the policy had been followed for six redundancy exercises and had been intended to be applied in two others

- payment of the enhanced terms had been virtually automatic from the employer's point of view, and

189

- all employees had a reasonable expectation that enhanced payments would be made.

In Harlow v Artemis International Corporation Ltd 2008 IRLR 629, QBD, the High Court allowed H's claim for enhanced redundancy pay on the basis that the enhanced redundancy policy was apt to be incorporated into his employment contract as an express term (see 'Express incorporation' above). It nonetheless went on to consider whether an entitlement to enhanced redundancy pay could alternatively have been implied by custom and practice. Following Albion Automotive Ltd v Walker and ors (above), it considered the following facts to be significant: that the policy was published and readily available on the company website; that the company had paid enhanced redundancy payments for many years; and that the policy was dealt with in the same section as other contractual terms. Furthermore, employees had a reasonable expectation that enhanced payments would be made to them and, indeed, most other employees facing redundancy were compensated in accordance with the policy. These factors all supported a finding that entitlement to an enhanced redundancy payment could be implied by custom and practice.

6.28 By way of contrast, in Quinn and ors v Calder Industrial Materials Ltd 1996 IRLR 126, EAT, the Appeal Tribunal held that redundant employees had no implied contractual right to enhanced redundancy payments. The employer's policy of making such payments was not incorporated into any agreement and details of the policy had never been communicated to the employees – the EAT considered that a positive act of communicating the policy to employees would have indicated that the employer had intended to be bound by it. Furthermore, although the policy had been followed in every case over a period of seven years, there had only been four redundancy situations during that time. Thus, although seven years might in the abstract be considered a 'substantial' period, the application of the policy only four times during that period meant that it was not so substantial in the context of analysing whether the policy had become an implied contractual term. In addition, the EAT noted that, while the policy had been applied consistently, there was evidence that the employer did not apply it automatically, but rather made a decision in each case as to whether to make an enhanced redundancy payment.

The EAT similarly held that the claimant was not entitled to an enhanced payment in Pellowe v Pendragon plc EAT 804/98. In that case, the employer had for 20 years given redundant employees a payment greater than their statutory redundancy pay. However, the chart for calculating the amount was contained in a management manual that was not publicised to staff. Following a transfer of the business, the new employer made the claimant redundant but only gave him statutory redundancy pay. The EAT upheld the

190

tribunal's decision that the claimant had not acquired a contractual right, through custom and practice, to the enhanced payment. It had not been made known to staff that they would receive enhanced payments and so the term could not be said to be notorious.

Lord Justice Underhill undertook a useful review of the relevant principles in Park Cakes Ltd v Shumba and ors 2013 IRLR 800, CA. He clarified that, when Lord Coulsfield in Quinn and ors v Calder Industrial Materials Ltd (above) stated that the crucial question is whether the circumstances support the inference that the employer intended to be contractually bound, he was referring to the employer's intention as objectively evinced. In other words, what matters is not what the employer actually intended but what intention its words or conduct would reasonably communicate to the employees. Similarly, when considering whether a payment was made 'automatically', what matters is not whether the company, internally, believed that it was making a unilateral choice whether to grant the benefit or make the payment but whether that was what should reasonably have been understood by the employees. Underhill LJ went on to list some of the circumstances that will typically be relevant in an enhanced redundancy payment case when considering what, objectively, employees should reasonably have understood. These circumstances include:

6.29

- the number of occasions on which, and the length of the period over which, the benefits have been paid

- whether the benefits are always the same

- the extent to which the benefits have been publicised

- how the terms are described

- what is said in the express contract, and

- the equivocalness of the employer's actions (i.e. whether the employer's practice is equally explicable on the basis that it is pursued as a matter of discretion rather than legal obligation).

In the Shumba case, the employment tribunal held that the employees did not have an implied contractual right to enhanced redundancy payments because the employer had not specifically drawn the employees' attention to the relevant policy and had not made payments under it 'automatically' in previous redundancy exercises. The Court of Appeal held that the tribunal had erred. The question was not whether the employer had regarded the payments as automatic in every case, but what the employees would reasonably have understood about the nature of the payments based on the employer's conduct in this regard. Furthermore, the fact that the employer had not specifically drawn the employees' attention to the policy in question was not decisive, since there was evidence that the policy document was available to employees on request. Indeed, the extent to which the employer had published the policy was 'only part of a rather complex picture about what information was made available to the company's employees and their representatives'. The Court therefore remitted the case to a tribunal for further consideration of these points.

6.30 Two further examples:

• **Peacock Stores Ltd v Peregrine and ors** EAT 0315/13: the EAT applied the approach of the Court of Appeal in Park Cakes Ltd v Shumba and ors (above), noting that what matters is what the employees would reasonably have understood about the status of the enhanced redundancy payments based on both the employer's communications and its conduct, viewed objectively. On this basis, the EAT upheld an employment tribunal's finding that an employee was, by virtue of custom and practice, entitled to an enhanced redundancy payment calculated on the basis of his full service and salary rather than applying the statutory cap in respect of either criterion. This was so despite there being some evidence revealing a variation of practice. In the EAT's view, once it had been established that enhanced redundancy payments would be paid – which was the case here based on a consistent practice over the period 1971 to 1996 – there would need to be clear evidence that the implied term had been superseded for it no longer to apply. Any unilateral departure by the employer would represent a breach of contract unless knowingly agreed to by the affected employees. In this case, the EAT accepted the tribunal's finding that there were no circumstances from which it could properly be inferred that what had been agreed had been superseded

• **Common v Invista Textiles (UK) Ltd** ET Case No.1401150/13: in 2006, ITU Ltd had introduced a new redundancy scheme designed to align redundancy terms for all employees and remove any discriminatory impact in light of the Employment Equality (Age) Regulations 2006 SI 2006/1031. The scheme was expressed to be non-contractual, but it was agreed with the recognised trade unions and was widely publicised to the entire workforce at the time of its adoption. It was then applied consistently in nine redundancy exercises over a period of six years. When C was made redundant in 2013, ITU Ltd applied less generous terms in the calculation of his redundancy payment. C claimed that it was thereby in breach of contract, the 2006 scheme having become contractual through custom and practice. The tribunal took into account the original communication of the scheme and its subsequent application. It found that there was no evidence to support ITU Ltd's assertion that every redundancy exercise had involved consideration by management of whether the company should exercise its discretion to make payments under the scheme. Nor could it be said that ITU Ltd had consistently made it clear to employees that the scheme was intended to be non-contractual, or that employees would have been aware of any management discussions that did take place as to whether the scheme should be applied in particular redundancy exercises. Viewed objectively, the unwavering application of the scheme across nine redundancy exercises over six years was not consistent with the exercise of a discretion rather than compliance with a legal obligation. The tribunal therefore concluded that payment of the benefits under the 2006 scheme was a contractual benefit implied into C's contract by custom and practice.

The distinction between an express term that is found in an employee handbook **6.31** (or similar document) and a term that is incorporated into the contract from such a document can become blurred. In Allen and ors v TRW Systems Ltd 2013 ICR D13, EAT, for example, an enhanced redundancy pay policy had been agreed between the employer and the employee 'Advisory Council' and the employee handbook contained a promise that it would be applied whenever redundancies were required. However, although the standard statement of terms and conditions referred to the employee handbook for some terms – such as holiday pay – it did not mention redundancy, nor did it contain any general statement that terms and conditions were as described in the handbook. Nonetheless, the EAT held it is not uncommon to find that matters of contractual entitlement are dealt with by different documents, such as an employee handbook, or by custom and practice, or (particularly in small businesses) orally, and that the handbook in this case was capable of being a source of contractual obligations, despite the absence of any express incorporation. The EAT also noted that the key consideration for a tribunal in deciding whether a policy could be relied on was whether the circumstances in which the enhanced redundancy package had been made known, or had become known, supported the inference that the employer intended to become contractually bound by it. It was well established that that question had to be determined, not by an examination of the employer's private intentions, but by an objective examination of the circumstances. The EAT also noted that tribunals should bear in mind that provision for redundancy has become a widely accepted feature of employees' remuneration packages and so tribunals should scrutinise with care any argument that redundancy payments intended to be part of an employee's remuneration package, once promised and communicated, were merely matters of policy and discretion. The case was remitted to a fresh tribunal for reconsideration. (Although the employer appealed to the Court of Appeal against the EAT's analysis of how a legal obligation might arise, the claim was settled without need for a decision on this point – Allen and ors v TRW Systems Ltd 2013 EWCA Civ 1388, CA.)

Occasionally, reliance on custom and practice works the other way round, in that the employer seeks to show that a custom or practice has displaced the employee's apparent contractual right to enhanced payments. Such an argument was advanced – albeit unsuccessfully – by the employer in Solectron Scotland Ltd v Roper and ors 2004 IRLR 4, EAT, as a defence to employees' seeking to enforce enhanced redundancy terms. The EAT, upholding a tribunal's decision, ruled that, on the evidence presented, no custom or practice had come into being by which the employees' contractual entitlement had been removed. The practice relied upon was not certain (since different terms were applied in respect of each redundancy exercise carried out), reasonable (since it depended on the whim of the employer), or notorious (since there was no consistent application of any of the terms). The EAT observed that it was doubtful, in any case, whether a custom could ever vary existing contractual rights. But even if it could, the practice in question would have to be a very long-established one.

6.32 **Settlement agreements.** An employer that pays enhanced redundancy payments may well wish to make entitlement to such payments conditional upon the employee signing a settlement agreement, in which he or she waives any right to bring claims arising out of his or her employment or dismissal. Where the enhanced payment scheme is contractual, it is advisable for employers to include in the scheme an express provision imposing a requirement to sign a settlement agreement. In the absence of such a provision, an employee might argue that he or she has a contractual right to receive the enhanced payment in any event and therefore remains free to bring claims against the employer – for unfair dismissal or discrimination, for example.

If there is no express provision making payment of enhanced redundancy pay conditional on the employee signing a settlement agreement, it is possible that such a condition might be implied by custom and practice. This was the finding of the Court of Appeal in Garratt v Mirror Group Newspapers Ltd 2011 ICR 880, CA, where all employees made redundant since 1993 had complied with a requirement to sign a compromise agreement (the previous name for a settlement agreement) in order to receive an enhanced redundancy payment and it was common knowledge among the current workforce that this was company policy. However, when G was made redundant in 2006 he refused to sign a compromise agreement and was not paid an enhanced redundancy payment. The Court rejected his argument that the position had changed when a collective agreement, which had been reached in 2002, was incorporated into his contract of employment in 2005. The Court noted that the collective agreement clarified the manner of calculation of redundancy payments but made no mention of the compromise agreement condition. The Court further noted that the evidence was that the requirement for a compromise agreement was 'taken as read' when the collective agreement was negotiated, and gave the view that a term to that effect could be implied by the 'officious bystander' test. Accordingly, it could not be suggested that the agreement was intended to change the practice of requiring a compromise agreement, nor that it had this unintended effect. That said, the Court commented that the employer could have put the issue 'beyond argument' by publicising to the workforce that an enhanced redundancy payment would only be paid if the outgoing employee signed a compromise agreement.

194

Any claim by an employer that an employee's entitlement to an enhanced **6.33** redundancy payment is conditional on him or her signing a settlement agreement will be subject to strict judicial scrutiny. Two examples:

• **McMahon v Skipton Building Society** ET Case No.1806738/09: a tribunal found that each time the employer had conducted a redundancy exercise senior management had decided whether to exercise their discretion to make enhanced payments. When they decided they would, they communicated that fact to affected employees. In the tribunal's view, it had become an implied term of employees' contracts that once they had received confirmation that an enhanced payment would be made, then they were entitled to receive that payment. The tribunal therefore held that the employer had acted in breach of contract when – a month after having informed the employee that he would receive an enhanced redundancy payment – the employer sought to insist on him signing a compromise agreement as a condition of receiving that payment. The employee was entitled to the enhanced redundancy payment and this was not subject to any conditions

• **Patel v Walkers Snack Foods Ltd** ET Case No.1900866/12: a tribunal found that the employer's contractual redundancy policy provided for only one exception to the payment of enhanced redundancy payments and that related to their affordability. There was no affordability issue on the facts in this case and the tribunal held that the employer did not have the right unilaterally to vary the contractual term to make the enhanced payment dependent on the employee signing a compromise agreement.

Where an employer does make entitlement to an enhanced redundancy payment conditional on signature of a settlement agreement, this does not constitute age discrimination – ABN Amro Management Services Ltd and anor v Hogben EAT 0266/09. There, the employee sought to argue that the requirement to waive age discrimination claims in a settlement agreement was indirectly discriminatory, in that it had a disproportionate impact on older workers, who are more likely to bring such claims. The EAT upheld a tribunal's decision to strike out this argument on the basis that it had no reasonable prospect of success. The requirement to waive all claims did not put people in any age group at a particular disadvantage, but affected all dismissed employees in the same way. In any event, the EAT considered that if the requirement did have a disproportionate impact on older workers, this could 'plainly' be justified. Mr Justice Underhill, then President of the EAT, commented: 'Employers have a legitimate interest in achieving finality as regards all issues arising out of the dismissal of an employee. Offering a further payment to achieve a binding compromise of all such issues is plainly a proportionate means of achieving that aim. Its proportionality is unassailable because the choice always remains with the employee: if he thinks it is a bad deal he need not take the offer.'

6.34 **Avoiding payments by dismissing for reason other than redundancy.** In Jenvey v Australian Broadcasting Corporation 2003 ICR 79, QBD, an employee who had already been earmarked for redundancy was dismissed for asserting a statutory right. He brought a claim before the High Court, seeking damages representing the enhanced redundancy payment that he did not receive. The High Court held that had the employee not been dismissed for asserting a statutory right (an automatically unfair reason for dismissal), he would have been dismissed on the same date by reason of redundancy because his full-time position would have ended. The High Court judge – Mr Justice Elias – decided that in these circumstances a term should be implied into the employee's contract to the effect that, where an employer has decided to dismiss the employee by reason of redundancy, and where any other reason for dismissal would have the effect of depriving him or her of enhanced redundancy benefits, the employer would not dismiss him or her for any reason other than redundancy without good cause. In this case, where the employee was dismissed for an automatically unfair reason after it had been resolved to dismiss him for redundancy, he was entitled to recover damages for breach of contract as compensation for the loss of the enhanced benefits.

In a somewhat unusual case, Wills v RWE NPower plc ET Case No.2701870/13, the employee, W, was notified on 14 December 2012 that his employment would terminate by reason of redundancy on 31 March 2013. He was entitled to an enhanced contractual redundancy payment in excess of £30,000. However, on 18 February 2013, W was convicted of child pornography offences and on 11 March he was sentenced to two years' imprisonment. W had not informed his employer of his conviction, but the employer became aware of it on 11 March when the sentencing hearing was reported in the local newspaper. W had previously arranged with his employer that he would take annual leave from 11 March until his employment terminated on 31 March – the effect of which was that he was not required to attend work between the date of his sentence and the end of his notice period. On 13 March, the employer wrote to W stating that it considered his contract to be frustrated as a result of his imprisonment and that it would not be paying him any notice payment or the enhanced redundancy payment. A tribunal upheld W's claim for breach of contract. The tribunal noted that W was not required to attend work between his imprisonment and the termination of his employment. His imprisonment made no difference to the performance of his contract and the contract had therefore not been frustrated. The employer was ordered to pay W his enhanced redundancy pay and a payment in lieu of notice. (Note that on the facts of this case the employer may have been better able to defend its decision not to pay W's redundancy pay if, instead of alleging frustration of the contract, it had summarily dismissed him for gross misconduct upon discovery of his conviction and imprisonment.) For discussion of the rules governing frustration of contract, see IDS Employment Law Handbook, 'Contracts of Employment' (2014), Chapter 13, 'Termination by operation of law', under 'Frustration'.

196

Public sector exit payments. A programme of legislative change is currently 6.35
underway in relation to exit payments – including redundancy payments – in
the public sector. In particular, the Government intends to introduce a £95,000
cap on such payments. The power to introduce the cap is contained in the
Enterprise Act 2016, with details to be dealt with in regulations. The draft
Public Sector Exit Payments Regulations 2016 indicate that the cap will apply
to the vast majority of exit payments, including payments for voluntary or
compulsory redundancy. There will be an exemption where an employee's
contractual entitlement to a higher payment is a protected term following
a TUPE transfer. A waiver system will also be established to allow higher
payments in exceptional circumstances.

Most public bodies in Great Britain will be covered by the cap, although it will be
for the Scottish, Welsh and Northern Irish governments to decide whether they wish
the cap to apply to devolved bodies. Notable exceptions include publicly owned
financial bodies, such as the Royal Bank of Scotland, and public broadcasters such
as the BBC and Channel 4. However, the Government said in its response to the
initial consultation on the cap in November 2015 that it expects such organisations
to establish their own, commensurate, caps on exit payments to coincide with the
entry into force of the statutory cap. The draft Regulations suggest that the cap
might come into force in October 2016 and it was confirmed by HM Treasury in
May 2016 that it will not come into force before then.

The Government is also considering imposing a number of additional limits 6.36
that would apply to the calculation of public sector exit payments. Specifically,
it has proposed limits on: the number of weeks' pay per year of service that can
apply when calculating exit payments; the total number of months' pay that
can be awarded; the maximum salary to be used as a basis for such calculations;
the amount that can be awarded to individuals nearing retirement; and access
to employer-funded pension top-ups in cases of early retirement. Consultations
on these proposals in respect of the public sector in general and on similar
proposals in respect of the Civil Service Compensation Scheme closed on 3 and
4 May 2016 respectively and the Government's response is awaited.

In addition, the Small Business, Enterprise and Employment Act 2015
included provisions to enable the recovery of exit payments made to
individuals who return to the public sector after a short period of time. The
draft Repayment of Public Sector Exit Payments 2016 provide that public
sector employees who were earning in excess of £80,000 prior to their exit
and who re-enter employment in any part of the public sector within 12
months of receipt of an exit payment must repay all or part of that payment,
the amount repayable depending on how long the employee has spent out
of public sector employment. It is unclear when these Regulations are likely
to come into force.

197

6.37 Tax treatment of enhanced redundancy pay

As a general rule, payments under enhanced redundancy pay schemes are not subject to income tax, as they do not represent emoluments paid in return for services rendered by the employee by virtue of his or her employment – see Mairs (HM Inspector of Taxes) v Haughey 1993 IRLR 551, HL. However, to the extent that they exceed £30,000 they are treated as employment income and are therefore chargeable under S.403 of the Income Tax (Earnings and Pensions) Act 2003 (ITEPA). The Government announced in the March 2016 Budget that, from 2018, the excess above £30,000 will also be subject to employer's national insurance contributions. For a detailed discussion of the tax treatment of termination payments, see IDS Employment Law Handbook, 'Employment Tribunal Practice and Procedure' (2014), Chapter 3, 'Conciliation, settlements and ADR', under 'Taxation of payments on settlement'.

Where an employee receives a payment as compensation for a change to his or her contractual enhanced redundancy terms, that payment will be chargeable to tax under S.403 ITEPA – Colquhoun v Commissioners for HM Revenue and Customs 2010 UKUT 431, TCC. Since the £30,000 exemption applies not to the tax year in which a payment is received but to the employment in respect of which the payment is made, such a payment will reduce the amount of the exemption that will be available to the employee when his or her employment is subsequently terminated. In Colquhoun the employee had received a payment of £33,148.71 in return for agreeing changes to his contractual redundancy terms. The employer paid £30,000 of this payment free from tax and deducted tax from the remainder under PAYE. When the employee was made redundant some years later, HMRC treated his entire redundancy payment as taxable under S.403 ITEPA. The Upper Tribunal upheld HMRC's decision, taking the view that the earlier payment of £33,148.71 had been made to satisfy the employee's contingent right to a redundancy payment; it derived its character from the nature of the payment it replaced and had accordingly been correctly treated at the time as taxable under S.403. Thus, the employee had used up his £30,000 exemption at that time and the entire redundancy payment paid on termination was chargeable to tax.

6.38 Age discrimination

As set out above, under 'Statutory redundancy pay scheme – formula for calculating statutory redundancy pay', payments under the statutory scheme are determined in part by an employee's age and length of service. Enhanced redundancy pay schemes often use similar criteria, but not always. Such schemes can be divided into two groups: enhanced schemes modelled on the statutory scheme, and enhanced schemes not modelled on the statutory

198

scheme. All schemes that use age-related criteria raise questions of age discrimination, but different considerations apply depending on the type of scheme involved.

Statutory scheme   6.39

Given the statutory redundancy payment scheme's reliance on age-based factors, the Government reviewed the scheme prior to the introduction of the Employment Equality (Age) Regulations 2006 SI 2006/1031 ('the Age Regulations'). In its 'Coming of Age' consultation document, published in July 2005, it expressed an intention to remove the three age bands for calculating redundancy payments set out in S.162(2) ERA (see 'Statutory redundancy pay scheme – formula for calculating statutory redundancy pay' above). In the end, however, the Government decided to retain these bands. It considered there to be three groups benefiting from payments under the scheme – younger, prime age and older workers – which each represent a distinct economic category. At one end of the spectrum, younger workers tend not to be out of work for long and only experience a small drop in pay when switching jobs. Older workers, on the other hand, face difficulties in finding new jobs, experience a substantial fall in pay if they do find new employment, and are much more likely to become long-term unemployed. As a result, the Government felt that the practice of applying different 'multipliers' to different age bands so as to give greater financial assistance to older workers in a redundancy context was justified.

The Government similarly decided to retain the two-year qualifying period for claiming a redundancy payment, despite its indirectly discriminatory effect upon younger workers (see further Chapter 5, 'Qualifications and exclusions', under 'Qualifying service'). The statutory redundancy pay scheme thus largely survived with its age-based criteria intact.

However, the following age-based aspects of the statutory redundancy scheme   **6.40**
were repealed with effect from 1 October 2006:

- the lower and upper limits on the right to claim redundancy payments (previously 18 and 65) in Ss.211(2) and 156 ERA. So, for example, employees aged 65 and over who are made redundant are entitled to a redundancy payment

- the 'taper' provision in S.162(4) and (5) ERA under which an employee's redundancy payment was reduced by 1/12th for every month of service over the age of 64, and

- S.158 ERA, which excluded the right to a redundancy payment in certain circumstances where the employee was also entitled to claim a pension (together with S.162(8) ERA and the Redundancy Payments (Pensions) Regulations 1965 SI 1965/1932 made under that provision).

199

(Note that the Age Regulations were repealed and replaced by the Equality Act 2010 in October 2010. However, no substantive changes were made to the law on age discrimination, or redundancy, by the EqA.)

6.41 **Enhanced scheme modelled on statutory scheme**
An employee's enhanced redundancy entitlement is often calculated with reference to his or her age and/or length of service – both, on the face of it, age discriminatory criteria. However, when drafting the Age Regulations, the Government decided to include an exemption allowing employers, in certain circumstances, to continue with this practice. In this regard, Reg 33 of the Age Regulations set out an 'approved' scheme under which employers could still make enhanced redundancy payments that varied according to the employee's age, without needing to show objective justification. This scheme was replicated in para 13 of Schedule 9 to the Equality Act 2010 (EqA) and closely mirrors the statutory redundancy scheme, discussed under 'Statutory redundancy pay scheme' above.

Under para 13(3) of Schedule 9 EqA, enhanced payments can be made to the following types of 'qualifying employee':

- an employee who is entitled to a statutory redundancy payment

- an employee who would have been entitled to a statutory redundancy payment if he or she had attained the requisite two years' qualifying service, or

- an employee who agrees to the termination of his or her employment where, if he or she had been dismissed, he or she would have fallen into one of the above two categories – for example, an employee who takes voluntary redundancy.

6.42 The redundancy payment made to a qualifying employee must be calculated in accordance with the statutory scheme, using the same age bands. However, the employer may then enhance the amount paid by doing any or all of the following:

- ignoring the limit on a week's pay provided for by S.227 ERA, to which statutory redundancy payments are subject. The employer can apply its own limit on a week's pay above that contained in statute, or can base redundancy payments on employees' actual pay

- applying a multiplier to the amount of statutory redundancy pay allowed for each year of employment. So, for example, a year's service under the age of 22 might attract a week's pay under the enhanced scheme instead of half a week's pay under the statutory scheme. The respective multiplier for each age band must be in proportion to the relevant statutory multiplier. So, in this example, a year's service between the ages of 22 and 40 must attract two weeks' pay instead of one, and a year's service over the age of 41 must attract three weeks' pay instead of one and a half

- applying a multiplier to the total amount of the payment – para 13(5).

This exception is extremely limited and many enhanced redundancy payment schemes will fall outside its scope.

Enhanced scheme not modelled on statutory scheme   6.43

An employer who uses a method to calculate the amount of enhanced redundancy pay that diverges from the requirements set out in para 13 of Schedule 9 EqA (see 'Enhanced scheme modelled on statutory scheme' above) but still contains age-related criteria will have to objectively justify the scheme if challenged on age discrimination grounds (see 'Objective justification' below).

Note that para 10 of Schedule 9 allows employers to provide benefits based on employees' length of service. However, this exception does not apply to any benefit awarded to an employee by virtue of his or her ceasing to work for the employer, and thus does not cover enhanced redundancy payments, as para 10(7) makes clear. Therefore, enhanced redundancy schemes based on the indirectly discriminatory criterion of length of service (without also incorporating the age bands used by the statutory scheme) will fall foul of the legislation unless they can be objectively justified.

Of course, the safest course of action for an employer with an enhanced   6.44
redundancy scheme falling outside para 13 of Schedule 9 EqA is to amend it. However, if the scheme is contractual, renegotiating it might prove both difficult and expensive. For information about changing employees' terms and conditions, see IDS Employment Law Handbook, 'Contracts of Employment' (2014), Chapter 9, 'Variation of contract'.

Objective justification. As mentioned above, there is a 'justification defence'   6.45
available to employers facing claims of direct or indirect age discrimination in relation to their enhanced redundancy schemes. However, the Government stated in the 'Coming of Age' consultation document that 'the test of objective justification will not be an easy one to satisfy... treating people differently on grounds of age will be possible but only exceptionally and for good reasons'. In order to benefit from the defence, the employer must show:

- in a direct discrimination claim, that the less favourable treatment meted out to the claimant on the ground of his or her age was a proportionate means of achieving a legitimate aim

- in an indirect discrimination claim, that the provision, criterion or practice which placed persons of the claimant's age group at a disadvantage was a proportionate means of achieving a legitimate aim – Ss.13(1) and (2) and 19 EqA.

201

6.46   Case law highlights a variety of potentially legitimate aims. In MacCulloch v Imperial Chemical Industries plc 2008 ICR 1334, EAT, for example, the EAT cited the following aims that the employment tribunal had identified as potentially legitimate:

- encouraging and rewarding loyalty

- encouraging older workers to take up voluntary redundancy, thereby enabling more junior staff to progress in their employment, and

- protecting older workers – for whom finding new employment is typically more difficult – from additional labour market disadvantage.

The facts in MacCulloch were as follows. M was made redundant by ICI in October 2006. She was 36 years of age and had been employed by the company for seven years. ICI's redundancy policy, in use for 35 years, provided that upon dismissal by reason of redundancy an employee was entitled to 'a severance payment comprising a percentage or number of weeks of qualifying pay based on age and the period of employment by ICI'. The method of calculating the exact payment differed depending on whether an employee's length of service was more or less than ten years. An employee with more than ten years' service who had reached the age of 50 would receive 175 per cent of qualifying pay. Once the employee reached the age of 57, the rate of pay the employee was entitled to began to diminish until, at the age of 61 years and 11 months, he or she would only be entitled to 50 per cent of qualifying pay. ICI's explanation for the generous payments between ages 50 and 57, provided the employee had worked for it for at least ten years, was that it became more difficult to obtain employment as a person grew older. The reason for the diminishing rate from the age of 57 onwards was that employees at that point would be in the position to access the maximum pension under the company's final salary scheme.

6.47   M claimed that the scheme unlawfully discriminated against her on the ground of her age, as she would have been entitled to a higher redundancy payment had she been older and/or had longer service. A tribunal, however, accepted that encouraging and rewarding loyalty is a legitimate aim. Furthermore, it was legitimate to try to protect older employees by giving them a larger financial payment, as they were more vulnerable on losing their job than younger employees. The tribunal also accepted the employer's submission that it had to respect the contractual entitlements and legitimate expectations of its existing workforce (the company had actually consulted on changes to the scheme as a result of the Age Regulations, but the majority of employees had opted to keep the status quo); and that the scheme's generous payments encouraged good industrial relations, a further legitimate aim. Turning to the issue of proportionality, the tribunal noted the following: the scheme applied to the entire workforce and had been successfully in place for 35 years; it

202

avoided the need for compulsory redundancies; it helped manage change in a changing world; and the ten-year length of service cap was reasonable in rewarding loyalty. The tribunal also had regard to the costs involved in setting up an alternative scheme, and the contractual promises made. Given all this, the tribunal found that M's treatment under the scheme had been objectively justified and dismissed her claim. However, the EAT allowed M's appeal on this point and remitted the case to the same tribunal to weigh the reasonable needs of the undertaking with the discriminatory effect on the individual.

In remitting the claim, the EAT held that while the tribunal had identified certain legitimate aims of the scheme, it had not properly determined whether the measures adopted were proportionate ways of achieving those aims. The principal features that the tribunal appeared to consider were the generosity and general acceptance of the scheme. In the EAT's view, while these features may well be relevant in helping to achieve the aims of the scheme, they did not deal at all with the issue of whether the difference in treatment was justified. Nor was there any recognition of the degree of difference in payment made to M and the chosen comparator, and an assessment as to whether this was reasonably necessary to achieve the scheme's objective. While refusing to rule out the possibility that a scheme such as ICI's may be justified, the EAT concluded that the analysis needed to reach that conclusion was lacking from the tribunal's decision. Mr Justice Elias, then President of the EAT, gave his views on the circumstances that might give rise to objective justification. He endorsed the employer's objective of rewarding loyalty as the reason for linking payments to length of service. He also approved the tribunal's findings that encouraging turnover and creating opportunities for junior staff are, in principle, capable of being legitimate aims that might be furthered by increasing payments for older workers; and that it could be legitimate to pay more to older workers as they are particularly vulnerable in the job market. In Elias P's view, the tribunal had been entitled to draw on its own experience in this respect rather than looking to the employer for evidence of the obstacles faced by older workers.

On remission, the tribunal held that the scheme was proportionate and **6.48** dismissed M's claim. It noted that there was 'considerable judicial support' for the idea that older people do not find work as easily as younger people. Moreover, ICI had acknowledged the potentially discriminatory impact of the scheme and had tried to change it. However, a 'flatter' scheme was not acceptable to the workforce, many of whom presumably welcomed the potential financial safety net that the scheme could provide them in later life. The tribunal further found that changing the scheme to make it less discriminatory would have been detrimental to the legitimate aims of maintaining a contented workforce and promoting good industrial relations.

Acceptance by the workforce of the terms of an enhanced redundancy scheme was also a consideration in Richardson and ors v Business Link Northwest

ET Case No.2400506/11. There, the claimants argued that they had been discriminated against on the ground of their age when the employer – who had previously offered only statutory redundancy pay – introduced an enhanced scheme under which all redundant employees would receive a payment of two weeks' pay for each year of service. The claimants, who were all in their fifties, maintained that they were put at a disadvantage by the new scheme in that they were not entitled to higher payments than redundant employees aged below 41, which they needed to protect them against the likelihood that they would be out of work for longer than those younger employees. The claimants contended that the employer should have put in place an enhanced scheme that mirrored the statutory scheme in accordance with the exception to the age discrimination legislation under para 13 of Schedule 9 EqA. An employment tribunal dismissed the claim, however, holding that the claimants were not put at a disadvantage by the fact that the scheme did not provide higher payments for older employees. But if it was wrong on this point, it went on to hold that the scheme had a number of legitimate aims, including rewarding employee loyalty and service; spending limited public money responsibly and fairly; and supporting workforce morale. In the tribunal's view, the scheme was a proportionate means of achieving those aims. In this regard, it was relevant and significant that the employee forum, which represented the entire workforce, took no issue and agreed with the manner in which the redundancy payment was enhanced and it was also consistent with decisions taken by other employers.

6.49   *Preventing a windfall as a legitimate aim.* Many enhanced redundancy schemes contain 'tapering' provisions that provide for a reduction in the amount of redundancy pay an employee receives once he or she gets close to retirement age. The legitimate aim generally relied upon by employers in these circumstances is that older employees would otherwise enjoy a windfall from a redundancy in circumstances where they are shortly to retire. However, whether tapering is a proportionate means of achieving that aim will depend on the facts of the case. In Loxley v BAE Systems Land Systems (Munitions and Ordnance) Ltd 2008 ICR 1348, EAT, L brought a claim of direct age discrimination based on BAE's redundancy scheme, which gave an entitlement to a redundancy payment based mainly on length of service. However, only those under 60 were entitled to a redundancy payment, and those aged between 57 and 60 had their payments reduced according to tapering provisions. L was 61 at the time he agreed to take redundancy and was not entitled to the contractual redundancy payment. The rationale for excluding those over 60 was that, until 1996, employees were required to retire at 60 and could do so on a full pension. The tapering requirements and the exclusion of over-60s were designed to prevent those close to retirement from receiving a windfall in the event that they were made redundant. In 1996 the retirement age was raised to 65, although until 1 April 2006 employees could still take their pension at 60 without incurring a penalty to their accrued benefits. A tribunal rejected L's claim, finding that the scheme was justified by the need to prevent employees close to retirement receiving a windfall. The tribunal also thought that the fact that the scheme had been agreed in consultation with trade unions went some way to support the contention that it was justified. L appealed to the EAT.

Mr Justice Elias, then President of the EAT, concluded that the tribunal's analysis had been defective. The tribunal had mistakenly focused on related changes to the pension scheme, rather than the redundancy scheme, and so did not properly engage with the justification issue. Commenting on the aims of the scheme at issue, he held that excluding an employee entitled to immediate pension benefits from a redundancy scheme altogether, or reducing the benefits paid under it, may be justified, but that a tribunal would need to thoroughly assess the impact on the employee. Remitting the case, he stated that it might be that L's pension entitlement, even if taken earlier than he would otherwise have wished, would be far more valuable than any redundancy entitlement. However, although the tribunal appeared to have had a lot of financial information about the various benefits, it had failed to analyse that information. The EAT warned that the fact that a scheme is collectively agreed does not guarantee that it will be justified.

The Loxley case was referred to in Kraft Foods UK Ltd v Hastie 2010 ICR 1355, **6.50** EAT, where the Appeal Tribunal considered whether an enhanced redundancy scheme that capped payments at the amount the employee would have earned had he or she continued in employment until normal retirement age indirectly discriminated against a 63-year old employee on the ground of his age. H had taken voluntary redundancy and then brought a claim of indirect age discrimination after his redundancy pay was capped at £76,560 – the amount he would have earned had he remained in work until the normal retirement age of 65, and which was £14,000 less than he would have received without the cap. The EAT held that since the purpose of the scheme was to compensate employees for loss of the expectation of remaining in employment, imposing a cap to prevent an employee receiving a 'windfall' that was more than he or she could have earned until retirement was a proportionate means of achieving a legitimate aim and was therefore justified. Mr Justice Underhill, then President of the EAT, stated that he would have reached the decision on justification without reference to previous authority, but that he drew 'strong support' for his conclusion on objective justification from obiter (i.e. non-binding) comments made by Mr Justice Elias (his predecessor as President of the EAT) in Loxley to the effect that age-related provisions in contractual redundancy schemes properly directed at the prevention of a windfall are justifiable.

However, employers should not assume that the tapering of benefits will invariably be justified. In MacCulloch v Imperial Chemical Industries plc 2008

205

ICR 1334, EAT, for example, the tribunal at first instance commented that the tapering provision in ICI's redundancy policy, which reduced payments to employees between the ages of 57 and 62, was not a proportionate means of achieving a legitimate aim. The taper may have been justified when many of the employees were members of the final salary pension scheme – and thus would receive their maximum pension entitlement – but that was no longer the case as the final salary scheme had been closed. This part of the decision was not appealed. Employers should therefore seek to ensure that any cap (or taper) is clearly aimed at preventing a windfall to the employee and that it strikes the correct balance between the needs of the business and any discriminatory effect on the employee.

6.51 The same enhanced redundancy scheme as that in the MacCulloch case came up for consideration again in Clark v Terra Nitrogen (UK) Ltd ET Case No.2504785/08 but from the perspective of a man of 61 years of age who had been employed by the company for 37 years. When C was made redundant, his payment under the enhanced scheme was 55.9 per cent of qualifying pay. C claimed that the reduction in his payment amounted to age discrimination. The tribunal noted that the aims of the scheme were to recognise loyalty and service to the company. It was also an incentive to encourage employees to take up voluntary redundancy and thereby reduce the number of compulsory redundancies. In relation to those employees aged between 50 and 57, the aim was specifically to help those who might find it difficult because of their age to obtain alternative employment. With those employees aged 57 and over, the tribunal was satisfied that the aim of the scheme was to put redundant employees on the same footing as those who worked on to retirement. This was not only to prevent a windfall but also to prevent retained employees from being resentful. The company's aims were to achieve financial equality not only between employees who had been made redundant but also between redundant employees and retained employees. The tribunal was therefore satisfied that the company's aims were legitimate. In considering whether the aims were proportionate to the discriminatory effect on C, the tribunal had regard to the actual effect on C and weighed that against the business needs. It took account of the fact that the scheme was generous and had been accepted by the workforce as it had operated successfully in the past. Moreover, the trade unions were happy for the scheme to continue following the coming into force of the Age Regulations. The tribunal also noted that as the company's normal retirement age was 62, C was, in effect, losing only 11 months' employment with the company compared with someone aged 50, who would potentially be losing 12 years' employment. In these circumstances, the tribunal was satisfied that the company's aims were proportionate to the discriminatory impact on C and therefore dismissed his age discrimination claim.

The prohibition on age discrimination and the availability of the justification defence actually stem from the EU Equal Treatment Framework Directive

(No.2000/78) and – while not expressed in precisely the same terms as the domestic decisions – judgments of the European Court of Justice do lend some support to the view that tapering provisions can serve the legitimate aim of preventing a windfall. In Odar v Baxter Deutschland GmbH 2013 2 CMLR 13, ECJ, for example, the ECJ held that an employer's social plan, which used a different calculation of redundancy pay for employees aged over 54, resulting in a lower payment than that received by younger employees, served the legitimate aims of granting compensation for the future; protecting younger workers and facilitating their reintegration into employment while taking account of the need to achieve a fair distribution of limited financial resources; and preventing compensation on termination from being claimed by persons who were not seeking new employment but would receive a replacement income in the form of an occupational old-age pension. The scheme in issue in this case guaranteed that redundant employees aged over 54 would receive at least 50 per cent of the amount that they would have received under the normal calculation. The ECJ considered that this was objectively justified, as it was both proportionate and necessary to meet the identified legitimate aims.

However, the ECJ has been less accepting of a total exclusion of pension **6.52** age workers from eligibility for severance payments. In Ingeniorforeningen i Danmark v Region Syddanmark 2011 1 CMLR 35, ECJ, the ECJ held that a Danish law that excluded dismissed employees eligible for an old age pension from the right to a 'severance allowance' ordinarily given for long service was discriminatory on the ground of age. The law had legitimate aims – namely, rewarding long service and supporting redundant employees while they looked for alternative work. However, it prohibited an entire category of workers, defined on the basis of age, from temporarily waiving their right to an old age pension in exchange for a severance allowance, thus making it financially more difficult for such individuals to exercise their right to work, should they wish to do so. The provision was therefore not a proportionate means of achieving the relevant aims and could not be justified.

Achieving the legitimate aim. As noted above, an employer may rely on one **6.53** or more of a number of potentially legitimate aims to justify an otherwise age discriminatory enhanced redundancy scheme. However, it will be unable to successfully maintain a justification defence if it cannot demonstrate that the scheme actually achieves those aims and is a proportionate means of doing so.

In Galt and ors v National Starch and Chemical Ltd ET Case No.2101804/07, for example, an employer was able to show that its enhanced redundancy scheme had a legitimate aim, but could not establish that the scheme was a proportionate means of achieving it. The facts were that the employer decided to close its Warrington site and entered into discussions with the recognised trade union. As part of a package of measures, the workforce was

207

offered enhanced redundancy terms – employees would receive a payment of three weeks' gross pay for each year of service under 40 years of age, and four weeks' gross pay for each year after that age. G and a number of other redundant employees claimed that the enhanced scheme treated them less favourably than employees who were older, as some or all of the years that they were entitled to count for the purposes of the relevant calculation were worked when they were under 40. The tribunal held that G and his colleagues had been unlawfully discriminated against contrary to the Age Regulations. It accepted that the employer had a legitimate aim: 'The company clearly feared that, unless acceptable proposals were made to the employees in question, there was a possibility of industrial unrest. The purpose of offering the enhanced redundancy terms was to avoid such unrest and bring about an orderly and satisfactory closure of the Warrington site.' However, in the view of the tribunal majority, the less favourable treatment of the claimants was not a proportionate means of achieving that aim, as the claimants' treatment did not actually contribute to the pursuit of the legitimate aim. Paying different amounts of redundancy pay according to employees' ages did not actually ensure that the closure of the site would occur without the feared industrial unrest. It followed that there had been unlawful discrimination.

6.54 Similarly, while preventing employees receiving a windfall is a potential legitimate aim (see 'Preventing a windfall as a legitimate aim' above), the tribunal's decision in Ormerod v Cummins Engine Co Ltd ET Case No.2508268/09 illustrates that an employer needs to put forward a clear case as to what the windfall would be. A failure to do so may lead a tribunal to conclude that the aim of avoiding a windfall is not a legitimate one in the particular circumstances. Moreover, to be in a position to be able to demonstrate proportionality in such cases, an employer will need to put forward sufficient evidence showing how an employee would be better off with the windfall.

The main facts of the case are as follows. O, who had been employed since 1974, was made redundant in 2008 at the age of 63. A collective agreement contained redundancy terms under which employees aged between 51 and 64 years of age would receive a redundancy payment of four weeks' pay for each completed year of service. O's enhanced redundancy payment would have been £38,733, but the employer decided that, in view of the economic situation, all redundancy payments would be capped at the level of the gross earnings that would have been received had employees remained in employment until the normal retirement age of 65. This meant that O's payment was capped at £24,461 and then further reduced by his notice payment to £17,497. O claimed that he had been unlawfully discriminated against contrary to the Age Regulations and the tribunal upheld his claim. It found that O had been less favourably treated on the ground of his age as he had not received the full contractual entitlement to four weeks' pay for each completed year of service because he was approaching retirement. This amounted to both direct and indirect age discrimination.

208

Turning to the question of justification, the tribunal noted that avoiding a **6.55** windfall was a potential legitimate aim. However, it found that in the instant case the employer's aim to avoid a windfall was not legitimate due, in part, to the fact that the employer had made no attempt to advance a clear case as to what that windfall was. Indeed, the employer had not shown that O would, in fact, have received a windfall at all. O gave evidence that his redundancy and early receipt of pension would result in a £5,000 reduction in his pension lump sum and a £1,000 annual reduction in his pension, amounting to an actuarial loss of over £20,000. O's redundancy and early drawing of his pension had also deprived him of various other benefits; for example, the loss of the chance to work on and enhance his pension, the loss of the opportunity to work any overtime in 2009 and 2010, and the loss of any potential bonuses.

With regard to proportionality, the tribunal held that the employer had failed to show that its actions would in any event be proportionate as 'no effort had been made... actuarially or in any other way to calculate precisely how [O] would have been better off in receiving the enhanced payment up to the cap' rather than working to retirement age with the opportunity to receive various benefits as referred to above. It had not provided the tribunal with any evidence as to O's pension entitlement, including how that entitlement related to or compared with his enhanced redundancy entitlement, or the impact of the other financial provisions. In these circumstances, the tribunal held that it was not possible to conclude that the capping of O's redundancy payment was proportionate.

In seeking to justify a potentially discriminatory redundancy scheme, an **6.56** employer may be able to rely on statistical evidence as to the typical financial needs of employees at different ages. In Lockwood v Department for Work and Pensions 2014 ICR 1257, CA, L commenced employment with the DWP at age 18. However, in 2007, when she was 26, her position was declared surplus. At around the same time, the employer announced a voluntary redundancy programme, with a payment scheme that operated an age banding system under which older employees benefited more than younger ones. As a 26-year-old with almost eight years' service, L was entitled to a payment of £10,849.04. However, had she been over 35 at the time of leaving, with the exact same length of service, she would have received a further £17,690.58. L claimed that this disparity in payment amounted to direct age discrimination. The Court of Appeal upheld an employment tribunal's decision that L's treatment under the scheme was justified. The Court accepted that in approaching the establishment of a scheme such as this, an individual assessment of each employee's circumstances was not practicable; it was necessary for the employer to adopt a banding approach and this would inevitably involve disparate treatment between employees of different ages. In the Court's view, when considering the proportionality of the scheme, the tribunal had been entitled to rely on statistical evidence

209

which showed that individuals in younger categories and in their twenties, who typically had fewer financial and family obligations, could generally be expected to react more easily and rapidly to the loss of their jobs, and that greater flexibility could be expected of them.

6.57 Non-payment

Any issues relating to an employee's right to a redundancy payment or to the amount of such a payment fall within the jurisdiction of the employment tribunal – S.163(1). Furthermore, an employee may be able to bring an action in the civil courts where he or she alleges non-payment of a redundancy payment – and therefore breach of contract – under a contractual scheme. For further information, see Chapter 10, 'Enforcement'. An employer's inability to pay in the context of insolvency is discussed in Chapter 7, 'Payments from National Insurance Fund', under 'Entitlement to payment – employer's insolvency'.

Note that S.7 of the Employment Act 2008 enables employment tribunals to award additional financial loss to employees who have brought a successful claim for a redundancy payment where that loss is attributable to the employer's non-payment – see S.163(5) ERA. The amount that a tribunal can award under this head must be 'appropriate in all the circumstances'.

6.58 Tribunals also have the power under S.12A of the Employment Tribunals Act 1996 to impose a financial penalty of between £100 and £5,000, payable to the Secretary of State, where the employer is found to have breached an employee's employment rights and there are one or more aggravating features. The Act does not define 'aggravating features', but Government guidance indicates that these are more likely to exist where the employer has a dedicated human resources function, where the act was deliberate or malicious, or in the case of repeated breach. Financial penalties are discussed in greater detail in IDS Employment Law Handbook, 'Employment Tribunal Practice and Procedure' (2014), Chapter 20, 'Costs and penalties', under 'Penalties against employers'.

7 Payments from National Insurance Fund

Entitlement to payment

Procedure

Amount of payment

As a social protection measure, all EU Member States are required to offer a guarantee – albeit a limited one – to employees whose employer becomes insolvent. In this regard, Article 3 of the EU Insolvency Directive No.2008/94 (originally No.80/987) imposes a general obligation on Member States to 'take the measures necessary to ensure that guarantee institutions guarantee... payment of employees' outstanding claims resulting from contracts of employment or employment relationships, including, where provided for by national law, severance pay on termination of employment relationships'. In fact, well before the coming into force of the original Directive, UK legislation already provided for payments such as outstanding holiday pay, arrears of salary or wages (up to a certain limit), pay in lieu of notice and statutory redundancy payments to be made out of a central fund to employees left high and dry by the insolvency of their employer.

This chapter is concerned with the recovery of redundancy payments pursuant to this state guarantee. But, as we shall see, the circumstances in which such recovery can be made extend beyond where the employer is shown to be insolvent. The relevant UK statutory provisions also require a payment to be made out of a central fund where an intransigent employer refuses to pay up despite it being clear that a statutory redundancy payment is due.

Entitlement to payment

Section 166 of the Employment Rights Act 1996 (ERA) contains a scheme whereby an employee may apply directly to the Department for Business, Innovation and Skills (BIS) for a redundancy payment out of what was originally called 'the Redundancy Fund' and is now called the National Insurance Fund (NIF).

The statutory provisions in effect require two conditions to be satisfied. The employee must show that:

- the employer is 'liable' to pay him or her an 'employer's payment' – S.166(1), and

- one or other of the following two situations applies

  - he or she has taken all reasonable steps – short of legal proceedings – to recover the payment from the employer and the employer has refused or failed to pay, or has only made partial payment – S.166(1)(a), or

  - the employer is insolvent as defined and the whole or part of the payment remains unpaid – S.166(1)(b).

These two situations are discussed in detail below.

7.3 Liability to make an employer's payment

It is fairly self-evident that the Secretary of State will only be liable for an employer's payment under S.166 if the employer is itself liable to make one – see Crawford v (1) Secretary of State for Employment (2) Colmore Depot 1995 IRLR 523, EAT (discussed under 'Procedure' below).

An 'employer's payment' is defined in S.166(2) as:

- a statutory redundancy payment

- a payment owing under an Acas-conciliated agreement or a settlement agreement that was made in respect of a claim to a statutory redundancy payment, or

- a termination payment under an agreement to which an exemption order applies under S.157 (see Chapter 5, 'Qualifications and exclusions', under 'Contracting out').

7.4 In this chapter we are exclusively concerned with recovery of statutory redundancy payments. It goes without saying that, for such a payment to be payable, the employee must have been made redundant as defined by the ERA – see Chapter 2, 'Redundancy', for details.

7.5 Employer's refusal to pay

As mentioned above, one of the two situations that may trigger entitlement to a payment from the NIF is where an 'employer's payment' (which, as we have seen, includes a statutory redundancy payment) has not been paid by the employer despite the fact that the employee has taken all reasonable steps to recover the payment from the employer. S.166(1)(a) ERA provides that the employee may apply to the Secretary of State (for which read BIS) for a payment from the NIF where '[he or she] has taken all reasonable steps, other than legal proceedings, to recover the payment from the employer and the employer has refused or failed to pay it, or has paid part of it and has refused or failed to pay the balance'.

For these purposes, the phrase 'legal proceedings' does not include employment tribunal proceedings, but does include proceedings to enforce

212

an employment tribunal's decision – S.166(4) ERA. An employee is not therefore expected to take enforcement proceedings in the county court before being able to apply to the Secretary of State – but will be expected to bring a claim for a redundancy payment before a tribunal if there is any reasonable basis for doubting whether a statutory redundancy payment is, in fact, payable. This might be so, for example, if it is unclear whether or not the employee has been dismissed for redundancy, or whether the claimant in question is an 'employee' working under a contract of employment as opposed to an independent contractor. It may also be the case if there is a legitimate dispute about whether the employee has sufficient continuous service (currently two years) to be eligible for a statutory redundancy payment. However, whenever liability on the employer to pay a redundancy payment is clear cut, the cases suggest that the Secretary of State is not entitled to require the employee to commence tribunal proceedings against the employer before applying for a payment out of the NIF – see, for example, Jeffrey v Grey 1967 2 ITR 335, ET.

The question of whether an employee had taken 'all reasonable steps' to recover a payment before applying to the Secretary of State came up in some of the very first cases decided under the redundancy provisions. For example, in Williams v Black 1967 ITR 317, ET, the employer had disappeared and apparently left the country, making it impossible for the employee to serve a tribunal claim on him. The tribunal felt that it could not decide on the merits of the employee's claim but it did decide how much he would have been entitled to so that he could apply to the Secretary of State for payment out of what was then the Redundancy Fund. In the circumstances, the employee was found to have taken all the steps he could reasonably take.

7.6

In Jeffrey v Grey (above) the employer admitted liability but simply said that he was unable to pay. The tribunal said that the commencement of tribunal proceedings was not a necessary step to recover payment in these circumstances because they could not help the employee to get money from the employer.

In general, the importance of S.166(1)(a) is that, unlike other payments potentially payable from the NIF (such as holiday pay and payment in lieu of notice), it enables an employee to claim an 'employer's payment' even if the employer is not insolvent. It is often the case that an employer is unable or refuses to pay a redundancy payment in circumstances where, despite all appearances to the contrary, the employer is not actually 'insolvent' as defined by the relevant legislative provisions. And sometimes a payment is refused for no other reason than the employer's intransigence. In either case, provided the employee can satisfy the precondition of having taken all reasonable steps to recover the payment, he or she can look to BIS to recover the payment from the NIF.

7.7

213

7.8 **Employer's insolvency**

The second situation that triggers an employee's entitlement to claim a statutory redundancy payment from the NIF is where the employer is 'insolvent' as statutorily defined – S.166(1)(b).

7.9 **Individual employers.** By virtue of S.166(6) ERA, an individual employer is insolvent in this context if:

- he or she has been adjudged bankrupt or has made a composition or arrangement with creditors (in England and Wales), or sequestration of his or her estate has been awarded or he or she has executed a trust deed for creditors or has entered into a composition contract (in Scotland), or

- he or she has died and his estate falls to be administered in accordance with an order under S.421 of the Insolvency Act 1986 (in England and Wales), or he or she has died and a judicial factor appointed under S.11A of the Judicial Factors (Scotland) Act 1889 is required by that section to divide the insolvent estate among creditors (in Scotland).

7.10 **Corporate insolvency.** Where the employer is a company, then under S.166(7) ERA that company is insolvent if:

- a winding-up order or an administration order has been made, or a resolution for voluntary winding up has been passed, in respect of the company

- the company is in administration for the purposes of the Insolvency Act 1986

- a receiver or (in England and Wales only) a manager of the company's undertaking is duly appointed, or (in England and Wales only) possession has been taken of any company property by or on behalf of the holders of any debentures secured by a floating charge on that property, or

- a voluntary arrangement proposed in the case of the company for the purposes of Part I of the Insolvency Act 1986 has been approved.

A company for these purposes includes a charitable incorporated organisation – S.166(9).

7.11 It is important to note that a company will not be regarded as insolvent simply because it has ceased trading, cannot pay its debts or has otherwise fallen into some kind of financial difficulty. In Pollard and ors v Teako (Swiss) Ltd 1967 ITR 357, ET, a landlord sent in bailiffs to take possession of a company's premises. The business closed with no prospect of reopening and the sale of stock and furniture was insufficient to pay off the arrears of rent. The company, however, was not insolvent as defined. No steps were taken to put it into liquidation because there were no remaining assets to realise. The same principle has been confirmed by subsequent cases – see, for example, Secretary of State for Trade

214

and Industry v Key and ors EAT 1356/01 and Secretary of State for Business, Innovation and Skills v Coward and anor EAT 0034/11.

In Secretary of State for Trade and Industry v Walden and anor 2000 IRLR 168, EAT – a case concerning a claim for payment of arrears of pay from the NIF – the EAT ruled that an employment tribunal had erred in assuming that some kind of insolvency procedure must have occurred to explain the dissolution of a company that had got into financial difficulties. The EAT emphasised that the relevant statutory provisions set out an exhaustive list of events amounting to insolvency. The onus is firmly on the claimant seeking to make a claim against the Secretary of State to adduce direct evidence of one of those events. Absence of proof that one of the events has occurred is fatal to the claim. The EAT pointed out that documentary proof of the fact that one of the specified types of insolvency procedure has been commenced is obtainable from Companies House.

The limitations discussed above could be a major drawback for employees were it not for the fact that, in respect of statutory redundancy payments and the other type of 'employer's payment' defined by S.166(2) ERA, an employee is entitled to make a claim to BIS under S.166(1)(a) if he or she has taken all reasonable steps to recover the payment in question from the employer (see under 'Employer's refusal to pay' above). In other words, whereas the absence of insolvency proceedings is fatal to other types of claim potentially payable out of the NIF, this need not be the case where the relevant claim concerns a statutory redundancy payment. This point is neatly illustrated by Secretary of State for Business, Innovation and Skills v Coward and anor (above), where the employee claimed a redundancy payment and notice pay from the NIF when her employer ceases trading and eventually dissolved. The EAT found no proof that an event falling within S.183(3) ERA (or, by extension, within S.166(7), which is identical in terms) had occurred and set aside the tribunal's award of notice pay. However, it did not interfere with the award of a redundancy payment under S.166(1)(a) on the ground that the employee had taken all reasonable practical steps to recover the payment. **7.12**

Partnerships. Where the employer is a limited liability partnership (LLP), the partnership is judged to be insolvent under S.166(8) ERA if: **7.13**

- a winding-up order, administration order or a determination for a voluntary winding-up has been made with respect to the partnership

- a receiver or (in England and Wales only) a manager of the undertaking of the partnership has been appointed or (in England and Wales only) possession has been taken by or on behalf of the holders of any debenture secured by a floating charge of any of the partnership's property comprised in or subject to the charge, or

215

- a voluntary arrangement proposed in relation to the partnership has been approved under Part I of the Insolvency Act 1986.

It would seem that any other type of partnership can only be insolvent for the purposes of S.166(1)(b) if each and every partner is insolvent. In Secretary of State for Trade and Industry v Forde 1997 ICR 231, EAT, the Appeal Tribunal ruled that, for an employer comprising a partnership to be regarded as 'insolvent', it is necessary that each and every one of the individual partners has been adjudged personally bankrupt. The EAT reached this decision on the basis that an employee who is employed by a partnership as a whole (as distinct from employment by an individual partner in a personal capacity) must show that his or her 'employer' (i.e. the partnership) is insolvent in order to secure entitlement to payments by the Secretary of State from the NIF. In the EAT's view, a partnership as a whole cannot be insolvent, since it 'is not an entity which can be or would be adjudged bankrupt'. However, it is arguable that the Appeal Tribunal overlooked the provisions of Part V of the Insolvency Act 1986, which allow 'unregistered companies' to be compulsorily wound up. For this purpose, the Insolvent Partnerships Order 1994 SI 1994/2421 expressly includes a partnership in the definition of 'unregistered company' and makes provision for the partnership as a whole to be wound up as insolvent. It is not necessary under the 1994 Order for each partner to be individually insolvent, since the partnership is regarded as an entity in itself.

7.14 **Types of insolvency procedure.** A detailed analysis of the various insolvency procedures that apply to individual, corporate and partnership insolvency is beyond the scope of this Handbook. However, the topic is outlined in IDS Employment Law Handbook, 'Transfer of Undertakings' (2015), Chapter 6, 'Transfer of insolvent companies', under 'Types of insolvency procedure'.

7.15 ## Qualification

In order to rely on the provisions for payment from the NIF, the claimant must show that he or she is entitled to a redundancy payment, which means, in the case of a statutory redundancy payment, that he or she must have completed two years' continuous service. This is so even if the employee is claiming under a contractual scheme covered by an exemption order, irrespective of whether that scheme contains any requirement for two years' service – S.167(2) ERA. In such a case, however, the period of continuous employment must be *calculated* in accordance with the provisions of the contracted-out scheme and not with those of the ERA. (See Chapter 5, 'Qualifications and exclusions', under 'Contracting out', for a more detailed discussion of contracted-out schemes.)

The claimant must also be an 'employee' as defined by S.230 ERA. This means that he or she must be working or have worked under a 'contract of employment' (i.e. a contract of service or apprenticeship) – see Chapter 5, 'Qualifications and exclusions', under 'Employees and excluded employees'. In practice, most of the case law generated by the statutory provisions for payments from the NIF concerns the issue of whether or not the claimants have employee status. BIS will decline to make such payments if, in the view of its officials, there is a question mark over the employment status of the claimant. In such cases, claimants often end up challenging the refusal of the Secretary of State to make a payment by taking tribunal proceedings – see, for example, Secretary of State for Trade and Industry v Bottrill 1999 ICR 592, CA; and Nesbitt and anor v Secretary of State for Trade and Industry 2007 IRLR 847, EAT.

A rare form of disqualification is where the claimant's contract has become **7.16** frustrated by the time of the insolvency. This occurred in Collins v Secretary of State for Trade and Industry EAT 1460/99, where the claimant had, as a result of an injury to his hand, been off work for a considerable amount of time. At the beginning of 1999, the managing director offered him the choice of remaining on the books or taking a redundancy payment. Since he thought he might eventually be fit to return to work, he opted for the former. However, a couple of months later the company went into receivership and the claimant at that point sought a redundancy payment from the Secretary of State. This was rejected on the ground that the claimant's contract had, by the time of the redundancy, come to be frustrated by his inability to work over a protracted period. An employment tribunal ruled in favour of the Secretary of State and, on appeal, the EAT upheld the tribunal's decision. Owing to the fact that the contract had been frustrated, the claimant was not employed under a contract of employment at the relevant date. In so concluding, the EAT rejected the claimant's contention that, in a situation where both parties regard the employment as continuing, it was not open to a tribunal to conclude that the contract had in fact been terminated by frustration. For an in-depth consideration of the law on frustration of contract, see IDS Employment Law Handbook, 'Contracts of Employment' (2014), Chapter 13, 'Termination by operation of law', under 'Frustration'.

Procedure

7.17

When an employer fails to pay the statutory redundancy payment or is insolvent, the employee may apply to the Secretary of State for a redundancy payment – S.166(1) ERA. (He or she may, of course, bring a claim against the employer first. A tribunal decided in Barcza v Potomac Restaurants Ltd (in liquidation) 1968 ITR 234, ET, that it had jurisdiction to hear a redundancy payment claim when the employing company was in liquidation and the employee had made no application to the (then) Department of Employment for payment out of the (then) Redundancy Fund.) If the Secretary of State

217

disputes the employee's entitlement under S.166, a reference can be made to an employment tribunal for a resolution of the matter under S.170 – see 'Reference to tribunal' below.

7.18 Application to Secretary of State

In order to accept a claim under S.166 and make a payment from the NIF, the Secretary of State must be satisfied that:

- the employee is entitled to a redundancy payment

- the employee has taken all reasonable steps to recover the payment from the employer or the employer is insolvent, and

- the payment remains unpaid (either in whole or in part) – S.167(1) and (2).

Although there is no specific time limit for making an application to the Secretary of State, it should be noted that S.166(1) stipulates that an employee can only claim payment out of the NIF if his or her employer is 'liable to pay' an employer's payment. Where the particular payment in question is a statutory redundancy payment, the employer can only be said to be liable to pay if, within six months of the 'relevant date' (i.e. the date of termination of employment) the employee takes one or more of the steps listed in S.164(1) regarded as necessary to establish his or her right to claim a payment. The relevant steps are:

- the employee makes a written claim for the payment to the employer – S.164(1)(b)

- the question as to the employee's right to, or the amount of, the payment has been referred to an employment tribunal – S.164(1)(c). (Note that a claim is 'referred to a tribunal' when it is physically received at the tribunal office, not when it is posted – Secretary of State for Employment v Banks and ors 1983 ICR 48, EAT)

- the employee presents a claim of unfair dismissal to a tribunal under S.111 – S.164(1)(d).

7.19 These steps are discussed in detail in Chapter 10, 'Enforcement', under 'Statutory redundancy payments – time limits'. So long as the employee has a 'live' claim against the employer triggered by having taken one of the necessary steps within the applicable time limit, the employee is entitled to apply to the Secretary of State for payment from the NIF in the event that the employer is insolvent or has simply refused to pay up.

The Secretary of State is only liable for a statutory redundancy payment that an employer is liable to make. An employee is not entitled to a statutory redundancy payment from his or her employer if he or she fails to take one or more of the steps listed in S.164(1) within the prescribed time limits. In

218

those circumstances, since the employer is not liable to make the redundancy payment, the Secretary of State is under no liability to make it either – see Crawford v (1) Secretary of State for Employment (2) Colmore Depot 1995 IRLR 523, EAT. In that case, C failed to apply for a redundancy payment when his employer's business, which was in receivership, was sold. This was because all the parties assumed that there had been a transfer under the Transfer of Undertakings (Protection of Employment) Regulations 2006 SI 2006/246 (TUPE). Over a year later it became clear that there had not been a transfer and C applied to the Secretary of State for a redundancy payment, but was refused on the ground that his claim was out of time. The EAT agreed. It rejected C's claim that it should consider the spirit and intention of the legislation and that time should only begin to run against C when it became clear that there had been no transfer. The EAT recommended that employees of companies that become insolvent make provisional claims for a redundancy payment from the employer and the Secretary of State promptly to cover themselves in the event that the insolvent undertaking is not transferred to a third party under TUPE.

Information from employer. The Secretary of State may require the employer to provide such information and documents as he or she needs to determine the employee's entitlement – S.169(1) ERA. Failure to comply without reasonable excuse is a summary offence punishable by a fine not exceeding level 3 on the standard scale – S.169(2). Deliberately or recklessly providing false information is an offence punishable by a fine or imprisonment or both – S.169(3) and (4). There is no limit to the level of fine that can be imposed in these circumstances.

7.20

Reference to tribunal

7.21

The Secretary of State is not bound to pay up on an application by an employee under S.166. Where any question arises as to the employee's entitlement or the amount of the payment claimed or both, the matter should be referred to an employment tribunal – S.170(1). It is not necessary for the employer to be joined as a party to the proceedings – Jones v Secretary of State for Employment 1982 ICR 389, EAT. Even if there has been an earlier tribunal hearing that has awarded a redundancy payment to the employee, the Secretary of State, if dissatisfied with the claim, may require the case to be reheard on its merits – Secretary of State for Employment v Banks and ors 1983 ICR 48, EAT. This somewhat surprising decision shows that the Secretary of State is not bound by an earlier tribunal's determination against the employer as to the employee's entitlement to a redundancy payment. So, for example, a prior decision as to an employee's sufficiency of continuous service in respect of entitlement to a redundancy payment can be 'unpicked' by the Secretary of State if he or she has cause to argue that that decision was wrong.

For the purpose of any reference under S.170, an employee who has been dismissed will, unless the contrary is proved, be presumed to have been dismissed for redundancy – S.170(2).

7.22 Amount of payment

If the employee is claiming a statutory redundancy payment, then the amount to be paid from the NIF is a redundancy payment computed in the usual way, less anything that has actually been paid by the employer – S.168(1)(a) ERA. If the employee is claiming a sum owing under an Acas-conciliated agreement or a settlement agreement, the amount to be paid is either the amount owing under the agreement or the amount of any redundancy payment that the employer would have been liable to pay but for the agreement, whichever is the lesser amount – S.168(1)(aa).

Things are somewhat more complicated if the employee is claiming under a redundancy scheme covered by an exemption order made pursuant to S.157 ERA. This provision – which deals with rare instances where trade unions and employers have jointly agreed to operate a redundancy scheme that stands in the place of the statutory provisions for redundancy payments – is discussed in Chapter 5, 'Qualifications and exclusions', under 'Contracting out'. Where a payment is to be made from the NIF in respect of a scheme covered by an exemption order, it is necessary to compute both the amount due under the scheme and the amount that would have been due under the statutory redundancy scheme. In calculating the latter amount, however, the provisions of the exempted scheme relating to the computation of continuous employment and the determination of the 'relevant date' are deemed to override any conflicting statutory provisions – S.168(2) and (3). The amount thus computed is called the 'relevant redundancy payment'. What the employee is entitled to from the NIF is either the amount due under the contracted-out scheme or the 'relevant redundancy payment', whichever is the lesser – S.168(2).

7.23 Interest

Under the Employment Tribunals (Interest) Order 1990 SI 1990/479 simple interest at the prevailing rate per annum (currently 8 per cent) is payable on any compensation or monetary award made by an employment tribunal that remains unpaid. Interest begins to accrue from the day immediately following the relevant decision day, which for most purposes is the day the document is sent to the parties recording the tribunal's award. This means that, in most cases, interest will start to accrue from the day after the relevant decision is made. However, the interest accrued is not *payable* if payment of the full amount of the award is made within 14 days after the relevant decision day.

In light of the above, if an employer becomes liable to pay such interest on account of a failure to pay the redundancy payment as ordered by a tribunal, and the employee subsequently looks to the Secretary of State to make the payment from the NIF, the payment by the Secretary of State must include the interest that was owed by the employer. However, if the only relevant decision made by a tribunal is the decision requiring payment by the Secretary of State from the NIF – in other words, no prior relevant decision has been made against the employer – the Secretary of State will not be required to pay interest unless he or she him or herself fails to make payment within 14 days of the relevant decision day – see Secretary of State for Employment v Reeves 1993 ICR 508, EAT (which concerned an earlier version of the Order that provided that interest only began to accrue after 42 days).

Subrogation of rights and remedies by Secretary of State 7.24

Whenever a payment is made from the NIF, the employee's rights and remedies against the employer are transferred to and vest in the Secretary of State – S.167(3) ERA. Under the same provision, any decision of an employment tribunal ordering a redundancy payment to be paid by the employer to the employee will be treated as an order for the payment to be paid to the Secretary of State. If the Secretary of State is successful in recovering money from the employer, such money will then be paid back into the NIF – S.167(4).

8 Unfair redundancy

Redundancy is one of the potentially fair reasons for dismissal listed in **8.1** S.98(2)(c) of the Employment Rights Act 1996 (ERA). Accordingly, in many cases an employer's liability in respect of a redundancy dismissal will be fully discharged by the payment of statutory or, where appropriate, contractual redundancy pay. However, it remains open to an employee to argue that his or her 'redundancy' dismissal was unfair under the ERA for one of the following reasons:

- the dismissal was not by reason of redundancy, but was instead for a reason which is not potentially fair under S.98(1) or (2)

- although a redundancy situation existed, the employee was selected for redundancy for a prohibited reason, meaning that the dismissal was automatically unfair – S.105 and related provisions, or

- although a redundancy situation existed, and the employee was not selected for an automatically unfair reason, the dismissal was nevertheless unreasonable under S.98(4).

In addition, an employee might claim that the decision to select him or her for redundancy was an act of unlawful discrimination. Discriminatory redundancy selection is discussed in Chapter 9, 'Discriminatory redundancy', under 'Discriminatory selection'.

Occasionally a redundancy dismissal can also amount to a breach of **8.2** contract. In Keable v Imagedata Group Ltd ET Case No.1806353/09, for example, the claimant was employed under a contract of apprenticeship but was dismissed by reason of redundancy nine months before his apprenticeship was due to end. His employer had decided that in view of its financial situation it could no longer afford to employ trainees. However, his contract of apprenticeship could be terminated only with good cause. An employment tribunal upheld the claimant's claim of breach of contract. The employer had committed itself expressly to completing the apprenticeship and it would have been reasonably practicable to have kept him on, despite the difficult economic situation. Breach of contract claims are discussed in IDS Employment Law Handbook, 'Contracts of Employment' (2014), Chapter 10, 'Breach of contract'.

223

8.3 Reason for dismissal

Where an employee argues that his or her dismissal was not by reason of redundancy, but was instead for a reason which is not potentially fair under the ERA, the statutory presumption under S.163(2) ERA that a dismissal is for redundancy will not operate and it will fall to the employer to show the reason for dismissal.

For a dismissal to be by reason of redundancy, a redundancy situation must exist – see Chapter 2, 'Redundancy', under 'Definition of redundancy'. However, it must be stressed that it is not for tribunals to investigate the reasons behind such situations. In Moon and ors v Homeworthy Furniture (Northern) Ltd 1977 ICR 117, EAT, the employer closed a factory on the ground that it was not economically viable. The employees sought to demonstrate that the factory was viable and the dismissals unfair, but the EAT ruled that there was no jurisdiction to consider the reasonableness of the decision to create a redundancy situation. That would be akin to considering the merits of an industrial dispute, which, following the introduction of the Trade Union and Labour Relations Act 1974, the tribunal had no power to do.

8.4 In a number of decisions reached after the Moon case, including Orr v Vaughan 1981 IRLR 63, EAT, and Ladbroke Courage Holidays Ltd v Asten 1981 IRLR 59, EAT, the EAT required the employer to show that the decision to make redundancies was based on proper information and consideration of the situation. This approach can be justified on the ground that the absence of such information and consideration throws into question whether the dismissals are by reason of redundancy at all. In the Ladbroke Courage Holidays case the EAT went so far as to suggest that the employer should be able to show a strong economic case for redundancies. However, this rests unhappily with the Court of Appeal's decisions in Hollister v National Farmers' Union 1979 ICR 542, CA, and James W Cook and Co (Wivenhoe) Ltd v Tipper and ors 1990 ICR 716, CA. In the Hollister case, the Court held that a good commercial reason was enough to justify the decision to make redundancies, and in Tipper it stressed that tribunals are not at liberty to investigate the commercial and economic reasons behind a decision to close. It did accept, however, that tribunals could question whether the decision to dismiss was genuinely on the ground of redundancy, and could therefore require that the decision to make redundancies was based on proper information. In short, a tribunal is entitled only to ask whether the decision to make redundancies was genuine, not whether it was wise.

8.5 Retirement

Following the repeal of Schedule 6 to the Employment Equality (Age) Regulations 2006 SI 2006/1031 in April 2011, there is now no 'normal

224

retirement age', and 'retirement' is no longer one of the potentially fair reasons for dismissal under S.98 ERA. For further details of how Schedule 6 to the Age Regulations used to operate, see IDS Employment Law Handbook, 'Unfair Dismissal' (2015), Chapter 8, 'Some other substantial reason', under 'Retirement dismissals'.

Automatically unfair redundancy

8.6

There has been a significant rise in recent years in the number of circumstances in which a dismissal will be held to be automatically unfair – i.e. unfair without any consideration of reasonableness under S.98(4) ERA. The relevant statutory provisions amend the substantive law of unfair dismissal and are designed to afford a greater degree of protection to certain categories of worker, or to those who carry out specific functions that are related to their employment. Most, but not all, of the provisions dealing with automatically unfair redundancy are contained in S.105 ERA.

From an employer's perspective, a dismissal that is 'automatically' unfair can prove more costly than a 'standard' unfair dismissal, as in some cases the compensation cap normally applicable to such claims will be set aside. Furthermore, most of the provisions disapply the two-year qualifying period (or one-year qualifying period where the employment began before 6 April 2012) for unfair dismissal rights.

In most cases, a dismissal will be automatically unfair where the reason or principal reason for it falls into one of the prescribed categories – for example, the employee was absent on jury service (S.98B), was a health and safety representative (S.100), or had asserted a statutory right (S.104). The automatically unfair redundancy provisions of S.105, however, are subtly different. They proceed on the basis that the reason or principal reason for dismissal was redundancy – a potentially fair, and thus not automatically unfair, reason for dismissal. They go on to provide that such a redundancy dismissal will nevertheless be automatically unfair where the employee was selected for redundancy for an automatically unfair reason.

8.7

Relevant provisions

8.8

In this section we provide a list of the statutory provisions governing automatically unfair redundancy selection. This is followed by a brief discussion of each of these provisions. Reference should also be had to IDS Employment Law Handbook, 'Unfair Dismissal' (2015), Chapter 9, 'Automatically unfair dismissals'.

Section 105(1) ERA states that an employee who is dismissed shall be regarded as unfairly dismissed if:

225

- the reason (or, if more than one, the principal reason) for the dismissal is that the employee was redundant – S.105(1)(a), and

- it is shown that the circumstances constituting the redundancy applied equally to one or more other employees in the same undertaking who held positions similar to that held by the employee and who have not been dismissed by the employer – S.105(1)(b), and

- it is shown that 'any of subsections (2A) to (7N) applies' – S.105(1)(c).

8.9   Subsections (2A)–(7N) apply where the reason (or, if more than one reason, the principal reason) the employee was selected for redundancy was:

- a reason relating to jury service as specified in S.98B – S.105(2A)

- a health and safety reason as specified in S.100 – S.105(3)

- a reason relating to a shop worker's or betting worker's refusal to do Sunday work as specified in S.101 – S.105(4)

- a reason relating to the employee's rights under the Working Time Regulations 1998 SI 1998/1833; the Merchant Shipping (Working Time: Inland Waterways) Regulations 2003 SI 2003/3049; the Fishing Vessels (Working Time: Sea-fishermen) Regulations 2004 SI 2004/1713; the Cross-border Railway Services (Working Time) Regulations 2008 SI 2008/1660; or the Merchant Shipping (Hours of Work) Regulations 2002 SI 2002/2125, as specified in S.101A – S.105(4A)

- a reason relating to the employee's role as an occupational pension scheme trustee as specified in S.102 – S.105(5)

- a reason relating to the employee's role as an employee representative or candidate for the purpose of collective redundancies or a transfer of an undertaking as specified in S.103 – S.105(6)

- that the employee made a protected disclosure as specified in S.103A – S.105(6A)

- a reason relating to the employee's assertion of a statutory right as specified in S.104 – S.105(7)

- a reason relating to the employee's rights under the National Minimum Wage Act 1998 as specified in S.104A – S.105(7A)

- a reason relating to the employee's rights under the Tax Credits Act 2002 as specified in S.104B – S.105(7B)

- a reason relating to the employee's right to request flexible working as specified in S.104C – S.105(7BA)

- a reason relating to the employee's right to request study or training as specified in S.104E – S.105(7BB) (subject to an exemption for employers with fewer than 250 employees)

- that the employee took protected industrial action within the meaning of S.238A of the Trade Union and Labour Relations (Consolidation) Act 1992 (TULR(C)A) – S.105(7C)

- a reason specified in Reg 28(3) or (6) of the Transnational Information and Consultation of Employees Regulations 1999 SI 1999/3323 – S.105(7D)

- a reason specified in Reg 7(3) of the Part-time Workers (Prevention of Less Favourable Treatment) Regulations 2000 SI 2000/1551 – S.105(7E)

- a reason specified in Reg 6(3) of the Fixed-term Employees (Prevention of Less Favourable Treatment) Regulations 2002 SI 2002/2034 – S.105(7F)

- a reason specified in Reg 42(3) or (6) of the European Public Limited-Liability Company Regulations 2004 SI 2004/2326 – S.105(7G) (note that these provisions were repealed on 1 October 2009 but re-enacted in European Public Limited-Liability Company (Employee Involvement) (Great Britain) Regulations 2009 SI 2009/2401)

- a reason specified in Reg 30(3) or (6) of the Information and Consultation of Employees Regulations 2004 SI 2004/3426 – S.105(7H)

- a reason specified in para 5(3) or (5) of the Schedule to the Occupational and Personal Pension Schemes (Consultation by Employers and Miscellaneous Amendment) Regulations 2006 SI 2006/349 – S.105(7I)

- a reason specified in Reg 31(3) or (6) of the European Cooperative Society (Involvement of Employees) Regulations 2006 SI 2006/2059 – S.105(7J)

- a reason relating to the automatic enrolment of jobholders into a pension scheme as specified in S.104D ERA – S.105(7JA)

- a reason specified in Reg 46(2) or 47(2) of the Companies (Cross-Border Mergers) Regulations 2007 SI 2007/2974 – S.105(7K)

- a reason specified in Reg 29(3) or (6) of the European Public Limited-Liability Company (Employee Involvement) (Great Britain) Regulations 2009 SI 2009/2401 – S.105(7L)

- a reason relating to a trade union blacklist as specified in S.104F ERA – S.105(7M), or

- a reason specified in Reg 17(3) of the Agency Workers Regulations 2010 SI 2010/93 – S.105(7N).

There is one other provision not yet in force. This covers selection for redundancy

8.10

227

- of employees under the age of 18 for exercising, or proposing to exercise, their right to participate in education or training as specified in S.101B ERA – S.105(4B)). At the time of writing, a date for the coming into force of S.101B has not yet been appointed.

In addition to the protection afforded by S.105 ERA, other statutory provisions make it automatically unfair to select an employee for redundancy for reasons connected with pregnancy, maternity suspension, maternity leave, paternity leave, adoption leave, shared parental leave, unpaid parental leave, dependant care leave or 'keeping in touch' days – see Reg 20(2) of the Maternity and Parental Leave etc Regulations 1999 SI 1999/3312 ('the MPL Regulations'); Reg 29(2) of the Paternity and Adoption Leave Regulations 2002 SI 2002/2788 ('the PAL Regulations'); Reg 34(2) of the Additional Paternity Leave Regulations 2010 SI 2010/1055 ('the APL Regulations'); and Reg 43(2) of the Shared Parental Leave Regulations 2014 SI 2014/3050 ('the SPL Regulations'). Dismissal is also automatically unfair if the employee becomes redundant during or at the end of his or her maternity, paternity, shared parental leave or adoption leave and the provisions relating to offers of suitable alternative employment are not complied with under Reg 10 MPL Regulations, Reg 23 PAL Regulations, Reg 28 APL Regulations or Reg 39 SPL Regulations – Reg 20(1) MPL Regulations; Reg 29(1) PAL Regulations; Reg 34(1) APL Regulations; and Reg 43(1) SPL Regulations. (Note that, while the APL Regulations remain in force, the APL regime has been abolished for parents whose baby is expected on or after 5 April 2015, and has been replaced with shared parental leave. For details, see IDS Employment Law Handbook, 'Maternity and Parental Rights' (2015), Chapter 8, 'Shared parental leave and pay'.)

8.11 There are also two automatically unfair redundancy provisions contained in the Trade Union and Labour Relations (Consolidation) Act 1992 (TULR(C)A). These apply where the employee was selected for redundancy for a reason (or principal reason) relating to:

- his or her membership or non-membership of a trade union, or to his or her participation in trade union activities or use of trade union services – S.153 TULR(C)A, or

- trade union recognition or derecognition – para 162, Sch A1 TULR(C)A.

And finally, Reg 7(1) of the Transfer of Undertakings (Protection of Employment) Regulations 2006 SI 2006/246 (TUPE) provides that a dismissal (including a redundancy dismissal) will be automatically unfair where the sole or principal reason for the dismissal is the transfer itself.

8.12 **Qualifying periods.** Note that there is no qualifying period for any of the above claims of automatically unfair selection for redundancy, with the exception of claims under Reg 7(1) TUPE, which requires that an employee

228

have two years' continuous service at the date of dismissal (one year in the case of employees whose employment commenced before 6 April 2012).

Exceptions. The automatically unfair reasons for selection for redundancy listed above are virtually identical to the automatically unfair reasons for dismissal (for which see IDS Employment Law Handbook, 'Unfair Dismissal' (2015), Chapter 9, 'Automatically unfair dismissals', in the Appendix, 'List of automatically unfair reasons for dismissal'). There are two possible exceptions to this.   **8.13**

First, S.12 of the Employment Relations Act 1999 makes it automatically unfair to dismiss for a reason related to the statutory right to be accompanied at disciplinary or grievance hearings. However, it makes no provision for a selection for redundancy to be automatically unfair on this basis.

Secondly, dismissal because of a 'spent' conviction within the terms of the Rehabilitation of Offenders Act 1974 is likely to be automatically unfair, unless the employee falls into a statutorily excluded category – see S.4(3)(b) of that Act. The Act makes no provision for a selection for redundancy to be automatically unfair on this basis, although it is arguable that it would be, so long as the spent conviction plays a material part in the employee's eventual dismissal. See IDS Employment Law Handbook, 'Unfair Dismissal' (2015), Chapter 6, 'Conduct', in the section 'Criminal offences at work', under 'Previous convictions – spent convictions under the Rehabilitation of Offenders Act 1974'.   **8.14**

Same undertaking and similar position   **8.15**
The provisions of S.105 ERA set out above are concerned with selection from a group, as one of the conditions for demonstrating automatic unfair dismissal is that the redundancy circumstances 'applied equally to one or more other employees in the same undertaking who held positions similar to that held by the employee and who have not been dismissed' – S.105(1)(b). As the EAT pointed out in MacAskill v John G McGregor (Stornoway) Ltd EAT 705/79, the effect of the wording of S.105 is that it does not apply to an employee who holds a unique position within an undertaking – although the dismissal of such an employee on the ground of redundancy may still be unfair under S.98(4). Similar reasoning would apply to redundancy dismissals under Reg 20(2) MPL Regulations 1999; Reg 29(2) PAL Regulations 2002; Reg 34(2) APL Regulations 2010; Reg 43(2) SPL Regulations; and under the TULR(C)A, which use identical wording to that used in S.105 ERA.

This means that an employee who claims that his or her selection for redundancy was for an automatically unfair reason will have to point to another individual employed in a similar position within the same undertaking who was not dismissed – see S.105(1)(b) ERA; Reg 20(2)(b) MPL Regulations;

229

Reg 29(2)(b) PAL Regulations; Reg 34(2)(b) APL Regulations; Reg 43(2) SPL Regulations; and S.153(a) and para 162(a), Sch A1 TULR(C)A. In practice, the two issues of 'similar position' and 'same undertaking' are often blurred by tribunals, which simply refer to the pool of employees (holding similar positions in the same undertaking) from which the selection for redundancy was made.

8.16 **Employed in same undertaking.** The question of whether an individual is employed in the same undertaking as others arises where an employer runs a number of plants or sites. The ERA does not define 'undertaking', which is a question of fact for the tribunal and may be overturned by the EAT only on the ground of perversity.

Where 'undertaking' is defined by agreement, this will generally be accepted. Where there is no agreement, tribunals have tended to define 'undertaking' fairly widely, as comparisons will in any case be limited to those holding 'similar positions' within that undertaking. Factors such as location, flexibility of labour and the type of skill used have all been held to be relevant. Furthermore, a range of employer activities may be covered if some degree of central direction exists. In Kapur v Shields 1976 ICR 26, QBD, Mr Justice Phillips said, in a different context, that 'some evidence of organisational unity, e.g. common accounting, management, purchasing arrangements, insurance, and so on' would suggest the existence of an undertaking. And in Oxley and ors v Tarmac Roadstone Holdings Ltd 1975 IRLR 100, ET, the fact that two plants shared a works manager was seen as important by the tribunal. Common management at some higher level was inevitable among plants owned by a single organisation. But at this low level, and coupled with a common bonus scheme, labour flexibility and similar work at both plants, it was seen as indicating a single undertaking.

8.17 **Employees holding similar positions.** 'Position' is defined in S.235(1) ERA by reference to an employee's status, the nature of the work he or she does, and his or her terms and conditions of employment. The decisions do not show any marked degree of consistency in determining whether employees hold similar positions and the question tribunals tend to ask themselves is the general one of whether a claimant was unfairly selected from a pool of employees, the pool sometimes being chosen without specific reference to either the undertaking concerned or the position of other employees. In Powers and anor v A Clarke and Co (Smethwick) Ltd 1981 IRLR 483, EAT, for example, Class 1 drivers, who could drive articulated lorries as well as four-wheel vehicles, were, by reason of their skill, in a different 'position' from Class 3 drivers, who could drive only four-wheelers.

The position of employees is a question of fact and, as such, is for the tribunal to decide. The EAT can overturn a finding of fact on the basis that it is perverse

– that no reasonable tribunal could have reached it on the evidence available – but it is usually reluctant to interfere in this way. In Copeman and Sons Ltd v Harris EAT 792/86 a tribunal held that the selection of a 'picker' from only one department when there were pickers doing virtually identical jobs in another department who had less service than the employee dismissed was an unfair restriction of the pool. The employment tribunal's decision was overturned by the EAT on a different point, but it refused to interfere with the tribunal's finding that the restriction of the pool to one department was unfair.

There are, however, a number of cases where the EAT has expressly disagreed   **8.18**
with tribunals on the question of 'position'. In Wellworthy Ltd v Singh and ors EAT 79/88, for example, the EAT overruled an employment tribunal's decision that the restriction of the pool for redundancy selection to the department within which the redundancy situation arose was unfair. The tribunal had said that this restriction unfairly disadvantaged one group of employees, but the EAT pointed out that any criteria upon which a selection was based would disadvantage some employees.

The label attached to a particular job is not conclusive when it comes to assessing the employee's position. Similar job titles may conceal real differences between the status of employees or the nature of the work they do. In Twidale v The Thomas Hill Engineering Co (Hull) Ltd ET Case No.21874/86, for example, an employee solely concerned with sales was termed a 'draughtsman' in common with those who were draughtsmen in the ordinary sense. He was found not to occupy the same position as the rest. The same tribunal also found that an employee treated by the company as being in a different position from the others was in reality in the same position as them.

Note that the Court of Appeal has stated that, when comparing the   **8.19**
position of employees, regard should only be had to the relative positions of the redundant employees and that any protected activities should be disregarded, even if the employee concerned had a contractual right to undertake such activities – O Dea v ISC Chemicals Ltd t/a Rhône-Poulenc Chemicals 1996 ICR 222, CA. This case, which concerned a trade union representative selected for redundancy, is discussed under 'Selection for trade union reasons' below.

Selection for reason relating to jury service   **8.20**
Section 105(2A) ERA provides that the selection of an employee for redundancy will be automatically unfair if the reason or principal reason for the selection was one of the following reasons set out in S.98B(1):

• he or she has been summoned to attend for jury service under the Juries Act 1974, Part I of the Coroners and Justice Act 2009, the Court of Session Act 1988 or the Criminal Procedure (Scotland) Act 1995, or

231

- he or she has been absent from work because he or she attended court in pursuance of being so summoned.

However, S.98B(1) will not protect the employee if the employer can show that:

- the circumstances were such that the employee's absence on jury service was likely to cause substantial injury to the employer's undertaking

- the employer brought those circumstances to the attention of the employee

- the employee refused or failed to apply to the appropriate officer to be excused from attending court or for the obligation to attend to be deferred, and

- the employee's refusal or failure was not reasonable – S.98B(2).

The 'appropriate officer' is defined in S.98B(3), but is usually also identified in the letter accompanying the summons for jury service.

8.21 Selection for health and safety reasons

Section 105(3) ERA provides that the selection of an employee for redundancy will be automatically unfair if the reason or principal reason for the selection was one of the following reasons set out in S.100(1):

- that the employee carried out, or proposed to carry out, activities in connection with preventing or reducing risks to health and safety at work, having been designated by the employer to do so – S.100(1)(a)

- that the employee performed, or proposed to perform, the functions of a health and safety representative, or member of a safety committee, either in accordance with arrangements established by statute or after being recognised as such by the employer – S.100(1)(b)

- that the employee took part, or proposed to take part, in consultations with the employer in accordance with the Health and Safety (Consultation with Employees) Regulations 1996 SI 1996/1513, or in an election of employee safety representatives in accordance with those Regulations, whether as a candidate or otherwise – S.100(1)(ba)

- that the employee brought to the employer's attention, by reasonable means, circumstances connected with his or her work which he or she reasonably believed were harmful or potentially harmful to health and safety. (This only applies where there is either no health and safety representative or committee, or it was not reasonably practicable for the employee to raise the matter by those means) – S.100(1)(c)

- that the employee left, proposed to leave, or (while the danger persisted) refused to return to, his or her place of work or any part of the place of

232 ——

work in circumstances of danger which he or she reasonably believed to be serious and imminent and which he or she could not reasonably be expected to avert – S.100(1)(d)

* that the employee took, or proposed to take, appropriate steps to protect him or herself or other persons from danger which he or she reasonably believed to be serious and imminent – S.100(1)(e). (The question of whether the steps an employee has taken, or proposed to take, were appropriate is to be judged by reference to all the circumstances, including, in particular, his or her knowledge and the facilities and advice available to him or her at the time – S.100(2). If the employer shows that it was, or would have been, so negligent for the employee to take the steps that he or she took, or proposed to take, that a reasonable employer might have dismissed him or her for taking those steps, or proposing to take them, then the dismissal will not be regarded as unfair – S.100(3)).

Note that the statutory maximum compensatory award (currently £78,962 or one year's salary, if lower) does not apply to a claim brought under S.105(3) – S.124(1A). Furthermore, if an employee is selected for redundancy for one of the first two reasons above, a minimum basic award of, currently, £5,853 applies – S.120(1).

In Smiths Industries Aerospace and Defence Systems v Rawlings 1996 IRLR 656, EAT, a health and safety representative was selected for redundancy on the basis of a points system relating to performance at work. He argued that his dismissal was connected with his health and safety activities and was accordingly automatically unfair under S.105. An employment tribunal rejected the claim, holding that the employer's assessments had been carried out in good faith and that the employee's health and safety activities had not contributed in any material way to his selection for redundancy. The EAT upheld the decision. There was no evidence to suggest that the employee's selection was related to his activities as a health and safety representative. In particular, there was nothing to suggest that his absence from ordinary work duties in order to deal with health and safety matters or his insistence on compliance with health and safety requirements had caused the person carrying out the selection exercise to be biased against him.

8.22

The tribunal in Rawlings had, however, found that – although not automatically unfairly dismissed under S.105 – the employee was unfairly dismissed for redundancy under S.98(4) because, in carrying out the selection exercise, the employer had disregarded the employee's performance of his health and safety duties that took up one third of his working time. On appeal, the EAT overturned this decision, stating that 'the protection against dismissal in a redundancy exercise, afforded to health and safety representatives, is neutral. They must not be disadvantaged, for example… [by] (negative discrimination). Equally, they are not entitled to be advantaged over their fellow employees in

233

the selection pool (positive discrimination).' This approach was subsequently followed by the EAT in Shipham and Co Ltd v Skinner EAT 840/00 – a case concerning an employee who had been designated by his employer as a health and safety adviser. There, the EAT held that an employment tribunal had erred in considering that the employer ought to have taken into account the employee's health and safety duties as part of the redundancy selection exercise. The EAT agreed with the decision in Rawlings that protection under S.105 is neutral, and noted that this principle applied equally to persons who come within any of the subsections of S.100(1), i.e. a designated health and safety adviser under S.100(1)(a) should not be afforded greater protection than a health and safety representative under S.100(1)(b).

8.23 In the following cases, tribunals found that the claimants had been selected for redundancy for health and safety reasons:

- **Irish v Commercial Vehicle Auctions Ltd** ET Case No.2801157/08: I was one of three yard operatives. His role was to move vehicles and plant items to different parts of the site, and occasionally to collect customers' vehicles from their homes and deliver them to the site. In autumn 2007 CVA Ltd began to use an overflow site to store vehicles, and this could only be reached from the main site by using a public road. I became concerned that some of the vehicles he had to drive on the public road were not roadworthy. He raised his concerns with his employer. In February 2008, without any prior warning, I was dismissed as redundant. An employment tribunal found that on the evidence the principal reason for I's dismissal was that he had made a protected disclosure, which tended to show that the health and safety of the public was endangered. (Note that this case was also brought under S.105(6A) – see 'Protected disclosures' below)

- **Flynn v Bunzl Vending Services Ltd** ET Case No.3301922/09: F worked for BVS Ltd cleaning, servicing and filling vending machines. She submitted a grievance, saying that she was required to lift large containers filled with milk, weighing around 14 kilos, to about chest height. BVS Ltd did not respond to her grievance and shortly afterwards she was selected for redundancy. An employment tribunal found that there was a strong connection between F lodging her grievance concerning the health and safety issue and her selection for redundancy, both because of the timescale and because BVS Ltd did not reply to her grievance even though she was raising an urgent health and safety issue.

8.24 Selection for refusing to work on Sundays

The ERA contains the provisions relating to Sunday trading that were previously contained in the Sunday Trading Act 1994 and the Betting, Gaming and Lotteries Act 1963 (as amended by Schedule 8 to the Deregulation and Contracting Out Act 1994). The purpose of these provisions is to safeguard the employment rights of shop and betting workers who object to working on Sunday. They also define the impact of such objections on the employment relationship and on unfair dismissal rights. Briefly, if a worker can bring him or herself within the definition of a 'protected' shop worker or betting worker or an 'opted-out' shop worker or betting worker, he or she will have the right to refuse to do Sunday work. In these circumstances, any agreement or provision of an employment contract will be unenforceable in so far as it requires the employee to work on a Sunday, and any dismissal for a refusal or threatened refusal to do Sunday work is deemed to be automatically unfair.

Section 105(4) ERA, read in conjunction with S.101, provides that it is automatically unfair to select an employee for redundancy if the principal reason for the selection is that:

- the employee was a protected shop worker or an opted-out shop worker, or a protected betting worker or an opted-out betting worker, and the sole or principal reason for the employee's selection for dismissal was that he or she refused (or proposed to refuse) to do shop work, or betting work, on Sunday or on a particular Sunday – S.101(1), or

- the employee was a shop worker or a betting worker and the sole or principal reason for which the employee was selected for dismissal was that he or she gave (or proposed to give) an opting-out notice to the employer – S.101(3).

8.25 The definitions of 'protected' shop and betting workers and 'opted-out' shop and betting workers are central to the operation of this provision and are examined in detail below. Essentially, a protected worker is a worker who was already employed as a shop or betting worker (but not solely working on Sundays) when the Sunday trading provisions came into force, or a worker who cannot be contractually required to work on Sundays. An opted-out worker is a worker who has given his or her employer a written notice opting out of Sunday work.

Note that, in addition to the provisions in the ERA which relate to Sunday working, an employee selected for redundancy on the basis that he or she refused to work on Sundays could have a claim under the religion or belief provisions in the Equality Act 2010 – see IDS Employment Law Handbook, 'Discrimination at Work' (2012), Chapter 11, 'Religion or belief'.

8.26 **'Protected worker'.** Under S.36 ERA an employee will be a protected shop or betting worker if he or she meets one of two sets of criteria. The first set is as follows:

- the worker must have been in employment as a shop/betting worker on the day before the 'relevant commencement date' – S.36(2)(a). The relevant commencement date is 26 August 1994 for shop workers and 3 January 1995 for betting workers – the respective dates on which the Sunday Trading

235

Act 1994 and Schedule 8 to the Deregulation and Contracting Out Act 1994 came into force

- on that day, he or she must not have been employed to work only on Sunday – S.36(2)(a)

- the worker must have been continuously employed during the period beginning with the day before the relevant commencement date and ending with the 'appropriate date' – S.36(2)(b). (The 'appropriate date' means the effective date of termination for the purposes of S.101 – S.101(4). For discussion of the 'effective date of termination', see IDS Employment Law Handbook, 'Contracts of Employment' (2014), Chapter 14, 'Date of termination'), and

- he or she must have been a shop/betting worker throughout that period of continuous employment, or throughout every part of it during which the worker's relations with his or her employer were governed by a contract of employment – S.36(2)(c).

Note that S.36(4) deems an employee to be a protected worker for the purposes of S.36(2)(a), despite the fact that the employment relationship had ceased by the day before the relevant commencement date, if that employee's continuity of employment was preserved at the commencement date by virtue of S.212(3) or under S.219 (absence by reason of sickness, temporary cessation of work or arrangement or custom, or absence pending reinstatement/re-engagement of a dismissed employee); and, when the employment relationship ceased, that employee was a shop worker or betting worker and was not employed to work only on Sunday.

8.27 Alternatively, a worker may be a protected worker if, under the terms of his or her contract, he or she is not and cannot be required to work on Sundays, and could not be required to do so even if Part IV of the ERA (which deals with Sunday working) were disregarded – S.36(3). This provision applies regardless of whether the employee was in employment at the relevant commencement date. An employer's right to require an employee to work on Sunday is clearly a question of construction of the relevant contract of employment.

'Shop worker' and 'shop work' are defined in S.232. A 'shop worker' means an employee who is or may be required under his or her contract of employment to do shop work – S.232(1). 'Shop work' is defined as work in or about a shop on a day on which the shop is open for the serving of customers – S.232(2). 'Shop' includes any premises where any retail trade or business is carried on – S.232(3). 'Retail trade or business' includes the business of a barber or hairdresser, the business of hiring goods other than for use in the course of a trade or business, and retail sales by auction, but does not include a catering business or the sale of programmes, catalogues, etc at theatres or other places of amusement – S.232(6). (See further IDS Employment Law

236

Handbook, 'Unfair Dismissal' (2015), Chapter 9, 'Automatically unfair dismissals', under 'Dismissal for refusing to work on Sunday'.)

8.28 'Betting worker' and 'betting work' are defined in S.233. A 'betting worker' is defined as an employee who is required, or may be required, to do betting work under his or her contract of employment – S.233(1). 'Betting work' is defined as work at a track for a bookmaker, being work which consists of or includes dealing with betting transactions, and work in a licensed betting office at a time when the office is used for betting transactions – S.233(2).

8.29 **'Opted-out worker'.** An opted-out shop worker/betting worker is an employee who, under his or her contract of employment, is or may be required to work on Sunday, but is not employed to work only on Sunday, and who has given his or her employer a signed and dated 'opting-out' notice stating that he or she objects to working on Sunday. To satisfy the statutory requirements, opted-out workers must have been in continuous employment as a shop or betting worker during the period beginning with the day on which the opting-out notice was given and ending with the 'appropriate date' (i.e. the effective date of termination of the contract – see 'Protected worker' above) – Ss.40 and 41(1) ERA. Opted-out workers do not obtain the protection afforded by the Act until the expiry of three months after the opting-out notice was served – S.41(3), although this may be reduced to one month where the employer has failed to provide an explanatory statement of the worker's rights regarding Sunday working – S.42.

8.30 **Loss of 'protected' or 'opted-out' status.** Under S.36(5) a protected shop worker or betting worker will lose that status if, on or after the commencement date, he or she gives the employer an 'opting-in notice' and, after giving that notice, makes an express agreement with the employer to do shop work or betting work on Sundays or on a particular Sunday. An 'opting-in notice' is a signed and dated notice in which a worker states that he or she wishes to work on Sunday or does not object to Sunday working – S.36(6).

Similarly, under S.41(2) an opted-out shop worker or betting worker loses that status if he or she gives the employer an opting-in notice after previously giving an opting-out notice, and then expressly agrees to do shop work or betting work on Sunday or a particular Sunday.

8.31 'Express agreement' is not defined in either case and would therefore seem to encompass verbal as well as written agreements. However, the opting-in notice must be in writing – S.36(6).

Working time cases

8.32 Section 105(4A) ERA, read in conjunction with S.101A, provides that it is automatically unfair to select an employee for redundancy on the ground that the employee:

237

- refused (or proposed to refuse) to comply with a requirement which the employer imposed (or proposed to impose) in contravention of the Working Time Regulations 1998 SI 1998/1833 – S.101A(1)(a)

- refused (or proposed to refuse) to forgo a right conferred by those Regulations – S.101A(1)(b)

- failed to sign a workforce agreement for the purposes of those Regulations, or to enter into, or agree to vary or extend, any other agreement with the employer that is provided for in those Regulations – S.101A(1)(c), or

- performed (or proposed to perform) any functions or activities as a workforce representative for the purposes of the Regulations or as a candidate in an election of workforce representatives – S.101A(1)(d).

Where the last of the above reasons applies, the minimum basic award of, currently, £5,853 applies – S.120(1).

8.33 Full details of the 1998 Regulations can be found in IDS Employment Law Handbook, 'Working Time' (2013). The operation of S.101A is discussed in greater detail in Chapter 7 of that Handbook, 'Enforcement and remedies', under 'Complaints to tribunals – automatically unfair dismissal'.

8.34 **Selection of occupational pension scheme trustees**
Section 105(5) ERA protects employees who act as trustees of relevant occupational pension schemes which relate to their employment. S.105(5), read in conjunction with S.102, provides that it is automatically unfair to select an employee for redundancy on the ground that he or she performed (or proposed to perform) any functions as such a trustee. Employees who are directors of a company that is a trustee are also protected – S.102(1A).

A 'relevant occupational pension scheme' means an occupational pension scheme (as defined in S.1 of the Pension Schemes Act 1993) established under a trust – S.102(2).

Where an employee brings a successful claim under S.105(5) the minimum basic award of, currently, £5,853 applies – S.120(1).

8.35 **Selection of employee representatives**
A number of legislative provisions require the election of employee representatives. While in many cases these will be pre-existing trade union representatives, given that the majority of the UK workforce is non-unionised, there are a large number of non-union representatives. Such employees enjoy an extensive level of protection from detriment or dismissal as a result of exercising their duties as representatives, and this is reflected in the protections against selection for redundancy found in S.105 ERA.

238

The collective redundancy consultation procedures in the TULR(C)A (see Chapter 12, 'Collective redundancies') and the Transfer of Undertakings (Protection of Employment) Regulations 2006 SI 2006/246 both provide for consultation with employee representatives, and S.105(6) ERA, read in conjunction with S.103, provides that it is automatically unfair to select an employee for redundancy if the principal reason for selection is that the employee:

- being an employee representative for the purposes of collective consultation on redundancy or transfer of undertakings, or a candidate in an election for such representatives, performed or proposed to perform any functions or activities as such an employee representative or candidate – S.103(1), or

- 'took part in an election of employee representatives'. This provision would seem to extend protection to employees selected for redundancy on the grounds that they voted in or organised an election of employee representatives – S.103(2).

Note that where an employee succeeds under S.105(6), the minimum basic award of, currently, £5,853 applies – S.120(1).

Protected disclosures   8.36

Section 105(6A) ERA, read in conjunction with S.103A, provides that it is automatically unfair to select an employee for redundancy on the ground that he or she has made a 'protected disclosure' within the meaning of Part IVA of the ERA.

Part IVA (Ss.43A–43L) was inserted into the ERA by the Public Interest Disclosure Act 1998 (PIDA). It provides protection for workers who disclose information about their employers on matters such as the commission of a criminal offence, failure to comply with a legal obligation, a miscarriage of justice, danger to health and safety, and damage to the environment. The worker making the disclosure must have reasonable grounds for his or her belief as well as a reasonable belief that the disclosure is in the public interest. For further details of these provisions, see IDS Employment Law Handbook, 'Whistleblowing at Work' (2013).

An example of selection for redundancy under this head: 8.37

- **Pattenden and anor v Medway Council** ET Case No.1101213/08: the claimants, P and B, made protected disclosures in relation to a company which maintained the Council's housing stock. On 9 July 2007 the Council published restructuring proposals, and at about the same time the claimants' manager said that whistleblowers in the department might be subject to legal and disciplinary action. P and B were made redundant as a result of the restructuring on 15 January 2008. An employment tribunal upheld P's claim of

239

automatically unfair dismissal. Although there was a genuine reorganisation, the people who had most significantly influenced it were those against whom the protected disclosures were made, and the evidence did not support the decision to select P for redundancy. The Council failed to prove that he was not made redundant because he had made protected disclosures. However, B had been made redundant for 'independent sound reasons'.

Note that certain health and safety cases may give rise to claims both under this head and under S.100(1)(c) – see, for example, Irish v Commercial Vehicle Auctions Ltd ET Case No.2801157/08 (discussed under 'Selection for health and safety reasons' above).

8.38 While the provisions introduced by the PIDA are aimed at encouraging 'whistleblowing', the broad term 'failure to comply with a legal obligation' is not qualified. It might therefore be arguable that an employee who raises a complaint that his or her employer is not complying with its obligations under the contract of employment, and who is later selected for redundancy as a result of having made such a complaint, would be automatically unfairly dismissed – see Parkins v Sodexho Ltd 2002 IRLR 109, EAT; Cavendish Munro Professional Risks Management Ltd v Geduld 2010 ICR 325, EAT. These cases have not been overruled, but the definition of a 'qualifying disclosure' in S.43B ERA was amended by the Enterprise and Regulatory Reform Act 2013 to include a requirement that the employee reasonably believe the disclosure to be in the public interest – an amendment that was intended to reverse or at least restrict the scope of this strand of case law. However, the first cases to consider this requirement have set the threshold for establishing public interest relatively low – see, for example, Chesterton Global Ltd (t/a Chestertons) and anor v Nurmohamed 2015 ICR 920, EAT. This issue is discussed further in IDS Employment Law Handbook, 'Whistleblowing at Work' (2013), Chapter 3, 'Qualifying disclosures', in the section 'What amounts to a qualifying disclosure?', under 'Public interest – the public interest and private employment disputes'.

Note that the statutory maximum compensatory award, currently £78,962 or a year's salary, whichever is lower, does not apply to dismissals under S.105(6A) – S.124(1A).

8.39 **Selection for asserting a statutory right**

Section 105(7) ERA provides that it is automatically unfair to select an employee for redundancy on one of the grounds specified in S.104(1). Those grounds are that the employee:

- brought proceedings against the employer to enforce a relevant statutory right, or

- alleged that the employer had infringed a relevant statutory right.

240

It is sufficient that the employee, without specifying the right, made it reasonably clear to the employer what the right claimed to have been infringed was – S.104(3).

It is specifically stated that it is immaterial whether or not the employee actually has **8.40** the right and whether or not it has been infringed – but the employee's complaint must have been made in good faith – S.104(2). For example, in Philip Hodges and Co v Crush EAT 1061/95 C reluctantly agreed to a pay cut as an alternative to dismissal when her employer found her work performance disappointing. C consulted a legally qualified friend and a law centre, and the latter wrote to the employer claiming that her reduction in pay was an unlawful deduction from her wages, contrary to what is now S.13 ERA. C was dismissed when she told her employer about the advice she had received. An employment tribunal upheld her claim that she had been dismissed for asserting a statutory right. The EAT subsequently upheld this finding. C had made her claim in good faith and it was irrelevant that her rights under S.13 had not in fact been infringed.

Relevant statutory rights. Section 104 does not apply to all statutory rights **8.41** but only to the 'relevant' rights referred to in S.104(4). The rights covered are as follows:

- the right to receive a written statement of employment particulars, a statement of changes to particulars or an itemised pay statement – Ss.1, 4 and 8 ERA

- protection of wages rights – Ss.13, 15, 18 and 21 ERA

- the right to a guarantee payment – S.28 ERA

- protection from detriment rights (jury service; health and safety; Sunday working; working time; trustees of occupational pension schemes; employee representatives; paid time off for study or training; protected disclosures; maternity, paternity, adoption, shared parental leave and unpaid parental leave; time off for dependants; time off for adoption appointments or ante-natal appointments; tax credits; flexible working; study and training; and refusing an offer to become an employee shareholder) – Ss.43M–47G ERA

- the right to time off for public duties – S.50 ERA

- the right of redundant employees to paid time off to look for work or arrange training – Ss.52 and 53 ERA

- the right to paid time off for ante-natal care – Ss.55 and 56 ERA

- the right to time off to accompany a woman to ante-natal appointments – S.57ZE ERA

- the right to paid or unpaid time off to attend adoption appointments – Ss.57ZJ, 57ZK, 57ZL ERA

241

- the right to time off for dependants – S.57A ERA

- the right of pension scheme trustees to paid time off – Ss.58 and 59 ERA

- the right of employee representatives to paid time off – Ss.61 and 62 ERA

- the right to paid time off for a young person for study or training – Ss.63A and 63B ERA

- the right to make a request in relation to study and training, and have it properly considered by the employer – Ss.63D and 63F ERA

- the right to remuneration on suspension on medical grounds – S.64 ERA

- the right to alternative work and remuneration on maternity suspension – Ss.67 and 68 ERA

- the right to unpaid parental leave – S.76 ERA

- the right to make a request for flexible working and to have it properly considered – Ss.80F and 80G ERA

- the right to minimum notice – S.86 ERA

- the right to receive a written statement of reasons for dismissal – S.92 ERA

- the right not to be unfairly dismissed – S.94 ERA

- the right to a redundancy payment – S.135 ERA

- the right not to suffer unauthorised deductions from wages in respect of union subscriptions – S.68 TULR(C)A

- the right not to suffer unauthorised deductions from wages in respect of a union political fund – S.86 TULR(C)A

- the right not to be offered an inducement in relation to union membership or activities – S.145A TULR(C)A

- the right not to be offered an inducement in relation to collective bargaining – S.145B TULR(C)A

- the right not to be subjected to a detriment on grounds related to union membership or activities – S.146 TULR(C)A

- the right of union officials to paid time off for union duties – Ss.168 and 169 TULR(C)A

- the right of union learning representatives to paid time off for learning and training activities – Ss.168A and 169 TULR(C)A

- the right of union members to time off for union activities – S.170 TULR(C)A

- the rights conferred by the Working Time Regulations 1998 SI 1998/1833; the Merchant Shipping (Hours of Work) Regulations 2002 SI 2002/2125; the

Merchant Shipping (Working Time: Inland Waterways) Regulations 2003 SI 2003/3049; the Fishing Vessels (Working Time: Sea-fishermen) Regulations 2004 SI 2004/1713 or the Cross-border Railway Services (Working Time) Regulations 2008 SI 2008/1660, and

- the rights conferred by the Transfer of Undertakings (Protection of Employment) Regulations 2006 SI 2006/246.

Dismissal for asserting a statutory right is discussed further in IDS Employment Law Handbook, 'Unfair Dismissal' (2015), Chapter 11, 'Dismissal for asserting a statutory right'.

National minimum wage

8.42

Section 105(7A) ERA, read in conjunction with S.104A, provides that it is automatically unfair to select an employee for redundancy on the ground that:

- any action was taken, or was proposed to be taken, by or on behalf of the employee with a view to enforcing, or otherwise securing the benefit of, a right to the national minimum wage (NMW) or other rights under the National Minimum Wage Act 1998

- the employer was prosecuted for an offence under the 1998 Act as a result of action taken by or on behalf of the employee to enforce a right under that Act, or

- the employee qualifies, or will or might qualify, for the NMW or a particular rate of the NMW.

For full details on the National Minimum Wage Act 1998, see IDS Employment Law Handbook, 'Wages' (2016), Chapter 5, 'National minimum wage'.

Tax Credits Act 2002

8.43

Working tax credits are designed to top up the earnings of working people (employed and self-employed) on low incomes, including those who do not have children. They are made up of a number of elements depending on the circumstances of the worker concerned, including elements to support the costs of approved or registered childcare and to help working households in which someone has a disability. Payment of tax credits is made via the employer through normal pay except in respect of the childcare element, which is paid directly to the main carer.

Section 105(7B) ERA, read in conjunction with S.104B, provides that it is automatically unfair to select an employee for redundancy on the ground that:

- any action was taken, or was proposed to be taken, by or on behalf of the employee with a view to enforcing, or otherwise securing the benefit of, a right conferred on the employee by regulations made under S.25 of the Tax Credits Act 2002

- a penalty was imposed on the employer, or proceedings were brought against it, under the Act as a result of action taken by or on behalf of the employee for the purpose of enforcing, or otherwise securing the benefit of, such a right, or

- the employee is entitled, or will or may be entitled, to working tax credit.

8.44 It is immaterial whether or not the employee has the right or whether or not it has been infringed, but the employee's claim to the right, and (if applicable) the claim that the right has been infringed, must be made in good faith – S.104B(2).

Note that tax credits are gradually being phased out by the Government and replaced with Universal Credit. This transition is currently expected to be completed between 2018 and 2021. At the time of going to press, no legislation has been proposed to confer on Universal Credit recipients or claimants protection equivalent to that provided under S.104B ERA in respect of tax credits.

8.45 Flexible working

Under S.105(7BA) ERA, the selection of an employee for redundancy will be automatically unfair if the sole or principal reason was one of those specified in S.104C relating to the employee's statutory right to request flexible working. These are that the employee:

- made (or proposed to make) an application to work flexibly under S.80F

- brought proceedings against the employer under S.80H (alleging that the employer had failed to deal with his or her request in a reasonable manner or within the statutory time limit, that a refusal of his or her request was based on incorrect facts, or that the employer wrongly treated his or her application as having been withdrawn), or

- alleged the existence of any circumstance which would constitute a ground for bringing such proceedings.

The statutory right to request flexible working is set out in Ss.80F–80I ERA, read with the Flexible Working Regulations 2014 SI 2014/1398. For a full discussion of these provisions, see IDS Employment Law Handbook, 'Atypical and Flexible Working' (2014), Chapter 4, 'Flexible working'.

8.46 Study and training

An employee of a company employing at least 250 employees who has completed 26 weeks' continuous service has a right to request to undertake study and training. An employee is not entitled to have his or her request granted, but merely to have it considered seriously and for rejections to be made on legitimate grounds. The rules governing the operation of this right are found in Ss.63D–63K ERA; the Employee

Study and Training (Eligibility, Complaints and Remedies) Regulations 2010 SI 2010/156; the Employee Study and Training (Qualifying Period of Employment) Regulations 2010 SI 2010/800; and the Employee Study and Training (Procedural Requirements) Regulations 2010 SI 2010/155. S.104E ERA sets out the circumstances in which dismissal in relation to a request to undertake study and training will be automatically unfair and S.105(7BB) states that it will be automatically unfair to select an employee for redundancy for a reason specified in S.104E: namely, that the employee made (or proposed to make) an application for study and training; exercised or proposed to exercise a right under S.63F; brought proceedings under S.63I; or alleged the existence of any circumstances which would constitute a ground for bringing such proceedings.

For more information on how the right to request study or training operates in practice, see IDS Employment Law Handbook, 'Unfair Dismissal' (2015), Chapter 9, 'Automatically unfair dismissals', under 'Dismissal relating to study and training'.

Protected industrial action cases

8.47

Under S.238A TULR(C)A, a dismissal is automatically unfair if the principal reason for the dismissal is that the employee took official industrial action and the dismissal occurred:

- within the period of 21 weeks beginning with the day on which the employee started to take industrial action

- after the end of the 21-week period, but the employee had ceased to take part in the industrial action before the end of that period, or

- after the end of the 12-week period, but the employer had not taken such procedural steps as would have been reasonable for the purposes of resolving the dispute – S.238A(2).

Note that the 12-week period referred to above is extended if at any time during the 12 weeks the employee is locked out by the employer. (For an explanation of lock-outs, see IDS Employment Law Handbook, 'Industrial Action' (2010), Chapter 8, 'Industrial action dismissals', under 'Dismissal during "non-protected" official action – strikes, lock-outs and other industrial action'.)

Section 105(7C) ERA provides that it is also automatically unfair to select an **8.48** employee for redundancy in any of the above circumstances.

Full details of the protected industrial action provisions are contained in IDS Employment Law Handbook, 'Industrial Action' (2010), Chapter 8, 'Industrial action dismissals'.

245

8.49 ## Part-time and fixed-term work

Both the Part-time Workers (Prevention of Less Favourable Treatment) Regulations 2000 SI 2000/1551 ('the PTW Regulations') and the Fixed-term Employees (Prevention of Less Favourable Treatment) Regulations 2002 SI 2002/2034 ('the FTE Regulations') contain provisions protecting employees from being dismissed for exercising rights under the Regulations.

Sections 105(7E) and (7F) ERA state that an employee is automatically unfairly dismissed for redundancy where the reason for redundancy selection was one of the automatically unfair reasons for dismissal provided for in Reg 7 PTW Regulations or Reg 6 FTE Regulations. The reasons in the two sets of Regulations are similar but not identical. In both sets the following reasons for dismissal are automatically unfair:

- the employee brought proceedings against the employer under the Regulations, or gave evidence or information in connection with such proceedings brought by any worker

- the employee requested a written statement of the reasons for his or her less favourable treatment

- the employee has otherwise done anything under the Regulations in relation to the employer or any other person

- the employee alleged that the employer had infringed his or her rights under the Regulations. It does not matter if the allegation is false, provided it is made in good faith

- the employee had refused (or proposed to refuse) to forgo any of his or her rights under the Regulations, or

- the employer believes or suspects that the employee has done or intends to do any of these things.

8.50 In addition, the FTE Regulations provide that it will be automatically unfair to dismiss an employee where:

- he or she sought a written statement of the reasons for variation of a fixed-term contract

- he or she refused to sign a workforce agreement for the purposes of the FTE Regulations

- he or she performed or proposed to perform any functions or activities as a workforce representative or candidate for the FTE Regulations, or

- the employer believes or suspects that the employee has done or intends to do any of these things.

246

Note that while the PTW Regulations generally protect all workers, not just employees, it is only employees who are protected from unfair dismissal and unfair redundancy selection under Reg 7(1). Other workers must rely on the right not to be subjected to a detriment for one of the reasons listed above, contained in Reg 7(2).

Pension consultation dismissals 8.51

The Occupational and Personal Pension Schemes (Consultation by Employers and Miscellaneous Amendment) Regulations 2006 SI 2006/349 require employers to engage in an information and consultation process with employee representatives when seeking to make changes to occupational or personal pension schemes. S.105(7I) ERA provides that the selection of an employee for redundancy will be automatically unfair if the reason (or, if more than one, the principal reason) for his or her selection was one specified in para 5(3) or (5) of the Schedule to the 2006 Regulations. These reasons are that the employee:

* performed or proposed to perform the functions of a representative or a candidate for election as a representative under the Regulations

* exercised, proposed to exercise, or made a request to exercise, the right to paid time off under paras 2 or 3 of the Schedule, or a person acting on the employee's behalf made or proposed to make such a request

* made, or proposed to make, a complaint to an employment tribunal to enforce a right or secure an entitlement under the Regulations. (It is immaterial whether the employee actually had the right or entitlement, or whether it was infringed, provided the claim to the right, and (if applicable) the claim that it had been infringed was made in good faith – para 5(6))

* complained, or proposed to complain, to the Pensions Regulator over failures to comply with requirements of the Regulations

* stood as a candidate in an election for employee representatives

* attempted to influence by lawful means the voting in elections for representatives

* voted in such an election, or

* expressed doubts about whether such an election was properly conducted.

In respect of the last four of these reasons, para 5(5)(h) specifies that it will also be automatically unfair to select an employee for redundancy for proposing to do, failing to do, or proposing to decline any of these things. 8.52

Trade union blacklists 8.53

The Employment Relations Act 1999 (Blacklists) Regulations 2010 SI 2010/493 came into force on 2 March 2010 and introduced a further ground of automatically unfair dismissal, the detail of which is found in S.104F ERA. These Regulations are aimed at preventing the use of trade union 'blacklists' and to this end Reg 3 prohibits the compilation, use, selling or supply of a list which:

- contains details of persons who are or have been members of trade unions or persons who are taking part or have taken part in the activities of trade unions, and

- is compiled with a view to being used by employers or employment agencies for the purposes of discrimination in relation to recruitment or in relation to the treatment of workers.

Discrimination in this context does not refer to a breach of the Equality Act 2010, but to less favourable treatment on the grounds of trade union membership or trade union activities – Reg 3(3).

8.54 Regulation 4 sets out a number of exceptions to the general prohibition: namely, where the person supplying a list does not and could not be expected to know that it is a prohibited list; where the list is compiled, used or supplied in order to expose a breach or possible breach of Reg 3; where the list is compiled, used, sold or supplied to recruit to a post that reasonably requires either trade union membership or knowledge of trade union matters; where the action relating to the list is required by law; or where the list is used or supplied in connection with legal proceedings.

Section 105(7M) ERA, read in conjunction with S.104F, provides that it is automatically unfair to select an employee for redundancy where the selection relates to a prohibited list and either:

- the employer contravenes Reg 3 in relation to that list, or

- the employer relies on information supplied by a person who contravenes Reg 3 in relation to that list, and knows or ought reasonably to know that the information relied on is supplied in contravention of Reg 3.

8.55 For more information on the blacklisting provisions, see IDS Employment Law Handbook, 'Trade Unions' (2013), Chapter 12, 'Unfair dismissal', under 'Trade union blacklists'.

8.56 Agency workers

The Agency Workers Regulations 2010 SI 2010/93 (AWR), which came into force on 1 October 2011, give temporary agency workers the right, after 12 weeks on the same assignment, to equal treatment in comparison with permanent workers as regards basic working conditions. S.105(7N) ERA provides that the selection of an employee for redundancy will be automatically unfair if the reason (or, if more than one, the principal reason) for the selection was one specified in Reg 17(3) AWR.

248

The reasons specified in Reg 17(3)(a) are that the agency worker:

- brought proceedings under the Regulations

- gave evidence or information in connection with such proceedings brought by any agency worker

- made a request under Reg 16 for a written statement (relating to the agency worker's basic working and employment conditions)

- otherwise did anything under the Regulations in relation to a temporary work agency, hirer, or any other person

- allcgcd that a temporary work agency or hirer has breached the Regulations (unless the allegation is both false and not made in good faith – Reg 17(4)), or

- refused (or proposed to refuse) to forgo a right conferred by the Regulations.

It will also be automatically unfair to select an agency worker for redundancy on the ground that the hirer or temporary work agency believes or suspects that the agency worker has done or intends to do any of the above – Reg 17(3)(b).

8.57

By their very nature the 2010 Regulations apply not just to agency workers who are employees but also to those who are workers. However, the right to claim automatically unfair dismissal under Reg 17(1) and the right to claim automatically unfair dismissal for being selected for redundancy under S.105(7N) ERA apply only to employees. Interestingly, unlike Reg 17(1), S.105(7N) does not actually specify that the *complainant* has to be an agency worker, leading to the possibility that an employee who is not an agency worker but stands up for the rights of an agency worker may claim automatic unfair dismissal if he or she is selected for redundancy on this basis, but not if he or she is simply dismissed (in which case he or she would have to establish that the employer's actions were unreasonable under S.98(4) in the usual way – see 'Unreasonable redundancy' below).

Collective labour laws

8.58

Recent years have seen the following legislation enacted to comply with European collective labour laws:

- the Transnational Information and Consultation of Employees Regulations 1999 SI 1999/3323

- the Information and Consultation of Employees Regulations 2004 SI 2004/3426

- the European Cooperative Society (Involvement of Employees) Regulations 2006 SI 2006/2059

249

- the Companies (Cross-Border Mergers) Regulations 2007 SI 2007/2974, and

- the European Public Limited-Liability Company (Employee Involvement) (Great Britain) Regulations 2009 SI 2009/2401 (which replaced relevant provisions of the European Public Limited-Liability Company Regulations 2004 SI 2004/2326).

Each of these sets of Regulations envisages the election of employee representatives to sit on consultative bodies. In addition, they all provide protection from dismissal, both for employees sitting on such bodies and for employees exercising rights under the Regulations.

8.59 The various subsections of S.105 ERA that relate to these Regulations operate to extend the protection against dismissal found within the Regulations themselves to protection from selection for redundancy. The circumstances under which the Regulations render a dismissal unfair include:

- that the employee performed or proposed to perform the functions of a representative

- that the employee or a person acting on his or her behalf made or proposed to make a request to exercise an entitlement conferred on the employee by the Regulations

- that the employee voted in a ballot for representatives

- that the employee brought tribunal proceedings, or complained to the Central Arbitration Council or the EAT, in relation to rights conferred by the Regulations

- that the employee stood in an election for representatives, and

- that the employee sought to influence, by lawful means, an election held under the Regulations.

8.60 ## Family-friendly cases

The law governing what are often referred to as 'family-friendly rights' includes substantial protection against dismissal for a reason related to an employee taking his or her statutory entitlement to maternity leave, paternity leave, adoption leave, shared parental leave, unpaid parental leave, or dependant care leave. The starting point is S.99 ERA, which provides that a dismissal will be automatically unfair if:

- the reason (or principal reason) for it is of a prescribed kind, or it takes place in prescribed circumstances, and

- the reason or circumstances relate to pregnancy, childbirth or maternity; ordinary, compulsory or additional maternity leave; ordinary or additional

250

adoption leave; unpaid parental leave; paternity leave; shared parental leave; time off for adoption or ante-natal appointments; or dependant care leave (and may also relate to redundancy or other factors – S.99(3)).

'Prescribed' means prescribed by regulations and the relevant regulations for redundancy selection purposes are Reg 20(2) and (3) of the Maternity and Parental Leave etc Regulations 1999 SI 1999/3312; Reg 29(2) and (3) of the Paternity and Adoption Leave Regulations 2002 SI 2002/2788; Reg 34(2) and (3) of the Additional Paternity Leave Regulations 2010 SI 2010/1055; and Reg 43(2) and (3) of the Shared Parental Leave Regulations 2014 SI 2014/3050. These provisions, which are all drafted in similar terms, effectively provide that it is automatically unfair to select an employee for redundancy for a reason connected with: **8.61**

- the pregnancy of the employee

- the fact that the employee has given birth to a child (and the dismissal ends her maternity leave period)

- a relevant requirement or recommendation which gives rise to a maternity suspension within the meaning of S.66(2) ERA

- the fact that she or he took or sought to take ordinary or additional maternity leave, ordinary or additional paternity leave, ordinary or additional adoption leave, shared parental leave, unpaid parental leave, or time off to care for a dependant under S.57A ERA

- the fact that he or she made use of the benefits of ordinary or additional maternity leave, additional paternity leave, or shared parental leave

- the fact that she or he failed to return after a period of ordinary or additional maternity leave, additional adoption leave or additional paternity leave where the employer did not notify her or him of the date on which the period in question would end and she or he reasonably believed that the period had not ended, or the employer gave her or him less than 28 days' notice of the date on which the period in question would end and it was not reasonably practicable for her or him to return on that date

- the fact that she or he considered undertaking, or refused to undertake, work on 'keep-in-touch' days during a period of maternity leave, adoption leave, additional paternity leave, or shared parental leave within the meaning of Reg 12A MPL Regulations, Reg 21A PAL Regulations, Reg 26 APL Regulations or Reg 37 SPL Regulations

- the fact that the employer believed that he or she was likely to take ordinary or additional adoption leave, additional paternity leave or shared parental leave

- the fact that he or she declined to sign a workforce agreement for the purposes of the MPL Regulations, or

- the fact that the employee, being a representative of members of the workforce for the purposes of a workforce agreement on unpaid parental leave, or a candidate in an election in which any person elected will, on being elected, become such a representative, performed (or proposed to perform) any functions or activities as such a representative or candidate.

(Note that, although the APL Regulations remain in force, the APL regime has been abolished for parents whose baby is expected on or after 5 April 2015, and has been replaced with shared parental leave. For details, see IDS Employment Law Handbook, 'Maternity and Parental Rights' (2015), Chapter 8, 'Shared parental leave and pay'.)

8.62 **Suitable alternative employment.** As is addressed in some detail in Chapter 3, 'Alternative job offers', under 'Offer during period of family leave', an employee who is made redundant while on maternity, adoption, additional paternity leave or shared parental leave is entitled to be offered suitable alternative employment in preference to other employees – Reg 10 MPL Regulations, Reg 23 PAL Regulations, Reg 28 APL Regulations, and Reg 39 SPL Regulations. These regulations count as prescribing regulations for the purposes of S.99 ERA, meaning that a failure on the part of the employer to comply with these provisions will lead to a finding of automatically unfair dismissal.

8.63 **Discrimination.** Selection for redundancy or a failure to offer suitable alternative work on the ground of an employee's maternity leave, etc may also give rise to a discrimination claim. See further Chapter 9, 'Discriminatory redundancy', under 'Pregnancy and maternity leave'.

8.64 **Selection for trade union reasons**

Section 153 TULR(C)A deals with selection for redundancy on grounds related to trade union membership or activities. The section provides that it is automatically unfair to select an employee for redundancy for any of the reasons specified in S.152(1). Those reasons are that:

- the employee was, or proposed to become, a member of an independent trade union

- the employee had taken part, or proposed to take part, in the activities of an independent trade union at an appropriate time

- the employee had made use of, or proposed to make use of, trade union services at an appropriate time

- the employee had failed to accept an offer or inducement in relation to trade union membership or activities, or collective bargaining, made in contravention of the employee's rights under S.145A or S.145B TULR(C)A, or

- the employee was not a member of any trade union, or of a particular trade union, or of one of a number of particular trade unions, or had refused, or proposed to refuse, to become or remain a member.

An 'appropriate time' means a time outside the employee's working hours or within his or her working hours by arrangement with the employer – S.152(2).

Note that the minimum basic award of, currently, £5,853 applies in the case of a successful claim under S.153 – S.156 TULR(C)A.

Where employees spend a large proportion of their time on union activities, **8.65** and a correspondingly small proportion on the work they are employed to do, they often score badly on the usual criteria applied for redundancy selection, such as quantity of work and work abilities. If employees are dismissed in these circumstances, it is often very difficult to determine the true reason for their selection. Was it the union activities or the work performance? It seems from the cases that where employers permit their officials to spend so much time on their union duties that their work suffers as a result, any selection of those officials for redundancy is likely to be automatically unfair. Two examples:

- **Dundon v GPT Ltd** 1995 IRLR 403, EAT: D, a union official, was employed as an accounts clerk in a large organisation. When he was appointed senior union representative, his employer gave him a less demanding job so that he could devote more time to his union duties. However, when it was found that D was spending most of his day on union matters, the employer agreed with him that he would spend only half the day on such duties. The arrangement soon lapsed and D went back to spending most of his day on union matters. A few years later, the employer needed to reduce its workforce and drew up selection criteria. It instructed its assessors that employees who were involved in union activities were to be assessed in the same way as other employees, with an allowance made for reasonable time off for union duties. D was selected for redundancy because his work output was so low and because of his bad timekeeping. An employment tribunal found that although D's union activities were relevant to his selection, they were not the main reason for it because the employer had not objected to those union activities. It held, therefore, that the dismissal was not automatically unfair under S.153. On appeal, the EAT overruled the tribunal on the ground that it had construed S.153 too narrowly: selection for trade union reasons included cases where there was no conscious or malicious selection on union grounds. In the EAT's view, D was selected for redundancy because he spent too much time on union activities – but he had carried out those activities at 'an appropriate time', since he had been given tacit permission to carry them out at the time he did. The EAT held that D had been automatically unfairly dismissed for trade union reasons

253

- **Robertson v Rolls Royce plc** ET Case No.321/94: R, who was employed as a fitter, was also a shop steward for the AEEU. He spent some 70 to 80 per cent of his time on trade union duties and he seemed to be free to engage in those activities at any time during his working shift. This affected his work in so far as he tended to be given the shorter and less complex jobs. When R asked for more complex work he was told that he would not be given it because there was no guarantee that he would be there to complete it. A redundancy situation arose and the employer was advised that it must not base its selection of employees on their union activities. R was made redundant and he complained that he had been selected for union reasons. The employment tribunal found that the employer had not carried out a reasonable assessment of R's abilities as he had been assessed according to the work he actually carried out rather than the work he was capable of doing. It held that the dismissal was unfair on this ground. Turning to S.153, the tribunal also concluded that R had been selected because he had engaged in trade union activities.

8.66   In Herbert v Air UK Engineering EAT 575/97, however, H, a workshop tradesman, spent three and a half hours a day on his shop steward duties. A redundancy situation arose in the workshop, with the result that either H or another employee would be made redundant. The employer adopted three selection criteria: qualifications, attendance record and length of service. H and the other employee scored equally on attendance and service but H was selected for redundancy because he was significantly outscored on qualifications. H argued unsuccessfully before a tribunal that his dismissal fell within S.153 because he had had no chance to gain the relevant qualifications because of the time spent on his trade union activities. The EAT upheld the tribunal's decision on appeal. Whereas in the Dundon case, above, the employee had been selected for redundancy because the employer felt he was spending too much time on his union activities, in the instant case the employee's dismissal was genuinely due to his lack of qualifications. The tribunal's finding that the employee did not gain the qualifications because of his union activities was not at all inconsistent with the finding that he was fairly dismissed because he lacked those qualifications. The EAT also rejected the argument that some sort of weighting factor should have been applied to the qualification criterion to allow for time spent on union activities. It might be possible to incorporate a weighting factor into a criterion based on employees' output, but it was not so easy to do so in the case of a qualification criterion. In any event, an employer must be entitled to regard qualifications for a skilled job as a high priority. Important as trade union activities are, they could not be legitimately invoked to seek to compensate for lack of qualifications.

As discussed under 'Same undertaking and similar position' above, an employee claiming unfair selection for redundancy under S.153 TULR(C)A must show that the redundancy situation applied equally to one or more

254

employees who held positions similar to that held by the employee and who were not dismissed. 'Position' in relation to an employee is defined in S.235(1) ERA as meaning the following matters taken as a whole: his or her status as an employee, the nature of the work, and his or her terms and conditions of employment. Where an employee holds a unique position within an undertaking, a claim under this section is therefore unlikely to be successful. In such a case, the employee may have to rely for a remedy on the ordinary provisions for unfair dismissal.

In O'Dea v ISC Chemicals Ltd t/a Rhône-Poulenc Chemicals 1996 ICR **8.67** 222, CA, O's contract specified that he was employed as a technical services operator (TSO), although for many years he had worked as a packaging operator to enable him to carry out his functions as the senior shop steward for the TGWU. By the time he was made redundant he was spending half his time on union activities. When the redundancy situation arose, O was encouraged to apply for other vacancies within the company but was told that he would be treated as an 'ordinary employee' for these purposes – i.e. he would only be considered for vacancies on the basis that, in future, he would not be involved in union activities. When he was dismissed, O claimed that he had been selected for redundancy on the ground of his union membership, contrary to S.153. An employment tribunal decided that the principal reason for O's dismissal was redundancy and not his union activities. Even if these activities had led to his being selected for redundancy, there was no other employee who held a position similar to his and who was retained in employment. The other TSOs who were retained did that job all the time and O was in a unique position vis-à-vis the other employees. Accordingly, an essential criterion of S.153 had not been made out. However, the tribunal did find the dismissal unfair on procedural grounds. O's appeal to the EAT was dismissed and he appealed to the Court of Appeal.

With regard to the definition of 'position', the Court of Appeal stated that, when comparing employees, consideration should only be given to the relative positions of the redundant employees and the trade union activities should be disregarded, even if the employee concerned had a contractual right to undertake such activities. If the time spent by a shop steward on union activities could put him or her in a position dissimilar to other employees, that would defeat the purpose of S.153, which is to protect employees carrying out such activities. Accordingly, it was an error of law for the tribunal to take account of O's union activities when considering whether his position was unique. However, the Court rejected O's argument that the tribunal should have ignored the fact that O was not actually working as a TSO to enable him to spend half his working day on union matters. The Court concluded that such an interpretation of 'position' was unacceptable because it would require a tribunal to ignore not only what O did as a shop steward but also what work he did as an employee, as well as the terms and conditions of employment. The tribunal should, therefore, have limited its

255

consideration to O's status as a skilled manual worker, to the nature of his work as a packaging operator, and to his terms and conditions of employment as a TSO. On this basis, O had not shown that there were other employees who held similar positions to the one he held. His position was not comparable to that of the TSOs or even the packaging operators. Furthermore, the tribunal had not been satisfied that his selection for redundancy was for a trade union reason. O's appeal was dismissed.

8.68 It seems that S.153 is concerned only with dismissal of individual employees on account of what they have done or proposed to do. In Carrington and ors v Therm-A-Stor Ltd 1983 ICR 208, CA, redundancies were brought forward because the TGWU requested recognition and 'coincidentally' 20 union members were selected. S.153 was held to have no application because the reason for dismissal was the union's request for recognition, which had nothing to do with what individual employees had done or proposed to do. (Note, however, that such actions by an employer could be caught by the provisions on recognition – see 'Trade union recognition cases' below.)

Although union activity is protected under S.153, industrial action is not. This means that employers, when selecting for redundancy, are allowed to take into account the fact that certain employees remained loyal during a strike while others did not – Cruickshank and ors v Hobbs 1977 ICR 725, EAT. In that case the EAT pointed out that selection on this basis might be particularly appropriate where the industrial action itself had 'caused or aggravated the redundancy'. The fairness of such dismissals would then depend on the issue of reasonableness. (Note, however, the limited protection available under S.105(7C) ERA for employees who take official industrial action – see 'Protected industrial action cases' above.)

Trade union dismissals are discussed in greater detail in IDS Employment Law Handbook, 'Trade Unions' (2013), Chapter 12, 'Unfair dismissal'.

8.69 ## Trade union recognition cases
The Employment Relations Act 1999 introduced statutory procedures for the recognition and derecognition of trade unions for collective bargaining. The provisions are contained in Schedule A1 to the TULR(C)A.

Among other things, these provide for protection from dismissal and selection for redundancy for reasons connected with trade union recognition. Para 162 of Schedule A1, read in conjunction with para 161(2), provides that it is automatically unfair to select an employee for redundancy for the sole or principal reason that the employee:

*   acted with a view to obtaining or preventing recognition of a union (or unions) by the employer under the Schedule

256

- indicated that he or she supported or did not support recognition of a union (or unions) by the employer under the Schedule

- acted with a view to securing or preventing the ending of bargaining arrangements under the Schedule

- indicated that he or she supported or did not support the ending of bargaining arrangements under the Schedule

- influenced or sought to influence the way in which votes were to be cast by other workers in a ballot arranged under the Schedule

- influenced or sought to influence other workers to vote or to abstain from voting in such a ballot

- voted in such a ballot, or

- proposed to do, failed to do, or proposed to decline to do, any of the above.

However, the employee will not be protected if his or her act or omission was 'unreasonable' – para 161(3). **8.70**

Trade union recognition is discussed in greater detail in IDS Employment Law Handbook, 'Trade Unions' (2013), Chapter 5, 'Trade union recognition', and Chapter 6, 'Statutory recognition'.

Transfer of undertakings **8.71**

Briefly, the Transfer of Undertakings (Protection of Employment) Regulations 2006 SI 2006/246 (TUPE) provide that where there is a 'relevant transfer' – for which, see IDS Employment Law Handbook, 'Transfer of Undertakings' (2015), Chapter 1, 'Identifying a "relevant transfer"' – the employment contracts of the employees employed in the undertaking are automatically transferred from the transferor to the transferee (Reg 4(1)), together with all the transferor's rights, powers, duties and liabilities in respect of such contracts (Reg 4(2)). As a result, on a relevant transfer, there is no automatic dismissal and no redundancy situation.

Where, however, there are express dismissals, Reg 7(1) provides that they will be automatically unfair where the sole or principal reason for dismissal is the relevant transfer. All employees of both the transferor and the transferee are protected by this provision.

However, where the sole or principal reason for the dismissal is an economic, technical or organisational (ETO) reason entailing changes in the workforce, Reg 7(1) will not apply and the fairness of the dismissal will fall to be considered under S.98(4) ERA – Regs 7(2) and (3). In addition, Reg 7(3)(b) provides that, where there is an ETO reason, then the dismissal will be by reason of redundancy if S.98(2)(c) ERA is satisfied (i.e. if the employee is redundant within the meaning of S.139 – see Chapter 2, 'Redundancy', under 'Definition **8.72**

257

of "redundancy"'). Otherwise, the dismissal will be potentially fair for 'some other substantial reason' within the meaning of S.98(1)(b).

8.73 **Does redundancy constitute an ETO reason?** Unfortunately, neither the TUPE Regulations nor the EU Acquired Rights Directive (No.2001/23), which TUPE implements, provides an answer to the question of whether the classic redundancy situation involving a diminution in the requirement for employees can constitute an ETO reason. However, while the legislation does not offer a definition, there is a substantial body of case law on what amounts to an ETO reason (see IDS Employment Law Handbook, 'Transfer of Undertakings' (2015), Chapter 4, 'Unfair dismissal', under 'Dismissals potentially fair for an "ETO" reason – economic, technical or organisational reason', for more details).

If the transferee does not require the full complement of employees belonging to the transferor, the case law suggests that this would amount to an 'economic' or 'organisational' reason entailing changes in the workforce, so that Reg 7(1) would not apply to render the dismissals automatically unfair. Two examples:

• **Meikle v McPhail (Charleston Arms)** 1983 IRLR 351, EAT: McP took over the pub where M worked. M continued to be employed for a short time after the transfer but then McP realised that he had over-committed himself and M was therefore dismissed. The EAT accepted that the reason was an 'economic' one under what is now Reg 7(2), and went on to judge the dismissal fair under the ordinary reasonableness test set out in S.98(4)

• **Trafford v Sharpe and Fisher (Building Supplies)** Ltd 1994 IRLR 325, EAT: SF Ltd took over the builders supply merchants where T worked as an estimator. He also ran a department on how to adapt equipment for use by the disabled. SF Ltd soon realised that the business it had bought was substantially overstaffed and that it had to reduce the workforce in order to make the business viable. It did not want either an estimating service or a disabled equipment advisory service and T was made redundant. The EAT accepted that the employer had shown an 'economic, technical or organisational reason' for the dismissal. However, it upheld the finding that T had been unfairly dismissed under S.98(4) (for which, see 'Unreasonable redundancy' below) for lack of proper warning and consultation.

8.74 It is difficult to find any objection to the decisions in the above cases, which both involved genuine redundancy situations. But the decision of the House of Lords in Litster and ors v Forth Dry Dock and Engineering Co Ltd (in receivership) and anor 1989 ICR 341, HL, demands that any dismissal occurring prior to the transfer be made on genuine ETO grounds. If there is any suggestion that they are part of a collusive bargain made between the transferee and the transferor, then the pre-transfer dismissals will most likely be rendered automatically unfair by virtue of Reg 7(1).

258

In this context, it is also worth noting that a transferor employer cannot rely on the ETO reason of the transferee in order to carry out pre-transfer dismissals. In Hynd v Armstrong and ors 2007 IRLR 338, Ct Sess (Inner House), H, a corporate lawyer, was employed by Morison Bishop, a law firm with offices in Edinburgh and Glasgow, in its Glasgow office. The partners in the firm decided to dissolve the partnership with effect from 31 July 2002, with the intention of forming two new firms: an Edinburgh-based firm called Morisons and a Glasgow-based firm called Bishops. Since Bishops was to concentrate on property law and litigation, the Glasgow partners of Morison Bishop anticipated a reduced requirement for corporate lawyers. Acting with the authority of the other partners in the firm, they made H redundant on 31 July 2002 – the date on which the partnership dissolved. H claimed that his dismissal was automatically unfair under what is now Reg 7(1). The employment tribunal and the EAT held that Reg 7(1) did not apply, since Bishops' reduced demand for corporate lawyers was an ETO reason. On appeal, the Court of Session examined the Acquired Rights Directive and held that the ETO defence has to be limited to dismissals for reasons which entail changes in the transferor's own workforce. H's appeal was therefore allowed.

Even if, as appears to be the case, genuine redundancies can constitute **8.75** an ETO reason, it is nevertheless arguable that not all redundancies will invariably do so. This is because, for the reason for dismissal to constitute an ETO reason, the economic or organisational reason must 'entail' changes in the workforce. This equates with a requirement to show that the particular dismissal was 'necessary' at the time it was made. It is therefore open to tribunals to go behind the contention that there has been a diminution in the requirements of the business and ask themselves whether, in the circumstances, the dismissals achieved a proper commercial aim and whether the veracity of the employer's explanation for the need to reduce the numbers of the workforce has been undermined by subsequent events – see Berriman v Delabole Slate Ltd 1985 ICR 546, CA.

This contrasts with the position of redundancies in an ordinary context under S.139 ERA where tribunals are enjoined not to look behind the fact of the redundancy situation to question how this has arisen and whether other options apart from dismissal were viable – Moon and ors v Homeworthy Furniture (Northern) Ltd 1977 ICR 117, EAT. See further Chapter 2, 'Redundancy', under 'Reason for dismissal'.

Once the employer has surmounted the hurdle of showing an ETO reason **8.76** for dismissal, the tribunal must decide whether in the circumstances (having regard to equity and the substantial merits of the case as well as the size and administrative resources of the business) the employer acted reasonably in treating the ETO reason as a sufficient reason for dismissal – S.98(4). Failure by a tribunal to take this step – by presuming that an ETO reason

259

is sufficient by itself for concluding that the dismissal is fair – would be an error of law – McGrath v Rank Leisure Ltd 1985 ICR 527, EAT. The reasonableness test is applied in the usual way – see 'Unreasonable redundancy' immediately below.

8.77 ## Unreasonable redundancy

Even if not automatically unfair, a redundancy dismissal may still be unreasonable (and therefore unfair) under the general unfair dismissal provisions contained in S.98(4) ERA. This states that 'the determination of the question whether the dismissal is fair or unfair (having regard to the reason shown by the employer) – (a) depends on whether in the circumstances (including the size and administrative resources of the employer's undertaking) the employer acted reasonably or unreasonably in treating it as a sufficient reason for dismissing the employee, and (b) shall be determined in accordance with equity and the substantial merits of the case'.

A dismissed employee may complain, for example, that he or she was unfairly selected for redundancy; that it was unreasonable for the employer to have dismissed him or her for redundancy where alternative work was available; or that the employer's redundancy procedure was defective – perhaps owing to a failure to consult.

8.78 In Williams and ors v Compair Maxam Ltd 1982 ICR 156, EAT, the EAT laid down guidelines that a reasonable employer might be expected to follow in making redundancy dismissals. The EAT stressed, however, that in determining the question of reasonableness it was not for the employment tribunal to impose its standards and decide whether the employer should have behaved differently. Instead it had to ask whether 'the dismissal lay within the range of conduct which a reasonable employer could have adopted'.

The factors suggested by the EAT in the Compair Maxam case that a reasonable employer might be expected to consider were:

• whether the selection criteria were objectively chosen and fairly applied

• whether employees were warned and consulted about the redundancy

• whether, if there was a union, the union's view was sought, and

• whether any alternative work was available.

8.79 In this section, we start by looking at the rules pertaining to procedural fairness in redundancy dismissals. We then look in detail at the issues a tribunal will consider when assessing the reasonableness or otherwise of a redundancy dismissal, including the unit to which any selection criteria were applied – usually referred to as the 'pool for selection'; the selection criteria themselves; the manner in which the criteria were applied; and the manner in which the redundancy dismissals were implemented.

Procedural fairness and ruling in 'Polkey'

8.80

The House of Lords' ruling in Polkey v AE Dayton Services Ltd 1988 ICR 142, HL, substantially changed the law of unfair dismissal, its main impact being to firmly establish procedural fairness as an integral part of the reasonableness test now found in S.98(4) ERA. Their Lordships decided that a failure to follow correct procedures was likely to make an ensuing dismissal unfair unless, in exceptional cases, the employer could reasonably have concluded that doing so would have been 'utterly useless' or 'futile'. With regard to redundancy dismissals, this meant, in the words of Lord Bridge, that 'the employer will not normally act reasonably unless he warns and consults any employees affected or their representative, adopts a fair basis on which to select for redundancy and takes such steps as may be reasonable to avoid or minimise redundancy by deployment within his own organisation'.

The issue of procedural fairness in unfair dismissal cases was temporarily overhauled during the period 2004–09, when statutory dismissal and disciplinary procedures (DDPs) were enacted and in force making it open to an employer to argue that compliance with a fair procedure would, on the balance of probabilities, have made no difference to its decision to dismiss. However, following the repeal of the DDPs, the issue of procedural fairness in unfair dismissal cases is once more governed by the Polkey decision. Thus, an employer cannot avoid a finding of unfair dismissal simply by arguing that 'although our procedure was defective, we would have dismissed him/her anyway'. Rather, a procedural failure renders a redundancy dismissal unfair under S.98(4), and the question of whether the employee would have been dismissed even if a fair procedure had been followed will be relevant only to the amount of compensation payable – see IDS Employment Law Handbook, 'Unfair Dismissal' (2015), Chapter 16, 'Compensatory awards: adjustments', under 'Polkey reductions'. So, for example, in Arhin v Enfield Primary Care Trust 2010 EWCA Civ 1481, CA, the Court of Appeal upheld an employment tribunal's decision that, while the employee had been unfairly dismissed for redundancy as a result of being left out of a pool for competitive selection, she was not entitled to reinstatement, re-engagement or a compensatory award. Even if a competitive selection procedure had taken place, she had no chance of being retained or employed.

In Langston v Cranfield University 1998 IRLR 172, EAT, the Appeal Tribunal considered that the principles of law relating to unfair redundancy dismissals were 'encapsulated' in the words of Lord Bridge in Polkey. In the EAT's view, it was therefore 'implicit' that unless the parties had agreed otherwise, an unfair redundancy dismissal claim incorporates unfair selection, lack

8.81

261

of consultation and failure to seek alternative employment on the part of the employer, whether or not each of these issues was specifically raised before the employment tribunal. Thus, it was incumbent upon the tribunal to consider each issue, in much the same way as it would consider each of the three elements of the test in British Home Stores Ltd v Burchell 1980 ICR 303, EAT, in a case of dismissal for misconduct. While the burden of proof under S.98(4) ERA was neutral, the EAT considered that an employer could normally be expected to lead some evidence as to the steps it had taken to select an employee for redundancy, consult with him or her (and his or her union, if applicable), and to seek alternative employment for him or her. Furthermore, an employment tribunal could normally be expected to refer to these three issues on the facts of the particular case in explaining its reasons for concluding that the employer acted reasonably or unreasonably in dismissing the employee by reason of redundancy.

8.82 It is important to note, however, that the claimant in Langston was a litigant in person and the EAT's judgment indicates that he was an inexperienced advocate who had difficulty presenting his case – a factor that may have influenced the EAT's reasoning. Indeed, the general applicability of the approach advocated by the EAT in Langston was called into question by another division of the EAT in Remploy Ltd v Abbott and ors EAT 0405/14. This was a complex multiple claim concerning the fairness of the mass redundancies that resulted from the closure of some 60 of R Ltd's factories and plants in 2012 and 2013. The EAT held that an employment tribunal had erred in granting the claimants' late application to introduce further issues concerning the reasonableness of R Ltd's attempts to seek alternative employment for them. The tribunal had been wrong to assume that it was bound by the decision in Langston to investigate in any case of unfair redundancy dismissal, as implicit in that claim, that the unfairness incorporated unfair selection, lack of consultation and failure to seek alternative employment on the part of the employer, even if not specifically pleaded or raised as issues by the claimants. The EAT commented that Langston should not be taken as authority for the proposition that in any unfair redundancy dismissal case where a point such as failure to seek alternative employment on the part of an employer has not been raised, the tribunal is required to take the point of its own motion. The EAT accepted that there may be some cases where the pleadings are sparse and a point is so obvious that a tribunal should take the point even if it has not occurred to the parties, provided the tribunal brings this to the attention of the parties so they can deal with it. But this was not appropriate in a case such as the present, where the claims were supported by the claimants' trade unions; the claimants were legally represented and their claim forms had been professionally drafted; issues in the case had been identified by reference to the parties' pleadings and there had been extensive and detailed case management orders made on the basis of those issues, which would be derailed if the new issues were introduced.

Acas Code of Practice. It should be noted that the current Acas 'Code of   **8.83**
Practice on Disciplinary and Grievance Procedures' does not apply to
redundancies.

Contractually agreed procedures   **8.84**

If an employee is selected for redundancy in breach of a customary arrangement
or agreed procedure, an employment tribunal must determine whether that
selection was fair or otherwise under the general reasonableness test set out in
S.98(4) ERA. Accordingly, if it is to avoid making a finding of unfair dismissal
the tribunal must be satisfied that it was reasonable for the employer to have
departed from the relevant agreement or procedure. There is no legislative
provision that gives agreed procedures and customary arrangements a special
protected status, but an employer cannot simply ignore them.

Incorporation of redundancy procedures. Some of the factors the courts   **8.85**
will consider when deciding whether a redundancy procedure has been
incorporated into an employee's contract were discussed by the High Court
in Alexander and ors v Standard Telephones and Cables Ltd (No.2) 1991
IRLR 286, QBD. As a result of technological change STC Ltd considered
making redundancies. It took into account the following selection criteria:
length of service, skill, aptitude, performance, attendance record and work-
approach. The employees disputed that they had been lawfully dismissed for
redundancy, contending that it was a requirement of the collective agreements
that selection for redundancy should be carried out on the basis of length of
service alone. They claimed that the terms of the relevant collective agreement
were expressly incorporated into their individual contracts of employment –
or impliedly incorporated as a matter of contractual intent – and that in
failing to adhere to the selection procedure in the collective agreement, STC
Ltd was in breach of contract. The employees' statutory written statements
of particulars included a provision that 'the basic terms and conditions of
your employment by this company are in accordance with and subject to the
provisions of [listed] relevant agreements', although the statements made no
mention of redundancy terms.

The High Court summarised the principles to be applied in determining
whether a part of a collective agreement is incorporated into individual
contracts of employment as follows: it is the contractual intention of the
parties to the agreement – the employee and the employer – which must be
ascertained. In so far as that intention is to be found in a written document, that
document must be construed on ordinary contractual principles but, where
there is no document or where the document is incomplete or inconclusive,
the parties' contractual intention has to be ascertained by inference from the
other available material, including collective agreements. Where a document
is expressly incorporated by general words it is still necessary to consider

263

whether any particular part of that document is apt to be a term of the contract; if it is inapt, the correct construction of the contract may be that it is not a term of the contract. Where it is not a case of express incorporation, but a matter of inferring contractual intent, the character of the document and the relevant part of it and whether it is apt to form part of the individual contract are central to the decision as to whether or not the inference should be drawn.

8.86   In the case at hand, the wording of the statements of written particulars was not sufficient to show an express incorporation of the redundancy procedure agreements, particularly as the written statements did not specifically deal with redundancy matters, implying that these were not a 'basic' term or condition to which the statement referred. Nor was it possible to infer, as a matter of contractual intent, that the selection procedure contained in the collective agreements had been incorporated into the individual contracts of employment. Where none of the other clauses of the collective agreement were apt to be incorporated, it would require a cogent indication that the clause setting out the basis for redundancy selection was to have a different character and was to be incorporated for it to have that effect. Here, the wording of the relevant clause was too weak to support an inference of incorporation when considered in context. It followed that the selection of the employees for redundancy was not in breach of any term of their contracts of employment and their claim would therefore be dismissed.

Indeed the EAT has also emphasised that tribunals should not too readily accept that collectively agreed terms as to redundancy selection procedures have been incorporated into individual employment contracts. This was the point made by the EAT in LTI Ltd v Radford EAT 164/00 when it upheld an employment tribunal's decision that a collectively agreed redundancy selection procedure was intended to apply as between the employer and the trade union only. In the EAT's view, a redundancy selection procedure is more akin to 'the stuff of' a collective agreement than that of an individual employment contract. The tribunal had been correct to take into account the fact that such procedures are 'not of day-to-day significance' in the employment relationship and that, following Alexander, an inference that their terms should be incorporated into individual contracts will be difficult to sustain. The EAT noted that collective agreement provisions for enhanced redundancy payments were more likely to be regarded as incorporated into individual contracts, stating that such provisions 'are different in nature from provisions as to procedures for selection'.

8.87   The incorporation of collective agreements into contracts of employment is discussed further in IDS Employment Law Handbook, 'Contracts of Employment' (2014), Chapter 5, 'Incorporated terms', under 'Express incorporation – collective agreements', and IDS Employment Law

Handbook, 'Trade Unions' (2013), Chapter 9, 'Collective agreements', under 'Incorporation – implied incorporation'.

Where it is established that a contractually agreed procedure for selection applied, employment tribunals are likely to take a dim view of an employer that selects an employee for redundancy in breach of such a procedure. In Bassett v Augusta Westland Ltd ET Case No.1701132/12, for example, the contractually agreed selection procedure provided that selection criteria were to be applied by managers familiar with employees' work. In the event that a current manager was not well placed to assess an individual's work the manager was required to contact HR in order that the views of the previous manager could be obtained where practicable before completion of the final assessment. One of B's assessors was not familiar with his work but did not contact HR as required by the agreement and did not seek the views of a manager who knew B's work. That assessor scored B poorly and as a result he was selected for redundancy. The tribunal held that this was a significant breach of the agreed procedure as AW Ltd had not provided any evidence as to why it had not been practicable to obtain the views of a manager more familiar with B's work, and there was no real basis for the poor scores awarded to B by his current manager. The tribunal considered that had he not been made redundant, B would almost certainly have continued working for AW Ltd until retirement at the age of 65. Calculated on that basis, B's future loss exceeded the statutory cap on compensatory awards in unfair dismissal claims (at the time, £72,300), so the tribunal made the maximum award.

8.88 Furthermore, where it can be shown that an agreed redundancy procedure was incorporated into an employee's contract of employment, a departure from that procedure may give rise to an action for wrongful dismissal based on the employer's breach of contract. The normal remedy in such cases will be an award of damages. However, in exceptional circumstances, the courts may be prepared to grant an interlocutory (temporary) injunction (called an interim interdict in Scotland) to restrain the breach pending a full trial of the issue – i.e. to prevent the employer dismissing in contravention of the agreed procedure until the case has come to court. The issue of injunctions in redundancy selection cases is discussed in Chapter 10, 'Enforcement', under 'Contractual redundancy terms – enforcement of non-pay terms'.

Voluntary redundancies

8.89 An employer will not necessarily be acting unreasonably if it does not invite volunteers before making compulsory redundancies. In Lintin v Imagelinx UK Ltd ET Case No.2603643/08, for example, an employment tribunal found that an employer had acted within the range of reasonable responses in discounting making voluntary redundancies on efficiency grounds, given that it had kept an open mind during the consultation process. However,

265

the reasonableness of dismissal in such circumstances will depend on the particular facts of the case. In Stephenson College v Jackson EAT 0045/13, for example, the EAT upheld an employment tribunal's finding that an employer had acted unfairly by dismissing the claimant instead of a co-worker who had volunteered for redundancy. While the claimant had received the worst score in a redundancy selection process, his co-worker had only fared one point better, due to having an additional qualification. However, there was no evidence that the employer actually attached any real value to this qualification. Furthermore, the employer knew that the co-worker was unhappy in his job and was struggling with the work and it failed to provide a reason for refusing his application for voluntary redundancy. Similarly, in Levene v Moffat Publishing Co Ltd ET Case No.3201397/15 an employment tribunal held that the employer had acted unfairly by failing to consider asking for volunteers for redundancy among its sales team as an alternative to making L, the sales team manager, compulsorily redundant. The tribunal noted that one member of the sales team had been due to retire – and in fact did retire – at around the time that L's redundancy dismissal took effect, and three other members of the sales team resigned within the following two months. Accordingly, the tribunal considered it highly likely that voluntary redundancies would have been achieved among the sales team. L was competent to perform a sales team role and could have been offered such a role as an alternative to redundancy.

8.90   **Pool for selection**

In carrying out a redundancy exercise, an employer should begin by identifying the group of employees from which those who are to be made redundant will be drawn. This is the 'pool for selection' and it is to these employees that an employer will apply the chosen selection criteria to determine who will be made redundant. In assessing the fairness of dismissals, tribunals will first look to the pool from which the selection was made, since the application of otherwise fair selection criteria to the wrong group of employees is likely to result in an unfair dismissal. If an employer simply dismisses an employee without first considering the question of a pool, the dismissal is likely to be unfair – Taymech Ltd v Ryan EAT 663/94.

Of course, there will be some redundancy situations where, because of the complete closure of the workplace, business or unit, selection as such will not be necessary. For example, in Zeff v Lewis Day Transport plc EAT 0418/10 the EAT upheld an employment tribunal's finding that there was no question of selection, and thus no need for selection criteria to be applied, where the employer closed down its chauffeur desk. The manager and two controllers on the chauffeur desk were made redundant; two administrators who had previously been assigned to the chauffeur desk were moved to the car desk and continued the same jobs as before. Similarly, in Kirby v North Midland

266

Construction plc ET Case No.2602999/08 an employment tribunal dismissed a claim by a construction engineer who was manager of the rail department that he had been unfairly selected for redundancy because he should have been put into a pool with four other managers, whose jobs he could do. The tribunal considered that the employer had not acted unreasonably in concluding that there were real differences between K's job and those of the other managers, and that as the whole of K's department was being closed it had good reasons for dealing with him separately.

Range of pools available. Where there is a customary arrangement or agreed procedure that specifies a particular selection pool, the employer will normally be expected to adhere to it unless the employer can show that it was reasonable to depart from it – Russell v London Borough of Haringey, unreported, 12.6.00, CA. Where there is no customary arrangement or agreed procedure to be considered, employers have a good deal of flexibility in defining the pool from which they will select employees for dismissal – Thomas and Betts Manufacturing Co v Harding 1980 IRLR 255, CA. They need only show that they have applied their minds to the problem and acted from genuine motives. For example, sometimes it may be to an employer's advantage to draw the pool for selection as widely as possible. This will give it the flexibility to select less capable staff across a range of departments or job categories instead of losing valued employees from a more narrowly defined group. In other situations, it may be appropriate to draw the pool more narrowly. In Gilleard v Lupton Fawcett LLP ET Case No.1812120/09, for example, a solicitors' firm employed associate solicitors and assistant solicitors, the associate solicitors being more highly paid than the assistants. G was an associate solicitor. The firm decided to make redundancies among the associate solicitors since it was the more complex work that was drying up. The firm began consultations with the associate solicitors with a view to making them all redundant. They proposed taking a pay cut so that they would be no more expensive than the assistant solicitors, thus enabling the cuts to be made across both categories, but the firm said that the selection of the associates was on the basis of the nature of the available work. G and the other associates were dismissed as redundant, and an employment tribunal rejected G's unfair dismissal claim. The firm had sound business reasons for making the selection in this way. Associate solicitors would at some point get frustrated with the low level of the work available; and if there were no assistant solicitors being trained up there would be no employees ready to be promoted to associate solicitors if the market recovered. Furthermore, the loss of skills and experience involved in dismissing associate solicitors was not of concern since there was under-capacity among the firm's directors, who did have those skills and experience.

However, in all cases, the employment tribunal must be satisfied that the employer acted reasonably and, in considering whether this was so, the following factors may be relevant:

8.91

267

- whether other groups of employees are doing similar work to the group from which selections were made

- whether employees' jobs are interchangeable

- whether the employee's inclusion in the unit is consistent with his or her previous position, and

- whether the selection unit was agreed with any union.

8.92 As a result, the pool is usually composed of employees doing the same or similar work, and an employer risks a finding of unfairness if it includes in the pool a range of different job functions. In Contract Bottling Ltd v Cave and anor EAT 0525/12 CB Ltd decided to reduce its administrative staff. It created a single pool of all administrative staff, encompassing functions as diverse as accounts, sales and quality control, and applied a general scoring matrix with the intention of dismissing staff, whatever their function, who scored the lowest. This meant that employees who were kept on might be retrained to do work of a completely different kind from their own – for example, a warehouse manager retrained to do accounting work. Two accounts staff who were dismissed succeeded in complaints of unfair dismissal on the basis that the selection procedure was unreasonable. The EAT upheld this decision on appeal. Although it did not specifically cite the construction of the pool as a reason for the unfairness, the EAT did note that this was an unusual and 'surprising' approach.

A tribunal will judge the employer's choice of pool by asking itself whether it fell within the range of reasonable responses available to an employer in the circumstances. As the EAT put it in Kvaerner Oil and Gas Ltd v Parker and ors EAT 0444/02, 'different people can quite legitimately have different views about what is or is not a fair response to a particular situation... In most situations there will be a band of potential responses to the particular problem and it may be that both of solutions X and Y will be well within that band.'

8.93 Indeed, the identification of an appropriate pool for selection is an area in which tribunals must take care not to substitute their own view for that of the employer. In Family Mosaic Housing Association v Badmos EAT 0042/13, for example, the EAT held that an employment tribunal had erred in finding that the employer's decision as to the appropriate pool for selection in a redundancy exercise had been outside the range of reasonable responses. FMHA employed five Regional Development Managers (RDMs), three of whom worked on new business development and two who were responsible for the delivery of existing projects. Due to financial pressure, FMHA determined that it had to restructure and decided that the number of new business RDMs would be reduced from three to two. However, on the basis that they had interchangeable skills, it placed all five RDMs into a single pool for selection. It then gave the RDMs the opportunity to identify

268

which posts they were interested in – i.e. the new business posts, and/or the delivery posts. When only two of the RDMs expressed an interest in the new business posts, FMHA decided to slot them into those roles. The remaining three RDMs, who had expressed an interest in the delivery posts, were put through a selection process. B, who was one of the existing delivery RDMs, scored the lowest and was made redundant. His unfair dismissal and race discrimination claims succeeded before the tribunal, which held that it was unreasonable for FMHA to define the pool for selection as including all five RDMs, but then effectively create a smaller sub-pool based on the voluntary expressions of interest from the at-risk employees.

On appeal, the EAT disagreed, holding that it was clear that FMHA had genuinely applied its mind to the formulation of the pool and that its decision was not outside the range of reasonable responses. It was appropriate for FMHA to recognise that all five employees were competent to do either job and to put them all in the same pool. At the same time, it was also appropriate to allow the employees to express an interest as between the posts. Had they all expressed interest in both posts, FMHA would have had to carry out a selection process in respect of all five employees for both positions. However, as only two employees expressed an interest in the two new business roles, this exercise was not necessary. While the tribunal had been entitled to scrutinise FMHA's thinking, it had then gone too far and substituted its own view as to what would have been appropriate. Although the EAT disagreed with the tribunal's findings on the reasonableness of the pool for selection, it upheld its decision that B's dismissal was unfair and discriminatory on grounds of race due to other significant failings in the selection process.

That said, the following cases demonstrate that tribunals will not uncritically **8.94** accept an employer's reasoning for drawing the pool for selection in a particular way:

- **Kvaerner Oil and Gas Ltd v Parker and ors** (above): the EAT upheld an employment tribunal's decision that an employer's pool for selection fell outside the range of reasonable responses. As a result of an internal reorganisation, KOG was split into two separate business units with their own management and budget structures. Both business units operated from the same site, and, in the months leading up to the claimants' redundancies, undertook mostly the same work. When redundancies became necessary, KOG confined the pool for selection to a single business unit. Four of the workers who were made redundant challenged this decision, claiming that KOG had artificially restricted the pool in order to get rid of employees who were on more expensive terms. The tribunal noted that the two business units were separately accounted for and managed. But it concluded that the claimants 'did not appreciate these organisation distinctions', as, so far as they were concerned, they were working in the same location doing very similar work. The EAT upheld the tribunal's decision that both business units should have been identified as the applicable pool. KOG had adopted too narrow an approach in giving undue weight to the different financial and management structures of the two business units. A reasonable employer would have adopted a wider approach and would have brought into consideration other factors, such as, in particular, the interchangeableness of the work between the two units

- **Hendy Banks City Print Ltd v Fairbrother and ors** EAT 0691/04: the claimants worked for a printing company in its 'finishing' department. Their work involved many tasks, one of which was the use of a perfect-binding machine for which they had been specifically trained. In 2002, as a step in the implementation of a redundancy programme, the employer chose a pool comprising only those who worked on the perfect-binding machine. An employment tribunal ruled that the pool had been defined too narrowly, given that (i) the claimants were the most experienced workers and they undertook all aspects of finishing work; and (ii) they spent no more than one third of their time on the machine, with the other two thirds being spent doing the same work as other members of the finishing department. On appeal, the EAT rejected the employer's contention that the tribunal had wrongly substituted its view of the correct pool for that of the employer. The EAT accepted that the reasons given by the tribunal for coming to the conclusion that the selected pool was not a reasonable one were perfectly sound

- **Davies v JCB Transmission** ET Case No.2901458/08: JCB employed a number of workers on a contract which stated that they were on a temporary appointment of uncertain duration; that they were employed to cover peaks in demand; and that the contract would expire when demand reduced. By 2008 the company suffered a downturn in demand and decided to implement redundancies. It put all employees, permanent and those on the temporary contracts, into one pool for selection. However, an employment tribunal found that it was unreasonable to include the fixed-term employees in the same pool for selection as permanent employees. The fixed-term contracts were determinable upon the occurrence of a specific event – a downturn in demand – and JCB would not have faced a successful claim of treating the fixed-term employees less favourably by terminating their contracts because demand had reduced

- **Wiggett v Groundwise Searches Ltd** ET Case No.3200274/11: W was originally employed by R in 2006 as an administration assistant and was promoted to the post of accounts assistant in 2010; two new administration assistants were employed at that time. In summer 2010, it became apparent that GS Ltd was facing financial difficulties and redundancies would be necessary. The managing director decided to make five redundancies: one of the two administration assistants, one of three productions assistants and three other standalone posts, one of which was W's. When the proposed redundancies were announced, W asked if she could revert to her administration assistant role but her request was refused. GS Ltd decided, based on advice from an external HR consultant, that because W's current accounts assistant role was a standalone role, it was unable to consider pooling W with the other administration assistants who were at risk of redundancy. W successfully claimed that her redundancy dismissal was unfair. The tribunal found that GS Ltd's choice of redundancy pool as applied to W fell outside the band of reasonable responses. W had considerable experience in the company whereas the administrative assistants had been employed for only a few months and had been trained by her; W had previously carried out this role for many years, and jobs in GS Ltd tended to be interchangeable, with employees often covering for each other. GS Ltd had not properly applied its mind to the possibility of pooling W with the administration assistants, particularly as this had been raised as an option by W at the outset.

Same work. An employer will need to have justifiable reasons for excluding a particular group of employees from the selection pool where those in the excluded category do the same, or similar, work to those who are up for selection. Two examples:

- **British Steel plc (Seamless Tubes) v Robertson and ors** EAT 601/94: the employer excluded a group of craftsmen, described as 'multi-skilled', who had recently been trained in all the various skills required by the company but who had short service. Redundancies were actually made from a pool of long-serving mechanical maintenance engineers and electrical engineers on the basis of 'last in, first out'. The employment tribunal decided that the multi-skilled craftsmen should have been included in the pool for selection as they could undertake the work of those in the selected pool. The tribunal said that it could be fair in certain circumstances to exempt a group of craftsmen from redundancies, but in the present case it was unreasonable for the employer to have done so given that both groups did similar work. The EAT upheld this finding

- **Holland v C and G Concrete Ltd** ET Case No.2600735/09: H was employed as a concrete mixer driver and he delivered concrete four days a week and mortar one day a week. Another driver, X, was originally classed as a mortar mixer driver, but for the two years prior to his dismissal he had been a concrete mixer driver four days a week and a mortar mixer driver for only one day a week. Due to the effect of the recession on the construction industry, the company decided to make one mortar mixer driver and one concrete mixer driver redundant from the site where H and X worked. The company treated the two categories of driver as two separate pools. H was identified as the lowest scoring driver in the concrete mixer group and X was the lowest scoring driver in the mortar mixer group. Both were

8.95

271

made redundant. An employment tribunal found that H had been unfairly dismissed. It considered it manifestly unfair to H for the employer to put X in the mortar mixer pool rather than the concrete mixer pool. If he had been properly allocated to the concrete mixer pool, he would have scored lower than H, who would thus not have been selected for redundancy.

8.96 It may be unreasonable to exclude a group of employees doing similar work from the selection pool even where the employees in the pool would have to undertake some training before carrying out the work done by the excluded employees. In Thornley v JCT600 Ltd ET Case No.1800944/10 T was one of seven technicians employed by JCT600 Ltd in its specialist workshop. Five of the technicians, including T, worked on Ferrari and Maserati vehicles and two worked on Lotus vehicles. In October 2009 JCT600 Ltd decided to reduce the number of technicians by one and T was selected from among the five technicians working on Ferrari and Maserati cars. An employment tribunal held that he had been unfairly dismissed. JCT600 Ltd had acted unreasonably in excluding from the pool the two technicians working on Lotus cars. In a previous redundancy exercise the pool had consisted of all the technicians. There was no consideration at any stage of transferring one of the technicians working on Maserati and Ferrari cars to Lotus in the event that a Lotus technician was selected for redundancy, yet this would have required only ten days' training. In fact, all technicians worked on all of the cars from time to time. (Note that this case is also discussed under 'Mobility clauses' below.)

8.97 **Interchangeable jobs.** A fair pool for selection is not necessarily limited to those employees doing the same or similar work. Employers may be expected to include in the pool those employees whose work is interchangeable. In Blundell Permoglaze Ltd v O'Hagen EAT 540/84, for example, an employment tribunal found a dismissal unfair because the pool from which the selection was made was unreasonably restricted. BP Ltd employed six employees in their warehouse, three of whom were drivers and three of whom were warehousemen. The drivers could perform the warehousemen's jobs but the reverse was not true. BP Ltd decided to get rid of one lorry and one employee. After unsuccessfully seeking a volunteer for redundancy from all six staff, it applied a LIFO test among the drivers alone. Had the test been applied to all six workers, O'H would not have been dismissed. The tribunal found the choice of pool for the selection unreasonable as the drivers could have, and had in the past, performed warehouse work, and the employer had originally sought a volunteer for redundancy among all six men. (The tribunal accepted that, had the redundancy been needed from among the warehousemen, it would have been wrong to have included the drivers in the pool, since the warehousemen could not do the drivers' jobs.)

Similarly, in Thackeray v Blake UK Ltd ET Case No.2801016/12 T was employed by BU Ltd as a general assembler from 1997, assembling components for television aerials. In April 2011 BU Ltd lost a contract and believed it was necessary to make two redundancies from its factory staff. It decided that the appropriate pool for selection would be seven general assemblers, of whom T scored the lowest and was made redundant. T claimed unfair dismissal, alleging that BU Ltd should have included in the pool for selection four other assemblers who worked on different components, and U, a factory cleaner who also did some general assembly work. The employment tribunal upheld T's claim. Although it accepted that the exclusion from the pool of the four other assemblers was justified on the basis that they did specialist work which was not interchangeable with the work of the general assemblers, it found that a reasonable employer would have included U in the pool. The evidence showed that she was competent in most of the tasks carried out by the general assemblers, and it was clear that if she had been selected for redundancy another of the general assemblers could have taken on her cleaning duties.

However, in Lomond Motors Ltd v Clark EAT 0019/09 the EAT overturned an employment tribunal's decision that the pool should have included an extra person, on the ground that her role was not properly interchangeable with the others. C worked as a branch accountant for a car dealer. The dealer operated from two sites, one in Glasgow and one in Ayr. In 2006 it acquired two further sites, one in Edinburgh and one in Stirling, which were served by another branch accountant, G. G was given responsibility for the Edinburgh site, C was transferred to work at the Stirling site, and another employee became branch accountant for Glasgow and Ayr. By the end of 2007 it was decided that a single employee should cover both the Edinburgh and Stirling sites. C was selected for redundancy from a pool consisting of C and G, but not the branch accountant for Glasgow and Ayr. An employment tribunal found that it had been unreasonable for the employer not to include in the pool the branch accountant for Glasgow and Ayr. However, the EAT disagreed, noting that the tribunal had found as a fact that that accountant did not have the requisite experience to cover the Stirling site and the jobs were therefore not properly interchangeable. While the pool might have included all three, the employer did not act unreasonably in deciding to have a pool of two. **8.98**

'Bumping'. Job losses confined to one team can result in the dismissal of skilled and experienced staff who are of greater long-term value to the organisation than other individuals whose posts are not directly affected. One way round this problem is to define the pool for selection broadly so as to encompass a number of different teams or job titles. The lawfulness of such a course of action was confirmed by the House of Lords in Murray and anor v Foyle Meats Ltd 1999 ICR 827, HL (discussed in Chapter 2, 'Redundancy', under 'Diminishing need for employees'). In that case, their Lordships confirmed that there is no reason why a dismissal of an employee cannot be regarded as being 'attributable' to a diminution in the employer's need for employees to do work of a particular kind within the meaning of S.139 ERA (definition of **8.99**

273

redundancy), irrespective of the terms of the particular employee's contract or the function that he or she performs. This potentially allows so-called 'bumping' dismissals, whereby an employee, X, whose job is redundant, is redeployed to another job and the employee in that job, Y, is the one who is actually dismissed. Although Y's job may not be redundant, his or her dismissal is clearly attributable to redundancy in that it has been brought about by the diminished need for work of a particular kind; namely, the work previously done by X.

The question arises whether bumping is merely an option available to an employer when determining how to define the appropriate pool or whether, to ensure fairness, the employer is obliged to consider bumping. Many of the cases on the subject turn on the issue of seniority. In Dial-a-Phone and anor v Butt EAT 0286/03 the EAT approved a finding that the employer should have considered the possibility of bumping a more junior employee. In that case, the EAT rejected the idea that it is always necessary for a senior employee to tell the employer that he or she is willing to accept a more junior role or a pay cut before the employer is obliged to consider the possibility.

8.100 In Lionel Leventhal Ltd v North EAT 0265/04 the EAT gave more detailed guidance on the circumstances in which an employer should consider bumping. A senior editor was selected for redundancy because he was the company's most expensive employee. An employment tribunal found his dismissal unfair, partly on the basis that the employer should have considered making a more junior employee redundant and offering his or her job to the claimant rather than merely assuming that the claimant would be unwilling to accept the resulting drop in salary. On appeal, the EAT was referred to case law, including the Court of Appeal's decision in Thomas and Betts Manufacturing Co v Harding 1980 IRLR 255, CA, which established that it can be unfair for an employer to fail to consider offering alternative employment to a potentially redundant employee, even in the absence of a vacancy. In the view of the EAT in Leventhal, whether or not such a failure is unfair is a question of fact for the tribunal, which should consider matters such as:

• whether or not there is a vacancy

• how different the two jobs are

• the difference in remuneration between them

• the relative length of service of the two employees, and

• the qualifications of the employee in danger of redundancy.

The EAT accepted that the tribunal had been entitled, on the facts, to hold that the employer's failure to take the initiative in considering the above matters rendered the claimant's dismissal unfair.

274

The factors set out in Leventhal were referred to with approval by another division of the EAT in Fulcrum Pharma (Europe) Ltd v Bonassera and anor EAT 0198/10. There B was recruited in January 2006 as a Human Resources Executive/Office Manager with responsibility for all HR matters and for managing a team of administrative staff. After a year, as a result of rapid growth in the business, B had given up her supervisory duties and become HR Manager. By mid-2008, C had joined as HR Executive, in a supporting role to B. In 2009, however, FP Ltd decided to reduce its HR function to one executive role, which was the role being carried out by C, intending to use an external consultancy for more complex HR issues. B was advised that her role was at risk of redundancy. B argued that both she and C should have been put at risk, and that C should have been made redundant because B had more experience and had performed both roles. FP Ltd maintained that C's role was not directly affected as it intended to continue to operate with an HR Executive role. B was dismissed, and brought a claim for unfair dismissal. The employment tribunal, in holding that B had been unfairly dismissed, considered that as the HR function was being reduced from two to one, the pool for selection should have been two, namely B and C. **8.101**

FP Ltd appealed to the EAT, which agreed with the tribunal that FP Ltd had been wrong to conclude, without any further or meaningful consultation as to the size of the pool, that the pool was one person simply because it was the manager's role that had to go. However, the tribunal had erred in finding that the pool should necessarily have consisted of two employees without any further analysis. The facts that B had previously carried out C's role, and that C had 'acted up' during B's sick leave, were not by themselves sufficient to determine that both B and C should be in the pool. The tribunal should have considered the approach taken in the case authorities, such as the Leventhal case.

But it would be wrong to conclude on the basis of Leventhal that an employer must consider bumping to avoid a finding of unfair dismissal. Indeed, in another decision the EAT held that an employment tribunal had correctly concluded that a dismissal was not rendered unfair by an employer's failure to consider dismissing a well-established junior employee in order to retain a more highly experienced senior employee – Byrne v Arvin Meritor LVS (UK) Ltd EAT 239/02. These cases suggest that the duty to act reasonably does not impose an absolute obligation to consider bumping as an option but that, in particular circumstances, the failure to do so may fall outside the band of reasonable responses. **8.102**

Previous experience in role. In Fulcrum Pharma (Europe) Ltd v Bonassera and anor (above) the EAT noted that the fact that the claimant had previously carried out a more junior role did not, by itself, determine that both roles should be included in the pool for selection. However, in Martin v Pepperl and Fuchs Ltd ET Case No.2410568/09 an employment tribunal considered **8.103**

275

that because M, a UK Sales Manager, had in the past done the role of Project Sales Manager, both roles should have been included in the pool. Evidence that a senior employee has previous experience in a more junior position may be relevant to whether or not 'bumping' should be considered, but this is a matter for the tribunal to decide on the facts of the case.

8.104 **Pool of one.** In Capita Hartshead Ltd v Byard 2012 ICR 1256, EAT, B, an actuary, no longer had enough work owing to a decline in the number of pension funds she managed (through no fault of her own). Although there were three other actuaries, she was treated as being in a pool of one. According to CH Ltd, this was because there was not enough work to sustain four actuaries and, given the personal nature of the work done by an actuary for a pension fund, there was a risk of losing clients if they were transferred between actuaries. When B was made redundant, she lodged an unfair dismissal claim, arguing that all four actuaries should have been included in the pool. An employment tribunal upheld that claim, finding that the risk of losing clients from reassigning actuaries was 'slight', and that the employer could not reasonably have concluded that including other actuaries in the pool would have been 'utterly useless'.

Upholding the tribunal's decision on appeal, the EAT rejected an argument that the statement in Taymech Ltd v Ryan EAT 663/94 that 'how the pool should be defined is primarily a matter for the employer to determine' meant that tribunals are precluded from holding that the choice of pool for selection by the employer is so flawed that the employee selected has been unfairly dismissed. That statement only applies where the employer has 'genuinely applied his mind to the problem' of selecting the pool. Even then, the EAT thought that an employer's decision will be difficult, but not impossible, to challenge.

8.105 An example of a case in which the employer was found not to have addressed the question of the appropriate pool is Cabral v Eville and Jones (UK) Ltd ET Case No.1102670/12. EJU Ltd employed meat hygiene inspectors and vets who provided services to the Food Standards Agency. C was employed as an Official Veterinarian (OV) in London and the south east and was the lead OV for two meat-processing plants. In May 2012 one of the plants closed down and EJU Ltd offered C the options of a meat inspector role in Guildford, temporary employment as an OV in London and the south east, or redundancy. C declined the alternative employment and was made redundant with effect from 4 September 2014. An employment tribunal accepted that there was a redundancy situation but found that C's dismissal was unfair because EJU Ltd had failed to give any meaningful consideration to whether C should have been placed in a pool with other OVs whose work would be reduced as a result of the plant closure. Rather than applying its mind to the question of what would be an appropriate pool for selection, EJU Ltd had simply taken the view that because C was the lead OV at the plant that closed he should be the one to face redundancy. The tribunal also found that the redundancy procedure was woefully inadequate, with no advance warning and no consultation. However, the tribunal considered that, had C been placed in an appropriate pool, there was still a 60 per cent chance that C would have been dismissed because he did not have the auditing skills that other OVs in the pool had.

An employer that *has* applied its mind to the question of a pool may still be challenged on its decision if the employment tribunal considers that it defined the pool in a particular way in order to ensure the dismissal of a particular individual. In Bottoms v Futuresource Consulting Ltd ET Case No.1200162/13, for example, the employment tribunal considered that the employer had made a deliberate decision to place B in a pool of one in order to ensure his departure from the company, and this made his dismissal unfair. B was one of four director-shareholders of FC Ltd. He had been intending to leave the company and had entered negotiations for the other three directors to buy out his shareholding. When the negotiations stalled, B indicated his intention to remain in the company if a satisfactory agreement for the purchase could not be reached. The company was undergoing a restructure at this time and it was decided that the management should consist of three directors and a CEO. The CEO consulted the company's HR adviser concerning the need to create a pool consisting of the four directors and to devise objective selection criteria. However, the CEO decided that B should be placed in a pool of one since he had been intending to leave the company in any event and the CEO thought that he would have come out the lowest if any objective scoring exercise had been conducted. The employment tribunal found that this was procedurally unfair: the decision not to create a pool was not an oversight or an unconscious decision given that FC Ltd had preselected B for redundancy with the intention of getting him out of the business. However, B's compensatory award would be subject to a 50 per cent Polkey reduction to reflect his failure to engage with the redundancy consultation process, which, in consequence, had prevented him from putting forward to FC Ltd his case that there should have been a pool and that he would not have scored the lowest of the four directors.

Another case involving a selection pool of just one employee was Halpin v Sandpiper Books Ltd EAT 0171/11. In that case the EAT concluded that it was not unfair for an employer to use a pool of one where an overseas office was being closed and H was the only employee who had been sent there from the UK. SB Ltd, a book distributor, asked H, an administrator/ analyst in its London office, to relocate to China to work in a sales role developing its business and raising its profile there. When H was first posted abroad, he continued to perform some of his administrative and analytical work, but in due course this was largely divided among staff in the UK. Subsequently, SB Ltd decided to close the China office, having concluded that

8.106

277

it was not financially viable and that the sales work carried out by H could be outsourced to a local agent. There was extensive consultation and, although H was offered alternative part-time administrative work in the UK, he turned this down and so was made redundant. In rejecting his unfair dismissal claim, an employment tribunal found that there was a genuine redundancy situation and concluded that H had been 'fairly selected in so far as he was in a pool of one given his unique position dealing solely with sales and based in China'.

Upholding the tribunal's approach on appeal, the EAT held that the decision as to the pool was one for SB Ltd to take and that limiting the pool to a pool of one was a logical decision that could not be easily overturned by a tribunal. H was on his own in China dealing with sales and SB Ltd had decided that the work he did there was no longer of interest to it. The fact that H had previously performed various administrative and analytical duties that were still mainly carried out by others did not alter the analysis. There were no other similarly qualified possible targets for redundancy and so a pool of one was appropriate. This case can be contrasted with Capita Hartshead Ltd v Byard (above), where the claimant was put in a pool of one when there were three other employees carrying out the same work. Moreover, as the employer in Capita Hartshead had not 'genuinely applied his mind' to the issue of who should be in the pool, this made it possible for the claimant to challenge the decision.

8.107 It is, however, worth noting the decision of another EAT, handed down a few months after that in Capita Hartshead, which suggests that an employer who omits to consider the question of pooling will not necessarily be acting unreasonably – Wrexham Golf Co Ltd v Ingham EAT 0190/12. There, I worked as Club Steward, responsible for managing the bar, cashing up and closing up in the evenings, and looking after the premises at weekends. WGC Ltd decided that, to save money, it would combine its bar and catering functions, and the Club Steward's duties could be divided among other staff, so I would be redundant. An employment tribunal held that the dismissal was unfair because WGC Ltd had failed to consider the issue of a pool, and whether other bar staff should have been placed at risk together with I. The tribunal was also critical of the information WGC Ltd provided to I and the extent of consultation undertaken. WGC Ltd successfully appealed to the EAT. Remitting the case for consideration by a fresh tribunal, the EAT noted that the word 'pool' is not found in S.98(4) ERA and 'there is no rule that there must be a pool: an employer, if he has good reason for doing so, may consider a single employee for redundancy'. Furthermore, in the EAT's view: 'There will be cases where it is reasonable to focus upon a single employee without developing a pool or even considering the development of a pool.' Accordingly, the question that the tribunal in the present case ought to have considered was whether, given the nature of the job of Club Steward, it was reasonable for WGC Ltd not to consider developing a wider pool of employees.

278

Multi-site redundancies. Difficulties can arise where a business is spread over a number of different sites. Should the employer treat employees working at different sites as separate groups for the purpose of redundancy selection? Or should the sites be lumped together?

8.108

As noted under 'Range of pools available' above, employers are allowed a certain degree of flexibility in determining the pool for selection. As a result, the make-up of the selection pool or pools in multi-site redundancy situations will vary, and much will depend upon the particular employer's business needs.

Take, for example, a nationwide employer with ten sites throughout the country. In addition to other staff, it employs 10–20 sales staff at each site (150 in all). The employer proposes to make 50 of the sales staff redundant nationwide. Its preference is to treat each site as an entity in itself, so that a number of redundancies are made out of the pool of sales staff at each particular site. This approach may be entirely reasonable. The employer may have good business reasons for treating each site separately – perhaps it wants to avoid closing any sites, but needs to retain some sales staff at each site for them to function properly.

8.109

But it will all depend on the facts. In Highland Fish Farmers Ltd v Thorburn and anor EAT 1094/94, for example, the EAT upheld an employment tribunal's decision that an employer was acting unreasonably by treating employees working at different sites as separate groups for the purpose of redundancy selection. The employer in question needed to make eight employees redundant out of its total workforce of about 50, which was spread over a number of different fish-farming sites in North Scotland. It decided to dismiss all three employees at the Torridon site, closing it down completely, and selected the other five from various other sites. Two of these were from the Aird site, which was only 40 minutes away from Torridon and shared some facilities with the business there. A majority of the tribunal decided that the pool of selection was unfair as it was not open to a reasonable employer to consider the Torridon and Aird sites in isolation. The EAT refused to interfere with this finding as it was a question of fact for the tribunal.

In different circumstances, however, it may be reasonable for the employer to concentrate its selection upon a single site. In Clews and ors v Liverpool City Council EAT 463/93 the Council operated two security forces, the Static Force and the Mobile Force. It made several attempts to amalgamate the two but these were resisted by the relevant trade unions. When the decision to make all nine supervisors in the Static Force redundant became known, the plan caused a great deal of industrial unrest, leading to a three-day strike and wide-scale picketing. An employment tribunal rejected the employees' contention that the pool for selection should have comprised both forces. It decided that it would have been unreasonable to combine them for the

8.110

279

purposes of a selection pool given the animosity between the two forces, which had deliberately been kept separate against the wishes of the employer, and the fact that the training of the Mobile supervisors was different from that of the Static supervisors. The EAT upheld this decision.

8.111 **Mobility clauses.** It could be argued that the existence of a mobility clause in an employee's contract of employment means that he or she could, or should, be included in a selection pool established in respect of a redundancy situation arising at a site to which he or she could be transferred; or, conversely, that he or she should be transferred out of a redundancy selection pool in reliance on such a clause. This argument was canvassed before the EAT in Lomond Motors Ltd v Clark EAT 0019/09. However, the EAT thought that there was 'considerable force' in the submission that mobility clauses are not relevant to an assessment of whether or not an employer has acted within the band of reasonableness in selecting the pool. As discussed in Chapter 2, 'Redundancy', under 'Closure of workplace – place of employment', a redundancy at the place where an employee in fact works is not rendered less genuine by the existence of a mobility clause which would have allowed the employer to send the employee elsewhere to work. The EAT in Lomond Motors extended this reasoning to the determination of the selection pool: 'It is not a question of considering what, historically, the position was... nor is it a matter of considering what, at some indefinite future date, the position might be. It is a matter of examining what actually is the position at the time of redundancy.' The employment tribunal had thus erred, to the extent that it was influenced in its decision as to the reasonableness of the employer's determination of the selection pool by the existence of a mobility clause in the claimant's contract of employment.

In Thornley v JCT600 Ltd ET Case No.1800944/10 (discussed under 'Same work' above) an employment tribunal considered that the likelihood that the Lotus operation was going to be relocated away from the main workshop did not justify the exclusion of the technicians working on Lotus cars from a pool for redundancy selection. T was one of seven technicians employed by JCT600 Ltd in its specialist workshop. Five of the technicians, including T, worked on Ferrari and Maserati vehicles and two worked on Lotus cars. In October 2009 JCT600 Ltd decided to reduce the number of technicians it employed by one and T was selected from among the five technicians working on Ferrari and Maserati cars as it was likely that the Lotus operation was going to be relocated away from the main workshop. The tribunal held that this was unfair dismissal. JCT600 Ltd acted unreasonably in excluding from the pool the two technicians working on Lotus cars.

8.112 Arguably, however, the existence of mobility clauses may be relevant where, in practice, employees do regularly work between different sites pursuant to such clauses. There may then be justification for including employees who are notionally based at different sites in one selection pool for redundancy purposes. For example, where an employer is intending to close down two out of ten sites, it would normally be reasonable for the redundancy selection to be concentrated on those two sites alone. However, where a particular type of employee – such as sales staff – move to a significant degree between sites in the course of their work, it may be reasonable for the sales staff to be selected from all ten sites for redundancy.

Pool for selection and collective consultation. It is worth noting here the distinction between the pool for selection in a multi-site redundancy situation and the concept of 'establishment' under the collective consultation provisions contained in S.188 TULR(C)A (discussed in Chapter 12, 'Collective redundancies'). The statutory duty to consult employee representatives arises under S.188(1) 'where an employer is proposing to dismiss as redundant 20 or more employees *at one establishment* within a period of 90 days or less' (our stress). The meaning of 'establishment' is critical here. An employer could contend that, where each site is treated as a separate pool for redundancy selection purposes, each should be regarded as a separate establishment for the purposes of S.188(1). Thus, even if it is proposing to make 20 or more employees redundant nationwide, fewer than 20 employees are being made redundant at each site and therefore the statutory duty to consult does not arise. **8.113**

We discuss the meaning of 'establishment' in Chapter 12, 'Collective redundancies', under 'Timetable for consultation – meaning of "establishment"'. Suffice it to say here that it is a legal concept defined by European and domestic case law that is entirely separate and distinct from the unfair dismissal provisions of the ERA, which give employers considerable latitude when choosing the pool for redundancy selection, provided they act within a range of reasonable responses. Take Mills and Allen Ltd v Bulwich EAT 154/99, for example, where the EAT held that members of a nationwide direct sales team, based in different offices, were a single team and therefore one 'establishment' for the purposes of S.188. That conclusion would have had no bearing on the appropriate pool for redundancy selection had the individual employees in that case brought unfair redundancy claims under the ERA.

Selection criteria
8.114

If the selection pool is reasonable, the employment tribunal will then consider the selection criteria applied by the employer to employees in the pool.

Criteria should be clear and transparent. It may well be unfair to score employees on a range of pre-advised selection criteria and then take into account additional factors of which the employees are unaware in deciding who to select for redundancy. In Watkins v Crouch t/a Temple Bird Solicitors 2011 IRLR 382, EAT, the selection criteria made known to the workforce were fee-earning ability, client-facing skills, knowledge of the firm's administrative procedures, availability **8.115**

281

for suitable work following any reorganisation, and adaptability. Each employee was given a mark against each criterion. W, a conveyancing secretary, and another employee were dismissed on the basis that they had the two lowest scores in the pool. However, W produced documents to the employment tribunal that showed that the firm's receptionist, who was also in the pool, had scored lower than her but had not been selected for redundancy. The firm sought to justify the receptionist's retention on the ground that she was too valuable an employee to lose. It argued that how employees scored against the five criteria was only one part of the decision-making process, and that the workforce knew that other factors would be taken into account, including the overall requirements of the business.

The EAT overturned the tribunal's decision that W had not been unfairly dismissed, on the basis that it had failed to address W's arguments. W's claim was remitted to a different tribunal, as it was possible that the tribunal would still have found her selection to be fair if it had found that the firm had made it clear to the workforce that scoring was subject to its right to retain a particular employee if that was what the future of the practice required, and if the firm's assessment of the receptionist could not be said to be flawed. However, the EAT noted that if the 'overall requirements of the business' were to be taken into account in deciding whether employees should be made redundant, it could well be argued that this should have been one of the advertised selection criteria on which all employees were scored, although it added that so subjective a criterion might not satisfy the requirement for selection criteria to be objective (see below).

8.116 It is also important to ensure that criteria are not unduly vague or ambiguous. In Odhams-Sun Printers Ltd v Hampton and ors EAT 776/86 the employer's criterion was LIFO, subject to the retention of a 'balance of skills' in each department. The EAT agreed with the tribunal that this was vague and imprecise and therefore flawed. Similarly, selection on the basis of a nebulous criterion – such as 'attitude to the work' – will usually be unreasonable. However, in Graham v ABF Ltd 1986 IRLR 90, EAT, the employer's criteria of 'quality of work, efficiency in carrying it out and the attitude of the persons evaluated to their work' narrowly passed the reasonableness test. G was selected for redundancy largely because of his attitude to the work allocated him – including obscene language and hostility – which had been the subject of complaint by colleagues and his manager. Although the EAT thought 'attitude to work' was 'dangerously ambiguous', it upheld the tribunal's finding that it was reasonable on the facts.

8.117 **Criteria must be objective.** In order to ensure fairness, the selection criteria must be objective; not merely reflecting the personal opinion of the selector, but being verifiable by reference to data such as records of attendance, efficiency and length of service. Some examples of criteria that were found to be insufficiently objective:

282

- **Williams and ors v Compair Maxam Ltd** 1982 ICR 156, EAT: the retention of employees who, in the manager's opinion, 'would keep the company viable' was ruled to be entirely subjective and unreasonable and the resulting dismissals unfair

- **KGB Micros Ltd v Lewis** EAT 573/90: the selection of salesmen based on a 'cost savings' criterion – those who cost most in terms of overheads but who generated least revenue were selected – was not an appropriate yardstick by which to assess employees' performance. The employer had failed to undertake any real appraisal of the employees and its selection process completely lacked objectivity

- **Everitt v Sealine International Ltd** ET Case No.1313646/09: the selection of employees on the basis of 'commitment' was found to be inappropriate. The employment tribunal considered that unless such a criterion is closely defined and measurable by agreed benchmarks it is subjective, and the fact that an employee forum had agreed the selection criteria did not make it any less so.

By contrast, 'attitude' was found not to be too subjective in Hill v Enterprise Management Services Ltd ET Case No.1313183/13. Although the employment tribunal in that case stated that it was 'greatly concerned' at the employer's reliance on this criterion because it appeared, on its face, to be highly subjective, ultimately the tribunal was satisfied that what the employer was actually trying to measure had its basis in fact – namely, the way in which work was carried out and the quality of the work, and that this had to be backed up by specific examples. The tribunal also expressed concern about criteria that involved managers' subjective perceptions of employees but held that, in this particular case, these were also based on objective facts.

8.118 In Howard v Siemens Energy Services ET Case No.2324423/08 an employment tribunal refused to criticise an employer for applying a selection criterion for redundancy purposes that reflected employees' adherence to the company's 'Values'. The tribunal found that the employer's use of the 'Values' – which were 'Accountable', 'Altogether' and 'Adaptable' – as a selection criterion was reasonable. However, the way in which adherence was assessed lacked objectivity and transparency. The 'Values' were a recent introduction and the tribunal found that the evidence showed that they had not been universally adopted within the company, nor had proper training been carried out on what they meant. Furthermore, there was no method of cross-checking or benchmarking different managers' assessments of the 'Values', which were necessarily subjective. Thus, there was no way of being certain that all managers applied the criterion in the same way. The claimant had therefore been unfairly selected for redundancy.

The fact that certain selection criteria may require a degree of judgement on the employer's part does not necessarily mean that they cannot be assessed objectively or dispassionately. In Mitchells of Lancaster (Brewers) Ltd v Tattersall EAT 0605/11 the EAT disagreed with an employment tribunal's conclusion that the criteria by reference to which an employee had been selected for redundancy were indefensibly subjective. T was employed as a property manager by ML Ltd, which owned various hotels and public houses. He was a member of a senior management team which comprised four other employees. ML Ltd had to make financial savings and the directors concluded that cutting T's post would have the least detrimental impact on the business because T's role was the least productive in revenue terms. The directors looked at the business skills of each manager and found that, other than T, they all had the relevant skills to bring in revenue. Finding that T had been unfairly dismissed, the tribunal held that the criteria by which he was selected for redundancy were unacceptable because they were 'wholly subjective and based solely on the views of the directors rather than being objective'. While the EAT upheld the finding of unfair dismissal on the basis of the unfair procedure followed by ML Ltd, it disagreed with the tribunal's criticism that the selection criteria were wholly subjective. In the EAT's view, it had not been inappropriate for a relatively small company in serious financial difficulty to use the criteria it did when deciding which one of the five senior managers to make redundant. The EAT stated that just because the criteria used were 'matters of judgement', it did not mean that they could not be assessed in an objective or dispassionate way. The chosen criteria would inevitably involve a degree of judgement, but that was true of almost all selection criteria other than the simplest criterion such as length of service or absenteeism. The EAT concluded: 'The concept of a criterion only being valid if it can be "scored or assessed" causes us a little concern, as it could be invoked to limit selection procedures to box-ticking exercises.' The criteria which ML Ltd had applied were, in the EAT's view, 'unexceptionable'.

8.119 In Swinburne and Jackson LLP v Simpson EAT 0551/12 a differently constituted EAT rejected the employer's submission that the EAT's comments in Tattersall on the validity of criteria that are 'matters of judgement' had changed the law in this area by removing or reducing the requirement for objectivity. The EAT stated that 'in an ideal world all criteria adopted by an employer in a redundancy context would be expressed in a way capable of objective assessment and verification. But our law recognises that in the real world employers making tough decisions need sometimes to deploy criteria which call for the application of personal judgement and a degree of subjectivity. It is well settled law that an employment tribunal reviewing such criteria does not go wrong so long as it recognises that fact in its determination of fairness.'

The prizing of objectivity above all other considerations led the employer into error in Mental Health Care (UK) Ltd v Biluan and anor EAT 0248/12.

There, the EAT upheld an employment tribunal's finding of unfair dismissal where the redundancy selection was based on assessment exercises of the kind usually used for recruitment. As such, the assessments did not take into account matters such as length of service, appraisal records, and the opinion of managers who knew the employees in the selection pool. Mr Justice Underhill observed that it is very unusual for an employer conducting a redundancy selection exercise primarily on the basis of competence to do so without any reference to past appraisals or the views of managers. Indeed, the employer, when giving evidence before the tribunal, had accepted that the procedure produced some surprises, in that some individuals who were perceived to be very good workers were selected, yet because the process was perceived to be transparent and free from bias, their redundancy was nonetheless confirmed.

Underhill J went on to make some comments that should give any HR professional or employment law practitioner pause for thought when undertaking or advising on a redundancy procedure. He acknowledged that the employer took a lot of trouble over and put a lot of resources into the redundancy selection, which was a matter for commendation, but noted that it had even so chosen 'an elaborate and HR-driven method which deprived it of the benefit of input from managers and others who actually knew the staff in question, and which by its very elaborateness was liable to be difficult to apply consistently'. The method produced surprising results but the employer persisted because the processes were thought to be so 'robust'. In the circumstances, Underhill J thought it entirely understandable for the tribunal to find that a blind faith in process – the *characteristic déformation professionelle* of HR departments – had led to the employer losing touch with common sense and fairness. He went on: 'The goal of avoiding subjectivity and bias is of course desirable but it can come at too high a price; and if the fear is that employment tribunals will find a procedure unfair only because there is an element of "subjectivity" involved, that fear is misplaced.' **8.120**

Extent of employer's discretion. Provided an employer's selection criteria are objective, a tribunal should not subject them or their application to over-minute scrutiny – British Aerospace plc v Green and ors 1995 ICR 1006, CA. Essentially, the task for the tribunal is to satisfy itself that the method of selection was not inherently unfair and that it was applied in the particular case in a reasonable fashion. Thus, employers are given a wide discretion in their choice of selection criteria and the manner in which they apply them and tribunals will only be entitled to interfere in those cases which fall at the extreme edges of the reasonableness band. **8.121**

Although this approach has been consistently approved by the higher courts for many years, the way in which tribunals deal with issues of fairness continues to provide fertile ground for appeals to the EAT. The outcome of these appeals shows that tribunals will rarely be justified in finding a dismissal unfair on the basis of the particular criteria adopted by the employer or the application of those criteria to the particular factual matrix. In Nicholls v Rockwell Automation Ltd EAT 0540/11, for example, the EAT held that an employment tribunal, having found that the employer's scoring system was fair and had been fairly applied, had erred in embarking upon a detailed critique of certain individual items of scoring for the purpose of determining whether it was reasonable to dismiss the claimant as redundant. Even if this exercise had been permissible, the tribunal had not made any findings as to why the managers responsible for scoring had marked the claimant as low as they had. Instead, the tribunal had substituted its own view as to the scores the claimant ought to have received for flexibility, administration and product knowledge. This was an error of law, and the tribunal's finding of unfair dismissal could not stand.

8.122 Similarly, in LTI Ltd v Radford EAT 164/00 the EAT held that the employment tribunal fell into error when it concerned itself with its own view of what selection criteria should have been applied rather than maintain focus on the employer's criteria. In that case, the employer had devised and applied a skills-based test under which those in the pool for selection had to perform a series of tasks within a set period for which they were assessed. The tribunal considered that this particular test not only disadvantaged the claimant but also failed to achieve the employer's stated aim of retaining those who had the most flexible skills. However, as the EAT observed, it was for the employer to decide how to make an assessment of skills. The tribunal's task was simply to consider whether a reasonable employer could have chosen the assessment method adopted in the particular case. Furthermore, in the absence of evidence that the skills test was an unfair measure of ability, the finding that the test had placed the claimant at a particular disadvantage indicated that the tribunal had wrongly focused on what was fair to the claimant and not on whether the employer had acted reasonably overall.

By contrast, in East Lancashire Masonic Hall Co Ltd and ors v Buckley EAT 0447/14 the EAT upheld an employment tribunal's decision that the selection process adopted by the employer fell outside the range of reasonable responses, in part due to the employer's choice of selection criteria. It had sought to reduce the number of assistant managers it employed from two to one due to financial pressures. B, the assistant manager who was selected for redundancy, successfully claimed that her dismissal was unfair. One of the aspects of the retained assistant manager's role was marketing, but the employer did not adopt skill or experience in marketing as a criterion for selection. In addition, the criterion that related to competence in IT was assessed in a subjective manner, based on documents and publications produced by each employee, whereas it would have been possible for the employer to obtain objective information on the ability of the two employees in this area; for example, by investigating the employees' specific knowledge of particular software

286

packages. The majority of the tribunal had been entitled to find that these failings, combined with the fact that members of the selection committee had been unduly influenced in their marking by a complaint made against the claimant by a colleague and had taken into account matters that had never been put to her, took the selection process as a whole outside the range of reasonable responses.

Length of assessment period. The length of the assessment period is likely to be important when it comes to determining the reasonableness of the application of selection criteria, as a short assessment period may not show the true picture. And employers will normally be expected to make allowances where an employee's assessment period is truncated by maternity leave, disability or other statutory absences, to ensure that he or she is scored fairly as against other employees. Two examples: **8.123**

- **Eurocasters Ltd v Greene** EAT 475/88: the selection criteria (productivity, absenteeism, attitude to work and cooperation with requests to work extra hours) were applied over a period of two years, during one of which G had been absent on maternity leave. She scored badly and was made redundant without consideration of the fact that her record had been exemplary prior to her maternity leave. The EAT found that the dismissal was unfair, the reasonable selection criteria having been unfairly applied

- **Vij-Solanki v IDT Global Ltd** ET Case No.2203531/08: V finished a period of maternity leave in March 2008, although she did not return to work until late April, having taken accrued holiday. In June 2008 the employer had to make redundancies and V was selected. An employment tribunal found that it was unreasonable for the employer to use only the period commencing in January 2008 to assess those at risk, as V had been away from work for much of this time. The decision to limit her assessment period to two and a half months was one which no reasonable employer could have reached. There were other options open to the employer which could have mitigated any unfairness (actual or perceived), including adding in a period of four months prior to V's maternity leave; simply scoring her on the six months prior to her maternity leave; or even taking a three-month assessment period for all staff from May to July 2008.

Protected activities and selection criteria. As we saw under 'Automatically unfair redundancy' above, employees who carry out trade union and other activities are protected in that their dismissal will be automatically unfair if they are selected for redundancy on account of those activities. That does not mean, however, that such employees should receive special treatment in a redundancy selection exercise. Thus, in Smiths Industries Aerospace and Defence Systems v Rawlings 1996 IRLR 656, EAT, an employee who spent approximately one third of his working time on his duties as a health and safety representative was selected for redundancy under a system based on **8.124**

287

seven criteria related to performance. The employee argued that his dismissal was unfair because the employer had failed in the selection process to take account of the skills and qualities that were entailed in the performance of his health and safety functions. Although the tribunal accepted that contention, on appeal the EAT rejected it, holding that the protection afforded to such representatives in a redundancy exercise is neutral. That is, while they are entitled not to be discriminated against on the ground of their health and safety activities, equally they are not entitled to be given more favourable treatment than their fellow employees in the pool for redundancy selection. Taking a representative's performance of health and safety duties into account when conducting a redundancy exercise would result in discrimination in that employee's favour.

Nor will the fact that the time spent on protected activities has hampered the employee's ability to match certain criteria necessarily assist the employee. In Herbert v Air UK Engineering EAT 575/97 a workshop tradesman who spent three and a half hours a day on his shop steward duties was selected for redundancy because he was less qualified than a colleague. The employee argued before a tribunal that his dismissal was unfair because he had had no chance to gain the relevant qualifications on account of the time spent on his trade union activities. The EAT upheld the tribunal's decision that the employee's dismissal was genuinely due to his lack of qualifications and was fair. The fact that the employee had not gained the qualifications because of his union activities made no difference. The EAT also rejected an argument that some sort of weighting factor should have been applied to the qualification criterion to allow for time spent on union activities. Whereas it might be possible to incorporate a weighting factor into a criterion based on employees' output, it was not so easy to do so in the case of a qualification criterion. In any event, an employer must be entitled to regard qualifications for a skilled job as a high priority. Important as trade union activities are, they could not be legitimately invoked to seek to compensate for lack of qualifications.

8.125 **Specific criteria.** Below, we discuss some of the more common criteria used by employers when selecting employees for redundancy. It should be pointed out, however, that the reasonableness of any particular criterion will always be a question of fact dependent on all the circumstances of the case.

8.126 **Last in, first out (LIFO).** LIFO was traditionally regarded as the easiest and the most obviously objective method of selection to administer and, until fairly recently, was the most common method used. However, its popularity has seen a steady decline owing to a number of factors: selection by service alone can have a detrimental impact on an employer's skills base; on average, women have shorter periods of service than men, meaning that the application of the criterion might constitute indirect sex discrimination; and, finally, the application of LIFO would appear to amount to indirect age discrimination

288

(for more on this, see Chapter 9, 'Discriminatory redundancy', under 'Age discrimination'). Practically speaking, any use of LIFO will now require objective justification in order to avoid contravening discrimination law.

In view of this, the standing of the historical case of Westland Helicopters Ltd v Nott EAT 342/88 must be called into question. There, the EAT considered that to ignore an employee's length of service, or to give it very little weight in the redundancy selection process, could be unreasonable for unfair dismissal purposes. The employer assessed employees for 'efficiency, proficiency and productivity', taking into account length of service only where scores were identical, and dismissed those with the lowest scores. The EAT suggested that a better policy would have been to add length of service to the calculations for all those employees whose scores were within the same bracket. These days, however, it is unlikely that a tribunal would find that an employer had acted outside the band of reasonable responses by failing to apply a potentially age discriminatory criterion.

Performance, skill and knowledge. It is very common for employers to select employees for redundancy on the basis of their performance at work. The potential stumbling block relates to how that performance is measured. For example, an organisation that sets employees targets and regularly reviews staff performance against those targets should have to hand objective and verifiable documentation on which to rank employees' performance. However, an employer that does not regularly monitor performance, and instead relies on the subjective opinion of the employee's manager at the time redundancy is considered, will be leaving itself open to the allegation that the criterion is either not objective or is not being applied in a fair manner. **8.127**

It is reasonable, not to mention sensible, for an employer to try to retain a workforce that is balanced in terms of skills and ability. Hence an individual's skill and knowledge are reasonable considerations, provided they are assessed objectively. The precise choice of factors and their relative weighting will be determined according to the current and future needs of the business. In Dresser UK Ltd v Burnett EAT 112/86, for example, the EAT held that the employer had acted reasonably in selecting the claimant for redundancy rather than a colleague, because the former's background was in sales and he lacked the engineering experience required for the post.

Employers using performance as a selection criterion also need to ensure that employees are compared fairly. In Griffiths v GEA Denco Ltd ET Case No.1316291/09 G was a sales engineer, employed to sell GEA products. These were difficult to sell, as there was no existing client base or reputation, the products had not been designed for the UK market, and the exchange rate made the price high. When the company suffered a reduction in turnover G was placed in a pool with other sales engineers, who all sold Denco products, **8.128**

289

which did not suffer from the same problems. G was selected for redundancy because on the selection criteria, which included performance, he scored lowest. An employment tribunal found that in comparing G's performance with that of the other sales engineers the company was not comparing like with like. The difficulties in selling GEA products impacted on G's scores and meant that the application of the scoring process was not reasonable.

8.129　**Flexibility.** Employers may wish to retain employees who are willing and able to be flexible in their approach to their job. However, employers should ensure that the criterion is necessary, can be applied in an objective manner and does not impact unfairly on particular employees. In Mole v Lamax Foods UK ET Case No.3303708/09, for example, M's selection for redundancy was found to be unfair in that one of the five criteria used was 'flexible approach', defined as willingness to work at the head office for two to three days per week and willingness to travel throughout the UK and overseas. This was outside the range of reasonable responses because M was originally employed as home-based and was only required to come into the head office once or twice a week, whereas the other two employees in the pool were employed on contracts which stated that their normal place of work was the head office. Furthermore, M did not need to travel in her role as much as the other employees.

Note that a requirement to be flexible in terms of hours or travelling is potentially indirectly discriminatory against women, who are more likely to have childcare or caring responsibilities. It may also impact unfairly on disabled employees. Employers relying on such criteria would therefore need to be able to objectively justify their use to avoid a finding of unlawful discrimination under the Equality Act 2010 – see further Chapter 9, 'Discriminatory redundancy'.

8.130　**Disciplinary records.** Employers are naturally inclined to take into account matters such as an employee's disciplinary record when selecting for redundancy. Provided the record is objective and similar offences are given the same weight, the use of such a criterion is likely to be fair.

One question that has arisen in the context of dismissal for misconduct is whether, in deciding to dismiss, an employer can take account of expired disciplinary warnings. In Airbus UK Ltd v Webb 2008 ICR 561, CA, the Court of Appeal reviewed case law on this question and concluded that it did not support the proposition that the conduct which was the subject of an expired warning must be ignored for all purposes when making the decision to dismiss. The Court did, however, indicate that its decision should not be read as encouraging reliance on expired warnings as a matter of course. Rather, the effect of Webb is to confirm that the use of an expired warning is a matter to be considered as part of the overall question of the reasonableness of dismissal.

290

While, in the context of redundancy, the decision in Webb does not outright **8.131** legitimise keeping expired warnings on file for the purposes of redundancy selection, it does confirm that there is no automatic or absolute bar on such use. However, it is likely that tribunals would consider it unfair for employers to take into account incidents that did not result in any disciplinary action being taken. In Meyer v Loftus Family Property ET Case No.3304813/09 M had been told that no disciplinary action was to be taken in relation to a particular incident, but that she would be dismissed if she repeated her actions. Although M submitted a grievance, this was not formally dealt with. An employment tribunal found that M was unfairly selected for redundancy because her employer took the incident into account in scoring her in respect of 'disciplinary record'.

Attendance records. It is generally unwise to make attendance the sole **8.132** criterion for redundancy selection. But where it is used as a criterion, there are conflicting authorities as to whether employers are required to look into the reasons behind employees' absences. In Paine and Moore v Grundy (Teddington) Ltd 1981 IRLR 267, EAT, the EAT found a dismissal unfair because of the employer's failure to investigate the reasons for an employee's absence. In Dooley v Leyland Vehicles Ltd, 1986 SC 272, Court of Session (Inner House), on the other hand, the Court of Session held that it was reasonable for employers to ignore the reasons behind absences because it was often impracticable for employers to discover them.

Where an employer is aware of the reasons behind an employee's absence, it may be held to have acted unreasonably if it does not then take them into account. In O'Neill v DGF Ltd ET Case No.1302373/09, for example, O's selection for redundancy was unfair because, in calculating his score under the attendance criterion, the employer had included absences when O's wife, who was about to give birth, had been up all night suffering from stomach pains; when he had had to take his child to the dentist; and when his wife had again been ill all night and they had been unable to find a babysitter. All these absences potentially gave O a right to take time off work under S.57A ERA (time off for dependants). If these absences had been ignored – in the same way as absences relating to maternity and paternity rights were – O would not have been selected for redundancy. (Note that in this case the employment tribunal may have been swayed by the fact that O was not given an opportunity to challenge his scoring.)

In Byrne v Castrol (UK) Ltd EAT 429/96 the EAT denied that Paine and Moore v **8.133** Grundy (Teddington) Ltd (above) established any inflexible rule that a tribunal will automatically fall into error if it fails to consider whether the employer, in using attendance as a criterion, has taken into account the reasons for the selected employee's absences. Whether or not the employer has done so is merely one of the factors that the tribunal may wish to consider in determining

291

the fairness of a redundancy dismissal. There was also a danger, said the EAT, that employers might make subjective judgements as to the merits or demerits of the reasons given by individual employees for their non-attendance.

It will not necessarily be unreasonable for an employer to take into account sickness absences that are the result of accidents at work – Bartholomew and ors v Mayor and Burgess of the London Borough of Haringey EAT 627/90. In that case it was argued that to include absences due to industrial injury at work under the criterion of absence due to 'sickness/injury' was unreasonable and unfair. The employment tribunal disagreed, holding that the criteria were reasonable in all the circumstances and applied equally and objectively to all employees. The EAT refused to interfere.

8.134 However, in Walsh v Homeserve Property Repairs ET Case No.1606356/09 a tribunal took the opposite approach. W was injured in a road traffic accident at work when travelling in a van driven by one of HPR's employees. He had to take 28 days off work and took further time off for subsequent treatment and medical examinations. He was later selected for redundancy, in part because of his high level of absence. The tribunal found that he had been unfairly dismissed, commenting that as HPR was vicariously liable for the accident and resulting time off work, it 'ill behoved them' to apply the scoring criteria for absence in a way that penalised W.

Whether or not a particular injury amounts to an 'industrial injury' may be a matter of dispute. However, so long as the employer's approach falls within the range of reasonableness, a tribunal is unlikely to interfere with it. For example, in Veitch v Kingspan Ltd ET Case No.1802555/09 V had an accident at work with a forklift truck in November 2007. He was discharged from hospital with painkillers but a few days later became distressed at work by flashbacks to the accident and his doctor signed him off work for 16 days with 'stress reaction'. Towards the end of 2008 K Ltd carried out a restructuring exercise and V was selected for redundancy. He claimed unfair dismissal on the basis that he had been given a low score for attendance primarily because of the time he had taken off suffering from stress, and that this should not have been taken into account because it was due to an industrial injury. However, the tribunal dismissed his claim. One reasonable interpretation of the term 'industrial injury' would be any injury sustained at work, but K Ltd's interpretation – that an industrial injury was a reportable injury under the Reporting of Injuries, Diseases and Dangerous Occurrences Regulations 1995 SI 1995/3163 – was not outside the range of reasonable interpretations. K Ltd acted reasonably in relying on the view of its safety manager that V's accident was not reportable because V had not sustained a physical injury that led him to being off work for three days or more.

8.135 The period over which attendance is assessed may also be a significant factor – see 'Length of assessment period' above. Although the question of what amounts to a reasonable period is a question of fact for the tribunal to decide in the particular case, the period should be substantial, particularly where long-serving employees are concerned. In Fleming v Leyland Vehicles Ltd ET Case No.S/1561/84 an employment tribunal criticised a six-month period as arbitrary and limited because it meant that an employee with 15 years' service was selected for redundancy while shorter-serving employees who had avoided sickness over the six-month period were retained. 18 months would have been a more suitable period.

Note that when using attendance as one of the selection criteria, employers must be mindful of discrimination law. Pregnancy-related absences should be discounted to avoid infringing the substantial legal rights afforded to pregnant workers – see Chapter 9, 'Discriminatory redundancy', under 'Pregnancy and maternity leave', and IDS Employment Law Handbook, 'Maternity and Parental Rights' (2015), Chapter 13, 'Discrimination and equal pay'. In addition, where an employee's absences are caused by a disability, selection on the ground of his or her attendance record might amount to disability discrimination under the Equality Act 2010 – see Chapter 9, 'Discriminatory redundancy', under 'Disability discrimination'.

Health. An employee's health (though not his or her disability) may be reasonably taken into account in the selection process. It may be reasonable to adopt criteria designed to retain the fittest workers, but employers should try to ensure that their facts are accurate so that they can make an informed decision rather than act on assumptions. Wherever possible, the employee should be consulted and the employer should consider offering him or her alternative employment. In Porter v Streets Transport Ltd EAT 274/86 the selection of P for redundancy on the ground that he suffered from a gastric ulcer was reasonable, but the EAT found that a failure to consult him had resulted in the employer's failure to offer him a vacant post and made the ensuing dismissal unfair. **8.136**

Note that where an employee's poor health amounts to a disability, selection of the employee for redundancy on health grounds might amount to disability discrimination under the Equality Act 2010 – see Chapter 9, 'Discriminatory redundancy', under 'Disability discrimination'.

Manner of selection
8.137

In order that dismissals on the basis of any particular selection criteria are fair, the application of those criteria must be reasonable. For example, in Eurocasters Ltd v Greene EAT 475/88 – see 'Length of assessment period' above – it was the inappropriate application of otherwise fair selection criteria that made the employee's dismissal unfair.

There have been numerous cases where the absence of consultation or the failure to offer alternative employment has made an otherwise fair dismissal

293

unfair, but the actual application of the criteria themselves may make a dismissal unfair even before the question of consultation is addressed. Some examples:

- **Lovell v Northampton College** ET Case No.1201910/10: an employment tribunal held that L was unfairly selected for redundancy from his job as a course coordinator at the College because his low score in the selection exercise had been based in part on concerns as to his performance that had never been raised with him and were not reflected in his prior performance appraisals, so he had never had the chance to defend himself. In addition, the tribunal considered that further errors in the scoring process, such as awarding points to L's colleagues for qualifications that they did not possess, demonstrated a lack of care on the part of the College that suggested an absence of good faith

- **Alexanders of Edinburgh Ltd v Maxwell and ors** EAT 796/86: selection was made on the basis of 'merit'. The selector was given no guidance and, although he did assess the employees under various headings, the tribunal found that there had been no systematic attempt to tabulate factors for comparison. The application of the selection criterion was therefore unfair

- **Boulton and Paul Ltd v Arnold** 1994 IRLR 532, EAT: selection of employees was to be made in accordance with an agreed procedure. The criteria were performance, length of service, discipline and attendance. In carrying out the exercise, the employer took every day of absence into account including, in the case of A, an authorised doctor's visit of half an hour. As a result, A scored only three out of a possible ten points in relation to absence despite having no unapproved short-term absence or lateness on her record. On the basis of this score, A was made redundant. An employment tribunal held, among other things, that not only had the employer radically departed from the agreed procedure but that treating a half-hour authorised absence to see a doctor as absence for the purpose of the redundancy assessment was unfair. The EAT upheld these findings.

8.138 However, while tribunals are entitled to consider whether selection criteria were applied fairly, they should not examine the actual scoring unless there has been bad faith or an obvious error – Dabson v David Cover and Sons Ltd EAT 0374/10. In that case, the claimant had been made redundant following a selection procedure in which his skills had been marked against the requirements for two different posts, transport manager and transport assistant. For the managerial job he had been given two points out of two under the heading 'Ability to plan routes', but for the less senior job only one point out of two for 'Ability to assist with route planning'. The EAT accepted that this did not clearly demonstrate error. Relying on the industrial experience of the lay members, it noted that the particular skills for a junior post may be different from those required for a senior post. For example, the

294

manager of a plumbing business may not be required to be a skilled plumber. It therefore rejected the claimant's argument that it was obviously inconsistent for him to be given different marks for essentially the same skill. (For further discussion of the extent to which a tribunal is entitled to appraise the fairness of an employer's scorings, see 'Analysing employee assessments' below.)

'Double' marking. It may be unreasonable for an employer to take the same matter into account in respect of more than one selection criterion. In Carclo Technical Plastics Ltd v Jeyanthikumar EAT 0129/10, for example, the EAT upheld an employment tribunal's decision that J's dismissal for redundancy was unfair on the basis of the selection criteria and the way they were applied. There were five criteria, including disciplinary warnings and quality of work. J's score for quality of work was reduced because she had received a verbal warning for unacceptable performance, but the same warning also reduced her score under the discipline criterion. The tribunal considered that this was neither proportionate nor fair and the EAT agreed, describing the use of one incident to double count as 'a fundamental and obvious error in the application of the procedure'. **8.139**

Discriminatory application of selection criteria. Potentially discriminatory factors in the application of seemingly objective criteria may also result in unfairness (not to mention a discrimination claim). For example, in British Sugar plc v Kirker 1998 IRLR 624, EAT, K, who was partially sighted, was selected for redundancy after 20 years' service. In the assessments he scored zero under two heads – performance and potential, despite never having been criticised for poor performance. The employment tribunal found that K had not been marked objectively as BS plc saw his poor eyesight as a problem and did not think he had a future with the company; his low scores therefore did not reflect the true position. The EAT upheld the tribunal's finding that this made the dismissal unfair. See further Chapter 9, 'Discriminatory redundancy', under 'Discriminatory selection – relationship between discrimination and unfairness'. **8.140**

Composition of selection panel. An employment tribunal may examine an employee's complaint that his or selection for redundancy is unfair because of his or her relationship or prior interactions with the person or persons responsible for applying the employer's selection criteria. However, this is a question of fact and provided the tribunal has given the issue proper consideration, the EAT will not interfere with its conclusions unless there is evidence of perversity. In Wess v Science Museum Group EAT 0120/14, for example, the EAT upheld an employment tribunal's decision that the fact that the selection panel included two managers against whom the claimant had previously raised grievances did not render her selection for redundancy unfair. The managers in question had only one vote between them, and the panel also included a member of the employer's HR team, and two independent directors with whom the claimant had no prior involvement. **8.141**

295

The tribunal had been entitled to find that the composition of the selection panel was not unreasonable and nor did it impact in any way on the fairness of the selection process.

The decision in Jebari v Enterprise Managed Services Ltd ET Case No.3301870/11 is an example of a case in which the composition of the selection panel was found to be unfair. There, EMS Ltd was facing a loss of contracts and decided it needed to make redundancies. At a late stage in the process, EMS Ltd decided that the claimant's role as manager of the health, safety and environmental team could be combined with that of B, the manager of the quality team. J, the director of the division that encompassed both teams, decided together with another director, S, that B was the better qualified of the two employees and should be retained. They then decided that the claimant was in a unique position so she did not need to be put in a pool with B. When the claimant attended her first consultation meeting she made it clear that she thought she should have been put in a pool of two with B. EMS Ltd therefore agreed to apply selection criteria to B and the claimant and compare their scores. The claimant received a lower score and was dismissed as redundant. However, the people who completed the selection matrices were J and S – the same people who had made the initial decision that the claimant should be made redundant. The employment tribunal considered that this was a very significant flaw in the process, as it was highly unlikely that J or S could have put their original decision out of their minds when applying the selection criteria. The dismissal was therefore unfair.

8.142 **Employer's responsibility for selection.** In one unusual case, a dismissal was found to be unfair because the employer had left the entirety of the selection procedure and consultation to the company to which the employee had been seconded. In Atlantic Power and Gas Ltd v More EAT 1125/97 M was employed by APG Ltd, a company providing services for rigs in the North Sea. The company had an agreement with a joint venture company, A/S Ltd, which was set up to provide services to Shell Oil. M and a number of other APG Ltd employees were seconded to A/S Ltd for the purpose of working on a particular rig. Shell's need for rig workers subsequently decreased and A/S Ltd began a selection process which led to M being 'de-seconded'. That in turn led to M's immediate dismissal for redundancy by APG Ltd. An employment tribunal found that the dismissal was unfair because the employer had no input whatsoever into the consultation and selection process, which was left completely to A/S Ltd, and the employer had taken no steps to satisfy itself that the selection made was reasonable. In the tribunal's view, this was a fundamental obligation of employers that could not be surrendered to any third party. The EAT upheld the tribunal's decision. It further pointed out that, even if the selection process carried out by A/S Ltd had been fair, the employer should at the very least have given M the chance to state why it should be somebody other than him who should be selected.

Analysing employee assessments

8.143

When selecting employees for redundancy, it is common practice for employers to decide upon a number of different criteria against which the employees in the pool for selection should be assessed and then to allocate marks for each employee under each of those criteria. Once the selection has been made, those selected might feel that the marking or grading was not carried out accurately and complain that the resulting dismissal was unfair. The question which then arises is whether, and to what extent, an employment tribunal can lawfully scrutinise the employer's assessments of all those in the pool in order to discover any evidence that would substantiate the employees' claims.

In Buchanan v Tilcon Ltd 1983 IRLR 417, Ct Sess (Inner House), the Court of Session ruled that, where an employee makes a general complaint of unfair selection, the employer does not have to prove to a tribunal that its grading of employees was carried out accurately. B was selected for redundancy mainly on account of his comparatively short service and poor attendance record. The employment tribunal found the dismissal unfair. To show reasonable selection, it said, an employer must prove the accuracy of the information on which it was based. On B's absenteeism, for example, the employer should have produced direct evidence of the retained employees' records, to satisfy the tribunal that their record was indeed not as bad as B's. The EAT, overturning this decision, held that the tribunal had imposed too high a standard of proof on the employer and so had erred in law. On appeal, the Court of Session held that where an employee's only complaint is unfair selection, all that the employer has to prove is that the method of selection was fair in general terms and that it was reasonably applied to the employee concerned. Where the tribunal, as here, had accepted that the senior official doing the selecting had made his decision fairly, using information he had no reason to question, to demand that he set up the accuracy of that information by direct evidence was unreasonable and unrealistic.

The Buchanan case was subsequently followed in Eaton Ltd v King and ors 1995 IRLR 75, EAT. There, four employees lodged complaints of unfair selection. One of the issues raised was the general fairness of the employer's application of the selection criteria. The manager, who was the only witness for the employer, had not carried out the assessments himself and was unable to explain in detail how the marks had been allocated to the employees concerned. In the employment tribunal's view, the absence of evidence as to how the marks had been arrived at made it impossible for it to decide that the selection criteria had been fairly applied to any of the claimants. Accordingly, it held that the employees had not been fairly selected. The EAT overturned the tribunal's finding. On a proper application of the principles established in the Buchanan case, all that the employer had to show was that it had set up a good system of selection which had been reasonably applied. In the EAT's view, there was no reason why the managers who took the decision

8.144

297

to dismiss should not have relied on the information supplied to them by the supervisors who carried out the assessments, and the managers could not be expected to be able to explain each marking. Furthermore, there was nothing in the tribunal's findings to suggest that the assessments were not carried out honestly and reasonably. The EAT considered that, while there may be cases where an inference could be drawn from the markings that there was something unfair about the application of the selection process, this was not such a case. The EAT concluded that the tribunal had fallen into precisely the error which had been identified in the Buchanan case, and ruled that all four employees had been fairly dismissed. (Note that the EAT's decision in this case was overturned on appeal by the Court of Session on another ground – King and ors v Eaton Ltd 1996 IRLR 199, Ct Sess (Inner House).)

The observations in the above cases, that an employer need only demonstrate that it had established a good system of selection which had been administered fairly, were expressly approved by the Court of Appeal in British Aerospace plc v Green and ors 1995 ICR 1006, CA. That case examined an employment tribunal's powers to order discovery of assessment forms by claimants who made general complaints about an employer's selection process. At that particular stage in the proceedings the claimants were not able to prove that the documents sought were relevant to an issue which had already been raised. The employees appeared to be seeking the information to go on a 'fishing expedition' for specific instances of unfairness. The Court, in refusing to grant an order for discovery, noted that if a system of graded assessment were to function effectively, its workings were not to be subjected to over-minute analysis. That was true both at the stage when the system was actually being applied and when its application was being questioned at a tribunal hearing. The Court added: 'To allow otherwise would involve a serious risk that the system itself would lose the respect with which it is at present regarded on both sides of industry, and that tribunal hearings would become hopelessly protracted.'

8.145 In Taylor and ors v (1) BICC Brand Rex Ltd (2) BICC Cables Ltd EAT 651/94 employees dismissed for redundancy complained to the EAT that an employment tribunal had made 'generic' findings (i.e. findings which applied equally to all the claimants) in coming to its conclusion that all had been fairly dismissed, and had failed to address the specific matters raised by the employees. In particular, a conflict of evidence over attendance and timekeeping records had not been resolved. This, in the employees' view, fell foul of the guidelines in Williams and ors v Compair Maxam Ltd 1982 ICR 156, EAT, that a tribunal should satisfy itself that it was reasonable to dismiss each individual employee and that the selection criteria had been applied fairly to each one of them. Again, the case turned on the degree of scrutiny required of the tribunal in such cases. Lord Justice Waite in the Green case (above) was quoted as saying: 'So in general the employer who sets up a system of selection which can reasonably be described as fair and applies

298

it without any overt sign of conduct which mars its fairness will have done all that the law requires of him.' The EAT thought it plain that, in order for the claimants to succeed in this case, there needed to be some sort of unfair conduct on the employer's part which could mar the fairness of the system, such as evidence of bad faith, victimisation or discrimination. In the instant case the dispute was over whether warnings had been given or had lapsed and the EAT concluded that the tribunal had made no error of law.

The difficulties that can arise where a tribunal subjects the employer's assessment of its employees to too great a scrutiny are well illustrated by the case of Semple Fraser LLP v Daly EAT 0045/09, in which the EAT overturned a tribunal's decision that D, a solicitor, had been unfairly dismissed for redundancy. Selection was between two solicitors, D and G. The employment tribunal had examined the selection criteria used by the employer and concluded that it could not be faulted. However, it adjusted G's score for mentoring (because, although appointed a mentor, G had not actually done any mentoring), and business development (because G had brought in one piece of business, which the tribunal did not think could constitute a 'strong track record' as required under the selection matrix). The adjusted scores meant that D and G scored equally, and the tribunal concluded that D was 'therefore' unfairly dismissed. The EAT disagreed – the tribunal had erred in subjecting G's scores to such minute scrutiny when there was no evidence of underlying unfairness in the application of the selection criteria. In any event, equal scores did not mean it was necessarily unfair to dismiss D; if it did, then it would have been equally unfair to dismiss G, but the tribunal had failed to recognise this 'inherent illogicality' in its approach. It should have asked whether, overall, no reasonable employer could have dismissed D, but instead, it had substituted its own view.

The principle that tribunals should not subject redundancy selection criteria **8.146** or the employer's application of them to undue scrutiny applies even where two groups of employees are scored separately and no system of moderation is used. In First Scottish Searching Services Ltd v McDine and anor EAT 0051/10 F Ltd acquired the business of two other companies, including SPH. TM and JM, who were formerly employed by SPH, transferred to F Ltd's employment. Before the acquisition, F Ltd indicated that it would probably need to make some redundancies after the transfer. The scoring matrix used by F Ltd in its subsequent redundancy exercise involved a mix of objective criteria – for example, disciplinary records and length of service – and subjective criteria such as interpersonal skills, performance, attitude and enthusiasm. F Ltd's employees (the 'pre-transfer employees') were scored by managers employed in F Ltd before the transfer while SPH employees, including TM and JM, were scored against the same matrix but by two SPH managers. TM and JM were identified as being at risk of redundancy whereas none of the pre-transfer employees was at risk.

The EAT overturned an employment tribunal's decision that F Ltd's selection process was fatally flawed because there had been no system for moderating the scores of the two groups of employees. It considered that the tribunal had fallen into the trap of engaging in 'microscopic' or 'over-minute' examination of the type warned against by the Court of Appeal in British Aerospace plc v Green and ors (above) and by the EAT in John Brown Engineering Ltd v Brown and ors 1997 IRLR 90, EAT (see 'Duty to disclose assessments to employees' below). Addressing the tribunal's main criticism that the method used by F Ltd did not incorporate a system for moderating the two sets of scores, the EAT observed that the tribunal had not explained what it meant when it referred to 'moderating' the scores, and nor was there any basis for the tribunal's assumption that moderation would have increased the scores of TM or JM. The EAT concluded that the tribunal had been wrong to find that identification of a risk in the system meant that the dismissals were unfair. The tribunal had substituted its own view for that of a reasonable employer in deciding that there was a need for moderation.

8.147 However, where there is clear evidence of unfair and inconsistent scoring, any subsequent dismissals are likely to be unfair. In Wardle v Killingholme Stevedoring Ltd ET Case No.1807464/09, for example, an employment tribunal found that W's selection for redundancy was unfair because three managers had carried out the scoring exercise on supervisors from three different parts of the workforce. It was clear on examining the marks that one manager had consistently scored people lower than the other two and there had been no attempt to ensure consistency in the scoring. The tribunal observed that the difficulty was that a large number of the criteria were 'very subjective'; but the HR department could have spent time talking to the managers, collectively, before the scoring exercise was carried out, and reviewed the scores afterwards. Examples could have been used as a scoring exercise and the three managers could have discussed beforehand how they would go about the task.

Furthermore, tribunals have quite often used unexplained quirks in scoring outcomes as a basis for inferring a prima facie case of discrimination – particularly in the context of age, disability and pregnancy/maternity discrimination claims. Such cases are explored in Chapter 9, 'Discriminatory redundancy'.

8.148 **Documentary evidence.** In FDR Ltd v Holloway 1995 IRLR 400, EAT, the EAT ruled that an employee dismissed for redundancy was entitled to be given access to documents relating to the assessments of other employees who had been retained. The main reason for this finding was that the employee's allegations of unfairness were specific, in that he was able to point to a particular employee whom he claimed should have been selected for redundancy instead of him. While he had been employed for over four years, another employee doing comparable work had been retained after only a few months' service.

300

He claimed that the employer had been in breach of the agreed procedure and that its selection criteria had either been unfairly applied or not applied in his case. The EAT held that the documents sought were clearly relevant to the issue of whether the employee had been unfairly dismissed and ordered the employer to disclose the information. Note, however, that the Court of Session has doubted (obiter) the correctness of this decision as, in its view, it is irreconcilable with the Court of Appeal's decision in British Aerospace plc v Green and ors (above) – King and ors v Eaton Ltd 1996 IRLR 199, Ct Sess (Inner House).

Nevertheless, there may be cases where the absence of documentary evidence indicates a lack of objectivity. In E-Zec Medical Transport Service Ltd v Gregory EAT 0192/08 G worked for a private ambulance service. An important part of the firm's business was transporting injured and sick holidaymakers who had been repatriated to the UK. During 2006 the company faced a downturn in this aspect of its work. It decided to restructure the site where G worked and to make four employees redundant out of a pool of 14. The selection process was supervised by the senior HR manager, W, who allocated marks for service, absence, sickness days, sickness occasions, and discipline. This was done by reference to employees' personnel files. The remaining selection criteria – performance, commitment and attitudes, skill base, and team working – were assessed by the regional manager, D. The company adopted a scoring matrix with definitions for the various criteria. However, D did not use any records or objective evidence in arriving at his scores but relied on his personal judgement as a line manager and his experience of working with the employees in the pool. G obtained one of the lowest scores and was made redundant.

The employment tribunal accepted that it was not its task to subject the marking system to microscopic analysis or to check that the system had been properly operated. While the choice of criteria fell within the range of reasonable responses, key aspects of the marking had been left to D's personal judgement; some of the criteria were not capable of measurement by reference to personnel records; and there was no evidence as to how the scoring had been arrived at. According to the tribunal: 'The absence of evidence before us as to how the scoring had been arrived at made it impossible for us to decide that the selection criteria had been fairly applied and accordingly the claimant had been unfairly selected.' The EAT upheld the tribunal's decision. **8.149**

Duty to disclose assessments to employees. The above cases were concerned with the evidence an employer must produce at an unfair dismissal hearing to show that it had fairly applied the selection criteria. However, the question of whether the employee has a right to know how he or she fared in the assessment process may well arise prior to dismissal. A failure to disclose to an employee selected for redundancy the details of his or her individual assessments may give rise to a finding that the employer failed in its duty to **8.150**

consult with the employee. In John Brown Engineering Ltd v Brown and ors 1997 IRLR 90, EAT, the EAT held that the employer's refusal, as a matter of policy, to disclose the marks of those selected for redundancy rendered its internal appeal process a sham. The employees' subsequent dismissals were accordingly unfair for lack of proper consultation. The EAT pointed out that a fair redundancy selection process requires that employees have the opportunity to contest their selection, either individually or through their union. See 'Collective consultation' and 'Individual consultation' below.

The Brown case does not go so far, however, as to hold that employees should be entitled to compare their own scores with those of employees who have been retained. On this question the courts, while demonstrating a clear understanding of an employee's desire to answer the question 'Why me and not somebody else?', have taken the view that to require the employer to review the assessments each time someone selected for redundancy challenges his or her own marks, or those of other employees, is an intolerable burden. Nor does the Brown case entitle employees to see interview notes and other documentation in the employer's possession. In Camelot Group plc v Hogg EATS 0019/10 the EAT pointed out that the Brown case was specific to its facts, of which the most salient were that the employees had been given no information at all about their individual assessments, not even their individual scores. In the EAT's view, the case 'is not authority for the proposition that if an employee intimates a broad, unspecific challenge to the application to him of redundancy assessment criteria, then he must be afforded the opportunity to see his interview notes (or any other documents) prior to any decision to dismiss'. In the present case, the EAT held that the employment tribunal had erred in finding that the claimant's request to see the notes of her redundancy selection interview should have put the employer on notice that she wished to challenge her score, and that it was therefore unfair of the employer to decide to dismiss her before providing the notes.

8.151 These decisions confirm the Court of Session's view in Buchanan v Tilcon Ltd 1983 IRLR 417, Ct Sess (Inner House), that, in general claims of unfair selection for redundancy, there is little scope for employees to challenge the fairness of an employer's decision to select a particular individual.

This logic was adopted in Boal and anor v Gullick Dobson Ltd EAT 515/92. There, employees complained that the consultation with them over their proposed dismissals for redundancy was rendered defective by the employer's refusal to disclose details of how their rivals for redundancy had been assessed. They argued that they could not challenge the decision to select them if they were unable to draw comparisons between the way in which they had been assessed and the way in which those retained had been assessed. In short, they could not answer the question 'Why me?' The EAT emphatically rejected these arguments. There was no legal authority for the proposition

302

that consultation had to be as detailed as the employees claimed. The duty on the employer was to act reasonably within the terms of S.98(4) ERA. It could not be said that an employer was under a duty to provide an employee selected for redundancy with all the information on which the decision to dismiss had been based so that the employee could examine it, point out any mistakes that might have been made and require the employer to go through a revision exercise. If this were required, the employer would not be able to carry out the redundancy exercise at all; it would lead to an 'intolerably protracted and utterly impracticable process'. Moreover, the disclosure of such information to employees would involve breaches of confidentiality and would destroy the morale of both workers and management.

Collective consultation
8.152

As explained in Chapter 12, 'Collective redundancies', S.188 of the Trade Union and Labour Relations (Consolidation) Act 1992 (TULR(C)A) places employers under a statutory duty to consult 'appropriate representatives' – i.e. trade union representatives or, where no union is recognised, employee representatives – where collective redundancies are proposed. While this duty is not strictly relevant to unfair dismissal claims, it has nonetheless been taken into account by tribunals considering the question of reasonableness under S.98(4) ERA.

In Williams and ors v Compair Maxam Ltd 1982 ICR 156, EAT, the EAT stated that trade union consultation was a factor in assessing the reasonableness of a dismissal but that a failure to consult would not, of itself, render a dismissal unfair. The EAT stressed in Hough and ors (including APEX) v Leyland DAF Ltd 1991 ICR 696, EAT, that a finding of failure to consult in breach of S.188 did not automatically lead to a finding of unfair dismissal. But, it said, it was reasonable for the tribunal in that case to decide that, had the union been consulted, there was a possibility that the redundancy dismissals might never have occurred.

While fair and proper consultation is a necessary ingredient of a fair dismissal, whether the consultation is adequate in all the circumstances is a question of fact for the tribunal. However, some guidance as to what constitutes 'fair consultation' was provided in R v British Coal Corporation and Secretary of State for Trade and Industry ex parte Price and ors 1994 IRLR 72, Div Ct. Lord Justice Glidewell said that fair consultation means consultation when the proposals are still at the formative stage, adequate information, adequate time in which to respond, and conscientious consideration by an authority of the response. Putting it another way, Glidewell LJ stated that consultation 'involves giving the body consulted a fair and proper opportunity to understand fully the matters about which it is being consulted, and to express its views on those subjects, with the consultor thereafter considering those
8.153

views properly and genuinely'. Although Glidewell LJ's comments were made in the context of the duty to consult collectively under S.188 TULR(C)A, they have been applied by the EAT in Rowell v Hubbard Group Services Ltd 1995 IRLR 195, EAT, and Pinewood Repro Ltd t/a County Print v Page 2011 ICR 508, EAT, and by the Court of Session in King and ors v Eaton Ltd 1996 IRLR 199, Ct Sess (Inner House), all of which are unfair dismissal cases.

In the King case the Court of Session applied Glidewell LJ's definition of 'fair consultation' to the facts of the case before it and overturned an employment tribunal's finding that there had been proper consultation with the unions. The Court found that, although there had been several meetings with the unions over the redundancies, these had taken place after the employer had formulated its proposals. There was no indication that the unions had had time to respond to the issues raised or that their views would have been considered. Nor had there been any specific reference at the meetings to the method of selection and this was a further pointer to the fact that the consultation had been flawed. The Court ruled that the redundancy dismissals were unfair for lack of consultation and because the employer had not shown that its method of selection was fair.

8.154　The question is always one of what is reasonable in the circumstances. In a small workplace fewer formalities may suffice. In Milne v Distillers Company (Cereals) Ltd EAT 692/87, for example, all but one of the staff were members of the General, Municipal, Boilermakers and Allied Trades Union, with whom the employer had agreed the redundancy selection procedure. The claimant challenged his dismissal for redundancy on the ground that his union, the Transport and General Workers' Union, had not been consulted. The EAT upheld an employment tribunal's rejection of the claim. Given the small size of the plant, the claimant must have been aware from an early stage of the redundancy situation. He had not asked his union to intervene and, moreover, had been individually consulted about his dismissal.

Just because a redundancy process is agreed with employee representatives does not mean that it is necessarily fair, even if it is based on suggestions made by those representatives. In Swan v DB Schenker Rail (UK) Ltd ET Case No.1607553/09 the employee representatives made a suggestion during consultations, adopted by management, that there should be no selection between employees in one location because there were matching vacancies for each employee. The outcome of this was that the claimant was left in a pool of one. Had the employer not accepted this proposal, the claimant would have been able to compete with another employee for a vacancy. His dismissal was therefore unfair.

8.155　**Individual consultation**

Dismissals are more likely to be unfair for lack of individual rather than collective consultation. The importance of following proper procedures

304

was made resoundingly clear by the House of Lords in Polkey v AE Dayton Services Ltd 1988 ICR 142, HL. In that case Lord Bridge stated that: 'In the case of redundancy... the employer will normally not act reasonably unless he warns and consults any employees affected or their representative, adopts a fair basis on which to select for redundancy and takes such steps as may be reasonable to avoid or minimise redundancy by redeployment within his own organisation.' Below, we summarise the facts in Polkey and another case to illustrate the point:

- **Polkey v AE Dayton Services Ltd** (above): P was dismissed for redundancy without his employer having made any attempt to consult him. An employment tribunal faulted the employer's breach of procedural fairness but decided that P had not been unfairly dismissed because he would have been dismissed even if the company had consulted him. The EAT and the Court of Appeal dismissed P's appeal but the House of Lords ruled that he had been unfairly dismissed. The question for the tribunal was whether the employer had acted reasonably in deciding that the reason for dismissing the employee was sufficient, not whether the employee would have been dismissed even if warning or consultation had taken place. Only if the employer could reasonably have concluded at the time of dismissal that consultation would be utterly futile and the decision to dismiss would be unaffected by any consultation with the employee could a dismissal in breach of procedural fairness be reasonable

- **De Grasse v Stockwell Tools Ltd** 1992 IRLR 269, EAT: D was made redundant from his position as machinist in a very small company with no warning and no consultation. He gave evidence that, had he been consulted, he would have suggested being considered for a position of driver-handyman – a job he could have done and which was held by an employee with less service than he had. The employment tribunal appeared to apply the 'no difference rule', which Polkey had rejected, noting that the outcome would have been the same if a fair procedure had been followed and excused the employer's lack of adequate redundancy procedures on account of the size of the company. The EAT, applying Polkey, overturned this finding on the ground that the 'no difference rule' was no longer good law. Furthermore, consultation would have made a difference – D might have been considered for another post. Regarding the size and administrative resources of the company, the EAT acknowledged that S.98(4) ERA specifically referred to these factors as relevant to the determination of reasonableness. It accepted that size could affect the nature and formality of the consultation process but refused to accept that it could excuse a total absence of consultation.

Consultation 'futile'. The above cases confirmed, in general terms, that a procedural impropriety in carrying out a dismissal would render the dismissal unfair. The only escape available to an employer was where it could reasonably

8.156

have concluded that a proper procedure would be 'utterly useless' or 'futile'. Whether or not this was the case was for the employment tribunal to answer in the light of the circumstances known to the employer at the time of the dismissal. In Polkey, Lord Bridge expressed the view that such cases would be 'exceptional'. In practice, such 'exceptional' cases have generally (but not always) been those where, for various reasons, the employer has been bound to operate under some measure of secrecy. Two examples:

- **Hammond v BTB Mailing Services Ltd** ET Case No.7129/88: H was made redundant after returning from sick leave. During his absence his job was made surplus by the installation of a computer and his employer, after consideration, decided that there was no alternative work available for him. The dismissal was found to be fair despite the lack of consultation as the employer had decided not to worry H with the issue of redundancy on account of his ill health. The employer had also decided, as it was entitled to on the facts known at the time, that consultation would have been futile

- **Speller v Golden Rose Communications plc** EAT 1360/96: S returned from her holiday to find that she had been dismissed from her post of marketing manager with a commercial radio station. An employment tribunal found that there were special circumstances justifying the complete lack of warning or consultation. The station was in dire straits, with all its advertising revenue frozen; there was a need for secrecy to avoid a knock-on effect on another station run by the company; and the employer had considered alternative employment but concluded that there was nothing available. The EAT could find no grounds for overturning the tribunal's decision that the dismissal was fair.

8.157 Two examples where the defence failed:

- **Poat v Holiday Inn Worldwide** EAT 883/93: the employer made P, a secretary, redundant without consultation when it reorganised its business in such a way that it no longer needed secretarial staff. There were no other suitable vacancies for her and a tribunal accepted the employer's argument that consultation would have made no difference to the decision to dismiss. The EAT overturned this finding, however, on the ground that the employment tribunal had erred in failing to apply Polkey. The EAT mentioned the various practical purposes which consultation could have but also said that it was 'courteous and humane to consult people when you are thinking of making them redundant'

- **University of Glasgow v (1) Donaldson (2) McNally** EAT 951/94: D and M were made redundant when their fixed-term contracts, which were funded by an external body, came to an end. The university had a policy of not carrying out formal consultations in relation to externally funded posts, even though they generally consulted the relevant unions over impending redundancies. An employment tribunal found the dismissals unfair. The fact that the employees' posts were externally funded did not excuse the lack of consultation and the circumstances of the case did not amount to 'exceptional' circumstances as envisaged by Polkey. The EAT upheld that finding, saying that there was nothing in Polkey to suggest that consultation did not apply to fixed-term contracts – the fact that a contract is fixed term is only one factor to be taken into account in determining reasonableness. Nor could it be said that consultation would have been futile when there were vacancies in the university at the time of the dismissals.

One question that has arisen over the interpretation of Polkey is whether an employer must make a conscious decision that consultation would be futile in order to act reasonably. In Polkey itself, Lord Mackay said that if the employer could reasonably have concluded in the light of the circumstances known to it at the time that consultation or warning would be utterly useless, it might well be acting reasonably in failing to consult. One interpretation of this dictum is that the employment tribunal must consider what a reasonable employer might have done in the circumstances – the objective test. However, Lord Bridge, while agreeing with Lord Mackay, expressed the exception in different terms. He said that a dismissal might be fair despite the lack of proper procedure if 'the employer himself, at the time of dismissal, acted reasonably in taking the view that, in the exceptional circumstances of the particular case, the procedural steps normally appropriate would have been futile'. This seems to suggest that the employer must have made a deliberate decision not to consult the employee, and on reasonable grounds – a subjective test. **8.158**

In Robertson v Magnet Ltd (Retail Division) 1993 IRLR 512, EAT, the EAT took the view that, on the basis of Lord Bridge's speech, the exception would normally apply only where the employer had considered and rejected the possibility of consultation. However, the Court of Appeal in Duffy v Yeomans and Partners Ltd 1995 ICR 1, CA, took a different view. Lord Justice Balcombe refused to accept that a redundancy dismissal must, as a matter of law, be unfair unless the employer has taken a deliberate decision not to consult. In his view, neither the wording of S.98(4) ERA nor the judgment of Lord Bridge supported that proposition. The tribunal must judge what the employer did and not what it might have done. It was what a reasonable employer could have done which had to be tested, so the tribunal must ask whether an employer, acting reasonably, could have failed to consult in the given circumstances.

Relationship with collective consultation. An employer should not assume that individual consultation is unnecessary where consultation with the appropriate representatives (see 'Collective consultation' above) has taken place. In Alexanders of Edinburgh Ltd v Maxwell and ors EAT 796/86 unions had been consulted on impending redundancies, but a dismissal was **8.159**

307

nevertheless unfair for lack of individual consultation. There was evidence that the shop stewards involved in negotiations had been more concerned with protecting their own interests than those of the other union members. However, even in the absence of such evidence, the EAT has stressed in a number of cases that employers should not assume that employees are privy to consultation with their union over redundancies, and that they should themselves ensure that the staff are aware of what is going on – see, for example, T and E Neville Ltd v Johnson EAT 282/79 and Huddersfield Parcels Ltd v Sykes 1981 IRLR 115, EAT.

This will be particularly important where collective consultation is carried out in secret. In Williams v Nationwide Building Society ET Case No.1700172/10 NBS began a redundancy process in March 2009. The process was agreed with a union, but it was also agreed that it would be kept secret to protect the business and managers had to sign non-disclosure agreements. W was called to a meeting on 17 September 2009 during which she was advised that following selection her post was redundant. An employment tribunal found that W was unfairly dismissed because she was told of her dismissal in advance of any genuine consultation – consultation carried out with the union did not help her because it was subject to the non-disclosure agreement.

8.160 Even where an employee is involved in the collective negotiations as a representative, the employer should not neglect to consult that employee as an individual if he or she is to be made redundant. In Walls Meat Co Ltd v Selby 1989 ICR 601, CA, the Court of Appeal found the dismissal of a shop steward unfair because the employer had not given him the opportunity to negotiate his own position after he had agreed, as a union representative, the application of a LIFO procedure. The Court stated that good industrial practice involved a two-stage consultation – first with the trade union about the procedure to be adopted, and then with the individuals chosen under that procedure.

The relationship between collective and individual consultation was considered by the EAT in Mugford v Midland Bank plc 1997 ICR 399, EAT. In that case the employer was planning a major reorganisation which would result in some 3,000 redundancies. M was given a series of briefings on the details of the proposed reorganisation and on the criteria to be used in redundancy selection. M was subsequently selected for redundancy. There followed a number of meetings to discuss the possibility of redeployment but they came to nothing and M was dismissed. The employment tribunal found that, although there had been no real individual consultation with M, there had been full consultation with the union and that on balance the employer had fulfilled its obligation to consult and M's dismissal was fair. On appeal, the EAT noted that collective consultation often concentrated on such matters as selection criteria and general arrangements for redeployment and that unions seldom wanted to be involved in the actual selection of individuals for redundancy. The EAT added that, once individuals had been identified for redundancy, consultation between the employer and the individual employees became important, even if there had already been extensive consultation on a collective level. Nevertheless, the EAT pointed out that it was a question of fact and degree for a tribunal to decide whether the consultation that had taken place was so inadequate as to render the dismissal unfair. In the instant case the tribunal had been critical of the lack of individual consultation but had decided that such consultation as had taken place was adequate in all the circumstances. Although the EAT suggested that it might have taken a different view, there were no grounds for overturning the tribunal's decision. To rule that the tribunal had made an error of law would, said the EAT, have raised the need for individual consultation prior to a decision to dismiss into a prerequisite for a fair dismissal. In the EAT's view, there were no grounds for taking such a restrictive approach.

The Mugford case made it plain that the simple fact that the employer carries out collective consultation does not, of itself, excuse a failure to conduct individual consultations. Nevertheless, tribunals appear to be more willing to tolerate an attenuated process of individual consultation if the employer has already consulted with a trade union or workplace representatives. In Unipart Eberspacher Exhaust Systems Ltd v Keenan EAT 1473/00, for example, the EAT overturned an employment tribunal's finding that an employer should have conducted individual consultation regarding the selection criteria in addition to the collective consultation that had already been carried out over the same matter. The employer had agreed the criteria with an established employee forum that regularly discussed workplace matters with management. In those circumstances, the EAT held that the tribunal's decision on this point was perverse. **8.161**

However, tribunals' tolerance of such limited individual consultation is unlikely to extend to cases in which the subject matter of the collective consultations did not cover the individual employee's situation. In Davies v Delta Display Ltd ET Case No.3303205/12, for example, T was employed as a customer services supervisor, having worked for DD Ltd since 2003. In July 2012 DD Ltd informed employees that it had to reduce its headcount for financial reasons. 80 redundancies were envisaged and employee representatives were elected. They were informed by DD Ltd of the selection criteria to be used, but no thought was given to the situation where there might be a pool of just one person. DD Ltd decided that D was in a pool of one, since her post would no longer exist in the new organisational structure. She was informed of this on 14 August and told that she would be invited to consultation meetings to discuss redeployment and go through redundancy calculations. She asked several times during the consultation period why her role no longer existed and how the new structure would work but received no response. On 31 August she was made redundant. She appealed against that decision, but her appeal was dismissed. An employment tribunal found the dismissal unfair, holding that consultation had been wholly inadequate. The collective consultation meetings were 'of no assistance whatsoever' because the way in which D was selected for redundancy was not anticipated during those discussions. The tribunal also considered that DD Ltd's failure to share with D the details of the new organisational structure led to the individual consultation meetings 'lacking any meaning whatsoever', as it meant that D could not understand why her position no longer existed and was not made aware of the positions that did exist in the new structure and for which she might have wished to apply.

8.162 **Subject matter of consultation.** If individual consultation is generally expected of an employer, the inevitable question arises: consultation about what? To some extent, the subject matter will depend upon the specific circumstances, but best practice suggests that it should normally include:

- an indication (i.e. warning) that the individual has been provisionally selected for redundancy

- confirmation of the basis for selection

- an opportunity for the employee to comment on his or her redundancy selection assessment

- consideration as to what, if any, alternative positions of employment may exist, and

- an opportunity for the employee to address any other matters he or she may wish to raise.

The purpose of consultation is not only to allow consideration of alternative employment or to see if there is any other way that redundancies can be avoided, it also helps employees to protect themselves against the consequences of being made redundant.

8.163 While the question of what constitutes fair and proper consultation in each individual case is a question of fact for the tribunal, the EAT provided some general guidance in Rowell v Hubbard Group Services Ltd 1995 IRLR 195, EAT. In that case R was warned in a memorandum from her employer that redundancies would have to be made and it set out the selection criteria to be used. She then received a letter informing her that she had been selected and offering her the opportunity 'to discuss any matters arising from [the] letter'. When R claimed unfair dismissal, the employment tribunal held that the invitation to discuss the contents of the letter provided sufficient opportunity for consultation. On appeal, however, the EAT said that the letter could not be read as anything approaching consultation. In the EAT's view, there was no real consultation with R, nor any invitation to consult at any stage in the process. Since this was contrary to the procedural

310

requirements laid down in Polkey, it overturned the tribunal's decision and held that R's dismissal was unfair.

In the course of its judgment, the EAT also referred to the comments of Glidewell LJ in R v British Coal Corporation and Secretary of State for Trade and Industry ex parte Price and ors 1994 IRLR 72, Div Ct (see 'Collective consultation' above), including the comment that consultation 'involves giving the body consulted a fair and proper opportunity to understand fully the matters about which it is being consulted, and to express its views on those subjects, with the consultor thereafter considering those views properly and genuinely'. The EAT took the view that those comments on the meaning of fair consultation were 'of assistance to employers when they have to consult with staff in the context of dismissal for redundancy or dismissal'. Although there were no invariable rules and the outcome of each case depended on its own facts, the EAT stated that 'when the need for consultation exists, it must be fair and genuine, and should... be conducted so far as possible as the passage from Glidewell LJ's judgment suggests'.

The Court of Session in King and ors v Eaton Ltd 1996 IRLR 199, Ct Sess **8.164** (Inner House), similarly adopted Glidewell LJ's definition. It was also quoted with approval by the EAT in John Brown Engineering Ltd v Brown and ors 1997 IRLR 90, EAT. In that case the EAT stated that what is required in each case is a fair process which gives each individual employee the opportunity to contest his or her selection, either directly or through consultation with employee representatives. The EAT suggested that this involved allowing employees selected for redundancy to see the details of their individual redundancy selection assessments.

Where an employee has been identified as the only employee at risk of redundancy, a failure to consult properly with him or her as to whether a more junior employee should be included in the pool for selection may render his or her dismissal unfair, even if the employer had considered the matter – Fulcrum Pharma (Europe) Ltd v Bonassera and anor EAT 0198/10. In that case, the EAT agreed with the employment tribunal that the employer had been wrong to conclude, without any further or meaningful consultation as to the size of the pool, that the pool was one person because it was the manager's role that had to go. Although notes prepared by the employer clearly showed that it had considered the issue of pooling, this had not been discussed with the employee who was at risk. More than this was required in terms of consultation. For example, the EAT thought that it might be for the employer to determine within the consultation process whether the more senior employee would be prepared to consider the more junior role at a reduced salary. (This case is also discussed under 'Pool for selection – bumping' above.)

311

8.165 Some examples of cases where there was insufficient consultation:

- **Clark v Business Angels Bureau Ltd (t/a Advantage Business Aims)** ET Case No.1307384/07: C was employed by BAB Ltd as investment manager. During his absence on holiday in August 2007 BAB Ltd acquired another company and e-mailed staff stating that there would be changes in the way that the company was run, and that the job of the investment manager would change. C saw the e-mail for the first time on his return from holiday and at a meeting on his first day back at work he was told about the changes, but no mention was made of redundancy. On 3 September he was told by e-mail that his old job had disappeared, and that his new role was to be discussed with him the next day. At that meeting he was told that the basic salary for the new job would be considerably less than what he had been receiving. Following unsuccessful negotiations, C refused the alternative offer and was made redundant. The employment tribunal accepted BAB Ltd's contention that it was not incumbent on it to consult with C over the business decision, but held that there was still a requirement that it consult adequately and properly at an individual level as to how that decision would impact on C's position. C had been unfairly dismissed

- **McLeod v Thresher Group Ltd** ET Case No.3301163/08: M was employed as branch manager of TG Ltd's off-licence in Finchley. By 1 November 2007 TG Ltd had decided to close the Finchley branch. On 14 January 2008 M was instructed to arrange a meeting with all staff on 16 January, but was given no indication of the purpose of the meeting. At the meeting TG Ltd announced that the store was under threat of closure and invited consultation on alternatives. TG Ltd mentioned to M that there was a vacancy for a manager at another store but M knew that that store was also under threat of closure. There were weekly bulletins giving details of vacancies but not all posts were included. M was informed at a meeting on 15 February that he was redundant and the store closed the next day. The employment tribunal accepted that TG Ltd was entitled to take its own business decision about closure of the store and was not obliged to consult staff on that decision, but it was not reasonable or fair to tell staff they were being consulted about a decision that had already been taken. If employees had been informed in late 2007 that the branch was to be closed, consultation would have concentrated on possible alternative employment. There would then have been vacancies that would have been acceptable to M

- **Hampton v Yakult UK Ltd** ET Case No.3300509/10: H was employed as a field representative by Y Ltd in the UK. Field representatives in Ireland were made redundant and in August 2009 Y Ltd drew the attention of its UK employees to these redundancies and stated that a review of the UK operation was 'currently under way'. In fact, by this time it had decided that the role of field representative should cease and be replaced by a different type of work. On 14 October the UK field representatives were summoned to meetings where they were told they were redundant. The employment tribunal upheld H's claim of unfair dismissal. The single line notice stating that a review of operations was under way could not amount to a warning that redundancies were likely

- **TNS UK Ltd v Swainston** EAT 0603/12: S was made redundant from her role as Business Development Director for the employer's 'DetailMed' service when the employer decided that this service was not sufficiently profitable. Although it disagreed with the employment tribunal's view that there was no redundancy situation because the decision to delete S's role was based solely on commercial considerations, the EAT upheld the tribunal's decision that the dismissal was unfair because the consultation process was wholly inadequate. Consultation only commenced after the final decision to dismiss S as redundant had been taken, thus depriving her of any opportunity to challenge the commercial need for her redundancy, or the employer's figures on which it assessed her performance in terms of its financial benefit to the business

- **Haq v Bromley College of Higher Education** ET Case No.1100111/13: H was selected for redundancy from her role as an ICT lecturer on the basis of the College's selection criteria; she was informed of her score on 7 September and was told that the College would contact her shortly to agree a date and time for her formal notice of redundancy meeting. H made it clear that she did not accept that she was redundant and believed the marking process was fundamentally flawed. The College provided more information on the scoring, but insisted that the next stage was the notice of redundancy meeting. Ultimately this was fixed for 31 October and H's employment ended on that day. H appealed but her appeal was unsuccessful. The employment tribunal found that H's dismissal was unfair: a meaningful consultation would have included a discussion with H about her scores, whereas the first thing that H was told at her meeting was that she was dismissed as redundant. The appeal hearing was not capable of remedying this defect. However, the tribunal made a 100 per cent Polkey reduction on the basis that even if there had been adequate consultation it was clear that H would have been made redundant in any event.

8.166 By contrast to the above cases, in Russell v DSG Retail Ltd ET Case No.2605368/09 the employment tribunal found that a relatively minor flaw in the consultation process was not such as to make the dismissal unfair. The claimant was not expressly told in the letter advising him of his redundancy that he had the right to appeal, although it was mentioned in an employee support guide supplied to him and all other employees at risk of redundancy.

8.167 *Information to be provided.* In Pinewood Repro Ltd t/a County Print v Page 2011 ICR 508, EAT, the EAT underlined the importance of providing an employee with adequate information in order to give him or her the opportunity to challenge a selection for redundancy. There, P, who had worked as an estimator for PR Ltd for 23 years, was told that he was at risk of redundancy. He was placed in a pool with two other employees and they each received a copy of the scoring matrix together with the standards and qualities that each level represented. However, P did not receive his actual scores. He scored the lowest and was invited to a consultation meeting at which he was given his scores. He raised a number of queries in relation to these, but was not provided with an explanation as to how they had been calculated. When his appeal against his redundancy selection was dismissed, P brought an unfair dismissal claim before an employment tribunal.

The tribunal found that P's redundancy dismissal was unfair on the basis that he did not have an opportunity during the consultation process to challenge his scoring since PR Ltd had not explained how the scores had been arrived at. On appeal, the EAT upheld this finding, stressing – after referring to Glidewell LJ's comments in R v British Coal Corporation and Secretary of State for Trade and Industry ex parte Price and ors (above) – that fair consultation involves the provision of adequate information on which an employee can respond and argue his or her case. This did not happen in the instant case. P should have been given the opportunity to challenge his scoring in relation to flexibility – particularly since this was an entirely subjective area.

8.168 However, the EAT did go on to note that further explanation of scoring may not be necessary in every case, especially where the scores relate to issues such as attendance, timekeeping, conduct and productivity. In essence, it is for the employment tribunal to decide whether an employee has been given sufficient information to challenge the scores given in a redundancy selection exercise. The EAT observed that in the modern climate much of this information would hopefully have been available to an employee via a previous appraisal process.

The Scottish EAT in Camelot Group plc v Hogg EATS 0019/10 held that there was no duty on the employer to provide notes of the claimant's redundancy selection interview. H had not suggested, when requesting the notes, that she intended to challenge her interview score, or indeed her score under any of the other selection criteria. The EAT considered that no rule of law requires that if an employee intimates a broad, unspecific challenge to the way in which redundancy assessment criteria have been applied, he or she must be afforded the opportunity to see his or her interview notes (or any other documents) before the decision to dismiss is taken. It also noted that the employment tribunal had been wrong to suggest that whenever an employee who is at risk of redundancy makes any request for information, an ensuing dismissal will be unfair if that request has not been acceded to. In asking to see a document that was bound to contain a wide range of information, H was seeking to embark on a fishing expedition. In the absence of a specific complaint about the way she had been scored, the employer was under no duty to respond.

Length and timing of consultation. Case law suggests that concern over the **8.169**
adequacy of consultation is likely to be particularly acute if an employee is
kept in the dark until very late in the redundancy process. Three examples:

- **Air 2000 Ltd v Mallam** EAT 0773/03: following a review of its IT
  department (in which M was employed as the e-solutions manager), A Ltd
  decided to advertise for the position of head of IT. M did not apply for the
  post. He was subsequently informed that his position was to be integrated
  with the senior position, and consultations took place as to whether there
  was an alternative position available. At a meeting in December 2002 he
  was told that he had been unsuccessful in his application for an alternative
  job and that, as a result, he was to be made redundant with immediate
  effect. His complaint of unfair dismissal was upheld by an employment
  tribunal on the ground that A Ltd had failed adequately to warn him of the
  possibility of redundancy during the departmental review, and had failed
  to consult him at that point about the deletion of his post. On appeal, the
  EAT observed that the fact that there has been adequate consultation in
  respect of one stage in a redundancy process – in this case, consideration for
  suitable alternative employment – did not necessarily mean that the tribunal
  was bound to find that consultation had been adequate overall. Nor was
  it the case that an employer is never under a duty to consult the employee
  about the commercial decision to delete his or her post but only about the
  consequences of that decision. The tribunal's conclusion in this case – that
  fairness required the employer to have consulted prior to the decision being
  taken to delete M's job – was one to which it had been entitled to come

- **Mofunanya v Richmond Fellowship and anor** EAT 0449/03: M was
  employed to work on the night-shift for a charity providing residential care
  for people with mental health problems. One of the patients in the care
  home, P, was a female who required intimate care and, for that reason,
  M's co-worker on the night-shift had always been female. The charity ran
  into financial difficulties and it was proposed that the number of night
  staff be reduced. Discussions took place over a substantial period – always
  during the day, when M was not at work – and eventually it was resolved
  that M should be made redundant rather than his co-worker, owing to P's
  need to be looked after by a female employee. Only then was M informed
  about the proposal, and, following a second meeting shortly afterwards,
  he was dismissed. An employment tribunal rejected his argument that his
  dismissal was unfair on account of the employer's failure to consult prior
  to making the decision to dismiss. On appeal, however, the EAT overturned
  that finding. At no stage during the lengthy consideration of the redundancy
  proposal did the employer take any steps to have personal discussions with
  the two people – M and his co-worker – who were intimately involved in
  the process. And when the decision to dismiss was eventually made, matters
  were thereafter rushed. There was no period of reflection to enable M to

315

take in and assess what was being put to him and to consider his various options. The employer's decision did not, therefore, fall within the band of reasonable responses

- **Vose v Cert Octavian plc** ET Case No.3301548/09: V was given one hour's notice of a meeting following his return from leave, and was not told what the meeting was about. The meeting lasted for seven minutes: V was told he was redundant, asked to return company property and was told to leave immediately. A client was told that day that V had left and a notice was posted saying that he and some others had left the business. He was only invited to a consultation meeting after he wrote to CO plc complaining of unfair dismissal. At the time there was a vacancy that would have been suitable for him. He raised it with CO plc at the meeting and was told he could apply for the post. When he asked why he could not simply be offered the job, he was told this was not possible as CO plc was in the middle of an internal recruitment process. CO plc conceded that V's dismissal was unfair. The employment tribunal noted that CO plc's failure to consult prevented any proper discussion of the alternatives and led to a breakdown of trust and confidence.

8.170 The extent and length of consultation necessary will depend on the facts. In Hilton v BAT Building Products Ltd EAT 787/87, for example, the EAT upheld the decision of an employment tribunal that H's dismissal was fair despite the fact that there had been only one and a half days' consultation with him before the decision to dismiss was taken. He had chosen not to work out his month's notice and had made it clear that he was not prepared to be downgraded in order to remain in employment. In the circumstances, the tribunal was therefore entitled to reach the decision that it did. Similarly, in Dudson v Deepdene School EAT 674/97 a school teacher received little consultation before being informed that she had been selected for redundancy. The employment tribunal nevertheless found her dismissal fair because the dismissal did not take effect for a further seven months, during which period the employee made no effort to apply for any alternative posts that were available within the school. The EAT upheld the tribunal's decision. It stated that, while consultation before dismissal is highly desirable and its absence will very often be critical, it is only one of many factors to be taken into account. According to the EAT, 'where there is ample opportunity for consideration after a decision as to redundancy but before its actual implementation, the weight to be attached to the absence of prior consultation may obviously be reduced'.

Note that the scope of the duty to warn and consult extends only to those employees who are the target of the proposed redundancy. An employer will not be penalised for failing to consult an employee at an earlier stage if the employee was not at risk of redundancy at that time but only becomes so as a result of subsequent knock-on effects of the original redundancies. In Byrne

316

v Arvin Meritor LVS (UK) Ltd EAT 239/02 the employee accepted a new role having been made fully aware that the position was unlikely to last for more than a year. Once he was in his new role, his old job disappeared following a restructuring exercise, during which redundancies were made. At the same time, the employer's requirements for the work carried out by the employee in his new job disappeared sooner than expected. Although efforts were made to find alternative employment, none was found and he was made redundant. An employment tribunal rejected his contention that he should have been consulted at the time of the original restructuring and, on appeal, the EAT upheld that finding. No duty to consult arose in regard to someone who might in the foreseeable future be affected by a redundancy/restructuring. To impose such a duty would place much broader obligations on an employer to consider the potential economic consequences of redundancy than are required under the reasonableness test in S.98(4) ERA.

Appeals. Case law has established that a failure by the employer to consult an employee before dismissal can be cured at an appeal hearing after the date of dismissal – Lloyd v Taylor Woodrow Construction 1999 IRLR 782, EAT. In that case, L was one of two quantity surveyors employed by TWC at a site in South Wales. In September 1997, owing to a reduction in workload, TWC decided that one of the surveyors would have to be made redundant. It decided upon L on the basis of ad hoc selection criteria. It did not consult with L about the selection criteria but informed him at a meeting that he was 'potentially redundant'. He was dismissed in October. Eight weeks later L requested a meeting with management and he was informed for the first time of the primary selection criteria used, namely length of service, attendance, disciplinary record and capability/suitability for the post. In the light of this meeting, L appealed against the decision to dismiss him and a final appeal was heard in April 1998. Both appeals were treated by TWC as rehearings of L's case, and on both occasions the original decision to dismiss L was upheld. L claimed unfair dismissal.

8.171

The employment tribunal found that the consultation process was defective in that L was not informed of the selection criteria before TWC took the decision to dismiss him. Nevertheless, the tribunal decided that – despite the procedural defect – there had been no unfair dismissal because the defect had been corrected by TWC at the later appeal hearings, when L was given the opportunity to contest the criteria. L appealed to the EAT, arguing that, where a dismissal is on the ground of redundancy, a failure by the employer to consult with the affected employee about the selection criteria before dismissal cannot be cured by consulting at a later date and then holding appeal hearings. The EAT dismissed L's appeal, stating that the tribunal had been entitled to find that the defect in consultation prior to dismissal had been cured by the rehearing at the appeal stages. It cited Whitbread and Co plc v Mills 1988 ICR 776, EAT, as clear authority for the proposition

317

that a procedural defect at the dismissal stage may be cured at the appeal stage. In doing so, it rejected L's argument that a case of dismissal by reason of redundancy was distinguishable from cases of dismissal for conduct or capability such as occurred in the Whitbread case.

8.172   Note that the EAT in Whitbread held that procedural defects could only be cured where the appeal amounted to a complete rehearing of the matter, not simply a review of the original decision. However, this part of its decision was subsequently overruled by the Court of Appeal in Taylor v OCS Group Ltd 2006 ICR 1602, CA. In that case the Court held that it is irrelevant whether the appeal hearing takes the form of a rehearing or a review as long as the appeal is sufficiently thorough to cure the earlier procedural shortcomings – see IDS Employment Law Handbook, 'Unfair Dismissal' (2015), Chapter 6, 'Conduct', under 'Disciplinary proceedings – right of appeal'.

8.173   Alternative employment

The consideration of alternative employment for employees selected for redundancy will often be an important part of a fair and reasonable redundancy procedure. While the statutory mechanism for offering alternative or renewed employment is dealt with in detail in Chapter 3, 'Alternative job offers', we consider below some of the circumstances in which a failure to offer such employment can lead to a redundancy dismissal being rendered unfair.

8.174   **Extent of obligation.** In Thomas and Betts Manufacturing Co v Harding 1980 IRLR 255, CA, the Court of Appeal ruled that an employer should do what it can so far as is reasonable to seek alternative work. This does not mean, however, as the EAT pointed out in MDH Ltd v Sussex 1986 IRLR 123, EAT, that an employer is obliged by law to enquire about job opportunities elsewhere and a failure to do so will not necessarily render a dismissal unfair. Two examples:

- **Kilgallon and ors v Pilkington United Kingdom Ltd** EAT 0771/03: P Ltd sought to avoid compulsory redundancies by offering secondments to Spain on terms that each secondee would accept voluntary redundancy at the end of the secondment period. Following negotiations with the recognised trade union, a clause was inserted into the secondment agreement providing that 'should there be any other opportunities for further employment with [P Ltd] at the end of your secondment, you will have the opportunity to be given full consideration' (the consideration clause). K and others accepted secondment in September 1999 but were made redundant in September 2001 without any attempt being made to redeploy them pursuant to the consideration clause. They adduced evidence to show that during the secondment period, P Ltd had filled vacancies for professional engineers and other jobs had been taken by ex-apprentices in accordance with the priority accorded to them under a recruitment policy agreed with the union.

The claimants unsuccessfully claimed that their dismissals were unfair as P Ltd had failed to consult about and offer alternative employment both in 1999 and at the end of the secondments. On appeal, the EAT held that the question of alternative employment did not arise in 1999 because the claimants had agreed to be seconded to Spain as an alternative to being made redundant. As for the position in September 2001 when their secondments ended, the employment tribunal had been entitled to find that the breach by P Ltd of its obligation under the consideration clause made no difference to the outcome in view of (i) the agreed policy favouring the recruitment of ex-apprentices, and (ii) the fact that the claimants were not suited to the other available positions

- **Amazon.co.uk Ltd v Hurdus** EAT 0377/10: following a reduction in the volume of recruitment of managerial and IT staff, A Ltd decided that it would reduce the number of recruiters it employed from two to one. H was selected for redundancy. He applied for a permanent position as Labour Manager – a post that was at that time being filled on a temporary basis by D, a fixed-term employee. H and D were both interviewed for the permanent position, but it was awarded to D. H successfully claimed that his dismissal was unfair on the basis that A Ltd had not done enough to find him an alternative role. The EAT overturned the employment tribunal's decision, holding that the question was whether A Ltd had taken reasonable steps to find alternative employment for H so that he could retain his employment. Even if H had no realistic prospect of securing the Labour Manager's position because the job had been effectively promised to D if her six-month fixed-term employment in the post went well, that did not render his dismissal by reason of redundancy unfair. A Ltd could only have been found to have acted unreasonably in this context if there was a vacant post for which H was suitable but for which he was not considered.

8.175 These cases show that, in certain circumstances, an employer may be excused a failure to make efforts to redeploy employees rather than make them redundant. However, as a general rule, tribunals will expect an employer with sufficient resources to take reasonable steps to ameliorate the effects of redundancy, including giving detailed consideration to whether suitable alternative employment is available. This may include allowing an at-risk employee the opportunity to demonstrate his or her suitability for a vacant position, even if the employer is doubtful about this because the employee lacks prior relevant experience. In O'Brien v Riverside Group Ltd ET Case No.2404843/11 an employment tribunal found that the claimant, a neighbourhood liaison officer, was unfairly dismissed as redundant in circumstances where she had wanted to apply for a vacant sales position but, despite accepting that her CV looked good, RG Ltd had refused to even offer her an interview because she had no previous sales experience and it did not accept her assertion that her skills were transferable.

In Fisher v Hoopoe Finance Ltd EAT 0043/05 the EAT suggested that an employer's responsibility does not necessarily end with drawing the employee's attention to job vacancies that may be suitable. The employer should also provide information about the financial prospects of any vacant alternative positions. A failure to do so may lead to any later redundancy dismissal being found to be unfair. Furthermore, when informing an employee of an available alternative position, the employer should be clear about any eligibility criteria for the role, and the terms on which the role might be offered. In Mayers v The Foundling Museum ET Case No.2203567/12 an employment tribunal found that M's dismissal for redundancy was unfair because her employer had told her that she would be guaranteed an interview for an alternative role only if she met the role's essential criteria. One of the criteria was the requirement to have an arts degree. M's degree was in archaeology and she decided there was no point in her applying. M was also put off from applying because the role was described as full time, whereas M's redundant role was part-time. In its evidence to the tribunal, the employer indicated that it would have interviewed M for the role despite the fact that her degree was not an arts degree, and that it would have considered employing two part-timers on a job-share basis. However, neither of these points was made to M at the time and this rendered the redundancy dismissal process unfair.

8.176 Even if an employer considers that an employee would not accept an alternative post, it may be unreasonable to exclude him or her from consideration for it without consulting him or her first. In Ward and anor v Mahle Filter Systems UK Ltd ET Case No.3102701/09 an employment tribunal found that the claimants' dismissals were unfair because a short-term post had arisen in a different part of the country and it was offered to one of the claimants' colleagues. It was only due to continue for a month, but in the event was extended for a further three months. The tribunal held that it was unfair to exclude the claimants from consideration for the post, without consultation.

The potential consequences for an employer who entirely fails to consult or even consider the possibility of alternative employment are well illustrated by Stanco Exhibitions plc v Wright EAT 0291/07. W was unfairly dismissed from his post as an electrical foreman. At the liability hearing the employment tribunal concluded that, though the company no longer employed electricians under contract (as opposed to sub-contract), W's history of being an employed electrician meant there was a possibility that he would have been kept on as an employed electrician, on a salary of £24,500, and that he should be compensated accordingly. On appeal to the EAT, the employer argued that the tribunal had erred in finding that the company ought to have created a new position of employment for W, when the company had in fact given up employing electricians directly. However, the EAT refused to interfere with the tribunal's decision, concluding that it had to consider whether on the balance of probabilities it was likely that W would have found a job within the company. Its conclusion was 'a realistic proposal' in the light of the evidence, including the fact that the company had originally employed electricians directly and that W was experienced.

It is also worth noting that the fact that it subsequently transpires that **8.177** the employee would not have accepted the alternative employment even if it had been offered to him or her will not prevent a finding of unfairness (although this may be a factor taken into account when the tribunal considers compensation). Thus, in Brown v Gavin Scott t/a Gavin Crawford EAT 149/87 the employment tribunal decided that there was no unfair dismissal, despite a failure to offer available alternative employment, because it found that B would not have accepted the offer in any event. The EAT overturned the decision and held that the dismissal was unfair for lack of consultation. Citing the decision in Polkey v AE Dayton Services Ltd 1988 ICR 142, HL (see 'Individual consultation' above), the EAT stated that the dismissal was unfair as the employer could not reasonably have decided at the time of the dismissal that consultation with B would have been 'utterly useless'.

Objectivity required? It should be noted that, when considering employees for **8.178** alternative employment, it would seem that there is no need to adopt the strict objectivity that is so important in the process of selection for redundancy. In Akzo Coatings plc v Thompson and ors EAT 1117/94 a redundancy situation was created when the employer closed a depot where 45 employees worked. Most of the employees applied for alternative employment at two other depots. The employer drew up selection criteria for the available vacancies in consultation with the employees' union. Each employee completed a questionnaire and was interviewed by a panel. The candidates with the highest scores were offered the alternative jobs. Those who had not been offered alternative employment brought claims of unfair dismissal. An employment tribunal found that the criteria used to select the employees for alternative employment were insufficiently objective, fair and reasonable. For example, the procedure included a subjective assessment by each employee's immediate manager; there was no independent observer present at the panel interviews; and the selection criteria used differed from those originally published. The tribunal therefore concluded that the dismissals were unfair. The EAT overruled the tribunal, holding that it had misdirected itself by applying the guidelines set out by the EAT in Williams and ors v Compair Maxam Ltd 1982 ICR 156, EAT. Those guidelines were concerned with the formulation and application of objective criteria related to selection for dismissal from a pool where some employees would be retained and others would be dismissed. The guidelines did not apply to selection for alternative employment, where the issue was whether the employer had taken reasonable steps to find alternative employment for the employees. It was clear on the facts of this particular case that the employers had taken such reasonable steps and the EAT substituted a finding that the dismissals were fair.

321

Similar findings to that in Akzo were subsequently reached by other divisions of the EAT in the following cases:

- **Darlington Memorial Hospital NHS Trust v Edwards and anor** EAT 678/95: an employment tribunal found dismissals for redundancy unfair because, in offering alternative employment, the employer had not followed similar principles of fairness to those that apply to selection for redundancy. The EAT overturned this decision on the same grounds as Akzo. However, it added some gloss to that decision, noting that the employer is at least obliged to conduct the selection process in good faith and give proper consideration to the redundant employees' applications

- **Look Ahead Housing and Care Ltd v Odili and anor** EAT 0437/07: in written tests and an interview for alternative posts, O and M fell well short of the required mark, but an employment tribunal considered that the employer ought to have offered them the posts because, among other factors, it had failed to take into account their past performance and because the interview process was subjective. The EAT overturned the tribunal's decision. The evidence did not entitle the tribunal to find that the jobs were so similar that any reasonable employer would have had regard to past performance. It also became too embroiled in the interview process. The EAT recognised that an interview process is always going to be to some extent a subjective exercise, but the evidence was that there had been a discussion beforehand about the questions to be posed and the kind of answers that the employer was looking for. The case was remitted to a fresh tribunal for reconsideration

- **Jones v Northumberland County Council** EAT 0482/08: J challenged the fairness of an interview process for a newly created post, claiming that there should have been a pre-existing template or set of model answers, and that the interviewing panel should have been differently composed. However, the EAT upheld the employment tribunal's decision that the process was not unfair. It had found that proper assessments were made based on the answers given by both candidates. The questions were based on the job description and person specification, and raised for consideration issues pertinent to the job. The tribunal considered the lack of model answers, but did not find that this made the process unfair: it pointed out that it is impossible, if two people are being interviewed for the same job, completely to remove any subjectivity from the process.

8.179 However, while the strict objectivity required when selecting for redundancy is not necessary in relation to offering alternative employment, a degree of objectivity is nevertheless important. In Ralph Martindale and Co Ltd v Harris EAT 0166/07 two senior management posts – held by H and E – were to be deleted and a new position created. Both H and E applied for the new role, while applications were also sought from other internal candidates whose posts were not at risk of redundancy. E was appointed after the application of a matrix of subjective criteria drawn up by a director of RMC Ltd, and on the basis that his was a 'less insular' management style. An employment tribunal decided that, owing to its subjective nature, the process of offering alternative employment was not fair, and further that no reasonable employer would have opened the new post up to candidates other than H and E. On that basis it determined that H's dismissal was unfair. On appeal, the EAT concluded that the tribunal's decision was not at odds with Akzo Coatings plc v Thompson and ors (above), and noted that the decision in Darlington Memorial Hospital NHS Trust v Edwards (above) supported the contention that minimum standards of fairness will apply. Tellingly, the EAT did not disapprove of the tribunal's criticism of the subjective nature of E's selection for the post.

Nevertheless, even where an employer fails to adhere to its own job description and person specification, and deviates from its stated interview process, in making a new appointment, a tribunal may still be entitled to conclude, on the evidence, that the process was fair – Morgan v Welsh Rugby Union 2011 IRLR 376, EAT. In that case M was employed by WRU to manage the development of premier-level rugby union football coaches. In 2008 WRU conducted a reorganisation, which involved amalgamating M's post with that of S, whose role had been to manage the development of community-level coaches. A new single post was created, for which M and S both applied. The job description and person specification provided that the appointee 'will be qualified to at least WRU Level 4 or equivalent' and that he or she 'will have an established reputation of developing elite coaches and within the field of coach education'. Following an interview process, S was appointed, and M was dismissed for redundancy. He brought a claim of unfair dismissal, which was dismissed, and he appealed to the EAT. He argued that in deciding to interview S, the appointment committee did not adhere to the job description or person specification. S was not qualified to the appropriate level and, unlike M, had no recent experience of training elite coaches. Furthermore, the committee did not adhere to the notified interview format. S was allowed to give an extended presentation, setting out a plan and vision for the post as opposed to addressing the agreed topic. As a result, he was not asked individual questions. The committee gave overall scores but did not score the presentation or questions individually.

8.180 The EAT observed that where an employer has to decide which employees from a pool of existing employees are to be made redundant, the criteria will reflect a known job, performed by known employees over a period. Where, however, an employer has to appoint to new roles after a reorganisation, the employer's decision has to be forward-looking, centring on the ability of the individual to perform in the new role. This sort of selection is more likely to involve an interview process. An employment tribunal considering whether the process of appointment to a new role is fair simply has to

323

apply S.98(4) ERA – as the tribunal did in Ralph Martindale and Co Ltd v Harris (above). The EAT stressed that a tribunal is entitled to consider how far an interview process was objective, but it should keep in mind that an employer's assessment of which candidate will best perform in a new role is likely to involve a substantial element of judgement. In the instant case the majority of the tribunal did not commit an error of law in taking the view that WRU was not bound to adhere to the job description and person specification slavishly or precisely. If the appointment of a new manager had been external, the employer would not have been so bound. If a candidate had emerged who was outstanding but did not meet some aspect of the person specification, the employer would have remained entitled to appoint that candidate. Although this might seem unfair to other candidates who did meet the person specification, it would not follow that the employer's decision was unreasonable. In the EAT's view, WRU was entitled to interview internal candidates even if they did not precisely meet the job description, and it was entitled to appoint a candidate who did not precisely meet the person specification. Nor did the EAT think that the tribunal had erred in its approach to the interview process WRU had followed. Like the tribunal, the EAT criticised the panel's failure to mark the candidates in accordance with the original plan, but considered this a matter for the tribunal to take into account in its assessment under S.98(4), which it had done.

8.181 The EAT's 'lucid summary of the relevant principles' in Morgan was adopted in Samsung Electronics (UK) Ltd v Monte-Cruz EAT 0039/11. One of the redundant employee's complaints was that instead of using the person specification as the basis of assessment when considering him and another candidate for an alternative job, the employer applied ten 'core competencies' designed for use in the annual appraisal process. In finding that M-C had been unfairly dismissed, the employment tribunal held that it would have been preferable if the employer had used the person specification, and that the core competencies were nebulous and open to subjective interpretation. Given the weaknesses of the core competencies, the managers conducting the interviews should have determined before the interviews how the criteria would be interpreted to avoid inconsistencies of approach. Allowing the employer's appeal, the EAT held that, while it is good practice for interviewers to discuss the approach to be followed and to establish what they understand by any assessment criteria and what would be good answers to the questions asked, a failure to take these steps will not of itself render the interview decision unfair. The failures identified did not result in the claimant suffering any serious substantial unfairness. Furthermore, the EAT dismissed as incorrect the tribunal's finding that it was unreasonable of the employer not to use past performance in appraisals when assessing the employee for the new role. The assessment tools to be used in an interview of this kind – which was not a redundancy selection exercise – were a matter for the employer's discretion. If

324

the tools used had been plainly inappropriate that might have been influential when determining the fairness of the dismissal, but that was not the case here. The post in question was a new job, despite similarities it might have had with the employee's previous role. Accordingly, it was understandable that the employer should choose to interview for it on a forward-looking basis.

Shortly after the decision in Samsung Electronics, a differently constituted EAT in Cumbria Partnership NHS Foundation Trust v Steel EAT 0635/11 held that an employer's decision not to follow its own procedure for appointing an employee to an alternative position within its organisation was not compliant with S.98(4). S's job was removed in a reorganisation and he applied for a newly created role within the same team. The Trust's Management of Organisational Change policy, which contained a commitment to avoid compulsory redundancies, set out various ways in which existing employees could be found alternative employment. S was eligible for 'competitive slotting-in', whereby employees affected by a reorganisation were moved to a new post following competitive interview. S was interviewed for the new role but was rejected for failing to achieve at least 50 per cent of the available marks. When he was made redundant he complained to an employment tribunal of unfair dismissal. The tribunal upheld the claim, finding that there was no provision in the Trust's policy for a 'competency bar' (i.e. the 50 per cent pass mark), nor any evidence that this had been past practice. It was not therefore reasonable for the Trust to impose such a bar in respect of existing employees in a procedure that was used as a method of avoiding compulsory redundancies. While a competency bar would be entirely justified in the recruitment policy, it was not appropriate for the 'slotting-in' process under the reorganisation policy. The EAT dismissed the Trust's appeal against the tribunal's decision.

8.182 While an employer may be perfectly entitled to select candidates for new roles based entirely upon their performance in a competitive interview process, a failure to inform the candidates of this may render the process unfair. In Newcastle City Council v Ford and ors EAT 0358/13, for example, the EAT upheld an employment tribunal's decision that F's dismissal for redundancy was unfair in circumstances where she had performed poorly at an interview for one of the new roles the Council had created. F had not been informed that the selection decision would be based entirely upon the interviews and the Council would not be taking account of its prior knowledge of candidates, or of the written forms the candidates had completed expressing their interest in and suitability for the new roles. Thus, she had been unfairly denied the chance to sell herself for the role at interview.

It is important to note that while the same level of objectivity may not be required in appointing redundant employees to alternative posts, as compared with selecting them for redundancy in the first place, subjectivity in the

325

process is more likely to raise questions of discrimination. In Kinch v Capita Registrars Ltd ET Case No.1100769/12, for example, K, who suffered from bi-polar affective disorder, went on long-term sick leave in February 2011. During her absence CR Ltd adopted a new digitised system, which resulted in K's role ceasing to exist. There was one alternative vacancy for which K applied but she was not offered an interview because the recruiting manager believed she was over-qualified: the role was junior and would have entailed a cut in K's pay; and the business required an immediate start, which the manager assumed would not be possible owing to K's illness. An employment tribunal held that K's redundancy dismissal was unfair as it was unreasonable for CR Ltd not to offer K an interview for the alternative position for which she was clearly qualified. The question of status and pay was for K to decide, and a reasonable employer would have at least enquired whether K was capable of an immediate start in the role. The refusal to offer an interview also amounted to discrimination arising from K's disability, contrary to S.15 of the Equality Act 2010. Discrimination could be inferred from the fact that an existing employee who was qualified for the job was rejected without interview while suffering from a disability which had caused her to be absent from work for some time, and CR Ltd had presented no evidence to dispel this inference.

Discrimination in the context of redundancy is extensively discussed in Chapter 9, 'Discriminatory redundancy'.

8.183 **Group companies.** It may sometimes be appropriate for employers to consider the availability of alternative employment not only within the particular company in which the employee is employed but also within other companies in the same group. In Euroguard Ltd v Rycroft EAT 842/92 GTS Ltd, a security company, had two subsidiary companies, E Ltd and CIT Ltd. R worked as a personnel officer for E Ltd and was based in Glasgow. GTS Ltd had two other personnel officers in Scotland, one in Glasgow and one in Edinburgh. One of the three had to be made redundant and R was chosen. At the time of the redundancy CIT Ltd was looking for a personnel officer. R expressed an interest in the post and was interviewed but was not successful. Other candidates for the job underwent more rigorous assessment and psychometric testing before the selection was made. The employment tribunal took the view that E Ltd had a duty to take reasonable care to consider R for any other posts which might have been suitable and, on the facts, R's application for alternative employment with CIT Ltd had not been adequately considered. His dismissal was unfair for that reason. E Ltd appealed on the ground that E Ltd and CIT Ltd were independent companies, but the EAT took the view that there might be circumstances in which it would be appropriate to look beyond the immediate employer to other companies within the group when considering the availability of alternative employment. The affairs of the company in this particular group, at least in regard to the appointment and

326

redundancy of staff at R's level, were closely integrated: the same individuals were involved and the same policy applied. The EAT concluded that the tribunal had been entitled to find R's dismissal unfair.

However, where there is evidence that the companies within a group operate autonomously, it will not be open to a tribunal to conclude that an employer should have allocated an employee to a vacant position within an associated company – Parfums Givenchy Ltd v Finch EAT 0517/09. In that case F was engaged on the beauty counter of PG Ltd's franchise in Selfridges department store in London. Separately branded, but part of the same group of companies, were Christian Dior and Guerlain. A single HR manager presided over the HR functions of the three perfume divisions. On 28 August 2008 PG Ltd's franchise closed down. F applied for alternative vacancies within the group, but she was unsuccessful. She alleged that the HR managers had colluded in denying her a role. However, the EAT overturned an employment tribunal's decision to uphold F's unfair dismissal claim. It was not open to the tribunal on the evidence to find that PG Ltd had power to allocate F to a position in Guerlain or Christian Dior. The three companies operated autonomously, with their own HR and line managers, and it was the line managers who interviewed F. The highest it could be put was that PG Ltd was under a duty to assist F and to consider alternative work. The EAT remitted the case to a fresh tribunal.

Inferior position. It will not necessarily be unreasonable for an employer to assume that an employee would not wish to accept an inferior position. The EAT suggested in Barratt Construction Ltd v Dalrymple 1984 IRLR 385, EAT, that 'without laying down any hard and fast rule' a senior manager who was prepared to accept a subordinate post rather than being dismissed should make this known to his or her employer as soon as possible. This case does not relieve employers from the obligation to consult employees, however, and in Hall v Times Furnishing Co Ltd EAT 267/87 a different division of the EAT found that the dismissal of a senior manager was unfair for lack of consultation. After failing to find him a position equivalent to that which he had held before, his employer dismissed him without discussing the possibility of offering him one of the inferior positions available.

8.184

Whether an employer's failure to offer an at-risk employee an inferior position will render a dismissal unfair will depend on the circumstances of the case. In Shipton v Ametek Airtechnology Group Ltd ET Case No.2703300/11, for example, AAG Ltd carried out a restructuring in which S's financial accountant role was removed. S was unsuccessful in his application for a new role of assistant financial controller and was dismissed as redundant. An employment tribunal found that S's dismissal was unfair because AAG Ltd had acted unreasonably in failing to inform S that a more junior position of accounts payable supervisor had not been filled internally in the course of

327

the restructuring and that S could have applied for it. It was clear that S had the skills required to carry out this role and although it would have involved him taking a £20,000 cut in pay, the tribunal considered that S would have accepted this as he was only two years away from retirement.

8.185 **Unreasonable terms.** Where an alternative job is offered on unreasonable terms, the dismissal of an employee who refuses that offer will probably be unfair. In Elliot v Richard Stump Ltd 1987 ICR 579, EAT, the employer refused the employee a trial period in a new job. The EAT ruled that the ensuing dismissal was unfair, as it was unreasonable of the employer to offer the alternative job on those terms. This was despite the fact that, as a matter of law, the employee was entitled to a trial period (see Chapter 3, 'Alternative job offers', under 'Trial periods'). The EAT held that, where the terms of an alternative job offered were prima facie unreasonable, the employee's dismissal on refusing it would justify a finding of unfair dismissal.

In Sun Valley Poultry Ltd v Mitchell and ors EAT 164/96 E and her two colleagues worked as administrators. The employer embarked upon a large-scale reorganisation that involved the merging of administrative departments and the loss of administrative jobs. The administrative jobs that would be available after the reorganisation were advertised internally, with employees from a number of departments being invited to apply. The stated qualifications for the new jobs included a requirement of A-level English and, if possible, another language. As E did not have A-level English she decided she had no chance of getting the job and sought employment elsewhere. Some time later, however, she learnt that the A-level requirement was a mistake. An employment tribunal upheld the employee's claim of unfair dismissal. Upholding that decision, the EAT held that the tribunal had been entitled to find that the employer acted unfairly and outside the bounds of reasonableness in imposing the requirement for A-level English. Moreover, the removal of the requirement had come too late, as the employee had already secured employment elsewhere.

8.186 By contrast, if the employer imposes a condition on alternative employment which is reasonable, dismissal of the employee for refusing to accept it may be fair. In Bickerton v Central Office Ltd ET Case No.16132/95 B had a 'spiky' haircut and wore T-shirts, torn trousers and a heavily studded belt. The employer tolerated this style of dress but tried to keep him away from customers, some of whom had complained about his appearance. When the employer had to reorganise its business owing to severe financial pressure, B was made redundant. He was offered alternative work, but on the condition that he wore company livery. B refused and the employer modified the condition to his wearing 'suitable' clothing. B still refused and was dismissed. The employment tribunal found the dismissal fair as the employer's request was reasonable.

328

Assessment at time of dismissal. The question of timing is important here. **8.187** Since the reasonableness of a dismissal is dependent on the situation known to the employer at the time of the dismissal, the appearance of an alternative job after the employee has been dismissed cannot make the dismissal unfair. In Octavius Atkinson and Sons Ltd v Morris 1989 ICR 431, CA, work became available only hours after the employee was dismissed on account of redundancy. The Court of Appeal held that this made no difference to the question of fairness. However, where an employer knows that work will become available in a short time it may be unreasonable to dismiss an employee for redundancy.

In Maguire v London Borough of Brent EAT 0094/13 the EAT held that an employment tribunal had been wrong to find that M's dismissal was fair where the employer had not offered M an alternative position on the basis that the position was 'under review' at the time of M's dismissal for redundancy. The alternative position had previously been occupied by another employee, A, who had given three months' notice of his resignation in April. A's employment therefore terminated and the position became vacant in July, while M was still serving his notice period. During the redundancy consultation process, M had queried whether he could move in to the position when A left, and the employer had accepted that it could be a suitable alternative position given M's skills and experience. The employer had also confirmed that it was reviewing the position, but it expected to have concluded the review in June, well before M's notice period was due to expire. In fact, that review took longer than anticipated and it was still ongoing both when M's notice expired and at the time of the unfair dismissal hearing. The tribunal had therefore considered that the position was not a 'vacancy' at the time M's redundancy took effect and his dismissal was fair. The EAT subsequently concluded that the tribunal had fallen into error. Remitting the case for consideration by a fresh tribunal, it noted that the time to consider the reasonableness of the dismissal is the time the dismissal occurred. In view of the facts in existence when M's employment came to an end, the tribunal had erred in failing to make findings as to the reasons why the review was delayed, why the position was not considered vacant while it was under review, why M's departure date was not or could not be deferred pending completion of the review, or why the employer considered that M could not occupy the position pending completion of the review.

329

9 Discriminatory redundancy

Sham redundancies

Victimisation

Discriminatory selection

Pregnancy and maternity leave

Age discrimination

Disability discrimination

Discrimination against part-time workers

Discrimination against fixed-term employees

In addition to claiming unfair dismissal (discussed in Chapter 8, 'Unfair **9.1** redundancy'), an employee selected for redundancy may argue that his or her dismissal was discriminatory. Most discrimination claims are brought under the Equality Act 2010 (EqA), although special provisions exist in respect of part-time and fixed-term workers (see 'Discrimination against part-time workers' and 'Discrimination against fixed-term employees' below). In this chapter we set out the main issues that can arise in the context of a redundancy claim. However, it is not intended to provide a comprehensive exposition of the law on discrimination, which is outside the scope of this Handbook. For detailed discussion of discrimination law under the EqA, see IDS Employment Law Handbook, 'Discrimination at Work' (2012).

The EqA does not contain any provisions that relate specifically to redundancy. However, an employee may seek to rely on the Act where:

- the redundancy was a 'sham', in that the dismissal was not by reason of redundancy, but was instead by reason of age, disability, gender reassignment, marital or civil partnership status, pregnancy or maternity, race, religion or belief, sex or sexual orientation (the 'protected characteristics') and thus constituted direct discrimination

- the employee's selection for redundancy constituted victimisation for his or her bringing a discrimination claim or taking other action protected under the Act, or

- the application of the selection criteria, the failure to offer alternative employment, or any other aspect of the redundancy process, was influenced by a protected characteristic and thereby amounted to direct or indirect discrimination.

9.2   Note that whereas the rights to claim redundancy pay and unfair dismissal are limited to employees as defined by S.230 of the Employment Rights Act 1996 (ERA) (see Chapter 5, 'Qualifications and exclusions', under 'Employees and excluded employees'), discrimination claims under the EqA can be brought by a more broadly defined category of worker – see IDS Employment Law Handbook, 'Discrimination at Work' (2012), Chapter 28, 'Liability of employers, employees and agents'.

9.3   **Uncapped compensation.** Unlike compensation for unfair dismissal, where there is a limit of (currently) £78,962 or a year's salary, whichever is lower, on the compensatory award, compensation for discriminatory dismissal is uncapped. In addition, tribunals may make an award for injury to feelings. Under the guidelines initially set out in Vento v Chief Constable of West Yorkshire Police 2003 ICR 318, CA, and updated in Da'Bell v National Society for Prevention of Cruelty to Children 2010 IRLR 19, EAT, and Simmons v Castle 2013 1 WLR 1239, CA, such awards generally range from £660 to £33,000.

An example of just how costly a discriminatory redundancy selection can be is afforded by Abbey National plc and anor v Chagger 2010 ICR 397, CA. In that case C, who was of Asian ethnic origin, was made redundant in a procedure that breached all of the Compair Maxam guidelines (see Chapter 8, 'Unfair redundancy', under 'Unreasonable redundancy'), as well as the (now repealed) statutory dismissal procedure. In addition, his employer failed to respond to a race discrimination questionnaire, had not followed the Commission of Racial Equality's Code of Practice on workforce monitoring (since superseded by the Equality and Human Rights Commission's Code of Practice on Employment), and had given no satisfactory explanation for facts which the tribunal found presented a prima facie case of race discrimination. The employment tribunal initially ordered that C be reinstated, but when the employer refused, it awarded C £2,855,659. Had the selection for redundancy merely been unfair on procedural grounds and not discriminatory, the maximum C could have recovered would have been £63,000 (the upper limit at the time). (The Court of Appeal subsequently remitted the case to the same tribunal to reconsider C's compensation on the ground that it had erred in failing to look at whether the award should be reduced to reflect the chance that C would have been dismissed in any event. However, it also went on to say that C could, in principle, recover 'stigma damages' to reflect the fact that employers – unrelated to the respondent – were unwilling to employ him because he had brought a discrimination claim.)

9.4   ## Sham redundancies

When determining the fairness of a redundancy dismissal tribunals are not normally entitled to investigate the reasons behind the redundancy situation. There is no need for employers to demonstrate that they were forced into

332

making redundancies by economic circumstances: it will be sufficient if they have their own good commercial reasons for making the changes. This does not mean, however, that tribunals will always take the employer's stated reasons for the dismissal at face value. As discussed under 'Discriminatory selection – reverse burden of proof' below, where an employee establishes facts from which discrimination can be inferred, the tribunal will look to the employer to provide a non-discriminatory explanation for those facts. Where consultation has been minimal, selection less than transparent and little effort made to offer the employee alternative employment, claims that a 'redundancy situation' was a sham – and the dismissal discriminatory – will be harder for an employer to rebut.

Some cases where tribunals have found 'redundancies' to be fabricated and discriminatory: **9.5**

- **Catton v Rye Street Coachworks Ltd** ET Case No.3201204/08: on 7 February 2008 C told the daughter of her employer's proprietor that she was pregnant. On 11 February C was told that, because of a 'reshuffle', she was redundant. There had been no indication that there might be redundancies and no sign of any downturn in work. The employer claimed that the decision to make C redundant had been taken in December, but she had not been offered employment at another branch where a new employee was taken on in January 2008. In the absence of any evidence from the proprietor or his daughter, the tribunal found that the employer knew that C was pregnant when it made the decision to dismiss. There was no true redundancy situation and C was dismissed because she was pregnant. This was an act of sex discrimination

- **Birchall v Rapide Reprographics Ltd** ET Case No.2401876/09: while off work due to illness B discovered she was pregnant, and informed her employer on 31 October 2008. Later the same day the employer delivered a letter to her home saying it was commencing a 14-day consultation period for redundancy due to a downturn in business. The letter said the employer was considering making about 11 people redundant, but in the event B was the only person dismissed. Although she was still off work ill she was fit to attend a meeting, but was not invited to do so. On 18 November she received a letter dismissing her. A tribunal found that the timing of the letter warning her of redundancy, the failure to meet her or consider alternative work and the fact that she was the only person made redundant all indicated that pregnancy was the true reason for dismissal

- **Lantsbury v Ebara International Corporation** ET Case No.2301433/09: L, who was aged 58, was employed as a field service engineer. EIC experienced a fall in orders and also wanted to reduce overheads in its UK operation, and so decided to lose one of its three field service engineers. It assessed the engineers and because L's score was lowest decided to select him for redundancy. He was called to a consultation meeting on 22 December 2008, where he was told he would be redundant with effect from 31 December. A tribunal concluded that the redundancy situation was not genuine: the need for UK-based engineers had not ceased or diminished. In any event the dismissal would have been unfair since EIC had decided who should be made redundant before the consultation period commenced and neither of the other engineers was called to a consultation meeting. There was no consideration of alternatives to dismissal or of alternative work. L was substantially older than the other two engineers and EIC had recruited a much younger engineer in the USA in September. The tribunal drew the inference that L's dismissal was linked to his age and was discriminatory.

9.6   Sometimes it is not the assertion of a redundancy situation that is found to be a sham but the timing of redundancy dismissals and/or the process put in place for dealing with them. For example, in Bartlett v Grafters Group Ltd ET Case No.1402747/10 the claimant was informed in April 2010 of specific targets she was expected to meet over a 12-week period in view of concerns about her performance. After suffering a miscarriage a month later she was called to a meeting to be told that the part of the business in which she was employed had been closed down. She rejected an offer of alternative employment on the ground that it was not suitable and subsequently brought a claim of sex discrimination. The employment tribunal found that there was no tangible evidence to explain why the performance review process had suddenly been accelerated and on that basis concluded that the decision to make the claimant redundant had been tainted by a discriminatory motivation in that it was precipitated by her pregnancy/miscarriage. A similar approach was taken in Clark v The Plumbing Academy UK Ltd ET Case No.2300415/14, where the employer, having commenced general consultation regarding prospective redundancies, suddenly accelerated that process in respect of the claimant after discovering that she was pregnant and was likely to experience medical complications associated with her pregnancy. Upholding a claim of pregnancy discrimination, the employment tribunal found that, although there was a genuine redundancy situation, it was the fact of the claimant's pregnancy that precipitated the timing of her dismissal and that the redundancy process had thus become a sham.

It should be stressed, however, that simply because redundancy is found to be a sham reason for dismissal, or because the process used to effect a genuine redundancy is a sham, does not necessarily mean that the claimant will have been discriminated against. He or she will still have to show that the employer's treatment was discriminatory or, in the case of maternity/pregnancy, that she suffered unfavourable treatment. Obviously, if the employer has advanced nothing but a sham reason for its actions, a tribunal may well decide that an inference can be drawn to the effect that the real reason related to a protected characteristic, in which case the onus is then on the employer to disprove any discriminatory element. However, the EAT has cautioned in analogous contexts – such as whistleblowing claims – that tribunals should not leap automatically from the finding that the reason for dismissal advanced by the employer lacks any foundation to a conclusion that the real reason must be the alternative reason advanced by the claimant – see, for example, Kuzel v Roche Products Ltd 2008 ICR 799, CA, and University of Bolton v Corrigan EAT 0408/14. Similar reasoning would undoubtedly apply to discrimination claims.

Victimisation

9.7

Victimisation is a self-contained form of discrimination under the EqA. S.27(1) provides that 'a person (A) victimises another person (B) if A subjects B to a detriment because (a) B does a protected act, or (b) A believes that B has done, or may do, a protected act'. 'Protected acts' for this purpose are any of the following:

- bringing proceedings under the EqA

- giving evidence or information in connection with proceedings under the EqA

- doing any other thing for the purposes of or in connection with the EqA, or

- making an allegation (whether or not express) that A or another person has contravened the EqA – S.27(2).

'Detriment' is not defined by the EqA but, according to the Equality and Human Rights Commission's Code of Practice on Employment, it would be 'anything which the individual concerned might reasonably consider changed their position for the worse or put them at a disadvantage' (para 9.8). It is clear that selection for redundancy could constitute a detriment, as the following cases demonstrate:

- **Fitness First Clubs Ltd v Drysdale** EAT 0195/08: the EAT upheld an employment tribunal's decision that an employee's selection for redundancy had been affected by her submission of a questionnaire under the Equal Pay Act 1970 (now the EqA)

- **Marshall v Veolia ES (UK) Ltd** ET Case No.2801214/09: on 23 September 2008 M and her manager had an argument. She gave evidence that he had launched into a tirade of abuse, including sexist language. She was signed off work suffering from stress and depression and did not return. She lodged a grievance, as a result of which her manager was given a written warning. M said she could no longer work with the manager, since she feared a repetition of the incident. On 12 December she was informed that she was at risk of redundancy. M was scored lowest of the people in the

335

pool and she was dismissed. However, an employment tribunal found that M's selection for redundancy was an act of unlawful victimisation. M had done a protected act by complaining about her line manager and he was substantially involved in the redundancy process. She established a prima facie case that the decision to put her in a pool with two administrators even though she was a sales coordinator (and thus did not have the same skills) could have been made by reason of her protected act and her employer failed to prove the contrary

• **Hill v Smith Emmerson Ltd and ors** ET Case No.2601657/08: H was practice manager for SE Ltd. In September 2007 SE Ltd invited her to become a partner in SEA LLP. The next day S informed SE Ltd that she was pregnant. In November SE Ltd offered her the choice of remaining an employee of SE Ltd or resigning and becoming a salaried partner with SEA LLP, with a consequent reduction in maternity entitlement. She elected to remain an employee of SE Ltd. Later that month SEA LLP asked H to relinquish her non-salaried LLP partner status to enable them to bring another partner into the business. H was distressed by this turn of events and made it clear that she wanted the status quo to remain. Notwithstanding her view, SEA LLP drew up an agreement to admit new partners and for H to resign as a partner. She made it clear that she thought this action was being taken because she was pregnant and submitted a grievance. She was removed as a partner in SEA LLP and on her return from maternity leave on 29 May, she was informed by SE Ltd that she had been provisionally selected for redundancy. She unsuccessfully applied for another role and was dismissed. An employment tribunal found that H was unlawfully victimised by SE Ltd because she had made an allegation of discrimination.

9.8 It is perfectly feasible for a tribunal to reject a complaint of discrimination regarding a redundancy process while at the same time upholding a victimisation claim. For example, in Barr v Country Land and Business Association Ltd ET Case No.2602698/11 B was made redundant from her job as Head of Sponsorship for CLBA's annual Game Fair. An employment tribunal rejected B's claim of indirect sex discrimination, which had been based on the fact that, as a single parent, she had been particularly disadvantaged by a proposed reorganisation and change of business location. The tribunal found that any discriminatory impact there had been was proportionate. But it upheld B's claim of victimisation, which was based on the fact that when she had set up her own consultancy following her redundancy, CLBA had e-mailed instructions to its employees not to have any dealings with her in negotiations with potential future sponsors for the Game Fair. In the tribunal's view, CLBA had not countered the inference that the issuing of the e-mail had been prompted by the protected act of B bringing a discrimination complaint.

336

For a fuller discussion of victimisation claims under the EqA, see IDS Employment Law Handbook, 'Discrimination at Work' (2012), Chapter 19, 'Victimisation'.

Discriminatory selection 9.9

Even where there is a genuine redundancy situation, a claim may arise where the employee considers that some aspect of his or her selection for redundancy was discriminatory. This may be because of the manner in which consultation was conducted (or because it was not conducted at all); because the employer failed to offer a suitable alternative vacancy to the employee; because of the application of discriminatory selection criteria; or for some other reason.

The two main forms of discrimination are direct discrimination and indirect discrimination. These are discussed in detail in IDS Employment Law Handbook, 'Discrimination at Work' (2012). Briefly, direct discrimination occurs where the employer treats an employee less favourably than it treats other employees because of a protected characteristic – S.13 EqA. For example, the employer selects an employee for redundancy because of his or her race. Indirect discrimination occurs where, instead of selecting an employee for redundancy on one of the prohibited grounds, the employer applies a provision, criterion or practice that puts an employee who has a particular protected characteristic at a particular disadvantage when compared with persons who do not share that characteristic and the use of the provision, criterion or practice cannot be justified – S.19. For example, the employer selects employees for redundancy on the basis of 'last in, first out'. This criterion is potentially indirectly discriminatory on the ground of age, as younger employees tend to have less service and are thus more likely to be selected for redundancy.

However, an employer may be able to justify an indirectly discriminatory 9.10 selection criterion (or any other indirectly discriminatory aspect of the redundancy selection process) if it can be shown to be a proportionate means of achieving a legitimate aim – S.19(2)(d). An example:

- **Ganesan v Opera Solutions Ltd** ET Case No.2203343/09: G worked for OS Ltd as a management consultant. Three redundancies needed to be made in the office in which G was based and he was selected. He claimed, among other things, that his selection amounted to indirect race discrimination because one of the criteria related to language skills. G was of Indian/Tamil origin and said that people not of his national and ethnic origin would be more likely to speak other European languages. During the hearing he withdrew the claim. However, the employment tribunal noted that since it was necessary for management consultants to have language skills of a high level for some of OS Ltd's projects, it would have found the inclusion of this criterion to be a proportionate means of achieving a legitimate aim.

337

We discuss below some issues that are generic to discriminatory redundancies, before briefly considering three specific protected characteristics that raise particular issues with regard to indirect discrimination: pregnancy/maternity, age and disability. This is not intended to provide a comprehensive account of the law in this area, but rather to highlight some of the issues involved. For detailed discussion of discrimination law under the EqA, see IDS Employment Law Handbook, 'Discrimination at Work' (2012).

9.11 Reverse burden of proof

As observed in Chapter 2, 'Redundancy', under 'Presumption of redundancy', where an employee is claiming a redundancy payment, there is a presumption that he or she has been dismissed for redundancy unless the contrary is proved – S.163(2) ERA. However, where the employee is claiming that his or her selection for redundancy was discriminatory this presumption is not relevant and the so-called 'reverse burden of proof' applies. This does not mean that, once an employee alleges that his or her selection for redundancy was discriminatory, the employer must disprove it. Rather, if an employee can prove facts from which the tribunal could infer that discrimination has taken place (i.e. establish a prima facie case of discrimination), then the burden shifts to the employer to provide a non-discriminatory explanation for those facts – see IDS Employment Law Handbook, 'Discrimination at Work' (2012), Chapter 32, 'Burden of proof', for details.

9.12 **Direct discrimination.** A simple allegation that an employee's selection for redundancy was discriminatory will be insufficient to shift the burden of proof. To put it another way, the mere possibility that an employer *could* have committed an act of discrimination is not sufficient to establish a prima facie case. This point was forcefully made by the EAT in Hammonds LLP and ors v Mwitta EAT 0026/10, when it allowed an employer's appeal against an employment tribunal's finding of race discrimination in the context of redundancy selection. The tribunal had wrongly held that an inference of discrimination could be made simply from the fact that the claimant (a female solicitor of mixed race) was of a different race from others who had not been selected for redundancy and had been provided with less work to do than her comparators, thus tending to show a pattern of marginalisation. Those facts merely showed a possibility that the claimant could have been discriminated against on the ground of race in the allocation of work but did not show that the employer had committed an act of race discrimination in the absence of a legitimate explanation. It was therefore an insufficient basis from which to draw an inference.

Similarly, in Hart v Anglia Newspapers Ltd ET Case No.1502625/08 a newspaper editor claimed that he was selected for redundancy on the ground of his age because he was the oldest editor in the group of newspapers and one of the oldest of the sub-editing staff. However, the tribunal found that even if H was the oldest editor, which was unproven, there was nothing to infer that age-related factors lay behind the redundancy. H offered no evidence to advance his suspicion that age was a factor in his dismissal and thus failed to make out a prima facie case sufficient to shift the burden of proof to the employer.

9.13 In essence, a tribunal will be looking for something more than the mere fact that there has been less favourable treatment between the claimant and his or her comparator and that the claimant has a protected characteristic which the comparator does not. Establishing that there is a difference in treatment is necessary before the reverse burden of proof rule can properly operate – see Essex County Council v Jarrett EAT 0045/15 – but as Hammonds LLP v Mwitta (above) shows, that is not enough. In Cooperative Centrale Raiffeisen Boerenleenbank BA v Docker EAT 0088/10 the requisite 'something more' comprised findings by the employment tribunal that not only was the claimant – a London-based global head of securities for a Dutch bank – of English nationality, whereas the person chosen for redeployment when the bank decided to relocate its securities team to Utrecht was Dutch; but also that the bank had not asked the claimant whether he was prepared to move to Utrecht, had not internally advertised the vacancy for the head of securities position there, and had not consulted the claimant about appointing a member of his London team to that position. In addition, the tribunal found that the appointment decision had been taken by the bank's Global Head of Financial Markets, who not only was Dutch himself but came from the same village as the appointee, and that the latter happened to be the only Dutch employee employed in the London securities team. The EAT held that, when taken together, these facts entitled the tribunal to shift the burden of proof on to the employer to disprove discrimination, and to conclude that as no satisfactory explanation was forthcoming the claimant had been treated less favourably on the ground of race.

Once an employee has proven facts from which discrimination can permissibly be inferred, employers are likely to find it harder to establish a non-discriminatory explanation for those facts in circumstances where they have failed to adopt a transparent and objective selection process (see also 'Sham redundancies' above). Two examples:

- **Obikwu and anor v British Refugee Council** ET Case No.1502553/07: an employment tribunal found that the employer had abandoned its own policies in the way it selected people for redundancy and that the way in which interviews were scored was 'eccentric and lacking in transparency'. After the redundancy selection there were no black workers, and two white females were retained without undergoing a selection process. The employer failed to prove the absence of discrimination and so the claims of direct race discrimination were upheld, although the tribunal was satisfied that there was no conscious discrimination

- **Shaw v Symphony Group plc** ET Case No.2400697/09: S worked for SG plc as a business account manager and in April 2008 was one of its highest performers. S told SG plc in April that she was pregnant. She was not due to go on maternity leave until October but SG plc began to transfer her accounts to other employees in July. S told SG plc she was unhappy about this and she decided to take her annual leave immediately before her maternity leave, making her last day at work 28 August. The market for SG plc's products deteriorated rapidly over the summer and on 24 September it decided to make up to 25 employees redundant nationwide. S was selected for redundancy and was dismissed on 24 October. An employment tribunal upheld her sex discrimination claim. In certain respects SG plc's criteria lacked objectivity, clarity and consistency. S was one of the top performers but was selected for redundancy before people who performed less well and SG plc failed to satisfy the burden of proving a non-discriminatory reason for dismissal.

9.14 **Indirect discrimination.** Where the statutory burden of proof rules are relied on in the context of an indirect discrimination complaint, it is necessary for the claimant to establish within the terms of S.19 EqA that the employer has applied a 'provision, criterion or practice' (PCP) that both disadvantaged others with the same protected characteristic as the claimant (e.g. sex or race) and created a particular disadvantage to the claimant – Dziedziak v Future Electronics Ltd EAT 0270/11. In Dziedziak, the claimant alleged that one of the reasons why she had been selected for redundancy was that she was often late arriving at work owing to childcare commitments. However, the EAT upheld an employment tribunal's rejection of her complaint of indirect sex discrimination: it correctly held that the burden of proof had not shifted so as to place the onus on the employer to disprove discrimination because the claimant had failed to establish that a PCP regarding timely arrival at work had been applied as one of the criteria on which redundancy selection was made.

In Magoulas v Queen Mary University of London EAT 0244/15 the claimant contended that, where an employer fails to appreciate that its criteria for redundancy selection are indirectly discriminatory, its consequent failure to consider alternatives to the discriminatory PCP precludes a finding that it has discharged the burden of proof. This contention was based on the observation of Lord Mance in R (on the application of E) v Governing Body of JFS and ors 2010 IRLR 136, SC, to the effect that justification could prove difficult to show where an employer has not appreciated that a PCP was indirectly discriminatory. However, Mrs Justice Elisabeth Laing, sitting in the EAT, held that Lord Mance's remarks – made in the entirely different context of judicial review – did not amount to a rule of law and that there was no binding authority obliging a tribunal to hold that an employer could not discharge the burden of proof if it had not considered alternatives to the PCP. In that particular case, the application of an indirectly age discriminatory criterion

340

governing consideration for redeployment into newly created research posts as part of a redundancy exercise was held to be justified by the twin aims of expanding research opportunities for younger staff and reducing costs. The EAT held that just because the employer had failed to consider alternatives to the age-tainted PCP did not preclude a finding, once the burden of proof had shifted, that the application of the indirectly discriminatory PCP was a proportionate means of achieving legitimate aims.

Relationship between discrimination and unfairness 9.15

A dismissal that is discriminatory will almost certainly also be unfair under S.98(4) ERA. Although the tests of discrimination and unfair dismissal are different, it is difficult to see how an employer could act 'reasonably' for ERA purposes while contravening discrimination legislation. An example of a redundancy dismissal that was both discriminatory and unfair can be found in British Sugar plc v Kirker 1998 IRLR 624, EAT, where K, who was partially sighted, was selected for redundancy after 20 years' service. In the assessments he scored zero under two heads – performance and potential. The tribunal found that K had not been marked objectively as his low scores did not reflect the true position. This made the dismissal unfair. The tribunal also found that the employer's attitude towards K's eyesight coloured its judgement of him in the redundancy selection process. It held that K had been treated less favourably as a result of the employer's prejudice and awarded him damages of just over £100,000 under the Disability Discrimination Act 1995 (now the EqA). The EAT upheld these findings and the award.

The reverse is not necessarily the case, however: unfair dismissals are not invariably discriminatory. In Igen Ltd (formerly Leeds Careers Guidance) and ors v Wong 2005 ICR 931, CA, the Court of Appeal held that, while it was open to the employment tribunal to draw an inference of discrimination on the facts of that case based on the unexplained unreasonable conduct by the employer, it cautioned tribunals 'against too readily inferring unlawful discrimination on a prohibited ground merely from unreasonable conduct where there is no evidence of other discriminatory behaviour on such ground'. Having said that, where an employee's selection for redundancy has been found to be unfair, and discrimination is also alleged, the employer may find it harder to convince a tribunal that discrimination did not occur.

Positive discrimination 9.16

It should be stressed that while the EqA prohibits discrimination against employees on one of the protected grounds, it does not sanction preferential treatment on the basis of any of the protected characteristics. An employer who positively discriminates in favour of an employee because he or she has a protected characteristic will leave itself open to discrimination claims from other employees who do not share that characteristic and were thereby

341

disadvantaged (except in the case of disability discrimination, which does not 'work both ways' – i.e. an employee cannot claim protection under the EqA on the ground that he or she is *not* disabled).

Nowhere was this more aptly demonstrated than in Eversheds Legal Services Ltd v De Belin 2011 ICR 1137, EAT, where the EAT upheld a claim of direct sex discrimination brought by a man selected for redundancy from a pool of two. The other employee was a woman on maternity leave, who had been awarded a notional score for 'lock-up', a measure of how quickly employees secured payment from clients for work completed. He received an actual score of 0.5 points for lock-up, and 27 points overall, while she was given the maximum two points for lock-up, and scored 27.5 points overall. The EAT upheld the tribunal's finding that the claimant had suffered less favourable treatment on the ground of his sex. The Appeal Tribunal rejected ELS Ltd's argument that it had a defence under S.2(2) SDA (now S.13(6)(b) EqA), which provides that no discrimination arises out of 'special treatment afforded to women in connection with pregnancy or childbirth'. The EAT decided that S.2(2) did not create a blanket exemption. The obligation could not extend to favouring pregnant employees or those on maternity leave beyond what was reasonably necessary to compensate them for the disadvantages occasioned by their condition. Given that there were less discriminatory ways of achieving a fair result, such as scoring both candidates as at an earlier date when they were both at work, awarding a notional maximum score was disproportionate.

9.17 Similar considerations arose in Obikwu and anor v British Refugee Council ET Case No.1502553/07. Two women on maternity leave were 'ring-fenced' for retention. The tribunal observed that 'those on maternity leave must take their selection or otherwise jointly with the rest of the workforce and be treated equally', commenting that the employer seemed to have got confused with the requirement to give preferential treatment in offering alternative work to women on maternity leave who have been made redundant (see directly below).

9.18 **Alternative employment and positive discrimination.** Preferential treatment is possible, in limited respects, when offering suitable alternative employment to employees who have been made redundant. First, as discussed under 'Pregnancy and maternity leave' below (and in detail in Chapter 3, 'Alternative job offers', under 'Offer during period of family leave'), employers have a statutory responsibility to offer suitable alternative employment initially to any employees made redundant while on maternity, adoption or shared parental leave – even if this means that another employee who is not on such leave but who is also redundant is thereby denied it.

In addition, given that a non-disabled person cannot benefit from the provisions of the EqA, moving a disabled employee to the head of the queue for redeployment in a redundancy situation (but behind any employees on maternity leave, etc) will not incur liability in discrimination law, whereas moving people of a particular race or sex would. A tribunal might, in fact, consider it a reasonable adjustment to offer a disabled employee preferential treatment. In Kent County Council v Mingo 2000 IRLR 90, EAT, the Appeal Tribunal held that a policy which gave preferential treatment to redundant or potentially redundant employees by prioritising them for redeployment over employees who suffered incapability or ill health was discriminatory. In the EAT's view, the Council could have made a reasonable adjustment to the policy to ensure that disabled employees received the benefit of priority consideration for deployment along with employees liable to be made redundant.

For more on disability discrimination, see 'Disability discrimination' below, and IDS Employment Law Handbook, 'Discrimination at Work' (2012).

Failure to offer alternative employment

9.19

Even where an employee's selection for redundancy is non-discriminatory, a failure to offer him or her a suitable alternative post may give rise to a successful discrimination claim. This may be in part because, as we discussed in Chapter 8, 'Unfair redundancy', in the section 'Unreasonable redundancy', under 'Alternative employment – objectivity required?', a competitive selection process for a new role does not have to meet quite the same stringent standards of objectivity as selection for redundancy from a pool – and this may thereby leave more room for discrimination to 'creep in', or at least be more readily inferred and harder to rebut. For example, in Rivkin v Mott MacDonald Ltd ET Case No.2408125/09 an employment tribunal found that although R's dismissal for redundancy was not on the ground of his age and was not unfair, the decision not to appoint him to an alternative post did amount to age discrimination. The fact that the manager claimed not to have known that R was 60 before the interview despite the notice of appearance indicating to the contrary, and the fact that there had been a discussion during the interview about R's age and the time it would take to train him up, led the tribunal to infer that age was a factor in the decision not to offer R the alternative post.

As mentioned under 'Positive discrimination – alternative employment and positive discrimination' above and 'Pregnancy and maternity leave' below, an employer will in some circumstances fall under a statutory duty to offer suitable alternative employment to an employee who has been made redundant. A failure to comply with this duty will lead to a finding of automatic unfair dismissal and may also be discriminatory.

9.20 ## Pregnancy and maternity leave

Selection of a woman for redundancy for a reason related to pregnancy or childbirth will amount to an automatically unfair dismissal – see Chapter 8, 'Unfair redundancy', under 'Automatically unfair redundancy'. It will also constitute direct discrimination under S.18 EqA, which provides that an employer will be taken to have discriminated against a woman if it treats her unfavourably during the protected period of her pregnancy because of the pregnancy or an illness resulting from it, or because she is on compulsory maternity leave, or because she is exercising or seeking to exercise (or has exercised or sought to exercise) the right to ordinary or additional maternity leave.

Employers need to be particularly aware of the risk of treating employees on maternity leave as 'out of sight, out of mind', as this can lead to discriminatory selection. In Pickard v BSS Group plc t/a Buck and Hickman ET Case No.1310103/09, for example, P went on maternity leave in August 2008 and another employee covered some aspects of her work. However, by the end of 2008 changes in working processes meant that more junior staff had time on their hands and they took on some of P's work. In February 2009 the employer decided to make redundancies and P was selected for redundancy because the employer believed there was no longer a need for her role. An employment tribunal found that P's absence on maternity leave had a significant influence on the employer's decision-making. If she had remained at work her duties would not have been dispersed around the team and it would have become apparent to the employer that the roles of other team members had diminished more than P's had.

9.21 Similarly, in Chagger v Mullis and Peake LLP ET Case No.3201677/09 an employment tribunal held that the claimant (C) had been discriminated against when she was selected for redundancy while on maternity leave without being included in the departmental restructure that led to the redundancy selection. C had contacted her employer several months before she was due to return to work indicating her preference for returning on a part-time basis. When, shortly afterwards, she was invited to a redundancy consultation meeting she reminded the employer of her wish to work part time and made it clear that she would consider a more junior position. The employment tribunal held that the employer had adopted an 'out of sight, out of mind' approach that reflected the fact that it did not want C to return on a part-time basis. Although the tribunal found that the redundancy scoring process was ostensibly fair and reasonable based on criteria which included 'flexibility', 'performance' and 'future potential', the majority concluded that the employer had been influenced by C's taking maternity leave and having future childcare requirements.

344

However, not all pregnant employees dismissed as redundant will automatically succeed in a claim of unfair dismissal or discrimination. An employee will not succeed if she is selected for redundancy for a reason which is genuinely unconnected with her pregnancy. In one unusual case, Sewell v McCowen EAT 569/94, the office manager of a very small and unsuccessful firm took maternity leave and, during her absence, the employer found that it could manage without her. In view of the company's worsening financial difficulties, she was dismissed for redundancy without consultation because the employer was certain she would not have wanted to do any of the other jobs within the company. The EAT upheld the tribunal's conclusions that a genuine redundancy situation existed and that the employee's maternity absence was not a relevant factor in her dismissal. Moreover, she had not been discriminated against on the ground of sex. It also found that the lack of consultation did not render the dismissal unfair because consultation would have been utterly useless. However, the EAT did add that this was an exceptional case.

In Maksymiuk v Bar Roma Partnership EATS 0017/12 the claimant alleged **9.22** that she had been selected for redundancy because of her pregnancy. Although she had only six months' service, she relied on the fact that her selection had been made a few days after she had informed her employer that she was pregnant as a basis for asserting that the employment tribunal should infer that pregnancy influenced the decision to dismiss. The tribunal rejected her claim and, on appeal, the EAT held that it had been entitled to do so. The Appeal Tribunal observed that the claimant could not hope to show that she had been dismissed or selected for redundancy because of her pregnancy unless she could show that (a) there was no genuine redundancy, (b) the criteria for redundancy lacked proper objectivity, or (c) the scoring of the matrix used to determine selection was itself not objective, but was influenced by pregnancy. It was not sufficient for her simply to establish that she was dismissed and was pregnant to the knowledge of the employer. In the event, the tribunal had held that the employer was already a long way down the road towards effecting a redundancy process before learning of the claimant's pregnancy, which militated against a finding that the redundancy was a sham. It also held – correctly so in the EAT's view – that the criteria for selection used by the employer were unobjectionable. This left only the question of whether the selection for redundancy owed anything to the claimant's pregnancy. Regarding this, despite her contention that she was underscored in relation to some of the criteria, the tribunal had accepted either that no such underscoring occurred or, if it had, it was explicable for reasons other than the claimant's pregnancy. The EAT found that this conclusion had been open to the tribunal on the evidence before it and therefore dismissed the claimant's appeal.

9.23   **Application of discriminatory selection criteria**

Employers may need to give thought to adapting redundancy selection criteria to avoid indirectly discriminating against women on maternity leave. For example, pregnancy-related absence is commonly and properly disregarded in selection based on attendance. Some consideration should also be given to the way in which flexibility is rewarded, since those with childcare responsibilities – predominantly women – may be adversely affected.

Employers also need to be wary of making assumptions about pregnant women or women on maternity leave. In Denysenko v Credit Suisse Securities (Europe) Ltd ET Case No.3200840/08 D was vice president responsible for Ukraine. In order to ensure her market was covered while she was on maternity leave she recruited a new employee, K. When D returned to work a year later there had been considerable management changes and D was told that K was to continue in his post, and that at first they were both to cover the role. However, she was subsequently selected for redundancy while K was retained. The tribunal found that during the redundancy selection process the employer commented on D's lengthy absence (on maternity leave) and made assumptions about D's ability as a mother to travel and work long hours when necessary. This amounted to direct discrimination.

9.24   Employers must also be alert, however, to the danger of disadvantaging male employees in adapting potentially discriminatory selection criteria. In Eversheds Legal Services Ltd v De Belin 2011 ICR 1137, EAT (see 'Positive discrimination' above), the more favourable treatment of a woman on maternity leave in the redundancy selection exercise amounted to sex discrimination against the male claimant.

9.25   **Alternative employment**

As discussed in detail in Chapter 3, 'Alternative job offers', an employee who is made redundant while on maternity, adoption or shared parental leave is entitled to be offered suitable alternative employment in preference to other employees – Reg 10 Maternity and Parental Leave etc Regulations 1999 SI 1999/3312 ('the MPL Regulations'), Reg 23 Paternity and Adoption Leave Regulations 2002 SI 2002/2788 and Reg 39 Shared Parental Leave Regulations 2014 SI 2014/3050. The employee does not have to 'apply' for such employment. In Bottomer v Chamberlains Estate Agents and ors ET Case No.1307016/08 four office managers were at risk of redundancy, but there was only one vacancy, for which all could apply. B, who was on maternity leave, did apply and was interviewed, but was not successful. The employer conceded that the failure to offer her the alternative post rendered her dismissal automatically unfair under the MPL Regulations, and the tribunal found that it also amounted to an act of discrimination.

A failure on the part of the employer to comply with these provisions will lead to a finding of automatically unfair dismissal, and, frequently (but, as noted below, not necessarily), also to a finding of discrimination under the EqA. Two further examples:

- **Hibbert v Mawdsley Brooks and Co Ltd** ET Case No.2411347/09: after H returned from maternity leave she was made redundant. A tribunal found that she was unfairly dismissed pursuant to the MPL Regulations and her dismissal amounted to sex discrimination. Her employer had restructured and had created a new post that incorporated part of H's job and was very similar to it. The employee who had covered H's maternity leave applied for and obtained the new post in H's absence. The employer treated H less favourably on the ground of her maternity leave by failing to offer her the opportunity to apply for the new post

- **McKeith-Wellington v Denial London Ltd and anor** ET Case No.3303074/10: M-W told D Ltd's director that she was pregnant in January 2010. In April D Ltd undertook a review of the business and decided that the line on which M-W worked should be discontinued, as it was not profitable. She was informed that her job was at risk of redundancy. At a consultation meeting D Ltd mentioned the possibility of creating a new sales manager role and gave M-W one day to indicate whether she was interested in being considered for it. However, D Ltd wrote to M-W while she was on maternity leave saying it did not think she would be suitable for the role mentioned and she was given notice of dismissal and offered a much more junior role. A tribunal found that M-W was entitled to be offered the sales manager role under the MPL Regulations. The director wanted someone who could start immediately and so did not want to wait until M-W returned from maternity leave. The dismissal was therefore also discriminatory on the grounds of M-W's pregnancy and/or maternity leave.

9.26 However, it must not be assumed that just because there has been a breach of the MPL Regulations leading to a finding of unfair dismissal, that automatically means that the claimant has been discriminated against. In Sefton Borough Council v Wainwright 2015 ICR 652, EAT, the EAT emphasised that there is a difference in how unfair dismissal protection is afforded under Reg 10 of the MPL Regulations and how protection is afforded against discriminatory (i.e. unfavourable) treatment because of pregnancy/maternity under S.18 EqA. The latter requires a finding of unfavourable treatment because of pregnancy or maternity leave, whereas under the MPL Regulations, a woman is entitled during the protected period of her pregnancy and maternity leave to special protection regarding offers of alternative employment and is be treated as automatically unfairly dismissed if her rights in the matter are denied. In the instant case, by not being offered a suitable available vacancy the employee had been treated unfavourably, but the employment tribunal

347

had failed to ask whether or not her absence on maternity leave was the *reason* for the unfavourable treatment, which it was obliged to do. The EAT therefore remitted that matter to the same tribunal for reconsideration.

9.27 **Discriminatory assumptions.** It is important that employers do not make discriminatory assumptions as to what alternative employment an employee will or will not accept, as the following cases demonstrate:

- **Smulczyk v Eutopia Solutions Ltd** ET Case No.3303068/08: when S went on maternity leave in December 2007 she knew the division in which she worked was not economically viable. At a meeting with ES Ltd in July 2008 she was told that two of her colleagues were transferring to Dubai. She assumed that she might also be offered a transfer to Dubai and she discussed the matter with her husband, who was favourably disposed to moving to Dubai as his firm had a branch there. ES Ltd wrote to S on 1 August inviting her to a meeting to discuss the fact that her division had now closed and the possibility of her role being made redundant. At that meeting she was told she was to be dismissed as redundant. She informed ES Ltd that she was willing to be transferred to Dubai, which seemed to take the employer aback. ES Ltd wrote to confirm her redundancy terms, but made no mention of the possibility of a transfer to Dubai. S appealed, and in response ES Ltd stated that it had not offered her a job in Dubai because 'it was not considered that you would want to move there with your family'. An employment tribunal found that the decision to dismiss S was taken while she was on maternity leave without considering the option of a transfer to Dubai. The reason ES Ltd gave for not considering this was revealing and was discriminatory on its face

- **Morgan-Iqbal v Minster Care Management Ltd** ET Case No.1306805/08: M-I worked as regional manager of four care homes. She was also acting manager of one of the homes. On 7 February 2008 that home was inspected and given a very poor rating. On 3 March M-I told MCM Ltd she was pregnant and shortly afterwards was off work for a week with a pregnancy-related condition. On her return she discovered that another manager had been moved into the home and she was increasingly sidelined. In May M-I was told she was at risk of redundancy. She was only offered jobs as a nurse in homes for which she had previously had responsibility. An employment tribunal drew an inference that MCM Ltd assumed M-I was not competent to perform as a manager because she was pregnant. There was a vacancy for a home manager at the time she was being consulted about redundancy but she was not even considered for it. The tribunal held that she had been discriminated against and she was awarded £15,000 for injury to feelings.

9.28 **Avoiding reverse discrimination against men.** Given that a woman who is pregnant or on maternity leave at the time a redundancy situation arises receives special protection from unfair dismissal under Reg 10 of the MPL Regulations by being given priority in respect of suitable alternative employment, the question arises as to whether a man who loses out as a result has any legal protection. In particular, can he claim to have suffered sex discrimination as a result of the favouritism shown to the woman? It was made clear in Eversheds Legal Services Ltd v De Belin 2011 ICR 1137, EAT, that, Reg 10 aside, any *disproportionate* favouring of a woman who is pregnant or on maternity leave could give rise to discrimination against a man who is adversely affected by the employer's disproportionate actions. That case concerned a sex discrimination claim brought by a male employee who had been made redundant following a redundancy exercise aimed at eliminating one of the two positions occupied by him and a female colleague on maternity leave. One of the criteria used for selection measured the length of time between undertaking a piece of work and receiving payment from the client (known as 'lock-up'). The man's lock-up score was at the lowest end of the scale. However, since the woman was absent on maternity leave at the measurement date, no score could be attributed to her because she had no client files. Consequently, and in accordance with the employer's policy for those at risk of redundancy who were on either maternity leave or sabbatical, she was awarded the maximum score. This resulted in the woman having a slightly better overall score than the claimant, as a result of which he was selected for redundancy. The man brought a claim of direct sex discrimination and, in defending the claim, the employer relied upon what is now S.13(6)(b) EqA, which provides that, for the purposes of applying the definition of direct discrimination, no account should be taken of any special treatment afforded to women in connection with pregnancy or childbirth. However, an employment tribunal upheld the claim, concluding that the different scoring methods applied to the female and male employees for lock-up constituted unlawful sex discrimination.

9.29 The matter reached the EAT, which ruled that, to the extent that a benefit extended to a woman who is pregnant or on maternity leave is disproportionate, there is no reason why a colleague who is correspondingly disadvantaged should not be entitled to claim for sex discrimination. The exemption from liability provided for by S.13(6)(b) must be construed in a way that incorporates the principle of proportionality, meaning that it must be read as referring only to treatment accorded to a woman in so far as it constitutes a proportionate means of achieving the legitimate aim of compensating her for the disadvantages occasioned by her pregnancy or maternity leave. Applying this principle, the EAT held that the means that had been adopted by the employer to resolve the problem caused by the female employee's absence were not proportionate because they went beyond what was reasonably necessary. There were alternative ways of removing the maternity-related disadvantage without unfairly disadvantaging the male colleague, the most satisfactory of which would have been to measure the performance of both the candidates for redundancy as at the last date that the female employee was at work.

The pregnant employee would have lost no legitimate advantage in having her performance measured in this way. What she was entitled to was to have her performance scored, notwithstanding her maternity absence, on a basis that reflected her capability, and an assessment at the earlier date would have achieved that.

The problem for employers is that, in some redundancy situations, they may have little option but to prioritise a woman who is pregnant or on maternity leave in order to avoid a finding of automatically unfair dismissal under Reg 10 of the MPL Regulations. In Sefton Borough Council v Wainwright 2015 ICR 652, EAT, W was employed by the Council as Head of Overview and Scrutiny. As part of a reorganisation, the Council proposed to abolish W's role and that of P, a man, and replace them with the combined role of Democratic Service Manager (DSM). W and P were both notified that they were at risk in July 2012. At that time, W had just begun maternity leave. The Council interviewed both P and W for the role in December 2012 and decided that P was better qualified. It therefore offered him the position and dismissed W as redundant in April 2013. W claimed that the dismissal was automatically unfair because the DSM role was a suitable available vacancy, which the Council was obliged to offer her under Reg 10, and that it was also discriminatory under S.18 EqA. An employment tribunal upheld both claims: it accepted that W's dismissal was automatically unfair by reason of the employer's breach of Reg 10 and, apparently assuming that such a breach must automatically be discriminatory, it also upheld her claim of pregnancy/maternity discrimination under S.18 EqA.

9.30 Although, on appeal, the EAT overturned the tribunal's decision on discrimination, it upheld the finding of automatically unfair dismissal. The Council had argued that the obligation to favour W for redeployment had only arisen after she had been given notice of redundancy and that such notice could only properly be served once a decision had been made not to offer her the DSM role. Only then did she enter the redeployment pool and become eligible to be prioritised for any available suitable alternative vacancies. The EAT, however, rejected that argument, noting that the danger with it was that it relied on terms such as 'displaced' and 'redeployment' rather than engaging with the term used by the MPL Regulations, namely 'redundancy'. The correct approach was that laid down by the EAT in Secretary of State for Justice v Slee EAT 0349/06 – i.e. that 'redundancy' is to be defined for Reg 10 purposes as it is under S.139 ERA. Once an employee's position is 'redundant', the obligation under Reg 10 arises. The fact that, in this case, the Council could have slotted either W or P into the newly-created position without any wider competition taking place did not mean that their previous positions were not 'redundant'. Furthermore, although Reg 10 does not define the word 'vacancy' and does not expressly oblige an employer to offer every suitable vacancy or, indeed, any particular vacancy if more than one might be

350

suitable, this did not prevent the DSM position from being a 'vacancy' within the terms of Reg 10 simply because it was not open or available to a pool wider than W and P. The term 'vacant' would normally be understood as 'not presently occupied' and so the fact that a job is only open to a limited pool does not mean that it is not 'vacant'. On the facts of this case, the tribunal was entitled to conclude that there was a vacancy and – given the Council's concession – that it was 'suitable' for W. It therefore should have been offered to W in priority over P.

In so concluding, the EAT did not ignore the problem thrown up by Eversheds Legal Services Ltd v De Belin (above). The Council had sought to argue that its interpretation of the right to special treatment under Reg 10, by which the right would not be engaged until it had decided who was the best candidate for the DSM role, was a 'proportionate' approach that recognised the varying interests of W, P and the Council. In the EAT's view the answer to this was that, although the Council might not have wanted to give the DSM vacancy to W in preference to P, it was obliged to do so unless it was in a position to offer W some other suitable available vacancy. In order to afford W the protection to which she was entitled under Reg 10 once her position was redundant – which, on the tribunal's finding, was in July/August 2012 – the Council was obliged to assess what available vacancies might have been suitable and to offer one or more of them to W without requiring her to engage in some form of selection process. Whether that meant that the Council had to offer the DSM position or whether it could have found some suitable alternative was for it to assess and, at that stage, it would have been open to the Council to have taken into account P's interests and its own desire to appoint the best person to the new role of DSM. It might not have been proportionate to have required the Council to have offered W a particular vacancy if something else would also have been suitable and had been offered. However, on the facts, the Council offered W nothing notwithstanding the availability of a suitable vacancy, i.e. the DSM position.

So where does this leave employers struggling to balance the competing **9.31** interests of parties affected by a redundancy to which Reg 10 potentially applies? It would seem that, where there is to be a merger of two roles into one, then, unless other suitable vacancies exist, the employee who is pregnant or on maternity leave *must* be offered the new role (assuming it is suitable) in favour of the other person. If that person is a man, he will not succeed in a claim of sex discrimination based on Eversheds Legal Services Ltd v De Belin (above) because offering the role to the woman who is pregnant/on maternity leave will be regarded as 'proportionate'. That is the clear message of the EAT's ruling in Sefton Borough Council v Wainwright (above).

More problematic is where the redundancy comprises a reduction in the number of the same or similar roles, leaving fewer such roles in place. What is the position, for example, where a pregnant woman works in the same role as ten others, and the employer is proposing to reduce the overall number of such roles to five? In this scenario it seems likely that the Reg 10 obligation is not triggered until the employer has gone though a redundancy selection process and determined whether the woman is to be selected and whether, therefore, any duty arises to consider her for a suitable alternative vacancy. In undertaking this process, the EAT's decision in Eversheds Legal Services Ltd v De Belin (above) is relevant in that it informs the relative treatment of employees within the redundancy pool. The employer's criteria and processes must be seen to be proportionate – i.e. sufficient (but no more than that) to offset any disadvantages that the woman encounters by reason of her being pregnant or on maternity leave. If the employer fails to offset these disadvantages, it risks being the subject of a claim of unfavourable treatment because of pregnancy/maternity under S.18 EqA. However, any disproportionate favouring of the woman at this stage could give rise to discrimination liability regarding a male employee who ends up adversely affected by the employer's disproportionate actions. Assuming a proportionate selection process is undertaken, then if the pregnant woman is nevertheless selected for redundancy, it is at that stage that the employer's obligation under Reg 10 kicks in: she will be entitled to be prioritised regarding any other suitable alternative vacancies that exist within the employer's or an associated employer's organisation.

9.32 Age discrimination

Traditionally, age was considered a legitimate factor to take into account in a redundancy exercise. Indeed, the right to claim a redundancy payment or unfair dismissal was subject to an upper age limit of 65. However, the prohibition on age discrimination – initially introduced by the Employment Equality (Age) Regulations 2006 SI 2006/1031 ('the Age Regulations') and now contained in the EqA – and the abolition of the upper age limit at the same time made many employers re-evaluate their redundancy policies. A redundancy selection criterion or a selection process that directly or indirectly discriminates on the ground of age will be unlawful unless the employer can show that it is objectively justified – see 'Objective justification' below.

Ensuring that the terms of a redundancy policy do not fall foul of the prohibition on age discrimination is, however, simply the beginning. Employers must also ensure that the policy is applied in a non-discriminatory manner. In Mayor and Burgesses of the London Borough of Tower Hamlets v Wooster 2009 IRLR 980, EAT, for example, W, a long-serving Council employee, was on secondment to a registered social landlord, EEH. When his work there came to an end, the Council gave him 12 weeks' notice of dismissal for redundancy but reassured him that that period would be used to try to find him alternative employment. EEH then offered to extend W's secondment until his 50th birthday, when he would become entitled to an early retirement pension. This offer was rejected by M, the Council's director of housing management, with the words: 'If you are going to pay his salary then you can pay his bloody pension when he is 50. If he goes now we do save the pension.' W unsuccessfully applied for vacancies at the Council before taking voluntary redundancy. A tribunal upheld his unfair dismissal and age discrimination claims, finding that M's refusal even to countenance extending the secondment and her comments to EEH about 'saving the pension' showed that W's pensionable age was the 'tipping point' in the decision to dismiss him. Furthermore, had the Council followed a fair redundancy and redeployment procedure, W would have obtained a permanent post. The Council appealed against the tribunal's finding on age discrimination but the appeal was dismissed by the EAT.

Objective justification

9.33

As mentioned above, there is a 'justification defence' available to employers facing claims of direct or indirect age discrimination. However, the Government stated in the 'Coming of Age' consultation document on the draft Age Regulations that 'the test of objective justification will not be an easy one to satisfy... treating people differently on grounds of age will be possible but only exceptionally and for good reasons'.

In order to benefit from the defence, the employer must show:

• in a direct discrimination claim, that the less favourable treatment meted out to the claimant because of age was a proportionate means of achieving a legitimate aim – S.13(1) and (2) EqA

• in an indirect discrimination claim, that the provision, criterion or practice which placed persons of the claimant's age group at a disadvantage was a proportionate means of achieving a legitimate aim – S.19 EqA.

Although the wording of the two justification tests is almost identical, the Supreme Court in Seldon v Clarkson Wright and Jakes (A Partnership) 2012 ICR 716, SC, held that it is an error to regard the tests as one and the same. Having reviewed ECJ jurisprudence, the Court held that the justification test for direct age discrimination is narrower than for the indirect form: direct discrimination can only be justified by reference to legitimate objectives of a public interest nature, rather than purely individual reasons particular to the employer's situation, such as cost reduction or improving competitiveness. In this respect, the ECJ had identified two categories of legitimate social policy objective: 'inter-generational fairness' and 'dignity'. (It should be pointed out that the Supreme Court's decision in Seldon, while of great significance, does not necessarily invalidate the body of domestic case law that has built up on the question of justification of direct age discrimination, as the legitimate aims identified in those cases have largely coincided with the two categories identified by the ECJ.)

9.34

In practice, the success of an age discrimination claim in the context of redundancy selection often turns on the employer's ability to establish the justification defence. Below, we look at some examples of cases where employers have – with varying degrees of success – sought to argue that the adoption of an age-discriminatory criterion when making redundancy selections was a proportionate means of achieving a legitimate aim.

9.35 **'Last in, first out' and length of service.** Traditionally, one of the most common methods of selecting employees for redundancy has been the 'last in, first out' (LIFO) method. As explained in Chapter 8, 'Unfair redundancy', under 'Unreasonable redundancy – selection criteria', what this means is that employees with the shortest length of service are selected for redundancy first. From an employer's perspective, LIFO carries the benefit of minimising the level of redundancy payments which are, of course, determined by length of service.

While LIFO does not directly discriminate on the ground of age – it does not automatically follow that an employee with ten years' service will be older than an employee with three years' service – it clearly constitutes a provision, criterion or practice (PCP) which will, generally speaking, adversely impact on younger workers. It follows, therefore, that an employer seeking to use LIFO as part of a redundancy selection exercise must be prepared to demonstrate that its use is objectively justified. If it cannot do so, the use of LIFO will be unlawful indirect discrimination. For example, in Catchpole and ors v DB Schenker Rail (UK) Ltd ET Case No.2509588/09 C and one other employee scored jointly in a redundancy selection exercise and the employer decided to use length of service as a tie-breaker to decide who should be made redundant. The other employee had longer service than C and so C was selected for redundancy. A tribunal upheld his claim of age discrimination. C was aged 34 and the other employee was 60. They were thus in quite different age groups and on the face of it the criterion of length of service was discriminatory. In the employment tribunal's opinion, the employer failed to justify its use as a proportionate means of achieving a legitimate aim. It used the criterion as a tie-breaker because it was administratively convenient to do so, and that was not enough.

9.36 For the purposes of the justification defence in this particular context, examples of what might arguably constitute a legitimate aim might include:

- encouraging and rewarding staff loyalty
- retaining skills and knowledge of the business that have been developed over time, and
- minimising costs in order to keep a company afloat.

It would be fair to assume that where LIFO or some similar length of service criterion is used as a part of a selection matrix that objectively takes into

354

account the various qualities of staff considered for redundancy, it will be less of a challenge to show that its use and application is justifiable. This proposition draws support from the Court of Appeal's decision in Rolls-Royce plc v Unite the Union 2010 ICR 1, CA, where the Court considered whether the use of length of service as a redundancy selection criterion was a proportionate means of achieving a legitimate aim. RR plc's redundancy policy, agreed collectively with the union, stipulated that an employee's length of service was a factor that would be taken into account in a redundancy selection exercise. In November 2007 RR plc announced that it was to start a redundancy consultation in its Derby factory. Concerned at the prospect of employees dismissed for redundancy bringing claims of indirect age discrimination in the employment tribunal, RR plc sought a declaration from the High Court that the length of service criterion could not lawfully be relied upon. Mr Justice Morison, sitting in the Queen's Bench Division, accepted that the criterion indirectly discriminated against younger workers. However, he decided that its inclusion was justified by the legitimate aim of bringing about redundancies peaceably.

The Court of Appeal, by a majority, upheld this decision. The Court held **9.37** that the employer's legitimate aim in applying the criterion was to reward loyalty and create a stable workforce in the context of a fair redundancy selection process, and that the means adopted were proportionate. Lord Justice Wall thought that the most important factor indicating that the means were proportionate was that length of service was just one of many criteria used and was not determinative of the selection. The union's statement that all workers were supportive of the policy, the younger ones being aware that they were likely to benefit from it at some point in the future, was also a factor that carried weight.

Wall LJ was also satisfied that the length of service criterion qualified as 'legitimate employment policy' and a 'labour market objective' in accordance with Article 6 of the EU Equal Treatment Framework Directive (No.2000/78), which identifies specific circumstances in which age discrimination may be justified. He commented that 'to reward long service by employees in any redundancy selection process is, viewed objectively, an entirely reasonable and legitimate employment policy and one which a conscientious employer would readily and properly negotiate with a responsible trade union'.

Experience. While relying on experience as a criterion for selection may, on the **9.38** face of it, appear sensible and uncontroversial, tribunals are likely to scrutinise its relevance to ensure that any consequent indirect discrimination caused to younger workers is objectively justifiable. Discrimination can arise because the opportunity to gain experience tends to correlate with longer service and a PCP that requires relevant experience may therefore disproportionately and adversely affect younger workers.

355

In Hannell v Rydon Group Ltd ET Case No.2376701/11, for example, H, a director of RG Ltd, was 38 years old and had worked in the construction industry since leaving university 15 years previously. He had worked for the company for 11 years and was highly regarded and had been identified as a potential leader. In 2011 RG Ltd decided to reduce the number of construction directors from two to one and following a process of selection it chose to dispense with H in favour of the other director. H was not told why that choice had been made or informed of the selection criteria underpinning it. However, it subsequently emerged that while the criteria included a range of competencies, 40 per cent of the scoring was accredited to 'relevant project delivery experience'. The other director, who was aged 55, scored highly on that criterion because of his longer service but H could not have scored as highly in view of the comparatively short period of his employment with the company. An employment tribunal held that, in the absence of satisfactory evidence as to why the use of the project experience criterion was a proportionate means of achieving a legitimate aim, RG Ltd had unjustifiably indirectly discriminated against H in respect of his age.

9.39 **Cost considerations.** In Mayor and Burgesses of the London Borough of Tower Hamlets v Wooster 2009 IRLR 980, EAT, the claimant succeeded with his direct age discrimination claim where the employer's decision to make him redundant instead of redeploying him was motivated by a wish to avoid the additional costs of his becoming entitled to an early retirement pension. Surprisingly, the employer made no attempt to put forward a justification defence in that case and the EAT did not therefore have to determine whether the need to keep costs down could amount to a legitimate aim and whether dismissing an employee to avoid such costs is a proportionate means of achieving that aim.

This issue cropped up again in Woodcock v Cumbria Primary Care Trust 2011 ICR 143, EAT, the facts of which were very similar to those found in Wooster. In Woodcock, W was employed in the public sector. His role was redundant and he would have been entitled to early retirement and enhanced pension benefits if employed at 50. Upon discovering the cost of these pension benefits – estimated to be between £500,000 and £1,000,000 – the Trust accelerated the redundancy process, bypassing the consultation stage entirely, and gave W 12 months' notice of dismissal shortly before his 49th birthday. W complained of direct age discrimination, among other things. The employment tribunal found that W had been directly discriminated against on the ground of his age. However, it went on to hold that the discrimination was justified as a proportionate means of achieving a legitimate aim – that of avoiding the additional costs that would be incurred if W reached pensionable age, coupled with depriving him of a 'windfall' (see Chapter 6, 'Redundancy payments', under 'Age discrimination – enhanced scheme not modelled on statutory scheme', for a discussion of this factor as a legitimate aim). W appealed.

356

Before the EAT, W argued that the tribunal had found his discrimination to be **9.40** justified purely on the basis of cost and that this was contrary to the decision of the EAT in Cross and ors v British Airways plc 2005 IRLR 423, EAT (a case which went to the Court of Appeal on other grounds). The EAT found that, on the contrary, the tribunal had followed the 'costs plus' approach set out in Cross – i.e. that cost is an admissible factor in determining whether discrimination is justified, but may not be taken alone. The perceived cost of delay was not the only justification advanced for the Trust's decision to give notice before the consultation meeting. There was also the consideration of preventing W receiving a 'windfall' – i.e. a benefit which he had no legitimate right to expect. Accordingly, ensuring that W was not employed when he turned 50 – and avoiding the corresponding loss to the Trust – was a legitimate aim going beyond the mere wish to reduce costs.

Mr Justice Underhill then went on to set out the Appeal Tribunal's thinking on the 'costs plus' orthodoxy and although his comments were obiter and are not binding on tribunals, they will no doubt carry some weight in future cases given that they were made by the then President of the EAT. The EAT accepted that as a matter of both principle and common sense, considerations of cost must be admissible in considering whether a PCP that has a discriminatory impact may nevertheless be justified. Furthermore, it saw no principled basis for a rule that such considerations can never by themselves constitute sufficient justification. The adoption of such a rule would tend to involve parties and tribunals in an artificial game of 'find the other factor', producing arbitrary and complicated reasoning. Underhill P noted that deciding where 'cost' stops and other factors start is not always straightforward.

The Court of Appeal rejected the claimant's further appeal in Woodcock v **9.41** Cumbria Primary Care Trust 2012 ICR 1126, CA, and expressed its own doubts on the continued correctness of the 'costs plus' orthodoxy. The Court noted that there is 'some degree of artificiality' in an approach to justification that renders cost inadmissible as a factor on its own, but admissible if linked to a non-cost factor. The Court observed that every decision an employer takes is likely to involve the question of cost in some way and that the wording of the discrimination legislation then in force did not exclude cost considerations – it merely required that the treatment be a 'proportionate means of achieving a legitimate aim', as S.19 EqA does now. However, the Court summarised the effect of ECJ case law as being that 'an employer cannot justify discriminatory treatment "solely" because the elimination of such treatment would involve increased costs'. Accordingly, while the wider implications of Cross have now been doubted at a higher level, its general principle survives.

Cost considerations also influenced redundancy selection in HM Land Registry v Benson and ors 2012 ICR 627, EAT, although in that case the employees claiming age discrimination did so because they were *not* selected

357

for redundancy. There the employer needed to reduce headcount and offered a voluntary redundancy/early retirement scheme. Having more applicants than could be accommodated within the £12 million budget allocated to the project, the employer adopted selection criteria that involved choosing those whom it would cost least to dismiss, so as to maximise the number of redundancies achievable within the budget. This had the effect of excluding from consideration employees aged between 50 and 54, because they would have been entitled to early retirement on an unreduced pension if selected. An employment tribunal upheld indirect age discrimination claims from five such employees, finding that the employer could have afforded to select them, albeit that this would have cost an extra £19.7 million.

9.42 Overturning that decision on appeal, the EAT held that the budget of £12 million was an intrinsic part of the employer's legitimate aim, which was to achieve the maximum number of redundancies possible within the budget. The tribunal had erroneously treated the limit on the budget as an aspect of the 'means' adopted by the employer to achieve more broadly defined aims. The tribunal's finding that the extra £19.7 million was not 'unaffordable' implied that it thought the employer could find the funds without becoming insolvent. That was to treat the language of 'real need', in the context of objective justification, as connoting a requirement of absolute necessity. This was the wrong approach. The task of the employment tribunal is to accept the employer's legitimate decision as to the allocation of its resources as representing a genuine 'need', but to balance it against the impact complained of. Had the tribunal done that here, it would have found the employer's means proportionate, since it was evident that there was no other available means of achieving the aim.

Since the decision in Woodcock v Cumbria Primary Care Trust (above) there have been a number of cases confirming that, in the context of reorganisations and redundancies, the application of indirectly discriminatory PCPs that are intended primarily to achieve cost-cutting can potentially be objectively justified as a proportionate pursuit of a legitimate aim. In Edie and ors v HCL Insurance BPO Services Ltd 2015 ICR 713, EAT, for example, the employer, faced with heavy financial losses, sought to introduce new terms and conditions that reduced or removed certain benefits including annual leave and enhanced redundancy pay. The employer's stated aim was to seek to balance the books on a year-by-year basis going forward. The EAT agreed with the employment tribunal's finding that the requirement to agree to new terms and conditions constituted the application of a PCP that had disproportionate adverse effect on old workers because, through longer service, the value of the benefits affected was higher. However, it went on to hold that the indirect discrimination involved was objectively justified. In the EAT's view, once a PCP is found to have a disparate and adverse impact on a protected group, a critical evaluation was required of whether the employer had a real need for

358

it and, if so, of the seriousness of the disparate impact on affected employees and of whether the measures were proportionate, balancing the needs of the employer against the effect of the PCP on the employees. In the instant case the tribunal had properly evaluated that matter, having found that it was legitimate for a business to seek to break even every year and to make decisions about the allocation of resources. It was clear that the tribunal had balanced the importance of that aim against the impact of the PCP on affected employees and had dealt adequately with proposed alternatives. Accordingly, it had been entitled to conclude that the requirement to accept the new terms to remain in employment was necessary to achieve the employer's legitimate aim and was a proportionate means of doing this.

Costs as justification for direct age discrimination. The extent to which an **9.43** employer can rely on cost considerations to justify a selection criterion that *directly* discriminates because of age must now be considered in the light of the Supreme Court's decision in Seldon v Clarkson Wright and Jakes (A Partnership) 2012 ICR 716, SC. As mentioned under 'Objective justification' above, the Court in that case expressly ruled out cost reduction as a legitimate aim for the purposes of justifying direct discrimination. Instead, to justify such discrimination an employer must identify an aim consistent with either 'inter-generational fairness' or 'dignity'. On the face of it, this would seem to lessen the scope for an employer to use age as a selection criterion if the cost of continuing to employ an individual is its primary concern. However, we should not overlook the observation of the Court of Appeal in Woodcock v Cumbria Primary Care Trust (above) that every decision an employer makes is to some extent influenced by cost. If the ultimate aim of the cost-saving falls within the categories of 'inter-generational fairness' or 'dignity', and the selection criterion was both an appropriate means of achieving that aim and necessary to that end, justification is likely to be established.

This view is borne out by the Court of Appeal's decision in Lockwood v Department of Work and Pensions 2014 ICR 1257, CA, when upholding an employment tribunal's decision that direct age discrimination in the terms for redundancy payments under the Service Compensation Scheme was objectively justified. The Court accepted that an age-banding formula whereby redundant employees aged 35 or under received lower termination payments than those over 35 constituted less favourable treatment because of age. However, after taking into account the decision in Seldon v Clarkson Wright and Jakes (A Partnership) (above), the Court ruled that, in approaching the establishment of a compensation scheme directed at applying a limited pot of money towards meeting what the employer assessed to be the different needs of employees at different ages, it was necessary to adopt a banding approach that would involve disparate treatment of employees of different ages. This was the case even though the individual claimant's personal circumstances – as a cohabitee in her twenties with family and mortgage responsibilities – were more typical

359

of employees over the age of 35. The employment tribunal had been entitled to hold that the disparate treatment was a proportionate means of achieving the legitimate aim underlying the banding policy – namely, to produce a proportionate financial cushion for people made redundant until alternative employment was found, or to act as a bridge to retirement and the receipt of a pension.

9.44 However, in Sturmey v Weymouth and Portland Borough Council EAT 0114/14 His Honour Judge Richardson sounded a general note of caution about what was and was not decided by the Court of Appeal in Woodcock v Cumbria Primary Care Trust (above). In the Sturmey case the claimant had been placed in a redeployment pool following a reorganisation of a local authority's job roles. Coinciding with this was a temporary freeze on recruitment, which meant that the opportunities for redeployment were stayed for an eight-week period. Normally employees would have been retained within the redeployment pool for a longer period than was normal pending the ending of the recruitment freeze, but in this particular case such a delay would have meant that the claimant would attain the age of 55 and thereupon have become eligible for expensive early retirement options under the terms of the local authority pension scheme. Accordingly, the employer decided to bring forward her notice of redundancy to ensure that these pension options were not triggered. The EAT allowed an appeal against the employment tribunal's finding that the considerations of cost justified the age discriminatory decision to dismiss the claimant before she attained 55. Before the tribunal, the employer had successfully relied on Woodcock as authority for the proposition that cost considerations can be taken into account to justify age discrimination provided they are not used as the sole basis for justification. However, the EAT concluded that the tribunal had not fully considered the discriminatory effect of reducing the period during which the claimant was kept in the redeployment pool. According to HHJ Richardson: 'Where the issue of justification arises, it is for the respondent to place before the employment tribunal the material on which it relies to show that its less favourable treatment because of age is justified: that is to say, that the treatment was a proportionate means of achieving a legitimate aim… If, therefore, an employer wishes to omit or elide stages in a redundancy and redeployment process because of age, what it must justify is not the redundancy itself but the discriminatory treatment. It is not the game it must justify; it is the moving of the goalposts. I do not think Woodcock sets out… any general principle as to whether omitting or eliding stages in the redundancy process to save pension costs will always achieve a legitimate aim or will always be a proportionate means of doing so.'

In remitting the case to a freshly constituted tribunal for reconsideration the EAT observed that the Court of Appeal in Woodcock had itself recognised that that case had turned on its own 'very particular circumstances'. It

360

was therefore wrong, in the EAT's view, for the tribunal in the instant case effectively to treat it as decisive of the issue of proportionality.

Other grounds for justification. Employment tribunals are often faced with claims that an employer has either deliberately or inadvertently allowed considerations of age to determine the outcome of who is and is not selected for redundancy. In Brunel University v Killen EAT 0403/13 the then President of the EAT, Mr Justice Langstaff, remarked that: '[I]n general if it is shown that of two applicants for a post one has a protected characteristic that the other does not, that person is not appointed and that person is on the face of it likely to be better qualified than the other, there is sufficient to call for an explanation.'   **9.45**

As discussed under 'Discriminatory selection – reverse burden of proof' above, in order to trigger the 'reverse burden of proof' rule so as to shift the onus onto the employer to disprove a prima facie case of discrimination, it is not sufficient simply to show a difference in treatment between one person who has a protected characteristic, and one who does not: something more needs to be shown. In the Brunel case this additional element consisted of – on its face – the surprising outcome that an employee at a university was not appointed to one of five newly created roles following a reorganisation. She was of a higher grade and therefore impliedly better qualified for the available positions than any of the successful colleagues. But the EAT ruled that, although the employment tribunal had not erred in shifting the burden of proof, it had fallen into error when taking into account factors that should have played no role in the decision to reverse the burden of proof and had also failed to get to the bottom of exactly why the claimant was not redeployed and, in particular, whether the reason for this was her age or sex (as she had alleged).

Where age discrimination is alleged, tribunals will scrutinise the explanations put forward by employers for their redundancy selection choices to determine whether these are tainted in any way. Some examples: **9.46**

- **Walker and ors v DCE Consulting Ltd and anor** ET Case No.2301417/09: DCE Consultants Ltd was headed by a 38-year-old managing director who wanted to make changes to the business. At a meeting to discuss his ideas he referred to the company as being top heavy with 'older, grey-haired consultants'. Redundancies were subsequently announced and the employer applied a matrix to determine who should be selected for redundancy, which went through seven versions before finally being used to select the claimants, who were all in their 50s. Another consultant, who was in his 40s, had scored much lower in relation to performance indicators, but was retained. The claimants were dismissed as redundant. An employment tribunal drew the inference that the employer had changed the matrix to get the result it wanted and held that, on the basis of the comments made by the managing director, the claimants were targeted for redundancy because of their age

361

- **Thompson v Bombardier Transportation UK Ltd and ors** ET Case No.2603778/11: T, who began working for BTUK in 1996, was employed as a PA to a senior director. In early 2011 BTUK faced a downturn in its business, having lost a major contract at the same time as a number of existing projects were coming to an end. All PAs were warned of redundancy and, following a scoring exercise, T was selected and made redundant. She brought a claim of age discrimination on the basis that she should have been given higher marks in the scoring process and that another PA, half her age, who also scored low enough to be considered for redundancy, had had her marks increased by the person deputed to verify the scoring. An employment tribunal upheld T's claim because BTUK had been unable to provide a satisfactory (non-discriminatory) explanation for the verifier's actions

- **Shiret v Credit Suisses Securities (Europe) Ltd** ET Case No.3202676/11: S began working for a predecessor of CSS in 1993. A redundancy exercise was commenced around the time that one of his colleagues, who had ambitions to succeed to S's more senior role, had indicated that he would resign if S continued in employment for another year. S, who was aged 55, was scored low on certain selection criteria in comparison with other colleagues in the redundancy pool who were significantly younger. This affected the overall result because such low scores were necessary to place him at risk of selection in view of his acknowledged competencies and unrivalled experience in his particular area of expertise. After being made redundant S brought a claim of age discrimination. An employment tribunal found that CSS's explanation for S's low scores was not credible. For example, he had been awarded no points at all for 'potential' despite his excellent skills and unrivalled contacts. The tribunal concluded that the reason for S's selection was his age and he had therefore been directly discriminated against.

9.47 However, not all ostensibly age-related redundancy decisions are discriminatory. In King v Richard Lees Steel Decking Ltd ET Case No.3500039/09, for example, K was a highly skilled draftsman in his early 60s. When the company had to make redundancies the marking system included employees' ability to use draftsmen's tools. One such tool was the Tekla system, on which K had been trained but had only used for about a month before being transferred to another job where he did not use it. He therefore had very little experience of using Tekla and when the selection criteria were applied he received a low score. He was selected for redundancy and claimed that the selection exercise was tainted by age discrimination: of the ten draftsmen in the department, he, along with four other people in their 50s and 60s, was selected for redundancy while five people in their 20s and 30s were retained. The employment tribunal dismissed his claim. Tekla was made available to the entire workforce and the employer made serious efforts to ensure everyone was trained. However, three of the older employees did not want to go on the courses and the issue was allowed to lie. This was not age discrimination; it was part of the workforce not wanting to improve their skills.

Exclusion of liability: statutory authority   9.48

Paragraph 1(1) of Schedule 22 to the EqA provides that an employer does not discriminate against an employee because of the employee's age if the employer does anything that it is obliged to do pursuant to 'a requirement of an enactment'. An enactment for these purposes includes Acts of Parliament, legislation produced by the devolved administrations in Scotland and Wales, and secondary legislation such as statutory instruments and ministerial orders. Para 1(3) clarifies that 'enactment' includes Measures of the General Synod of the Church of England, and that enactments passed or made on or after the date on which the EqA was passed are included.

The Explanatory Notes that accompanied the EqA make it clear that the statutory authority defence applies only where the employer has no choice under legislation but to discriminate. Examples of this given in the Notes include where an employer dismisses a disabled employee because health and safety regulations leave it with no other choice, or where an employer refuses to employ someone who is not old enough to hold an LGV licence to drive a large goods vehicle. Guidance given in cases decided under the antecedent discrimination legislation such as that set out by the House of Lords in Hampson v Department of Education and Science 1990 ICR 511, HL, is also likely to be of relevance. Although that case considered S.41 of the Race Relations Act 1976, which has not been fully re-enacted into the EqA, the wording of that provision clearly inspired para 1 of Schedule 22 in so far as it allowed for an exception where the employer acted in pursuance of an enactment, requirement or condition. Their Lordships in Hampson restricted the S.41 RRA exception to acts done in necessary performance of an express obligation. Accordingly, they refused to allow the exception to excuse discrimination where the Crown, a local authority or another statutory body was given discretion to act under an enactment, and chose to exercise that discretion in a way that had discriminatory effects.

In Heron v Sefton Metropolitan Borough Council EAT 0566/12 the issue   9.49
was whether the terms of the Civil Service Compensation Scheme (CSCS) – which had been established pursuant to a statutory power contained in the Superannuation Act 1972 – required a local authority employer to treat an employee aged over 60 less favourably than younger colleagues in the calculation of redundancy payments. The EAT held that the CSCS was an 'enactment' within the meaning of para 1(1) of Schedule 22 to the EqA. However, the terms of the CSCS had been incorporated into the employee's contract by the local authority when she was transferred to it from a central government department in accordance with the Transfer of Undertakings (Protection of Employment) Regulations 2006 SI 2006/246. Thus, the terms were contractual, not statutory. As a result, any 'requirement' under the scheme in relation to the employee was not a requirement of an enactment; it was a requirement of a contract, which incorporated the terms of an enactment. Consequently, the employer could not

363

rely upon the statutory authority defence for the less favourable treatment that the claimant suffered because of her age.

However, in Palmer v Royal Bank of Scotland plc EAT 0083/14 the employer met with greater success. In that case the EAT upheld an employment tribunal's decision that an employee who was 49 had not suffered age discrimination when, in the midst of a restructuring exercise, the employer allowed employees aged between 50 and 55 an opportunity to consider whether to opt for redeployment, voluntary redundancy or early retirement. The employer had provided the older employees with this opportunity because it had lowered the age at which an employee could take early retirement without an actuarial reduction for early receipt of pension from 55 to 50 – this being the minimum age permitted by the Finance Act 2004. It followed that the claimant and her comparators were in materially different circumstances: she could not claim voluntary early retirement at the projected date of her dismissal, while her comparators could. The circumstance was not caused by any unlawful discrimination on the ground of age but by the lawful discrimination allowed by statute. Accordingly, the claimant's claim of direct age discrimination failed.

9.50 Disability discrimination

As identified in Chapter 8, 'Unfair redundancy', under 'Unreasonable redundancy – selection criteria', there are potential pitfalls in using health and attendance records as a means of selecting employees for redundancy, since doing so may infringe the disability discrimination provisions of the EqA. These prohibit, inter alia, direct and indirect disability discrimination and discrimination arising from a disability. They also impose a duty on employers to make reasonable adjustments. In this section we briefly explain what is meant by discrimination arising from a disability before considering the application of the duty to make reasonable adjustments in a redundancy context. For a full discussion of disability discrimination law generally, see IDS Employment Law Handbook, 'Discrimination at Work' (2012), in particular Chapter 6, 'Disability'; Chapter 20, 'Discrimination arising from disability'; and Chapter 21, 'Failure to make reasonable adjustments'.

9.51 Discrimination arising from disability

Section 15 EqA introduced the concept of 'discrimination arising from disability'. This, unlike the concept of disability-related discrimination that had previously applied under the Disability Discrimination Act 1995, does not require the disabled person to establish that his or her treatment was less favourable than that experienced by a comparator. It provides that a person (A) discriminates against a disabled person (B) if A treats B unfavourably because of something arising in consequence of B's disability, and A cannot show that the treatment is a proportionate means of achieving a legitimate aim. In view of this provision, employers will obviously need to be particularly careful when applying redundancy selection criteria that could adversely affect disabled employees.

Such caution was exercised by the employer in Espie v Balfour Beatty Engineering Services Ltd EAT 0321/12, when E, who suffered from depression, was made redundant after scoring lowest in the selection exercise, which was due to him being graded 'poor' for attendance. It was not disputed that E was unable to attend work between October 2009 and July 2010 because of his depression, and he consequently claimed, under S.15 EqA, that BBES Ltd had unlawfully taken this period of absence into account when scoring and, ultimately, dismissing him. The EAT rejected the claim, holding that BBES Ltd had, in fact, disregarded his period of absence for depression but had counted the time he was off work for an appendectomy, which did not amount to a disability. Accordingly, his low attendance score was not something 'arising in consequence of [his] disability', for the purposes of S.15, but rather as a result of the problems he had with his appendix.

In IPC Media Ltd v Millar 2013 IRLR 707, EAT, the question arose whether, **9.52** for the purposes of a S.15 claim, the claimant (M) had raised a prima facie case of unfavourable treatment because of something arising in consequence of her disability such as to cause the burden of proof to be shifted on to the employer to show that the claimant's disability played no part in M's dismissal for redundancy. In that case the redundancy consultation was overseen by a manager, O, who was also responsible for helping to determine whether there were any suitable alternative roles for M. In the event, no vacancies were identified at that stage and M was eventually notified that she was to be made redundant. However, during her internal appeal details emerged of certain vacancies, including a manifestly suitable alternative role. Notwithstanding this, M's appeal was unsuccessful and her dismissal confirmed.

M subsequently brought claims of disability discrimination contending that the reason she had not been offered the alternative role was her record of sickness absence related to her osteoarthritis. Although her claim of direct discrimination was dismissed, the employment tribunal upheld her S.15 claim on the basis that an inference of disability discrimination could be drawn from the fact that there was no good reason why M had not been offered the suitable alternative vacancy and that, subject to clear evidence to the contrary, it was reasonable to assume that the failure to do so was due to her absence record associated with her disability. However, on appeal by the employer, the EAT held that the tribunal had fallen into error. In its view, no prima facie case of discrimination could arise in this case based on an inference of discrimination unless it could be shown that O, the manager who conducted the consultation, knew of M's history of absences. That was because a person could not be influenced (either consciously or subconsciously) by something

365

of which he or she was unaware. In this case, the tribunal had made no finding as to O's knowledge; but had it done so it would inevitably have found that she did not have any knowledge of M's sickness absences or of her disability. The EAT accordingly dismissed M's S.15 claim.

9.53　For a more detailed discussion of S.15 EqA, see IDS Employment Law Handbook, 'Discrimination at Work' (2012), Chapter 20, 'Discrimination arising from disability'.

9.54　Reasonable adjustments

Under S.20(3) EqA an employer is under a duty to make reasonable adjustments where a provision, criterion or practice (PCP) of the employer's puts a disabled person at a substantial disadvantage in comparison with persons who are not disabled. A failure to comply with that duty will amount to discrimination – S.21.

Section 18B(2) of the Disability Discrimination Act 1995 used to contain a non-exhaustive list of examples of what might amount to a reasonable adjustment. For example, in the context of redundancy selection the list included 'modifying procedures for testing or assessment' and 'transferring [the employee] to fill an existing vacancy'. However, the list has not been reproduced in the EqA and instead, the Equality and Human Rights Commission's Code of Practice on Employment ('the Employment Code') (which contains statutory guidance on the EqA) states that what is a reasonable step for an employer to take will depend on the circumstances of each individual case (para 6.29). But although the EqA does not specify any particular factors that should be taken into account, the examples previously given in S.18B(2) DDA are likely to remain relevant in practice, particularly as those examples are now listed in para 6.33 of the Employment Code. The Code also suggests some further examples of reasonable steps that did not appear in the DDA, including adjusting redundancy selection criteria.

9.55　In addition to the examples contained in S.18B(2), S.18B(1) DDA set out a number of factors tribunals should consider when determining reasonableness, including the effectiveness of a proposed step. These factors have not been replicated in the EqA but are likely to continue to be relevant, given that the majority of them are now listed in para 6.28 of the Employment Code as examples of factors that a tribunal *might* take into account when considering reasonableness. In other words, it will not automatically be an error of law for a tribunal to fail to consider, for example, the effectiveness of an adjustment, so long as it has adequately considered whether the proposed adjustment would be reasonable.

However, it is unlikely to be 'reasonable' to alter redundancy selection criteria if the alteration would still result in the claimant being selected – Lancaster

v TBWA Manchester EAT 0460/10 (discussed under 'Omitting or altering selection criteria' below). The difficulty for employers, of course, is that it is often not until the reasonable adjustment has been applied that it is possible to know if the employee would still be selected for redundancy; so the ratio in Lancaster should probably not be relied upon to excuse taking action, unless the outcome has been researched and can safely be predicted. However, an employer may rely upon the case at tribunal to avoid an injury to feelings award being made against it.

Even if dismissal for redundancy would not have been avoided by adjustments **9.56** that would otherwise be reasonable, this is not to say that they can be overlooked if the benefit of them would avoid other substantial disadvantage being caused to a disabled employee. In Dominique v Toll Global Forwarding Ltd EAT 0308/13, when rejecting the claimant's reasonable adjustments claim, an employment tribunal concluded that the adjustments sought to the redundancy scoring exercise would not have prevented the claimant from being dismissed for redundancy. However, the EAT accepted that the S.20(3) EqA duty on the employer went further than this. In the words of Mrs Justice Simler: '[W]e agree, that whilst in an ideal world a complainant… may seek to avoid a scoring process or a redundancy process that leads to his [or her] dismissal, there are lesser detriments that he or she might seek to avoid and, in particular, the detriment of being placed at a disadvantage as a consequence of unlawful or potentially unlawful discrimination.'

Similarly, in Menezes v Coin Street Community Builders ET Case No.2374924/11 the claimant suffered from depression and was disposed to self-harming (a fact of which the employer was aware). On being informed that her position was redundant, the claimant was told that if she wished to apply for any suitable alternative vacancies she would have to follow the normal recruitment procedure, including completing an application form. Although she did this, she was unsuccessful and was eventually dismissed as redundant. Regarding the claimant's disability discrimination claim under S.21 EqA, the employment tribunal concluded that the employer had failed to make the reasonable adjustment of securing professional support for the claimant during the redundancy process. Although this would not have prevented the loss of her job, it would have reduced the deterioration of her mental health.

Below we discuss various reasonable adjustments that have been proposed in **9.57** the context of redundancy selection and the extent to which these have been considered by tribunals to be relevant to the employer's compliance with the duty under S.20(3) EqA.

Discounting disability-related absences. It seems safe to assume that **9.58** discounting disability-related absences when selecting for redundancy could amount to a reasonable adjustment, given that the Employment Code suggests

367

adjusting redundancy selection criteria as an example of a reasonable step. Two cases brought under the DDA:

- **Cox v City Centre Training (Northern) Ltd** ET Case No.2504232/06: C was diagnosed as suffering from diabetes in 2004. In 2005, CCT Ltd began a redundancy consultation and C was selected following the application of selection criteria that included attendance, despite C's having been off sick with an ingrown toenail for the duration of the consultation exercise. At a meeting, C expressed the view that the problems with his toenail were a result of his diabetes and offered to obtain medical advice to prove it. CCT Ltd, however, proceeded to dismiss C later that week. A tribunal found that the problems with C's toe and the ensuing absence were both related to his disability. In the circumstances, the tribunal took the view that a reasonable adjustment would have been to discount the absences which were related to C's disability. In addition, it formed the view that fatigue caused by diabetes had impacted negatively on C's performance, thus harming his scores in the selection process. In the tribunal's view, CCT Ltd had ignored the issue of C's disability, had displayed an ignorance of the effects of the condition, and had carried out a dismissal that was both discriminatory and unfair from beginning to end

- **Robson v Domino UK Ltd** ET Case No.1400506/09: R was employed as a salesman. In autumn 2006 he was diagnosed as diabetic and he also began to suffer from what was later diagnosed as chronic fatigue syndrome. He had a long period of absence from April 2007 to January 2008. He came back on a phased return for two months and was not given any sales targets for five months. In October 2008 D UK Ltd began consulting its employees about redundancy. R was selected on the basis of the scoring criteria. His scores were adversely affected by his absence: D UK Ltd had only looked back over the previous 12 months, during which R had been either absent or doing reduced work for much of the time. His manager told him that his drive and energy had been reduced since his illness and that D UK Ltd needed the best people to cope with the extra work resulting from the cuts in the workforce. R's disability discrimination claim was upheld. The tribunal found that the effects of his disabilities reflected adversely upon his work prior to selection and that it would have been a necessary and reasonable adjustment for the employer to increase his scores to remove the disadvantage.

9.59 **Trial period.** It may be a reasonable adjustment to offer an employee a trial period in a new role. In Lee v University of Westminster ET Case No.2201292/08 L, who suffered from epilepsy, was assessed as being unsuitable for redeployment into a new role that was being considered. The University offered him redeployment on a trial period as an alternative to redundancy. However, he was then absent for some months due to substantial ill health. When he recovered he asked to be put on the trial period, but the

University decided that because of his absence he was even more unskilled for the role and that it would be too much of a business risk to put him in it. His employment was terminated with effect from 31 March 2008. An employment tribunal upheld his claim of disability discrimination. The tribunal was hesitant about whether offering a trial period on the employee's return to work could be a reasonable adjustment, but accepted the parties' shared view that it was.

Delaying consultation pending health assessment. In Aubury v SP Group Ltd **9.60** ET Case No.1316697/09 A fell ill in June 2008 with a neurological condition. In September 2008 he returned to work on a phased basis, resuming full-time work in February 2009. An occupational health report in January stated that he was fit to fulfil his role, but without overtime or unusual hours, and that he should be fully fit within three to six months. By June 2009 the employer had to embark on a redundancy programme. A was selected for redundancy and he claimed that he was discriminated against on the ground of his disability because he was still not functioning fully as a result of his illness and this was not taken into account. His claim was upheld in part: the employer applied the selection criteria and then considered A's objections to his scoring without having an up-to-date assessment of his health. The employer should have made a reasonable adjustment by delaying the consultation and decision-making process until such a report was obtained so the full impact of his disability could be considered. However, the employer had made a reasonable adjustment in assessing A over a period of nine months rather than 12, and in comparing his scores against a period of 12 months before his illness and attributing an extra mark to him as a result. So, even had the employer obtained a report, he would still have been selected for redundancy. A was awarded £2,000 for injury to feelings.

(Note that, following the EAT's decision in Lancaster v TBWA Manchester (above), the tribunal's finding in the Aubury case that it would have been a reasonable adjustment to delay the consultation and decision-making process until a health report was obtained is questionable, given that on the facts it would have made no difference to his selection. However, we suggest that taking such action may well be considered a reasonable adjustment in a case where such a report might have an impact on the employee's selection.)

Omitting or altering selection criteria. In Lancaster v TBWA Manchester **9.61** (above) L, a senior art director at an advertising and marketing agency, suffered from a panic and social anxiety disorder that amounted to a disability for the purposes of the DDA (now EqA). Following the loss of a major contract, L was at risk of redundancy. He was placed in a pool of three and scored against selection criteria about which he had not been consulted. L's initial score was 198, compared to 298 and 299 for the other two senior art directors. Following his dismissal for redundancy, L brought

369

various claims, including one of disability discrimination. The basis of this was that the application of three of the redundancy selection criteria – all of which required communication skills and relied on the subjective views of the scorers – was a provision, criterion or practice (PCP) which placed him at a substantial disadvantage due to his disability. He therefore contended that TBWA was obliged to make a reasonable adjustment to the selection process by omitting those criteria. As an alternative argument, L identified the PCP that disadvantaged him as the entirety of the selection criteria, and argued that the adjustment TBWA should have made was adopting a more objective set of criteria such as attendance and length of service. The tribunal rejected both contentions: since L had failed to establish that either of his proposed adjustments would or could have prevented his being selected for redundancy, they could not be considered reasonable.

L appealed to the EAT, arguing among other things that the tribunal gave undue regard to the question of whether the two proposed adjustments would have removed the disadvantage L suffered. The EAT held that the tribunal had been entitled to find that the removal of the three offending selection criteria would not have been a reasonable adjustment. When considering whether an adjustment is reasonable, a tribunal was obliged by S.18B(1)(a) DDA to take into account the extent to which that adjustment 'would prevent the effect in relation to which the duty is imposed'. The tribunal had done so, and concluded that the removal of the criteria would not have made a difference because L would still have scored the lowest of the candidates. As for the second proposed adjustment – the replacement of all selection criteria with purely objective measures – the EAT held that the tribunal had been entitled, in light of the creative and senior level of the post held by L, to find that the wholesale replacement of selection criteria could not have prevented his redundancy. (Note that S.18B(1)(a) was not re-enacted in the EqA. However, as previously mentioned, most of the factors listed in that subsection, including the one referred to by the EAT, are now listed in para 6.28 of the Equality and Human Rights Commission's Code of Practice on Employment, which contains statutory guidance on the EqA.)

9.62 Although the employee was unsuccessful in the Lancaster case, there will be circumstances where adjustments to selection criteria would go some way towards helping disabled employees remain in employment, as opposed to being made redundant, and would therefore be seen as reasonable. Two examples:

- **Kelly v Land Rover** ET Case No.1311339/09: K, who had worked for LR since 1984, suffered from physical disabilities to his neck and back and as a result had two long periods of sickness absence, one in 2006 and the second from April 2007 to September 2008. In January 2009 LR embarked upon a restructuring process as a result of which redundancies became necessary.

The selection criteria included performance over the past three years. K did not score well because he had been absent for much of the three-year period and as a result there was a dearth of people with relevant knowledge of his skills and experience. Following his eventual dismissal for redundancy he brought various claims including a complaint under S.21 EqA regarding the failure to make reasonable adjustments. An employment tribunal upheld that claim on the basis that K had been put at a substantial disadvantage when compared to any of his non-disabled colleagues who were not absent during the assessment period. The tribunal took the view that LR could have carried out a number of reasonable adjustments such as extending the three-year assessment period in his case, extending the timescale over which the process was carried out and allowing K a full interview process as part of the selection procedure

- **Doolan v Interserve Facilities Management Ltd** ET Case No.2300082/12: D, who was autistic, worked in IFM's mail room. In September 2011 he was invited to a group redundancy consultation meeting but owing to his disability he had little or no understanding of the serious risk to his continued employment. The employer wrote to him the next day confirming the prospect of redundancy but that letter was only read two weeks later by D's father when the whole family was about to leave for a holiday. A number of the selection criteria for redundancy impacted directly on D because of his autism – including job flexibility, versatility, initiative, and the quality of work relationships. After a decision was made that D should be selected for redundancy, his father wrote to IFM pointing out that his son would always 'fail' in a process structured in favour of an average (non-autistic) person. Although D's father was invited to attend subsequent consultation meetings, D was eventually dismissed as redundant on 17 November 2011. An employment tribunal upheld his S.21 EqA claim on the basis that IFM had adopted a single set of criteria and applied these to all employees in a wide range of jobs within the redundancy pool. In doing so it had failed to make the reasonable adjustment of assessing D against the specific mail-room post he had worked in. He was placed at a very substantial disadvantage by being assessed by reference to attributes and skills that were directly and adversely affected by his disability.

Alternative work. As discussed under 'Discriminatory selection – failure to offer alternative employment' above, a disabled employee may have grounds for arguing that it would amount to a reasonable adjustment for him or her to be prioritised for alternative available employment. Even if that is not the case, employers should always consider the possibility and in doing so should be careful not to make assumptions about a disabled employee's ability to perform alternative work without first consulting him or her. In Steers v S Walsh and Sons Ltd ET Case No.3201805/09 an employment tribunal upheld an employee's claim that his selection for

9.63

371

redundancy amounted to unlawful direct discrimination on the ground of his disability because, among other things, his employer had failed to discuss with him the possibility of alternative employment and offered work to another employee that he could have performed because it made assumptions about his multiple sclerosis without checking whether those assumptions were correct.

In Redcar and Cleveland Primary Care Trust v Lonsdale EAT 0090/12 L initially worked as a senior occupational therapist, which was a band six role within the Trust. However, in 2008 she suffered a significant deterioration in her vision, making it impossible for her to continue in that role, and she was redeployed to a band four post. In 2010 the Trust embarked on a restructuring exercise. Under stage one of the restructuring plan, employees could apply for posts within their existing band, or one band above. Only at stage two of the exercise could they apply for other posts, to the extent that these remained unfilled. Consequently, when L's band four role was identified as being at risk of redundancy, she was not permitted, at stage one, to apply for the band six job she was interested in. She was also unable to apply for it at stage two, as it had already been filled by someone else. Following her eventual dismissal for redundancy, L lodged a number of claims in the employment tribunal, including that the employer had failed to make reasonable adjustments by not permitting her to apply for the band six role. The tribunal upheld this claim and its decision was subsequently approved by the EAT. It held, among other things, that had L not become disabled she would have remained in her original band six role, which would in turn have meant that she could have applied for another band six role under the restructuring plan at stage one. She was disadvantaged by not being able to apply for that role. In all the circumstances, it was not unreasonable to make an exception to the restructuring plan to allow for L's disability.

9.64   Two further examples:

- **Phillips v Great Western Ambulance Service NHS Trust** ET Case No.1400567/12: P brought a grievance against the respondent Trust which was put on hold when she suffered a nervous breakdown and was signed off work. Some months later she was referred to occupational health, which confirmed that she was well enough to be contacted and take part in the grievance procedure. P's grievance was investigated and rejected and her appeal was dismissed. At a subsequent meeting she told the Trust that she was fit for work but could not contemplate returning to work with any of the people involved in her grievance. In practice, this appeared to rule out any return to the Trust. Occupational health confirmed that this position was likely to be permanent and raised the possibility of a transfer to a different Trust. Soon afterwards, however, P determined that she could return to her original role, but by then the employer had decided that that role should be deleted as it had not been performed for two years and was considered to be obsolete. P was put on special leave while the employer implemented a redundancy procedure and a few months later she was formally dismissed as redundant. P brought a number of tribunal claims, including a complaint of failure to make reasonable adjustments. It was accepted that she was disabled as result of the long-term effects of her nervous breakdown. The employment tribunal held that the Trust had failed to make the reasonable adjustments of exploring the possibility of an interim and phased return to work in a different role, rather than placing her on special leave; discussing with her what support she needed and how her return to work might be managed; and giving her time to consider what options for alternative work she might consider

• **Callaghan v I-Smart Consumer Services Ltd and ors** ET Case No.1201004/11: C suffered from attention deficit with hyperactivity disorder (ADHD) and was on medication that allowed her to cope at work provided she could avoid stressful situations or sudden changes to her routines. One evening ICS Ltd (her employer) phoned her at home and told her that, as one of the best performers in her team, she was being transferred into the sales team. She attended a meeting the next day to discuss the business reorganisation during which she became very upset about the lack of notice of the change. It was apparent, however, that ICS Ltd would not alter its decision. The following day C informed her employer about her disability and the effect that sudden change had on her but, despite this, she was told that her original job was no longer available. She went on sick leave and then wrote to ICS Ltd saying that, as her role was obsolete, she was prepared to accept redundancy with immediate effect. ICS Ltd chose to treat this as a resignation on C's part. C brought claims of unfair constructive dismissal, discrimination arising from a disability under S.15 EqA, and failure to make reasonable adjustments, all of which were upheld by an employment tribunal. It found that, while ICS Ltd had a potentially fair reason for dismissal – business reorganisation – it had behaved completely unreasonably and this was because of something related to her disability. Furthermore, the employer had failed to make the reasonable adjustment of seeking to avoid the effect on C of a requirement to move to a new role suddenly by offering a staged transfer with close mentoring.

Competitive interviews and assessments. One issue that often arises is whether   **9.65** adjustments should be made to competitive processes for determining who should be offered vacancies by way of suitable alternative employment. Case law shows that an employer may well be expected to make adjustments in this context in order to eliminate the disadvantage that the competitive nature of such processes causes to disabled employees as a result of their disability.

In London Borough of Southwark v Charles EAT 0008/14 C was placed in a redeployment pool in May 2011 following the elimination of his job for LBS

373

as an Environmental Enforcement Officer (grade 9). While in the pool his GP signed him off sick for three months due to 'sleep paralysis agitans' – a condition that meant that C woke up at night, paralysed, and so felt unable to go back to sleep. This led to him suffering from depression. The receipt of C's sick note was the first that LBS knew of his disability and its cause. On 17 June LBS's occupational health adviser, A Ltd, advised that, as a result of C's disability, he was not fit to attend administrative meetings. Following receipt from C's doctor of a further sick note, LBS agreed to extend the period in which it would allow C to remain in the redeployment pool. On 11 August A Ltd tried to telephone C while he was still off sick to ask whether he was well enough to attend an interview for a particular vacancy (Noise Support Officer (grade 7)) for which he had previously expressed some interest. After unsuccessfully making further attempts to contact him, LBS wrote to C recording that it had received 'no indication as to whether you are able to attend interviews' and notifying him that his employment would therefore terminate the following day 'in the absence of receiving an expression of interest from you regarding vacancies'.

9.66 C subsequently brought claims for unfair dismissal and disability discrimination (failure to make reasonable adjustments and discrimination arising from disability). An employment tribunal held that he had been dismissed for redundancy and that his dismissal had been fair following adequate consultation and the opportunity to apply for other jobs. However, it upheld his claims of disability discrimination. The tribunal found that, since LBS had been aware from 17 June onwards that C suffered from a disability that prevented him from attending administrative meetings (which included redeployment interviews), it had failed to make reasonable adjustments by dispensing with the need for him to attend an interview. As a result he was placed at a substantial disadvantage by being dismissed. The tribunal noted the suggestions made by C's trade union representative that an interview could have taken place at C's home, or information could have been required from him in advance, or a less formal interview process could have taken place. It also noted that, as C had been an employee since May 2008, managers could have been consulted for an assessment of his abilities for a post that was two grades below his current post.

LBS's appeal to the EAT against the employment tribunal's decision was unsuccessful. With specific regard to the tribunal's decision that LBS had failed to make reasonable adjustments, the Appeal Tribunal held that the tribunal had been entitled to find: (i) that LBS had applied a PCP in the form of a practice requiring those in the redeployment pool to attend for interview for potential redeployment posts; (ii) this had put C at a substantial disadvantage because he could not attend an interview, which in turn meant that he could not demonstrate that he was qualified for any of the jobs for which he might have applied (in particular, for the post of Noise Support Officer, for which he had indicated a qualified expression of interest); and (iii) LBS knew that C suffered from a significant disability in the form of an inability to attend administrative meetings. In the EAT's view, the tribunal had 'understandably and sensibly' concluded that such meetings embraced interviews for new jobs.

A similar conclusion was reached in Wilebore v Cable and Wireless Worldwide **9.67** Services Ltd ET Case No.3304124/10, where W was employed by CWWS as a field operations manager. In July 2008 he was diagnosed with a rare form of cancer requiring removal of his aorta and he was off work until May 2009. During his absence CWWS reorganised its field services division and W's role was deleted and replaced by a new role, field services manager (FSM). He was told about the reorganisation but assured that, in view of his excellent record, he would naturally be appointed to the new role, although he would have to go through an assessment. Upon his return to work, CWWS financed counselling sessions for W as he was finding his condition highly stressful, and engaged occupational health to try to ensure that he was fit to undergo the assessment, which took place on 26 March 2010. There were five candidates but only one attained the pass mark for the assessment. Although, at that point, W decided not to continue with the selection process, CWWS nonetheless offered him the role of acting FSM for three months during which he would be coached on areas where he had proved weak. The role would then be readvertised at the end of W's trial period at which point he would have to go through another assessment. W went off work suffering from stress and depression and contacted CWWS on 17 April to ask for redundancy figures. On 2 May he wrote saying that the uncertainty surrounding his role had impacted on the stress he was suffering and that he felt he had no option but to take redundancy. He subsequently brought claims of unfair dismissal and failure to make reasonable adjustments, both of which were upheld by the employment tribunal. It found that CWWS had failed to make the reasonable adjustment of offering the role of FSM to W without the need for a competitive assessment: the offer of that role could have been coupled with a development plan, which would have helped him overcome the substantial disadvantage caused by his cancer, especially in view of the fact that, prior to the onset of his illness, he was already performing key aspects of the FSM role very proficiently. The employer was aware that W was suffering from high levels of stress as a result of his medical condition and the need to go through a competitive process heightened his feelings of insecurity. His stress and anxiety caused him to underperform in the assessment process.

In the seminal case of Archibald v Fife Council 2004 ICR 954, HL, the House of Lords accepted that, in some circumstances, the duty to make reasonable adjustments under what is now S.20 EqA can require an employer to transfer a disabled employee to a vacant post at a slightly higher grade without requiring him or her to undergo a competitive interview. In so holding, Lady Hale (with whom their other Lordships agreed) observed that the statutory protections

375

relating to disability discrimination necessarily entail a measure of positive discrimination in the sense that employers are required to take steps to help disabled people which they are not required to take for others. However, neither that case nor any of the cases discussed above should be taken to mean that employees should be given favourable treatment requiring them to be redeployed to jobs well beyond their qualifications or experience. Everything will depend on the circumstances and what is reasonable. Confirmation of this point was provided in Wade v Sheffield Hallam University EAT 0194/12, where the EAT upheld an employment tribunal's decision that it would not have been a reasonable adjustment for the employer to waive its competitive interview process and appoint the redundant claimant to an entirely new role. The employer in that case had decided that the claimant failed to meet the essential requirements of the vacant post. That belief was genuine and was supported by evidence showing that she had failed to accept that the new role was in any way different from the post she had occupied before going on sick leave. In those circumstances, it could not be a reasonable adjustment simply to appoint her to a role for which she was not considered suitable.

9.68 **Postponing or delaying redundancy.** In Doran v Department for Work and Pensions EATS 0017/14 the EAT held that it was open to an employment tribunal to hold that an employer's duty to make reasonable adjustments was not triggered in circumstances where, at the point of dismissal, the disabled employee had been off sick for a long period, remained unfit to work and was unable to give any indication of when she might be able to return. However, in other cases where evidence demonstrates that an employee may be in a position to return to work in the not-too-distant future, tribunals have held that a postponement of the redundancy process can constitute a reasonable adjustment. Two examples:

- **Parvez v Mackenzie Tools and Productions Ltd** ET Case No.1301258/11: P was dismissed as redundant from his post as sales manager at a time when he was on a phased return to work following an accident at work which had resulted in a serious arm injury. Prior to the accident he had spent 80 per cent of his time on backroom management duties: during the phased return he undertook no shop floor duties partly because of the mental anxiety brought on by returning to the scene of his accident. An employment tribunal held that P's dismissal for redundancy was fair but that the employer had failed to make the reasonable adjustment of delaying the redundancy exercise to enable P to make a full return to work. Had this been done – and there were no immediate pressures to cut costs – there was a reasonable chance that P would have been able to overcome the substantial disadvantage caused by his injury and his mental reaction to it resulting in a resumption of activities on the shop floor. This, in turn, might have justified expanding the pool for selection or exploring possible adjustments to P's terms and conditions of employment, particularly in relation to salary, to enable dismissal for redundancy to be avoided

376

- **See v Westfield Shopping Towns Ltd** ET Case No.2200378/11: S, who was employed as commercial manager by WST Ltd, was informed on 14 June 2010 that his post was at risk of redundancy. He was noticeably shocked at the news, but informed WST Ltd that he had been signed off work for two weeks because of a recent bereavement. In the event he remained unfit to work due to severe depression. WST Ltd wrote to him on 2 July, drawing attention to some redeployment opportunities but telling him that if it did not hear from him by 5 July it would assume he was not interested. It also offered him the opportunity to meet to discuss further his possible redeployment, with flexibility as to venue and the opportunity for breaks or adjournments as necessary. S was not sufficiently well to respond and he was eventually dismissed. S wrote a lengthy letter in response explaining that while he was interested in the possibility of alternative employment, he had not been fit to apply for vacancies during his absence. In early September WST Ltd revoked his dismissal and resumed consultation, but the only alternative role S was told about was on a fixed-term contract and, for that reason, he decided not to pursue that option. S was dismissed again at the end of October, even though somebody had just resigned from a post that would have been a suitable alternative for him. An employment tribunal held that S had been unfairly dismissed and that WST Ltd had failed to make reasonable adjustments. In the tribunal's view, it would have been reasonable to have postponed S's redundancy as he was not able, by reason of his disability, to participate in the redundancy process during the summer of 2010 and WST knew that posts that might have been suitable for him were likely to be created in early 2011.

Discrimination against part-time workers

9.69

Employers in straitened circumstances may wish to make part-time workers redundant as it is usually more cost effective to make a part-time worker redundant than to cut the hours of a full-time worker. However, employers considering such action must ensure that they do not fall foul of the Part-time Workers (Prevention of Less Favourable Treatment) Regulations 2000 SI 2000/1551 ('the PTW Regulations'). These provide that a part-time worker has the right not to be treated by his or her employer less favourably than the employer treats a comparable full-time worker as regards the terms of his or her contract, or by being subjected to any other detriment by any act, or deliberate failure to act, by his or her employer – Reg 5(1). It applies where:

- the reason for the treatment is that the worker is a part-timer, and

- the treatment is not justified on objective grounds – Reg 5(2).

The right applies in addition to the right not to be unfairly selected for redundancy for exercising rights under the PTW Regulations found in

377

S.105(7E) of the Employment Rights Act 1996 (see Chapter 8, 'Unfair redundancy', under 'Automatically unfair redundancy – part-time and fixed-term work').

9.70 Redundancy selection

It is clear that the scope of the PTW Regulations embraces the right of part-time workers to be treated no less favourably than comparable full-timers with respect to redundancy selection, unless the different treatment is objectively justified. Two examples of cases in which employees successfully claimed discrimination on this basis:

- **McGuinness v North Estates Ltd** ET Case No.2400578/08: an employment tribunal found that a part-time administrator was selected for redundancy because she worked part time. Another administrator who worked part time was also made redundant, whereas a full-time employee doing similar work was retained, and there was no evidence that the employer had considered retaining the part-time employees

- **Clarke v Brookside (1998) Ltd t/a Nottingham Volkswagen and anor** ET Case No.2600301/09: C was employed as a fleet sales executive. Following a period of maternity leave she worked for three days a week. In April 2008 B Ltd recruited a new fleet sales manager to whom C was to report. The tribunal accepted C's evidence that he made comments about her being the 'part-time department' and 'a baby machine'. Following a downturn in business C was informed in October 2008 that she was at risk of redundancy. As she was pregnant she asked if she could bring forward her maternity leave and take a year's leave to give the market time to recover, but B Ltd rejected that proposal and she was dismissed as redundant later that month. An employment tribunal found that C was discriminated against on the grounds of her gender and part-time working arrangement.

9.71 However, in Vij-Solanki v IDT Global Ltd ET Case No.2203531/08 V's claim of less favourable treatment on the ground of part-time status was dismissed. In June 2008 V's employer had to make redundancies and V, who worked three days a week, was selected. She claimed, among other things, that in being selected for redundancy and dismissed she had been less favourably treated than her full-time colleagues. However, the employment tribunal found that apart from a remark that V did not show the same 'commitment' as the others in her pool, there was nothing in the selection exercise which could have led it to believe that V's status as a part-time worker was the reason for her treatment. The employer had demonstrated its willingness to accommodate flexible or part-time working in agreeing to V's two requests to reduce or change her hours following periods of maternity leave. The tribunal was satisfied, notwithstanding the comment regarding her commitment, that V's selection for redundancy was because she scored lower than her colleagues

378

and that there was no evidence that her scores were tainted by her part-time status. It noted that it would in fact have suited the employer's 'budgetary imperatives' to have selected a full-time worker rather than V for redundancy.

The Part-time Workers Regulations are considered at length in IDS Employment Law Handbook, 'Atypical and Flexible Working' (2014), Chapter 3, 'Part-time workers'.

Indirect sex discrimination   9.72

Prior to the introduction of the PTW Regulations, part-time workers who suffered discriminatory treatment on the ground of their part-time status had to rely on the discrimination legislation for a remedy, in particular on the Sex Discrimination Act 1975 (since repealed and superseded by the EqA). The rationale for such claims was that since most part-time workers were (and continue to be) women, the unequal treatment of such workers was likely to affect far more women than men. Therefore, unless a clear and objective explanation was provided, the discriminatory treatment of part-time workers was likely to amount to indirect sex discrimination and/or breach the principle of equal pay for equal work.

Although it might be thought that the introduction of the PTW Regulations completely eliminated the need to bring discrimination claims, in practice part-time claimants often bring claims under the Regulations and the EqA in the alternative. Indeed, where a claimant wishes to obtain an award for injury to feelings, he or she will need to claim under the EqA because this head of compensation is not available under the Regulations.

Employment tribunals often deal with indirect sex discrimination claims   9.73
arising in the context of redundancy selection where the claimants have been refused alternative employment because they are unable to meet a requirement to work full-time hours or at least the specified hours demanded by the employer. Here are two examples:

- **Chandler v American Airlines Inc** ET Case No.2329478/10: C, who worked as a lead agent for AA Inc, returned from maternity leave in April 2009 on an agreed part-time basis. However, in July AA Inc carried out a review of its passenger services and, as a result, the post of lead agent was abolished and post-holders were invited to apply for the posts of operational coordinator or team leader. C applied for the team leader position and was successful, but AA Inc informed her that that post was full time and that although it would honour her hours and roster pattern for a trial period of four months it would expect her to increase her hours to full time at the end of that period. She told AA Inc that she was not in a position to work full time and at the end of the trial period she was given a choice: to work full time, consider a job share or accept a redundancy

379

package. Under duress, she opted for the latter and brought a claim of sex discrimination. Upholding that claim, an employment tribunal found that, since significantly more women than men have primary responsibility for childcare, the requirement to work full time was to the detriment of women and it was not a proportionate means of achieving AA Inc's stated aim of improving management. The company accepted in evidence that the team leader position could have been undertaken otherwise than on a full-time basis, although not on the hours that C had previously been working. It followed that the provision, criterion or practice to work full time could not be justified

- **Meyer v Homebase Ltd** ET Case No.1101683/12: M worked for H Ltd on a part-time basis, organising her hours around the school day. In January 2012 H Ltd announced a redundancy/realignment process across their stores and as a result all employees had to be interviewed for revised roles and were warned that there would be changes to their terms and conditions in order to increase flexibility. The outcome of a protracted individual consultation process was that M was offered a post working from 4.30 pm to 8.30 pm three days a week. She was unable to do these hours due to her childcare commitments but by this time other roles that would have been suitable for her had already been distributed. As M was unwilling to accept the role offered, she was dismissed for redundancy. An employment tribunal held that H Ltd's requirement that M work the specified hours was indirectly sex discriminatory and did not constitute a proportionate means of achieving a legitimate aim. There were other daytime roles that she could have carried out; and the way that H Ltd had organised matters meant that employees were only able to voice their concerns about the hours they were offered after all the roles had been assigned. This was particularly disadvantageous to women with childcare commitments.

9.74 ## Discrimination against fixed-term employees

The Fixed-term Employees (Prevention of Less Favourable Treatment) Regulations 2002 SI 2002/2034 ('the FTE Regulations') provide specific protection for fixed-term employees. They provide that it is unlawful for an employer to treat a fixed-term employee less favourably than the employer treats a comparable permanent employee as regards the terms of his or her contract or by subjecting him or her to any other detriment by any act or deliberate failure to act, unless the difference in treatment can be objectively justified – Reg 3.

This means that fixed-term employees should not be selected for redundancy purely because they are on fixed-term contracts, unless this can be objectively justified. Where, for example, a fixed-term employee has been brought in specifically to complete particular tasks or to cover for a peak in demand, it is likely that an employer could objectively justify selecting him or her for redundancy at the end of the contract. Where length of service is the main criterion for redundancy selection, the same criteria should apply to fixed-term employees as to comparable permanent employees, unless differences are objectively justified.

In Hopkins v City University ET Case No.2204178/08 the employee failed **9.75** to establish that his selection for redundancy was on the ground of his fixed-term status. He was employed in a senior administrative capacity on a series of fixed-term contracts from 18 June 2007 to 30 September 2008. One of the main reasons for his appointment was to ensure oversight at a senior level of a reorganisation programme. A consequence of the reorganisation was that H's role was disestablished and replaced by a similar role of COO, which was advertised externally. Following the competitive recruitment procedure an external candidate was appointed and H's last fixed-term appointment was not renewed, meaning that he was dismissed for redundancy. He claimed that he had suffered a detriment on the ground of his fixed-term status when the University created the COO role, advertised the post externally, and subsequently dismissed him. However, an employment tribunal dismissed his claim. The decision to create the position of COO was part of the restructuring exercise and had nothing to do with H personally. H could not point to a valid comparator, but in any event the decision to advertise the COO role externally had nothing to do with H's fixed-term status: it was because the role was judged to be of critical importance and the University was anxious to ensure that the best possible candidate was appointed. The same policy applied to other COO roles in the University. His dismissal was the inevitable consequence of H losing the competition, and was not discriminatory. The tribunal concluded that even had it found discrimination under Reg 3, it would have held that H's treatment was justified. The University was entirely justified in seeking to recruit the best possible candidate for a senior role, and H had, at the time, given it every reason to think he agreed with the decision to advertise the role externally.

The right not to be treated unfavourably under Reg 3 is in addition to the right not to be unfairly selected for redundancy for exercising rights under the Regulations found in S.105(7G) of the Employment Rights Act 1996 (see Chapter 8, 'Unfair redundancy', under 'Automatically unfair redundancy – part-time and fixed-term work').

The FTE Regulations are discussed in detail in IDS Employment Law Handbook, 'Atypical and Flexible Working' (2014), Chapter 2, 'Fixed-term employees'.

10 Enforcement

Most redundancy payments are paid by the employer at the time of dismissal. **10.1**
But what happens if there is a dispute between employer and employee
as to the employee's entitlement to a redundancy payment, the amount
of redundancy pay due, or the legitimacy of the employee's selection for
redundancy? If the parties cannot come to an agreement on the matter, the
employee may be forced to bring proceedings in an employment tribunal to
settle the dispute. In this chapter we examine the procedural requirements for
bringing a statutory redundancy pay claim or for claiming unfair redundancy.
We also consider various procedural issues relating to claims for contractual
redundancy payments and the enforcement of other rights under contractual
redundancy schemes.

Statutory redundancy payments   10.2

Any question as to an employee's right to a statutory redundancy payment, or
as to the amount of any payment made, should be referred to an employment
tribunal under S.163 of the Employment Rights Act 1996 (ERA). Claims
for statutory redundancy payments fall under the exclusive jurisdiction of
employment tribunals and cannot be brought in the civil courts. While a
full examination of the procedural requirements for bringing tribunal claims
falls outside the scope of this Handbook, it is worth noting a couple of basic
points. First, all claims to employment tribunals must be made on a specified
form, the ET1, while all responses to claims must be on form ET3. Failure
to use the correct form will lead to the claim or response being inadmissible.
Secondly, claims for redundancy payments are one of the jurisdictions
under which an employment judge may sit alone (i.e. without lay members)
– S.4(3)(c) Employment Tribunals Act 1996 (ETA). Thirdly, claims for
redundancy pay, like most employment claims, must first be referred to the
Advisory, Conciliation and Arbitration Service (Acas) for conciliation before
an employment tribunal claim may be submitted – Ss.18 and 18A ETA.
Finally, a statutory redundancy pay claim is a 'Type A' claim for the purpose
of tribunal fees, attracting an issue fee of £160 and a hearing fee of £230 –
the Employment Tribunals and the Employment Appeal Tribunal Fees Order
2013 SI 2013/1893. A detailed exposition of employment tribunal procedure,
conciliation and fees can be found in IDS Employment Law Handbook,
'Employment Tribunal Practice and Procedure' (2014).

383

10.3   Time limits

Section 164 ERA sets out the time limits for presenting a claim under S.163. The general rule is that an employee will lose entitlement to a statutory redundancy payment unless one of the following four events occurs before the end of a period of *six months* beginning with the relevant date:

- the payment is agreed and paid – S.164(1)(a)

- the employee makes a written claim for the payment to the employer – S.164(1)(b) (see 'Written claim to employer' below)

- the question as to the employee's right to, or the amount of, the payment has been referred to an employment tribunal – S.164(1)(c). (Note that a claim is 'referred to a tribunal' when it is physically received at the tribunal office, not when it is posted – Secretary of State for Employment v Banks and ors 1983 ICR 48, EAT), or

- the employee presents a claim of unfair dismissal to a tribunal under S.111 ERA – S.164(1)(d) (see 'Unfair dismissal complaint' below).

The 'relevant date' in this context means the effective date of termination of employment (EDT) and is defined in three ways:

- where the employee's contract of employment is terminated by notice (whether given by the employer or the employee), it is the date on which the notice expires

- where the contract is terminated without notice, it is the date on which termination takes effect

- in relation to an employee who is employed under a limited-term contract which terminates by virtue of the limiting event without being renewed under the same contract (see Chapter 1, 'Dismissal', under 'Expiry of limited-term contract'), it is the date on which the termination takes effect – S.145(2).

10.4   There are two special features of the relevant date in the context of the time limit for tribunal claims:

- if the employee accepts an offer of alternative employment with a trial period and then leaves or gives notice or is dismissed during the trial period, the relevant date is the date the employment comes to an end and not, as in other contexts, the date the original contract ended – S.145(4)(a)

- if the employer dismisses summarily or with insufficient notice, the relevant date is the date on which the termination takes effect. It is not deemed to be the date upon which proper notice would have expired, as it is for certain other purposes by virtue of S.145(5). If an employee who is entitled to the maximum statutory notice of 12 weeks is summarily dismissed on 15 March, the six-month period still expires on 14 September. No account is taken for this purpose of the notice the employee ought to have been given.

384

It is crucial to note that a period of six months beginning with the relevant date *includes* that date. Thus, six months beginning with 15 March ends on 14 September and not, as the unwary often think, on 15 September.

Section 164(1) provides that one of the specified events must occur before the **10.5** end of the six-month period beginning with the relevant date. There seems no reason on this wording why the event should not take place before the relevant date itself so that an employee could, for example, make a claim for a redundancy payment while still working out his or her notice of dismissal. The EAT, however, held in Watts v Rubery Owen Conveyancer Ltd 1977 ICR 429, EAT, that a claim will be premature and invalid if it is made before dismissal takes effect. This decision was followed by another division of the EAT in Pritchard-Rhodes Ltd v Boon and anor 1979 IRLR 19, EAT.

The correctness of the Watts decision has long been the subject of debate – especially since S.111(3) now specifically permits an unfair dismissal claim to be presented during a notice period, and this is one of the events specified in S.164(1). However, the decision was endorsed by the EAT in Foster v Bon Groundwork Ltd 2011 ICR 1122, EAT, a case concerning issue estoppel. In the course of the proceedings, an issue arose as to whether the principle that a claim for a redundancy payment can only be pursued after the expiry of the notice period remained good law. In the EAT's view, it clearly did. According to Mr Justice Silber, 'Parliament has not changed the law on this when it could have done so when introducing the provision for unfair dismissal.' Although the employer appealed to the Court of Appeal – see Foster v Bon Groundwork Ltd 2012 ICR 1027, CA – the case was decided on other grounds and the Court declined to express an opinion on whether Watts remains good law.

Extending time limit. Under S.164, an employee's right to a redundancy **10.6** payment does not necessarily expire at the end of the six-month period if none of the specified events has taken place. If during the six months immediately following the initial six-month period he or she makes a written claim for payment to the employer or refers a redundancy pay claim to a tribunal or presents an unfair dismissal complaint to a tribunal, then the tribunal has a discretion to award a redundancy payment. This discretion is to be exercised if it appears to the tribunal to be just and equitable that the employee should receive a redundancy payment having regard to the reason shown by the employee for his or her failure to take any of the specified steps earlier and to all the other relevant circumstances – S.164(2) and (3).

Subject to three exceptions relating to mediation in cross-border disputes, early conciliation and death of the employee (discussed below), there is no discretion to extend the time limit beyond the second six-month period and a claim received even one day after the combined 12-month period will be irrevocably out of time. This is the case even where the employee is in no way

385

at fault. In Crawford v (1) Secretary of State for Employment (2) Colmore Depot 1995 IRLR 523, EAT, C failed to apply for a redundancy payment when his employer's business, which was in receivership, was sold. This was because all the parties, including the Secretary of State, assumed that there had been a transfer under what are now the Transfer of Undertakings (Protection of Employment) Regulations 2006 SI 2006/246 (TUPE). Over a year later it became clear that there had not been a transfer and C applied to the Secretary of State for a redundancy payment. This was refused on the ground that his claim was out of time. The EAT agreed. It rejected C's claim that it should consider the spirit and intention of the legislation and that time should only begin to run against C when it became clear that there had been no transfer. The EAT recommended that employees of companies that become insolvent should make provisional claims for a redundancy payment from the employer and the Secretary of State promptly to cover themselves in the event that the insolvent undertaking is not transferred to a third party under TUPE.

10.7 *'Just and equitable'.* In deciding whether it is just and equitable to award a redundancy payment outside the normal six-month time limit, a tribunal should take account of the reason for the employee's failure to present the claim in time and all other relevant circumstances – S.164(3)(b). The EAT considered this provision in Paul v C and J Stone Ltd EAT 209/80, where a tribunal had refused to consider a claim presented four days out of time. In the EAT's view, the statutory words involved the tribunal taking some account of the merits of the employee's claim – i.e. how likely he or she was to succeed in a claim for a redundancy payment if it allowed the claim to proceed – and there was certainly no error of law in it doing so. The EAT went on to say that 'the circumstances under which this Appeal Tribunal would feel able to interfere with a discretion exercised by [a] tribunal are rare indeed'. Thus, there will normally be no point in appealing against a tribunal's decision on this issue unless there has been a clear misdirection in law.

The EAT did find an error of law in Smith v Humber Ship Repairing Ltd and ors EAT 366/85. S's claim had been late because of faulty advice from his union. The tribunal relied on the case of Dedman v British Building and Engineering Appliances Ltd 1974 ICR 53, CA, and said simply that any remedy S might have lay against his union advisers. The EAT pointed out that the Dedman case concerned the time limit for an unfair dismissal claim. The statutory test for this is whether it was 'reasonably practicable' to have brought the claim in time, not the very different test of whether the tribunal considers it 'just and equitable' to award a redundancy payment outside the six-month time limit. The case was remitted for the tribunal to think again.

10.8 Four cases where late claims have been allowed:

386

- **Gadd v Maiseys (Kenilworth) Ltd** ET Case No.5994/78: the employer and the company accountants promised several times to do something about a redundancy payment but then refused to pay after the six-month time limit had passed. The employee referred her claim to a tribunal promptly after the refusal

- **Taylor v Secretary of State for Employment** ET Case No.14939/95: T, who was made redundant upon her employer's bankruptcy, applied to a tribunal for a redundancy payment just within the discretionary 12-month limit. The tribunal took account of the fact that T had been given incorrect advice and information and had waited patiently for the outcome of certain disputed matters

- **Ratcliffe v Chillingtons Developments (by the Official Receiver) and anor** ET Case No.27278/83: R, a company director, knew that the company was insolvent when he was dismissed for redundancy. He waited for the company to go into liquidation – which took about eight months – before claiming a redundancy payment from the official receiver. The tribunal thought it was reasonable for him to wait and see what happened when the company went into liquidation

- **Nixon v IMB Contractors Ltd** ET Case No.4733/85: N was employed for about five years on a succession of contracts in between which he was laid off. He did not claim a redundancy payment until ten months after the expiry of the last contract. A tribunal decided that he had been continuously employed and that it was just and equitable to award a redundancy payment because he expected to be re-employed and had kept in touch with the employer.

10.9 *Mediation in EU cross-border disputes.* Since 20 May 2011, the time limit for enforcing a redundancy payment claim may be extended where the parties are engaged in mediation to resolve a cross-border dispute and that mediation started before the time limit was due to expire – Ss.164(4) and 207A(5). If, in these circumstances, the normal time limit for bringing a tribunal claim under S.164(1)(c) or the extended time limit under S.164(2) would expire before the mediation ends or less than eight weeks after it ends, the time limit will be extended to the end of eight weeks after the mediation ends – Ss.164(4) and 207A(6). A cross-border dispute is one in which at least one of the parties is domiciled or habitually resident in a Member State of the European Union other than that of any other party – Article 2 EU Cross-border Mediation Directive (No.2008/52).

10.10 *Early conciliation.* Claims for redundancy pay are subject to the 'early conciliation' (EC) rules, which came into force on 6 May 2014. The EC rules require that anyone who is considering bringing a complaint to an employment tribunal must first contact Acas, be offered conciliation, and receive an EC certificate before being allowed to submit the claim to the tribunal – see Ss.18A and 18B of the Employment Tribunals Act 1996 (ETA) and the Employment Tribunals (Early Conciliation: Exemptions and Rules of Procedure) Regulations 2014 SI 2014/254. In addition, S.207B ERA makes provision for extending the time limits that apply to various ERA claims in order to facilitate conciliation, and S.164(5) provides that these provisions apply to redundancy pay complaints under S.164(1)(c) and (2).

Briefly, the effect of S.207B is twofold. First, the clock will stop when Acas receives the EC request and start to run again the day after the prospective claimant receives the EC certificate. Secondly, if a time limit is due to expire during the period beginning with the day Acas receives the EC request and one month after the prospective claimant receives the EC certificate, the time limit expires instead at the end of that period. This effectively gives the prospective claimant one month from the date when he or she receives (or is deemed to receive) the EC certificate to present the claim. For more details of the EC regime, see IDS Employment Law Handbook, 'Employment Tribunal Practice and Procedure' (2014), Chapter 3, 'Conciliation, settlements and ADR', under 'Early conciliation', and Chapter 5, 'Time limits', under 'Extension of time limit under early conciliation rules'.

10.11 *Death of employee.* If the employee dies during the period of six months beginning with the relevant date, the period is extended to one year beginning with the relevant date – S.176(7)(a). Where no claim has been brought on behalf of the deceased employee by the end of that period, it would seem possible, by virtue of S.164(2), for the tribunal to extend the time limit by an additional six months if it considers it just and equitable to do so. If the employee dies after the first six-month period, but before the end of the following six months, the second six-month period, during which the tribunal has a discretion whether or not to award a redundancy payment, is extended to one year – S.176(7)(b).

If there is no personal representative to pursue a claim on behalf of a deceased employee's estate, the tribunal has the power to appoint an 'appropriate person' for this purpose. This may be a person authorised to act in connection with the claim by the employee before his or her death. Alternatively, it may be the surviving spouse, civil partner, child, parent or sibling of the deceased – S.206(4) and (5).

10.12 **Subsequent claims.** Section 164 states that an employee will not be entitled to a redundancy payment unless one of the specified events has taken place before the end of the six-month period beginning with the relevant date. If one of the specified events has occurred within the six-month period, there is then no time limit for presenting a subsequent claim to a tribunal. Two illustrations:

• **Bentley Engineering Co Ltd v Crown and Miller** 1976 ICR 225, QBD: M was dismissed and paid a redundancy payment, based on eight years' service, within six months. Nearly two years after his dismissal he made a claim to a tribunal that the payment should have been based on 23 years' service. The High Court held that there was nothing in the wording of what is now S.164 ERA to prevent his doing so

- **Germain v Harry Taylor of Ashton Ltd** ET Case No.51738/95: G was made redundant in February 1974. He sent a letter to his employer five months later asking for his redundancy pay. He received a cheque for £580 but discovered, in June 1995, that he had been paid only half the amount to which he was entitled. A tribunal found that, since G had made a claim in writing for redundancy pay within six months of the relevant date, his claim could proceed to a full hearing.

Written claim to employer. One of the events that secures the right to a redundancy payment is where the employee has made a claim for the payment in writing to the employer within the six-month time limit – S.164(1)(b). Employees may not always frame written claims with legal precision, however. In Hetherington v Dependable Products Ltd 1971 ITR 1, CA, the Court of Appeal said that any notice in writing should be construed liberally in favour of the employee. In that case the only written communication within the time limit was a letter from a union representative to the employer asking 'when it would be convenient for me to come along and meet your Mr Ditchburn re the position of Mr Hetherington, who was made redundant whilst off on the sick'. The Court of Appeal said that – even on a liberal construction – this could not be construed as a claim for a redundancy payment. It appeared to be no more than a request to discuss the possibility of an ex gratia payment. The Court stated that it would have been different if the letter had asked for a meeting to discuss a redundancy payment to Mr Hetherington. **10.13**

In Price v Smithfield and Zwanenberg Group Ltd 1978 ICR 93, EAT, the Appeal Tribunal refined the Hetherington test and said that 'the test which ought to be applied is that the notice or the writing relied on must be of such a character that the recipient would reasonably understand in all the circumstances of the case that it was the intention of the writer or, if it is written on behalf of the employee, the employee to seek a redundancy payment'. In that case there had been a meeting with the employer at which, among other things, the employee's entitlement to a redundancy payment had been discussed. The notice relied on was a letter from the employee's solicitors to the employer saying: 'So far I have not heard from you in respect of Mr Price's claim for wrongful dismissal including his claim for a redundancy payment.' The EAT said that the letter was a sufficient indication that the employee was seeking a redundancy payment.

Unfair dismissal complaint. Another of the events that secures the right to a redundancy payment is the presentation of an unfair dismissal complaint within the six-month time limit – S.164(1)(d). 'Presentation' occurs when the **10.14**

claim form is actually delivered to the tribunal office, not when it is posted or e-mailed. However, the time limit for presenting an unfair dismissal complaint is actually three months, (unless the tribunal decides that it was not reasonably practicable to present the complaint in time and that it was presented within a reasonable period thereafter) – S.111(2) (see 'Unfair dismissal' below). The EAT has held that an unfair dismissal complaint presented outside the three-month limit will still entitle the employee to a redundancy payment if it was presented within the six months specified in S.164(1) – Duffin v Secretary of State for Employment 1983 ICR 766, EAT. Mr Justice Browne-Wilkinson thought that the normal limitation period of six months for redundancy payment claims should still apply where the claim has been mistakenly identified as an unfair dismissal claim, provided, of course, that the employee has actually been dismissed because of redundancy.

10.15 **Lay-off and short-time.** The normal statutory time limit does not apply when an employee's claim for a redundancy payment is based on a spell of lay-off or short-time working. The very different rules that apply to lay-off and short-time claims are fully explained in Chapter 4, 'Lay-off and short-time'. There are, however, circumstances in which a claim that is apparently based on a period of lay-off or short-time is in reality, or is converted into, an 'ordinary' redundancy claim:

- the statutory scheme for lay-off and short-time redundancies only applies when the employer has a contractual right to lay off or impose short-time working. If an employer has no contractual right, imposition of a lay-off or of short-time working will be a fundamental breach of contract entitling the employee to resign and claim to have been constructively dismissed for redundancy – see Chapter 1, 'Dismissal', under 'Constructive dismissal'

- the statutory scheme for lay-off and short-time redundancies does not apply at all if an employee has been dismissed – S.151. If an employee serves a notice of intention to claim based on a spell of lay-off or short-time working and the employer responds by dismissing him or her, the employee can only claim a redundancy payment on the basis of an express dismissal for redundancy.

In both these circumstances, the employee's claim will in fact be a 'normal' redundancy claim so that the normal time limit of six months will apply.

10.16 **Acas Code of Practice**

Since April 2009, the Acas 'Code of Practice on Discipline and Grievance' has applied to the majority of complaints that can be brought in an employment tribunal. The Code has statutory backing in that an employment tribunal may increase or reduce any award by up to 25 per cent to reflect either an employer's or an employee's unreasonable failure to follow the Code – S.207A Trade Union

390

and Labour Relations (Consolidation) Act 1992. While the Code itself states that it does not apply to redundancy dismissals, redundancy payment claims under S.163 ERA are covered. Thus, an employee's failure to initiate a grievance in accordance with the Code could mean that any redundancy payment he or she receives is reduced by up to 25 per cent. Likewise, an employer's failure to deal with the grievance as the Code requires could result in an increase of up to 25 per cent.

Non-payment

10.17

Section 163(5) ERA gives employment tribunals the power to award additional financial loss to employees who have brought a successful claim for a redundancy payment where that loss is attributable to the employer's non-payment. The amount that a tribunal can award must be 'appropriate in all the circumstances'.

Unfair dismissal

10.18

An employee aggrieved at his or her selection for redundancy may bring a claim of unfair dismissal. Like claims for redundancy payments, unfair dismissal claims fall under the exclusive jurisdiction of employment tribunals. The circumstances in which a redundancy dismissal may be unfair are discussed in Chapter 8, 'Unfair redundancy'. In this chapter, we briefly consider the time limit and other procedural requirements that apply to an unfair dismissal claim. For a more detailed discussion of the law governing unfair dismissal generally, see IDS Employment Law Handbook, 'Unfair Dismissal' (2015).

Time limit

10.19

Unlike claims for redundancy payments, where the time limit for bringing the claim is six months (see 'Statutory redundancy payments – time limits' above), claims of unfair dismissal must be brought within three months of the end of employment (unless not reasonably practicable). This is enshrined in S.111(2) ERA, which states that a tribunal will not consider a complaint of unfair dismissal unless it is presented:

- before the end of the period of three months beginning with the effective date of termination (EDT) – S.111(2)(a) (the rules governing the EDT are the same as those governing the 'relevant date' for redundancy payments – see 'Statutory redundancy payments – time limits' above), or

- within such further period as the tribunal considers reasonable in a case where it is satisfied that it was not reasonably practicable for the complaint to be presented before the end of that period of three months – S.111(2)(b).

These two provisions are subject to S.111(3), which states that, where a dismissal is with notice, tribunals may consider a complaint if it is presented before the notice period expires.

391

10.20 **Reasonably practicable.** As with redundancy payments, the time limit for unfair dismissal claims is subject to tribunals' discretion to extend time in certain circumstances. However, unlike redundancy payments, the discretion applies not where it is 'just and equitable' to extend time, but where it was not 'reasonably practicable' for the claimant to present the claim within three months of the EDT. A full consideration of the circumstances in which a tribunal can exercise this discretion falls outside the scope of this Handbook but can be found in IDS Employment Law Handbook, 'Employment Tribunal Practice and Procedure' (2014), Chapter 5, 'Time limits', under '"Not reasonably practicable" extension'.

10.21 **Cross-border mediation and early conciliation.** As with claims for redundancy payments, the time limit for bringing an unfair dismissal complaint may be extended to facilitate cross-border mediation or early conciliation – Ss.111(2A), 207A and 207B. These provisions are discussed briefly in the section 'Statutory redundancy payments' above, under 'Time limits – extending time limit'. For more details of the early conciliation regime, see IDS Employment Law Handbook, 'Employment Tribunal Practice and Procedure' (2014), Chapter 3, 'Conciliation, settlements and ADR', under 'Early conciliation', and Chapter 5, 'Time limits', under 'Extension of time limit under early conciliation rules'.

10.22 ## Qualifying service

As explained in Chapter 5, 'Qualifications and exclusions', under 'Qualifying service', the right to a statutory redundancy payment is limited to those employees who have at least two years' continuous service. By contrast, until fairly recently the right to claim unfair dismissal was subject to a qualifying period of only one year's continuous service for many years. This meant that employees who had between one and two years' service, though not entitled to claim a statutory redundancy payment, were able to challenge their selection for redundancy via the medium of unfair dismissal. For employers, this emphasised the importance of following a fair selection procedure and not simply selecting those employees who were ineligible for a statutory payment (see further Chapter 8, 'Unfair redundancy'). However, the Government's decision to increase the qualifying period for unfair dismissal rights from one to two years for employment commencing on or after 6 April 2012 has eliminated this distinction, although there are a number of circumstances giving rise to automatically unfair dismissal, in respect of which there is no qualifying period (see further IDS Employment Law Handbook, 'Unfair Dismissal' (2015), Chapter 9, 'Automatically unfair dismissals').

10.23 ## Compensation

Tribunal awards for unfair dismissal are normally split into two parts – the basic award and the compensatory award. However, in cases where a statutory redundancy payment has been made, and provided that the payment has been correctly calculated (see Chapter 6, 'Redundancy payments', under 'Statutory redundancy pay scheme'), an employee who successfully establishes that his or her redundancy was in fact unfair will not normally be entitled to the basic award element. The formula used to calculate the basic award is identical to that used to calculate redundancy payments and the statutory regime makes it clear that employees are only entitled to one, not both – see S.122(4). The compensatory award for unfair dismissal is generally subject to a statutory cap, currently set at £78,962 (as from 6 April 2016) or a year's salary, whichever is lower. There are, however, a number of types of automatically unfair dismissal where the cap does not apply, meaning that a claimant can recover the full extent of his or her loss – see further Chapter 8, 'Unfair redundancy', under 'Automatically unfair redundancy'.

For a full discussion of the principles that apply to the award of compensation consequent on a finding of unfair dismissal see IDS Employment Law Handbook, 'Unfair Dismissal' (2015), Chapter 13, 'Basic awards', and Chapter 14, 'Compensatory awards: types of loss'.

Reinstatement/re-engagement   10.24

Although most unfair dismissal claimants seek only compensation, it should not be forgotten that the ERA also makes provision for two other (mutually exclusive) remedies – reinstatement (under S.114) and re-engagement (S.115). Both types of remedy essentially involve the employer re-employing the dismissed employee, either in the same post from which he or she was dismissed or in a comparable role. S.112 ERA provides that, when a tribunal upholds an unfair dismissal claim, it must explain to the claimant that re-employment is an available remedy and ask if he or she wishes for such an order to be made – it is only if the claimant declines re-employment that the tribunal can go on to consider making an award of compensation. The unfair dismissal legislation therefore prioritises re-employment over compensation by providing that it should be the first remedy to be considered. Nonetheless, orders of reinstatement and re-engagement are very rarely sought and the overwhelming majority of successful unfair dismissal complaints result in an award of compensation.

The main factor that a tribunal must take into account when considering whether to make a re-employment order, if one is sought, is whether it would be 'practicable' for the employer to comply with such an order – S.116. Tribunals may give weight to employers' commercial judgement in deciding what is practicable and they may not make an order merely because it is possible for a dismissed employee to be accommodated. In Port of London Authority v Payne and ors 1994 ICR 555, CA, the Court of Appeal overturned a tribunal's re-engagement order made on the basis that the employer should

393

have invited applications for voluntary severance from the existing workforce. Thus, where there is a genuine redundancy situation and the dismissal was unfair on procedural grounds, the question of practicability is likely to tell against a re-employment order. In contrast, where the redundancy situation has not been established to the tribunal's satisfaction, re-employment may be more realistic – two examples:

- **United States Navy v Coady** EAT 275/94: C was purportedly dismissed for redundancy. A tribunal found that no redundancy situation in fact existed; the employer had simply replaced C with someone it considered better at the job. The tribunal ordered reinstatement, despite the employer's objection that this would cause overstaffing. The EAT upheld the decision. The services of the employee were not redundant and reinstatement would simply put matters back to where they were before the dismissal. Any resulting overstaffing would be the consequence, not of the reinstatement, but of the way in which the employer had gone about the management of the club in which C worked and the termination of his employment. It might be inexpedient for the employer to reinstate C but it was not impracticable

- **Carpenter v ABB Industrial Systems Ltd** ET Case No.1500/95: C, an engineer, was unfairly dismissed for redundancy. The employer failed to comply with the tribunal's order for reinstatement on the ground that it would have forced the company to make someone else redundant. However, during the course of the tribunal hearing, it emerged that the company had in fact, since the first practicability hearing, taken on a contract engineer from an agency and that this worker was still there. The tribunal held that, in the circumstances, reinstatement was certainly practicable.

10.25 Other factors that potentially have an impact on practicability include the employee's relationship with his or her ex-colleagues and whether there remains trust and confidence between the employee and the employer. Either of these factors may become relevant where a redundancy selection process has turned sour. In Arhin v Enfield Primary Care Trust 2010 EWCA Civ 1481, CA, A was found to have been unfairly dismissed for redundancy after the Trust failed to adopt a fair selection procedure. However, the employment tribunal refused to order re-engagement. On appeal, the Court of Appeal accepted that the tribunal had erred in relying on the 'strained relationship' between A and her line manager as a factor against re-engagement when the line manager had left the employer and emigrated shortly before the remedies hearing. However, it was satisfied that the tribunal's remaining factors against re-engagement, including the lack of a suitable job, the underlying need to economise and A's conduct in relation to an internal dispute, remained cogent. There was never a case for re-engagement despite evidence that A was well-liked and respected by a number of colleagues.

394

For a more detailed examination of the remedies of reinstatement and re-engagement, see IDS Employment Law Handbook, 'Unfair Dismissal' (2015), Chapter 12, 'Remedies', under 'Reinstatement and re-engagement'.

Contractual redundancy terms 10.26

Many employers offer enhanced redundancy pay as part of their benefits packages. However, if an employer declines to make such a payment, the employee will need to demonstrate that the enhanced scheme forms part of his or her contract of employment. It may be that the contract of employment expressly refers to the scheme, or it could be incorporated by implication. On the other hand, the employer may contend that the scheme is not contractual and simply indicates the employer's policy, subject to the exercise of discretion. A more detailed examination of enhanced redundancy pay schemes can be found in Chapter 6, 'Redundancy payments', under 'Enhanced redundancy pay'. For consideration of the general principles of contract law, including the incorporation of contractual terms, see IDS Employment Law Handbook, 'Contracts of Employment' (2014), Chapter 3, 'Contractual terms', and Chapter 5, 'Incorporated terms'.

Where an employer's enhanced redundancy scheme is contractual, an employee's entitlement to a payment under that scheme arises on the termination of employment. As a result, claims for contractual redundancy pay fall under employment tribunals' limited jurisdiction to hear contract claims granted by the Employment Tribunals Extension of Jurisdiction (England and Wales) Order 1994 SI 1994/1623 ('the 1994 Order'), as well as being actionable in the civil courts. Generally speaking, an employee will be better served bringing the claim in a tribunal as costs can only be awarded in limited circumstances, such as where the claim is misconceived or vexatious. However, there are some situations – for example, where the amount claimed exceeds £25,000 – in which a civil court claim may be preferable.

Time limits 10.27

There is a vast difference between the time limit for claims in employment tribunals and that for claims in the civil courts. An employee claiming a contractual redundancy payment in an employment tribunal must normally present his or her claim within three months of the effective date of termination (EDT) or, if there is no EDT, within three months beginning with the last day upon which the employee worked in the employment which has terminated – Article 7 of the 1994 Order. By contrast, an employee has six years from the date of breach of contract to lodge a claim in the county court or High Court in England and Wales – S.5 Limitation Act 1980; or five years to lodge a claim with the Sheriff Court or Court of Session (Outer House) in Scotland – S.6 Prescription and Limitation (Scotland) Act 1973.

395

10.28 **Effective date of termination.** The EDT for the purpose of a contractual redundancy pay claim is the same as for statutory redundancy pay claims, namely:

- where the employee's contract of employment is terminated by notice (whether given by the employer or the employee), it is the date on which the notice expires

- where the contract is terminated without notice, it is the date on which termination takes effect

- in relation to an employee who is employed under a limited-term contract which terminates by virtue of the limiting event without being renewed under the same contract, it is the date on which the termination takes effect. (Note, however, that the inclusion of contractual redundancy schemes in limited-term contracts is extremely rare.)

In most redundancy situations, the employee's contract will be terminated with notice, meaning that the time limit starts to run from the end of the notice period. This is the case so long as the employer gives notice – it does not matter if the employee is not expected to work for all of the notice period.

10.29 **Date of breach of contract.** If the contractual redundancy scheme specifies a date or event upon which any payments under the scheme will be made, then it is only once that date has passed that the employer could be said to be in breach of contract by not making the payment. Where the contract is silent as to when such a payment will be made, it falls to the court to determine when the obligation to pay arose. While there is significant scope for academic debate on when a breach occurs, in practical terms the entitlement to a redundancy payment arises upon the dismissal of the employee. Therefore, a court would be likely to find that the breach occurred either on or immediately after the employee's dismissal.

10.30 **Public sector cases.** In addition to the general contractual jurisdiction afforded by the 1994 Order, tribunals may have to consider claims made under contractual, as opposed to statutory, redundancy schemes in the public sector in two circumstances:

- where the claimants are Crown servants who are excluded from the statutory scheme but have the right to refer questions of entitlement under an analogous scheme to a tribunal – S.177 ERA

- where the claimants have rights under an alternative scheme because they have been contracted out of the statutory scheme through an exemption order – S.157 ERA.

The statutory time limits for redundancy payments do not necessarily apply in these circumstances. In Greenwich Health Authority v Skinner 1989 ICR 220, EAT, S was excluded from the statutory scheme as being a Crown servant and she received a contractual redundancy payment in December 1986. She presented a claim disputing the amount to a tribunal in January 1988. The employer objected that this was out of time. The terms of the contractual scheme imposed an obligation to claim from the employer within six months of the cessation of employment, but then simply said that if an employee was dissatisfied, the matter could be referred to a tribunal. The EAT held that the statutory time limit only applied to claims under the statutory redundancy scheme. The terms of S's contractual scheme, which was what governed her rights, did not impose any express time limit for a reference to a tribunal. It followed that the time limit for a claim was the general limitation period of six years for a contractual claim imposed by the Limitation Act 1980. It is probable that the same reasoning would apply in a case covered by an order under S.157. (Note that the corresponding limitation period in Scotland is five years, not six.)

Acas Code of Practice   10.31
Following the repeal of the statutory grievance procedures in April 2009, employers and employees are now expected to observe the grievance procedures contained in the Acas 'Code of Practice on Discipline and Grievance', which applies to breach of contract claims brought in employment tribunals. An unreasonable failure to comply with the provisions of the Code may result in an adjustment to the amount of compensation awarded of up to 25 per cent – S.207A Trade Union and Labour Relations (Consolidation) Act 1992.

Compensation limit   10.32
While employment tribunals have jurisdiction to hear breach of contract claims following termination of employment, there is a statutory limit of £25,000 on the amount of damages that they can order a party to pay – Article 10 of the 1994 Order. If an employee has a contractual right to a redundancy payment in excess of this figure, he or she is not prevented from pursuing a claim in the tribunal, but will not be able to recover any more than £25,000.

One option might be for the employee to attempt to recover any further amount owing in the ordinary civil courts. However, this course of action failed in Fraser v HLMAD Ltd 2006 ICR 1395, CA, where F succeeded in his wrongful dismissal claim in an employment tribunal and was awarded £25,000 in damages, although the tribunal had assessed his loss at £80,000. He applied to bring an action in the High Court to recover the amount by which his damages for wrongful dismissal exceeded the tribunal's statutory maximum but the High Court held that he was barred from doing so by 'cause of action estoppel' and struck out the claim. The Court of Appeal upheld the High Court's decision.

397

10.33 Thus, employees claiming contractual redundancy payments of over £25,000 should bring the whole claim in the county court or High Court (or the Sheriff Court or Court of Session in Scotland). An employee cannot claim the first £25,000 in the tribunal and then rely on the tribunal's finding of breach of contract to secure any monies outstanding in the civil courts, since the cause of action (in this case, breach of contract) will have been extinguished upon the tribunal's reaching its decision.

10.34 ## Enforcement of non-pay terms

While most breach of contract claims in a redundancy context involve disputes over entitlement to a contractual redundancy payment, a contractual redundancy scheme may provide for other benefits that cannot adequately be enforced or compensated by way of a damages claim. Most notably, contractual redundancy procedures often specify the criteria according to which employees will be selected for redundancy. In such cases, while a failure to observe the contractual procedure may give rise to an unfair redundancy dismissal, the employee may be more interested in preventing the dismissal in the first place by seeking an injunction (or 'interdict' in Scotland) to prevent the employer continuing with the redundancy process in breach of the contractual requirements. Injunctions are 'equitable remedies' and will only be granted at the discretion of the court where damages would not be an adequate remedy.

It is well established that injunctions are available to enforce compliance with a procedure laid down in an employment contract, although they are more commonly sought in conduct and capability cases than in redundancy cases. In the most recent high authority on the issue, Chhabra v West London Mental Health NHS Trust 2014 ICR 194, SC, the Supreme Court recognised that, as a general rule, it is inappropriate for the courts to step in and remedy minor irregularities in the course of disciplinary proceedings, but approved the use of injunctions in cases of more serious irregularity. The case concerned disciplinary proceedings against a doctor under the contractual procedure that applies in the NHS. In deciding that an injunction was appropriate, the Court considered that there had been a substantial and material departure from the contractual procedure and took into account the likely inadequacy of common law damages for dismissal.

10.35 The Supreme Court's approach in Chhabra sets a high threshold for intervening in a disciplinary matter and, in so far as the principles are transferable to contractual redundancy procedures, it is unlikely that many disputes over redundancy selection will be considered serious enough to warrant judicial intervention. There are, however, a few examples of employees seeking injunctions in relation to contractual redundancy procedures. In both Alexander and ors v Standard Telephones and Cables plc 1990 ICR 291,

ChD, and Anderson v Pringle of Scotland Ltd 1998 IRLR 64, Ct Sess (Outer House), employees were selected for redundancy in contravention of an agreed redundancy procedure and sought injunctions to restrain their dismissals until the case could come to trial. The crucial question for the courts was whether the employers had sufficient confidence in the abilities of the employees to do their jobs to delay dismissal until the issue could be fully tried. In Alexander, the High Court refused to grant an injunction – it considered that the employer did not have complete confidence in the employees selected, and it was also relevant that the relationship of employer and employee had broken down. In Anderson, in contrast, the Court of Session granted the injunction sought. The Court stated that it did not follow that, because the employer preferred to retain other employees, it no longer had trust and confidence in A (although the position would have been different if there had been any question of mistrust). The Court concluded that the balance of convenience favoured the preservation of the status quo.

While both Courts accepted that an injunction could only be granted in circumstances where trust and confidence has not broken down, they took different views as to what inferences should be drawn from the fact that an employee has been selected for redundancy in the first place. It is easy to see the force in both arguments. Once employees have been assessed according to particular criteria, there is some substance to the view that the employer would have less confidence in those employees who scored lower than in those who scored higher. On the other hand, there is clearly strength in the Court of Session's argument that selection for redundancy does not mean that the employment relationship has necessarily broken down. The work performance of an employee who has been selected for redundancy is unlikely to be so unacceptable that it would destroy the confidence the employer had in the employee, otherwise the employer would have considered dismissal on other grounds.

10.36 One factor that limits the practicality of an injunction is that it must be sought in the civil courts. The 1994 Order has no application in a case where employment has not yet terminated and, in any event, Article 3 only confers power on employment tribunals to award damages – an employment tribunal therefore has no power to grant the equitable remedy of injunction.

For a discussion of injunctions and equitable remedies more generally, see IDS Employment Law Handbook, 'Contracts of Employment' (2014), Chapter 10, 'Breach of contract', under 'Equitable remedies – injunctions'.

11 Time off during notice period

Who is protected?

Request for time off

Reasonable time off

Working hours

Right to be paid

Complaining to a tribunal

11.1

Section 52 of the Employment Rights Act 1996 (ERA) gives employees under notice of dismissal for redundancy a right to reasonable time off with pay during working hours, either to look for work or to make arrangements for training for future employment. A tribunal can make a modest financial award against an employer who unreasonably refuses to allow such employees time off or who allows time off but refuses to pay for it.

Who is protected?

11.2

The right to time off to look for work only applies to employees, so the self-employed are excluded.

Employees

11.3

Crown employees are specifically given the right to time off – S.191 ERA, as are Parliamentary staff – Ss.194 and 195. Certain categories of employee are not covered, however. They are:

* members of the armed forces – S.192

* merchant seamen and women and share fishermen and women – S.199(2) and (4) (although seafarers employed on ships registered under S.8 of the Merchant Shipping Act 1995 are covered provided that the ship is registered as belonging to a port in Great Britain, that under his or her contract the employee does not work wholly outside Great Britain, and that he or she is ordinarily resident in Great Britain – S.199(7) and (8))

* those in the police service, or having the powers and privileges of a constable – S.200.

Employees who 'under [their] contract of employment' ordinarily work outside Great Britain used to be excluded from the right to time off (and from other rights contained in the ERA, including the right to claim unfair dismissal) by

401

virtue of S.196. However, S.196 was repealed by the Employment Relations Act 1999, leaving the ERA silent with regard to its territorial scope. The House of Lords in Lawson v Serco Ltd and two other cases 2006 ICR 250, HL, cleared up some of the uncertainty by holding that the statutory right to claim unfair dismissal ordinarily covered 'employment in Great Britain'. It is strongly arguable that this test should also apply to the right to time off under S.52, along with all the other rights that used to be excluded by virtue of S.196. See Chapter 5, 'Qualifications and exclusions', under 'Employees and excluded employees – overseas employment', and IDS Employment Law Handbook, 'Employment Tribunal Practice and Procedure' (2014), Chapter 2, 'Tribunals' jurisdiction', under 'Territorial limitations – territorial reach', for further details.

11.4 Qualifying period

In order to qualify for the right to time off, employees must have been continuously employed for at least two years on whichever is the later of the following dates: the date when notice expired or the date notice would have expired if the statutory notice due under S.86(1) ERA had been given – S.52(2). Provided that an employee has at least two years of continuous employment, he or she will qualify for the right regardless of how many hours he or she works.

11.5 Notice of dismissal

As noted above, the right to time off applies to employees who are under notice of dismissal for redundancy. This means the employee must have received an indication of the actual date when the employment will terminate: a mere warning that redundancies are likely to occur will be insufficient. Also, the reason for the dismissal must actually be redundancy. If the employee loses his or her job for some other reason not involving a redundancy situation – for example, due to a reorganisation of the business – he or she has no statutory right to time off. However, the fact that the employee is not entitled to a redundancy payment (for example, because the employee has unreasonably refused an offer of suitable alternative employment) does not affect the right to time off – Dutton v Hawker Siddeley Aviation Ltd 1978 ICR 1057, EAT.

11.6 Request for time off

There is no formal procedure for claiming time off under the ERA. However, it seems that an employee must actually request the time off before he or she can be entitled to it (although there is no specific requirement to this effect in the Act itself). This point arose in Ryford Ltd v Drinkwater 1996 IRLR 16, EAT, albeit in the context of the right to take time off for trade union duties under S.168 of the Trade Union and Labour Relations (Consolidation)

Act 1992. There, D, who was due to work a night shift from 6 pm to 6 am, stopped work at midnight because he had to attend a meeting about pay at 10 am the following day. R Ltd deducted £30.66 from his pay for the six hours he did not work. The employer accepted that D's absence from work was for union duties. It did not, however, consider that it was in breach of its duty to allow him time off. Although D claimed to have put in his request two hours before he started the night shift, R Ltd said that it did not know that he had made such a request. D was supposed to get permission from C, the works director, but, according to C, D had not asked him for permission. The EAT held that an employer can only 'fail to permit' time off if it is aware that a request for time off has been made. Therefore the employee had to establish, on the balance of probabilities, that a request for time off was made, that it came to the notice of the employer's appropriate representatives, and that the employer either refused or ignored it.

Reasonable time off   11.7

The employee is entitled to 'reasonable' time off which the employer must not 'unreasonably refuse'. The ERA itself does not define what is meant by 'reasonable' (or 'unreasonable') but, essentially, a balance must be struck between the needs of the employee to seek work or arrange training against the needs of the employer to get the work done. The following factors are likely to be relevant:

- the length of the employee's notice period

- the purpose for which the time off is being requested

- when the employee put in the request for time off

- local difficulties in finding employment

- the provisions of any redundancy procedure agreement that deals with the question of time off

- the effect of the employee's absence on health and safety

- the effect of the employee's absence on the running of the business – for example, there may be production targets which might be affected by the employee's absence or, where large-scale redundancies are involved, the employer may wish to retain some control over how many employees have time off at any one time.

There do not appear to have been any instances where it has been held that the employer was reasonable in refusing any time off at all, even where the employer's business is in serious financial difficulties. Such difficulties, may, however, reasonably give rise to the imposition of restrictions as to when and how much time is taken off.

11.8   The time off must be for one of the following reasons:

- to look for new employment, or

- to make arrangements for training for future employment.

However, nothing in the ERA says that an employee must produce evidence of appointments, etc before being granted time off to look for work. Such evidence will be no more than a relevant consideration in deciding whether a refusal to grant a particular request for time off was reasonable – Dutton v Hawker Siddeley Aviation Ltd 1978 ICR 1057, EAT. A tribunal followed this approach in Hasler v Tourell Precision Engineers Ltd ET Case No.11431/83, holding that the employer acted unreasonably in making it a condition of taking time off that the employee had a firm lead to follow up. Such a rule, it said, would even prevent the employee from visiting a job centre in working hours during his or her notice period. Conversely, in Seldon v The Kendall Co (UK) Ltd ET Case No.14442/85 the tribunal rejected a claim under S.52 where the evidence showed that the employee had ignored job vacancies in his own area, preferring instead to travel further afield to make speculative enquiries. He had also refused extra work offered by his present employer. The fact that he had no definite lead to follow on his travels had fuelled his employer's suspicions that his search for work was not genuine and its refusal to allow time off was, therefore, reasonable.

11.9   ## Working hours

The right is to take reasonable time off during 'working hours', which are defined in S.52(3) ERA as being 'any time when, in accordance with [the employee's] contract of employment, the employee is required to be at work'. This means that an employer will not be able to require an employee simply to rearrange his or her hours or make up for lost time elsewhere – see, for example, Ratcliffe v Dorset County Council 1978 IRLR 191, ET.

In Hairsine v Kingston upon Hull City Council 1992 ICR 212, EAT, the Appeal Tribunal considered the meaning of 'working hours' in the context of the right to take time off work to perform union duties under what is now S.168 TULR(C)A. There, H worked a basic 39-hour week on a shift pattern. He applied for permission from the Council to attend a union-organised course for shop stewards. In a letter formally granting permission to attend the course, the Council stated that 'day release with pay will be granted where H would normally be at work'. The letter emphasised that, when not on the course, H was to report for work in the usual way. H's course fell on a day when he was rostered on a late shift, from 3 pm to 11 pm. The course ran from 9 am to 4 pm. Having attended the course, H travelled to work, arriving at 4.40 pm. He worked until 7 pm and then went home. The Council paid H from 3 pm until 7 pm (i.e. for four hours' work) but did not pay him for the hours from 7 pm to 11 pm, which he did not work. H argued that the course he attended was the equivalent of an eight-hour shift and he was therefore entitled to be paid for those eight hours whether or not he attended work in the evening.

The EAT held that H's contention could not be supported. It referred to what is now S.173 TULR(C)A, which states that 'working hours' should be taken to be 'any time when, in accordance with his contract of employment, [the employee] is required to be at work' (identical wording to that used in S.52(3) ERA). The EAT stated that if 'working hours' were intended to mean the mathematical number of hours which the employee was contracted to work during any given day, then the phrasing of this provision would have been quite different. In the instant case, the hours before 3 pm during which H attended the course did not constitute 'working hours' since his shift was not scheduled to start on the day of the course until that time. And the hours from 4 pm to 11 pm that he was required to work did not count because the course had ended by that time and time off during those hours was not therefore required to enable him to carry out trade union activities. **11.10**

Similarly, in Calder v Secretary of State for Work and Pensions EAT 0512/08, a case concerning time off for safety representatives under the Safety Representatives and Safety Committees Regulations 1977 SI 1977/500, C, a union-appointed safety officer, complained that her employer had failed to allow her time off to attend a health and safety course, contrary to Reg 4(2) of the Regulations. C worked Tuesdays to Thursdays and the course was held on Fridays. The EAT held that the case clearly could not get off the ground because there was no contention that the employer had refused to permit C to attend. Permission was not required since the course took place on Fridays. Since the course did not take place during C's working hours, Reg 4(2) did not come into play.

Cases on the definition of working time under the Working Time Regulations 1998 SI 1998/1833 may also be relevant. So, for example, employees who are required to be at the employer's premises while on call are likely to be entitled to time off to look for work during that period because it constitutes working time. However, employees who are not required to be on the employer's premises while on call will probably not be entitled to time off during that period because it does not constitute working time – see Landeshauptstadt Kiel v Jaeger 2004 ICR 1528, ECJ; Sindicato de Médicos de Asistencia Pública (SIMAP) v Consellería de Sanidad y Consumo de la Generalidad Valenciana 2001 ICR 1116, ECJ. A degree of caution needs to be exercised here, however, since statutory 'working time' is not necessarily the same as contractual 'working hours'. For more information as to the definition of 'working time' see IDS Employment Law Handbook, 'Working Time' (2013), Chapter 1, 'Scope and key concepts', under 'Working time'. **11.11**

11.12 ## Right to be paid

An employee who takes time off under S.52 ERA is entitled to be paid at the 'appropriate hourly rate' for that time off (subject to a maximum overall entitlement). The appropriate hourly rate is the amount of a week's pay divided by:

- the number of normal working hours in a week as specified in the contract of employment – S.53(2), or

- where the number of normal working hours varies from week to week, the average number of normal working hours, calculated by dividing by 12 the total number of the employee's normal working hours during the 12-week period ending with the last complete week before the day on which notice was given – S.53(3). The calculation date for this purpose is the date on which the employer's notice was given – S.225(2).

For more information about 'a week's pay' and 'normal working hours', see IDS Employment Law Handbook, 'Wages' (2016), Chapter 9, 'A week's pay'.

11.13 The maximum entitlement during the whole of the employee's notice period is two fifths of one week's pay (i.e. 40 per cent) – S.53(5), and an employee will have no further entitlement to paid time off once that maximum has been reached. There is, however, no ceiling on the amount of a week's pay as there is when, for example, calculating redundancy pay (where the current limit on a week's pay is £479 as of April 2016) – S.227. It follows that if an employee earns £1,200 per week, his or her maximum entitlement for time taken off during the notice period is £480.

Note that S.52 does not place any limit on the amount of time off that may be taken, provided that the time off is reasonable. It is only the payment for that time that is subject to the two-fifths maximum. In theory, then, an employee may be entitled to more than two fifths of a week off to look for work (provided the request is reasonable). In practice, however, an employee who has already taken two fifths of a week off would not have an effective remedy if refused further time off as it is not possible to claim compensation once the maximum entitlement due under the ERA has been paid (although the employee could still seek a declaration).

11.14 ## Complaining to a tribunal

If an employer unreasonably refuses to allow time off or fails to pay what is due, the employee may complain to a tribunal – S.54(1) ERA. The complaint must generally be presented within three months of the day on which it is alleged that time off should have been allowed, although a tribunal may extend this time limit by a further reasonable period if it is satisfied that it was not reasonably practicable for the complaint to be presented in time – S.54(2). (The time limit may also be extended to facilitate cross-border mediation or early conciliation – Ss.54(2A), 207A and 207B.)

If the employee's complaint is successful, the tribunal must make a declaration to that effect and order the employer to pay the amount which it finds to be due to the employee – S.54(3). If the employer has allowed time off but refused to pay for it, the amount due is the appropriate hourly rate for the time off (subject to the maximum discussed under 'Right to be paid' above). If the employer has unreasonably refused time off, the amount due is that which the employee would have received if the request had been granted. This means that an employee who was refused time off and who stayed at work can be paid twice for the same period of time, once for working and once under the tribunal's award. As the tribunal said in Hasler v Tourell Precision Engineers ET Case No.11431/83, this is in the nature of a bonus for the employee and a penalty for the employer. If the employer does pay some of the amount due, it goes towards discharging the employer's liability and the tribunal can only award the amount by which it falls short of the appropriate sum – S.53(7). However, the amount awarded should not be affected by the fact that the employee receives a contractual redundancy payment which is more generous than the statutory redundancy entitlement.

11.15 Finally, S.203 invalidates any provision that purports to exclude or limit the right to time off (unless incorporated into a valid settlement agreement or an agreement reached under the auspices of an Acas conciliation officer) – see further IDS Employment Law Handbook, 'Employment Tribunal Practice and Procedure' (2014), Chapter 3, 'Conciliation, settlements and ADR'.

12 Collective redundancies

Scope of duty to consult

Timetable for consultation

The consultation process

'Appropriate representatives'

Special circumstances defence

Complaints about breach of S.188

Protective awards

Notification

The statutory duty on employers to inform and consult their workforce about **12.1** proposed redundancies, which is contained in S.188 of the Trade Union and Labour Relations (Consolidation) Act 1992 (TULR(C)A), was introduced in order to implement the mandatory provisions of the EU Collective Redundancies Directive (No.75/129), which was subsequently replaced by the EU Collective Redundancies Directive (No.98/59). S.188 was significantly amended by the Trade Union Reform and Employment Rights Act 1993 and the Collective Redundancies and Transfer of Undertakings (Protection of Employment) (Amendment) Regulations 1995 SI 1995/2587 ('the 1995 Regulations') in order to bring it further into line with the provisions of the Directive. The 1995 Regulations were introduced in response to the ECJ's ruling in Commission of the European Communities v United Kingdom 1994 ICR 664, ECJ, that the UK provisions failed properly to implement the 1975 Directive on a number of points. The most significant finding of the ECJ was that the UK provisions were in breach of the Directive in that they did not require an employer to consult where there was no recognised trade union.

Although the 1995 Regulations purported to fill the gaps in the UK consultation requirements, they were highly controversial, not least because they permitted employers to bypass consultation with a recognised union and consult instead with 'employee representatives'. Moreover, there were many who argued that S.188 remained in conflict with the 1975 Directive in that the provisions for the consultation of 'employee representatives' were insufficiently detailed and permitted an employer to evade its obligations to consult. Although a legal challenge on these grounds failed in R v Secretary of State for Trade and Industry ex parte UNISON and ors 1996 ICR 1003, Div Ct, the Government nonetheless decided to make further amendments to the consultation provisions. Among other things, these amendments – which were introduced by the Collective

409

Redundancies and Transfer of Undertakings (Protection of Employment) (Amendment) Regulations 1999 SI 1999/1925 ('the 1999 Regulations') – compelled an employer to consult with a recognised trade union where there is one. The amendments also tightened up the provisions on the election of employee representatives.

12.2   Statutory references in this chapter are to sections of the TULR(C)A, as amended, unless otherwise stated, while references to 'the Collective Redundancies Directive' are to the 1998 Directive, which is in effect a consolidation of the 1975 Directive as amended by Directive 92/56. References to 'BIS' are references to the Department for Business, Innovation and Skills, which was created by the merger of the Department for Innovation, Universities and Skills and the Department for Business, Enterprise and Regulatory Reform in June 2009, and thereby became the competent Government department in respect of collective redundancy matters.

12.3   Scope of duty to consult

Section 188(1) TULR(C)A states that 'where an employer is proposing to dismiss as redundant 20 or more employees at one establishment within a period of 90 days or less, the employer shall consult about the dismissals all the persons who are appropriate representatives of any of the employees who may be affected by the proposed dismissals or may be affected by measures taken in connection with those dismissals'.

Before a change of wording introduced by the 1999 Regulations, the duty was to consult only the representatives of the employees whom the employer proposed to dismiss. Now the duty is to consult with any employees who *may be affected* by the proposed dismissals or by measures taken in connection with those dismissals, whether or not the employer proposes to dismiss them. The amendment recognised the fact that there are employees whose jobs are not directly threatened but who may nevertheless be either directly or indirectly affected by proposed redundancies.

12.4   Exclusion of small-scale redundancies
An employer's duty to consult only arises where it is proposing to dismiss 20 or more employees at one establishment within a period of 90 days. The meaning of 'establishment', and questions concerning the number of proposed redundancies, are discussed under 'Timetable for consultation' below.

12.5   Employees only
The obligation to consult on collective redundancies only arises in respect of 'employees' as defined by S.295(1) TULR(C)A. This includes apprentices but excludes Crown employees, those serving in the armed forces, House

410

of Lords and House of Commons staff, those in police service, and share fishermen and women – Ss.273, 274, 277, 278, 280, and 284.

'Police service' means service as a member of a constabulary maintained by virtue of an enactment, or service in any other capacity by virtue of which a person has 'the powers or privileges of a constable' – S.280(2). By virtue of S.200 ERA, an identical exclusion applies for the purposes of claims under the ERA, such as unfair dismissal. S.200 ERA (and thus by extension S.280 TULR(C)A) has been held to be wide enough to cover constables with limited powers, such as parks constables – see Redbridge London Borough Council v Dhinsa and anor 2014 ICR 834, CA.

12.6 In London Borough of Wandsworth v Vining and ors 2016 ICR 427, EAT, the trade union UNISON argued that its inability to claim a protective award on behalf of parks constables for failure to consult infringed its freedom of association and assembly rights under Article 11 of the European Convention on Human Rights. The EAT accepted that Article 11 was engaged, but observed that Article 11(2) allows 'the imposition of lawful restrictions on the exercise of these rights by members of the armed forces, of the police or the administration of the State'. The Appeal Tribunal stated that it was in no position to express a view on the proportionality of the apparent exclusion by S.280 of parks constables, as Article 11(2) requires. It noted that evidence and submissions on proportionality would be a matter for the Secretary of State, who had not been joined to these proceedings. However, the EAT went on to set out its view that, even if Article 11 was breached, it would not be possible to read S.280 TULR(C)A so as to allow the claims to proceed. (Note that UNISON has reserved the right to seek a declaration of incompatibility pursuant to S.4 of the Human Rights Act 1996 and the claimants have reserved the right to contend to a higher court that Redbridge London Borough Council v Dhinsa and anor (above) was wrongly decided.) The jurisdictional aspect of this case relating to unfair dismissal is discussed in IDS Employment Law Handbook, 'Unfair Dismissal' (2015), Chapter 2, 'Exclusions from right to claim', under 'Specific categories of worker – police'.

12.7 **Fixed-term employees.** Those employed under a fixed-term contract – i.e. a contract that terminates on expiry of a specific term, on completion of a particular task, or on the occurrence or non-occurrence of a specific event – are excluded from an employer's duty to consult on collective redundancies unless the employer is proposing to dismiss the employee as redundant before the expiry of the term, the completion of the task or the occurrence or non-occurrence of the event – S.282 (which came into effect on 6 April 2013).

12.8 **Overseas employees.** It should be noted that the provision in S.285 excluding employees working overseas from the right to be consulted was repealed by the Employment Relations Act 1999. Therefore, any affected employees

411

who work overseas must be included in the consultation process. However, employers are not under a duty to notify the Secretary of State of proposed redundancies in respect of employees who ordinarily work outside Great Britain – see 'Notification' below.

12.9 **Collective Redundancies Directive covers 'workers'.** While the collective consultation obligations under the TULR(C)A apply only in respect of employees, the equivalent obligations under the EU Collective Redundancies Directive (No.98/59) apply in respect of the broader category of 'workers'.

In Balkaya v Kiesel Abbruch- und Recycling Technik GmbH 2015 ICR 1110, ECJ, the ECJ held that the concept of a 'worker' cannot be defined by reference to the legislation of the Member States but must be given an autonomous and independent meaning under EU law. It adopted a broad definition, stating that the central feature of the relationship is that, for a certain period of time, a person performs services for and under the direction of another person, in return for which he or she receives remuneration. Thus, both a company director who was not also a shareholder in the company and a trainee whose training placement was paid for by a national public authority were workers and had to be counted towards the threshold when determining whether the obligation to consult on collective redundancies was triggered.

12.10 Executive board members of companies in Great Britain are often also employees so are generally covered by S.188 TULR(C)A in any event. However, 'a person who performs services for and under the direction of another person, in return for which he or she receives remuneration' might be thought to refer not only to employees, but also to the wider category of 'workers' who enjoy a number of rights under UK employment law, including rights under the Working Time Regulations 1998 SI 1998/133. The term 'worker' for these purposes encompasses not just employees but all those working under any other contract 'whereby the individual undertakes to do or perform personally any work or services for another party to the contract whose status is not by virtue of the contract that of a client or customer of any profession or business undertaking carried on by the individual'.

If a claimant were to successfully argue that the S.188(1) threshold for the duty to consult is triggered by the dismissals of workers, not just employees, the inevitable consequence would be that more employers would be obliged to collectively consult on redundancies. It might even mean that the decision not to offer further shifts to a worker on a zero-hours contract would count as a dismissal for the purposes of the collective consultation thresholds. Such a state of affairs could increase the appeal of fixed-term contracts, the non-renewal of which are specifically excluded from the consultation requirements by S.282(2) – see 'Fixed-term employees' above.

412

Meaning of 'employer'   12.11

Under S.188(1), the obligation to consult falls on 'the employer'; that is, the 'person by whom the employee… is employed' – S.295(1). Thus, it is the employer who actually employs the employees affected by any proposed redundancies who is responsible. This is the case even if the decision on redundancies is taken by another company controlling the employer; for example, where the employer is part of a group of companies. In Akavan Erityisalojen Keskusliitto (AEK) ry and ors v Fujitsu Siemens Computers Oy 2010 ICR 444, ECJ, the ECJ clarified that the obligation to consult will always lie with the subsidiary company which employs the workers and never with the parent company irrespective of whether the decision in connection with collective redundancies was made by the parent or the subsidiary – see further '"Proposing to dismiss" – who proposes to dismiss?' below.

The case of Mayor v Herencia Yacente de Rafael de las Heras Dávila 2010 2 CMLR 22, ECJ, draws attention to the fact that the Collective Redundancies Directive presupposes that there is an employer to carry out the consultation. In that case the employer, a natural person whose company did not have a separate legal identity, had died. The European Court held that Article 1(1) of the Directive did not preclude national legislation from providing that the termination of contracts of workers whose employer was a natural person as a result of the death of that employer did not amount to a collective redundancy situation. Nor did the Directive preclude national legislation that allowed for different compensation depending on whether the workers lost their jobs as a result of the death of the employer or as a result of a collective redundancy.

Transfer of undertaking. As noted above, the general rule is that it is the   12.12 employer that must carry out the consultation. However, there is an exception where the redundancy dismissals are consequent on a transfer of a business to which the Transfer of Undertakings (Protection of Employment) Regulations 2006 SI 2006/246 (TUPE) apply. Under the TUPE Regulations, where a business or part of a business changes hands, the new owner (the transferee) becomes liable for the contracts of employment of those employed by the seller (the transferor) and assigned to the business or part of the business transferred. Since it is not uncommon for a transferee employer to need to make redundancy dismissals when it acquires the new workforce, it makes practical sense to allow the transferee to consult the affected employees about the redundancies *before* the transfer, even though the employees at that stage are still employed by the transferor. This is made possible by Ss.198A and 198B TULR(C)A, which were inserted by the Collective Redundancies and Transfer of Undertakings (Protection of Employment) (Amendment) Regulations 2014 SI 2014/16 with effect from 31 January 2014.

Under S.198A, where:

- there is or is likely to be a transfer to which the TUPE Regulations apply

- the transferee is proposing to dismiss 20 or more employees at one establishment within 90 days, and

- employees who are or who are likely to be transferred include one or more employees who may be affected by the proposed dismissals or by related measures

the transferee may elect to consult representatives of affected transferring employees before the transfer takes place – S.198A(1) and (2). However, the transferee may only make such an election if it gives written notice to the transferor and the transferor agrees – S.198A(3). If the pre-transfer consultation goes ahead then Ss.188–198 TULR(C)A apply as if the transferee were already the transferring employees' employer and modifications are made to the collective redundancy provisions to allow for this – Ss.198A(4)(a) and 198B. The transferor may provide information or other assistance to the transferee to help the transferee meet the consultation requirements – S.198A(4)(b).

12.13 The transferee can cancel the pre-transfer consultation at any time by written notice to the transferor – S.198A(5). In these circumstances, Ss.188–198 no longer apply and anything done under those sections has no effect – S.198A(6)(a) and (b). Anyone originally notified of the election or proposed dismissals must be notified of the cancellation as soon as reasonably practicable – S.198A(6)(c). The transferee cannot make another election in relation to the proposed dismissals – S.198A(6)(d).

12.14 Definition of 'dismissal'

For the consultation obligations to apply, it must be shown that the employer is actually proposing to 'dismiss' at least 20 employees. 'Dismiss' and 'dismissal' are to be construed in accordance with S.95 of the Employment Rights Act 1996 (ERA) – S.298 TULR(C)A. Accordingly, an employee will be treated as dismissed if:

- his or her contract of employment is terminated by the employer with or without notice, or

- he or she has been constructively dismissed (a constructive dismissal occurs when an employee resigns, with or without notice, because of a repudiatory breach of contract by the employer.

Note that S.95 ERA also states that there has been a dismissal where the employee is employed under a limited-term contract and the contract expires by virtue of the limiting event without being renewed under the same.

414

However, S.282(2) TULR(C)A makes it clear that the expiry of a limited-term contract does not count towards the number of 'dismissals' for the purposes of the collective redundancy procedures unless the contract has been terminated early by reason of redundancy. This provision is discussed under 'Employees only – fixed-term employees' above and 'Definition of "redundancy"' below).

Business transfer. In circumstances where it is proposed that an undertaking, or part of an undertaking, is to be transferred to another employer, then – provided the TUPE Regulations apply – there will be no dismissals, although the separate duty to consult contained in those Regulations will arise. However, if TUPE does not apply, then employees' contracts are likely to be terminated on the transfer and so a proposal for a transfer will potentially give rise to the obligation to consult on redundancy.   **12.15**

Alternative employment. It has been established that redeployment may amount to a 'dismissal' for the purposes of the collective consultation provisions – Hardy v Tourism South East 2005 IRLR 242, EAT. There, the employer decided to close one of its offices as part of a restructuring, but initially estimated that, of the 26 employees at that office, only 12 would be made redundant with the rest being redeployed. An employment tribunal held that the employer's hope that some of the employees would be redeployed meant that it had not been proposing to dismiss 20 or more employees in total, and hence that the collective consultation provisions had not been triggered. The EAT, however, overturned the tribunal's decision on appeal. In its view, an employer proposes to 'dismiss' an employee if, on an objective consideration of what it says or writes, it is proposing to withdraw the existing contract from the employee, or to depart so substantially from it that it amounts to a withdrawal of the whole contract. The EAT thought it sufficiently clear from the tribunal's findings of fact that this test was met in this case, and so substituted a decision to that effect. The EAT in Hardy did not have before it extensive details of the redundant employees' existing contracts. However, it did note that there was no suggestion on the employer's part that the employees were subject to a mobility clause. It was therefore clear that any redeployment could not be within the terms of the existing contracts, and so would be tantamount to a dismissal.   **12.16**

By contrast, in Home Office v Evans and anor 2008 ICR 302, CA, the Court of Appeal held that an employer was entitled to rely upon a mobility clause in employees' contracts in order to relocate them within the terms of their existing contracts, thus avoiding making them redundant upon the closure of their place of work. E and L were employed by the Home Office as immigration officers based at Waterloo International Terminal (WIT). In 2004 the Home Office decided that immigration control was no longer required there and initially considered applying its redundancy procedures (which largely reflected the obligations under the TULR(C)A). Having taken legal advice, however, it

415

decided to enforce the mobility provisions contained in employees' contracts of employment. E and L were informed that they would be transferred to Heathrow. They resigned and claimed unfair constructive dismissal.

12.17 In the tribunal's view, the closure of immigration control at WIT automatically triggered a 'redundancy notice' under E's and L's contracts, together with the relevant consultation obligations. It conceded that the Home Office had a choice between invoking the mobility provisions and making redundancies. However, that choice had to be made at the time the obligation to consult arose and, once made, the employer could not then change its mind. The Court of Appeal disagreed, holding that the employer had not 'dodged' between implementing contractual redundancy procedures and invoking the mobility clause. From the time of its announcement that the employees' workplace was to close, the employer made it clear that it would relocate the affected employees in accordance with their contracts. Accordingly, there had been no proposal to dismiss the claimants as redundant and the Home Office had not acted in breach of contract in respect of consultation. E and L had not been constructively dismissed and their claims were rejected.

12.18 **Voluntary redundancies.** Voluntary redundancies can amount to 'dismissals' for collective consultation purposes. In Optare Group Ltd v TGWU 2007 IRLR 931, EAT, for example, the Appeal Tribunal upheld a tribunal's finding that employees who applied and were accepted for voluntary redundancy were 'dismissed' and so should have been included in the total number of employees whom the employer proposed to dismiss as redundant. Their inclusion raised the total number of redundancy dismissals to 20, meaning that the employer's failure to consult collectively was a breach of S.188. It must be stressed, however, that this decision turned very much on its own facts – it is for tribunals to decide whether there has been a consensual termination of employment, in which case there would have been no proposal to 'dismiss', or whether, as here, the employees have volunteered *to be dismissed* as redundant, in which case they must be included in the calculation under S.188.

The Optare case can be contrasted with Khan v HGS Global Ltd and anor EAT 0176/15, which, although not a case concerning the collective redundancy provisions, considered the question of whether an employee's acceptance of voluntary redundancy constituted a dismissal. K managed a team of employees working in Chiswick that carried out a project for one of HGSG Ltd's clients, D Ltd. When D Ltd decided to in-source the work carried out by K's team the provisions of the TUPE Regulations came into play. During the consultation process relating to the transfer, employee representatives raised concerns about the extra distance employees transferring to D Ltd would have to travel. Responding to those concerns, HGSG Ltd announced that those who would face a journey time in excess of 1.25 hours would have the option of

416

(1) relocating to D Ltd's employment at High Wycombe, (2) applying for any available roles within HGSG Ltd, or (3) potential redundancy.

K was one of those facing a journey time of over 1.25 hours if he transferred to D Ltd. In individual consultation meetings it was made clear he had the three options outlined above. K opted for redundancy and his employment ultimately terminated on the date other employees transferred to D Ltd. An employment tribunal found that K's acceptance of voluntary redundancy was not a dismissal, but that his employment had ended by mutual consent. The EAT upheld this decision. It said that a termination by mutual consent requires freedom of choice on the part of the employee. If there is no real choice the termination will be a dismissal. However, an element of voluntarism on the part of an employee does not necessarily give rise to termination by way of mutual agreement. A volunteer for redundancy dismissal may volunteer freely but is still volunteering to be dismissed. The employment tribunal had heard evidence as to the actual nature of the choice offered to K and plainly considered that this provided the relevant context. The default position was that K's team would transfer to D Ltd. If none of them took the redundancy option, none of them would be dismissed. The fact that there might be a redundancy situation at some future point did not mean K was volunteering to be dismissed as part of such an exercise at that time.

12.19

'Proposing' to dismiss

12.20

Note that the collective consultation obligations arise where an employer is 'proposing' to dismiss 20 or more employees as redundant. This raises the question of when exactly the obligation kicks in. This is discussed in detail under 'Timetable for consultation – proposing to dismiss' below.

Definition of 'redundancy'

12.21

The proposed dismissals must be on the ground of redundancy, as defined in S.195(1) TULR(C)A, in order for the duty to consult to arise – S.188(1). For the purposes of proceedings brought under the redundancy consultation provisions, there is a presumption that a dismissal, or proposed dismissal, is for redundancy – S.195(2).

It is important to be aware that, as a result of amendments introduced by the Trade Union Reform and Employment Rights Act 1993, the definition of 'redundancy' for collective consultation purposes differs significantly from the ERA definition for the purpose of individual claims for redundancy payments or unfair dismissal – for which see Chapter 2, 'Redundancy', under 'Definition of "redundancy"'. S.195(1) provides that 'references to dismissal as redundant are references to dismissal for a reason not related to the individual concerned or for a number of reasons all of which are not so related'. This broadly echoes the definition to be found in Article 1 of the Collective Redundancies Directive.

417

12.22   The difference between the definitions of individual and collective redundancy has potentially important implications. If, for example, an employer wants to introduce a change in terms and conditions but cannot secure the agreement of employees to the change, the usual course is to terminate existing contracts and issue new ones incorporating the desired variation. These facts would be unlikely to fall within the ERA definition of 'redundancy', and so would not give rise to statutory redundancy payments (although they may give rise to unfair dismissal claims). Under the S.195 definition of 'redundancy', on the other hand, such dismissals – not being related to the individuals concerned – would trigger the S.188 statutory consultation procedure, requiring the employer to negotiate with the appropriate representatives of the employees with a view to reaching an agreement before imposing the new contracts. In GMB v Man Truck and Bus UK Ltd 2000 ICR 1101, EAT, the employer gave employees notice of dismissal and then offered them re-engagement under new terms. The EAT held that the duty to consult applied despite the fact that the employer never intended the employees to lose their jobs and that the employees continued to work uninterrupted throughout.

In University of Stirling v University and College Union 2015 ICR 567, SC, the Supreme Court held that the dismissal of four employees on fixed-term contracts, at the point when their fixed term expired, was not for a reason related to the individuals concerned. Baroness Hale, giving the lead judgment, explained that the non-renewal of a fixed-term contract is likely to be for a reason related to the individual if the employer still needs the work to be done but decides that the specific employee is not the right person to do it. However, the end of a research project or a particular undergraduate course would not be a reason related to the individual employee but a reason related to the employer's business, since the business no longer has a need for someone to do the research or teach the course. Even the ending of a fixed-term contract for maternity or sickness cover would be for a reason relating to the employer's business because the reason is that the person who normally does the job is returning to work, which is not a reason related to the individual employee.

12.23   In reaching its decision the Supreme Court overturned the Court of Session, which had upheld the decision of the EAT that the employees had not been dismissed as redundant. However, in doing so the Supreme Court cited with approval the 'admirable' test laid down by the EAT (2012 ICR 803, EATS). According to the EAT, '[a] reason relates to the individual if it is something to do with him such as something he is or something he has done. It is to be distinguished from a reason relating to the employer, such as his – or in the case of insolvency, his creditors' – need to effect business change in some respect'. The EAT's error had been to place the dismissals at issue into the first rather than the second category

418

The effect of this decision is rather limited since the TULR(C)A has now been amended to exclude the expiry of fixed-term contracts from the collective consultation obligations (although the EAT test cited by the Supreme Court continues to have general relevance). The EAT had held that dismissal on expiry of a fixed-term contract was always for a reason related to the individual concerned, and thus never for redundancy under the TULR(C)A. The Government decided to put this decision on a statutory footing and introduced an amendment to S.282 TULR(C)A with effect from 6 April 2013. S.282(2) now provides that termination of fixed-term contracts is expressly excluded from the collective consultation rules set out in Ss.188–198 TULR(C)A unless the fixed-term employment in question is terminated by reason of redundancy before the expiry of the term, the completion of the task or the occurrence or non-occurrence of the event specified in the contract.

12.24 As explained under 'Definition of "dismissal"' above, the term 'dismissal' in S.188 should be taken to include a constructive dismissal. In Pujante Rivera v Gestora Clubs Dir SL and anor 2016 ICR 227, ECJ, the European Court held that where an employee seeks the termination of his or her employment in response to a pay cut imposed by the employer for economic reasons unrelated to the individual employee, the termination counts as a 'redundancy' for the purpose of the collective consultation obligations imposed by Article 1(1)(a) of the Collective Redundancies Directive.

Note that the consultation requirements will still apply even if the employees concerned are not entitled to redundancy payments by reason of an agreement to that effect – Association of University Teachers v University of Newcastle-upon-Tyne 1987 ICR 317, EAT.

12.25 **Concurrent consultations.** The broader definition of 'redundancy' under S.195(1) means that there might be circumstances in which an employer is required to run more than one type of consultation; for example, where an employer wishes to make changes to its final salary pension scheme. In these circumstances, provided it employed 50 or more employees, the employer would be required to consult under the pension consultation requirements – see the Pensions Act 2004 and the Occupational and Personal Pension Schemes (Consultation by Employers and Miscellaneous Amendment) Regulations 2006 SI 2006/349. The employer would probably also need to consult under the collective redundancy regulations – assuming the change affects 20 or more employees – as the situation is likely to trigger S.195 redundancies (termination and re-engagement as a result of changes to terms and conditions). Rather than undergo two lots of consultation under the respective regulations, the consultations can be carried out concurrently as a single consultation process, provided both sets of statutory requirements are complied with.

12.26 Timetable for consultation

To reiterate, S.188 TULR(C)A provides that an employer proposing to dismiss as redundant 20 or more employees at one establishment within a period of 90 days or less must consult the appropriate representatives of the employees affected by the redundancies. Consultation must begin 'in good time' and must in any event begin:

- where 100 or more redundancies are proposed at one establishment within a 90-day period, at least 45 days before the first of the dismissals takes effect (90 days where the proposals to dismiss were made before 6 April 2013), and

- otherwise, at least 30 days before the first dismissal takes effect – S.188(1A).

12.27 'In good time'

The requirement under S.188(1A) to begin consultation 'in good time' derives from Article 2(1) of the Collective Redundancies Directive, which does not set out any specific time limits. It was introduced by the Collective Redundancies and Transfer of Undertakings (Protection of Employment) (Amendment) Regulations 1995 SI 1995/2587 ('the 1995 Regulations') in place of the previous requirement to consult 'at the earliest opportunity'. In Newspaper Publishing plc v NUJ EAT 1064/97 the EAT thought that there was unlikely to be any significant distinction between the two phrases, holding that, on the facts of the case, both would require consultation to begin within 24 hours of the date that redundancy dismissals were proposed. However, in Dewhirst Group v GMB Trade Union EAT 0486/03 the EAT appeared to accept that the change was a deliberate move by the Government to reduce the obligation on employers to the bare minimum required by the Directive, and that 'in good time' is therefore a less stringent requirement than 'at the earliest opportunity'.

A comparison of the following two cases – one decided before and one after 1995 – seems to support the view that the change of wording is significant. In a pre-1995 case, GKN Sankey Ltd v National Society of Metal Mechanics 1980 ICR 148, EAT, the employer decided at the end of May to close its factory on 15 September. It began consultation with the union on 5 June, thus providing for the statutory 90 days. The EAT found that, in the circumstances, consultation had not begun 'at the earliest opportunity', i.e. at the end of May, and the employer was therefore in breach of S.188, even though it had observed the applicable statutory consultation period. In the post-1995 case, Amicus v Nissan Motor Manufacturing (UK) Ltd EAT 0184/05, on the other hand, redundancies were initially proposed in October but consultation with appropriate representatives did not begin until January. The EAT accepted

420

that 'in good time' means no more or less than time sufficient for fair consultation to take place, working back from the final date, which is the first date for dismissal. Furthermore, this should not involve a mechanistic, arithmetical or calendar approach – what is 'good time' depends on many factors, including the number of staff and unions involved, and what is a reasonable amount of time for unions to be able to respond to proposals and make counter-suggestions. On the facts of the case, counting back from the date of the eventual dismissals the following June, the EAT was satisfied that consultation had taken place 'in good time'.

In any event, employers should ensure that they begin the consultation process early enough to enable meaningful consultation to take place. In complex cases, this may mean allowing for more time than the applicable statutory consultation period before the first dismissals take effect (see 'Minimum statutory consultation periods' below) in order to be 'in good time'. **12.28**

Minimum statutory consultation periods
12.29

As explained under 'Timetable for consultation' above, while employers are under an overriding duty to begin consultation 'in good time', S.188(1A) sets out *minimum* periods of consultation. To recap, these are:

- where 100 or more redundancies are proposed at one establishment within a 90-day period, at least 45 days before the first of the dismissals takes effect (90 days where the proposals to dismiss were made before 6 April 2013), and

- otherwise, at least 30 days before the first dismissal takes effect.

These minimum periods are intended to ensure that the parties have sufficient time within which to consult by specifying a date by which consultation must have started. They do *not* dictate how long the consultation should take. In other words, the 30-, 45- or 90-day requirements do not require that the parties consult for 30, 45 or 90 days. It is therefore possible for collective consultation to take place over a shorter period of time. However, the employer's proposals must still be at a formative stage when consultation begins and the union must be given sufficient time to make a meaningful contribution. For example, in Amicus v Nissan Motor Manufacturing (UK) Ltd (above) the EAT held that the employer, which started consultation well before the applicable 30-day minimum requirement, complied with S.188(1A), even though consultation with the trade union effectively lasted only two weeks.

But where the employer has reached agreement with the appropriate representatives before the end of the minimum consultation period, it should not be tempted to then bring forward the date of any agreed dismissals. If it dismisses before the statutory consultation period is up, it will be in breach of **12.30**

421

S.188. (The only exception is if there are 'special circumstances which render it not reasonably practicable' for the employer to comply, but in this situation the employer must still comply to the extent that it is reasonably practicable to do so in the circumstances – see 'Special circumstances defence' below.)

12.31 **'Proposing to dismiss'**

The duty to consult arises where the employer is 'proposing to dismiss' for redundancy. Historically, courts and tribunals have taken the view that this phrase implies that some sort of decision must have been made. For example, in Association of Patternmakers and Allied Craftsmen v Kirvin Ltd 1978 IRLR 318, EAT, the Appeal Tribunal stated that, for it to be said that an employer is 'proposing to dismiss', 'the employer must have formed some view as to how many are to be dismissed, when this is to take place and how it is to be arranged'. In that case the employer was in financial difficulties and attempts were made to sell the business. When the last prospective purchaser withdrew, a receiver was appointed who immediately gave redundancy notices to the workforce. The union argued that the duty to consult arose when the employer contemplated, or should reasonably have contemplated, the possibility of redundancies. The EAT, however, held that the employer only proposed to dismiss on the day the last potential purchaser vanished and the receiver was appointed. Before that, redundancies were merely a contemplated possible event, so there was no breach of the consultation requirements.

However, while the TULR(C)A imposes the duty to consult at the point that an employer *proposes* collective redundancies, Article 2(1) of the Directive requires consultation where an employer is *contemplating* collective redundancies. In MSF v Refuge Assurance plc and anor 2002 ICR 1365, EAT, the Appeal Tribunal accepted that the difference in wording makes the TULR(C)A more restrictive than the Directive – 'proposing to dismiss' refers to a state of mind that is much more certain and further along in the decision-making process than mere contemplation. The EAT thus confirmed that the TULR(C)A does not comply with European law in this regard.

12.32 The EAT's conclusion in the MSF case is supported by the European Court of Justice's decision in Junk v Kühnel 2005 IRLR 310, ECJ. This case focused on the timing of consultation in relation to the notice of dismissal (on which see 'Timing of dismissal notices' below), but the ECJ also considered the point at which the duty to consult arises. It noted that 'the case in which the employer "is contemplating" collective redundancies and has drawn up "a project" to that end corresponds to a situation in which no decision has yet been taken'. It went on to state that the wording of the Directive indicated that 'the obligation to consult and to notify arose prior to any decision by the employer to terminate contracts of employment'. Thus, as a matter of European law, the obligation to consult arises before the employer has set its mind on dismissal. This interpretation of the Directive is unimpeachable as a matter of common sense – any consultation that takes place once an employer has already decided to dismiss would be little short of a sham – but creates something of a dilemma for UK courts and tribunals, which have to resolve the conflict between conflicting clearly worded EU and UK legislation.

In this regard, the EAT has attempted to give the wording of S.188 some degree of 'purposive' construction. In Scotch Premier Meat Ltd v Burns and ors 2000 IRLR 639, EAT, for example, it held that a company considering two possible courses of action as to its future, one of which would involve effecting redundancy dismissals, the other of which would not, was 'proposing to dismiss' for S.188 purposes. According to this interpretation, it would seem that while the duty under the TULR(C)A does not arise until there is some specific proposal for dismissals, it can arise (as the Directive requires) before the employer's mind is committed to a definite course of action. However, more recently the EAT has required something more specific in order for dismissals to be 'proposed' for collective consultation purposes. In UK Coal Mining Ltd v NUM (Northumberland Area) and anor 2008 ICR 163, EAT, Mr Justice Elias, then President of the EAT, noted that the collective consultation duty will not arise 'when the closure is mooted as a possibility but only when it is fixed as a clear, albeit provisional, intention'. This interpretation seems to be closer to the wording of the TULR(C)A than to the ECJ's clear statement of principle in Junk v Kühnel (above). However, Elias P considered all of the relevant case law – including Junk – on the point so his comments can be taken to hold some authority.

The European Court revisited the question of when an employer can be said to **12.33** be 'contemplating' collective redundancies in Akavan Erityisalojen Keskusliitto (AEK) ry and ors v Fujitsu Siemens Computers Oy 2010 ICR 444, ECJ. There the Court held that an employer's duty to consult under Article 2(1) of the Directive is triggered once a strategic or commercial decision compelling it to contemplate or to plan for collective redundancies has been taken and not when such a decision is merely contemplated. In the ECJ's view, there were clear disadvantages to a premature triggering of the obligation; for example, restricting the flexibility available to undertakings when restructuring and causing unnecessary uncertainty for workers about their job security. The ECJ also considered that, should consultation begin when decisions that may lead to redundancies are merely contemplated, the relevant factors to be taken into account during the course of that consultation would not be known. In such circumstances, the objectives of the consultation listed in Article 2(2) of the Directive – avoiding termination of employment contracts, reducing the number of workers affected and mitigating the consequences – could not be achieved. The ECJ also held that the obligation to start consultation was not dependent on the employer being able to supply to workers' representatives information of the type listed in Article 2(3)(b), such as the reasons for the

423

projected redundancies, the numbers and categories of employees to be made redundant, the period over which the projected redundancies are to be effected and the selection criteria to be used. In the ECJ's view, the wording of the Directive clearly envisaged such information being provided during consultations, but not necessarily at the time they start.

Unfortunately the decision in Akavan is not without its problems and at certain points the ECJ appears to blur the distinction between the triggering of the obligation to consult and the obligation to start consultation. This was recognised by the Court of Appeal in United States of America v Nolan 2011 IRLR 40, CA, and as a result the Court decided that a reference to the ECJ was necessary to clarify when the consultation obligation under the Directive arises. While the ECJ had already addressed the issue in Akavan, the Court of Appeal considered that decision to be 'unclear'.

12.34   In Nolan, the commanding officer of a US army base in Hampshire informed the civilian workforce on 24 April 2006 that the base would close at the end of September 2006. In early June management wrote to the Local National Executive Council, which represented the employees, stating that final decisions on redundancies would be made at the end of June, following consultation. On 30 June, around 200 civilian employees received notice of dismissal and the dismissals took effect at the end of September. One of those made redundant, N, made a claim for a protective award on the basis that workforce representatives had not been consulted as required by S.188. An employment tribunal upheld her claim, finding that, as the decision to close the base inevitably meant mass redundancies, consultation should have commenced before the decision was made, given that there could be no meaningful consultation afterwards. According to the tribunal, this view was reinforced by the EAT's decision in UK Coal Mining Ltd v NUM (Northumberland Area) and anor (above), handed down after the tribunal's initial deliberations. On appeal, the EAT took the view that the UK Coal Mining case required consultation over the decision to close a workplace where it would inevitably lead to redundancies and upheld the protective award. However, it remitted the case to the same tribunal on other grounds. The USA again appealed, arguing, among other things, that the ECJ's decision in Akavan Erityisalojen Keskusliitto (AEK) ry and ors v Fujitsu Siemens Computers Oy (above), handed down after the EAT's decision in UK Coal Mining, showed that the latter decision had interpreted the consultation obligation under the Directive too widely.

In deciding to refer the matter to the ECJ, the Court of Appeal stated that it found the reasoning in Akavan 'difficult to follow'. In the Appeal Court's view, it was not clear whether the ECJ had stated that the consultation obligation arises (i) when an employer proposes, but has not yet made, a decision that will foreseeably or inevitably lead to collective redundancies; or (ii) only when such a decision has actually been made and the employer is proposing consequential redundancies. The Court was able to cite parts of the ECJ's judgment supporting each of these constructions. Since the issue at stake was too important to risk adopting the wrong interpretation, the Court concluded that a reference to the ECJ was necessary to clarify when the consultation obligation arises under the Directive. On 22 March 2012, Advocate General Mengozzi issued his opinion that the obligation to consult is triggered, within a group structure, when a body or entity that controls the employer makes a strategic or commercial decision which compels the employer to contemplate or to plan for collective redundancies. The Advocate General considered that this analysis, which he derived from Akavan, could apply to the closure of a military base, entailing collective redundancies of civilian staff, where the strategic decision had been taken at a much higher level. However, when the ECJ came to give its ruling (United States of America v Nolan 2013 ICR 193, ECJ), it decided that it had no jurisdiction to decide the matter because of Article 1(2)(b), which excludes from the Directive's scope 'workers employed by public administrative bodies or by establishments governed by public law'. Although the domestic legislation, i.e. S.188 TULR(C)A, makes no such exemption, the ECJ can only rule on the interpretation of the Directive, which simply did not apply in this case.

12.35 When the case returned to the Court of Appeal, the Court ordered a further hearing on the question of when the consultation obligation arose by reference purely to the domestic provisions. The USA then appealed against that decision to the Supreme Court – United States of America v Nolan 2015 ICR 1347, SC. It argued that the TULR(C)A did not apply to the actions of a foreign state. It also argued that the 1995 Regulations, which amended the scope of S.188 TULR(C)A so as to cover employees working at an establishment without trade union representation, were ultra vires in that they purported to extend the consultation obligation to public administrative bodies or public law establishments.

The Supreme Court (by a majority of 4:1) dismissed the appeal. It held that the TULR(C)A, as amended, should be interpreted as covering the closure of a military base such as occurred in this case. Even though such closure was not a situation foreseen by the legislature, this was not a reason for reading into clear legislation a specific exemption that would not reflect the scope of any exemption in EU law, especially when the foreign state could have invoked state immunity but failed to do so in time. The Supreme Court also rejected the argument that the 1995 Regulations were ultra vires and remitted the case to the Court of Appeal for a decision on when the duty to consult arose. At the time of writing, this decision is still awaited.

12.36 In many cases the difference between 'propose' and 'contemplate' will be of little more than semantic interest, since an employer under a duty to consult

425

does not necessarily have to start consulting immediately. Now that employers are obliged to consult 'in good time' rather than 'at the earliest opportunity', the need to pinpoint the precise moment at which the duty to consult arises is diminished. This is because deciding whether consultation was undertaken 'in good time' is likely to involve focusing on the date of dismissal, and looking at what happened up to that date, rather than on the date on which the duty to consult was triggered. In fact, as noted under '"In good time"' above, the EAT endorsed this approach in Amicus v Nissan Motor Manufacturing (UK) Ltd EAT 0184/05. Thus, there is support for the proposition that so long as the consultation process does not begin so late that proposals for dismissal have effectively been cast in stone, there should be no grounds for complaint to a tribunal that the process did not begin until some time after the possibility of mass redundancies was first mooted. This must, however, be subject to the overriding requirement that consultation be 'meaningful'.

Note that, as we discuss in 'The consultation process – subject matter of consultation' below, following the decision of the EAT in UK Coal Mining Ltd v NUM (Northumberland Area) and anor (above), employers are obliged to consult over the economic reasons behind a redundancy situation. Thus, 'in good time' indicates that consultation must begin early enough for representatives to be able to have a real opportunity to affect the decision to make redundancies.

12.37 **Who proposes to dismiss?** Aside from the rather ephemeral issue of the difference between 'contemplation' and 'proposal', there are some more practical issues to consider. The legislation is couched in terms of the employer's contemplating or proposing dismissal, with no clarification of who, in a corporate entity, is to be taken as doing the thinking.

The EAT considered this issue in Leicestershire County Council v UNISON 2005 IRLR 920, EAT, highlighting the difference, in some organisations, between 'officers' who propose courses of action and 'politicians' who decide on them. In that case, a tribunal had found that a 'proposal' within the meaning of S.188 had been made by officers of the Council nearly a month before being ratified by a formal political decision of the Council's employment committee. The tribunal, after considering the reality of proposing and deciding on redundancies within the Council, concluded that not only the proposal but also the decision to dismiss had been made by the Council officers prior to the confirmation by the employment committee. The EAT upheld this decision. (Note that part of the EAT's decision was appealed to the Court of Appeal – 2006 IRLR 810, CA – but this aspect of its judgment was untouched.)

12.38 Similarly, in Dewhirst Group v GMB Trade Union EAT 0486/03 an employer's decision to close one of its manufacturing sites constituted a proposal to dismiss, notwithstanding that in order to be carried out, the proposal needed to be approved by the company group of which the employer formed a part.

426

Parent company. In Akavan Erityisalojen Keskusliitto (AEK) ry and ors v   **12.39**
Fujitsu Siemens Computers Oy (above), the ECJ considered how a parent
company's involvement in the process that leads to collective redundancies can
impact on the employer's obligation to consult. Article 2(4) of the Collective
Redundancies Directive makes it clear that the obligation to consult only
applies to the employer and not the parent company controlling the employer.
According to the ECJ, this means that where the decision that will lead to
redundancies is taken by the parent company, the obligation does not arise
until such time as the parent company identifies the subsidiary that will be
affected by the redundancies. In the Court's view, to conclude otherwise would
be to strip the obligation to consult of any meaning: until the subsidiary
is identified, it is not possible to identify means of avoiding, reducing the
number of, and mitigating the consequences of, collective redundancies. That
said, where the parent company has identified the subsidiary which is likely
to shed jobs and fails immediately and properly to inform it of a decision that
may or will lead to collective redundancies, it is the subsidiary that must bear
the consequences. Furthermore, in light of the decision in Junk v Kühnel 2005
IRLR 310, ECJ (see 'Timing of dismissal notices' below), the consultation
procedure must be concluded by the subsidiary affected by the collective
redundancies before that subsidiary, on the direct instructions of its parent
company or otherwise, terminates the contracts of the employees who are to
be affected by those redundancies.

Company wound up. In some cases where a financial crisis is the cause   **12.40**
of the redundancies there may be a question as to whether S.188 applies
at all. In the case of In re Hartlebury Printers Ltd and ors (in liquidation)
1992 ICR 559, ChD, it was held that the duty to consult did not arise where
redundancies were the result of a court order requiring the winding up of the
company, contrary to the wishes of the administrators. In such circumstances
it could not be said that the dismissals were ever 'proposed' within the
meaning of S.188. Mr Justice Morritt emphasised, however, that S.188 did
apply to circumstances where the administrator of an insolvent company
proposes dismissals. This is because an administrator acts as an agent of the
employer, so that the administrator's proposals must be regarded as having
been made by the employer. This is confirmed by the decision in Claes and ors
v Landsbanki Luxembourg SA (in liquidation) 2011 ICR 1364, ECJ, where
the European Court held that, until the legal personality of an establishment
ceases to exist, the obligations under Articles 2 and 3 of the Directive had
to be fulfilled by the management of the establishment, where it was still in
place, or by the liquidator, where the management had been taken over in its
entirety by a liquidator.

In MSF v Refuge Assurance plc and anor 2002 ICR 1365, EAT, Mr Justice
Lindsay, then President of the EAT, commented that the interpretation of
S.188 in In re Hartlebury Printers Ltd and ors (in liquidation) (above) 'may

427

be vulnerable as representing a construction of the Directive so as to make it consistent with the domestic legislation rather than, as is required, the other way round'. Having said that, Hartlebury has not been expressly overruled, and so the possibility still remains of an employer escaping liability under S.188 where the decision to close down a company's operations is made by a court.

12.41 ## Ascertaining the number of redundancies

In determining how many employees an employer is proposing to make redundant within the meaning of S.188, no account can be taken of any employees in respect of whom consultation has already begun – S.188(3). Thus, if an employer is already consulting on 70 proposed redundancies (which, as noted above, would require a minimum 30-day consultation period) and a further 30 redundancies are proposed a few days later, it is not possible to add the two groups together and claim that the threshold of 100 proposed redundancies has occurred and the 45-day minimum consultation period applies to all. If, however, consultation has not started in respect of the 70 employees, the two groups may be added together. S.188(3) would not apply in these circumstances and the company would have 'proposed' 100 redundancies – see, for example, TGWU v Nationwide Haulage Ltd 1978 IRLR 143, ET. As noted under 'Scope of duty to consult' above, in ascertaining the number of proposed dismissals account must be taken of *all* those affected, which could include some employees whom the employer has no intention of dispensing with; for example, those whose terms and conditions might be changed as a result of any reorganisation (Hardy v Tourism South East 2005 IRLR 242, EAT), or those whom it is proposed should be dismissed and immediately re-engaged (GMB v Man Truck and Bus UK Ltd 2000 ICR 1101, EAT).

Where the employer staggers proposed dismissals (and has not yet begun consulting), the question arises as to whether – provided they occur within a 90-day period – the dismissals should be aggregated. If, for example, the employer proposes to make over 100 employees redundant but, for a variety of reasons, decides that the employees should leave gradually in batches, the obligation is to consult with the employees at least 90 days before the first dismissal takes effect. If, however, the employer did not intend to make a second batch of redundancies when the first batch was initially proposed, the circumstances may not be caught by S.188 where each batch involves fewer than 20 employees.

12.42 Three examples:

• **Rae and ors v Beaumont Legal** ET Case No.1810229/08: the downturn in the housing market had a detrimental impact on BL's workload and on 4 April 2008 it dismissed four employees by reason of redundancy and announced three days later that it expected to make a further ten employees

428

redundant. In the event, nine employees left by the end of May. In June, BL decided that an additional 12 employees were to be made redundant. The employees argued that BL was now under an obligation to consult collectively. The tribunal disagreed. In its view, BL conducted two discrete redundancy exercises. The first took place in April and concluded by May, at which stage BL did not contemplate making any further redundancies. The subsequent decision that more jobs needed to go was triggered by the impact of the fall in the housing market on the company's cash flow. The tribunal found that BL was not trying to evade its obligations under the TULR(C)A

- **Jones and ors v Sunlight Service Group Ltd** ET Case No.1200582/09: SSG Ltd, which suffered a downturn in business in 2009, announced that it was to close its plant at Wellingborough with a loss of 89 jobs, which triggered a 30-day consultation period. However, the tribunal found that the company had deliberately reduced the number of employees being made redundant, and thereby brought down the consultation costs, by making ten staff redundant immediately after the decision to close the plant was taken. This was a calculated breach of its S.188 duty

- **Elligate and ors v MZ Realisations 1 Ltd (formerly Modelzone Ltd)** ET Case No.3101597/13: MZR1 Ltd had 47 stores in the UK with over 300 employees. On 26 June 2013 joint administrators were appointed for the business, which was insolvent but in a position to continue trading with a view to a sale, if possible. An e-mail was sent to all employees on 27 June stating that 'there may be redundancies and store closures [...] if that were to be a proposal that arises from the urgent review that we are undertaking, we would wish to consult about this with all affected staff at the relevant time. We are also mindful of the possibility that one potential route for the business is a sale.' The next day, 28 June, 18 staff from head office were made redundant. It later proved impossible to find a buyer for the business as a going concern and on 17 July the first store was closed. Further store closures followed and the resulting redundancies, or the overwhelming majority of them, were completed by the end of August. Six of the employees made redundant on 28 June claimed that MZR1 Ltd had failed to comply with its duty to collectively consult. The tribunal disagreed. Relying on Mr Justice Elias's comment in UK Coal Mining Ltd v NUM (Northumberland Area) and anor 2008 ICR 163, EAT, that the collective consultation duty will not arise 'when the closure is mooted as a possibility but only when it is fixed as a clear, albeit provisional, intention' (see '"Proposing to dismiss"' above), it held that the closure of the stores was not MZR1 Ltd's state of mind on 28 June, or indeed at any time prior to the appointment of employee representatives on 17 July for consultation in relation to the later redundancies. The phrasing of the notice to staff was in terms of the possibility of redundancies. As at 28 June, the focus was on saving the

429

business by finding a buyer. There was, at that date, no proposal to make collective redundancies.

12.43 Meaning of 'establishment'

In order to engage the consultation obligations under S.188(1) TULR(C)A, the requisite number of dismissals must be proposed 'at one establishment'. The leading decision on the meaning of 'establishment' is Rockfon A/S v Specialarbejderforbundet i Danmark 1996 ICR 673, ECJ, where the ECJ held that 'establishment' is a term of Community law and cannot be defined by reference to the laws of the Member States. Rather, in every jurisdiction it must be understood as meaning, depending on the circumstances, the unit to which the redundant workers are assigned to carry out their duties. It is not essential for the unit in question to have a management which can independently effect collective redundancies.

The employer in Rockfon was seeking to evade the consultation requirements by centralising the responsibility for dismissals so that all employees could be considered as working at one establishment, as, under Danish law, the larger the workforce in a particular establishment, the higher the number of proposed redundancies needed to trigger collective consultation. Such an approach would be of no use to UK employers seeking to avoid the consultation requirements, since the UK legislation has adopted the alternative formula provided by Article 1(1) of the Directive for defining collective redundancies, whereby the consultation requirement is triggered if 20 employees are to be made redundant at one establishment, regardless of the size of the workforce at that establishment. Thus UK employers would be prone to argue not that all the employees are employed at a single establishment, but that the redundant employees were in fact employed at different establishments. Nevertheless, the principle of the ECJ's decision suggests that any attempt by a UK employer to artificially divide the employees' 'establishment' for the purposes of S.188 will be as unsuccessful as the Danish employer's attempts at aggrandisement.

12.44

Rockfon was subsequently endorsed in Athinaiki Chartopoiia AE v Panagiotidis and ors 2007 IRLR 284, ECJ, where the European Court confirmed, among other things, that:

- the term 'establishment' is to be defined broadly so as to limit the instances of collective redundancy to which the Directive does not apply

- an establishment, in the context of an undertaking, may consist of a distinct entity, having a certain degree of permanence and stability, which is assigned to perform one or more given tasks, and which has a workforce, technical means and a certain organisational structure allowing for the accomplishment of those tasks

430

- the entity in question need not have any legal, economic, financial, administrative or technological autonomy in order to be regarded as an establishment

- it is not essential for the unit in question to be endowed with a management that can independently effect collective redundancies in order for it to be regarded as an establishment.

Both Athinaike and Rockfon A/S v Specialarbejderforbundet i Danmark (above) were subsequently endorsed in USDAW and anor v Ethel Austin Ltd and ors 2015 ICR 675, ECJ (more commonly referred to as the 'Woolworths case'), and Lyttle and ors v Bluebird UK Bidco 2 Ltd 2015 IRLR 577, ECJ, where the ECJ confirmed that the 'establishment' is the unit to which the redundant employees are assigned to carry out their duties. The ECJ also held that it is not necessary to aggregate the dismissals across all of an employer's establishments for the purposes of determining whether the protections in the Directive apply – see 'Woolworths case' below for more details.

Unit to which employees assigned. The test for determining 'establishment' **12.45** formulated by the ECJ in Rockfon A/S v Specialarbejderforbundet i Danmark (above) was applied by the EAT in the following cases (with differing results):

- **Mills and Allen Ltd v Bulwich** EAT 154/99: B was employed by MA Ltd from 1993 until her dismissal for redundancy in 1998. She was based in the company's Manchester office and was a manager in the direct sales team, which sold poster sites to businesses. MA Ltd planned a reorganisation of the sales force in which it was initially envisaged that the entire direct sales team staff would be dismissed as redundant. In the event the company dismissed 24 employees around the country, all members of the direct sales team. A tribunal held that MA Ltd had breached S.188 by failing to undertake consultation and the EAT upheld that decision. While the company had treated the Manchester direct sales department as a distinct entity, the redundancies were directed solely to that department nationwide, and so the tribunal had been entitled to find that the department was a single establishment in which more than 20 employees were made redundant. The nationwide team was capable of constituting the 'unit to which the workers made redundant are assigned', within the meaning of Rockfon

- **MSF v Refuge Assurance plc and anor** 2002 ICR 1365, EAT: although a tribunal found that redundant insurance field workers were assigned to their local branch offices, it concluded that the establishment in question was not the individual branch office, but the entire field staff. The EAT, however, overturned that decision, as it did not accord with the principle laid down in Rockfon that 'establishment' means the unit to which workers are assigned

- **Renfrewshire Council v Educational Institute of Scotland** 2013 ICR 172, EATS: the Appeal Tribunal overturned a tribunal's decision that redundant

431

teachers were assigned to the Council's Education and Leisure Service Department, rather than the individual schools at which each taught. According to the EAT, the tribunal's finding that a school, whose operation, funding and staffing fell within the Department's control, was not a distinct entity was fundamentally flawed. A school was capable of being a 'unit', and whether it was the teacher's 'establishment' depended upon whether the teacher was actually assigned to it, not who had powers of control over it. Moreover, the unit to which an individual is 'assigned' refers to the factual, not the contractual, position. The link with the place of work is dependent upon where the employment is 'at', not where the contract may otherwise provide for the work to be performed. Therefore, mobility clauses in the teachers' contracts did not mean that the school, designated as their place of work in the contract, could not be the unit to which they were assigned. The case was remitted to the tribunal to consider the question of establishment afresh. If the teachers were found to be assigned to their individual schools, there would be no breach of S.188.

12.46 These cases demonstrate that the decision is ultimately one for the tribunal to reach on the facts of the particular case. Some tribunals have tended to adopt a broad definition of 'establishment' – as advocated by the European Court in Athinaiki Chartopoiia AE v Panagiotidis and ors (above) – where employers have tried to avoid their obligations under S.188 in cases of multi-site redundancies. Two examples:

• **Tierney-Rymer v Sainsbury's Supermarkets Ltd** ET Case No.1803829/09: T-R worked for SS Ltd, a national chain of supermarkets, as a community food and health adviser. All advisers promoted healthy eating to a variety of community-based groups in a particular geographical area. They were given a large supermarket in that area as their 'home store' for Inland Revenue purposes and to allow them access to office facilities, but they were not managed in any way by the store. In 2008, SS Ltd made 34 advisers, including T-R, redundant but decided that it was not required to carry out collective consultation. The tribunal disagreed, finding that the advisers were effectively organised as a national team and thus a distinct entity within SS Ltd; they were not subject to the branch management structure and only had a tenuous link to their home stores. Accordingly, SS Ltd had made more than 20 employees redundant at one establishment

• **Fairhurst v Stephens LLP** ET Case No.2406673/09: S, a firm of solicitors, proposed to dismiss as redundant up to 60 employees across its five offices. It argued that each office was a separate establishment, which meant that its S.188 duty was not triggered. The tribunal noted, among other things, that management decisions were made centrally, e.g. by a staff committee attended by senior partners and employees from all the offices, and found that the firm as a whole formed one establishment for the purposes of S.188.

432

Woolworths case. The position under domestic law was thrown into **12.47** considerable uncertainty by the EAT's decision in USDAW and anor v Ethel Austin Ltd and ors 2013 ICR 1300, EAT (more commonly referred to as the 'Woolworths case'), where the Appeal Tribunal held that the words 'at one establishment' in S.188(1) must be deleted to ensure compliance with the Collective Redundancies Directive. The cases arose out of the liquidation of retail chains Woolworths and Ethel Austin in 2008 and 2010, which resulted in the loss of several thousand jobs. The recognised trade unions brought claims alleging that the administrators failed to comply with their duty under S.188, which were upheld by employment tribunals. However, in making protective awards under S.189 TULR(C)A, the tribunals treated each individual store as a discrete 'establishment' for the purposes of S.188 and decided that there was no duty on the administrators to consult on redundancies at any store with fewer than 20 employees. Accordingly, the tribunals only made protective awards where 20 or more employees were dismissed at one store. This meant that around 4,400 workers – 1,210 at Ethel Austin and 3,233 at Woolworths – did not receive protective awards. The unions appealed to the EAT, arguing that this construction of S.188 was contrary to the Directive's objective of protecting workers' rights on redundancy.

The EAT, hearing the appeals together, began by looking at Article 1 of the Directive, from which the duty to consult over collective redundancies is derived and which gave Member States a choice, upon transposing the Directive, as to when the duty to consult will be triggered under domestic law. Whereas the option in Article 1(1)(a)(i) looked to the size of the existing workforce and the establishments in which employees worked, the one chosen by the Government, in Article 1(1)(a)(ii), required an employer to consult collectively where, over a period of 90 days, the number of redundancies was 'at least 20, whatever the number of workers normally employed in the establishments in question'. In the EAT's view, ECJ case law showed that the term 'establishment' could be given a broad or a narrow construction, as long as it gave effect to the Directive's core objective of improving workers' rights. But while the meaning of the term was critical for determining whether the duty to consult was triggered under option (i), there was no need to construe the term in any particular way for the second option because the duty under (ii) applied 'whatever' establishments the employees work in. In imposing a site-based restriction on the number of proposed redundancies that can trigger the duty to consult, S.188(1) was therefore more restrictive than the Directive.

As it was clearly Parliament's intention to implement the Directive correctly, **12.48** the EAT held that it was entitled to construe S.188 so as to give effect to the consultation obligation as set out in the Directive. Applying the principles on statutory interpretation as derived from Ghaidan v Godin-Mendoza 2004 2 AC 557, HL, and EBR Attridge LLP ((formerly Attridge Law and anor) v Coleman 2010 ICR 242, EAT, the EAT decided that compliance with the Directive

433

could be achieved by deleting the words 'at one establishment' from S.188(1). Accordingly, in the EAT's view the duty to consult over collective redundancies arose where 20 or more employees were to be dismissed, irrespective of where they worked. Thus, on the facts of each case, all employees, including those working in stores where fewer than 20 redundancies took place, were entitled to protective awards for breach of the TULR(C)A.

In reaching its decision, the EAT did not consider it necessary to ask the ECJ for clarification on the meaning of 'establishment' for collective redundancy purposes. However, in Lyttle and ors v Bluebird UK Bidco 2 Ltd IT Case No.555/12, a decision pre-dating the Woolworths case, an industrial tribunal in Northern Ireland took the opposite view. In that case, the tribunal considered the meaning of 'establishment' for the purposes of collective redundancy consultation obligations imposed under Article 216 of the Employment Rights (Northern Ireland) Order 1996, which mirrors S.188(1) TULR(C)A, and decided that it was not clear whether 'establishment' in that provision should be defined in the same way as in Article 1(1)(a)(i) or whether the phrase 'at least 20' in Article 1(1)(a)(ii) referred to the number of redundancy dismissals across all of an employer's establishments or to the number of dismissals per establishment. An authoritative ruling on these issues from the ECJ was therefore required.

12.49 In January 2014, the Court of Appeal heard an appeal in the Woolworths case (USDAW and anor v Ethel Austin Ltd and ors 2014 EWCA Civ 142, CA) and decided that it, too, should make a reference to the ECJ, and although the cases were not formally joined the Advocate General dealt with them together when he gave his opinion on 5 February 2015. He considered that the 'establishment' is the unit to which the redundant employees are assigned to carry out their duties and that it is not necessary to aggregate the dismissals across all of an employer's establishments for the purpose of determining whether the protections in the Directive apply.

In USDAW and anor v Ethel Austin Ltd and ors 2015 ICR 675, ECJ, the ECJ followed the Advocate General's opinion and confirmed that the Directive does not require all 'establishments' to be aggregated for the purpose of the 20-employee threshold. The ECJ referred to its judgment in Rockfon A/S v Specialarbejderforbundet i Danmark (above) to the effect that the term 'establishment' means the unit to which the workers made redundant are assigned to carry out their duties. It is not essential in order for there to be an 'establishment' that the unit in question is endowed with a management that can independently effect collective redundancies. The term 'establishment' was further clarified in Athinaiki Chartopoiia AE v Panagiotidis and ors (above) where the Court confirmed that an 'establishment' may consist of a distinct entity having a certain degree of permanence and stability. Thus, an 'establishment' may be a part of a whole undertaking, and where an undertaking comprises several entities meeting the criteria for an 'establishment', it is the entity to which the workers made redundant are assigned to carry out their duties that constitutes the 'establishment' for the purposes of the Directive.

As for the facts in the Woolworths case, the ECJ noted that since the dismissals **12.50** were effected within two large retail groups carrying out their activities from stores situated in different locations throughout the UK, each employing in most cases fewer than 20 employees, the employment tribunals had taken the view that the stores to which the employees affected by those dismissals were assigned were separate 'establishments'. It would be for the Court of Appeal to establish whether that was a proper interpretation in the light of the ECJ's clarification of the Directive.

Thus, although the ECJ did not conclusively determine that each individual store should be considered a separate establishment, its judgment clearly suggested that this was a permissible approach for the tribunals to take. The case subsequently returned to the Court of Appeal, which allowed the appeal by consent, overturning the EAT's decision that the words 'at one establishment' in S.188(1) should be disregarded.

Two weeks after its decision in the Woolworths case, the ECJ in Lyttle and ors **12.51** v Bluebird UK Bidco 2 Ltd 2015 IRLR 577, ECJ, again followed the Advocate General's opinion and held that the 'establishment' is the local unit to which the redundant employees are assigned to carry out their duties. The ECJ ruled that the term 'establishment' in Article 1(1)(a)(ii) of the Directive must be interpreted in the same way as the term in Article 1(1)(a)(i). This definition requires that account be taken of the dismissals effected in each establishment considered separately. In the ECJ's view, the Directive does not require all 'establishments' to be aggregated for the purpose of the 20-employee threshold and so Article 216 of the Employment Rights (Northern Ireland) Order 1996, which mirrors S.188(1) TULR(C)A, is not incompatible with the Directive in this regard. On 24 September 2015, the case returned to the industrial tribunal in Northern Ireland, which determined that each individual store was to be considered a separate 'establishment' and where each establishment consisted of fewer than 20 redundant employees the collective consultation duty did not apply – Lyttle and anor v Bluebird UK Bidco 2 Ltd IT Case No.555/12.

Bringing forward the dismissal date   **12.52**

The EAT has been astute to avoid a potential problem that might arise in respect of the statutory periods of consultation where the redundant employees choose to leave early. Suppose, for example, that an employer proposing to dismiss over 100 employees starts consultation the statutory 45 days before the date it is proposed that the first dismissal will take effect, but some or all of the employees volunteer to leave before that date. If the

435

employer allows them to do so, is it in breach of its consultation duties? After all, consultations have now started less than 45 days before the first dismissal. The EAT has held that in these circumstances there is no breach because the relevant date in S.188(1A) is the date proposed for the first dismissal to take effect, and not when the first employee actually leaves – E Green and Son (Castings) Ltd and ors v ASTMS and anor 1984 ICR 352, EAT; TGWU v RA Lister and Co Ltd EAT 436/85.

12.53 **Timing of dismissal notices**

One matter that often causes confusion is the relationship between the employer's duty to consult under S.188 and the duty to give proper notice to the employees to terminate their employment contracts. These are, of course, separate issues: redundancy dismissals must be effected in accordance with both the statutory consultation procedure and with the provisions as to notice contained in statute or employees' individual contracts.

The UK courts and tribunals have long insisted that consultation must begin before dismissal notices are sent out – see NUT v Avon County Council 1978 ICR 626, EAT. Furthermore, it is generally held that an employer cannot legitimately send out dismissal notices on the day after consultation began. For example, in TGWU v Ledbury Preserves (1928) Ltd 1985 IRLR 412, EAT, the Appeal Tribunal said that 'there must be sufficient meaningful consultation before notices of dismissal are sent out. The consultation must not be a sham exercise; there must be time for the union representatives who are consulted to consider properly the proposals that are being put to them.' But this approach still leaves open the possibility that in a long consultation procedure (i.e. 45 days), so long as the consultation has reached a meaningful stage, notice of dismissal can be given towards the end of the consultation process but before it actually finishes. So, an employer undertaking a 45-day consultation might validly give two weeks' notice of dismissal after 31 days, so that dismissals take effect at the end of the statutory consultation period but no later.

12.54 The ECJ considered the issue in Junk v Kühnel 2005 IRLR 310, ECJ, where the Court was asked to rule on the meaning of 'redundancy', as it appears in the Collective Redundancies Directive, in the context of German law. The relevant provisions of domestic legislation used two words for termination of employment: 'Kündigung', referring to a party's declaration of intention to terminate the employment relationship; and 'Entlassung', referring to the actual cessation of the employment. The existence of a legal distinction between the two meant that, under German law, a redundancy did not occur on the date on which the employer declared its intention to terminate the contracts of employment, but on the date when the individual periods of notice of redundancy expired. Accordingly, an employer was able to enter

436

consultation (and notify the relevant authority) after declaring its intention to terminate employment, since it would be doing so before the actual cessation of employment. The Berlin Labour Court queried whether this was compatible with the Directive.

The ECJ held that it was not. It considered that Articles 2–4 of the Directive must be construed as meaning that the event constituting redundancy consists of the declaration by an employer of its intention to terminate the contract of employment. An employer is not entitled to give notice of termination until *after the conclusion* of the consultation procedure set out in Article 2, and after notification of the projected collective redundancies to the competent public authority as provided for in Articles 3 and 4 (see 'Notification' below). The ECJ took the view that notification to a worker that his or her contract of employment has been terminated is the expression of a decision to sever the employment relationship, and the actual cessation of that relationship on the expiry of the period of notice is no more than the effect of that decision. Thus, for the purposes of the timing of the consultation procedure set down in the Directive, a redundancy dismissal must be deemed to take place on the day the employer gives notice, and not on the day that that notice expires. In other words, running the consultation period alongside the notice period is incompatible with the Directive.

At first glance, the Junk decision has significant implications for UK law. However, as we noted above, while the TULR(C)A sets down minimum consultation periods, the Directive does not. All the Directive requires is that consultation begins 'in good time' and with a view to reaching an agreement. With this in mind, Acas, in its guidance, 'Handling large-scale redundancies' (April 2014), states that 'redundancy notices must not be issued until collective and individual consultation has been completed' but that they may be given before the end of the minimum period, if the consultation is genuinely complete, so long as the dismissal itself does not take effect until the minimum period has expired and individual notice periods have been observed. In other words, there is no reason why an employer cannot give notice of dismissal, taking effect at the end of the minimum period, once the actual substance of the consultation has been completed. Take the example given above of an employer undertaking a 45-day consultation. If, by the 30-day point, all possibilities of avoiding redundancy have been explored and exhausted, the employer may still issue notices of dismissal taking effect 15 days later. The Directive, as interpreted by Junk, is satisfied because the substantive consultation and the notice period do not coincide. Moreover, the employer will also have abided by its TULR(C)A obligations – consultation began at least 45 days before the first dismissal 'takes effect' for S.188 purposes. To clarify, Acas takes the view that, regardless of Junk, the date on which a dismissal 'takes effect' under S.188 is the date of termination rather than the date on which notice of dismissal is given.

12.55

437

The same principle would presumably apply where an employer is undertaking a 30-day consultation (i.e. where it is proposed to dismiss as redundant between 20–99 employees within 90 days). However, unless employees' notice periods are very short and the consultation is over very quickly, there will inevitably be overlap between the notice period and the substantive consultation process, such as to render the procedure incompatible with the Directive. In these cases, it might be safer to hold off on issuing notices of dismissal until consultation has run for 30 days. While this will result in added expense for the employer at a bad time, avoiding the risk of a protective award arguably makes that a price worth paying – see 'Protective awards' below.

12.56 ## When does consultation end?

The TULR(C)A does not expressly set out when consultation is deemed to finish, which left the EAT to grapple with this issue in Vauxhall Motors Ltd v TGWU 2006 IRLR 674, EAT. In that case, VM Ltd proposed in January 2003 to dismiss 400 'temporary' employees engaged on 12-month fixed-term contracts at one of its plants, with the first dismissal taking effect on 25 April 2003 and the last on 5 September 2003. On 24 January 2003, VM Ltd gave notification of its intentions to the Secretary of State on the standard form HR1 (for which, see 'Notification' below); wrote to the TGWU, enclosing a copy of that form and providing further information about the proposals; and began consultation (all as required by Ss.188 and 193 TULR(C)A). The consultation was successful, with the temporary employees' contracts being extended and the proposed redundancies thus avoided. However, 46 of the temporary employees remained at risk of redundancy and, on 11 March 2004, VM Ltd successfully applied to the Department for Trade and Industry (DTI) for a six-month extension to the HR1 registered the year before. On 23 September the company told the union that there was no redundancy situation in relation to the remaining temporary employees. However, four days later it wrote to the DTI, explaining that the planned termination dates for the temporary employees was, by agreement with the union, extended to 22 October to allow for further consultation. With that letter the company lodged a new HR1, identifying 345 permanent staff for redundancy. The union was not given a copy of this. The company subsequently refused to add the remaining 46 temporary employees at risk of redundancy to the consultation process for the proposed 345 redundancies. On 26 November 2004 the temporary employees were dismissed.

On a complaint by the union, a tribunal found VM Ltd in breach of S.188. In its view, the relevant date for the purpose of considering whether VM Ltd had complied with its S.188 obligations was 27 September 2004, when the second HR1 was sent to the DTI. VM Ltd's refusal to include the 46 remaining temporary employees in the larger redundancy exercise meant that it had failed to engage in meaningful consultation or to provide the union

438

with relevant information, as required by S.188. The EAT overturned that decision on appeal. It was common ground that the requirement to provide information to the union was complied with in January 2003, along with the S.193 duty to send an HR1 to the DTI. The question was whether there came a time when the S.188 compliance was spent. The EAT agreed with the tribunal that S.188 does not have an unlimited shelf-life. Where, for instance, a company in grave financial difficulties serves a S.188(4) letter on a union and consultation begins, but redundancies are prevented because the company receives a large order, consultation ends at that point. If a year later the order is fulfilled with nothing to replace it, so that the employer needs to consider redundancies again, the original S.188 notice is spent and a fresh round of consultation is required.

However, the situation in the instant case was very different. The tribunal **12.57** had in fact found that there had been an ongoing dialogue between the company and the union about the status, extension and transfer of the temporary employees from January 2003 up until their eventual dismissals in November 2004. The tribunal, however, had confused matters and accordingly misdirected itself by holding that a second wave of consultation should have begun when the second HR1 was sent to the DTI in accordance with S.193. Had it confined its deliberations to the requirements of S.188, as it should have done, it would have found that there had been a seamless and meaningful consultation process from January 2003 right up until the date of the eventual dismissals; the 'elastic' of the S.188 compliance had not, therefore, been broken.

The Vauxhall decision should not be taken as laying down a general principle that a consultation procedure remains valid for a considerable period. Rather, it emphasises that tribunals' focus should be on the substance of a consultation rather than the timetable within which it takes place. The reference to 45 days in the TULR(C)A does not mean that, if consultation extends beyond that period, it must restart. So long as the consultation is meaningful, and deals with the same employees and the same prospective redundancies, there should be no grounds for finding a breach of S.188 simply because the dismissals only take effect some time after the procedure was instituted.

The consultation process

12.58

The nature of the consultation required of employers under S.188 TULR(C)A was changed by the Trade Union Reform and Employment Rights Act 1993 (TURERA) to bring that section into line with the Collective Redundancies Directive. S.188(2) now provides that the consultation must include consultation about ways of:

- avoiding the dismissals

439

- reducing the numbers of employees to be dismissed, and

- mitigating the consequences of the dismissals

and must be undertaken by the employer 'with a view to reaching agreement with the appropriate representatives'.

12.59 Meaningful consultation

The final requirement – that the objective of the consultation must be agreement – does not mean that both parties have to end up entirely satisfied with the outcome. The final decision on redundancies is one for the employer to take, and economic factors will often have to prevail over employees' interests. However, this requirement does mean that the consultation must at least be meaningful. In Susie Radin Ltd v GMB and ors 2004 ICR 893, CA, an employer found to be 'going through the motions' of consultation was held to be in breach of S.188, which, in the words of Lord Justice Peter Gibson, imposes an 'absolute obligation on the employer to consult, and to consult meaningfully'. The ECJ in Junk v Kühnel 2005 IRLR 310, ECJ, took a similar view, based on the same wording in Article 2(1) of the Directive, holding that the words 'with a view to reaching an agreement' connote an obligation to negotiate.

The Acas guidance, 'Handling large-scale redundancies', states that it is 'not necessary for the parties involved to reach agreement for the consultation to be complete. As long as there has been genuine consultation "with a view to reaching agreement", an employer can end the consultation' but this should be done only when it can demonstrate that it has 'listened and responded to the views and suggestions raised'. This means allowing enough time to discuss issues at a formative stage and giving real consideration to counter-proposals or suggestions. For employers and representatives to show that they have acted reasonably throughout their dealings, and as a matter of good practice, signed copies of any meeting minutes should be kept.

12.60 Substance of consultation

The amendments made to S.188 by the TURERA fundamentally changed the basis on which consultation takes place. Courts and tribunals tended to take a fairly narrow view of the sort of consultation employers were required to undertake under the unamended S.188. Although the EAT insisted that consultation must not be a 'sham' – see, for example, TGWU v Ledbury Preserves (1928) Ltd 1985 IRLR 412, EAT – consultation was largely restricted to the procedure for handling redundancies which the employer had already decided upon.

Since 1995, however, courts and tribunals have not shied away from imposing progressively more onerous consultation obligations on employers. One of the

440

leading cases on the substantive requirements of S.188(2) since the TURERA amendments, Middlesbrough Borough Council v TGWU and anor 2002 IRLR 332, EAT, established that the three features of redundancy consultation set out in S.188(2) – namely, consultation about ways of avoiding the dismissals, of reducing the numbers to be dismissed and of mitigating the consequences of the dismissals – are to be viewed disjunctively as three separate, mandatory duties of consultation. So, while an employer might genuinely consult with the unions about ways of reducing the number of employees to be dismissed and mitigating the consequences of those dismissals, it may still fail in its duty to engage in genuine consultation on the question of whether or not to declare redundancies at all, and so breach S.188. Furthermore, it is not open to an employer to argue that consultation about ways of avoiding the dismissals would, in the circumstances, be futile.

In Kelly and anor v Hesley Group Ltd 2013 IRLR 514, EAT, the EAT **12.61** stipulated that it is for the employer to address each of the matters listed in S.188(2). It is not enough for the employer simply to provide the opportunity for the employee representatives to raise their concerns.

Reasons for redundancies. It was long thought that consultation need not **12.62** be concerned with the economic background to the redundancy situation. In Securicor Omega Express Ltd v GMB 2004 IRLR 9, EAT, for example, the Appeal Tribunal held that there was no breach of S.188 when an employer did not consult with trade unions over redundancies arising from workplace closures until the decision to close the workplaces had already been taken. The employer had satisfied S.188 by consulting about ways of avoiding the dismissals that could result from the closures, reducing the number of employees to be dismissed, and mitigating the consequences of those dismissals. Although the consultation had to be fair and meaningful, and not a sham, there was no obligation on the employer to consult about the necessity of closing the workplaces in the first place.

However, this view – that the reasons behind a redundancy situation do not need to feature in employers' negotiations with employee representatives – was rejected by the EAT in UK Coal Mining Ltd v NUM (Northumberland Area) and anor 2008 ICR 163, EAT. There, an employer's decision to close a coal mine gave rise to an obligation to consult under the TULR(C)A. Although some consultation was instigated, the employer gave the union representatives a misleading reason for the closure, citing health and safety considerations rather than the economic concerns that were the true motivating factor. A tribunal found that there was a breach of S.188. The employer appealed, arguing that, since cases such as Securicor had established that there was no duty to consult about the reasons for a redundancy situation, giving a misleading reason for the closure could not affect the validity of the consultation procedure. The unions resisted that

441

argument and cross-appealed, asserting that the authorities were wrong to rule out consultation about the reasons for redundancy.

12.63 The EAT agreed with the unions. In its view, Article 2(2) of the Collective Redundancies Directive clearly requires consultation over a decision to close a plant, and had the Directive been properly implemented then the TULR(C)A would say this. The EAT recognised that there was an issue over whether the TULR(C)A could be interpreted to incorporate this requirement. However, it felt that the obligation to consult over avoiding proposed redundancies 'inevitably involves engaging with the reasons for the dismissals, and that in turn requires consultation over the reasons for the closure'. The EAT went on to note that, strictly, it is the proposed dismissals that are the subject of consultation rather than the closure itself, and that if the employer planned a closure but believed that redundancies could be avoided then there would be no obligation to consult under the TULR(C)A over the closure. Realistically, however, this would be an exceptional case, and where closure and dismissals are inextricably linked (as they almost always are), the duty to consult over the reasons for the closure arises.

Although the focus of the UK Coal Mining ruling was on workplace closures, there is no reason why the logic of the decision should not extend to any case of restructuring that might lead to multiple redundancies. As noted under 'Scope of duty to consult – definition of "redundancy"' above, 'redundancy', within the meaning of the TULR(C)A, is not limited to instances where there is a reduced need for work of a particular kind and can include fundamental changes in terms and conditions tantamount to a dismissal. In such cases, following the UK Coal Mining case, the reasons for such changes will have to be open to scrutiny. It is also worth noting that the lay members of the EAT in UK Coal Mining expressed the view that, in practice, the decision would not alter industrial arrangements very much, since most employers already inform union representatives about their reasons for considering the need to close a plant and are prepared to respond to union observations on the matter.

12.64 The decision in UK Coal Mining Ltd v NUM (Northumberland Area) and anor (above) has recently come under scrutiny in United States of America v Nolan 2011 IRLR 40, CA, which concerned the USA's decision to close a military base in Hampshire. The USA argued that, following the ECJ's decision in Akavan Erityisalojen Keskusliitto (AEK) ry and ors v Fujitsu Siemens Computers Oy 2010 ICR 444, ECJ, the Collective Redundancies Directive did not require consultation over a decision (including the reasons) to close a plant. The Court of Appeal accepted that, if Akavan is indeed authority for a narrower interpretation of the Directive, it followed that the UK Coal Mining decision was wrongly decided. However, as fully explained under 'Timetable for consultation – "proposing to dismiss"' above, the Appeal Court found the reasoning of the European Court

442

in Akavan 'difficult to follow' and therefore decided to make a reference to the ECJ to clarify its ruling. On 22 March 2012, Advocate General Mengozzi issued his opinion that the obligation to consult is triggered, within a group structure, when a body or entity that controls the employer makes a strategic or commercial decision which compels the employer to contemplate or to plan for collective redundancies. The Advocate General considered that this analysis, which he derived from Akavan, could apply to the closure of a military base, entailing collective redundancies of civilian staff, where the strategic decision had been taken at a much higher level. However, when the ECJ came to give its ruling, it decided that it had no jurisdiction to decide the matter because of Article 1(2)(b), which excludes from the Directive's scope 'workers employed by public administrative bodies or by establishments governed by public law'. Although the domestic legislation, i.e. S.188 TULR(C)A, makes no such exemption, the ECJ can only rule on the interpretation of the Directive, which simply did not apply in this case – United States of America v Nolan 2013 ICR 193, ECJ.

When the case returned to the Court of Appeal, the Court ordered a further hearing on the question of when the consultation obligation arose by reference purely to the domestic provisions. The USA then appealed against that decision to the Supreme Court, arguing that the collective consultation obligations under the TULR(C)A should not apply to the actions of a foreign state and that the Transfer of Undertakings (Protection of Employment) (Amendment) Regulations 1995 SI 1995/2587, which amended the scope of S.188 TULR(C)A in 1995, were ultra vires – United States of America v Nolan 2015 ICR 1347, SC. As discussed under 'Timetable for consultation – "proposing to dismiss"' above, these arguments were unsuccessful and the Supreme Court dismissed the appeal. The question of when consultation must start is therefore set to return to the Court of Appeal for further consideration.

It should be noted that the Acas guidance, 'Handling large-scale redundancies', does not state that employers must consult about the background reasons for the redundancies, but states that 'genuine consultations about the business reasons behind the proposed redundancies are more likely to produce creative solutions'. **12.65**

Disclosure of information **12.66**

Meaningful consultation between the employer and the appropriate representatives about a collective redundancy situation presupposes that the representatives have some knowledge of the employer's plans. As the Acas guidance, 'Handling large-scale redundancies' notes, certain information must be disclosed to the appropriate representatives 'so that they can play a constructive part in the consultation process'.

Section 188(4), which closely resembles Article 2(3) of the Directive, sets out the information that the employer must give to the representatives for

443

the purposes of the consultation. It states that the employer must disclose in writing to the appropriate representatives:

- the reasons for its proposals (but see 'Substance of consultation – reasons for redundancies' above)

- the numbers and descriptions of employees it proposes to dismiss as redundant

- the total number of employees of that description employed at the establishment in question

- the proposed method of selecting the employees who may be dismissed

- the proposed method of carrying out the dismissals, with due regard to any agreed procedure, including the period over which the dismissals are to take effect

- the proposed method of calculating the amount of any redundancy payments to be made (other than statutory redundancy pay) to employees who may be dismissed

- the number of agency workers working temporarily for and under the supervision and direction of the employer

- the parts of the employer's undertaking in which those agency workers are working, and

- the type of work those agency workers are carrying out.

12.67 The final three categories of information were added by the Agency Workers Regulations 2010 SI 2010/93 with effect from 1 October 2011. Employers use temporary agency workers for a number of reasons, often to cover for short-term absences among its permanent staff but also to fill job vacancies on a longer-term basis. The use of agency workers in the employer's business will usually be a topic for discussion when the parties come to consult about ways to avoid or mitigate any proposed dismissals – with appropriate representatives likely to suggest that the number of temporary staff should be reduced before the dismissals of any permanent staff are considered.

12.68 **Recipients of information.** In order to comply with S.188(4), the information must be given to the appropriate representatives. However, as we will discuss under 'Appropriate representatives' below, there is one exception to this. S.188(7B) provides that, if the employees have been invited to elect representatives but have failed to do so within a reasonable time, the employer must instead give the information required under S.188(4) directly to each affected employee.

12.69 **Timing of disclosure.** Section 188 does not expressly state when the information must be given, and it was thought initially that it must be disclosed

444

before the consultation begins – E Green and Son (Castings) Ltd and ors v ASTMS and anor 1984 ICR 352, EAT. However, the EAT revisited this issue in Securicor Omega Express Ltd v GMB 2004 IRLR 9, EAT. Considering S.188(4) in the light of Article 2(3) of the Directive, which requires the information to be given 'in good time during the course of the consultations', the EAT concluded that, in so far as the Green case requires a S.188 notice to be given before consultation begins, the judgment should not be followed. In its view, 'the service of a S.188 notice should not be a question of procedural or substantive bar wholly, but should form part of the wider question as to whether there has, in a particular case, been fair consultation'.

The issue of when, for the purposes of Article 2(3) of the Directive, the necessary information should be supplied to workers' representatives was considered by the ECJ in Akavan Erityisalojen Keskusliitto (AEK) ry and ors v Fujitsu Siemens Computers Oy 2010 ICR 444, ECJ. There, the European Court stressed that the wording of the Directive clearly envisioned such information being provided *during* consultations – the obligation to supply all the information required does not necessarily have to be fulfilled at the moment when consultation begins. Moreover, the rationale behind the provision was to enable workers to participate in the consultation process as fully as possible, which meant that the employer had to keep workers informed of developments and supply them with all the relevant information that became available at different times during the consultation process.

Adequacy of information. In MSF v GEC Ferranti (Defence Systems) Ltd (No.2) 1994 IRLR 113, EAT, the EAT held that there is no rule that failing to provide full and specific information under each of the S.188(4) heads must in all cases be treated as non-compliance with the statute. The EAT suggested that the headings are not necessarily of equal importance in every case and could not necessarily be treated as separate and distinct. The seriousness of the default, and whether it is such as to amount to non-compliance with S.188, is a question of fact for the tribunal. The later judgment in Securicor Omega Express Ltd v GMB (above) suggests that, in any event, even if a failure to provide adequate information amounts to non-compliance, the remedy may be adjusted to reflect the seriousness of the default. There, the S.188(4) notice was inadequate in that it contained no mention of the total number of employees at the establishment in question or the proposed method of calculating the redundancy payments. However, these were technical failures and the EAT decided that a nominal protective award of one day's pay was appropriate in the circumstances.

12.70

Nevertheless, the EAT in Kelly and anor v Hesley Group Ltd 2013 IRLR 514, EAT, made it clear that S.188(4) demands literal compliance. In that case, the employer's letter stating that the collective consultation related to its proposal to terminate the contracts of employment of employees who had

445

not agreed to new terms and conditions, to which 96 per cent had agreed, was insufficient. It did not, for example, contain the reasons for the proposed dismissals and it was not enough to say that the recipients would have known the reasoning from oral communications.

12.71 Section 188(4) does not lay down any guidance as to how specific and detailed the information must be. Article 2(3) of the Directive, however, says that the purpose of providing the employees with the information is to 'enable workers' representatives to make constructive proposals'. This suggests that a fairly high level of detail is required. Employers will be reluctant to disclose information that they consider sensitive, especially information that pertains to their financial circumstances. However, following the ruling in UK Coal Mining Ltd v NUM (Northumberland Area) and anor 2008 ICR 163, EAT, to the effect that employers must consult over the reasons behind a redundancy situation, they may have little choice. Furthermore, as Mr Justice Elias, then President of the EAT, noted in that case, the Information and Consultation of Employees Regulations 2004 SI 2004/3426, which impose general information and consultation obligations on all businesses with 50 or more employees, arguably require a similar level of disclosure.

It has been suggested that the S.188(4) list of information that the employer is required to provide may not be exhaustive. Article 2(3) of the Directive requires that employers shall, in good time during the course of consultations, provide representatives with 'all relevant information' but there is no comparable requirement in the TULR(C)A. However, in GMB v Amicus and ors and another case 2003 ICR 1396, EAT, the Appeal Tribunal opined that the draftsman can be taken to have assumed that 'all relevant information' would be contained in the matters set out in S.188(4) and that perhaps the reason for the omission was a wish for precision and clarity. If the EAT is correct about this, then this suggests that tribunals should resist the urge to attempt to interpret S.188(4) purposively and so read in notification requirements that are not set out in black and white.

12.72 **Adequacy of HR1 notice.** In MSF v GEC Ferranti (Defence Systems) Ltd (No.2) (above) the employer claimed to have satisfied the requirements of S.188(4) when it sent the union a copy of the HR1 form used to notify the Secretary of State of redundancies under S.193 – see 'Duty to give representatives copy of HR1' and 'Notification' below. The HR1 indicated the total number of proposed redundancies, the occupational groups affected and the number by which each group would be reduced, although the employer stressed that these figures were 'a best estimate only' and could change dramatically. In meetings with management, the union emphasised the importance of knowing what categories of employees would be affected and two weeks later, on 26 September, the union was given a more detailed breakdown of the redundancies by sector. On 7 October the employer issued the union with a list identifying the numbers and descriptions of the persons to be made redundant by reference to job category and location. An employment tribunal held that consultations began when the union received the HR1. On appeal, the EAT stressed that the question of whether sufficient information had been supplied depended on the facts and circumstances of the particular case. However, it stated that the tribunal had failed to give any proper consideration to the question and had not provided any reasons for its decision. The Appeal Tribunal went on to hold that the information in the HR1 was inadequate and that the employer only complied with S.188(4) when it provided the further information on 26 September.

Delivery of information. The information should be either given to the appropriate representatives or posted to an address notified by them to the employer or, in the case of trade union representatives, posted to the main or head office of the union – S.188(5). The question of what constitutes effective delivery of the information arose in National Association of Local Government Officers v London Borough of Bromley EAT 671/91. In that case the information regarding proposed redundancies was delivered to the union's office by hand on 19 December. When the employer's messenger entered the office he found it occupied by a woman who said that the relevant union officer was not in but that she would pass the delivery on to him when he returned. In the event, the union officer did not receive the information until 31 December. No explanation for the delay could be found and the identity of the woman to whom delivery was made could not be established. The EAT held that the information had nevertheless been properly delivered when it was handed into the union's office, not when it finally reached the relevant official. A delivery is effected for the purposes of S.188(5) when the information is given to an individual whom the deliverer reasonably believes has authority to receive it. **12.73**

Duty to give representatives copy of HR1 **12.74**
There is one further information right enjoyed by employee/trade union representatives. Whenever an employer is proposing redundancies on a scale that triggers the consultation procedures of S.188, it will be under a duty to notify the Secretary of State of those redundancies – S.193(1) and (2) (see 'Notification' below). In addition to notifying the Secretary of State, S.193(6) provides that the employer must give a copy of the notice (usually termed an HR1 form) to each of the representatives who are to be consulted under S.188. There does not appear to be any remedy in the case of an employer who fails to comply with this requirement, however.

Access to employees and facilities **12.75**
Finally, in relation to the consultation process, note that an employer must allow the representatives with whom it is consulting access to the affected

447

employees and must afford those representatives such accommodation and other facilities as may be appropriate – S.188(5A). This requirement is also important as a matter of good practice and as a means of achieving meaningful consultation. The Acas guidance, 'Trade Union representation in the workplace' (March 2014), states that 'employers should, where practical, make available to union representatives the facilities necessary for them to perform their duties efficiently and to communicate effectively with their members, other representatives and full time officers'. Included within the guide are examples of the sorts of facilities that might be appropriate, including office space and accommodation for meetings, noticeboards, telephones, and use of electronic media such as e-mail, intranet and internet. It states that 'the provision of fully equipped temporary office space will be particularly beneficial in helping [representatives] discharge their duties, especially where a large number of employees are affected directly and indirectly'.

12.76 'Appropriate representatives'

The Collective Redundancies Directive requires Member States to introduce legislation obliging employers who are contemplating redundancies to consult with 'workers' representatives'. However, S.188 TULR(C)A originally required employers to consult only where the employees were members of a recognised trade union. Therefore, an employer who did not recognise a trade union did not have to comply with the statutory consultation requirement. This was declared unlawful by the ECJ in Commission of the European Communities v United Kingdom 1994 ICR 664, ECJ, and accordingly the Collective Redundancies and Transfer of Undertakings (Protection of Employment) (Amendment) Regulations 1995 SI 1995/2587 ('the 1995 Regulations') amended S.188 so that employers were placed under a duty to consult with the 'appropriate representatives' of the affected employees. One aspect of this amendment which raised many eyebrows at the time was that it had the effect that, even where the employer recognised a trade union, it was able to bypass that union and consult instead with employee representatives if it saw fit. This controversial aspect of the consultation provisions was subsequently removed by amendments introduced by the Collective Redundancies and Transfer of Undertakings (Protection of Employment) (Amendment) Regulations 1999 SI 1999/1925 ('the 1999 Regulations'), which ensure that a recognised trade union can no longer be lawfully left out of the consultation process.

Section 188 now defines the 'appropriate representatives' of the affected employees with whom the employer must consult as follows:

- if the employees are of a description in respect of which an independent trade union is recognised by the employer, then the 'appropriate representatives' are the representatives of the trade union – S.188(1B)(a)

- in any other case (i.e. where the employees are not represented by a union recognised by the employer), the employer can choose to consult either: (i) employee representatives who were appointed or elected by the affected employees for a purpose other than redundancy consultation but 'who (having regard to the purposes for and the method by which they were appointed or elected) have authority from those employees to receive information and to be consulted about the proposed dismissals on their behalf'; or (ii) employee representatives elected by the affected employees for the purposes of redundancy consultation (the election must be in accordance with S.188A(1) – see 'Election of employee representatives' below) – S.188(1B)(b).

We shall consider each of these categories of representatives in turn. However, **12.77** in determining the 'appropriate representatives' within their organisation for the purposes of redundancy consultation, employers may find it useful to consider the following, necessarily sequential, questions:

(1) is an independent trade union (or more than one) recognised in respect of *all* the affected employees? If the answer is 'yes', the employer must consult with the recognised union(s)

(2) if the answer to (1) is 'no', is an independent trade union (or more than one) recognised in respect of some of the affected employees? If the answer is 'yes', the employer must consult with the recognised union(s) and either existing employee representatives who have authority to consult on behalf of affected employees who are not represented by a union or with employee representatives specially elected for that purpose

(3) if the answer to (2) is 'no' because there is no independent trade union recognised at the employer's workplace, the employer must either consult with existing employee representatives who have authority to consult on behalf of affected employees or with employee representatives specially elected for that purpose.

Trade union representatives

12.78

The effect of S.188(1B) is that, if affected employees – or, to use the words of the statute, employees 'of a description' – are represented by a recognised, independent trade union, the employer must inform and consult representatives of that trade union, as opposed to other employee representatives. The Acas guidance, 'Trade Union representation in the workplace', confirms this, stating that 'where a trade union is recognised, consultation... must be with the union representatives.'

'Independent' and 'recognised' trade union. Section 188(1B) does not compel **12.79** an employer to consult with the representatives of a trade union unless that union is 'independent' and 'recognised'. Both concepts are discussed in detail in IDS

Employment Law Handbook, 'Trade Unions' (2013), but for present purposes it suffices to set out the basic statutory requirements that must be met.

12.80 *Independence.* The law acknowledges that, for trade unions to carry out their functions properly, they must be truly independent of employers. There is a statutory definition of 'independence', found in S.5 TULR(C)A, which provides that a union is independent if it is not under the domination or control of an employer, and not liable to interference by an employer (arising out of the provision of financial or material support or by other means) tending towards such control.

Note that a listed trade union – that is, one found on the list of unions maintained by the Certification Officer – may apply to the Certification Officer under S.6(1) TULR(C)A for a certificate stating that it satisfies the statutory definition of independence.

12.81 For further consideration of trade union independence, see IDS Employment Law Handbook, 'Trade Unions' (2013), Chapter 1, 'Trade unions', under 'Independence'.

12.82 *Recognition.* Put simply, 'recognition' is the process by which an employer accepts a trade union as being entitled to act on behalf of a particular group (or groups) of workers for some purpose. S.178(3) TULR(C)A provides that a recognised trade union is one that is recognised 'by an employer, or two or more associated employers, to any extent, for the purposes of collective bargaining'. 'Collective bargaining' encompasses negotiations relating to or connected with one or more of the following:

- terms and conditions of employment, or the physical conditions in which any workers are required to work

- engagement or non-engagement, termination or suspension of employment

- allocation of work between workers or groups of workers

- disciplinary matters

- a worker's membership or non-membership of a trade union

- facilities for trade union officials, and

- machinery for negotiation or consultation, and other procedures, relating to any of the above matters, including the recognition by employers or employers' associations of the right of a trade union to represent workers in such negotiation or consultation or in the carrying out of such procedures – S.178 TULR(C)A.

Recognition can be either voluntary on the part of the employer or compulsory under the complex statutory scheme contained in Schedule A1 to the TULR(C)A.

450

See IDS Employment Law Handbook, 'Trade Unions' (2013), Chapter 5, 'Trade union recognition', and Chapter 6, 'Statutory recognition', for further details.

No need to be member of recognised union. It is important to note that S.188(1B) does not stipulate that a trade union representative can only be an 'appropriate representative' for the purposes of redundancy consultation where the affected employees are, in fact, members of the union. Instead, the provision makes it clear that the affected employees must be 'employees... of a description' in respect of which the union is recognised by the employer. It is therefore the class or category of employees that the union represents that is relevant here, not whether any particular employee is a member of the union. **12.83**

It follows from this that an employer may be obliged to consult a union even if the employees to be dismissed or otherwise affected by the dismissals are not actually members of that union. In Governing Body of the Northern Ireland Hotel and Catering College and anor v NATFHE 1995 IRLR 83, NICA, the employer recognised two independent trade unions for collective bargaining purposes in respect of its college lecturers, the NATFHE and the NASUWT. When two lecturers at one of the employer's colleges faced redundancy, the employer consulted with their union, which was the NASUWT. The NATFHE argued that it should have been included in the consultation because it was recognised by the employer in respect of employees 'of a description' whom it proposed to dismiss, i.e. college lecturers, even though it had no members at that particular college. The Court, examining the relevant Northern Ireland provision that mirrored S.188(1B) (but which has since been repealed), agreed. In its view, if Parliament had intended to limit the requirement to consult to a case where the employee was a member of the recognised union, it would have been simple to state that in clear terms. Moreover, the Court pointed out that, even though the union may not be concerned to protect individual non-members, it may be interested in preserving the jobs being made redundant. The NATFHE should accordingly have been consulted over the proposed redundancies.

Union 'representatives'. Any consultation must take place with 'representatives' of the trade union, which are defined by S.196(2) as officials or other persons authorised by the trade union to carry on collective bargaining with the employer. Employers should therefore ensure that they are consulting with persons who have the appropriate authority to conduct negotiations for the trade union. This could be a shop steward, a district union official or a national or regional official. **12.84**

In GMWU v Wailes Dove Bitumastic Ltd 1977 IRLR 45, ET, a tribunal held that an employer fully complied with S.188 when it consulted a shop steward about redundancies, and other union officials had no right to any further consultation. In that case the employer consulted the recognised shop steward with whom it customarily negotiated. Some time later it notified the union's regional organiser that redundancies were anticipated. The regional organiser demanded a meeting with the employer but this was refused because consultation had already taken place with the shop steward. The tribunal held that consultation with the shop steward was sufficient and that there was no need for the employer to have consulted the regional organiser as well.

12.85   Employee representatives

Where there is no recognised union, or the affected employees are not of a description in respect of which an independent trade union is recognised, the employer must consult with 'employee representatives' – S.188(1B)(b). As mentioned under 'Appropriate representatives' above, the employer has a choice between consulting existing employee representatives or employee representatives that have been elected by the affected employees specifically for the purposes of the consultation. Regardless of which route the employer decides to take, the employee representatives must be employed by the employer at the time of their election or appointment – S.196(1) TULR(C)A.

12.86   Existing employee representatives

One option, then, is for the employer to inform and consult 'employee representatives appointed or elected by the affected employees otherwise than for the purposes of [redundancy consultation], who (having regard to the purposes for and the method by which they were appointed or elected) have authority from those employees to receive information and to be consulted about the proposed dismissals on their behalf' – S.188(1B)(b)(i) TULR(C)A.

The employer may therefore consult through an existing consultative body, such as a staff council, even though the existing employee representatives were not appointed or elected for the specific purpose of being consulted about proposed redundancies. What matters is that these employee representatives have suitable authority from the affected employees to consult about that issue on their behalf. The Acas guidance, 'Handling large-scale redundancies', states that any existing body – and it gives the example of a body formed for the purposes of the Information and Consultation of Employees Regulations 2004 SI 2004/3426 (the ICE Regulations) – 'must have a broad enough remit to discuss redundancy issues'.

12.87   The importance of the statutory wording in determining whether members of an existing consultative body are 'appropriate representatives' for the purposes of S.188(1B)(b)(i) was emphasised by the EAT in Kelly and anor v Hesley Group Ltd 2013 IRLR 514, EAT. The employer in that case chose to consult the existing 'joint consultative committee' (JCC), which was set up as an advisory body to communicate the views of staff to management and vice versa. Representatives were elected following nomination, although the employer also co-opted members onto the committee. The JCC's constitution expressly stated that it did not have a negotiating function. The EAT held that an employment tribunal had erred in concluding that members of the JCC were appropriate representatives for the purpose of S.188(1B)(b)(i) because it had failed to deal specifically with the matters that it was required to consider under the statute. In particular, it had not established whether the JCC had the employees' authority to represent them for the purpose of collective redundancies.

In United States of America v Nolan 2011 IRLR 40, CA, the employer argued that N was not an 'appropriate representative' for TULR(C)A purposes because, having been elected to the Local National Executive Council (LNEC) following the announcement of redundancies, she had not been elected by the affected employees 'otherwise than for the purposes of [S.188]'. Rather, she had been specifically elected for that purpose, which meant that she fell within S.188(1B)(b)(ii) and her election would then have to satisfy the detailed electoral requirements set out in S.188A (see 'Election of employee representatives' below). As those requirements had not been met, she had no standing to claim a protective award under S.189 (see 'Complaints about breach of S.188' below). The EAT was not convinced that this was what actually happened in the case. It thought that, while it was overwhelmingly likely that the LNEC's work from the date of N's election would be concerned with the proposed redundancies, N might have been elected to deal with a variety of matters relating to those redundancies, including but not limited to consultation under S.188, in which case her election as an employee representative would be valid. However, the tribunal had not made the necessary findings of fact to determine whether N had been validly elected for the purposes of S.188(1B)(b)(i), and the issue was remitted to the tribunal. On appeal, the Court of Appeal upheld the EAT's decision. (Note that this point did not form part of the USA's arguments in its appeal to the Supreme Court – United States of America v Nolan 2015 ICR 1347, SC.)

ICE Regulations. Employee representatives elected under the ICE Regulations will often satisfy the description of existing representatives set out in S.188(1B)(b)(i), provided, of course, that their remit is sufficiently broad. The ICE Regulations, which apply to businesses with at least 50 employees, give free rein to employers and employee representatives to agree the issues on which the representatives will be entitled to be informed and consulted. If, however, the agreement does not extend to redundancy and/or reorganisation, the representatives may not be competent to undertake consultation under the TULR(C)A. **12.88**

Although employers and employees are free to negotiate any type of information and consultation agreement under the ICE Regulations, there is a standard agreement that applies where such negotiations prove fruitless. The

453

standard agreement is set out in Regs 18–20 and expressly covers decisions likely to lead to a redundancy situation, as defined by the TULR(C)A – Reg 20(1)(c)(i). However, when the S.188 duty to consult arises, the employer is free to comply with its duties under the TULR(C)A instead of those under the ICE Regulations, provided that the employer notifies the ICE representatives in writing of its intention to do so – Reg 20(5). Thus, an employer may choose to conduct elections for employee representatives specifically for the redundancy consultation rather than go along with the default agreement in place under the ICE Regulations.

12.89 ## Election of employee representatives
If there are no trade union or appropriate employee representatives already in existence, then it will be necessary to elect employee representatives specifically for the purpose of redundancy consultation. The employer may also decide to elect new employee representatives where it does not want to use existing ones, perhaps because it is unsure as to whether the latter have authority to consult on behalf of the affected employees. Any election that ensues should be conducted in accordance with the detailed list of requirements for the election of employee representatives set out in S.188A.

Section 188A(1) provides that:

- the employer must make such arrangements as are reasonably practical to ensure that the election is fair – S.188A(1)(a)

- it is the employer's responsibility to determine the number of representatives to be elected. The employer must ensure that there are sufficient representatives to represent the interests of all the affected employees, having regard to the number and classes of those employees – S.188A(1)(b)

- the employer must determine whether the affected employees should be represented either by representatives of all the affected employees or by representatives of particular classes of those employees – S.188A(1)(c)

- before the election the employer must determine the employee representatives' term of office. The term of office must be long enough to enable the information and consultation process to be completed – S.188A(1)(d)

- the candidates for election as employee representatives must, on the date of the election, be affected employees – S.188A(1)(e)

- no affected employee may be unreasonably excluded from standing for election – S.188A(1)(f)

- all those who are affected employees on the date of the election are entitled to vote – S.188A(1)(g)

- the employees may vote for as many candidates as there are representatives

454

to be elected to represent them or their particular class of employee – S.188A(1)(h)

- so far as is reasonably practicable, voting must be in secret and the election should be conducted so as to ensure that the votes are accurately counted – S.188A(1)(i).

Furthermore, S.188A(2) provides that if, following an election, one of the successful candidates ceases to act as an employee representative and any of the employees are no longer represented as a result, then another election must be held – in accordance with S.188A(1)(a), (e), (f) and (i) – to elect a new employee representative.

12.90

The legislation is silent as to how many representatives must be elected, but states that this will depend on the number and classes of affected employees. Given the use of the word 'representatives' in the plural throughout Ss.188 and 188A, it seems likely that a single representative will not be sufficient. To some extent, the number of employee representatives the employer chooses will depend on whether it decides that, in accordance with S.188A(1)(c), affected employees should be represented either by representatives of all the affected employees or by representatives of particular classes of employee who may be affected by the proposed dismissals. The latter may increase the overall number of employee representatives, but has the obvious advantage of ensuring that the interests of each group of affected employees is represented.

In Robson v Domino UK Ltd ET Case No.1400506/09 the tribunal found that the employer unreasonably excluded an employee from standing for election as a representative in breach of S.188A(1)(f). D Ltd proposed to make a number of redundancies across its business, triggering the S.188 duty to consult. It then invited all affected staff to apply for election as employee representatives. D Ltd wished to appoint two employee representatives for its sales team and R put himself forward. However, his application was rejected on the basis that D Ltd wanted the representatives to be from the Cambridge Head Office (R worked from home) because that was where most of the affected employees were likely to be based and where the consultation meetings would take place, and where photocopying and other facilities were more readily available, and it did not wish to take R out of the 'sales loop' while consultation was ongoing. The tribunal found, having regard to the company's statement that all affected employees were entitled to stand for election, that it was not reasonable for it to reject R's application. Furthermore, R was told to stop acting as a salesman during the consultation month, most of the company's sales staff were not based in Cambridge, and the tribunal did not think that the cost of the arrangement or the convenience of having people in head office could outweigh employees' rights under S.188A.

12.91

455

12.92   **No need to hold ballot.** The statutory requirement to 'elect' representatives pursuant to S.188A was scrutinised by the EAT in Phillips v Xtera Communications Ltd 2012 ICR 171, EAT. XC Ltd, a technology company, intended to close its Harold Wood site, thereby triggering the collective redundancy consultation obligations. It decided that two employee representatives would be needed and the staff provided the names of two volunteers. Another person then volunteered and the company agreed to proceed with three employee representatives. No staff objected to this process of selection. Following his redundancy, P complained that XC Ltd was in breach of its duty to consult under the 1992 Act because it failed to hold an 'election' for the employee representatives as required by S.188A.

The EAT rejected his complaint, holding that XC Ltd had complied with S.188A because the provision could not be interpreted as forcing an employer to hold a ballot where the number of candidates precisely matched the number of available places for elected representatives. The statutory scheme's aim is to ensure that in larger-scale redundancy situations the interests of the employees are collectively represented by those of their number whom they have chosen to represent them. The function of S.188A is to ensure a fair process for identification of those representatives by way of election. But it could not be said that Parliament intended to compel the employer to conduct a ballot in every circumstance. Where, as in this case, the number of candidates precisely tallies with the number of representatives to be elected, the employer would only expend valuable time and resources on a wholly unnecessary exercise. It therefore concluded that the statute does not require a ballot in an uncontested election.

12.93   The Appeal Tribunal did acknowledge that the absence of a requirement to hold a ballot may enable an employer to 'rig' the nomination process – for instance, by identifying favoured 'yes men' among its staff and encouraging them to stand for election and then creating a matching number of vacancies for employee representatives. That said, it was adamant that S.188A(1) itself contains sufficient protection against manipulation of this sort in that S.188A(1)(a) requires that the employer make arrangements 'to ensure that the election is fair'.

The Phillips case was distinguished in Akhbar and ors v Comet Group Ltd (in Creditor's Voluntary Liquidation) and anor ET Case No.1102571/12. There, the tribunal decided that since the representatives had not been elected, none were proper representatives for the purposes of consultation. There was no evidence to show that the representatives had 'authority from those employees to receive information and to be consulted about the proposed dismissals' and no information about how the representatives were appointed or elected or what their purposes were. It said that the reasoning in Phillips was premised on the employer's initial proposal to hold an election and established that where the number of candidates put forward matches the number of vacancies, there is no need to hold an actual ballot. However, the EAT in that case did not consider the position where the employer never proposed to hold an election at all. In the instant case, a majority of the representatives were effectively selected by management; they were asked or nominated by managers to stand. The tribunal considered that 'the system was wide open to abuse if managers had wished, contrary to their instruction, to abuse it'. The promise of a fair election provides a crucial safeguard for employees in such circumstances. More fundamentally, elections are a key ingredient of the statutory scheme for consultation in S.188 because they confer authority on representatives. There was no evidence that the selected representatives had authority to reach agreement on behalf of their constituents on the key statutory issues: avoiding, reducing, or mitigating the effects of proposed redundancies. Rather, their role was to receive information and to raise questions and proposals. The tribunal was not persuaded that the representatives nominated, largely by managers, had authority to represent the affected employees. As such the employer had not complied with S.188.

Delay in electing representatives. There are specific provisions for dealing with the potential delaying effect of having to elect representatives prior to consultation. S.188(7A) provides that where an employer has invited any of the affected employees to elect employee representatives, and the invitation was issued in time to allow the employees to elect the representatives before the date when the consultation is required to begin, the employer shall be taken to have complied with its obligations if it consults or informs as soon as is reasonably practicable after the election. What this means is that if the employer misses the applicable minimum consultation period because it is waiting for representatives to be elected, then this will not amount to a breach of S.188 so long as the employees have been given sufficient time to elect representatives and the employer has consulted as soon as possible after the election. No light is thrown on what is an appropriate time to allow for an election to take place, which will be a question of fact for the tribunal to decide. If other employee elections are conducted among the workforce, the timescale for these may be relevant here. **12.94**

Duty to inform individuals. Note that S.188(7B) provides that if affected employees, having been invited by the employer to elect representatives, fail to do so within a reasonable time, the employer must provide each affected employee with the information set out in S.188(4) (see 'The consultation process – disclosure of information' above). **12.95**

Statutory protection for appropriate representatives **12.96**

Elected employee representatives, and candidates for such elections, enjoy certain rights and protections under the Employment Rights Act 1996 (ERA).

457

These are the right to time off to fulfil their duties and the right not to be selected for redundancy, to be dismissed or to suffer a detriment for a reason connected with their status or activities as employee representatives – see Ss.47(1), 61–63, 103 and 105 ERA. Trade union representatives who are also employees enjoy similar rights under the TULR(C)A – see Ss.146, 152, 153 and 168 TULR(C)A.

In addition, S.47(1A) ERA gives employees the right not to be subjected to a detriment by any act, or any failure to act, by the employer done on the ground that the employee participated in an election of employee representatives. The wording of this provision appears wide enough to protect both the organisers of elections and those who vote in them, as well as the actual candidates.

12.97 Section 47 – the right not to suffer a detriment – does not apply if the detriment in question amounts to a dismissal – S.47(2). This is because dismissal is dealt with separately in S.103 ERA. S.103(1) provides that it is automatically unfair to dismiss an employee on the ground that he or she performed or proposed to perform any of the functions or activities of an elected employee representative or of a candidate in an election for such representatives. S.103(2) extends this protection to those participating in the election of representatives. It provides that a dismissal will be regarded as unfair if the principal reason for the dismissal 'is that the employee took part in an election of employee representatives' for collective redundancy purposes.

12.98 ## Special circumstances defence

There is a 'defence' open to employers that have failed to comply fully with the information and consultation requirements of S.188 TULR(C)A. S.188(7) provides that if there are 'special circumstances which render it not reasonably practicable' for an employer to comply with a requirement to:

- begin consultation in good time and within the applicable minimum period (S.188(1A))

- consult about ways of avoiding or reducing the dismissals and mitigating their consequences (S.188(2)), or

- disclose information to the appropriate representatives for the purposes of consultation (S.188(4)),

the employer need only take such steps towards compliance with that requirement as are reasonably practicable in the circumstances. The onus is on the employer to show both that there were special circumstances and that it took all reasonably practicable steps – S.189(6).

458

What are 'special circumstances'?

There is no definition of 'special circumstances' in the TULR(C)A. In Clarks of Hove Ltd v Bakers' Union 1978 ICR 1076, CA, the Court of Appeal held that a 'special circumstance' must be something 'exceptional', 'out of the ordinary' or 'uncommon'. Indeed, since the purpose of the consultation requirements is to allow planning for, and consultation on, a redundancy situation, in order to constitute special circumstances making it not reasonably practicable to consult fully, the situation must usually be unexpected or have very specific and unusual characteristics.

Even where special circumstances are shown, these do not absolve the employer from complying with the consultation requirements in respect of which compliance was reasonably practicable or which were not affected by the special circumstances. The employer must still take all steps towards compliance as are reasonably practicable in the circumstances of the case. In Shanahan Engineering Ltd v Unite the Union EAT 0411/09 SE Ltd, an engineering construction firm contracted to work on a new power station, was urgently required by its client, Alstom, to reduce the number of workers it had on site to alleviate health and safety problems caused by congestion and ground conditions. Within three days, SE Ltd had selected around 50 employees for redundancy according to agreed selection criteria and dismissed them with one week's notice. The EAT agreed with a tribunal's finding that 'special circumstances' applied to relieve the employer of the obligation to undertake the full 30-day consultation over collective redundancies, but that it should still have made some attempt at consultation. The EAT stated: 'The instructions given by Alstom made it inevitable that the workforce on the contract would have to be reduced; but it remained for Shanahan to decide whether employees should be dismissed for redundancy, how many employees should be dismissed, when they should be dismissed, and what if anything ought to be done to mitigate the consequences of dismissal. These were proper matters for consultation; it was the aim of the legislation that there should be consultation with a view to agreement if possible on these issues.'

Below we consider some of the more common situations in which employers plead special circumstances. It is worth noting that while some of these may not be 'special' enough to excuse lack of consultation, they may nevertheless be taken into account by a tribunal when considering the remedy for breach of S.188 – see 'Protective awards' below. There is one situation which will *never* amount to special circumstances and that is where the decision leading to the proposed dismissals is taken by 'a person' who controls the employer (e.g. a parent company) and that person fails to provide the employer with the necessary information. We deal with this exclusion from the scope of S.188(7) first.

Exclusion from defence. Although the TULR(C)A does not define 'special circumstances', it does specify one situation that *cannot* constitute a S.188(7) defence in respect of a failure to consult. This exception is contained in the second limb of S.188(7) and provides that where 'the decision leading to the proposed dismissals is that of a person controlling the employer (directly or indirectly)' and that person fails to provide 'information' to the employer, the employer cannot rely on that failure as a special circumstance excusing lack of compliance with S.188. This provision, which was introduced by the Trade Union Reform and Employment Rights Act 1993, derives from the Directive.

The scope of this exclusion from the 'special circumstances' defence was considered by the EAT in GMB v Amicus and ors and another case 2003 ICR 1396, EAT. Its key conclusion was that 'information' referred to in S.188(7) includes not only the specific information the employer is required to give to employee representatives under S.188(4), but also any information that an employer needs in order to begin a redundancy consultation process. The employer in that case therefore could not rely on the 'special circumstances' defence where there had been a delay in its receipt of information about a decision leading to proposed dismissals taken by a controlling undertaking.

12.102 The EAT set out a practical example to show how the exception operates. It described a hypothetical situation where a parent company decides that a wholly-owned subsidiary operating one plant with 100 employees must cease trading. The parent company makes that decision on day one, but does not inform its subsidiary until day 90. The subsidiary ceases trading on day 91 and dismisses all of its employees on that day. Owing to the operation of the exception contained in the second limb of S.188(7), the subsidiary would not be permitted to rely upon the parent company's delay in notifying it of its decision as a reason for non-compliance with its statutory consultation obligations. The EAT went on to explain that if the parent company's delay in informing its subsidiary were only 30 days, it would be only the delay of 30 days which would fall to be ignored for the purposes of the special circumstances defence. The EAT further explained that if, in this second situation, the dismissals could not be avoided before a further 60 days had elapsed (meaning that the 90-day consultation period could not have been achieved in any event), the parent company's decision to close the plant might still amount to 'special circumstances' rendering the subsidiary's compliance with S.188 not reasonably practicable.

12.103 **Insolvency and financial crises.** Many redundancies are the consequence of difficult financial circumstances, which may themselves lead to insolvency. In Clarks of Hove Ltd v Bakers' Union (above) the Court of Appeal pointed out that insolvency is not on its own a 'special circumstance'. Far from being 'exceptional' or 'out of the ordinary', insolvency is in fact a fairly common occurrence. In the Court's view, whether special circumstances exist will depend entirely on the cause of the insolvency. If, for example, sudden disaster strikes a company, making it necessary to close, then plainly that would be capable of being a special circumstance, and that is so whether the disaster is physical or financial. But where the insolvency is due to a gradual running down of the company, a tribunal is entitled to conclude that there are no special circumstances. In the Bakers' Union case the company was in financial difficulties and required about £100,000 to meet its obligations. Because of an adverse report on its affairs, a crucial loan was refused. The last hope that some of the company's shops might be sold off proved to be ill-founded and redundancy notices were sent out. The Court of Appeal upheld the tribunal's finding that these facts disclosed no special circumstances.

Similarly, in GMB v Messrs Rankin and Harrison (as joint administrative receivers of Lawtex plc and Lawtex Babywear Ltd) 1992 IRLR 514, EAT, the EAT held that the dismissal of workers to make an insolvent company more attractive to investors, and the subsequent closure of the workplace when no buyer came forward, were incidents common to any form of receivership or insolvency. They were by no means sufficiently unexpected or out of the ordinary as to constitute special circumstances excusing the employer's failure to consult. And in In re Hartlebury Printers Ltd and ors (in liquidation) 1992 ICR 559, ChD, it was held that the fact that a company is under an administration order is not in itself a special circumstance.

12.104 Even if redundancies do flow from a sudden, unexpected event, that event must be looked at in context to see if its ramifications justify dispensing with the requirements of S.188. For example, in Industrial Chemicals Ltd v Reeks and ors EAT 0076/04 the employer was not permitted to rely on the special circumstances defence where the reason for redundancy dismissals was the loss of a large contract for the supply of a particular chemical called 'SAP'. The chemical was produced at a plant by a workforce of 61 employees. The decision to withdraw the SAP contract was made on 7 August and in letters written on 15 August IC Ltd informed the workforce that it had taken the view that SAP production would have to stop on 16 August. It therefore considered that the majority of the employees would be made redundant immediately (albeit with notice), although some 19 staff would be retained for a short period in order to finalise some work on the contract. The employer cited the 'speed and critical nature of developments' culminating in the loss of the SAP contract as the reason why it had not been reasonably practicable to undertake TULR(C)A consultation. However, a tribunal – upheld by the EAT on appeal – considered that the chronology of events and the employer's circumstances fell a long way short of the special circumstances envisaged by S.188(7). It noted that although IC Ltd had trade debts of £5 million, the company held large amounts of assets and had a turnover of £62 million per year. In the tribunal's view, IC Ltd had reached an entirely commercial decision to cut all future loss flowing from the SAP plant at the earliest opportunity and had proceeded on the assumption that the sudden cessation of production excused its consultation obligations. However, the company had provided insufficient information to the tribunal to justify that assumption.

461

There are cases, however, where financial crises have been held to constitute special circumstances. In Hamish Armour (Receiver of Barry Staines) v ASTMS 1979 IRLR 24, EAT, for example, a company ran into financial difficulties and, having already received one government loan, applied for another in December. On 12 January this was refused, although an alternative source was suggested. When this too was refused on 3 February the company went into receivership. Four days later the receiver dismissed the workforce without notice. The EAT held that there were special circumstances. It thought that an application for a second government loan in these circumstances was sufficiently special to make it not reasonably practicable to provide the information required by S.188(4) until the outcome of the application was known.

12.105 In USDAW v Leancut Bacon Ltd (in liquidation) 1981 IRLR 295, EAT, the Appeal Tribunal followed the Hamish Armour approach and held that special circumstances existed where a withdrawal of a takeover offer by a third party led to a bank immediately placing an ailing company into receivership. Although receivership might not be unusual in such circumstances, the financial deterioration was sufficiently sudden to be a special circumstance.

12.106 **Unexpected loss of work.** In Howlett Marine Services Ltd v AEEU EAT 253/98 a tribunal found that special circumstances existed where the employer was entirely unexpectedly told by the contractor to whom it provided labour that staff cuts would be needed. The tribunal found that the decision made by the contractor was out of the ordinary, exceptional and uncommon. This was particularly so as the project on which the employees were engaged was expected to last for several months more and the amount of work involved had increased rapidly since the start of the project, to the point where overtime was being worked. However, the contractor then repeated its instruction to de-man a week later. The tribunal found that, in respect of that second instruction, special circumstances could not be said to apply – in the light of the first order from the contractor to cut staffing levels, the second order could not have been entirely unexpected. The EAT upheld this approach on appeal.

12.107 **Ignorance.** The employer's mistaken belief that it is not obliged to consult is not a special circumstance, even when it relies on Government advice – UCATT v H Rooke and Son (Cambridge) Ltd 1978 ICR 818, EAT.

12.108 **Consultation would be futile.** In Amicus v GBS Tooling Ltd (in administration) 2005 IRLR 683, EAT, the Appeal Tribunal commented (obiter) that if consultation were genuinely futile, perhaps because the future of the business is out of the employer's hands to the extent that there is simply no time for consultation to take place at all, that might be relevant to making out a 'special circumstances' defence.

12.109 **Keeping closure or takeover secret.** In NUJ v The Western Times Company Ltd ET Case No.7819/87 a tribunal held that the employer's need to keep

462

the closure of a newspaper secret, in order to avoid a considerable loss of immediate advertising revenue, was not a special circumstance. The tribunal said that most trading companies faced with large-scale redundancies could apply the same argument.

Problem industries. In some industries – like construction and shipbuilding – workers are sometimes taken on for specific jobs in the knowledge that when the job is completed redundancies will be necessary. In Amalgamated Society of Boilermakers, Shipwrights, Blacksmiths and Structural Workers v George Wimpey ME and C Ltd 1977 IRLR 95, EAT, a case concerning redundancies at a building site, the impossibility of forecasting exactly when redundancies would occur was held to be a special circumstance excusing failure to consult. **12.110**

National security. In United States of America v Nolan 2015 ICR 1347, SC, the Court of Appeal conjectured that a decision not to consult over an operational decision of military sensitivity – in that case, the closure of a military base – would probably enable a sovereign state to plead the 'special circumstances' defence. However, the Court did not have to decide the issue because the USA had not advanced the defence and when the case came before the Supreme Court, Lord Mance – giving the majority judgment – took a somewhat different view. He considered that, while S.188(7) could conceivably be of assistance to the USA in resisting a claim that it had breached the S.188 consultation obligations on the facts due to issues of feasibility, it was 'much less obviously designed for situations where consultation might be thought to be incongruous for high policy reasons'. **12.111**

Complaints about breach of S.188 **12.112**

A complaint that an employer has failed to comply with S.188 TULR(C)A should be brought under S.189 TULRC(A), as amended by the Collective Redundancies and Transfer of Undertakings (Protection of Employment) (Amendment) Regulations 1999 SI 1999/1925 ('the 1999 Regulations'). If a tribunal finds that the employer has acted in breach of S.188, it *must* make a declaration to that effect and *may* make a 'protective award' – S.189(2) (see 'Protective awards' below).

Under the amended provisions, the persons entitled to bring a complaint seeking a declaration and a protective award are:

- in the case of a failure relating to the election of employee representatives, any of the affected employees or any of the employees who have been made redundant – S.189(1)(a). In these circumstances it is for the employer to show that the S.188A requirements for election have been satisfied – S.189(1B)

463

- in the case of any other failure relating to employee representatives, any of the employee representatives to whom the failure related – S.189(1)(b)

- in the case of failure relating to representatives of a trade union, by the trade union – S.189(1)(c), and

- in any other case, by any of the affected employees or by any of the employees who have been dismissed as redundant – S.189(1)(d).

12.113   If there is disagreement as to whether an individual was an appropriate representative for the purposes of S.188, the employer has the burden of satisfying the tribunal that the individual had the authority to represent the affected employees – S.189(1A).

A complaint under S.189 must be made either before the date on which the last of the dismissals takes effect or during the period of three months beginning with that date. However, tribunals have a discretion to allow complaints within such further period as they consider reasonable if it was not reasonably practicable to present the complaint within three months – S.189(5). The reference to 'reasonably practicable' echoes the language used by the ERA in relation to time limits for bringing, among other things, unfair dismissal claims. The case law on reasonable practicability in that respect will therefore be highly relevant to claims under the TULR(C)A – see IDS Employment Law Handbook, 'Employment Tribunal Practice and Procedure' (2014), Chapter 5, 'Time limits', under '"Not reasonably practicable" extension'.

12.114   **Acas conciliation.** The Acas early conciliation scheme contained in S.18 of the Employment Tribunals Act 1996 (ETA) (which requires a claimant to contact Acas before instituting tribunal proceedings) applies in respect of any complaint concerning a failure to comply with a requirement of S.188 or S.188A – S.18(1)(a) ETA. In these circumstances, S.292A TULR(C)A applies to extend the time limits in S.189(5) to facilitate conciliation before the institution of proceedings – S.189(5A). For further information about the Acas early conciliation scheme, see IDS Employment Law Handbook, 'Employment Tribunal Practice and Procedure' (2014), Chapter 3, 'Conciliation, settlements and ADR', under 'Early conciliation'.

12.115   **Right to claim**
As will be obvious from the different categories set out in S.189(1) (see 'Complaints about breach of S.188' above), whether or not an individual has standing to bring a claim in respect of an employer's failure to observe the requirements of S.188 depends on the kind of failure at issue. The relationship between failures related to employee representatives, under S.189(1)(a) and (b), and failures 'in any other case' under S.189(1)(d), was considered by the Court of Appeal in Mercy v Northgate HR Ltd 2008 ICR 410, CA. There, M, who was dismissed as redundant, brought a claim for a

protective award in respect of the employer's failure to provide information to the elected employee representatives. The tribunal made the award but, on appeal, the EAT overturned that decision on the basis that M had no standing to claim under S.189. In so doing, it rejected M's argument that the failure was within the 'any other case' category of S.189(1)(d). Rather, the failure was one relating to employee representatives and so fell within S.189(1)(b), meaning that only the employee representatives could bring a claim. The Court of Appeal approved the EAT's decision. Where a complaint under S.189 relates to the election of an employee representative, any affected employee (including, in this case, M) would have standing under S.189(1)(a). However, where employee representatives are appropriately in place – as they were here – a complaint about a failure relating to them can only be brought by them. The proper approach would have been for M to raise his complaint with the employee representatives, who, if they could obtain no redress from the employer directly, could have brought the claim.

This interpretation would appear to accord with the Collective Redundancies Directive. In Mono Car Styling SA v Odemis and ors 2009 3 CMLR 47, ECJ, the European Court held that the Directive's provisions on consultation were essentially 'collective' in nature and therefore intended to be enforced by employee representatives rather than by the employees themselves. Thus, provided employee representatives (assuming they exist) can bring a claim, it would seem that national provisions limiting or setting conditions on an individual employee's right to do so will not contravene the Directive.

Impact on protective award. Section 189(1) is also relevant to the extent of the tribunal's power to make a protective award for breach of S.188 (see 'Protective awards' below). Such an award may only be made in favour of those who have been dismissed as redundant *and* in respect of whom a complaint under S.189 has been proved. Since a trade union can only bring a claim in respect of those employees it represents, the protective award which results only benefits those employees – TGWU v Brauer Coley Ltd 2007 ICR 226, EAT. The Appeal Tribunal noted that where there are non-union employees, representatives of whom have also not been consulted, they must make their own claims, although there is nothing to stop a claim being made simultaneously by a trade union and individual employees. **12.116**

Similarly, if a protective award is made in favour of an individual claimant, it cannot be extended to other employees who, although affected by the employer's failure to consult, were not party to the proceedings brought by that claimant. In Independent Insurance Company Ltd v Aspinall and anor 2011 ICR 1234, EAT, II Co Ltd went into provisional liquidation in June 2001 and made 351 employees – including A and his fellow claimant – redundant at the company's offices in Cheadle. In accordance with Ss.188 and 188A, II Co Ltd was obliged to consult and provide information to either employee or trade union representatives, and to arrange for the necessary elections, but it failed to do so. It followed that those employees faced with redundancy were entitled to a protective award under S.189. A large number of claims were stayed because of proceedings in the Companies Court, and when an application for a protective award made by some of the dismissed employees was finally heard, a number of them were struck out, settled or dismissed.

12.117 When A made his claim, he did not attempt to seek an award in respect of his fellow employees in a similar situation, and nor did his fellow claimant. Nevertheless, the employment tribunal made a protective award that applied to the claimants and all employees at the Cheadle office. At a subsequent review of its decision, the tribunal did not accept the employer's contention that the claimants lacked standing to bring what amounted in effect to a representative action, noting that S.189(3), which defines what a protective award comprises, states that it is an award in respect of 'one or more descriptions of employees'.

II Co Ltd appealed to the EAT. Relying on TGWU v Brauer Coley Ltd (above) among other things, it argued that it was necessary to construe the phrase 'description of employees' in the case of an individual claimant as referring to that individual only, rather than an entire class of which he or she was one. The EAT agreed. Ss.188–189 give representative rights to trade unions and elected representatives only. The effect of the tribunal's decision was hopelessly anomalous, as it would enable other employees – whose cases were dismissed, struck out, or not even brought – to benefit. Furthermore, it would be impossible for an employer to defend proceedings or to consider which defences might arise in relation to different individual employees. The statute had to be read in its context and regard had to be paid to the fact that Parliament would not have intended to produce such anomalies. Accordingly, II Co Ltd's appeal was allowed and the tribunal's protective award in respect of employees other than the claimants was set aside.

12.118 These cases demonstrate that anyone with legal standing to bring a claim under S.189 can only obtain a protective award to benefit those he or she properly represents – either individually or collectively. However, what of those employees who, although represented for the purposes of S.188, are excluded from the scope of a protective award for one reason or another? Are they able to bring their own claims under S.189 in these circumstances? Or do they have any other course of redress? These issues were considered by the EAT in Harford and ors v Secretary of State for Trade and Industry EAT 0313/07. WF Ltd was placed in administrative receivership and its employees dismissed between 3 and 26 May 2006. The GMB union, which represented all of WF Ltd's manual workers, obtained a protective award in respect of employees who were dismissed on 3 or 5 May 2006 only – the dates on which its members were dismissed. A number of employees who were dismissed on other dates subsequently made an application to the Secretary of State for payment of a protective award out of the National Insurance Fund (see Chapter 7, 'Payments from National Insurance Fund'). The application was refused, and they brought a claim against the Secretary of State before an employment tribunal.

The same employment judge who sat alone in the GMB case heard the claim. He found that the employees were not covered by the protective award already granted by him in the GMB case. Furthermore, he deduced from the documents before him that the employees were not manual workers (or union members), and could accordingly not benefit from the protective award made in the GMB's favour. For this reason, he refused to review, or extend the scope of, the original award.

On appeal, the EAT took issue with the judge's finding that the employees **12.119** were not manual workers, and thus not represented by the GMB union for the purposes of S.188. The judge appeared to have assumed that they were managerial or technical staff without raising this issue with their representative. The question of whether all or some of them were manual workers was accordingly remitted to the same judge.

The Appeal Tribunal went on to note that the protective award in the GMB case was limited in scope: only manual workers dismissed on 3 or 5 May 2006 could take advantage of it. The employees in question, assuming that they were indeed manual workers, could therefore not benefit from the award, as they had been dismissed on other dates. Their options in these circumstances seemed limited – particularly as they were by then out of time to make a free-standing claim under S.189(1)(a) or (d) (subject to being granted an extension of time). However, the EAT doubted in any event whether either provision would be available to employees who were represented by a trade union. Once a trade union was recognised in respect of any affected employees, S.189 appeared to require that only that union could bring a claim under the section. That said, the EAT thought it unnecessary to decide the point.

Instead, the EAT held that the employees who had missed out under the **12.120** terms of the protective award could apply to the employment tribunal under rule 10(2)(r) of the Employment Tribunal Rules of Procedure, contained in Schedule 1 to the Employment Tribunals (Constitution and Rules of Procedure) Regulations 2004 SI 2004/1861 (now rule 34 of the Employment Tribunal Rules of Procedure, contained in Schedule 1 to the Employment Tribunals (Constitution and Rules of Procedure) Regulations 2013 SI 2013/1237), for the judge to allow them to be joined (out of time) as parties to the GMB case because they had an interest in the outcome of the proceedings. They could then apply, under rule 34 of the Tribunal Rules (now rule 70), for the decision in that case to be reviewed in the interests of justice so as to cover dismissals

467

on other dates, and for any consequent protective award to be recoverable from the Secretary of State.

Although the majority of employees are likely to be dismissed at the same time as a company becomes insolvent, it is not uncommon for a small number of employees to be kept on for a short period in order to conclude the company's business and assist the representatives of the receivers. Any protective award obtained by the appropriate representatives in respect of the initial redundancies only would therefore leave those who have been dismissed later in the unenviable position of having to apply to the tribunal themselves to rectify the scope of the original award.

12.121 Protective awards

As explained above, if a tribunal finds that an employer has acted in breach of S.188 TULR(C)A, it *must* make a declaration to that effect and *may* make a 'protective award' – S.189(2). A protective award is an award of pay to those employees who have been dismissed as redundant, or whom it is proposed to dismiss as redundant, and in respect of whom the employer has failed to comply with the requirements of S.188 – S.189(3). There seems to be something of an anomaly here. S.189(3), which was not altered by the 1999 Regulations, makes it clear that for an employee to be covered by an award, he or she must be an employee whom the employer has dismissed or has proposed to dismiss as redundant. Yet an important change introduced by the 1999 Regulations is the extension of the right to consultation to all 'affected' employees. That is, an employer is now required to consult not only in respect of employees whose jobs are threatened, but also in respect of those who are otherwise 'affected' by the redundancy situation – see 'Scope of duty to consult' above. Thus it would seem that, as the legislation currently stands, an 'affected' employee who does not fall within the scope of S.189(3) has the right to be consulted and the right to bring a complaint of failure to consult, but no right to receive a protective award.

The protective award will be calculated by reference to a 'protected period', which is of whatever length the tribunal decides is 'just and equitable', up to a maximum of 90 days – S.189(4) (see 'Length of "protected period"' below). The rate of remuneration is one week's pay for each week of the protected period – S.190(2) (see 'Quantification of protective award' below).

12.122 Length of 'protected period'
The award is for a 'protected period', beginning with the date on which the first of the dismissals to which the complaint relates takes effect, or the date of the award (whichever is the earlier) (see 'Start date of "protected period"' below), and continuing for however long the tribunal decides is 'just

468

and equitable' – S.189(4). The Act gives tribunals no guidance as to how to exercise their discretion over the length of the protected period, or whether to make an award at all, except to say that they should have regard to the 'seriousness of the employer's default'. However, there is a maximum limit on the protected period of 90 days.

The protective award is subject to the 90-day maximum in all cases. This is the result of an amendment made by the 1999 Regulations. Previously, S.189(4) related the protected period to the numbers of employees that the employer proposed to dismiss, so that an award of 90 days was only possible in cases where 100 or more employees were to be dismissed. In all other cases, the protected period was limited to 30 days. The amendment removed that distinction for the purpose of the protective award. In Newage Transmission Ltd v TGWU and ors EAT 0131/05 the EAT expressly rejected the contention that, despite the amendment, the maximum award in a 30-day consultation period should still be 30 days. The employer there argued that if a 90-day protective award is proportionate to an employer's breach of the 90-day consultation period, then the same maximum award is disproportionate where the consultation period is 30 days. The EAT rejected that argument, noting that a protective award is punitive rather than compensatory, and so should be subject to the maximum compensation permitted by Parliament.

12.123 Before 2004 courts and tribunals were unclear as to the purpose of the protective award, and hence of how to calculate the protected period. Most leading authorities inclined towards the view that the award was designed to be compensatory in respect of the failure to consult. However, that still left room for uncertainty as to exactly what the award was meant to compensate, especially in cases where employees suffered no actual loss. Thankfully, that debate has been conclusively laid to rest by the Court of Appeal's decision in Susie Radin Ltd v GMB and ors 2004 ICR 893, CA, where the Court made it clear that the protective award is designed to be punitive rather than compensatory.

12.124 **Award is punitive, not compensatory.** In Susie Radin Ltd v GMB and ors (above), a tribunal found that the respondent employer had failed in its duties in respect of a collective redundancy situation when it had provided none of the information required under S.188(4) and had simply 'gone through the motions' of the consultation. The tribunal made an award for a protected period of 90 days. The employer appealed unsuccessfully to the EAT, and again to the Court of Appeal, against the level of the award, arguing that the purpose of the award was to compensate employees and that, in the circumstances, consultation would not have made any difference. The Court of Appeal rejected that argument, endorsing the tribunal's approach, and went on to give guidance on how tribunals should exercise their discretion under S.189. It noted that S.188 imposes an absolute obligation on employers to consult meaningfully over proposed redundancies, and that S.189 is designed

469

to ensure that such consultation takes place by providing a sanction against a failure to comply. Nothing in the TULR(C)A links the award to any loss suffered by employees. Thus, the focus should be on the employer's default and its seriousness.

12.125   **Relevant factors.** The Court in Susie Radin condensed the above principles into five factors that tribunals should have in mind when applying S.189:

- the purpose of the award is to provide a sanction, not compensation

- the tribunal has a wide discretion to do what it considers just and equitable, but the focus must be on the seriousness of the employer's default

- the default may vary in seriousness from the technical to a complete failure both to provide the required information and to consult

- the deliberateness of the failure may be relevant, as may the availability to the employer of legal advice about its obligations under S.188, and

- how the tribunal assesses the length of the protected period is a matter for the tribunal, but a proper approach where there has been no consultation is to start with the maximum period of 90 days and reduce it only if there are mitigating circumstances justifying a reduction to an extent to which the tribunal considers appropriate.

In the years since Susie Radin was decided, this case has been applied many times by tribunals and courts without being greatly expanded. It therefore remains the definitive guidance on S.189. Attention should be drawn, however, to the EAT's decision in Amicus v GBS Tooling Ltd (in administration) 2005 IRLR 683, EAT, in which it considered the issue of 'deliberateness' in some detail. In that case, GBS Ltd had made efforts to give the union sufficient information and keep it informed in general terms of the economic circumstances that eventually gave rise to collective redundancies. However, employees were dismissed the day after the proposal to dismiss was crystallised with no consultation whatsoever. Following Susie Radin, the tribunal made a 70-day protective award, finding that efforts made by GBS Ltd to involve the union before the proposal to dismiss arose amounted to a mitigating factor justifying a reduction from the maximum. The EAT refused to interfere with that decision on appeal. It held that GBS Ltd's efforts at keeping the union informed 'put [it] into a different category from the employer who had either deliberately, or recklessly, or even negligently, taken no steps whatever to inform the employees or the unions of the problems that might and/or were imminently going to arise'. So, in assessing deliberateness, tribunals should consider whether an employer has been secretive, misguided, or has simply failed to disclose information at the right time and in the right context.

12.126   Two other points are worth noting from the GBS Tooling decision. First, the EAT confirmed that a tribunal can take into account the employer's actions before the duty to consult arises. It expressly rejected the union's argument that the only mitigating factors that a tribunal can take into account are those arising during the statutory consultation period, i.e. after dismissals are 'proposed'. Secondly, the EAT underlined that futility – i.e. that consultation would have made no difference to the outcome – is not a factor to be taken into account under S.189. Rather, it thought that if consultation were genuinely futile, perhaps because the future of the business is out of the employer's hands, that might be relevant to making out a S.188(7) 'special circumstances' defence (see 'Special circumstances defence' above).

In Smith and anor v Cherry Lewis Ltd (in receivership) 2005 IRLR 86, EAT, the Appeal Tribunal identified some additional factors tribunals should not take into account. It overturned a tribunal's decision not to make a protective award on the basis that, since the employer would by reason of insolvency be unable to pay, the making of an award would be completely ineffective as a sanction against the employer. The tribunal had erroneously viewed the sanction as retributive rather than punitive or dissuasive. The EAT underlined the need for the tribunal to focus on the extent of the employer's default in exercising its discretion. The tribunal in the present case had therefore erred in taking into account the employer's inability to pay and the likelihood that the burden of paying the awards would fall onto the Government, both of which were irrelevant factors.

12.127 The EAT in E Ivor Hughes Educational Foundation v Morris and ors 2015 IRLR 696, EAT, reiterated the point made in Susie Radin Ltd v GMB and ors (above) that tribunals should focus on the seriousness of the employer's default. In the EAT's view, certain obiter (i.e. non-binding) comments made in Sweetin v Coral Racing 2006 IRLR 252, EAT (a case concerning a failure to consult in relation to a TUPE transfer), could be seen as supporting the proposition that whether an employee has suffered loss consequent on a failure to consult may be relevant to the assessment of a protective award to the extent that 'the penal nature of such award, or the need to reflect any actual loss suffered, may justify fixing an award at a particular level'. However, the fact that one or more employees has not suffered actual loss as a result of the failure to consult could not constitute a mitigating factor justifying a reduction in the length of the protective award. In the present case, the employer's failure to consult was not deliberate, but arose from its 'reckless failure to consult legal experts on the employment implications' of its decision to close the school at which the employees taught. Since it had not even considered consultation at the time, the employer could not attempt to argue as a mitigating factor after the event that entering into consultation about possible closure would have sealed the school's fate as the information would have leaked and parents would have withdrawn their children. It was clear that the tribunal had considered all of the relevant circumstances and the EAT held that it had been entitled to set the protected period at 90 days.

471

Note that the main thrust of Susie Radin Ltd v GMB and ors (above) – that tribunals should start at a 90-day protected period and reduce this if there are mitigating circumstances – only strictly applies where there has been no consultation at all. Although Susie Radin underlines that tribunals have a wide discretion under S.189 to make an award that is 'just and equitable', and are therefore entitled to make a full 90-day award even where there has been some attempt at consultation, we would suggest that this will be a rare case. Mr Justice Elias, then President of the EAT, commented in UK Coal Mining Ltd v NUM (Northumberland Area) and anor 2008 ICR 163, EAT, that 'if there has been some consultation, however limited, then the tribunal is compelled thereby to reduce the compensation below the maximum. No doubt that is true where such consultation as does take place is more than minimal.' So, although the tribunal ultimately has a generous discretion to make such award as it thinks fit, it will generally have to 'give credit' for an employer's attempts to comply with S.188.

Below we give some further examples of factors that tribunals and courts have considered when determining the length of the protected period.

12.128 **Employer giving misleading reasons.** In UK Coal Mining Ltd v NUM (Northumberland Area) and anor (above), the employer falsely told the trade unions that a colliery was being closed for health and safety reasons, when the real reason was economic. The tribunal took the view that there had been a very serious and fundamental failure to consult, and that the limited consultation about various marginal issues did not in any material way mitigate the seriousness of the conduct so as to compel it to reduce the protected period below the maximum 90 days. On appeal, the EAT refused to interfere with the tribunal's exercise of its discretion.

12.129 **Employer's willingness to negotiate.** In Leicestershire County Council v UNISON 2006 IRLR 810, CA, a tribunal found that there had been an intentional and total failure to consult in respect of one group of employees who were to have their pay downgraded, and so awarded the full 90 days. By contrast, in respect of a second group, whose rights to pay supplements and overtime were to be adversely affected, the tribunal noted that the Council had eventually offered to consult with the union, but the union had failed to take up that offer. Because of this, the tribunal limited the protected period for the latter group to 20 days. On the Council's appeal, the EAT held that the tribunal had failed fully to take into account the mitigating circumstances in respect of this group – the evidence of the Council's approach to the group was impressive, in that it did not seek simply to consult, but also to negotiate with a view to avoiding the dismissals. The EAT therefore substituted a protected period of ten days. However, the Court of Appeal allowed a further appeal by the union against the EAT's reduction of the protective award. Neither view – ten or 20 days – was perverse. Although a different tribunal might have awarded ten days, the tribunal in the instant case had correctly applied Susie Radin Ltd v GMB and ors (above) and so its decision should not have been disturbed.

Trade union's reluctance to cooperate. In GMB and anor v Lambeth Service   **12.130**
Team Ltd and anor EAT 0127/05 the EAT held that a tribunal was entitled
to take a union's obstructive approach to statutory consultation into account
when assessing the correct protected period. The tribunal had found evidence
of the union's refusal to cooperate and, unlike in Susie Radin Ltd v GMB and
ors (above), this was not a case of an employer wholly failing to discharge its
duty to consult. The company's initial failure to supply information had been
quickly rectified and the union had chosen not to respond to the information
provided. In the EAT's view, the Susie Radin guidance did not require the
tribunal to focus solely on the employer's default but rather to take into
account 'all the circumstances' in order to make an award that was 'just and
equitable' under S.189(4).

Trade union's acquiescence. In Lancaster University v University and College   **12.131**
Union 2011 IRLR 4, EAT, the Appeal Tribunal upheld a tribunal's decision
to reduce a protective award in respect of an employer's failure to undertake
collective redundancy consultation where the failure had effectively been
condoned by the recognised trade union. The redundancies, which arose from
the expiry of fixed-term contracts, had happened regularly for over ten years
and the union had only recently begun to complain about the consultation
procedure. According to the EAT, the tribunal was in effect saying that,
because of the history, the employer may not have been fully alert as to the
need for collective consultation and only became aware over a period of time.
In other words, it had been 'lulled into a false sense of security' by the union.
It had not been unreasonable for the tribunal to take that into account. The
EAT therefore declined to interfere with the tribunal's decision to make a
reduced protective award of 60 days' pay. It was relevant that the EAT placed
weight on the fact that the employer's failure to consult was not deliberate.
The EAT was less convinced that a union's previous acceptance – even if long-
standing – would, by itself, be a mitigating factor, if the employer was well
aware of its obligation to consult.

Attitude of employer. If an employer not only fails to consult but also acts   **12.132**
in an uncooperative and obstinate way, a maximum award is likely to result.
In General and Municipal Boilermakers Trade Union and ors v Swan Hunter
Shipbuilding and Engineering Group (in administrative receivership) ET Case
No.39135/94 a tribunal found that there had been a 'total and wilful' default
and made a maximum award of 90 days.

Partial compliance. In TGWU v Purnell Colours Ltd COET 1130/99 the   **12.133**
employer wrote to the union saying redundancies would be inevitable but,

473

because of special circumstances (see 'Special circumstances defence' above), it was impossible to give exact details or to consult as S.188 required. The tribunal found there to be no special circumstances, but that the letter was a partial compliance with S.188. This, it concluded, should be taken into account when making the protective award. Similarly, in NUT and anor v South Glamorgan County Council ET Case No.37142/93 the local authority conceded that it had breached S.188. Nevertheless, the tribunal found that there had been several meetings with affected employees and union representatives and that the union was partly responsible for the failure to commence the statutory consultation process. The tribunal considered these circumstances were significant mitigation and made an award of 28 days rather than the maximum 90.

It would seem that the partial compliance can take place before the actual duty arises. In Amicus v GBS Tooling Ltd (in administration) 2005 IRLR 683, EAT, GBS Ltd had made efforts to give the union sufficient information and keep it informed in general terms of the economic circumstances that eventually gave rise to collective redundancies. However, employees were dismissed the day after the proposal to dismiss was crystallised with no consultation whatsoever. The tribunal made a 70-day protective award, finding that efforts made by GBS Ltd to involve the union before the proposal to dismiss arose amounted to a mitigating factor. The EAT refused to interfere with that decision on appeal. It held that GBS Ltd's efforts at keeping the union informed 'put [it] into a different category from the employer who had either deliberately, or recklessly, or even negligently, taken no steps whatever to inform the employees or the unions of the problems that might and/or were imminently going to arise'. It expressly rejected the union's argument that the only mitigating factors that a tribunal can take into account are those arising during the statutory consultation period, i.e. after dismissals are 'proposed'.

12.134 **Third party pressure.** In Shanahan Engineering Ltd v Unite the Union EAT 0411/09 the EAT held that the tribunal had failed to justify its reasons for granting a protective award of 90 days. SE Ltd, an engineering construction firm contracted to work on a new power station, was urgently required by its client, A, to reduce the number of workers it had on site to alleviate health and safety problems caused by congestion and ground conditions. Within three days, SE Ltd had selected around 50 employees for redundancy according to agreed selection criteria and dismissed them with one week's notice. While those 'special circumstances' (see 'Special circumstances defence' above) did not entirely excuse the failure to consult, they still operated as a mitigating factor, which the tribunal should have taken into account in assessing the seriousness of the default and in deciding the level of the protective award. The tribunal should also have had regard to the fact that consultation could have taken place over a shorter period of time, although the EAT stressed that this did not mean that the award should be tailored to the length of time consultation would have taken. The EAT remitted the case to the same tribunal to reconsider the length of the protective award.

Insolvency. In AEI Cables Ltd v GMB and ors EAT 0375/12 the EAT held that in making a protective award of 90 days in respect of AEIC Ltd's total failure to consult, the employment tribunal had not had sufficient regard to the company's insolvency. Between 17 and 20 May 2012, AEIC Ltd was warned by a firm of accountants that unless it reduced its costs quickly or acquired new funding, it risked trading while insolvent, meaning that the directors would become personally liable for any obligations then incurred by the company. AEIC Ltd therefore requested an overdraft extension from its bank. However, when this request was refused on 25 May, the company decided that its cable plant should be closed immediately and that approximately 124 employees who worked there should be made redundant. An employment tribunal found that there were no special circumstances to excuse AEIC Ltd's total failure to consult and made a protective award of 90 days.

12.135

On appeal, the EAT held that the tribunal had erred in envisaging that there could have been a 90-day consultation period starting in May. This would have meant that the company would have had to trade while insolvent, against the advice of its accountants. In light of the fact that a 90-day consultation period was simply not possible, the EAT considered that the appropriate level of award was 60 days and reduced it accordingly. This took into account the fact that some consultation could have taken place in the limited time available between 17 May and 25 May, bearing in mind that it was only on 27 May that the dismissal letters went out.

Note that, in certain circumstances, insolvency can constitute a 'special circumstance' justifying a failure to consult, meaning that no liability under S.188 arises. This is discussed under 'What are "special circumstances"? – insolvency and financial crises' above. In the AEI Cables case, the tribunal's finding that the insolvency did not constitute a 'special circumstance' was not appealed.

12.136

Start date of 'protected period'

12.137

The 'protected period' starts when the first of the dismissals takes effect or from the date of the award if this is earlier – S.189(4). There have been conflicting interpretations of this provision. In GKN Sankey Ltd v National Society of Metal Mechanics 1980 ICR 148, EAT, the Appeal Tribunal considered that the period began when the first dismissal actually took place, irrespective of the original proposed date. This meant that if an employer persuades an employee to leave before the proposed date of dismissal, the protected period starts then. In theory, the protected period could therefore end before the other employees were made redundant on the original proposed date.

475

However, another division of the EAT, in TGWU v Ledbury Preserves (1928) Ltd (No.2) 1986 ICR 855, EAT, considered this to be a wrong approach. In that case, the proposed date of termination of the employees' contracts of employment was 31 December but one employee left on 28 October. The tribunal held that the 30-day protected period began to run on 28 October, which meant that it ended before the other employees were dismissed. The EAT overruled the decision and held that the protected period should begin when the first dismissals were expected to occur in accordance with the original proposals. (This view is supported by another EAT decision, E Green and Son (Castings) Ltd and ors v ASTMS and anor 1984 ICR 352, EAT.)

12.138 The difference between the two approaches should be of much less significance now that the S.190(3) set-off provisions have been repealed. Previously, the problem with the GKN Sankey approach was that it enabled an employer to lessen the impact of a protective award by persuading an employee to leave early. Since double payment was not allowed, the effect of a protective award would be largely nullified because the period of the award would coincide with the period during which the remaining employees continued to be employed and paid under their contracts. Following the removal of S.190(3), together with the punitive approach now applied to protective awards (see 'Length of protected period' above), there are far narrower grounds on which an award may be reduced and so identifying the actual period in respect of which the award is made has become much less important.

12.139 Quantification of protective award

Where a protective award has been made, remuneration must be paid to all employees who have been, or are to be, made redundant and who are of a description specified by the tribunal – S.190(1) TULR(C)A. The rate of remuneration is one week's pay for each week of the protected period – S.190(2). A week's pay is calculated in accordance with Ss.220–229 of the Employment Rights Act 1996 (ERA) – S.190(5) (see IDS Employment Law Handbook, 'Wages' (2016), Chapter 9, 'A week's pay'). There is no ceiling placed on the amount of a week's pay for these purposes. If an employee would not have received any pay under the contract while employed, he or she is not entitled to anything under the protective award – S.190(4). This would apply to employees who are on unpaid leave or on strike – see, for example, Cranswick Country Foods plc v Beall and ors 2007 ICR 691, EAT.

In Canadian Imperial Bank of Commerce v Beck EAT 0141/10 the EAT held that, for the purpose of calculating a protective award, a week's pay should refer only to the employee's basic salary and not to any discretionary bonus. B had argued that the discretionary bonus constituted the bulk of his remuneration package and that to exclude it from the concept of 'a week's pay' would be to largely deprive the protective award of any real deterrent effect.

Although S.221(2) ERA provides that a week's pay for these purposes is 'the amount which is payable by the employer under the contract of employment', B had contended that the effectiveness of EU law would not be guaranteed unless account was taken of his discretionary bonus. The EAT accepted that there might be cases in which an employee's basic salary is so small that it could be said that failing to include a discretionary bonus or commission payments in a week's pay would deprive a protective award of any deterrent effect. However, it did not consider that any such principle applied in B's case. It could not be said that the protective award of £45,000 in this case did not penalise the employer. The EAT noted that B's basic annual salary of £125,000 was 'not an insignificant sum', even if it was much less than he might ultimately have received as a remuneration package in respect of that year had he remained in employment. Moreover, at the time of his dismissal he had not yet become entitled to have any decision made as to whether he should receive a bonus, let alone how much that bonus should be or what form it should take.

Note that the set-off provisions once contained in S.190(3) were repealed **12.140** by the Trade Union Reform and Employment Rights Act 1993. Under those provisions, where the employee received any payment from the employer under his or her contract of employment, or by way of damages for breach of that contract, for any part of the protected period, that payment went towards discharging the employer's liability to pay remuneration under the protective award. Conversely, the protective award could go towards discharging the employer's contractual liability in respect of the protected period. The effect of S.190(3) was that a three-month payment in lieu of notice could wipe out a maximum protective award altogether, thus allowing an employer to disregard the statutory provisions. The ECJ in Commission of the European Communities v United Kingdom 1994 ICR 664, ECJ, held that these set-off provisions deprived the protective award of its practical effect and deterrent value and were in breach of the Directive.

Losing protective award   **12.141**
Where an employee is employed during the protected period and he or she is fairly dismissed for a non-redundancy reason, or unreasonably terminates the employment contract, then he or she is not entitled to remuneration under the award in respect of any period during which he or she would otherwise have remained employed – S.191(1). Note that it is the wider definition of redundancy in S.195(1) that applies here, so that an employee will not be deprived of the award if the dismissal was for a reason or reasons 'not related to the individual concerned' – see 'Scope of duty to consult' above. Furthermore, if an employee unreasonably refuses an offer of suitable alternative employment, then he or she loses the protective award for the period during which he or she would, but for the refusal, have been employed – S.191(2) and (3). If the employee accepts

477

such an offer, he or she has four weeks (or longer, if agreed in writing) to try out the new job. If the employee reasonably leaves during that time, he or she will still be entitled to the protective award – S.191(4)–(7). For more details on an employee's right to refuse alternative employment, see Chapter 3, 'Alternative employment', under 'Suitability and reasonableness'.

Note that if an employee to whom a protective award relates dies during the protected period, the protected period for that employee is treated as ending on his or her death – S.190(6).

12.142 **Enforcing protective award**
An employee in respect of whom a protective award is made may bring a complaint under S.192 if his or her employer fails, wholly or in part, to pay the amount awarded – S.192(1). Note that it is the employee, not the representatives, who must enforce the protective award.

12.143 **Time limits.** Section 192(2)(a) provides that the complaint must be made 'within three months beginning with the day (or, if the complaint relates to more than one day, the last of the days) in respect of which the complaint is made of failure to pay remuneration'. Where a tribunal is satisfied that it was not reasonably practicable for the complaint to be presented within that three-month period, the complaint will be allowed to proceed where it is presented within such further period as the tribunal considers reasonable – S.192(2)(b). The time limit may also be extended to facilitate early conciliation – S.192(2A).

In Howlett Marine Services Ltd v Bowlam and ors 2001 ICR 595, EAT, the EAT confirmed that, where nothing has been paid for any part of the protected period, the three-month limitation runs from the last day of that period. It does not run from the date the protective award is made. Having said that, the EAT acknowledged that it is essential that at the date when the S.192 complaint is presented to an employment tribunal, there must have been a failure to pay. There cannot be a failure to pay without there being a legal obligation to pay and there is no legal obligation to pay until a protective award has been made under S.189(2). Therefore, a protective award must actually have been made in order for a S.192 complaint to be made. Subsequently, the EAT recognised that there could be circumstances in which the end of the three-month limitation period running from the last day of the protected period could pre-date the date that the protective award is actually made, meaning that any enforcement complaint would already be out of time.

12.144 However, the EAT held that a complaint under S.192 is not time-barred unless neither S.192(2)(a) nor (b) is satisfied – these subsections are alternatives. The test of reasonable practicability under S.192(2)(b) is applicable to the period

478

of three months that ends with the S.192(2)(a) expiry dates. Once the delay goes on after that, the question is not expressly whether it was not reasonably practicable to present a claim within the further period but simply whether the delay in the further period was reasonable or unreasonable. Therefore, where, as was the case here, the whole of the S.192(2)(a) period has expired before the protective award is made, the question of reasonable practicability is at no stage the test. Instead, the tribunal is only required to decide whether the delay during the further period was or was not reasonable.

Turning to the facts of the case, the EAT held that the claimants had not unreasonably delayed in bringing their claims under S.192 by waiting to see whether the Secretary of State was going to seek recoupment of jobseeker's allowance (JSA) from their protective awards. Payments under a protective award are treated as earnings for the purposes of social security legislation so an employee who is entitled to payment under such an award (or an enforcement order pursuant to S.192) is disqualified from claiming JSA for the same period. However, because the award may not be made until some time after dismissal the employee is entitled to claim JSA (or income support) and, if and when a protective award is made, the amount paid out can be recouped from the money due under the award.

The EAT noted that Reg 7 of the Employment Protection (Recoupment of Benefits) Regulations 1996 SI 1996/2349 has the effect of postponing relevant awards in order to enable the Secretary of State to initiate recoupment. Any payment of remuneration to which an employee would otherwise be entitled under a protective award is treated as stayed (or in Scotland, sisted) until the Secretary of State has either served a recoupment notice on the employer or has notified the employer in writing that he or she does not intend to serve a recoupment notice. That being said, Reg 7(3) provides that the stay (or sist) is without prejudice to the right of an employee to present a complaint under S.192(1). Therefore the claimants in this case could have presented their S.192(1) complaints without waiting for the Secretary of State's decision. The stay (or sist) would simply take effect in respect of any such complaint or any order made under S.192(3) until the position in relation to recoupment had been determined. Nevertheless, the EAT held that it is not necessarily unreasonable for an employee to await the Secretary of State's recoupment decision before launching enforcement proceedings under S.192(1). Until the recoupment position is known, the employee would not know, or may well not know, whether he or she should launch proceedings for £5, £50, £500 or, indeed, possibly nothing at all. A continuing state of indecision or unknowingness as to recoupment is a factor which an employment tribunal can properly take into account when judging the reasonableness of the delay in the 'further period' described in S.192(2)(b). However, the EAT made it clear that it was not to be taken as saying that it will invariably be the case that delay in order to find out the position regarding recoupment will be considered reasonable delay within S.192(2)(b).

12.145

479

12.146 **Enforcing awards on insolvency.** The issues of insolvency and redundancy commonly coincide, as the former will often lead to the latter. Employees made redundant upon their employer becoming insolvent will inevitably face difficulties recovering back pay, redundancy payments and protective awards from the insolvent company. In so far as protective awards are concerned, it has been established that such awards are 'provable' debts in liquidation, meaning that they can be claimed against the insolvent company out of its remaining assets – Day v Haine and anor 2008 ICR 1102, CA. Under the Insolvency Rules 1986 SI 1986/1925, debts are provable whether they are 'present or future, certain or contingent' as at the date of liquidation – rule 12.3(1). The Rules specifically state that debts that arise after the date of liquidation can only be claimed against the company if they arise 'by reason of [an] obligation incurred before that date' – rule 13.12(1). The Court of Appeal in Haine held that, where there has been a failure to consult under S.188, the tribunal realistically has no discretion not to make a protective award. Therefore, a failure to consult gives rise to a contingent liability at the time the failure occurs, even though no actual award is made until a tribunal determines the matter.

Note that Part XII of the Employment Rights Act 1996 (ERA) offers some protection to employees of an insolvent company by permitting them to apply to the Secretary of State for payment of certain debts owed to them by their insolvent employer out of the National Insurance Fund. These provisions are primarily designed to allow employees to claim arrears of pay, but 'pay' for these purposes is defined to include awards made in respect of a protected period – S.184(1)(a) and (2)(d) ERA. The amount that the Secretary of State can be obliged to pay is, however, limited to eight weeks' pay, capped at £479 per week (as of April 2016).

12.147 Notification

The statutory duty to notify the Secretary of State of proposed redundancies is imposed by S.193 TULR(C)A. If an employer proposes to dismiss as redundant 100 or more employees at one establishment within 90 days or less, it must give notice in writing to the Secretary of State of its proposals before giving notice to terminate an employee's contract of employment in respect of any of those dismissals and at least 45 days before the first of the dismissals takes effect (90 days where the proposals to dismiss were made before 6 April 2013). If it proposes to dismiss 20–99 employees at one establishment within such a period, the notice must be given before giving notice to terminate an employee's contract and at least 30 days before the first dismissal takes effect – S.193(1) and (2). Notice must be given using the prescribed form – HR1 – and, where there are representatives to be consulted under S.188, a copy must be given to each representative – S.193(4)(c) and (6).

The requirement for an employer to give notice to the Secretary of State before giving notice of termination to an affected employee was inserted into S.193 by the Collective Redundancies (Amendment) Regulations 2006 SI 2006/2387 with effect from 1 October 2006. This amendment was made in response to the ECJ's decision in Junk v Kühnel 2005 IRLR 310, ECJ, that, for the purposes of the Collective Redundancies Directive, a redundancy occurs when an employer gives notice of termination of employment contracts, and not when that notice expires. The amendment therefore makes it clear that an employer may not wait until the notice period has already begun to run before notifying the Secretary of State.

Notification is not necessary in respect of redundancies affecting Crown employees, those serving in the armed forces, House of Lords and House of Commons staff, those in police service and share fishermen and women – Ss.273, 274, 277, 278, 280 and 284. Furthermore, since 6 April 2013, S.282 excludes employment under a fixed-term contract – being a contract that terminates on expiry of a specific term, on completion of a particular task, or on the occurrence or non-occurrence of a specific event – unless the employment is terminated by reason of redundancy before the expiry of the term, the completion of the task or the occurrence or non-occurrence of the event. These individuals are also excluded from the obligation to collectively consult – see 'Employees only' above. Employees who ordinarily work outside Great Britain are also excluded under the notification requirements – S.285. However, unlike the other categories of individuals listed above, overseas employees must be included in the consultation process if they are affected by the proposed redundancies. **12.148**

Where an employer has already notified the Secretary of State of one set of redundancies, those redundancies do not count again if a further set of redundancies is notified – S.193(3). If, for example, an employer notifies the Secretary of State of a proposal to dismiss 70 employees for redundancy and then finds it necessary to dismiss a further 35, this counts as two separate proposals to dismiss, each of which requires 30 days' notification, and not as a proposal to dismiss 105 in total, which would require 45 days' notification. Where there are representatives to be consulted under S.188, the notice must identify those representatives and state the date when consultation began – S.193(4)(b).

The prescribed form – HR1 – can be obtained from the Redundancy Payments Office or downloaded from the government website. The completed notice can be returned by post or e-mail to the addresses provided on the form – S.193(4)(a). After receiving the notice, the Secretary of State may by written notice require the employer to produce further information – S.193(5). **12.149**

If there are special circumstances which make it not reasonably practicable for the employer to comply with its obligations under S.193, it should take

481

such steps as are reasonably practicable – S.193(7). Ignorance of the law is not a 'special circumstance' that will excuse a failure to comply – Secretary of State for Employment v Helitron Ltd 1980 ICR 523, EAT. Nor, where the decision leading to the proposed dismissals is that of a person controlling the employer (either directly or indirectly), is a failure by that person to provide the necessary information to the employer – S.193(7). 'Special circumstances' for these purposes will be defined by reference to the same defence available in respect of a failure to consult under S.188 – see 'Special circumstances defence' above.

12.150 **Offence of failure to notify.** Failure to give notice to the Secretary of State as required by S.193 is a criminal offence punishable on summary conviction by a fine not exceeding level 5 on the standard scale – S.194(1). (Level 5 on the standard scale was previously capped at £5,000 but this cap was removed by the Legal Aid, Sentencing and Punishment of Offenders Act 2012, which means that where a 'level 5' offence is committed on or after 12 March 2015, the possible fine is unlimited.) However, failure to provide the appropriate representatives with a copy of the S.193 notification seems to have no consequences.

In 2015 the Department for Business, Innovation and Skills (BIS) brought criminal proceedings against three former directors of City Link Ltd, alleging that they had failed to notify the Secretary of State of proposed redundancies in breach of S.193 – BIS v Smith, Peto and Wright, unreported. In late 2014, the directors of CL Ltd were considering various options, such as a sale or a restructuring, as the company had been trading at a loss for some time. Proposed funding was withdrawn on 22 December 2014 and the directors concluded that CL Ltd would become insolvent by mid-January 2015. The directors decided at a board meeting on 22 December that the company should go into administration. The proposal to make more than 2,700 employees redundant was made by the administrator on 24 December when it took over the company. Subsequently, on 26 December, the administrator gave notice to the Secretary of State under S.193(1) and (7).

12.151 The key issue was whether there was a duty on the directors to notify the Secretary of State on 22 December. The prosecution case was that the directors' decision to put CL Ltd into administration made the large-scale redundancies inevitable or almost inevitable. The case came before Deputy District Judge David Goodman at Coventry Magistrates' Court and his verdict and reasons were given on 13 November 2015. The three defendants were acquitted. The court accepted the defendants' evidence that they genuinely believed that a sale in administration was not only possible but quite probable. There had been interest from national companies and an offer had been made before the administrator was appointed. The court concluded that no proposal to make the workforce redundant had been formed by the defendants on 22 December. Nor, on the evidence given to the court, was there an inevitability or near-inevitability that redundancies would flow from the decision to go into administration. Although dismissing the charge, the judge warned that the decision was very fact-specific and no employer should take his conclusion to be a precedent for the proposition that an employer can avoid its responsibilities under S.193 simply by going into administration.

Case list

(Note that employment tribunal cases are not included in this list.)

A

A Dakri and Co Ltd v Tiffen and ors 1981 ICR 256, EAT	4.12
ABN Amro Management Services Ltd and anor v Hogben EAT 0266/09	6.33
AEI Cables Ltd v GMB and ors EAT 0375/12	12.135
Abbey National plc and anor v Chagger 2010 ICR 397, CA	9.3
Air Canada v Lee 1978 ICR 1202, EAT	3.28, 3.30
Airbus UK Ltd v Webb 2008 ICR 561, CA	8.130
Akavan Erityisalojen Keskusliitto (AEK) ry and ors v Fujitsu Siemens	
Computers Oy 2010 ICR 444, ECJ 12.11, 12.33, 12.34, 12.39, 12.64, 12.69	
Akzo Coatings plc v Thompson and ors EAT 1117/94	8.178
Albion Automotive Ltd v Walker and ors 2002 EWCA Civ 946, CA	6.27
Alexander and ors v Standard Telephones and Cables plc 1990 ICR 291, ChD	10.35
Alexander and ors v Standard Telephones and Cables Ltd (No.2) 1991	
IRLR 286, QBD	8.85
Alexanders of Edinburgh Ltd v Maxwell and ors EAT 796/86	8.137, 8.159
Allen and ors v TRW Systems Ltd 2013 ICR D13, EAT; 2013 EWCA Civ 1388, CA	6.31
Allinson v Drew Simmons Engineering Ltd 1985 ICR 488, EAT	4.17
Amalgamated Society of Boilermakers, Shipwrights, Blacksmiths and	
Structural Workers v George Wimpey ME and C Ltd 1977 IRLR 95, EAT	12.110
Amicus v GBS Tooling Ltd (in administration)	
2005 IRLR 683, EAT	12.108, 12.125, 12.133
Amicus v Nissan Motor Manufacturing (UK) Ltd EAT 0184/05	12.27, 12.36
Amos and ors v Max-Arc Ltd 1973 ICR 46, NIRC	2.56
Anderson v Pringle of Scotland Ltd 1998 IRLR 64, Ct Sess (Outer House)	10.35
Archibald v Fife Council 2004 ICR 954, HL	9.67
Arhin v Enfield Primary Care Trust 2010 EWCA Civ 1481, CA	8.80, 10.25
Arkley v Sea Fish Industry Authority EAT 0505/09	6.24
Arnold Clark Automobiles Ltd v Mak EAT 0052/13	2.37
Association of Patternmakers and Allied Craftsmen v Kirvin Ltd	
1978 IRLR 318, EAT	12.31
Association of University Teachers v University of Newcastle-upon-Tyne	
1987 ICR 317, EAT	12.24
Athinaiki Chartopoiia AE v Panagiotidis and ors 2007	
IRLR 284, ECJ	12.44, 12.46, 12.49
Atlantic Power and Gas Ltd v More EAT 1125/97	8.142
Autoclenz Ltd v Belcher 2011 ICR 1157, SC	5.7
Aylward and ors v Glamorgan Holiday Home Ltd t/a Glamorgan	
Holiday Hotel EAT 0167/02	2.50

B

BBC v Farnworth EAT 1000/97	2.41, 2.54, 2.55
Babar Indian Restaurant v Rawat 1985 IRLR 57, EAT	2.89
Balkaya v Kiesel Abbruch- und Recycling Technik GmbH 2015 ICR 1110, ECJ	12.9
Barnes and ors v Leavesley and ors 2001 ICR 38, EAT	1.52
Barnes v Gilmartin Associates EAT 825/97	2.48, 2.49

C

D

487

488

489

Kelly and anor v Hesley Group Ltd 2013 IRLR 514, EAT — 12.61, 12.70, 12.87
Kennedy v Werneth Ring Mills Ltd 1977 ICR 206, EAT — 3.44
Kenneth MacRae and Co Ltd v Dawson 1984 IRLR 5, EAT — 4.2, 4.12
Kent County Council v Mingo 2000 IRLR 90, EAT — 9.18
Kentish Bus and Coach Co Ltd v Quarry EAT 287/92 — 2.22, 3.29
Kerry Foods Ltd v Lynch 2005 IRLR 680, EAT — 1.23
Khan v HGS Global Ltd and anor EAT 0176/15 — 1.70, 12.18
King and ors v Eaton Ltd 1996 IRLR 199, Ct Sess
(Inner House) — 8.144, 8.148, 8.153, 8.164
Kingwell and ors v Elizabeth Bradley Designs Ltd EAT 0661/02 — 2.4
Kinmond v Rushton Connections Ltd EAT 799/97 — 1.18
Kitching v Ward and ors 1967 3 KIR 322, Div Ct — 3.9
Kleboe v Ayr County Council 1972 ITR 201, NIRC — 2.16
Knox v Biotechnology and Biological Services EAT 0066/06 — 5.39
Kraft Foods UK Ltd v Hastie 2010 ICR 1355, EAT — 6.50
Kuzel v Roche Products Ltd 2008 ICR 799, CA — 9.6
Kvaerner Oil and Gas Ltd v Parker and ors EAT 0444/02 — 8.92
Kykot v Smith Hartley Ltd 1975 IRLR 372, QBD — 2.47

L

LTI Ltd v Radford EAT 164/00 — 8.86, 8.122
Ladbroke Courage Holidays Ltd v Asten 1981 IRLR 59, EAT — 8.4
Laing v Thistle Hotels plc 2003 SLT 37, Ct Sess — 3.40
Lambe v 186K Ltd 2005 ICR 307, CA — 2.12, 2.56
Lancaster University v University and College Union 2011 IRLR 4, EAT — 12.131
Lancaster v TBWA Manchester EAT 0460/10 — 9.55, 9.60, 9.61
Landeshauptstadt Kiel v Jaeger 2004 ICR 1528, ECJ — 11.11
Langston v Cranfield University 1998 IRLR 172, EAT — 8.81
Lassman and ors v Secretary of State for Trade and Industry
and anor 2000 ICR 1109, CA — 5.22
Lawson v Serco Ltd and two other cases 2006 ICR 250, HL — 2.28, 5.14, 11.3
Lees v Imperial College of Science, Technology and Medicine EAT 0288/15 — 1.43
Leicestershire County Council v UNISON 2005 IRLR 920, EAT;
2006 IRLR 810, CA — 12.37, 12.129
Leonard v Strathclyde Buses Ltd 1998 IRLR 693, Ct Sess (Inner House) — 2.72
Lewis v A Jones and Sons plc EAT 776/92 — 2.16
Leyland Vehicles Ltd v Reston and ors 1981 ICR 403, EAT — 6.11
Lignacite Products Ltd v Krollman 1979 IRLR 22, EAT — 5.37
Lincoln and Louth NHS Trust v Cowan EAT 895/99 — 3.38
Lionel Leventhal Ltd v North EAT 0265/04 — 8.100
Litster and ors v Forth Dry Dock and Engineering Co Ltd (in receivership)
and anor 1989 ICR 341, HL — 1.57, 8.74
Little v Beare and Son Ltd EAT 130/80 — 3.49
Lloyd v Taylor Woodrow Construction 1999 IRLR 782, EAT — 8.171
Lockwood v Department for Work and Pensions 2014 ICR 1257, CA — 6.56, 9.43
Lomond Motors Ltd v Clark EAT 0019/09 — 8.98, 8.111
London Borough of Haringey v Reynolds EAT 1070/98 — 1.50
London Borough of Southwark v Charles EAT 0008/14 — 9.65
London Borough of Wandsworth v Vining and ors 2016 ICR 427, EAT — 12.6
Lonmet Engineering Ltd v Green 1972 ITR 86, NIRC — 3.12

492

IDS Handbook • Redundancy

T

U

Index

A

Acas
early conciliation, 10.10, 10.21

Acas Code of Practice on Discipline and Grievance
contractual redundancy payments, 10.31
generally, 10.16
unreasonable redundancy, 8.83

Age
disqualification from redundancy payments, 5.31

Age discrimination
cost justification, 9.36, 9.39–9.44
examples, 9.46
exclusion of liability, 9.48–9.49
experience justification, 9.38
generally, 6.38–6.56, 9.32
last in, first out, 9.35, 9.36
objective justification, 9.33–9.34, 9.36–9.38
qualifications, 9.45
reverse burden of proof, 9.45–9.46
statutory authority to act, 9.48–9.49
training opportunities, 9.47

Agency workers
automatically unfair redundancy, 8.9, 8.56, 8.57
exclusions from right to statutory redundancy payment, 5.7

Alternative employment
see also **Trial periods**
acceptance of offer, 3.15
alternative to redundancy, 2.59–2.62
assessment at time of dismissal, 8.187
benefits, 3.44–3.45
collective redundancies, 12.16
communication of offer, 3.14
constructive dismissal, 3.56
contents of offer, 3.8–3.13
death of employee after offer, 3.66
death of employer after offer, 3.60–3.62, 3.66
different work offered, 2.58
disability discrimination, 9.63
discrimination, 9.19
extent of obligation, 8.174–8.177
extra job content, 3.43
family-friendly rights, 9.25–9.31
family leave, 3.67–3.71, 8.62
financial prospects, 3.11
form of offer, 3.8–3.10
generally, 8.173
group companies, 8.183
inferior position, 3.41, 3.42, 8.184
instructions to report for work, 3.12
job content, 3.41, 3.42, 3.43
job prospects, 3.51, 3.52
lay-off, 4.33
multiple offers, 3.11
not genuine offer, 3.52
objectivity, 8.178–8.182
offer, 2.58, 3.1, 3.2
offer and acceptance, 3.3–3.5
option to accept redundancy payment, 3.55
pay, 3.44, 3.45
pay protection, 3.45
positive discrimination, 9.19
pregnancy discrimination, 9.21–9.27
re-employment in pursuance of offer, 3.16
reasonableness, 3.38–3.40
relevant date, 10.4
shift patterns, 3.46
short-term working, 4.33
statements of intent to find alternative employment, 3.12
status, 3.41, 3.42, 8.184
statutory ambiguity, 3.3–3.5
substantial change in job content, 3.43
suitable employment, 3.33–3.58
test for redundancy, 2.59–2.62
time off to look for work, 3.57
timing of offer, 3.6, 3.7, 3.53, 3.54
unreasonable refusal, 2.58, 3.33–3.53
unreasonable terms, 8.185, 8.186
working hours, 3.46
workplace change, 3.47–3.50

Annual leave
lay-off, 4.14

Anticipatory breach
variation in contract of employment, 1.23, 1.46

499

IDS Handbook · Redundancy

500 ─────────────────────────

503

507

511